Early American Nature Writers

Early American Nature Writers

A Biographical Encyclopedia

Edited by
Daniel Patterson

Roger Thompson and Scott Bryson,
Contributing Editors

Greenwood Press
Westport, Connecticut • London

Library of Congress Cataloging-in-Publication Data

Early American nature writers : a biographical encyclopedia / edited by Daniel Patterson; Roger Thompson and
    Scott Bryson, contributing editors.
        p. cm.
    Includes bibliographical references and index.
    ISBN: 978–0–313–34680–4 (alk. paper)
1. American literature—Bio-bibliography—Dictionaries. 2. Nature in literature—Bio-bibliography—Dictionaries.
3. Authors, American—Biography—Dictionaries. 4. Natural history—United States—Historiography—Dictionaries.
5. Natural history—United States—Bio-bibliography—Dictionaries. I. Patterson, Daniel, 1953– II. Thompson, Roger,
1970– III. Bryson, J. Scott, 1968–
PS163.E18 2008
508.092'2—dc22   2007027958
[B]

British Library Cataloguing in Publication Data is available.

Library of Congress Catalog Card Number: 2007027958
ISBN: 978–0–313–34680–4

First published in 2008

Greenwood Press, 88 Post Road West, Westport, CT 06881
An imprint of Greenwood Publishing Group, Inc.
www.greenwood.com

Printed in the United States of America

The paper used in this book complies with the
Permanent Paper Standard issued by the National
Information Standards Organization (Z39.48–1984).

10 9 8 7 6 5 4 3 2 1

For my parents
Jerry Bruce Patterson
and
Carol Hale Patterson
ne plus ultra

Contents

Contents

Preface

The North American continent called a new literature into being when Europeans began to visit its shores, explore its interior, and establish new settlements. They had never seen anything like it, and they said so repeatedly in letters, reports, and promotional tracts. That literature evolved over time and became quite diverse, but always central to it is the continent itself: the varieties of landscape, the native plant and animal species, the phenomena of climate and seasons, and the human response to it all. Of all national literatures, no other is more responsive to its physical place on Earth than American literature.

Early American Nature Writers: A Biographical Encyclopedia tells the stories of the lives and careers of more than 50 of the writers who helped write young America into the imaginations of readers. This is a motley group, including explorers, naturalists, sportsmen, travelers, farmers, preachers, essayists, philosophers, artists, editors, musicians, educators, poets, and carpenters—but they all wrote nonfiction prose about nature in America.

Our cultural appetite for nature writing has, perhaps ironically, increased over the past several decades as the global environmental crises have continually worsened. Today most people would agree that of all the issues we must confront and deal with, the one needing most urgent action is the health of the environment. Over the past half century or so, writers like Rachel Carson, Barry Lopez, Annie Dillard, Loren Eiseley, and Chet Raymo have contributed to the cultural work of guiding us to a relationship with the natural world that is sustainable into the future. The writers treated in this volume are their predecessors, reflecting the evolving conceptions of and attitudes toward nature in the nation's earlier centuries—a body of past thought about nature from which we can draw insights and inspiration today.

It should be noted that not all of the "American" nature writers included in this volume were American citizens. For several of the earliest authors, there was not in their lifetimes an "America" of which to be a citizen. But to exclude William Byrd II and John Lawson would be to exclude important early representations of regions of what was yet to become a nation separate from the Great Britain of their nativity. Even after the founding of the new nation, numerous Europeans found themselves drawn to the American vastness and astounding biodiversity. To exclude a naturalist like Thomas Nuttall who spent 28 years in the United States but retained his British citizenship throughout his life would be to exclude an ornithology that is as "American" as Audubon's *Birds of America*. Audubon himself had barely any clear citizenship at all, since he was of illegitimate birth and was born on a Caribbean island colonized by France, until he took American citizenship at age 27 (on July 3,

1812). Of all the writers included, the one whose stay in the United States was briefest is Isabella Lucy Bird, but her account of her travels in the American Rocky Mountains is an important early representation of the Rockies and to omit it would be to misrepresent the literary history of those mountains. Thus, legal American citizenship was not required to be included in this volume. What was required was that the author have made a significant contribution to the literature of the American environment. Crèvecoeur, who referred to Americans in 1782 as "this promiscuous breed," would have been pleased with this editorial decision.

Following the Introduction, the author entries are arranged alphabetically by author's last name. At the end of each article, the reader will find a complete list of each author's publications (the Primary Bibliography) and a list of sources and scholarly works consulted in the writing of the entry (the Secondary Bibliography). Nature writing has many aspects with important implications for the understanding and interpretation of American culture; therefore, much has been written about it. The list of Further Readings at the rear of this volume is intended as a guide into that body of work that has grown up around early American nature writing.

Acknowledgments

To all the contributors to this volume much credit is due. No one had scheduled time to research and write about one of the early American nature writers on my list, yet all of them managed—sooner or later—to make the time to do so. They are excellent scholars, and I am grateful to them all.

Before I came to this project, Roger Thompson and Scott Bryson (whose *Twentieth-Century American Nature Writers: Prose* was published in 2003) did some of the initial work. They recruited scholars for and edited eight of the entries included herein and compiled a list of additional readings, largely relied upon for the list printed in the backmatter of the present volume. I am grateful for their excellent contributions.

Central Michigan University has provided institutional support while I developed this volume. My colleagues in the Department of English Language and Literature have shown a gratifying and sustaining interest in my work in the earlier periods of American nature writing. I am fortunate in this regard. I am especially grateful to Mary Obuchowski, Linda Peterson, and Peter Koper.

I am also fortunate to have known over the years generous and supportive colleagues and friends in the Association for the Study of Literature and Environment who in both tangible and intangible ways have helped shape this and several other works. I most want to mention Joni Adamson, Lorraine Anderson, Mike Branch, Larry Buell, John Calderazzo, John Elder, Cheryll Glotfelty, Christoph Irmscher, Rochelle Johnson, John Knott, Paul Lindholdt, Bernie Quetchenbach, Susan Rosen, Sheryl St. Germain, and Scott Slovic.

I wish here also to acknowledge an object on my desk that I made constant use of during the production of this book: a revolving book stand built for me by my brother, David. When he saw a photograph of the one Thomas Jefferson designed and had built for himself, David thought, "My brother should have one of those," so he made me one. All my friends now want him for a brother.

For walking and paddling with me hither and yon, time and again, I most affectionately thank my sons, Shane and David. And for accompanying me through this project and all our adventures, my wife, Alison Miller, knows how I feel.

I have dedicated this volume to my parents. If my mother had not sailed to France in 1952 to join my father, whom the United States Air Force had sent to Fontainebleau, I would have amounted to little in this life. As it was, I was born forty weeks after they embraced dockside, and that has made all the difference.

Introduction: The Rise of American Nature Writing

Daniel Patterson

The renaissance of literary environmental writing underway in the United States since the 1960s is a remarkable cultural phenomenon that has not been exceeded in any period of the nation's literary history. As the array of environmental crises worsened and as public awareness of them broadened in the 1950s and 1960s, the culture was being prepared for new kinds of writing about the world. Not only was the larger readership forming, but also the new authors were being born into and acquiring their first knowledge of the ecological world during these decades. "Nature writing" would become arguably the most vital literary movement in America in the last decades of the twentieth century, and its purpose would be fundamentally subversive—that is, it took on the work of critiquing and realigning the culture's predominately anthropocentric and exploitative relationship to the physical environment. It is also true of American literature, however, that probably no other national literature has ever devoted so much of its energy to representations of the land and to considerations of the relationship between the land and its human inhabitants. Since the very first European accounts of the "new world," the need to represent the physical environment in language has been continuous. When Henry Thoreau considered the difference between British and American literature in his *Journal*, he characterized the former as essentially "tame & civilized"; the American continent would insist, as it were, on having its wildness expressed: "There was need of America" (January 10, 1851). The roots of American nature writing thus reach deeply into the past. This past is the subject of this volume.

To contextualize the "early American nature writers" treated in this volume, one could profitably begin by looking at the "new philosophy" of Francis Bacon and the institution of that worldview in the Royal Society, founded in 1662. Bacon saw his world, which was both British and imperious, as stultified and blinkered by long traditions of Aristotelian thought. Since Aristotle's deductive habits of mind never allowed him to see the actual natural world, Bacon believed, any account or representation of natural phenomena by Aristotle or those who shared his epistemology would be inaccurate, misleading, and unhelpful to the advance of culture. Human culture would advance only so far as it achieved the control of nature. At the center of the Royal Society's mission was the perfection of humankind's ability to manipulate nature and exploit its potential contributions to human life and culture.

The Royal Society's epistemology was radically empirical. The much disparaged

Aristotelian reliance on deduction rather than on empirical observation as a means of knowing the world was seen as coercing observers to see only what they had been taught to expect. The new emphasis was on the direct observation of cause and effect in natural phenomena. To discover the cause of a phenomenon was to discover a natural law, which subsequently would lead to further discoveries and an inevitably growing body of the laws of nature. The new science envisioned a sequence through which knowledge would be acquired: particular facts would lead observers to minor laws; those minor laws would accumulate and thereby point the way to major laws. This progress of science would continue across the future generations of humans, each new generation enjoying the benefits of the cumulative knowledge of past generations. Guided always, of course, by the rational faculty of the human mind, the five senses could be relied upon as the means by which humans came to know the world around them. The new naturalist thus admirably unified in one person both the empirical and the rational faculties. The new naturalist was also helping lay the scientific foundation necessary for the formation of a true philosophy to guide and shape human culture. Because human culture would be based on an empowering knowledge of the physical universe, it would be an actively creative culture conducive to the fulfillment of the human potential in both the arts and the sciences. No limit to this progress was imagined.

Clearly, in such an agenda there is much potential for the secularization of the sciences, and voices arose in the ongoing discussion of how religion and science would stand in relation to one another. As the new science moved away from the earlier faith in the essential teleology of the world's phenomena, it also abandoned the analogy of God as an artist creating works of beauty and substituted the analogy of a skilled craftsman or engineer manufacturing exquisitely detailed machines. Although the divorce of science from theology would not be complete

until approximately the middle of the nineteenth century, a new tension was perceived in England in the seventeenth century. The materialist and atheistic tendencies apparent in this time were countered by the "physico-theologians," who would argue for keeping the natural sciences in a subservient position to theology.

Probably the most eloquent and influential voice among the physicotheologians was that of John Ray (1627–1705), whose *The Wisdom of God Manifested in the Works of Creation* appeared first in London in 1691, after which Ray enlarged the work through three editions before his death; thereafter the book was published in more than 20 later editions by the year 1846. Most significant for the purposes of the present volume are Ray's calls for a new kind of literature about nature and for a broader interest among readers in the new books thus produced. For Ray, one of the chief ends of humankind—that is, "part of our business and employment in Eternity"—was "to contemplate the Works of God, and give him the Glory of his Wisdom, Power and Goodness manifested in the Creation of them." Thus nature study—even when empirically driven and focused on the causes of phenomena—becomes a form of worship, and natural history is kept within the compass of theology. Indeed, the empirical study of nature could be seen as a "Preparative to Divinity." Ray complained that his culture's interests were in need of realignment:

> Let us then consider the Workes of God, and observe the Operations of his Hands: Let us take notice of and admire his infinite Wisdom and Goodness in the Formation of them: No Creature in this Sublunary World is capable of so doing beside Man; and yet we are deficient herein: We content our selves with the knowledge of the Tongues, and a little skill in Philology, or history perhaps and Antiquity, and neglect that which to me seems more material, I mean Natural History and the Works of Creation.

Because the works of natural history that he wanted to see published would be imbued with his philosophy of nature, the language would not aspire to scientific objectivity; rather, the prose of the new literature should be evocative and eloquent—worthy of acts of worship. Nature writers have always been faced with the challenge of interesting readers in books without plots, books in which little more than natural phenomena are represented. Ray recognized this cultural barrier in his day and encouraged a new readership:

> If Man ought to reflect upon his Creator the glory of all his Works, then ought he to take notice of them all, and not to think any thing unworthy of his Cognizance.

"I wish that this might be brought in Fashion among us," he wrote.

Thus, the rise of the new science was accompanied by a call for a new literature of nature. The more empirical approach to nature study and the cultural goal of taming and subduing nature also impelled much of the European exploration and colonization of the newly discovered regions of the planet. This age of intensified European exploration produced its own new literature, of course, one of the chief challenges of which was how and to what purpose to represent the new places in words. A broad array of different purposes brought about a broad array of types of writing about the "new world" at a time when it can be seen now that a number of new conditions were arising that would allow the rise of American nature writing by the last decades of the eighteenth century.

A humbler, less purely anthropocentric ethic was emerging in Europe even in the height of European exploration and colonization. By the late eighteenth century, this somewhat more biocentric ethic would appear in the earliest works now recognizable as "nature writing" and continue as a characteristic strain in American nature writing through both the nineteenth and twentieth centuries.

The early manifestations of this humbler ethic (as Keith Thomas explains in *Man and the Natural World: A History of the Modern Sensibility* [1983]) appear in religious contexts. John Calvin, for example, in the sixteenth century, though he had a completely anthropocentric worldview, was a voice for a biblical stewardship. God placed animals in subjection to humankind, but, Calvin wrote, "he did it with the condition that we should handle them gently." In this line of thinking, cruelty to animals could be seen as sinful, as a violation of divine trust. Before the Civil War in England, bear-baiting, cock-throwing, cock-fighting, and the ill treatment of domestic animals were opposed on these theological grounds.

Another Puritan argument against the cruel animal sports held that animals had no spirit of ferocity before Original Sin. Their ferocity, then, was a reminder of human sinfulness and ought not be a source of pleasure. Macaulay once joked that the Puritans opposed bear-baiting not because of the suffering of the bear but because the spectators were enjoying themselves. After the Restoration of 1660, the Puritan opposition to cruelty to animals was sustained by Quakers and Dissenters, and then in the eighteenth century by Methodists and Evangelicals.

A parallel secular opposition to these sports was also rising. Montaigne wrote against them, as did Addison and Steele. By the eighteenth century, this combination of religious arguments and the opposition of an educated middle class made it increasingly difficult, if not impossible, to *openly* condone the killing of animals for mere sport. What was happening was a major change from Christian anthropocentric traditions. The idea that the world did not exist exclusively to benefit humankind was finding ever broader acceptance. This subtle cultural shift would inform many of even the earliest works of American nature writing.

Eighteenth-century developments in the natural sciences, most importantly botany, also influenced how America's first generation of nature writers conceived of nature and how they represented plant and animal species and natural phenomena in their writings. Between 1740 and 1790 (as James Larson explains in *Interpreting Nature: The Science of Living Form from Linnaeus to Kant*

[1994]), botanists in Europe and the Americas moved away from an older teleological conception of nature and toward a more ecological conception, that is, toward a model of nature that took into account the complex web of relationships existing among plant and animal species in a given region. Linnaeus's binomial system of plant classification (published in its earliest form in 1735) became a giant step toward the natural system of taxonomy that naturalists wanted. The Linnaean taxonomy was also so simple that amateurs on both sides of the Atlantic were able to take up botany as a passionate hobby, professional naturalists revised the national floras, and the landed gentry rearranged and enhanced their gardens and collections. The field botanists focused ever more on observable causation in nature and ever less on theological suppositions about the mind of God. A humbler science emerged as naturalists became more satisfied with working toward the more attainable goal of representing what their senses told them and what their minds could infer therefrom. Botanists also began working as a community of laborers, combining their findings more so than ever before. Liberated, as it were, from earlier strictures, they were able to consider afresh the implications of this increasing body of data and advance toward the more complex, ecological model of the natural world. Throughout the nineteenth century, the new botany would appear in American nature writing as the life science that most often wedded the scientific and the literary, as "the beautiful science," in Elizabeth C. Wright's phrase.

Following the American Revolution, a number of geopolitical, scientific, and literary developments influenced the rise of American nature writing. First of all, a cluster of publications suggests that the transatlantic world was ready for a new cultural focus on the natural world. Crèvecoeur's *Letters from an American Farmer* (1782) attracted wide interest because of its early and largely pastoral representation of the world's newest nation in its first attempts to establish an agrarian economy and culture. Thomas Jefferson's patriotic *Notes on the State of Virginia* (1784), in rendering a selection of the new republic's natural history and landscape, became an early voice for applying current aesthetic theory to representations of American landscapes and entered forcefully into international natural history debates. Gilbert White's *The Natural History and Antiquities of Selborne* (1789) was so widely read and revered that it showed many later writers the way to bringing detailed nature observation into the realm of literary pastoralism. A full 60 years after this publication, Susan Fenimore Cooper would aspire to have her *Rural Hours* (1850), the first book-length work of literary nature writing by an American woman, placed on readers' shelves beside their copies of White's *Natural History*. William Bartram's *Travels* (1791) is a rangy compilation of travel narrative, natural history, ethnography, and literary meditations on nature observations that became a favorite of many of the leading Romantic poets as well as of many of the most accomplished nature writers since then. It is a telling cultural fact for the history of American nature writing that all of these works have been in almost continuous publication since their original appearance more than 200 years ago.

In 1802, when Thomas Jefferson wrote his instructions for The Corps of Discovery, he not only created the planet's first government-funded scientific expedition and set in motion the first transcontinental exploration of the regions west of the Mississippi, but he also ordered the first of what would become many written accounts of the vastly fascinating American West through all the decades of the nineteenth century. The Louisiana Purchase of 1803 doubled the size of the United States and quite suddenly settled into the imaginations of the new Americans as a continental interior as unknown as it was immense. This single geopolitical development is probably the most influential factor in the rise of American nature writing in the first half of the nineteenth century. This vast unknown interior called not only for exploration, settlement, and development but also to be written. Among America's early nature writers are several naturalists and government agents who, in following their professions, found themselves writing these new American places into the imaginations of readers back East.

The ongoing discussion among nature philosophers and natural history writers in the early nineteenth century informed the manner of representing natural phenomena in words. Laura Dasso Walls describes the two chief views of nature that were available to America's early nature writers during the period of literary and scientific Romanticism. One view conceived of nature as a divine, harmonious whole that transcended its physical manifestation in the form of the sensory world of human experience. From this perspective—which Walls refers to as "rational holism"—nature can be most accurately and fully comprehended in the human mind, where any worldly observation of natural phenomena becomes merely a means to the contemplation of the mind of God. This conception of nature comes to the United States from the German idealist philosophers, Johann Wolfgang von Goethe, and Samuel Coleridge, and finds its fullest and most enduring expression in the "Transcendentalist" philosophy of Emerson and in the special creationism of Louis Agassiz. The alternative model of nature was more empirical and held that nature could be comprehended only by attending to the causes of observable phenomena and by thereafter inferring and describing the network of systems that govern the physical environment. This understanding of nature is essentially ecological; Walls refers to it as "empirical holism." Proponents of this view were Alexander von Humboldt, Charles Lyell, Charles Darwin, and Thoreau in his later years. (See Walls's account of these conceptions of nature in *Seeing New Worlds: Henry David Thoreau and Nineteenth-century Natural Science* [1995], 3–52.) The difference between these two theories of nature can be seen in small in two parallel phrases: in Emerson's *Nature* (1836), the chief Transcendentalist characterizes the observing self as "part and particle of God," whereas Thoreau, in the opening of "Walking" (1851), describes his more worldly self as "part and parcel of Nature." Every early American nature writer has a vision of nature that can be usefully viewed as placed on a spectrum somewhere between these two orientations.

The term "nature writing" cannot be properly said to describe a literary genre; the phrase serves, however, as a needed, convenient way to refer to the mélange or menagerie of types of writings about nature that emerge and thereafter ramify in the late eighteenth and early nineteenth centuries. Thomas J. Lyon, one of the first and most accomplished scholars of American nature writing, found that even from its origins, the American literature of nature could not be neatly classified: "nature writing is not in truth a neat and orderly field." To facilitate the new interest in the formal study of this literature that was rising in the 1980s, Lyon proposed "A Taxonomy of Nature Writing," but rather than a hierarchy or family tree of discrete types of writings, Lyon uses the device of a spectrum because it effectively allows the blurred boundaries and overlappings of form that characterize the relations among the works of this literature. (See Lyon's *This Incomperable Land: A Book of American Nature Writing* [1989], 3–7.) Contributing to the ramifying diversification of American nature writing was an active debate about how nature should be represented. On one extreme of this debate were those naturalists who believed that poetry or literary art should be kept separate from science. In all works intended to represent nature usefully and accurately, the observer, the perceiving self, should be removed in order to maintain strict "objectivity." The premise here is that a "subjective" rendering of natural phenomena could not advance one's knowledge or understanding of the world. The tenets of Romanticism fueled a healthy resistance to such a reductionist view of perceiving and representing the world. Thoreau, for example, considered this theory of objective science as "inhuman" (*Journal*, May 1,

1859)—indeed, as impossible: "There is no such thing as pure *objective* observation." On this side of the representation debate, Romanticism granted to the perceiving self—that is, to the mind of the observer—a powerful, creative function that Agassiz, Asa Gray, and others denied. In the very act of engaging the world in an act of perception, the mind becomes the agent of meaning, the site where meaning is made. The world is knowable only through the medium of the human mind, and these writers on the Left Bank of American Romanticism (following Goethe and Coleridge) saw not only legitimacy but also a cultural need for a literature that gave voice to nature according to what was emerging as a new epistemology. The most valuable writing about nature would reflect this epistemology in a sort of dance between object and subject, between natural phenomenon and perceiving self. Quite opposed to the theory that the observer should remove himself from the written representation, Thoreau suggested that science should be biography:

> The sum of what the writer of whatever class has to report is simply some human experience, whether he be poet or philosopher or man of science. The man of most science is the man most alive, whose life is the greatest event. (*Journal*, May 6, 1854)

With such disparate epistemological options available, the field of American nature writing was sure to be a mazy place.

There were also other, more tangible social or cultural conditions that influenced the rise of the nature essay in the nineteenth century. Lawrence Buell has shown that by approximately the middle third of the century, the following three developments were increasing the likelihood that authors would turn to environmental nonfiction:

> a specialization in the branches of natural science to the point that exposition for laypersons seemed necessary; a degree of urbanization sufficient to produce substantial numbers of readers regretful about being cut off from nature; and a sufficient array of literary media

(lecture forums, magazines, book production and distribution networks) to provide belletristic writers with a decent hearing if not a fortune. (*The Environmental Imagination: Thoreau, Nature Writing, and the Formation of American Culture* [1995], 398)

That the literary nature writing of Alexander Wilson and John Godman precede these conditions makes their accomplishments all the more impressive, suggesting the passionate dedication of artists with original visions. The same can be said of Crèvecoeur and William Bartram to some extent. Nevertheless, the appearance of the personal nature essay is one of the most significant developments in the early history of American nature writing. Following the publication and success of Susan Cooper's *Rural Hours* (1850) and Henry Thoreau's *Walden* (1854), American literary culture had accepted a new genre. That even a small, obscure publishing house, M. Doolady, would take on the financial risks of a prose treatise on nature by an all-but-unknown author, Elizabeth C. Wright's *Lichen Tufts* (1860), further suggests that publishers were aware of a new readership.

The later into the nineteenth century one looks, the more evidence there is of the widening divide between science and religion. The physicotheologians took on the task of reconciling the two in the seventeenth century. Two hundred years later, the findings of Charles Lyell and Charles Darwin made the reconciliation much more challenging. In his *Principles of Geology* (1830–1833), Lyell argues from fossil evidence that Earth is incalculably older than the common Christian claim of approximately 6,000 years and that the geologic processes that produced the state of the planet in the present age are still and always at work. Creation, that is, was not completed in the biblical six days; there is as much creation ahead of us in time as ever there was behind us. By deepening his contemporaries's conception of the age of the planet, Lyell made it more difficult to argue that a Christian God created the world for the sole benefit of a single species. Darwin, even more dramatically, offered challenges to Christian views of human exceptionalism. With the publication and broad discussion of *On the Origin of Species* (1859), the cultural consideration of how the lone human being relates to nature took on a new heftiness. Darwin's theory of speciation by variation and natural selection also showed the prevailing models of nature to be overly simple and pointed the way to a conception of nature that encompasses its ecological complexities. Many would find cause for pessimism or even despair in what looked like determinism in Darwin's findings, but others would embrace the more dynamic conception of nature as a means to a deeper apprehension of nature's most profound principles and thereby as a means to a new kind of beauty in the physical environment and in the human relation to it. "There is grandeur in this view of life," Darwin wrote. John Burroughs saw the need to coach his culture in accepting the deeper view:

> To many good people evolution seems an ungodly doctrine, like setting up a remorseless logic in the place of an omnipresent Creator. But there is no help for it. Science has fairly turned us out of our comfortable little anthropomorphic notion of things into the great out-of-doors of the universe. We must and will get used to the chill, yea, to the cosmic chill, if need be. (*Time and Change* [1912], 2)

This is not to suggest, however, that the simpler, more anthropomorphic view of nature did not continue a healthy existence throughout the century; it certainly did and has remained a continuous (if diminishing) thread even to the present day in environmental writing.

Of course, all of the cultural changes and influences described here develop more or less gradually over time and manifest themselves in mottled patterns across our literary history. All of the authors treated in this volume, however, produced their contributions to American nature writing amid these (and surely other) conditions. The recent interest in formal ecological literary analysis (often referred to as "ecocriticism") gave rise to this volume, and our hope is that *Early American Nature Writers: A Biographical Encyclopedia* will in turn enable and inspire the continued study of how our literature mediates between a living world and a yearning human consciousness.

Nota bene: In the interest of efficiency, specific references to primary and secondary sources are omitted throughout this volume; however, all the sources used in the preparation of each chapter are included in the primary and secondary bibliographies.

Daniel Patterson
Blanchard, Michigan

Elizabeth Agassiz
(December 5, 1822–June 27, 1907)

Jennifer Dawes Adkison

As the writings of a writer and a naturalist, Elizabeth Agassiz's work was undervalued in her lifetime. Agassiz, herself, failed to appreciate her own contribution to the nineteenth-century understanding of the natural world. Elizabeth Cary Agassiz spent much of her adult life in the shadow of her famous husband, Swiss naturalist Louis Agassiz. Characteristic of Elizabeth Agassiz's self-effacement was her anxiety that her voice in the Agassizes' collaboration *A Journey in Brazil* might lend a "sentimental" tone to Louis Agassiz's work. In a letter to her sister, Sarah G. Cary, she writes:

> ...I am conscious that what is beautiful and picturesque in his studies interests me more than what is purely scientific, and sometimes I am afraid that in my appreciation of that side of the subject I shall weaken his thought and give it a rather feminine character.

Her accomplishments—among them books and articles on natural history as well as the founding of Radcliffe College—however, contradict her own uncertainty about her abilities.

Born on December 5, 1822, to Thomas and Sarah Cary, Elizabeth Cabot Cary was a child of privilege among the Boston elite, surrounded by a large circle of relatives. The second of seven children, she also grew up in close proximity to her numerous cousins.

Elizabeth Cary was educated both at home by her governess and in later years at Elizabeth Peabody's Historical School in Boston. Although she did not exhibit a particular interest in science or natural history in her early years, her association with Louis Agassiz as an adult would lead her to the central work of her life.

In 1846, Elizabeth Cary met Louis Agassiz at a dinner given by her sister Mary and Mary's husband, Harvard professor Cornelius Conway Felton. Louis Agassiz, who had made a name for himself as a naturalist and popular speaker, was in Boston presenting a series of lectures at the Lowell Institute. Louis Agassiz's wife, Cécile, who had stayed behind with their children in Switzerland, died during his absence, and in 1850, he and Elizabeth Cary married. Elizabeth Agassiz was a devoted stepmother to Louis Agassiz's three motherless children. She developed a particularly strong bond with Alexander, who was 13 years old at the time of his father's marriage. Elizabeth Agassiz would in later years write a book of natural history with her stepson as well as raise his children upon the death of his wife.

In marrying Louis Agassiz, Elizabeth Agassiz embarked upon what was to become the central mission of her life. She took on the responsibility not only of running the Agassiz household but also of assisting her husband as his editor and secretary, transcribing his lectures, and later producing detailed descriptions of their journey to Brazil and his work there. Elizabeth Agassiz authored two books of natural history as well as a series of articles for *Atlantic Monthly*. Her accomplishments as a nature writer and popularizer of scientific observation were not fully understood or acknowledged in her own lifetime. More recent critical reevaluation of her contribution to science writing has even established her own contribution to several texts publicly attributed to her husband. In *American Women of Letters and the Nineteenth-Century Sciences: Styles of Affiliation*, Nina Baym asserts that 21 articles published in *Atlantic Monthly* under Louis Agassiz's name were actually written by Elizabeth Agassiz and that these articles were revised into Louis Agassiz's *Methods of Study in Natural History*, *Geological Sketches*, and *Geological Sketches, Second Series* by Elizabeth herself.

There is no indication that Elizabeth Agassiz had any interest in natural history prior to her marriage. In the early years of her marriage, however, racked with debt, she founded a school for girls in 1855 where she first became captivated by natural history and scientific observation. Because her husband's salary as chair of zoology and geology at Harvard University did not substantially cover the debt the family accrued—particularly Louis Agassiz's extensive acquisition of natural history specimens—Elizabeth Agassiz started her school, with the enthusiastic assistance of her husband and two older stepchildren, to supplement their income. The Agassiz School for girls featured lectures from Harvard professors, most prominently Louis Agassiz himself. At her school, Elizabeth Agassiz was herself both teacher and de facto student. She attended lectures and made careful notes of each subject. In 1863, relieved of the debt that had haunted their early years, the Agassizes closed the school. Elizabeth Agassiz felt both freedom and a tinge of sadness in closing the school, but it had done more than accomplish its purpose. Not only were the Agassizes in better shape

financially, but Elizabeth Agassiz had also found a calling.

Based on her newfound interest, during the years when the school was still in session, Elizabeth Agassiz had published her first book, *A First Lesson in Natural History* in 1859 using the pseudonym Actaea. (The six editions of the text that followed were all published under her own name.) In her book, Elizabeth Agassiz popularizes the science she had learned from her husband and presents sea life in clear and simple language suitable for the instruction of children. The book was written as letters addressed to her niece and nephew, Lisa and Connie Felton, and contained illustrations by her stepson. Agassiz uses as a premise for her book the idea that she is writing in response to questions by the children about the natural world. She begins with the details of the lives of sea creatures, then gives the scientific information for each species. She weaves the information about marine life into a kind of storytelling directly addressed to the children: "I hope that the Sea-Anemone has interested you so much, that you will like to hear about some other animals of the same kind, which live also in the sea, and of which I have a strange and wonderful story to tell you." She uses the Nahant, Massachusetts, shore marine life as subject matter for her text, particularly the kinds of creatures children might encounter. In focusing upon the familiar, Agassiz hoped to inspire curiosity about nature among her young audience. Significantly, her awareness of voice and audience in appealing to the children allowed her to demystify scientific observation by encouraging their own involvement with the natural world.

A second book, *Seaside Studies in Natural History. Marine Animals of Massachusetts Bay. Radiates*, published in collaboration with Alexander Agassiz, appeared in 1865. In both this and her previous text, Elizabeth Agassiz brings the study of marine animals to a popular audience. Her graceful prose and rich description are evident in this passage on sea anemones from *Seaside Studies*:

They may be found in any small pools about the rocks which are flooded by the tide at high water. Their favorite haunts, however, where they occur in greatest quantity are more difficult to reach; but the curious in such matters will be well rewarded, even at the risk of wet feet and a slippery scramble over rocks covered with damp sea-weed, by a glimpse into their more crowded abodes. Such a grotto is to be found on the rocks of East Point at Nahant. It can only be reached at low tide, and then one is obliged to creep on hands and knees to its entrance, in order to see through its entire length; but its whole interior is studded with these animals, and as they are of various hues, pink, brown, orange, purple, or pure white, the effect is like that of brightly colored mosaics set in the roof and walls.

In this passage, the reader is obliged to come into the grotto with her and see for him- or herself the wonder of the animal "mosaic." Agassiz places her readers into her text and, with Agassiz herself as their guide, allows them to feel the water and slippery rocks on their feet. The immediacy of her writing insists that the readers participate in the experience of the natural world and assures that for their participation they will be amply rewarded.

In her text, Agassiz includes compelling descriptions not just of the creatures themselves but also of the expeditions to view such creatures. These accounts add a sense of drama to her writing. She describes one such night expedition on which the party sets out in boats in search of jellyfish. Out of the "still surface of the water unbroken," they pull the nets full of jellyfish. Agassiz exclaims,

> What genie under the sea has wrought this wonderful change? Our dirty, torn old net is suddenly turned to a web of gold, and as we lift it from the water heavy rills of molten metal seem to flow down its sides and collect in a glowing mass at the bottom.

The colorful jellyfish break the silence of the night and punctuate it with their vivid glow. The sea creatures transform the old net into a vision of radiance. She describes other such nights when "there is something wild and weird in the whole scene, which at once fascinates and appalls the imagination." She tells how the greenish glow of light on water against the darkly outlined land combines to form a mystical scene that tempts her readers out upon the water. Agassiz's ability to capture these experiences in vivid detail distinguishes her writing from dry scientific textbooks. She brings to life the painstaking practice of scientific observation.

Despite her conversational style, Agassiz's writing is thorough and concise. Agassiz's science is not compromised by her desire for mass appeal. Her entry for the Campanella is representative; after calling it a "pretty little Jelly-fish," Agassiz goes on to describe it and its life cycle in scientifically accurate language:

> There are but four chymiferous tubes in the Campanella, and four stiff tentacles, which in consequence of the peculiar character of the veil appear, when the animal is seen in profile, to start from the middle of the disk.

Another jellyfish, the Lucernaria, is called "One of the prettiest and most graceful." Illustrations, many of which were drawn by stepson Alexander Agassiz, accompany her text. She concludes her text by going further afield in a chapter where she explores marine life in various other geographic areas and argues that the same geographic distributions that characterize terrestrial flora and fauna of specific earthly zones may be usefully applied to marine life. Through her careful observation of the Nahant shore and in contrasting the aquatic creatures there with other regions, Agassiz maintains that zones may be equally applied to the sea as to the earth.

Responses to and assessments of Elizabeth Agassiz's natural history texts have varied. Nina Baym points out that Agassiz deemphasized her own role: "...either effacing her own contribution or pointedly contrasting it to Louis's achievements as the product of a weaker feminine versus stronger masculine intellect." Agassiz's biographer Lucy Paton claimed that in order to fully appreciate

Agassiz's contribution one must realize that she had no formal scientific education and that the science behind her texts was that of her husband. Truly undercutting Agassiz's accomplishment and abilities, Paton states, "They [Agassiz's books] are admirable expressions of her peculiar ability, which lay in the power of presenting second-hand knowledge accurately as if it were the result of her own scientific observations." In contrast, Vera Norwood, in her 1993 study *Made From this Earth: American Women and Nature*, explains the novelty of Agassiz's approach:

> There is a new language in Agassiz's book, one that [botanist Almira] Phelps did not contemplate. Rather than finding value in nature study as a way to develop reverence for the Creator, Agassiz reveres the magical world itself for its surprises as well as its familiarity. In the writing of Elizabeth Agassiz, we begin to see nature brought to life, not with a stylized list of canned emotions gleaned from poets' projections onto flowers or a set of labels learned from a male biology professor, but from immersion into concrete details.

Norwood sees Agassiz as foundational to American women's nature writing, with her attention to detail and ability to transmit to her audience her own enchantment and fascination with the natural world. In Agassiz's work, nature itself inspires admiration, and her genius lies in the way that she uses language to convey the inherent value of the natural world, not for what it inspires, but for what it is.

In her natural history texts, Elizabeth Agassiz both brings a sense of immediacy to the natural world as the reader experiences what she describes and fulfills Louis Agassiz's imperative to his students for detailed description to accompany and support their observations. Unlike her husband, Elizabeth Agassiz avoided the essentialist philosophies that caused him to condemn evolution and promote the idea that distinctions between races of humans were permanent and irrevocable. Although nothing in her work directly contradicts that of her husband, whom she revered, Elizabeth Agassiz takes a much broader view. In her biography of her husband, Elizabeth Agassiz describes his views but does not substantially comment upon them. Instead, she uses his own words from his final article, "Evolution and Permanence of Type." Calling it Louis Agassiz's "last word upon science," Elizabeth Agassiz excerpts portions of the text in order to illustrate his unwavering support of the distinctions between "types." In a brief introduction to these passages, Elizabeth Agassiz writes, "He maintained that this law acts within definite limits, and never infringes upon the great types, each one of which is, in his view, a structural unit in itself." Agassiz's refusal to evaluate the accuracy of his views perhaps becomes a tacit evasion of them.

In 1865 and 1866, the Agassizes undertook a trip to Brazil where Louis Agassiz hoped to find evidence to support his claim that each species had developed independently of all others. In stark contrast to Darwin's theories, Louis Agassiz argued for the distinction between species and even viewed the races as separate, distinct, and biologically incapable of intermingling. The journey yielded no conclusive evidence to prove or disprove Louis Agassiz's theories. As Linda Bergmann suggests in "A Troubled Marriage of Discourses: Science Writing and Travel Narrative in Louis and Elizabeth Agassiz's *A Journey in Brazil*," Louis Agassiz's "...overconfident anticipation of what he [would] discover," in part, weakened his own claims about the success of the venture. The experiences of the Agassizes in Brazil formed the basis of their travel narrative *A Journey in Brazil*. During their travels, Elizabeth Agassiz kept a journal of daily events and Louis Agassiz's scientific observations and wrote letters home that she used as the basis for the narrative. Although Louis Agassiz's supplementary notes accompany the text and authorship is credited jointly, the bulk of the writing was her own. Bergmann sees the narrative as two documents with differing purposes—a travel narrative and science writing—and argues that Elizabeth Agassiz's contribution to the text overshadows her husband's own

...precisely because it is a better example of its own kind of discourse. Elizabeth's voice undermines her husband's because on this particular expedition her "delicate observations from the picturesque" are more convincing than her husband's "scientific observations."

Nina Baym counters this assertion by claiming that Elizabeth Agassiz's contribution to *A Journey in Brazil* "...unselfconsciously and unvaryingly deploys a vernacular version of his taxonomy." According to Baym, the racial distinctions of Agassiz's portrayal of the Brazilian people seem to support her husband's scientific observations.

Agassiz uses the travel narrative as the basis for her writing in *A Journey in Brazil*, but, like her natural history writing, she also records in detail the people and places she encounters. She observes and records her observations with a keen eye for the beauty and fascination of the place. Using language reminiscent of her writing about marine life on the Nahant shore, Agassiz writes, "Today we have seen numbers of flying-fish from the deck, and were astonished at the grace and beauty of their motion." Although the rainforest she encounters is "impenetrable" in its "density, darkness, and solemnity," she works to familiarize herself with the landscape. Despite Agassiz's desire to see and know the land, her vision of logging the rain forest, as Bergmann notes, seems contradictory to modern readers. Agassiz writes,

> The abundance and variety of timber in the Amazonian Valley strikes us with amazement. We long to hear the saw-mill in these forests, where there are several hundred kinds of woods, admirably suited for construction as well as for the finest cabinetwork.

In this passage, Agassiz uncharacteristically values the rainforest for what it is worth in a practical sense rather than what it inspires.

The Agassizes' narrative was well received, and, several years later, Louis Agassiz encouraged Elizabeth to keep a journal of their experiences on board the *Hassler*, a steamship on a deep-sea dredging expedition to California. During this journey, the Agassizes retraced Darwin's steps in *The Voyage of the Beagle* in Louis Agassiz's continued attempts to disprove Darwin's theories. In December 1871, they set sail for California by way of the West Indies, Rio de Janeiro, Monte Video, through the Straits of Magellan, and ended the voyage at San Francisco. Along the way, she read Darwin's account of the same places and remarked that she was surprised to find differences from and variations of his descriptions in her own observations. Leaving the ship and traversing into the depths of the Amazonian rain forest, Elizabeth Agassiz found that, in contrast to Darwin's depiction of the forests as "dusky," "Every trunk, every branch, every fallen log, every stone was cushioned deep in bright green moss." Elizabeth Agassiz's writings about the expedition, although never published in their entirety, were crafted into a series of articles for the *Atlantic Monthly*.

A little over a year after the Agassizes returned from the *Hassler* expedition, Elizabeth Agassiz experienced dual tragedies. Louis Agassiz died unexpectedly, after an illness that had lasted only two weeks. Eight days after Louis Agassiz's death, Alexander's wife, Anna, died, leaving their three young children motherless. Elizabeth Agassiz's attention turned to two consuming tasks—a biography of her late husband and the care and raising of Anna and Alexander's children.

Upon her husband's death, Elizabeth Agassiz began a new chapter in her life. In 1885, she published the biography it had taken her nearly nine years to write, *Louis Agassiz: His Life and Correspondence*, in two volumes. It was also during this period of her life that Elizabeth Agassiz helped establish Radcliffe College. Identifying a need for a school for girls and remembering Elizabeth Agassiz's own previous work on such a school, in 1879, a group of Cambridge women nominated her to chair a committee to sponsor a girl's school affiliated with Harvard. The resulting school became Radcliffe College in 1894, named for one of its early benefactors, and Elizabeth Agassiz became its first president, a position she held until 1903.

An illness in 1904 left Elizabeth Agassiz an invalid, although she still enjoyed reading and recording her thoughts in her daily journal. On June 27, 1907, Elizabeth Agassiz died. It is impossible to completely identify Elizabeth Agassiz's contribution as a nature writer since so much of what she wrote has been folded into and subsumed by Louis Agassiz's own work. Their relationship was without doubt a symbiotic one, which opened up a whole new world for Elizabeth. She had lived thirty years after her husband's death, and although the arc of his career shaped her own early life, her accomplishments, both before and after his death, stand on their own merit.

PRIMARY BIBLIOGRAPHY

Books

A *First Lesson in Natural History*, as Actaea (Boston: Little, Brown, 1859; revised edition, Boston: Ginn & Heath, 1879).

Seaside Studies in Natural History. Marine Animals of Massachusetts Bay. Radiates, by Agassiz and Alexander Agassiz (Boston: Houghton Mifflin, 1865).

A *Journey in Brazil*, by Agassiz and Louis Agassiz (Boston: Ticknor & Fields, 1868).

Louis Agassiz: His Life and Correspondence, 2 vols. (Boston: Houghton Mifflin, 1885).

Selected Periodical Publications— Uncollected

"An Amazonian Picnic," *Atlantic Monthly* 17 (March 1866): 313–23.

"A Dredging Expedition in the Gulf Stream," *Atlantic Monthly* 24 (October 1869): 507–17; 24 (November 1869): 571–78.

"The Hassler Glacier in the Straits of Magellan," *Atlantic Monthly* 30 (October 1872): 472–78.

"In the Straits of Magellan," *Atlantic Monthly* 31 (January 1873): 89–95.

"A Cruise through the Galapagos," *Atlantic Monthly* 31 (May 1873): 579–84.

Biographies

Lucy Allen Paton, *Elizabeth Cary Agassiz: A Biography* (Boston: Houghton Mifflin, 1919).

Louise Hall Tharp, *Adventurous Alliance: The Story of the Agassiz Family of Boston* (Boston: Little, Brown, 1959).

SECONDARY BIBLIOGRAPHY

References

Nina Baym, "Elizabeth Cary Agassiz and Heroic Science," *American Women of Letters and the Nineteenth-Century: Styles of Affiliation* (New Brunswick, NJ: Rutgers University Press, 2002), 91–112.

Linda Bergmann, "A Troubled Marriage of Discourses: Science Writing and Travel Narrative in Louis and Elizabeth Agassiz's A Journey in Brazil," *Journal of American Culture* 18 (Summer 1995): 83–88.

Linda Bergmann, "Widows, Hacks, and Biographers: The Voice of Professionalism in Elizabeth Agassiz's *Louis Agassiz: His Life and Correspondence*," *a/b: Auto/Biography Studies* 12, no. 1 (1997): 1–21.

Vera Norwood, *Made from This Earth: American Women and Nature* (Chapel Hill: University of North Carolina Press, 1993).

Elizabeth Wagner Reed, "American Women in Science Before the Civil War," dissertation, University of Minnesota, 1992.

Papers

The majority of Elizabeth Agassiz's letters and diaries are held in the Schlesinger Library at Harvard University. Other letters are held in Harvard's Houghton Library and the Library of the Museum of Comparative Zoology.

Louis Agassiz
(May 28, 1807–December 14, 1873)

Christoph Irmscher

History has not been kind to Louis Agassiz. For a considerable period of time, he was one of the world's most renowned scientists, equally famous as a paleontologist, ichthyologist, and geologist. He founded and ran a natural history museum and wrote extensively about science, not only for a limited circle of specialists but also for a wider audience, which he hoped would include fishermen and farmers as well as "the students in our colleges" and the "learned professions" (Jules Marcou's biography lists over 400 articles published between 1828 and 1880). "Since Benjamin Franklin," observed his one-time student William James, "we had never had among us a person of more popularly impressive type." In his capacity as professor of Natural History and Geology at Harvard's Lawrence Scientific School, Louis Agassiz, the former protégé of the likes of Alexander von Humboldt and Georges Cuvier, lionized by polite Boston society and admired by scientists abroad, put American biology on the map. Nowadays he is remembered, if at all, for his stubborn resistance to Darwinism and for his assertion, worn thin by repetition, that humans of different races, like different species, should not "interbreed." By the mid-1870s, even the more devoted of his students, including his own son Alexander, had deserted their increasingly embattled master. Two years after his death, the German biologist-philosopher Ernst Haeckel denounced Agassiz as the "most ingenious and most active charlatan in the entire field of science." Modern historians have shown even less compassion for the Harvard scientist, describing him not only as "retrograde" but also intellectually ill-equipped for his forays into realms beyond the boundaries of zoology, "into philosophical regions whose ontological bogs and epistemological swamps had swallowed up better men than he" (Mary Winsor). In Louis Menand's recent assessment, Agassiz spent his life compiling mountains of data on top of which his ideas precariously perched like unfinished buildings ready to topple. Agassiz's science, wrote Menand, "wasn't theoretical and his theory wasn't scientific."

Such negative responses tend to obscure some of the original contributions Agassiz did make, especially in the field of science writing, as Guy Davenport has pointed out. Jean Louis Rodolphe Agassiz was born on May 28, 1807, in a parsonage in Motier, Switzerland, surrounded by the Bernese Alps and the Jura Mountains, in a landscape that continued to inspire him long after his immigration to the United States. As an adolescent, he read Jean-Baptiste Lamarck and Cuvier, compiling extensive notes about the birds, insects, and freshwater fishes he saw and collected in the neighboring woods, lakes, and meadows. An avid hiker and swimmer, Agassiz showed similar determination also in his academic pursuits, defying his parents' wish that he join his uncle's trading company or become a respectable physician. After briefly studying medicine in Zurich, Agassiz transferred to Heidelberg in 1826, where he first learned to use a microscope and encountered the recapitulation theory of the German *Naturphilosophen* (the notion that an individual's fetal life repeats the history of the order to which it belongs). In 1827, Agassiz left Heidelberg for Munich, where, determined to become "the first naturalist of his time," he studied with the embryologists Ignatius Döllinger and Lorenz Oken as well as philosopher Friedrich Schelling, rising to such distinction within a mere year that he was asked to describe and classify the fishes collected from the Amazon River system during the journey his botany professor Karl Friedrich Philipp Von Martius had undertaken with the zoologist Johann B. de Spix from 1817 to 1820. Never shy in matters of self-promotion, the 21-year-old naturalist confidently informed his sister: "Will it not seem strange if the largest and finest book in Papa's library is one written by his Louis?" In May 1829, *Brazilian Fishes,* written in Latin and characterized in Agassiz's own preface as the "first literary essay of a young man," appeared in print, with a timely dedication to Georges Cuvier. On the basis of this book and a mere 18 months after his arrival in Munich, the faculty of the University of Munich awarded Agassiz the title of a Doctor of Philosophy. In April 1830, he dutifully passed both the oral and written examinations in medicine.

Later the same year, Agassiz, who now retained his own natural history illustrator, returned home, with plans for a monograph on all the freshwater fishes of central Europe and a second work, even more comprehensive, on fossil fish and their classification. In the winter of 1831 he traveled to Paris, to consult collections of the Musée d'Histoire Naturelle and to profit from Cuvier's advice on comparative anatomy. Cuvier died of cholera a short time later, anointing Agassiz as a worthy successor by leaving his fish specimens to him. A personal gift from Alexander von Humboldt, who continued to take an interest in Agassiz's career although they would later part ways over Agassiz's racial politics, allowed Agassiz to stay in Paris even after Cuvier's death.

Agassiz was now the most brilliant new star in the crowded skies of European science. Under the influence of Cuvier, his theoretical stance had solidified. Species had to be classified inductively rather than deductively, he believed, through close observation, description, and analysis. But such intensive empirical study would automatically lead the naturalist to appreciate God's direct impact, through special and separate acts of creation, on the order of nature. God's plan for the entire world was established when "man," as Agassiz would later put it, "existed only in the intellectual conception of his Maker."

With a little help from Humboldt, Agassiz secured an appointment as professor of Natural History in Neuchâtel, Switzerland, which also placed him in charge of a newly founded natural history museum. Academically, these were Agassiz's most productive years, although much of his time was taken up with his continuing study of fossil fishes, not completed until 1843. A monumental description and analysis of 1,700 ancient specimens, newly classified on the basis of their scales, *Recherches sur les poissons fossiles* ("Investigations into Fossil Fishes") was dedicated to Agassiz's mentor, Alexander von Humboldt. Agassiz also completed a monograph on the embryology and anatomy of the salmon family (with lithographic plates hand colored after living specimens), compiled a bibliography of books and articles on natural history, and released the *Nomenclator zoologicus,* an index and dictionary of zoological terminology. He began to take an interest in invertebrate animals, describing first the echinoderms of Switzerland and then turning his attention to mollusks. Finally, inspired by a visit to the glaciers of the Rhône Valley and a subsequent trip to the mountains of Scotland, Agassiz developed his theory of the

"Ice Age," a time during the Pleistocene epoch when an advancing sheet of ice covered the world from the North Pole to the borders of the Mediterranean and Caspian seas, wiping out all life on Earth. Retreating north, the ice masses left the world barren, strewn with telltale traces of their existence, such as boulders, striated rocks, and gravel. No one, then, could claim any continuity between ancient and recent forms of life. In a volume intended as a supplement to *Poissons fossiles,* a description of the fish fossils of the "Old Red Sandstone" ("Vieux Grès Rouge") in Scotland and Russia, Agassiz did present an argument that looked as if it confirmed the dreaded notion of "transmutation." He showed that the embryonic stages of recent fish specimens recalled the disposition of the fins in the primitive fossils of the "Red Sandstone." But the assumed coincidence of geological succession, fetal development, and zoological creation depended, Agassiz insisted, not on any "material connection" but solely on "intellectual coherence"—further proof of the wonderful comprehensiveness of God's plan for the world. The full text of the Book of Nature, with all its parallels, quotations, and allusions, was present only in the divine mind. However, patient readers like Louis Agassiz could come close to deciphering it.

In 1840, Agassiz set up an observation post on the glacier of the Aar, which soon became known as the "Hôtel de Neuchâtelois," where he and a growing party of friends spent considerable periods of time surveying, measuring, and analyzing the ice. Agassiz's many commitments had led him to create a veritable "scientific factory" in Neuchâtel, as one of his collaborators said, with a small army of assistants (naturalists, draftsmen, clerks) and a printing press at his disposal. But as would happen many times more in his life, his reach exceeded his grasp. The printing press foundered, and so did his marriage to Cécile Braun, the sister of a German fellow student. Unhappy about her husband's obsessive work habits and suspicious of the increasing influence of his private secretary

Desor on her husband, Cécile departed in 1845, taking her two daughters Ida (born 1837) and Pauline (born 1841) with her back to Carlsruhe, leaving only her ten-year-old son Alexander behind in Neuchâtel. Agassiz was unperturbed:

> Whatever befalls me, I feel that I shall never cease to consecrate my whole energy to the study of nature....I shall always sacrifice everything to it; even the things which men usually value most. (to Charles-Lucien Bonaparte, July 1845)

Relief came in the form of a grant from the Prussian king, Frederick Wilhelm IV, who gave Agassiz $3,000 to study the natural history of the New World. What was intended to be a temporary stay turned into a new career. In the winter of 1846, thousands vied for seats in Boston's Tremont Temple to hear the handsome professor with the charming accent lecture on "The Plan of the Creation, especially in the Animal Kingdom." Eagerly they soaked up the lecturer's message that the entire history of creation, starting with the smallest radiated animal and ending gloriously with man, had been carefully planned by God himself. Agassiz set up house in East Boston, where many of his former collaborators joined him (zoologist Charles Girard, artist Jacques Burkhardt, lithographer Auguste Sonrel), sharing space with turtles, a tame bear, and a family of opossums. Agassiz was elated at the opportunities that life close to the shore offered him, where, for the first time, he was able to observe many of his beloved marine animals "in their natural conditions of existence" (to Elie de Beaumont, August 31, 1847).

Carrying out a long-hatched plan, the president of Harvard University, Edward Everett, persuaded the industrialist Abbott Lawrence to donate $50,000 to found a school of science at Harvard and to sponsor, along with it, a new professorship, intended specifically for the "big-geologico-everythingo-French-Swiss gun," as one contemporary called him. In the fall of 1847, Agassiz accepted the appointment and moved to Cambridge. A few months later, Cécile Agassiz died of tuberculosis in Freiburg. Agassiz's second, "American" marriage to Elizabeth Cary in 1850 opened the doors of upper Boston society to him.

His American colleagues were not prepared for the full power of Agassiz's presence, the mixture of scholarship, ambition, and chutzpah he brought to everything he touched. At the 1849 meeting of the American Association for Advancement in Science in Cambridge, MA, Agassiz delivered no fewer than 27 papers in five days, on topics ranging from geology to comparative embryology. Emerson, who would later rank Agassiz next to Carlyle as one of "my men," was intrigued by the foreign professor's charisma, which he compared to the power of "gravitation over upraised bodies." In the classroom, Agassiz encouraged his students to see for themselves rather than accept knowledge secondhand, and long after his death stories circulated about how he would force his students to continue studying a fish even as it was decomposing before their very eyes, because they had not yet *begun* to describe it (for an example, see Ezra Pound's *ABC of Reading*). Van Wyck Brooks would later call him the "Johnny Appleseed" of American science, but Agassiz might more appropriately be understood as a kind of "benign Captain Ahab of American natural history" (Irmscher). His Barnumesque acquisitiveness soon spanned the entire country. For example, when he announced his intention to publish a "Natural History of the Fishes of the United States," over 6,000 circulars were distributed instructing citizens in the proper mode of collecting and then properly shipping fish to Cambridge.

During these years, Agassiz also explored the links between natural history and anthropology he had pondered ever since visiting the haphazard collection of skulls, the "American Golgotha," compiled by the Philadelphia doctor and self-styled craniologist Samuel Morton. Convinced that human races were "zoologically distinct" like animal species, Agassiz declared at the 1850 meeting of the American Association for the Advancement of Science in Charleston, SC, that people of different skin color "did not originate from a common centre, nor from a single pair." His friend, the poet Henry Wadsworth Longfellow, after listening to one of his public lectures mocked Agassiz's argument: "He thinks there were several Adams and Eves." To prove his claims about the real differences between black and white, Agassiz "pioneered" the use of the camera for pseudo-anthropological purposes: in 1850, he commissioned the Charleston photographer Joseph T. Zealy to produce daguerreotypes of 15 slaves in the nude—a gallery of racial "types" intended to teach the viewer a lesson in racial "inferiority."

Along with Agassiz's politics, his science further hardened into ideology. He was not prepared to meet the challenge of Darwin's *Origin of Species*, sent to him by the author shortly after its publication in 1859, and could not effectively respond to the arguments of Darwin's supporters in America, among them his own colleague, the botanist Asa Gray, who had resented Agassiz's "impulsive character" since 1848. Agassiz's *magnum opus*, the *Contributions to the Natural History of America*, which Agassiz had intended to be a complete account, in ten volumes, of the "mode of life of all our animals" and for which he had garnered some 2,500 subscribers, never got past the turtles and the jellyfish, though the four volumes that were published are among the most beautifully illustrated zoological works of the nineteenth century. Most of Agassiz's energy now went into the Museum of Comparative Zoology, which he had established at Harvard in 1859 and whose burgeoning collections were intended to illustrate his belief that the diversity of life on earth reflected divine creation, not evolution.

Agassiz, who had now become an American citizen, remained active also as the author of popularly written articles on science, becoming one of the busiest contributors to *The Atlantic Monthly*. The time had come, he believed, "when scientific truth must cease to be the property of the few, when it must be woven into the common life of the world." Now the results of science touched "the very problem of existence." Science was not intended, "like the learning of the Egyptians," for an "exclusive priesthood who may expound the oracle according to their own theories, but should make a part of all our intellectual culture and of our common educational systems." Agassiz's essays typically originated in public lectures, and he purposely retained, as he explained in the preface to a collection of his *Atlantic Monthly* articles, titled *Geological Sketches* (1865), "the familiarity induced by the personal relation of a lecturer to his audience, so different from the more distant one of the author to his reading public." Talking as a friend among friends, Agassiz frequently would ask his readers to join him in imaginative exercises requiring an unusual suspension of disbelief. In *Geological Sketches*, for example, he would take his mesmerized American audience back into a time when the Old World was not so old and the New World was not so new. If Europe was then just beginning to rise up out of the Azoic waters, America, though now "so recent in culture and civilization," had been around for much longer. In fact, she was the "first-born" among the continents:

> Hers was the first dry land lifted out of the waters, hers the first shore washed by the ocean that enveloped all the earth beside; and while Europe was represented only by islands rising here and there above the sea, America already stretched an unbroken line of land from Nova Scotia to the Far West.

The global vision of the history of creation offered here became tangible in the cosmopolitan figure of the writer-lecturer himself. What reader would not have followed Agassiz in his or her imagination when invited to stroll with him "along the Silurian beach," back to a time when "the earliest animals and plants" were just being created?

A virtuoso on the blackboard—several photographs show the "Prof" posing next to just completed chalk drawings showing eggs, invertebrate animals, or the metamorphosis of insects—Agassiz also developed a firm, richly illustrative American prose style. One only needs to compare the assertive nature of Agassiz's sentences with the tentative, brilliantly convoluted meanderings of Darwin's "long argument" to recognize that the difference between the two men was not just one of scientific method and temperamental makeup but also of style. "Perhaps my readers will pardon the digression," Agassiz writes in his chapter on "The Growth of Continents" in *Geological Sketches*, "if I interrupt our geological discussion for a moment, to offer them a word of advice, though it be uncalled for." Explaining that he has often been asked about the best way to enter Switzerland, Agassiz offers the following recommendation for the discerning tourist:

> Enter it in the afternoon over the Jura. If you are fortunate, and have one of the bright, soft afternoons that sometimes show the Alps in their full beauty, as you descend the slope of the Jura, from which you command the whole panorama of the opposite range, you may see, as the day dies, the last shadow pass with strange rapidity from peak to peak of the Alpine summits.

So rapidly will this shadow leap from one elevation to the next that it seems "like the step of some living spirit of the mountains." But then, as the brilliant glow of the setting sun over the mountain vanishes, "the strangest effect of all" takes place: a sudden "ashy paleness" grasps the mountains, giving them "a ghastly, chilly look." However, the final sight greeting the American traveler's rapt eye will be "a faint blush that dies gradually into the night." Note Agassiz's subtle use of syntax, whose qualifications mirror the reader's gradual involvement in the dramatic visual spectacle that is unfolding before her eyes. This remembered theater of light ("the glory, the death, the softly succeeding life") over the mountains of Agassiz's childhood becomes a meditation on the timelessness of God's creation, manipulating the reader into accepting a deeper connection between geology and theology. As the complex description of the setting sun demonstrates, change in Agassiz's world is not process. It happens in stages, each of them different from the ones preceding it, each of them infused with the Creator's spirit.

There was no doubt in Agassiz's mind that God himself had dictated the Good Book of Nature. Take his comments on the fossils of crinoids, known as "sea-lilies," in *Methods of Study* (1863), also based mostly on articles published in *The Atlantic Monthly*. In their sheer variety, these small marine animals seem "like the productions of one who handles his work with an infinite ease and delight, taking pleasure in presenting the same thought under a thousand different aspects." Agassiz leisurely contemplates their transformations, "from a close cup to an open crown, from the long pear-shaped oval of the calyx in some to its circular or square or pentagonal form in others" and delightedly imagines the forms yet unknown specimens might take, which he then finds to be just so:

> Since I have become intimate with their wonderful complications, I have sometimes amused myself with anticipating some new variation of the theme, by the introduction of some undescribed structural complication, and then seeking for it among the specimens at my command, I have rarely failed to find it in one or the other of these ever-changing forms.

Agassiz eliminates the element of surprise from the study of natural history; the scientist finds in nature only what he already knows must be there. Appropriately, Agassiz compares the relation between the scientist and nature to that of a child with his puzzle:

> The world is the geologist's great puzzle-box; he stands before it like the child to whom the separate pieces of the puzzle remain a mystery till he detects their relation and sees where they fit, and then his fragments grow at once into a connected picture beneath his hand.

If thought and study are needed to unravel the facts of life, then "it must have required an intelligent mind" to create these facts.

As *Methods of Study* shows, Agassiz was genuinely enthralled by the beauty of his specimens, admiring, for example, the gradual expansion of a holothurian (a sea cucumber), whose coloring he thinks is more beautiful than the plumage of a tropical bird or a butterfly's wing:

> Slowly, almost imperceptibly, as it becomes accustomed to its new position, it begins to elongate; the fringes creep softly out, spreading gradually all their ramifications, till one end of the animal seems crowned with feathery, crimson sea-weeds of the most delicate tracery.

Nature has its humorous side, too. By the same token, though, most readers will only reluctantly follow Agassiz when entreated to "try to forget" such beautiful animals "in their individuality" and think about the place of holothurians within God's well-ordered taxonomic whole. In Agassiz's writings, the stubborn peculiarity of the objects described—a beautiful sunset, a jellyfish, a glacier—always exceeded the framework of the ordering system Agassiz wanted to impose on it, just as the specimens in his museum continued to elude his grasp, where, to the despair of his son and successor, "Alex" Agassiz, barrels of unclassified objects were piling up in the basement.

In April 1865, Agassiz, supported by a grant from the wealthy businessman Nathaniel Thayer and accompanied by a party of volunteers that also included the 23-year-old William James, Agassiz traveled to Brazil to find evidence of Pleistocene glaciation, collect large numbers of freshwater fish, and thus prove, once and for all, that species really did not change or migrate. Significantly, the results of the trip were shared with the readers back home chiefly in a popular book written by his wife Elizabeth, *Journey in Brazil*. In his wife's admiring vignettes, Louis Agassiz is portrayed as a kind of latter-day, steam-propelled Columbus, the eager harbinger of American superiority on the Amazon river, surrounded by hordes of devoted natives proffering natural history specimens.

A different story emerges from William James's letters home, which represent the Harvard professor as a somewhat pompous "General Sherman" in command of lackluster troops and morbidly fascinated by the specter of Brazilian miscegenation, which he attempted to document in numerous photographs. In an appendix to *Journey in Brazil* about "Permanence of Characteristics in Different Human Species," Agassiz applied what he termed the "natural history method" to humans of different races, darkly warning his readers in postslavery America once again of the dangers of racial "interbreeding."

The last decade of Agassiz's life was marked by growing health problems and constant haggling for museum funds, though he characteristically also embarked on a new project, the Penikese summer school in natural history, which took place in Buzzard's Bay, Massachusetts, from May to July 1873 and became the subject of John Greenleaf Whittier's poem, "The Prayer of Agassiz." In 1871, Agassiz and his wife departed for their last expedition in search of proof against Darwin. At the behest of Benjamin Peirce, head of the U.S. Coast Survey, the *Hassler,* a deep-draft, doubled-hulled experimental research ship that frequently broke down, took Agassiz's party down the eastern seaboard and along the Atlantic Coast of South America, retracing Darwin's famous *Beagle* voyage. Agassiz visited the Galapagos, where he found nothing explained and the "mystery of change, with such marked and characteristic differences between existing species" only deepened (to Peirce, July 29, 1872). He remained staunchly resistant to Darwinian theory, as long as it involved the "transition of one species into another" and the idea that variations could be transmitted from parent to offspring. In his last essay, "Evolution and Permanence of Type," Agassiz declared that the facts of nature were as "sacred as a moral principle." The question of the origin of life was still open, Agassiz observed. Darwin's theory was "conjectural," perhaps not even "the best conjecture possible in the present state of our knowledge." One month before

his essay appeared, a worn-out Agassiz died, aged only 66. He was laid to rest in Mount Auburn cemetery in Cambridge. The most appropriate tribute from a contemporary came not from a fellow scientist but from poet James Russell Lowell. In a long commemorative poem dripping with sentiment ("Uprooted is our mountain oak"), Lowell offered one pertinent observation: Agassiz had had a "poet's eye," he said, which "takes a frank delight in all it sees."

PRIMARY BIBLIOGRAPHY

Selected Books/Monographs

Selecta genera et species piscium: quos in itinere per Brasiliam annis MDCCCXVII-MDCCCXX jussu et auspiciis Maximiliani Josephi I...peracto collegit et pingendoes curavit Dr. J.B. de Spix...digessit descripsit et observationibus anatomicis illustravit Dr. L. Agassiz (Munich: C. Wolf, 1829–).

Recherches sur les poissons fossiles, 5 vols. of texts and 5 atlases [18 parts] (Neuchâtel: Petitpierre, 1833–1843).

Monographies d'échinodermes, vivans et fossiles (with Edouard Desor and G. Valentin), 4 parts (Neuchâtel: aux frais de l'auteur, 1838–1842).

Histoire naturelle des poissons d'eau douce de l'Europe centrale (with Carl Vogt). Atlas of 41 plates and 2 vols. of text (*Embryologie des Salmones; Anatomie des Salmones*) (Neuchâtel: aux frais de l'auteur, 1839–1845).

Études sur les glaciers (Neuchâtel: Jent et Gassmann, 1840).

Études critiques sur les mollusques fossiles, 2 parts (Neuchâtel: Petipierre; Wolfrath, 1840–1845).

Nomenclator zoologicus, 26 parts (Solothurn: Jent et Gassmann, 1842–1846).

Monographie des poissons fossiles du Vieuz Grés-rouge ou Système Dévonien [Old Red Sandstone] *des îles Britanniques et de Russie,* 3 parts (Neuchâtel: A Sonrel, 1844–1845).

An Introduction to the Study of Natural History (New York: Greeley and McElrath, 1847).

Nouvelles études et experiences sur les glaciers actuels, leur structure, leur progression et leur action physique sur le sol (Paris: V. Masson, 1847).

Principles of Zoology: Touching the Structure, Development, Distribution, and Natural Arrangement of the Races of Animals, Living and Extinct (with A. A. Gould) (Boston: Gould and Lincoln, 1848).

Bibliographia zoologicae et geologicae: A General Catalogue of All Books, Tracts, and Memoirs on Zoology and Geology, ed. H.E. Strickland, 4 vols. (London: Ray Society, 1848–1854).

Twelve Lectures on Comparative Embryology, Delivered before the Lowell Institute, in Boston, December and January, 1848–1849 (Boston: Henry Flanders, 1849).

Lake Superior: Its Physical Character, Vegetation, Animals, Compared with Those of Other and Similar Regions (with J. Elliot Cabot et al.) (Boston: Gould, Kendall and Lincoln, 1850).

Contributions to the Natural History of the United States of America, 4 vols. (Boston: Little, Brown, and Co., 1857–1862).

An Essay on Classification (London: Longman, Brown, Green, etc., 1859).

Methods of Study in Natural History (Boston: Ticknor and Fields, 1863).

Geological Sketches (Boston: Ticknor and Fields, 1866).

The Structure of Animal Life: Six Lectures Delivered at the Brooklyn Academy of Music in January and February, 1862 (New York: Charles Scribner, 1866).

A Journey in Brazil (with Elizabeth Agassiz) (Boston: Ticknor and Fields, 1868).

Geological Sketches: Second Series (New York: James R. Osgood, 1876).

Selected Articles in Periodicals

"The Diversity of Origin of the Human Races," *Christian Examiner* 49 (July 1850): 110–45.

"Prof. Agassiz on the Origin of Species," *American Journal of Science and Arts* 30 (July 1860): 142–55.

Letters

Elizabeth Cary Agassiz, ed., *Louis Agassiz: His Life and Correspondence*, 2 vols. (Boston: Houghton Mifflin, 1886).

Elmer Charles Herber, ed., *Correspondence between Spencer Fullerton Baird and Louis Agassiz, Two Pioneer Naturalists* (Washington, DC: Smithsonian, 1963).

SECONDARY BIBLIOGRAPHY

Biographies

Lane Cooper, *Louis Agassiz as Teacher* (Ithaca, NY: Comstock, 1917; revised ed. 1945).

Edward Lurie, *Louis Agassiz: A Life in Science* (Baltimore: Johns Hopkins University Press, 1960).

Jules Marcou, *The Life, Letters, and Works of Louis Agassiz*, 2 vols. (New York: Macmillan, 1896).

Louise Hall Tharp, *Adventurous Alliance: The Story of the Agassiz Family of Boston* (Boston: Little, Brown, and Co., 1959).

References

Van Wyck Brooks, *The Flowering of New England* (New York: E.P. Dutton, 1952).

Guy Davenport, ed., *The Intelligence of Louis Agassiz: A Specimen Book of Scientific Writings* (Boston: Beacon, 1963).

Ralph Waldo Emerson, *Emerson in His Journals*, ed. Joel Porte (Cambridge, MA: Harvard University Press, 1982).

Ernst Haeckel, *Ziele und Wege der heutigen Entwicklungsgeschichte* (Jena: H. Dufft, 1875).

Christoph Irmscher, *The Poetics of Natural History: From John Bartram to William James* (New Brunswick, NJ: Rutgers University Press, 1999).

William James, "Louis Agassiz," *Science*, N.S. 5 (19 February 1897): 285–89.

Samuel Longfellow, ed., *The Life of Henry Wadsworth Longfellow, with Extracts from His Journals and Correspondence*, 3 vols. (Boston: Houghton Mifflin, 1891).

James Russell Lowell, "Agassiz," *The Atlantic Monthly* 33 (May 1874): 586–96.

Louis Menand, *The Metaphysical Club: A Story of Ideas in America* (New York: Farrar, Straus, and Giroux, 2001).

Ezra Pound, *The ABC of Reading* (London: Faber, 1934).

Mary P. Winsor, *Reading the Shape of Nature: Comparative Zoology at the Agassiz Museum* (Chicago: University of Chicago Press, 1991).

Manuscripts

The major repository of Agassiz's papers is Harvard University, with significant collections held by the Houghton Library, the University Archives, and the Museum of Comparative Zoology. The official Letter Books of the Museum of Comparative Zoology at Harvard contain some 1,300 letters by Agassiz. His "ethnographic" albums of photographs taken in South Carolina and Brazil are in the archives of the Peabody Museum at Harvard University.

John James Audubon
(April 26, 1785–January 27, 1851)

Deborah Lawrence

Audubon was an artist, a hunter, a scientist, and a nature lover. Although he did not think of himself as an accomplished writer, Audubon's journals, letters, autobiographical essays, and volumes of natural history are a significant contribution to American nature writing. With his regard for anatomical correctness and precision, he distinguished himself by his scrupulous attention to detail. Remarkably neglected by scholars of nineteenth-century American literature, Audubon's writings are a pioneering effort to define our American wild lands.

The only written work Audubon intended for publication was *The Ornithological Biography*. Never republished in its original form, it was edited by Audubon's wife, Lucy, and his Scottish collaborator William MacGillivray. His granddaughter Maria Audubon wrote out her own edited version of Audubon's journals and then burned the originals. Only three of the original journals survive. These surviving manuscripts, however, cover pivotal episodes in Audubon's career. The first journal begins on October 12, 1820, just after he boarded a flatboat bound from Cincinnati to New Orleans. During the course of this trip, the 35-year-old Audubon changed his bird-sketching avocation into a vocation. By the end of 1821, Audubon was a determined artist. Not published until 1967, the second surviving journal manuscript is the one he kept from 1826 until 1829. It details another leave taking from his family, this time to go to England, Scotland, and France to arrange for the publication of the Double Elephant Folio *Birds of America*. The third journal he kept from 1840 until 1843 while he worked to secure a sound financial future for his family while completing the smaller Octavo edition of *Birds of America*. Audubon was a compulsive correspondent, and a large number of his letters survive, especially from the years 1826 to 1840, the period when he worked on *The Birds of America* and *Ornithological Biography*. These unedited letters demonstrate his conversational, anecdotal, and uninhibited style. Frequently confessional, they are filled with strong emotion, alternating between despair and giddy enthusiasm.

Audubon's life is the epitome of Romanticism. He was born in Les Cayes, Santo Domingo, in 1785 to Jean Audubon, French sea captain and trader, and one of his mistresses, Jeanne Rabin, a French chambermaid who died six months after giving birth. When he was three years old, Audubon accompanied his father to Nantes, France, where his father's wife, Anne Moynet Audubon, raised him. In 1803, the year Meriwether Lewis and William Clark were preparing to leave on their journey across the American continent, Audubon was 18 years old and in jeopardy of being drafted into the Napoleonic

Wars. To escape conscription, Audubon was sent to America to oversee his father's farm, Mill Grove, in Montgomery County, 24 miles northwest of Philadelphia. Living the life of a country gentleman, Audubon spent his time walking in the woods, hunting, and drawing birds. He collected all kinds of wildlife specimens, which he preserved, wired in characteristic postures, and then sketched.

At the age of 20, Audubon returned to France for a year in order to gain his father's approval to marry Lucy Bakewell, the daughter of an Englishman who owned Fatland Ford, an estate adjoining Mill Farm. He returned to Pennsylvania in April 1806, accompanied by Ferdinand Rozier, a family friend from Nantes. The two young men decided to head west to make their fortunes. They traveled to Pittsburgh and then by flatboat down the Ohio River to Louisville.

While Rozier's account of the trip gives scant attention to the landscape, Audubon investigates the artistic potential of the nonfictional travel narrative by rendering a seductively charming landscape. Audubon is emotionally involved and caught up by the beauty of the place. He claims that his mind was "affected by strong emotions, and wandered far beyond the present moments." More typical of travel writing of the period, Rozier maintains an aloof and disengaged mentality by treating the experiences of the journey retrospectively. The sleeping accommodations at the taverns along the way were poor, the roads were miserable, and the flatboat was cumbersome. Contemptuous of travel, Rozier records the discomforts of the trip from a point outside the action and after the fact. In contrast, Audubon details the beauty of the sights and sounds along the shore from a position within the narrative. According to Audubon, night comes, "sinking to the darkness the broader portions of the river" and tinkling bells tell him that cattle in nearby valleys are in search of food. He hears the "hooting of the Great Owl, or the muffled noise of its wings" as it sails smoothly over the stream. The juxtaposing journey accounts clarify not only the differences between the partners, but the contrast between the early American traveler who affirms the safety and comfort of home and journeyers like Audubon who seize the opportunities offered by adventure and who affirm travel as an end in itself.

Audubon married Lucy on April 5, 1808, and on her wedding trip from Pennsylvania to Louisville, she, like Rozier, complained of the length of the trip and the deprivations along the way. Once arrived she was thoroughly disenchanted with the place. She was lonely, Audubon was always at the store, Louisville did not have a library or bookstore, and she did not care for Rozier. In contrast, Audubon's journal entries praise the abundance of the land and the hospitality of the people (*Audubon and His Journals* 1: 28). However, instead of standing behind the counter as Lucy had thought, he was frequently roaming the woods, shooting, and drawing birds. They were his passion. Lucy once ruefully admitted, "I have a rival in every bird." Later Audubon would reminisce about this period of his life:

> I spent much Money and One Year of My [sic] as Happy as the Young bird; that having Left the Parents sight carolls Merily, While Hawks of All Species are Watching him for an easy prey. (*Mississippi River Journal*, November 28, 1820)

Audubon's first son, Victor Gifford Audubon, was born in 1809. That same year, while tending his store, Audubon met Alexander Wilson. The artist-naturalist had come to Kentucky to get subscribers for his illustrated compendium of American birds, *American Ornithology*. In Audubon's sketch of their meeting in the episode titled "Louisville in Kentucky," he writes that he was about to sign his name to Wilson's list of subscribers when Rozier interrupted him in French and told him not to sign, saying, "My dear Audubon, what induces you to subscribe to this work? Your drawings are certainly far better, and again, you must know as much of the habits of American birds as this gentleman." Although "vanity" and the persuasion of his friend kept him from signing, their brief meeting inspired Audubon's growing passion for studying birds by sketching.

In 1810, Rozier and the Audubons moved to the rough frontier town of Henderson, Kentucky, to manage a general store. Wearing leather hunting shirt and pants and moccasins, Audubon again spent most of his time in the woods, hunting and drawing birds. In the winter of 1810, Rozier dissolved their partnership. Audubon opened a mill with his wife's brother, Tom Bakewell, as a partner. Audubon's second son, John Woodhouse Audubon, was born in 1812. That same year Audubon was awarded United States citizenship. In 1819, the mill failed; Audubon declared bankruptcy and was jailed briefly for debt. After working as a portraitist, art teacher, and taxidermist in Cincinnati, Ohio, he decided to launch a full-time pursuit of America's birds and their habitats. Audubon believed he could surpass Wilson's work by correcting his errors, cataloguing birds he had missed, and providing readers with more background detail. However, in order to comprehensively catalogue and document American wildlife, he needed to encounter his subjects personally whenever possible and in their natural habitat. To do so, he had to spend time in the woods, away from the distractions of civilization.

With his gun, his dog Dash, and a young apprentice, Joseph Mason, Audubon left his family to the charity of friends and took off down the Ohio and Mississippi rivers to New Orleans in search of birds. In his journal entry of October 12, 1820, Audubon wrote: "Without any Money My Talents are to be My Support and My enthusiasm my Guide in My Difficulties, the whole of which I am ready to exert to keep, and to surmount." Most important among the opportunities provided by the trip down the Mississippi is that Audubon has the time to increase his knowledge of the drawing and dissecting of birds. In his journal, he included a short autobiographical sketch for his sons Victor and John. In it, he attempted to justify his ambitious project and the resulting hardship to his family by claiming that he had this dream even as

a youth. "Ever since a Boy I have had an astonishing desire to see Much of the World & particularly to Acquire a true Knowledge of the Birds of North America," he wrote (*Mississippi River Journal*, November 29, 1820). From the beginning of his associations with Rozier, Audubon had felt keenly the conflict between the stifling effect of managing a business and developing his own drawing interests. The journey provided him with the freedom to turn his attention from the burdens of supporting a home and family to the opportunities of exploring his art.

Audubon's journal of his trip down the Mississippi documents his early career. Despite his failed business ventures, he reveals in his entries a stubborn determination to fulfill his dream of finding and painting every specimen of bird he comes across. His energy and originality make his journal entries, and his nature writing in general, pulse with life. He is rarely the detached observer. His details are filtered through his presence and the lens of his emotion. Seeing a flock of 50 swans leaves him indescribably "happy and void of care." When he examines the eggs of the Pewee Flycatcher, the parent birds allow him to come within a few yards of the nest. The initiator of bird-banding in North America, Audubon becomes so familiar with these birds that he is not only able to handle the young, but to attach silver threads around their legs.

In his writing, Audubon gives the birds human emotions. The Canada Goose is shy; the male Passenger Pigeon is pompous. After the turkey hens lay their eggs, the males are clumsy and slovenly. The mockingbird "approaches his beloved one, his eyes gleaming with delight, for she has already promised to be his one and only." As Audubon plots to kill the Golden Eagle, the bird sits defiantly from his "post of martyrdom."

Audubon attempts to recreate their bird-calls so that the armchair reader not only can see the birds but also can hear them from his drawing room. The crane's "kewrr, kewrr, kewrooh" is delightful to his ear. The Ivory-Billed Woodpecker utters a loud "pait, pait,

pait." The notes of the Passenger Pigeon "resemble the monosyllables kee-kee-kee-kee, the first being the loudest, the others gradually diminishing in power." And the great horned owl's call sounds "like the last gurglings of a murdered man."

Not only does Audubon strive to make his readers see and hear the birds, but also he sets them in the birds' environment. The biographical essay on the Ivory-Billed Woodpecker typifies Audubon's attention to background detail:

> I wish, kind reader, it were in my power to present to your mind's eye the favourite resort of the Ivory-billed Woodpecker. Would that I could describe the extent of those deep morasses, overshadowed by millions of gigantic dark cypresses, spreading their sturdy moss-covered branches, as if to admonish intruding man to pause and reflect on the many difficulties which he might encounter, should he persist in venturing farther into their almost inaccessible recesses.

Here is the heroism of the solitary naturalist who treads dangerous ground in order to provide a precise firsthand report of the birds and their habitat. Certainly before him in American literature there is nothing like Audubon's detailed, engaged, and emotional account. Seeking to create realistic depictions of birds in their natural setting, Audubon's explorations would eventually lead to the Dry Tortugas, Labrador, and the Gulf Coast from Florida to Texas. The years he spent tracking and painting birds culminated in his project, *The Birds of America.*

In 1826, after failing to find an American publisher for his work, Audubon went to England. Together with English engraver Robert Havell, he published his life-size Double Elephant Folio *Birds of America* (1827–1838). The publication featured sheets measuring 29 and 1/2 inches by 39 and 1/2 inches, which allowed Audubon to represent the birds in life size. Unquestionably the greatest work on birds ever produced, the four-volume classic illustrated 1,055 bird specimens from 489 species. Audubon's

desire to make his work more affordable led him to begin the first Octavo Edition, printed and hand-colored by J.T. Bowen in Philadelphia between 1840 and 1844.

Intended initially as descriptive text to accompany the engravings, *Ornithological Biography* (5 volumes, 1831–1839) was prepared in collaboration with the Scottish naturalist William MacGillivray, professor of comparative anatomy at Edinburgh University. The bird biographies evince Audubon's scrupulous eye for detail. He describes not only the appearance, habitat, movement, sounds, and anatomical measurements of each bird, but the discomfort and danger he has as a result of his attempts to procure his information for his readers. For example, in his essay on the Ivory-Billed Woodpecker, Audubon describes the "dangerous nature of the ground" he has had to tread. The many difficulties that he had to encounter in the woods in order to get to "almost inaccessible recesses" is little appreciated, Audubon complains, by the "idle fops" who bemoan the loss of a shilling as they saunter "through the Exhibition rooms of the Royal Academy of London, or any equally valuable repository of art." In the essay on the White-Crowned Sparrow, Audubon describes the dangers he experienced in a secluded glen near the Gulf of St. Lawrence. However, notes "so sweet, so refreshing, so soothing, so hope inspiring . . ." reward him for his discomfort. The self-portrait he gives us is that of the free-spirited artist-backwoodsman who is dedicated to the pursuit, understanding, and appreciation of unspoiled landscapes and abundant wildlife.

The bird biographies are particularly significant today because they detail species that are now extinct. One of Audubon's best-known passages concerns the flocks of passenger pigeons whose migrations would blacken the sky for days at a time. Repulsed by the farmers' ill-advised killing of the birds, Audubon describes one aftermath:

> The pigeons were picked up and piled in heaps, until each had as many as he could

possibly dispose of, when the hogs were let loose to feed on the remainder.

In a biography of another extinct species, he noted with alarm the rapid depletion of the Carolina Parakeet, the only parrot native to the United States. He wrote:

The Parakeets are destroyed in great numbers, for whilst busily engaged in plucking off the fruits or tearing the grain from the stacks, the husbandman approaches them with perfect ease, and commits great slaughter among them.

In the early editions of the *Ornithological Biography* Audubon interspersed 60 "Delineations of American Scenery and Manners," referred to by Audubon in a letter of December 3, 1834, as "episodes." Later, when he published the smaller octavo edition (1840–1844), the episodes were left out. Although these semiautobiographical, semifictional stories about pioneer life on the American frontier contain some of his most vivid writing, Audubon felt that they might ruin his reputation as a naturalist. Many of these short personal essays are taken directly from the journals, some are reminiscences of his early explorations in Kentucky and Louisiana, and a few are stories he had heard from acquaintances. Audubon was an avid reader of Scott, Cooper, and Irving, and his episodes have many characteristics of early American Romanticism. The authenticity of each portrait is derived by Audubon's insertion of himself in the scene. One episode, for example, recounts a meeting between Audubon and Daniel Boone. Before bedding down for the night, Boone tells Audubon a story of his being captured by Indians in Kentucky. Although Audubon probably never met Boone, and Boone's story of his capture by Indians was a well-known tale by the time Audubon tells it, the epsiode gains authenticity because Audubon is supposedly hearing it from Boone himself. His goal in the episodes, as in his other nature writing, was to capture not objective nature, but the dramatic in nature and thereby stimulate in his readers an excitement about birdlife and nature in

general. And this is his contribution to American nature writing. Audubon did not simply record data. He dramatized the wilderness by interweaving fact and autobiographical vignette. Readers of Audubon are able to enter the nineteenth-century American wilderness. He not only lets them see the great diversity of wildlife, but they can hear the voice of nature in his writing.

Audubon's 1826 journal was first published, together with his journals from 1827, 1828, and 1829, as part of the section titled "The European Journals" in *Audubon and His Journals* (1897). These journals record a genuine degree of posturing. To appeal to a European audience, Audubon adopted the pose of the American woodsman. His wolf-skin clothing, his long hair curling down about his shoulders, and his frontier vernacular reflected his deficient education and inferior social position. And yet significantly, Audubon contemplates the superiority of western life to the decadence and wealth of Europe. In a letter to his son Victor, he described the difference between America and the Old World:

The superfluity of refinement here is of itself a source of wonder inexhaustible, but the unbounded freedom of our beloved America will be for ever preferred by me.

In a letter to his wife, he assures her that he would never abandon his country, "rough as it is." He writes: "America will always be my land. I never close my eyes without traveling thousands of miles along our noble streams; and traversing our noble forests." While he found the meticulously ordered European gardens appealing, he preferred the freedom of the unkempt American wilderness. He complained that England's pears and apples were the size of American green peas and that London's zoological garden contained fewer natural wonders than he would be able to find in a single morning spent in an American swamp.

In addition to the posturing, the 1826 journal reveals a genuine tension between Audubon's desire for society and fame and his feelings of inferiority and loneliness for his family; it expresses his longing to return to the American woods before they were irreparably damaged and the wildlife destroyed. Audubon's journal entry, fictively addressed to Sir Walter Scott, is prophetic:

> Oh Walter Scott, where art thou? Wilt thou not come to my country? Wrestle with mankind and stop their increasing ravages on Nature, and describe her now for the sake of future ages. Neither this little stream, this swamp, this great sheet of flowing water, nor these mountains will be seen in a century hence as I see them now. Nature will have been robbed of her brilliant charms. (Ford, *1826 Journal*, 388–89)

Audubon recognized the necessity for writers such as Scott to record the beauty of the wilderness before it literally vanished. Whereas Audubon's later nature writing frequently lacks the spontaneity and intensity of his earlier prose, virtually all of the later work manifests his increasing concern for the vanishing wilderness. He saw the country's trend toward urbanization. Although he was a compulsive hunter, he was aware of the importance of the environment and the dangers of unlimited killing. In the first episode, "The Ohio," Audubon connects the need for an environmental literary history with the rapidity with which the wilderness is being destroyed:

> I feel with regret that there are on record no satisfactory accounts of the state of that portion of the country, from the time when our people first settled it. This has not been because no one in America is able to accomplish such an undertaking. Our Irvings and our Coopers have proved themselves fully competent for the task. It has more probably been because the changes have succeeded each other with such rapidity, as almost to rival the movement of their pen.

Audubon's ecological concerns are further illustrated in the episode "Scipio and the Bear." Audubon relates the story of a bear hunt that begins with an enthusiasm to kill a bear family in retaliation for the bears'

destruction of a field of corn. The vignette concludes with the juxtaposition of the narrator's description of the cruel killing of the bears and the comment that the hunters are more destructive to the fields than the bears.

Upon completion of his *Birds of America*, Audubon began his last project, *The Viviparous Quadrupeds of North America*. To research this work, he secured passage up the Missouri on a steamboat that departed in the spring of 1843. He was 58 years old, and he knew this would be his last long excursion. Significantly, it would lead him farther west than he had ever been. *The Missouri River Journal* records Audubon's travels from St. Louis up the river and into Indian and buffalo territory. On June 13, 1843, he arrived at Fort Union, a federal outpost close to the confluence of the Missouri and Yellowstone Rivers. Like his Labrador journal (1833), the *Missouri River Journal* is less dramatic than his earlier notebooks, but it is, nevertheless, valuable for its vivid descriptions. Although he and his men are caught up in hunting, he observed in his journal that the prairies were littered with the carcasses of buffalo and complained that this killing for sport would lead to their extinction. And yet, Audubon, toothless and aging, gets caught up in the excitement of the hunt. He records in his journal how he danced on his back to lure an antelope within gunshot: "I lay on my back and threw my legs up, kicking first one and then the other foot, and sure enough the Antelope walked towards us, slowly and carefully." Although Audubon admired the way the Indians were able to hunt the depleted buffalo, he did not romanticize them. In fact, he criticized writers and painters who glamorized the character of the Indian and the harshness of their existence. He called painter George Catlin's book "altogether humbug" for doing so.

The *Quadrupeds of North America* was issued as lithographs in both large portfolio in 1845–1848 and a smaller, multivolume edition in 1854. About half of the original drawings for the work were by Audubon; the rest were by his son John. Both sons, John and Victor, worked with John Bachman on the accompanying text. Audubon died on January 27, 1851, at his home on the Hudson. He is buried in Trinity Cemetery at 155th Street and Broadway in New York City. A tall runic cross marks his grave.

In 1886, Lucy Audubon's former student George Bird Grinnell, the editor of *Fish and Stream*, founded the first Audubon Society. A conservation-environmental group, the Audubon Society's mission is in part to promote interest in birds and their protection. In the past hundred years there have been more than a dozen Audubon biographies. He is a protagonist in Eudora Welty's short story "A Still Moment" and the subject of two book-length poetic sequences: Robert Penn Warren's *Audubon: A Vision* and Pamela Alexander's *Commonwealth of Wings: An Ornithological Biography Based on the Life of John James Audubon*. However, despite Audubon's lingering popularity, his nature writing has been remarkably overlooked.

PRIMARY BIBLIOGRAPHY

Books

The Birds of America, from the Original Drawings by John James Audubon, 4 vols. (London: Published by the Author, 1827–1838).

Ornithological Biography, or an Account of the Habits of the Birds of the United States of America, accompanied by descriptions of the objects represented in the work entitled The Birds of America, and interspersed with delineations of American scenery and manners, 5 vols. (Edinburgh: Adam and Charles Black, 1831–1839).

The Birds of America from Drawings made in the United States and its Territories, 7 vols. (New York and Philadelphia: the Author and J.B. Chevalier, 1840–1844).

The Viviparous Quadrupeds of North America, 3 vols., in collaboration with the Reverend John Bachman (New York: V.G. Audubon, 1845–1848).

Journal of John James Audubon Made During His Trip to New Orleans in 1820–1821, ed. Howard Corning (Boston: Club of Odd Volumes, 1929).

Journal of John J. Audubon Made While Obtaining Subscriptions to his "Birds of America," 1840–1843, ed. Howard Corning (Cambridge: The Club of Odd Volumes, 1929).

Letters of John James Audubon, ed. Howard Corning, 2 vols. (Boston: The Club of Odd Volumes, 1930).

The 1826 Journal of John James Audubon, edited by Alice Ford (Norman: University of Oklahoma Press, 1967).

Selected Editions

Maria R. Audubon, ed., *Audubon and His Journals*, 2 vols. (New York: Charles Scribner's Sons, 1897).

Alice Ford, ed., *The Bird Biographies of John James Audubon* (New York: The Macmillan Company, 1957).

Alice Ford, ed., *Audubon, by Himself: A Profile of John James Audubon, from Writings Selected, Arranged, and Edited* (New York: The Natural History Press, 1969).

Ben Forkner, ed., *John James Audubon: Selected Journals and Other Writings* (New York: Penguin, 1996).

Francis Hobart Herrick, ed., *Delineations of American Scenery and Character by John James Audubon* (New York: G.A. Baker and Company, 1926).

Christoph Irmscher, ed., *John James Audubon: Writings and Drawings* (New York: The Library of America, 1999).

Richard Rhodes, ed., *The Audubon Reader* (New York: Everyman's Library, 2006).

Scott Russell Sanders, ed., *Audubon Reader: The Best Writing of John James Audubon* (Bloomington: Indiana University Press, 1986).

SECONDARY BIBLIOGRAPHY

Selected Biographies

Alexander Adams, *John James Audubon* (New York: G.P. Putnam's Sons, 1966).

Stanley Clisby Arthur, *Audubon, An Intimate Life of the American Woodsman* (New Orleans: Harmanson, 1937).

Lucy Audubon, *The Life of John James Audubon*, ed. R. Buchanan (London: Sampson Low, Son & Marston, 1868).

Robert Buchanan, *Life and Adventures of Audubon, the Naturalist*, edited from material supplied by his widow (London: Sampson Low, Son & Marston, 1869).

John Burroughs, *John James Audubon* (Boston: Small, Maynard, 1902; Woodstock, NY: The Overlook Press, 1987).

John Chancellor, *Audubon: A Biography* (New York: Viking, 1978).

Alice Ford, *John James Audubon: A Biography* (New York: Abbeville Press, 1988).

Ella M. Foshay, *John James Audubon* (New York: Harry N. Abrams, 1997).

Francis Hobart Herrick, *Audubon the Naturalist*, 2 vols. (New York: D. Appleton and Co., 1917).

Clark L. Keating, *Audubon: The Kentucky Years* (Lexington: University Press of Kentucky, 1976).

Richard Rhodes, *John James Audubon: The Making of an American* (New York: Knopf, 2004).

William Souder, *Under a Wild Sky: John James Audubon and the Making of The Birds of America* (New York: North Point Press, 2004).

Shirley Streshinsky, *Audubon: Life and Art in the American Wilderness* (New York: Villard Books, 1993).

References

Pamela Alexander, *Commonwealth of Wings: An Ornithological Biography Based on the Life of John James Audubon* (Middletown, CT: Wesleyan University Press, 1991).

Edward H. Dwight, "The Autobiographical Writings of John James Audubon," *Bulletin of the Missouri Historical Society* 19 (October 1962): 26–35.

Michael Harwood and Mary Durant, *On the Road with John James Audubon* (New York: Dodd, Mead, and Company, 1980).

Alton A. Lindsey, *The Bicentennial of John James Audubon* (Bloomington, IN: Indiana University Press, 1985).

John Francis McDermott, ed., *Audubon in the West* (Norman: University of Oklahoma Press, 1965).

Gary A. Reynolds, *John James Audubon and His Sons* (New York: Grey Art Gallery and Study Center, 1982).

Barbara M. Stafford, *Voyage into Substance: Art, Science, Nature, and the Illustrated Travel Account, 1760–1840* (Cambridge, MA: MIT Press, 1984).

Robert Penn Warren, *Audubon: A Vision* (New York: Random House, 1969).

Margaret C. Welch, "John James Audubon and his American Audience: Art, Science, and Nature, 1830–1860" (PhD dissertation, University of Pennsylvania, 1988).

Eudora Welty, "A Still Moment," in *The Collected Stories of Eudora Welty* (New York: Penguin Books, 1983).

Papers

John James Audubon's letters, private papers, and manuscripts can be found principally at the American Museum of Natural History, New York; American Philosophical Society Library, Philadelphia; the Audubon Museum, Henderson, Kentucky; the Charleston Museum, Charleston, South Carolina; the Filson Club Historical Society, Louisville, Kentucky; Princeton University Library, Princeton, New Jersey; The Royal Scottish Academy, Edinburgh; Tulane University, Howard-Tilton Memorial Library, New Orleans, Louisiana; The Beinecke Rare Book and Manuscript Library, Yale University, New Haven, Connecticut; and the Field Museum, Chicago, Illinois.

Florence Merriam Bailey
(August 8, 1863–September 22, 1948)

Kandi Tayebi

Florence Merriam Bailey's work as an ornithologist and nature writer began in her early twenties and continued until she was 76 years old. While most of her work focuses on the observation of birds and their habits, she also wrote about the human inhabitants of the West and their cultures. Throughout her career, she combined the science of ornithology with a style that encouraged popular audiences to study and appreciate birds. Her *Handbook of Birds of the Western United States* became the standard text for ornithology for 25 years and was illustrated by one of the most famous nature illustrators of the time, Louis Agassiz Fuertes. As a lifelong lover of nature, she worked for more than 50 years to preserve the birds throughout the United States, developing local Audubon Societies, leading bird-watching classes for community members, and supporting ecological education for young people through Boy Scouts and other organizations. Critics in the past have focused on her latter more scientific works, ignoring her early writings, but critics currently are reexamining her works not only for their scientific interest but as a form of nature writing that built upon and challenged that being done by John Burroughs.

On August 8, 1863, Florence Merriam was born the youngest of four children in Locust Grove, New York, to Clinton Merriam, a Republican Congressman, and Caroline Hart Merriam, a Rutgers graduate and amateur astronomer. Her sister, Gertrude, died at the age of five the day before Florence was born. Reared on a rural farm in upstate New York and educated largely at home, Florence Merriam was encouraged by her family to pursue her interest in natural history. While her mother introduced her to astronomy, her brother Hart, who later was to become the chief of the U.S. Biological Survey, invited her to trap and collect animals and plants, thus teaching her anatomy and biology. Hart's collection of animal skins and bones grew so large his father had to build a three-story museum to house them. Florence's aunt Helen from her father's side lived nearby and collected plant specimens for her herbarium, encouraging Florence and her brothers to explore the woods. Her father also showed great interest in the wildlife surrounding their home and was a friend of naturalist John Muir, who shared his theory on glacial activity in Yosemite Park with Merriam's father in a letter. Walking in the woods and sitting patiently for hours watching the birds, she developed the instincts of a naturalist, and, at the same time, encouraged by her brother Hart, she began to write down her observations. This combination of appreciation of her natural surroundings and closely detailed observations serves as the basis for most of her nature writing.

In 1882, Merriam left home to attend Smith College. Because she lacked much formal schooling, she was allowed to enter Smith College only as a nondegree student. Although her passion remained natural history, the school offered few science classes, and therefore she took mostly courses in languages and literature. Yet she still showed a desire to write a thesis on Charles Darwin and evolution and identified Ralph Waldo Emerson as the most influential person on developing her philosophy. While at Smith, she became an ardent environmentalist after reading about birds killed to decorate women's hats. Millions of birds were killed during the 1880s to support this fashion craze, and Merriam decided to found the first Smith College Audubon Society in order to help educate women about the importance of birds. She recruited John Burroughs to lead student nature walks at Smith, sent out thousands of circulars attacking the use of birds and their feathers for decoration, and wrote articles protesting the killing of birds for fashion in the local papers. In three months, one-third of the campus or about 100 women had joined the Smith College Audubon Society.

By 1885, she became the first woman associate member of the American Ornithologists' Union, which was organized partly in order to protect bird species from extinction. In the same year, she wrote an article for the College Science Association about birds observed in the area and their habits, which was reprinted in part by two local newspapers. What began as articles in journals and newspapers would later be collected into her first book, *Birds Through an Opera Glass* (1889), which described how to recognize various birds and chronicled her experiences as a bird watcher. The book received excellent reviews in journals such as *Auk* and *The Atlantic Monthly* and became popular during the 1890s.

Merriam's first book would build the foundation on which her later work rested. Although popular, this book was classified by critics as children's literature, having been issued by Houghton Mifflin's Riverside Press in a series entitled "The Riverside Library for Young People." The book is modeled after Burroughs' *Wake-Robin*, but, unlike Burroughs, she critiques the methods of the predominantly male ornithological establishment. While Burroughs writes unapologetically about killing birds in order to study them, Merriam calls for observing live birds in their natural habitats. She encourages readers to observe the natural world and record their observations, advocates camouflage for scientific observation, and discusses the importance of interactions between humans and birds. During her lifetime, most ornithologists studied birds as specimens in public and private collections. In fact, many naturalists found that shooting the birds was the only way to ensure correct classification in various species. When confronted with difficult-to-observe birds, Merriam patiently watched with her opera glass, making herself as unobtrusive as possible. She found it profoundly absurd to shoot the bird in order to name it.

Like Charles Darwin and John Burroughs, Merriam anthropomorphizes the birds. Her first book compares bird watching to people watching and describes the bird's behavior as typical Victorian human behavior. Therefore, nesting goldfinches are described as a couple expecting its first baby, and the female black-throated blue warbler is described as a woman forced to take on her husband's name. Critics have focused much of their criticism of her works on this method of describing bird behavior.

Throughout her life, Merriam's health was fragile, and she sought a cure in the fresh air out West in Utah, California, and Arizona. Her travels resulted in a cure of what was probably tuberculosis as well as several books chronicling her travels and the birds she encountered. While traveling in Utah, she met with several Mormon women who lived in a community practicing polygamy and listened to their stories. This trip resulted in *My Summer in a Mormon Village* (1894), her first book that focused on a travel narrative instead of on educating people about birds, but which still combined descriptions of nature with social commentary. While recuperating at her uncle's ranch in San Diego County, she wrote *A-Birding on a Bronco* (1896), which described the wild birds of California. Her uncle's land was covered with wildflowers that attracted hummingbirds, a species that at the time was being killed and sold to collectors for their skins. She also observed the natural environment of southern California being changed by progress, as buildings were built over natural areas; yet, she was still able to document a wide range of birds. Riding on horseback, she found that the birds did not fly away but allowed her to approach unobserved. With this book, she began her long collaboration with the noted nature illustrator Louis Agassiz Fuertes. By this time, the bird population in California had declined to about half of what it had been 15 years earlier, so Merriam decided to write a book to educate children about birds. The resulting *Birds of Village and Field* (1898) suggested careful observation and that educating children was one method which could stop the indiscriminate killing of birds.

By this time, Merriam had made a name for herself in the world of ornithology. She was listed in *Who's Who in America* in 1900, and through her work with Hart at the Biological Survey, she had developed a friendship with Vernon Bailey, the chief naturalist working for Hart. They were married on December 16, 1899, and began their lifelong travels together. During the same time, her friend Frank Chapman created the popular journal of ornithology *Bird-Lore,* and Florence Merriam Bailey contributed several articles to it, along with most of the prominent American writers on birds. The newlywed couple traveled throughout the Southwest, studying wildlife, recording their observations, and producing articles for various journals. Vernon and Florence camped simply, without watch fires and out under the stars. One of Bailey's most popular articles "Meeting Spring Halfway," in *Condor,* described her travels with Vernon

through Texas from Texarkana to Corpus Christi to Brownsville and finally to the Mexico line and back into California. She detailed the plants, animals, and birds along the way. The article was finally serialized in 1916. In her writings, Bailey tries to keep the image of the real bird alive and not let it get lost in Latin terminology and scientific observation.

By 1900, Bailey had begun her most extensive writing project, *Handbook of Birds of the Western United States* (1902), which was her first work to include scientific terminology and precise descriptions of bird appearances, reproductive behavior, and distribution. Frank Chapman reviewed her book in *Bird-Lore,* stating that it was "the most complete textbook of regional ornithology" (November–December 1902). The popularity of the book among laymen and scientists sent the book into 17 editions and became a guide for later writers in the field, including Roger Tory Peterson.

In 1903, Bailey went to New Mexico to aid her husband in making a detailed biological survey of the Territory of New Mexico. Teddy Roosevelt wanted to protect the wild natural areas and create a forest preserve in the mountains north of Taos, and the survey was supposed to help justify the move. During this trip, Bailey began her work on what would become the 800-page *Birds of New Mexico* (1928). Critics view this work as her most significant contribution to ornithology. The original study was begun by Wells W. Cooke, who died. Bailey finished the work and published it under her own name with credit to Cooke in the introduction. The book begins with the first recorded account of birds by white men in the territory in 1540. Later, in 1961, when J. Stokley Ligon published his book on New Mexico's birds, he paid tribute to Bailey, calling her the "greatest American woman ornithologist." Her book covered many birds previously unknown before the publication of her work and earned her the American Ornithologists' Union's Brewster Medal for the most important book on birds of the western hemisphere and eventually an honorary doctorate from the University of New Mexico, in 1933.

In 1907, Bailey returned to California to San Juan Capistrano where she discovered a natural area already filling with people and machines. This trip would provide her with her first close look at water birds and would expose her to more indiscriminate hunting, which she despised. Although not completely against hunting, she, throughout her writings, shows a dislike of hunters who kill for no reason and who allow the birds to suffer. In honor of Bailey's work in ornithology, Joseph Grinnell in 1908 named a new subspecies of chickadee after her: *Parus gambeli baileyae*, the Pacific mountain chickadee. Years later, Randolph (Pat) Jenks named an unmapped volcanic formation sacred to the Arizona Indians after her: Bailey Crater. Her writings on birds would garner her a position as the first woman fellow in the American Ornithologists' Union, the "highest honor to which an American ornithologist can attain," according to Elliott Coues, another fellow, and an honorary bachelor's degree from Smith College in June 1921, 35 years after she left school.

Vernon and Florence Bailey not only traveled together but also collaborated on several books, the most comprehensive of which was *Wild Animals of Glacier National Park: The Mammals by Vernon Bailey, The Birds by Florence Merriam Bailey* (1918). Although she also contributed to Vernon's book *Cave Life of Kentucky Mainly in the Mammoth Cave Region* (1933), the couple usually traveled together but published separately. Most of Vernon's work was published as government documents while Florence's became journal articles and books. Over the course of their marriage and travels together, she published 11 books and more than 100 journal articles. They developed a pattern of wintering in Washington, D.C., where Florence hosted parties for local scientists and politicians, and summering all over the West doing fieldwork. Their travels took them to North Dakota, Texas, New Mexico, Oregon, California, and many other regions. She studied the birds while he focused on the mammals.

Always their relationship was intimately tied to nature. Acquaintances of the couple stated that they both greeted each other with imitations of songbirds' calls. Although the couple never was able to have children—Florence suffered several miscarriages—they were involved in the education of children through Boy Scouts, the Audubon Society, and Florence's writings aimed at young people. In 1942, Edward Preble in *Nature Magazine* would describe their relationship as based on "working together, and working for others, whether in natural-history studies, or in any field—social, educational, or humane—that called for cooperative effort."

Throughout her life, Bailey would continue to support her brother Hart's work at the Biological Survey. Because the Biological Survey was part of the Agriculture Department, it was necessary for some of the research to focus on how to help ranchers and farmers. Hart asked Bailey to research and report on economic ornithology, the usefulness of birds to farming. From 1896 until the end of her career, Bailey wrote articles for *Audubon* focusing on the benefits of birds for farming and ranching. She continually noted how progress in the West was encroaching on the habitat of birds and endangering their existence and that the birds were humankind's best hope of combating the insects that were killing crops. In Oregon in 1914, she observed the loss of habitat for the birds that occurred because of logging, and she saw her articles as a way not only to help classify species of birds but also to encourage an appreciation of the birds and thus a reason for protecting their environment. To educate people about the beneficial uses of birds, she published two articles in *Bird-Lore*, "The Red-headed Woodpecker" (1910) and "The Tufted Titmouse" (1913), which were later reprinted by the National Association of Audubon Societies as Educational Leaflets. She produced her largest series of magazine articles in 17 installments over five years in *Condor* about North Dakota birds, striving once again to introduce the general public to the birds she had learned to love. She advocated encouraging the growth of bird populations in order to attack the problem of insect infestations that at the time were damaging many crops in the United States, particularly in the West where the abundant vegetation often brought with it a vigorous insect world.

Her educational efforts would continue throughout her lifetime. She was the only female instructor for the Association of Ornithologists' Union classes open to the public. These classes were extremely popular when they were established in 1900, but continued to grow throughout the rest of the decade. Bailey also helped train teachers through the Audubon Society of the District of Columbia. She believed that training teachers was one of the most effective ways to ensure the education of schoolchildren.

In 1929, the Baileys were commissioned to do a study on the wildlife of the Grand Canyon, which resulted in her last book *Among the Birds in the Grand Canyon Country* (1939). In her usual manner, Bailey encouraged readers outside ornithology to appreciate and explore the birds of the region. At the age of 66, Bailey still walked throughout the canyon observing birds, but declined to take a trip with Vernon and a team from the University of Arizona to San Francisco Mountain near Flagstaff, writing to Hart that "it would be too strenuous for me to keep up with a lot of young folks." During this trip, she came to appreciate the other wildlife in the canyon and recorded observations of the behavior of the squirrels. The canyon contained two types of squirrel, the Abert squirrel on the South Rim and the Kaibab on the North Rim. Bailey was intrigued by the Abert squirrels who buried pine cones. She realized that this behavior was an important method of distribution of pine seeds and wrote her findings up in the *Journal of Mammalogy* (1932).

In 1933 Vernon Bailey retired from the Biological Survey, and the Baileys retired to a newly built homestead in southern California. They envisioned themselves continuing their work in the relatively comfortable space of their own land. Vernon Bailey worked on

developing a more humane trap called the VerBail trap. Florence was vehemently against the use of the steel trap and wanted its use abolished in favor of the more humane traps of her husband. Vernon received prizes from the American Humane Association for his invention. A year later, they returned to their Washington, D.C., house. Smith College planned Bailey's class's 50th reunion, which she would miss in order to take one last extensive trip through the West. She described her trip to her friends at Smith College:

> New Mexico and Arizona gave us fossil forests, the prehistoric ruins of Mesa Verde, Mexican adobes and Indian pueblos....The party left us in California in our home cabin where forty years ago I wrote "A-Birding on a Bronco."

Bailey would use this trip to pass on her love of the outdoors and her desire to study wildlife to her grandnieces.

In September 1940, Bailey and her husband were recognized for their contribution to the study of wildlife by *Condor*, which published their photograph with a caption that read, "Florence Merriam Bailey and Vernon Bailey, far known for their long time devotion to the study of birds and mammals." Margaret Rossiter in *Women Scientists in America* would rate the Baileys as one of the 49 most "notable couples in science before 1940."

Bailey would lose both her beloved brother Hart and, two months later, her husband in 1942. After her husband's death, she no longer took field trips to the West but continued to enjoy the birds on long walks by her home. On September 22, 1948, Florence Merriam Bailey died in her Washington, D.C., home.

Florence Merriam Bailey holds an important position in environmental writing, not only as a scientist but also as a nature writer. Her writings helped enfranchise women, children, and uneducated people in the world of science and thus reshaped the study of ornithology. She moved the study of birds from the museum and laboratory to the field, from dead specimens to living birds. Like Rachel Carson, who combined literature and science and who humanized the animal world, Bailey displayed an intuitive love of nature and a scientific understanding of its workings.

PRIMARY BIBLIOGRAPHY

Books

Birds Through an Opera Glass (Boston: Houghton Mifflin, 1890).

My Summer in a Mormon Village (Boston: Houghton Mifflin, 1894).

A-Birding on a Bronco (Boston: Houghton Mifflin, 1896).

Birds of Village and Field (Boston: Houghton Mifflin, 1898).

Handbook of Birds of the Western United States (Boston: Houghton Mifflin, 1902).

Bird Classes of the Audubon Society of the District of Columbia, 1898–1912 (Washington, D.C.: ASDC, 1912).

Wild Animals of Glacier National Park: The Mammals by Vernon Bailey, The Birds by Florence Merriam Bailey (Washington, D.C.: Government Printing Office, 1918).

Bird Classes of the Audubon Society of the District of Columbia, 1913–1922 (Washington, D.C.: ASDC, 1922).

Birds Recorded from the Santa Rita Mountains in Southern Arizona (Berkeley: Cooper Ornithological Club, 1923).

Birds of New Mexico (Santa Fe: New Mexico Department of Game and Fish, 1928).

Among the Birds in the Grand Canyon Country (Washington, D.C.: Government Printing Office, 1939).

Other

Vernon Bailey, "Birds," in *Cave Life of Kentucky Mainly in the Mammoth Cave Region* (Notre Dame: Notre Dame University Press, 1933; reprinted from *The American Midland Naturalist* 14.5 [1933]: 385–635).

Frank Chapman, "Biographical Sketches," in *Handbook of Birds of Eastern North America* (New York: D. Appleton and Co, 1895).

Mrs. L.W. Maynard, "Introduction," in *Birds of Washington and Vicinity* (Washington, D.C.: n.p., 1898).

Some Needs of Public Education in the District of Columbia (Memorial to Congress, Executive Council, Public Education Association of the District of Columbia. Washington, D.C.: Government Printing Office, 1905).

Selected Periodical Publications— Uncollected

"Our Smith College Audubon Society," *Audubon Magazine* 1 (1887): 175–78.

"Hints to Audubon Workers: Fifty Common Birds and How to Know Them," *Audubon Magazine* 1 (1887): 108–13, 132–36, 155–59, 181–85, 200–204, 224–26, 256–59, 271–77.

"Interesting Nesting Sites of a Winter Wren," *Auk* 7 (1890): 407.

"Our Piazza Boarder," *American Agriculturist* 49 (August 1891): 449–50.

"Around Our Ranch-House," *Observer* 7 (January 1896): 1–5.

"A Sensible Hummingbird," *Our Animal Friends* 23 (February 1896): 133–34.

"Notes on Some of the Birds of Southern California," *Auk* 13 (April 1896): 115–24.

"How Birds Affect the Farm and Garden," *Forest and Stream* 47 (August 1896): 103–4, 123–24, 144–45.

"A True Observer (Mrs. Olive Thorne Miller)," *Observer* 7 (1896): 291–295.

"The Snowbird at Home," *Observer* 7 (1896): 499–502.

"Trade Rats and Coyotes," *Forest and Stream* 2 (January 1897): 5.

"Clark's Crows and Oregon Jays on Mount Hood," *Bird-Lore* 1 (April 1899): 46–48.

"The Spring Migration of Birds," *St. Nicholas* 27 (May 1900): 644–45.

"How to Conduct Field Classes," *Bird-Lore* 2 (June 1900): 3, 83–87.

"The Scissor-tailed Flycatcher in Texas," *Condor* 4 (March 1902): 30–31.

"The Harris Hawk on His Nesting Ground," *Condor* 5 (May 1903): 66–68.

"Additional Notes on the Birds of the Upper Pecos," *Auk* 21 (July 1904): 349–63.

"A Dusky Grouse and Her Brood in New Mexico," *Condor* 6 (July–August 1904): 87–89.

"Additions to Mitchell's List of the Summer Birds of San Miguel County, New Mexico," *Auk* 21 (October 1904): 443–49.

"Breeding Notes from New Mexico," *Condor* 7 (March 1905): 39–40.

"Notes from Northern New Mexico," *Auk* 22 (July 1905): 316–318.

"A Nest of *Empidonax difficilis* in New Mexico," *Condor* 8 (September 1906): 108.

"Nesting Sites of the Desert Sparrow," *Condor* 8 (September 1906): 111–12.

"White-throated Swifts at Capistrano," *Condor* 9 (November 1907): 169–72.

"Memories of a Frontierswoman," *Outlook* 95 (July 30, 1910): 744–47.

"An Irrigated Ranch in the Fall Migration," *Condor* 12 (September 1910): 161–63.

"The Red-headed Woodpecker," *Bird-Lore* 12 (March–April, 1911): 86–89.

"The Oasis of the Llano," *Condor* 13 (March–April 1911): 42–46.

"Haymakers of the Rock Slides," *Forest and Stream* 76 (April 8, 1911): 530–31.

"Birds of the Cottonwood Groves," *Condor* 14 (July–August 1912): 113–16.

"With Asio in the Greenwood," *Bird-Lore* 15 (September–October 1913): 285–90.

"The Tufted Titmouse," *Bird-Lore* 15 (November–December 1913): 394–97.

"A Family of North Dakota Marsh Hawks," *Bird-Lore* 17 (November 1914): 431–38.

"Characteristic Birds of the Dakota Prairies," *Condor* 17 (September–October 1916): 173–79; 17 (November 1916): 222–26; 18 (January 1917): 14–21; 18 (March 1917): 54–58.

"Feeding the Birds," *Oregon Sportsman* 4 (January 1916): 22.

"Meeting Spring Half Way," *Condor* 18 (July 1916): 151–55.

"Birds of River, Forest and Sky," *Mazama* 5 (December 1916): 41–47.

"Red Letter Days in Southern California," *Condor* 19 (September 1917): 155–59.

"A Return to the Dakota Lake Region," *Condor* 20 (January 1918): 24–37; 20 (March 1918): 64–70; 20 (May 1918): 110–14; 20 (July 1918): 132–37; 20 (September 1918): 170–78; 21 (January 1919): 3–11; 21 (May 1919): 108–14; 21 (July 1919):157–62; 21 (September 1919): 189–93; 21 (November 1919): 225–30; 22 (January 1920): 21–26; 22 (March 1920): 66–72; 22 (May 1920): 103–8.

"Cactus Wrens' Nests in Southern Arizona," *Condor* 24 (September 1922): 163–68.

"Christmas Thoughts of the Birds," *Every Child's Magazine* (December 1924): 282.

"Some Plays and Dances of Taos Indians," *Natural History* 24 (1924): 84–95.

"Red Willow People of the Pueblos," *Travel* 45 (September 1925): 10–13.

"Plumage of the Black Swift," *Murrelet* 12 (March 1931): 2, 55.

"Abert Squirrel Burying Pine Cones," *Journal of Mammalogy* 13 (May 1932): 2, 165–66.

"Birds of the Southwest," *Nature Magazine* (February 1934): 76–80.

SECONDARY BIBLIOGRAPHY

References

Julie Dunlap, "Florence Merriam Bailey," in *Notable Women in the Life Sciences: A Biographical Dictionary*, ed. Benjamin F. Shearer and Barbara S. Shearer (Westport, CT: Greenwood Press, 1996), 27–31.

Felton Gibbon and Deborah Strom, eds., *Neighbors to the Birds: A History of Birdwatching in America* (New York: Norton, 1988).

Jen Hill, "The Best Way Is the Simplest: Florence Merriam and Popular Ornithology," in *Such News of the Land: U. S. Women Nature Writers*, ed. Thomas S. Edwards and Elizabeth A. DeWolfe (Hanover: University Press of New England, 2001), 110–19.

Harriet Kofalk, *No Woman Tenderfoot: Florence Merriam Bailey, Pioneer Naturalist* (College Station: Texas A&M University Press, 1989).

Harriet Kofalk, "Florence Merriam Bailey," in *American Nature Writers*, ed. John Elder (London: Charles Scribner's Sons, 1996), 53–62.

Paul H. Oehser, "Florence Augusta Merriam Bailey," in *Notable American Women*, ed. Edward T. James (Cambridge, MA: Harvard University Press, 1971).

Edward A. Preble, "Vernon Bailey Passes," in *Nature Magazine* (June–July, 1942), 329.

Margaret W. Rossiter, *Women Scientists in America* (Baltimore: Johns Hopkins University Press, 1982).

Beverly Seaton, "Florence Merriam Bailey," in *American Women Writers*, ed. Lina Mainiero (New York: Frederick Ungar Publishing Company, 1979), 91–93.

Deborah Strom, ed., *Birdwatching with American Women* (New York: W.W. Norton, 1986).

Papers

Florence Merriam Bailey Papers (82/46), in Bancroft Library, University of California at Berkeley.

Letters, Class of 1886, 1886–1947, in Smith College, Northampton, MA.

John Bartram
(May 23, 1699–September 22, 1777)

Tom J. Hillard

John Bartram is remembered as one of the first and greatest botanists of colonial America. Spanning a career of more than 40 years, his work with plants profoundly influenced eighteenth-century American scientific communities. Among his many claims to fame, he served as a founding member of the American Philosophical Society, and he corresponded with an impressive international network of renowned scientists and thinkers. Some consider his identification of reproductive structures in plants to be his greatest contribution to botany. Despite these notable accomplishments, it is important to note that John Bartram never had any literary pretensions; to him, writing was primarily a means of communication—scientific or otherwise. Because of this, literary scholars have largely passed him over. Ironically, his importance as a literary naturalist has also been overshadowed by the literary successes of his famous son, William Bartram. Regardless of these critical hurdles, his contributions to natural history writing reflect an important period of writing about the natural world. In his lifetime, two travel diaries containing his naturalist observations were published in England, and he wrote a number of brief articles for contemporary scientific journals. Bartram's voluminous correspondence (recently collected in an 800-page edition) offers more conclusive evidence of his importance and influence among eighteenth-century thinkers. Moreover, biographer Thomas P. Slaughter has argued rightly that

> John Bartram's garden, the plants he collected, the journals he wrote, his correspondence, and, most importantly, his personal style and patient instruction of others in the ways of nature made him the most beloved American naturalist of his day.

Bartram's grandparents were Quaker followers and admirers of William Penn, and they sailed from Derbyshire, England, to Philadelphia in 1683. His father William was one of the children accompanying them on the voyage. Upon arrival in the colonies, his grandparents helped found the small village of Darby just west of Philadelphia, and there the elder Bartram (John's grandfather) purchased 300 acres, began a prosperous farm, and soon became a respected leader in the community. On March 22, 1696, the son William Bartram (John's father) married Elizah Hunt, a daughter of neighbors who owned land at Kingsessing. John Bartram, their first child, was born on May 23, 1699, near their farm at Darby, Pennsylvania.

Relatively little is known about John's earlier years, but the information available suggests a difficult and often sad childhood. The young Bartram was a sensitive child who, according to biographers Edmund and Dorothy Berkeley, not only suffered from chronic "indigestion and heartburn," but also feared thunderstorms—a fear that remained with him throughout his life, despite his lengthy travels and time spent outdoors. In October 1701, his mother Elizah died from complications several weeks after the birth of her second child, James. His father remarried in 1707, to Elizabeth Smith, whose father was "out of unity" with Darby Meeting (the local congregation of Quakers); consequently, William Bartram was likewise declared so in 1708. This falling out with the Darby Quakers prefigures similar troubles that John Bartram would himself have in later life. William later left Pennsylvania for Carolina with his wife and his newborn daughter Elizabeth; together they moved to a Quaker settlement in Bath County. Ironically, it was good fortune that John was left behind. Tensions on the Carolina frontier were high, and Indians attacked the region on September 22, 1711. William was killed, and Elizabeth and her two children (William, Jr., was born in June 1711) were taken captive, to be ransomed later in 1712.

Despite these traumatic experiences, John Bartram led an otherwise ordinary, Quaker childhood. He attended Quaker school in Darby, which had become compulsory in 1692. There he received a practical education. His interest in science began at an early age, but he struggled from lack of a knowledgeable teacher and no textbooks. He dreamed of learning and working in the areas of "Physick" and surgery, but the close ties between plants and medicine soon led him toward botany. Consequently, the family farm life agreed with him.

In 1723 John Bartram married a young Quaker woman named Mary Maris, and they soon had two children: Richard (1724) and Isaac (1725). Tragedy struck again, however, when both Mary and young Richard died in the same year, 1727. In the meantime, Bartram had inherited a large estate from his grandmother, and even though he claims in his writing to be poor, he lived well and

prosperously. After the loss of his wife and son, he purchased even more land: 112 acres in Kingsessing, on the west bank of the Schuylkill River (near Philadelphia). There he established an impressive homestead, enlarging the house on the property and eventually creating what has now become the oldest living botanical garden in the United States (Bartram's Gardens is now operated by the John Bartram Association). Bartram's early years at the Kingsessing home were characterized by a hard work ethic; there he practiced and learned impressive farming skills. He also learned to carefully observe the natural systems of the region, noting particularly the relationships between soil and plants, land use and erosion—observations that indicated the direction he would head in life, and ones that anticipate the science of ecology long before such a discipline was formally named. Such themes would also often appear in his writing.

With the success of his farm and his remarriage, to Ann Mendenhall, in 1729, Bartram soon needed to expand his estate. Over the next decades he continued to enlarge his landholdings, which aided the rapidly growing family. The couple eventually had nine children together: James (1730), Moses (1732), Elizabeth (who died as an infant, 1734), Mary (1736), twins Elizabeth and William (1739), Ann (1741), John (1743), and Benjamin (1748).

Bartram's career as botanist and scientist really began in 1733, when a mutual friend introduced him to Peter Collinson, a London textile merchant with a passion for plants and gardening. Collinson, working in England, stood at the forefront of British interest in exotic plants; his network of merchants shipped specimens from all over the world, but Collinson had long lacked a trustworthy American supplier. When they met through correspondence in 1733, Collinson and Bartram became long and fast friends; it soon became clear to Collinson that Bartram, having already gained a reputation as a botanist, was just the man to do his collecting on the American continent. Bartram and Collinson never met face to face, but their correspondence was frequent and lengthy, so much so that the vast majority of Edmund and Dorothy Berkeley's *The Correspondence of John Bartram, 1734–1777* contains letters exchanged between these two men. Their epistolary relationship would last over 35 years. This important friendship with Collinson helped Bartram in two primary ways. First, it gave Bartram an entrée into the larger international scientific community of the eighteenth century, to which Collinson was already well connected. Bartram would eventually befriend such intellectual notables as Carolus Linnaeus, Cadwallader Colden, Mark Catesby, John Gronovius, Peter Kalm, John Fothergill, Hector St. John de Crèvecoeur, and Benjamin Franklin. Second, the collecting assignments provided Bartram with employment beyond his farming. He first began collecting seeds and plant specimens for Collinson on behalf of Robert James, 8th Baron Petre, who shared horticultural interests with both Collinson and Bartram. By the late 1730s, Bartram was collecting an annual salary to cover travel expenses for his botanizing missions. During these years he traveled extensively both locally and afar, including a journey to the source of the Schuylkill River (1736) and trips to Maryland and Virginia into the Shenandoah Valley (1738). In 1738 he gained international attention when he discovered ginseng along the Susquehanna River, which had until then been known to grow only in the Far East. All the while, at home and abroad, Bartram was observing and studying the natural world, enlarging his knowledge any way he could, and making a reputation for himself along the way.

John Bartram's first and most famous "literary" production originated from one of these collecting voyages in which he traveled into present-day New York and Canada in 1743. The volume bears the title *Observations on the Inhabitants, Climate, Soil, Rivers, Productions, Animals, and other matters worthy of Notice. Made By Mr. John Bartram, In his Travels from Pensilvania to Onondago, Oswego and the Lake Ontario In Canada.* Diplomat and translator Conrad Weiser was leading a group to Onondaga (the Iroquois "capital") for peacekeeping purposes. Encouraged by Collinson, Bartram accompanied this party (as did cartographer Lewis Evans) because he had long desired to explore the relatively uncharted Indian land to the north. The voyage began on July 3, 1743, and lasted roughly two months. Bartram scrupulously kept a daily journal of his observations of plants, animals, landforms, and Native cultural practices. When the voyage ended, Collinson distributed Bartram's journal among his friends, who were eager to read the naturalist accounts of America. Bartram had no intention to publish this manuscript, but nevertheless Collinson sent it to the printers without his knowledge. Consequently, John Bartram unknowingly became the author of his first book in 1751.

Bartram's *Observations* is a slender volume, and compared to many other accounts of eighteenth-century natural history and travel, it does lack a certain literary refinement. In the "Preface" to the original edition, Richard Jackson notes that Bartram's "stile is not so clear as we could wish, however, in every piece of his, there are evident marks of much good sense, penetration, and sincerity, join'd to a commendable curiosity." In spite of this common criticism of Bartram's prose, the book provides powerful examples of this important moment of pre-Revolutionary natural history. For example, his entries are often brimming with the rhetoric of use. In the lands yet unsettled by England, Bartram imagines a future of cities, towns, and other developments— even though he knew those areas had long been settled by Native Americans. Observing the settlement of Oswego, he comments that "a good englishman cannot be without hopes of seeing these great lakes become one day accustomed to *English* navigation." And although the book's daily entries typically offer a spare, chronological account, some of Bartram's observations are especially noteworthy to the genre of natural history writing, such as this one made on July 15:

We set out on a N. E. course, and passed by very thick and tall timber of beach, chesnut, linden ash, great magnolia, sugar-birch, sugar-maple, poplar, spruce and some white pine, with ginseng and maidenhair; the soil black on the surface, and brown underneath, the stones a brown grit, the way very uneven over fallen trees, abundance of hollows, and heaps of earth, turned up by the roots of pros-trate timber: hence it is that the surface is principally composed of rotten trees, roots, and moss, perpetually shaded, and for the most part wet, what falls is constantly rotting and rendring the earth loose and spungy, this tempts abundance of yellow wasps to breed in it, which were very troublesome to us through-out our journey....

In a move typical of his writing, Bartram begins with a standard catalogue of natural resources and then hints at a related natural process (in this case of soil formed from fallen trees). He then mentions how those plants and soil types create a habitat for a particular species: the yellow wasp. In this way, Bartram links animals to places, processes to plants. In so doing, *Observations* demonstrates—as Bartram had been doing for years in his own farming practices—an awareness of natural systems and complex interdependencies.

Bartram acquired even more attention with a second publication in 1751. When Thomas Short was putting together a third edition (and first American edition) of his *Medicina Brittanica*, a compendium of medici-nal knowledge, Bartram supplied a brief preface about the history and uses of plants as medicine. He also wrote an appendix as well as copious notes throughout the book about ways to use and prepare medicinal plants. Though less influential in the literary world, Bartram's work in the *Medicina Brit-tanica* has left a lasting impression in the medical field; modern critics have noted that some of his suggestions about plants are still used in medicine even today.

In addition to these first two book publica-tions, in the 1740s Bartram also began to publish regularly in contemporary scientific journals. Many of these articles, usually no more than a page or two in length, were first directed to Peter Collinson, who often pre-sented them before the Royal Society in Lon-don. Later, several appeared in the Royal Society's *Philosophical Transactions*, in Lon-don's *Gentleman's Magazine*, and in Benjamin Barton's *Medical and Physical Journal*. Nota-bly, few of Bartram's periodical publications concerned botany, which is a testament to his far-ranging scientific abilities. The articles cover such varied topics as wasps, mayflies, rattlesnake teeth, mussels, earth-quakes, and even the phenomenon of aurora borealis. In fact, his theories about river for-mation, ancient flooding, and his concept of a "geologic survey" have caused Francis D. West to call him, deservedly, the "first American-born geologist." Taken together, Bartram's articles demonstrate the breadth of his inquisitive mind and help situate him in the international scientific community of the mid-eighteenth century.

At the same time he was publishing in this variety of fields, Bartram's seed collecting business was also expanding rapidly. By the early 1850s he was regularly shipping out "seed boxes" overseas, and among the patrons supporting these ventures were some of "England's, Ireland's, and Scotland's most influential and wealthy men, able to afford elaborate and extensive gardens," according to the Berkeleys' biography. By this time, word of exotic southern plants enticed him, and Bartram at last was able to make two journeys to the Carolinas between 1760 and 1762. While there, he toured gardens, made important contacts, and gathered a host of new specimens and seeds. As could be expected of one so motivated, the more Bar-tram traveled, the more he collected, and the more widely his sphere of influence fell. In fact, after years of botanical service to En-gland, in 1765 he at last received the official recognition that he had wanted for so long: King George III named Bartram "the King's Botanist." It was thus—as Royal Botanist for the King of England—that John Bartram made his famous journey into Florida (which had recently been acquired from France) in 1765. At 66 years old, with his sight beginning to fail him, and assisted by his son William, he traveled as far south as St. John's River. The mission of the father and son, according to a *Pennsylvania Gazette* article printed in the Berkeleys' biography, was to "discover the curious and most valuable vegetable and mineral Productions of these Countries."

During Bartram's lifetime, the journal he kept on that voyage was printed in two different versions. The first was published in *Gentleman's Magazine* in 1767 and incorrectly credited to his son William as "An extract of Mr. Wm [sic] Bartram's Observations in a journey up the River Savannah in Georgia, with his son, on discoveries." That same year another version of the same journal appeared as an addendum to the second edition of William Stork's *An Account of East-Florida with a Journal, Kept by John Bartram of Philadelphia, Botanist to His Majesty for the Floridas; upon a Journey from St. Augustine up the River St. John's.* Again, interestingly enough, Bartram intended for neither of these accounts to be published. The first had been sent to press by Collinson, who had received a copy of the journal, and the second was the work of Governor James Grant, of Florida. The longer version in *An Account*, critics generally agree, was heavily edited and thus does not quite reflect Bartram's actual journal. Still, it represents a similar narrative as his *Observations* of 1751, one that aims to take stock of natural resources in a previously unknown region. But, unlike Bartram's first book, *An Account* lacks much of the anecdotal detail of the earlier work; in fact, some critics have characterized it by these very silences. Even so, the book was met with much enthusiasm (and reprinted twice more within the next decade).

In his final years, Bartram continued to maintain his foreign correspondence, even after the advent of the Revolutionary War in 1775. He spent much of his time in his garden, which showcased the fruits of a lifetime of cultivation. Bartram had almost singlehandedly introduced countless European plant species in the New World, and likewise his efforts helped spread American plants to many parts of Europe. Bartram's Gardens, as it is known, became more and more the focus of his cultivating projects as he began to travel less and less, until 1775 when his business was shut down because of halted trade with England. In 1777, Bartram had the profound, final pleasure of listening to the stories of his son William, who had returned that January from extensive travels in the South (the same voyages he later narrated in his famous *Travels* [1791]). Bartram had not seen his son in years, and now at last he heard with delight the tales that proved young Billy had adopted the mantle of botanist. Later that year, on September 22, John Bartram died from a sudden illness. True to form, he never stopped working in his garden until his final day.

John Bartram will likely never be considered a great writer by any conventional scholarly definition, but current critical trends demonstrate that his writings do present valuable insights about British colonial representations of nature. His descriptions of landscapes and the natural resources of the eastern American continent are often typical of the colonial enterprise: cataloguing and describing in terms of utility and potential settlement. Equally often, Bartram's words show us a more human side of eighteenth-century science, a mind afire with the excitement of discovery and the importance of a mission to understand how nature functions.

PRIMARY BIBLIOGRAPHY

Books

Observations on the Inhabitants, Climate, Soil, Rivers, Productions, Animals, and other matters worthy of Notice. Made By Mr. John Bartram, In his Travels from Pensilvania to Onondago, Oswego and the Lake Ontario In Canada. To which is annex'd, a curious Account of the Cataracts at Niagara. By Mr. Peter Kalm, A Swedish Gentleman who travelled there (London: Printed for J. Whiston & B. White, 1751).

An Account of East-Florida with a Journal, Kept by John Bartram of Philadelphia, Botanist to His Majesty for the Floridas; upon a Journey from St. Augustine up the River St. John's, with William Stork (London: W. Nicoll & G. Woodfall, 2nd ed., 1767); enlarged as *A description of East-Florida kept by John Bartram of Philadelphia, botanist to His Majesty for the Floridas; upon a journey from St. Augustine up the River St. John's*, with William Stork (London: W. Nicoll & G. Woodfall, 3rd ed., 1769; 4th ed., 1774).

Collection

Helen Gere Cruickshank, ed., *John and William Bartram's America: Selections from the Writings of the Philadelphia Naturalists* (New York: The Devin-Adair Company, 1957).

Other

Richard Saunders [Benjamin Franklin], "Indian Physick," in *Poor Richard's Almanac* (Philadelphia: Ben Franklin, 1741).

Thomas Short, *Medicina Britannica*, preface and appendix by Bartram, 3rd ed. (Philadelphia: Ben Franklin, 1751).

Selected Periodical Publications— Uncollected

"A Letter from John Bartram, M.D. to Peter Collinson, F.R.S. concerning a Cluster of small Teeth observed by him at the Root of each Fang or great Tooth in the Head of a Rattle Snake, upon dissecting it," *Philosophical Transactions* 41 (1740): 358–59.

"Extract of a Letter from Dr. John Bartram, to Mr. Peter Collinson, F.R.S. containing some Observations concerning the Salt-Marsh Muscle, the Oyster-Banks, and the Fresh-Water Muscle, of Pensylvania," *Philosophical Transactions* 43 (1744): 157–59.

"An Account of some very curious Wasps Nests made of Clay in Pensilvania; by Mr. John Bartram: Communicated by Mr. Peter Collinson, F.R.S.," *Philosophical Transactions* 43 (1745): 363–66.

"A Description of the Great Black Wasp, from Pensylvania, as communicated from Mr. John Bartram to Mr. Peter Collinson, F.R.S.," *Philosophical Transactions* 46 (1749): 278–79.

"Some Observations on the Dragon-Fly or Libella of Pensilvania, collected from Mr. John Bartram's Letter, communicated by Peter Collinson, F.R.S.," *Philosophical Transactions* 46 (1750): 323–25.

"A further Account of the Libellae of May-flies, from Mr. John Bartram of Pensylvania, communicated by Mr. Peter Collinson, F.R.S.," *Philosophical Transactions* 46 (1750): 400–402.

"Of the Great Black Wasp of Pennsylvania, communicated to the Royal Society, by Mr. P. Collinson, F.R.S., being an Extract of his Friend, Mr. John Bartram's Letter," *Gentleman's Magazine* 21 (1751): 101.

"Some Remarks on Dr. Alston's Dissertation on the Sexes of Plants by two celebrated botanists of North America, both dated June 10, 1755," *Gentleman's Magazine* 25 (1755): 407–8.

"A Letter from Mr. John Bartram of Pensylvania, to P. Collinson, Esq., F.R.S., in which there is a remarkable Conformity of Sentiments with the Author of some Physico-mechanical Conjectures on the Propagation of the shocks of Earthquakes (see p. 221) tho' it is impossible they could borrow from one another," *Gentleman's Magazine* 26 (1756): 474–75.

"Extract of a Letter from Mr. John Bartram, of Philadelphia, to Benjamin Franklin, LL.D. F.R.S. relating to a remarkable Aurora Borealis," *Philosophical Transactions* 52 (1762): 474.

"Observations made by Mr. John Bartram, at Pensilvania, on the Yellowish Wasp of that Country: In a Letter to Mr. Peter Collinson, F.R.S.," *Philosophical Transactions* 53 (1763): 37–38.

"An extract of Mr. Wm [sic] Bartram's Observations in a journey up the River Savannah in Georgia, with his son, on discoveries," *Gentleman's Magazine* 37 (1767): 166–68.

"Notices of the Epidemics of Pennsylvania and New-Jersey, in the Years 1746, 1747, 1748, and 1749," ed. B.S. Barton, *Medical and Physical Journal* 1, pt. 1 (1804): 3–5.

"Additional Observations on the Cicada Septendecim. By the late Mr. John Bartram. From a MS. in the possession of the editor," ed. B.S. Barton, *Medical and Physical Journal* 1, pt. 1 (1804): 56–59.

"Memorandums concerning the Earthquakes of North America," ed. B.S. Barton, *Medical and Physical Journal* 1, pt. 1 (1804): 65–67.

"Native American or Indian Dogs," ed. B.S. Barton, *Medical and Physical Journal* 1, pt. 2 (1805): 18–19.

"Diary of a Journey Through the Carolinas, Georgia, and Florida from July 1, 1765, to April 10, 1766," ed. Francis Harper, *Transactions of the American Philosophical Society*, new series 33 (1942): 1–120.

Letters

Edmund Berkeley and Dorothy Smith Berkeley, eds., *The Correspondence of John Bartram, 1734–1777* (Gainesville: University Press of Florida, 1992).

William Darlington, ed., *Memorials of John Bartram and Humphry Marshall* (Philadelphia: Lindsay and Blakiston, 1849; facsimile, New York: Hafner, 1967).

SECONDARY BIBLIOGRAPHY

Biography

Edmund Berkeley and Dorothy Smith Berkeley, *The Life and Travels of John Bartram: From Lake Ontario to the River St. John* (Tallahassee: University Presses of Florida, 1982).

References

Rose Marie Cutting, *John and William Bartram, William Byrd II and St. John de Crèvecoeur: A Reference Guide* (Boston: G.K. Hall, 1976).

Ernest Earnest, *John and William Bartram: Botanists and Explorers* (Philadelphia: University of Pennsylvania Press, 1940).

Thomas Hallock, *From the Fallen Tree: Frontier Narratives, Environmental Politics, and the Roots of a National Pastoral, 1749–1826* (Chapel Hill: University of North Carolina Press, 2003).

Josephine Herbst, *New Green World* (New York: Hastings House, 1954).

Christoph Irmscher, *The Poetics of Natural History* (New Brunswick: Rutgers University Press, 1999).

Thomas P. Slaughter, *The Natures of John and William Bartram* (New York: Alfred A. Knopf, 1996).

Francis D. West, "John Bartram: Geologist," *Quaker History* 47.1 (1958): 35–38.

Papers

Important collections of John Bartram's papers and publications are held at the Historical Society of Pennsylvania, the Academy of Natural Sciences of Philadelphia, The American Philosophical Society Library, and the British Library.

William Bartram
(April 20, 1739–July 22, 1823)

John D. Cox

Sometimes called the father of American nature writing, William Bartram produced only one significant work during his long life, *Travels Through North and South Carolina, Georgia, East and West Florida*. Published in 1791, the book describes Bartram's journey of almost four years, from March 1773 until January 1777, through the southeastern region of the newly forming nation. The book is generally regarded as a classic of both travel literature and nature writing, as its almost poetic descriptions of magnificent flora and fauna, numerous lists of Latinate nomenclature, and enthusiastic expression of the author's response to the wonders of nature have captivated readers since its publication. Although not immediately acclaimed upon its publication in the United States, Bartram's *Travels* was quickly published in England and Ireland and was translated into both German and French by the end of the eighteenth century. The book was popular enough in both England and France to require second printings within ten years, at least partly due to its popularity with English and European Romantics, such as Samuel T. Coleridge, William Wordsworth, and Francois-Rene de Chateaubriand. Thus, even though *Travels* was not republished in the United States during William Bartram's lifetime, it has long been considered an important work. *Travels* has enjoyed particular success in recent years, as a renewed interest in early American nature writing has resulted in a number of new editions. With the Library of America's publication of the superb volume, *Travels and Other Writings* (including Thomas Slaughter's newly researched chronology, from which much of the following information was taken), Bartram's place in the canon of American literature, particularly American nature writing, is certainly secure.

Bartram came to the study of nature easily, for his father, John Bartram, was perhaps the greatest botanist in North America during the mid-eighteenth century. John Bartram influenced his son's views in a variety of ways, and William's representations of nature, both as a young visual artist and as a mature artist and writer, reflect a complex, often contradictory relationship with the natural environment, perhaps as a result of a similarly complex relationship with his famous father. John was an important figure in colonial America; along with his friend Benjamin Franklin, for instance, he was a founding member of the American Philosophical Society, and he was acquainted with many of the best-known political and intellectual figures of the time. John's career as a botanist was secured in 1728 when he purchased a 112-acre farm on the banks of the Schuylkill River near Philadelphia, for here he created one of the English colonies' first botanical gardens. As a botanist and a businessman, John Bartram spent much of his time and energy either cultivating interesting plants in his own gardens or traveling through the American wilderness in search of undiscovered species. John was particularly adept at locating specimens previously unknown in Europe, and he is generally credited with finding and identifying at least one quarter of all unnamed plants sent to Europe during the colonial period. Although he did appreciate the beauty of "God's creation," John was largely interested in nature's usefulness to society. During his trips, frequently accompanied by his son William, John often described the environments he encountered in terms of their potential for future development. For instance, he tended to describe the soil in terms of its fertility and probable suitability for crops and even measured streams by the number of mills they might be able to support. Clearly an Enlightenment scientist and an early adherent of Linnaeus's binomial system, John traveled with an eye toward measurement, classification, and collection.

In 1733, John began to send seeds and other specimens of plants and animals to English patrons, most notably fellow Quaker Peter Collinson, a merchant, botanist, and member of the Royal Society. This business and personal relationship, which lasted until Collinson's death in 1768, played a large role in John's eventual fame throughout Europe as a botanist. Collinson introduced a number of English botanists, professional and amateur, to John's collections and, most importantly, helped secure in 1765 John Bartram's appointment as the King's Botanist in the North American colonies. Collinson was important to John Bartram's son as well, for he encouraged the young William's interest in drawing and circulated amongst his aristocratic friends some of William's earliest sketches.

Little is known of William's infancy and early childhood. Born along with his twin sister, Elizabeth, on April 20, 1739, William was one of nine children of John Bartram,

the grandson of William and Elizah Bartram, and the great-grandson of John and Elizabeth Bartram, who had emigrated from England in 1683 during one of the first periods of Quaker immigration into the new colony of Pennsylvania. Ann Mendenhall, William's mother and John Bartram's second wife, was the daughter of Benjamin Mendenhall, an English Quaker wheelwright who had immigrated to Pennsylvania around the same time as John's grandparents. Although the Bartram family had long been associated with the Quakers, both William's father and his grandfather had their official ties severed; in 1708, William's grandfather, William, was declared "out of unity" with the Darby Monthly Meeting of the Religious Society of Friends, and his father, John, was disowned by the Darby Monthly Meeting in 1758 for denying the divinity of Christ, although he continued to attend Meeting regularly. As for William himself, while his adult beliefs did not correspond perfectly with those of the Society of Friends, his Quaker background exerted a tremendous influence on his relationship with, and representations of, the natural environment, as several later commentators have shown.

Unlike his father, who had little formal education, William did receive schooling in his youth. In 1754, he began to attend the Academy of Philadelphia, later to become the College of Philadelphia, where he studied a variety of academic subjects, including Greek, Latin, English, rhetoric, history, geography, mathematics, astronomy, and natural philosophy, all of which are evident in his later writings. No doubt William's education also benefited from the numerous visitors who came to his father's gardens over the years. For instance, Peter Kalm, a Swedish botanist and disciple of Linnaeus, visited the Bartrams on several occasions, beginning in 1748, when William was only nine years old. In later years, many of the nation's most famous figures, including George Washington and Thomas Jefferson, would not only purchase seeds and plants from the Bartrams but also make personal visits to the famous gardens.

At some point during these years, William Bartram had also begun to draw birds and plants, for by 1753, his father had sent some of William's sketches to Collinson in England. In the summer of that year, Collinson included in a package a "little token" for John's son, "whose pretty performances please me much." Although these first sketches by "Billy" are not particularly life-like, the young artist's skill was obvious, and his abilities increased rapidly. Later that same year, Collinson again included a gift for the young Bartram, whose drawings had been "much admired and better than could be expected for his first trials." About this same time, William began accompanying his father on collecting trips, a practice that would continue for years. In September 1753, for instance, John and William went on an expedition to the Catskill Mountains of New York, to which they returned in the summer of 1754; in 1755, they searched for botanical specimens in Connecticut and New York. William was apparently an observant, curious traveler and artist, for during these and subsequent trips, the young William managed to sketch birds that the famous naturalist-artist Mark Catesby had neglected or missed. What is perhaps even more noteworthy about these early sketches, however, is William's practice of depicting his subjects in relation to their natural environments. Earlier artists had generally drawn natural subjects completely isolated from their surroundings; while Catesby had included other natural objects, these additions did not necessarily bear any direct relationship to his primary subject. William, on the other hand, generally included in these early sketches the environment most closely associated with the birds being drawn. For instance, an early sketch of a sanderling shows the bird on a beach surrounded by seashells and plants found in the bird's natural habitat. Following his father's lead, William attempted to represent not simply a single example of a plant or animal isolated from its environment but the connections amongst various species of flora and fauna within all of nature. This early focus on the unity of nature continued throughout William's life and greatly influenced all of his subsequent sketches and writings.

Although the young William was clearly recognized as a talented artist and botanist, his father felt he needed a more secure profession than his art would provide. Thus, as the son of this somewhat demanding and increasingly famous botanist and businessman, William spent much of his life struggling to find a means of earning a living, to earn the respect of his father, and to create his own individual identity. As a result, before William finally settled into the life for which he is most commonly known, he attempted a number of professional endeavors, all of which seemed somehow doomed from the start. His father's friend, Benjamin Franklin, offered in 1756 to take William on as an apprentice, but John Bartram believed printing too difficult a trade in which to succeed; that same year, William himself declined an offer to apprentice with the physician Alexander Garden, although he did become an apprentice to James Child, a Philadelphia merchant. This apprenticeship lasted until 1761, when John Bartram helped establish William as a merchant on the Cape Fear River in North Carolina, where he lived with his uncle, Colonel Bartram. William must have been particularly unsuited to life as a businessman, for he gathered debts during this time that haunted him for years; only in 1783 did he finally settle debts first accrued during this period. This first phase of his life as a merchant in North Carolina came to a close in 1765 when his father, newly appointed as the King's Botanist for the North American colonies, asked William to sell his stock, close his business, and accompany him on a trip through the Florida lands recently acquired by England.

With his new title of Royal Botanist, John Bartram also received from King George III a yearly stipend of £50, which allowed John a degree of freedom to travel and to explore that he had long desired. The stipend also allowed John to bring along on his southern journey his floundering son William. The pair traveled from July 1765 until March 1766 and covered much of the coastal regions of southern North Carolina, Georgia, South Carolina, and northern Florida. They also traveled up the Savannah River to Augusta and searched in Florida for the source of the St. Johns River, covering much of the territory that William would further explore by himself just a few years later.

Once the trip was completed, John could not, or would not, support his son permanently, so William continued to search for a vocation that would allow him the freedom to pursue his real passions—exploring wild terrain, sketching flora and fauna, and describing the natural environments around him. Thus, when John Bartram finished his journey in Florida and set out for Charleston, William remained behind to become a plantation owner, hoping to grow rice and indigo on land along the St. Johns River that his father had purchased for him. Although John seems to have believed the attempt futile, he did once again financially support his son's professional endeavor, even purchasing and sending to William six slaves, tools, and provisions necessary for a new plantation. By autumn of that year, however, William had suffered a serious illness and made very little progress on his plans. Henry Laurens, a family friend and later president of the Continental Congress, visited William twice and subsequently wrote John a sympathetic letter outlining William's difficulties and the unsuitability of the land for raising crops. John again advised his son to stop the business in which he was involved, to sell the plantation, and to return home. In November 1766, Bartram did abandon the plantation and set sail from St. Augustine for Philadelphia. On the trip home, however, he was shipwrecked off the coast of Florida, so he returned to St. Augustine, worked briefly on surveying projects, and wrote to Collinson in London to see about finding work as an illustrator. The following fall, he returned to Philadelphia, where he worked periodically as a day laborer and a merchant.

During these years that William searched in vain for a suitable profession, he did not neglect his art, however, for in 1756 he sent drawings to Collinson and dried specimens of birds to George Edwards, an English author and illustrator. In 1758, the London journal *Gentleman's Magazine* published two of William's drawings of turtles. Several years after this publication, his father forwarded to Collinson many of the drawings and paintings William had created during their southern trip in 1765–1766. William's first substantial work as a professional nature artist came after William had returned to Philadelphia from Florida, however, when Collinson informed him in 1768 that the Duchess of Portland had commissioned Bartram for a fee of £21 to sketch all American marine shells, "from the very least to the greatest." In addition, after Collinson's death in August, Dr. John Fothergill took over the role of assisting William, commissioning him to draw mollusks and turtles for another £21. William sent a number of drawings to these two patrons in the years following.

At about this same time, however, William's debts were beginning to catch up to him, so he fled Philadelphia in 1770 in order to avoid his creditors. He returned to North Carolina, hoping to collect some old debts that were owed to him, but he was apparently unable to secure enough of them to pay off his own bills. The following year, his father informed him that George Bartram, William's brother-in-law, had settled with William's creditors for £100; William finally settled his remaining debts with the £200 he received after his father's death in 1777. In 1772, William wrote to his parents that he was planning once again to abandon his business in North Carolina so that he could return to Florida to resume his career as a nature artist, writing that he wanted to "retreat within myself to the only business I was born for, and which I am only good for (If I am intitled to use that phrase for any thing)." He also wrote to Fothergill in London asking him to sponsor a collecting and drawing trip to Florida. Although his father opposed William's return to the region and explained that he would not fund such a venture, John Bartram was apparently placated once Fothergill agreed to the plan. In October, Fothergill sent William detailed instructions for collecting and sending seeds and live specimens and for making drawings; as payment, William would receive a yearly salary of £50, plus expenses. Late in 1772, William returned to Philadelphia to prepare for his travels, and, on March 20, 1773, he left home for what would become his famous four-year journey through the southeast.

Bartram's travels during these four years are somewhat difficult to trace accurately, for his accounts are often confusing, and he seems to have lost track of time at some point during this period, gaining a year and believing that he returned to Philadelphia in early 1778. He apparently maintained throughout his life that his travels had continued until 1778, so many later writers describing William's journey have been mistaken about the exact dates of his trip. (Because John Bartram died in September 1777, some commentators —believing William's account of the dates of his journey—have suggested that William never made his peace with his father, returning to Philadelphia only after John Bartram's death. However, as Thomas Slaughter points out, William did, in fact, return several months before John died; also William incorrectly identified the year of John's death as 1778, so there is little evidence of the antipathy between dying father and adult son that some critics have claimed.) In addition to the confusion over exact dates because of inaccuracies within *Travels*, William's published account of his journey frequently contradicts his two-part report to Fothergill, not published until 1943. Until that time, when his report to Fothergill was published in the *Transactions of the American Philosophical Society*, readers interested in Bartram's life had little to go on but *Travels*. *Travels* is generally regarded as the less accurate of the two accounts, but the contradictions between the texts often do little to clear up confusion over Bartram's exact movements during this time. The commentary in Francis Harper's invaluable "Naturalist Edition" of *Travels*, recently republished by The University of Georgia Press, as well as the chronologies included in *William Bartram: Botanical and Zoological Drawings* and the Library of America's edition of *Travels*, edited by Joseph Ewan and Thomas Slaughter, respectively, are all particularly useful references for the reader desiring more detailed knowledge of Bartram's specific movements.

After sailing from Philadelphia to Charleston in March 1773, receiving money from Dr. Lionel Chalmers, with whom Fothergill had arranged payment for Bartram, and staying briefly with Thomas Lamboll in Charleston, Bartram traveled in April to Savannah, Georgia. Returning to a site he had seen with his father, William wanted to revisit a colony of *Franklinia alatamaha*, a species of tree discovered, named, and first described by the Bartrams. After this brief sojourn, Bartram returned to Savannah and shortly thereafter befriended Lachlan McIntosh and his son John, of Darien, Georgia. Bartram managed to witness treaty negotiations with Creek Indians at Augusta, Georgia, and then traveled through the northeastern region of the state with a large surveying party that included his new friend, John McIntosh.

This trip, described in some detail in both his *Travels* and his report to Fothergill, figuratively illustrates botany's sometimes unwitting role in the process of colonization during this period, for by participating in the accumulation of knowledge about a specific environment, botanists such as Bartram encouraged development to proceed more smoothly and easily. In *Travels*, Bartram describes the "caravan" with which he traveled as consisting of

> surveyors, astronomers, artisans, chain-carriers, markers, guides, and hunters, besides a very respectable number of gentlemen, who joined us, in order to speculate in the lands, together with ten or twelve Indians, altogether to the number of eighty or ninety men.

In his generally more concise report to Fothergill, Bartram added that he frequently traveled at the head of this large surveying party:

> having more time and opportunity to make my observations, & for the better availing myself of this advantage, I chose to keep a small distance ahead of the Main body; by which I avoided the heat & dust rais'd by such a Number of People; & at the same time had leisure & opportunity to pick up any curiosities within view.

Significantly, Bartram immediately precedes into the wilderness these surveyors, land speculators, and others who hope to make use of the land only recently purchased from the native inhabitants.

After visiting the Oconee River and the mouth of the Tugaloo River, Bartram returned to Savannah in 1773 and apparently spent most of his fall and winter in or around that city. By March 1774, however, William was on his way to Florida, for in mid-April, he traveled by boat up the St. John's River to Spalding's Lower Store, a trading post run by Charles McLatchie, with whom Bartram became friends. Around this time Bartram visited the Alachua Savanna, a landscape to which he seemed particularly attracted and which drew from Bartram some of his most enthusiastic descriptions of the natural environment. Bartram frequently reveled in the natural sights he encountered, and *Travels* is filled with exuberant expressions of delight and joy at the wonders of nature; however, few sites received the kind of response Bartram provides of the Alachua Savanna.

Approaching from the south, Bartram writes in *Travels*, he first encountered a small lake at the edge of the larger savanna:

> This little lake and surrounding meadows would have been alone sufficient to surprise and delight the traveller; but being placed so near the great savanna, the attention is quickly drawn off, and wholly engaged in the contemplation of the unlimited, varied, and truly astonishing native wild scenes of landscape and perspective, there exhibited: how

is the mind agitated and bewildered, at being thus, as it were, placed on the borders of a new world! On the first view of such an amazing display of the wisdom and power of the supreme author of nature, the mind for a moment seems suspended, and impressed with awe.

Passages such as this one have encouraged the common view of Bartram as a proto-Romantic writer, a predecessor of Henry David Thoreau and his contemporaries. However, as the reader of *Travels* can hardly help notice, Bartram's poetic descriptions of nature are frequently juxtaposed with more scientific lists of the species he has encountered, a rhetorical strategy that results in an almost dizzying combination of discourses. For instance, just prior to the description above, Bartram explains that he entered a grove

> consisting of various kinds of trees, as the Magnolia grandiflora, Corypha palma, Citrus Aurantium, Quercus sempervirens, Morus rubra, Ulmus sylvatica, Tilia, Juglans cinerea, Æsculus pavia, Liquidambar, Laurus Borbonia, Hopea tinctoria, Cercis, Cornus Florida, Halesia diptera, Halesia tetraptera, Olea Americana, Callicarpa, Andromeda arborea, Sideroxilon sericium, Sid. tenax, Vitis labrusca, Hedera arborea, Hedera quinquefolia, Rhamnus volubilis, Prunus Caroliniana (pr. flor. racemosis, foliis sempervirentibus, lato-lanceolatis, acuminatis, serratis) Fagus sylvatica, Zanthoxilon clava Herculis, Acer rubrum, Acer negundo, Fraxinus excelsior, with many others already mentioned.

Although Bartram's scientific nomenclature was not always accurate, these listings have encouraged many readers to view Bartram as primarily a scientific, rather than a literary, writer.

During the same period that Bartram was visiting the Alachua Savanna, he also came to know a number of Seminole Indians, who gave him the name "Puc Puggy," meaning "Flower Hunter." Bartram's relationship with and representations of Native Americans are as complex and as fascinating as his pictures of the natural world. Although he spends the last section of *Travels* attempting to adhere to his Enlightenment impulses by classifying native customs and societies, he generally seems to view Native Americans as equals rather than simply as objects of study. In fact, in several passages that describe interactions between himself and individual Native Americans, Bartram explicitly states that the two of them are equal in God's eyes. Even though they do not have the benefits of a formal education, Bartram explains, Native Americans do enjoy an innate understanding of right and wrong:

> It is certain they have not the assistance of letters, or those means of education in the schools of philosophy, where the virtuous sentiments and actions of the most illustrious characters are recorded, and carefully laid before the youth of civilized nations: therefore this moral principle must be innate, or they must be under the immediate influence and guidance of a more divine and powerful preceptor, who, on these occasions, instantly inspires them, and as with a ray of divine light, points out to them at once the dignity, propriety, and beauty of virtue.

In other sections of the text, Bartram has a tendency to romanticize Native Americans, but he also seems to have been interested in learning from them and in building stronger ties between the native tribes and people of European descent. For example, Bartram argues in the introduction to *Travels* that "men of ability and virtue" should be sent by the government into tribal towns in order to learn their language, record their customs, and understand their culture. According to Bartram,

> These men thus enlightened and instructed would be qualified to judge equitably, and when returned to us, to make true and just reports, which might assist the legislature of the United States to form, and offer to them, a judicious plan for their civilization and union with us.

William clearly had a very different view of Native Americans from that of his father, who held a lifelong grudge against "Indians" for killing his father, William's grandfather, when John Bartram was 12.

After spending the autumn and winter of 1774–1775 in Florida and Georgia, William Bartram returned to his base, Charleston, in March 1775. Bartram left Charleston for Augusta on April 22, just after the battles of Lexington and Concord had initiated the Revolutionary War but before news of those events had reached Charleston. Traveling alone for much of this time, William journeyed north into South and North Carolina but decided not to enter Cherokee territory, heading instead south into Georgia and then westward toward Alabama. He reached Mobile, Alabama, in July and sailed to Pensacola, Florida. Here he was granted permission from the British governor to collect botanical specimens in West Florida, but he then returned to Mobile and continued westward. During his trip to Louisiana, Bartram developed a serious problem with his eyes, perhaps the result of either poison ivy or even scarlet fever, and stayed at "Pearl Island" in Louisiana for several weeks in order to recover. After his recovery, he visited Baton Rouge and other parts of Louisiana and returned to Mobile in November, when he again fell ill. Bartram briefly traveled to a Creek Indian settlement in Alabama, then went on to Georgia, where he spent the spring and summer of 1776. At this time, Bartram may have taken a brief break from his travels to volunteer with his friend General Lachlan McIntosh's troops, who were preparing for a British attack on Florida that never materialized, but he soon resumed his travels. Late in the year, William shipped the last of his plant specimens to Fothergill in London. His southern travels ended in late November when Bartram left Charleston to visit Wilmington, North Carolina, and then travel overland to his father's home in Philadelphia, where he arrived in January 1777.

When Bartram had convinced Fothergill in 1773 to finance his southern travels, his patron had been explicit in his expectations. In addition to instructing William to make sketches of the flora and fauna he encountered and to collect and forward both seeds and live specimens, Fothergill had told William that he should keep a journal of his travels throughout the southeastern colonies. Although William had not been a particularly conscientious employee, he had eventually sent to Fothergill numerous dried plant specimens, 59 drawings, and a two-part written report. After returning to Philadelphia, however, Bartram went to work on a much more significant project, revising the journal of his four years into what was finally published in 1791 as *Travels*.

Bartram's revisions took years to get into print, although exactly how much time he took to complete these revisions is unclear. There is some evidence that *Travels* was completed by 1786, for in that year Enoch Story, Jr., a Philadelphia publisher, solicited subscriptions for an edition of Bartram's *Travels* to be dedicated to Benjamin Franklin; however, this edition was never published. In 1790 another Philadelphia publisher, James and Johnson, asked for new subscriptions for an edition of Bartram's *Travels*. Among those received were subscriptions from President George Washington, Vice President John Adams, and Secretary of State Thomas Jefferson. The book was deposited for copyright in August and finally published sometime in the fall, although the exact date is unknown. By the next year, the book had crossed the Atlantic, for in 1792 an edition was published in London by Joseph Johnson. After this, several additional editions were published throughout Europe within the following decade.

The contemporary response to *Travels* in the United States was not particularly positive. Although some early readers found the botanical lists and descriptions useful and impressive, most critics complained that these admirable sections were too often scattered amidst Bartram's emotional outpourings. Despite these early responses, however, *Travels* has not frequently been valued for its scientific accuracy but read instead as a sort of pre-Romantic prose-poem by an eighteenth-century man of nature. Bartram's influence on the Romantic and Transcendental poets has been well documented. Coleridge, for instance, drew heavily on *Travels* for images he incorporated into *Kubla Khan*, and Wordsworth, Thomas Carlyle, Ralph Waldo Emerson, and Thoreau all read Bartram's work. Thus, almost since its publication, criticism of *Travels* has been divided over the question of the author's place in American writing about the natural environment. On the one hand, many critics have seen Bartram as an early proponent of Nature and an important forerunner to such later figures as Thoreau and Emerson. Another group of critics, however, has downplayed Bartram's proto-Romanticism or proto-Transcendentalism, insisting that he is more like his father, John, than unlike, thus arguing that his exploitative tendencies outweigh his "environmentalist" sensibilities. As recent critics have pointed out, however, these readings tend to obscure the cultural work that Bartram's text might have accomplished, so critics have begun to view Bartram's writings as commentary on the contemporary political scene. For instance, Christopher Looby argues that Bartram and others utilized the structure of the Linnæan classification system as "a figure for social stability and...for an intensely desired end to the flux of revolutionary social-historical change." Douglass Anderson argues that in *Travels* Bartram hopes to present a vision of "measured skepticism as a corrective for patriotic fervor," and Philip Terrie argues that Bartram's view of nature "as alternating between the blissful and the fearsome" points more generally to his "profound skepticism concerning the character of human affairs." For many of these writers, Bartram's writings about nature in the American South are significant not only for what they might say about the natural environment but also for what they might tell readers about early American social and political movements and ideas.

William Bartram himself seemed to have had very little to say directly about the current events of his day. After *Travels* was published, Bartram spent most of the remaining 32 years of his life working in his father's garden, owned and operated by William's younger brother, John, after their father's death in 1777. William did maintain rather extensive correspondence with other botanists, particularly Benjamin Smith Barton, to whose *Elements of Botany* Bartram provided numerous illustrations and ample material, all unacknowledged. Also, Bartram published an occasional piece or gave an occasional talk on subjects pertaining to natural history. In 1804, he published a short biography of his father, "Some account of the late Mr. John Bartram," as well as a short essay, "Anecdotes of an American Crow," describing one of his pets. Furthermore, as Bartram became increasingly famous, there seems to have been a fairly steady stream of visitors to the garden. In addition, Bartram was invited by President Jefferson to serve as an advisor on an expedition up the Red River, but Bartram declined the offer, citing his age and infirmities. Several other occasional pieces by Bartram were published in the early nineteenth century, but Bartram was clearly interested in a less artistically active life during these years. William Bartram died from a ruptured lung artery on July 22, 1823, and was buried at an unrecorded location.

By almost all accounts, Bartram's *Travels* is a contradictory, beautiful, and impressive work. The work contains a multitude of rhetorical styles and discursive characteristics, for Bartram lists and classifies as well as waxes poetic; he attempts to understand nature objectively yet celebrates the mystical, unknown, and personal aspects of the natural world. The book thus reflects the many competing identities of William Bartram himself: Billy Bartram, son of an Enlightenment scientist; William Bartram, renowned artist of nature; and Puc Puggy, the gentle flower hunter adopted into a Seminole tribe. Rather than detracting from the text, however, these contradictions form the fascinating core of the book, for by reading *Travels*, one can

watch the author attempt to come to terms with his past in the very act of creating a new identity—an identity that both frees him from his earlier failures and reflects not only his Enlightenment ideals but also his proto-Romantic impulses.

PRIMARY BIBLIOGRAPHY

Book

Travels through North and South Carolina, Georgia, East and West Florida, the Cherokee Country, the Extensive Territories of the Muscogulges, or Creek Confederacy, and the Country of the Chactaws (Philadelphia: Printed by James & Johnson, 1791; London: Printed for J. Johnson, 1792).

Editions and Collections

John and William Bartram's America: Selections from the Writings of the Philadelphia Naturalists, ed. Helen Gere Cruickshank (New York: Devin-Adair, 1957).

The Travels of William Bartram: Naturalist's Edition, ed. Francis Harper (New Haven: Yale University Press, 1958).

William Bartram: Botanical and Zoological Drawings, 1756–1788, ed. Joseph Ewan (Philadelphia: American Philosophical Society, 1968).

Other

"Travels in Georgia and Florida, 1773–74: A Report to Dr. John Fothergill," ed. Francis Harper, *Transactions of the American Philosophical Society* 33 (November 1943): 121–242.

Travels and Other Writings, ed. Thomas Slaughter (New York: Library of America, 1996).

SECONDARY BIBLIOGRAPHY

Biographies

N. Bryllion Fagin, *William Bartram: Interpreter of the American Landscape* (Baltimore: Johns Hopkins University Press, 1933).

Ernest Earnest, *John and William Bartram: Botanists and Explorers* (Philadelphia: University of Pennsylvania Press, 1940).

Thomas Slaughter, *The Natures of John and William Bartram* (New York: Random House, 1996).

References

Charles H. Adams, "William Bartram's *Travels*: A Natural History of the South," *Rewriting the South: History and Fiction,* ed. Lothar Hönnighausen (Tübingen: A. Francke, 1993), 112–20.

Robert D. Arner, "Pastoral Patterns in William Bartram's *Travels,*" *Tennessee Studies in Literature* 18 (1973): 133–45.

Michael Branch, "Indexing American Possibilities: The Natural History Writing of Bartram, Wilson, and Audubon," *The Ecocriticism Reader,* ed. Cheryll Glotfelty and Harold Fromm. (Athens: University of Georgia Press, 1996), 282–302.

Edward J. Cashin, *William Bartram and the American Revolution on the Southern Frontier* (South Carolina University Press, 2000).

John D. Cox, "Traveling Texts: Southern Travel Narratives and the Construction of American National Identity" (dissertation, University of Mississippi, 2000).

Rose Marie Cutting, *John and William Bartram, William Byrd II, and St. John de Crevecoeur: A Reference Guide* (Boston: G.K. Hall, 1976).

Berta Grattan Lee, "William Bartram: Naturalist or 'Poet'?" *Early American Literature* 7 (1972): 124–29.

Christopher Looby, "The Constitution of Nature: Taxonomy as Politics in Jefferson, Peale, and Bartram," *Early American Literature* 22 (1987): 252–73.

Mary S. Mattfield, "Journey to the Wilderness: Two Travellers in Florida, 1696–1774," *The Florida Historical Quarterly* 45 (1967): 327–51.

Patricia M. Medeiros, "Three Travelers: Carver, Bartram, and Woolman," *American Literature, 1764–1789: The Revolutionary Years,* ed. Everett Emerson (Madison: University of Wisconsin Press, 1977), 195–211.

L. Hugh Moore, "The Aesthetic Theory of William Bartram," *Essays in Arts and Sciences* 12 (1983): 17–35.

Pamela Regis, *Describing Early America: Bartram, Jefferson, Crèvecoeur, and the Influence of Natural History* (Philadelphia: University of Pennsylvania Press, 1992).

John Seelye, "Beauty Bare: William Bartram and His Triangulated Wilderness," *Prospects: The Annual of American Cultural Studies* 6 (1981): 37–54.

Philip G. Terrie, "Tempests and Alligators: The Ambiguous Wilderness of William Bartram," *North Dakota Review* 59 (1991): 17–32.

Papers

The Historical Society of Pennsylvania houses the most extensive collection of Bartram materials, although the British Museum also has a collection. A number of Bartram's sketches and drawings are in private collections.

Isabella Lucy Bird
(October 15, 1831–October 7, 1904)

E. Frances Frame

Isabella Bird was a strong-willed, energetic, and courageous adventurer. She was the first woman to address the Royal Geographic Society and one of the group's first female fellows. She navigated a narrow road between Victorian restrictions on women and a desire to explore that required sure footing on the most precarious mountain path. Her success in negotiating that trail represents a significant achievement. Her chief contribution to American nature writing was *A Lady's Life in the Rocky Mountains*, which went through seven editions in three years and is still available today in both scholarly and popular editions. A new scholarly edition of Bird's letters to her younger sister, Henrietta, now facilitates examination of her early career, and recently scholars have begun exploring Bird's later work on Persia and East Asia. Bird's career illustrates the popularity female writers experienced among general readers, especially women, and their difficulty in gaining entry into professional, scientific societies reserved for men.

Born in Yorkshire, England, Bird was the first daughter of evangelical minister Edward Bird and his second wife, Dora Lawson. Bird was related to William Wilberforce, an intellectual evangelical who led the abolition movement in England, and her family exemplified Christian faith, education, and confident action on the world stage. She also counted several strong Christian women among her relatives, including missionaries to India and Persia. Bird's father instructed her in traditionally male subjects such as Latin and botany and often took his young daughter riding with him on his horse, teaching her to observe her surroundings closely. In 1835, after the birth of Henrietta, Bird developed a number of health problems, including a spinal malady, insomnia, nervousness, depression, and headaches, all possibly resulting from frustration at the limited outlets available for female energy and intellect.

Bird first traveled to America in 1854, and her report of a visit to Niagara Falls in *The Englishwoman in America* (1856) anticipates her later writing about Colorado. She discusses nature both as sublime creation and as human resource, a practice she continues in *A Lady's Life in the Rocky Mountains*. In her depiction of a walk behind the falls, she presents nature as a personal challenge and constructs her conquest of it as a victory not only over nature but also over her own apprehensions. She refers to nature as God's temple, insists upon her own moment of solitary contemplation (during which she reports feelings of transcendence), and remarks on the insufficiency of language to convey her experience. She describes the many colors of the sunset and consciously employs metaphor and personification. Her consternation at having to "do Niagara" according to a predetermined tourist agenda and her need for solitude to achieve the transcendence she desires reveal the motivations behind her later choices to explore less accessible places in more difficult seasons and to travel alone when at all possible.

During her visit in 1854, Bird met Washington Irving at a Gramercy Park reception and spent time with James Russell Lowell and Henry Wadsworth Longfellow. She returned to America in 1857 to collect information for her father on American religion and met Henry David Thoreau and Ralph Waldo Emerson. For several years, during which she suffered the deaths of her father (1858) and mother (1866), Bird limited her travels to the British Isles. In 1872, she traveled through a hurricane, which she found invigorating, and disembarked briefly in Hawaii to help a fellow traveler. She reveled in having no morning callers and going without stockings and started riding astride her horse instead of sidesaddle, a risky move for a Victorian lady concerned about her reputation but necessary for travel to remote regions. She clambered along a 2,500-foot cliff until the trail became so narrow she had to dismount her horse by sliding under him; she made it to the top by hanging on to his tail. She visited the crater of Kilauea and climbed over razor-sharp volcanic rock to reach the top of Mauna Loa at 13,650 feet. Bird drew upon her letters and journals for *Six Months in the Sandwich Islands* (1875), a hit that earned praise from the respected journal *Nature* for its botanical accuracy.

Bird's greatest contribution to American nature writing was *A Lady's Life in the Rocky Mountains*, published serially in *The Leisure Hour* in 1878 and in book form in 1879. The work takes the form of letters written to her sister, Henrietta, beginning September 2, 1873, at Lake Tahoe and concluding with a note at Cheyenne on December 12. In the book, Bird describes the landscape, plants, and animals, as well as humankind's relation to them.

She describes the lay of the land, including, in a single passage, "an upland valley," "glades and sloping lawns," "mountains breaking into pinnacles," a "single dell," "deep, vast canyons," and "pine-clad ranges." She often specifies sizes and distances in her descriptions of nature, but these measurements are usually prefaced with "around" or "about" or given as ranges. While she praises Estes Park for turning the beholder's thoughts toward God, she is irritated when features of the landscape seem "too artistically grouped," an observation that Vera Norwood sees as evidence of Bird's familiarity with shifts in what was valued in landscape from the eighteenth to the nineteenth centuries. On other occasions, however, Bird seems to appreciate scenes that are artistically arranged and views the lack of foreground in one landscape as a "great artistic fault." She laments the destruction wrought by mining, which proceeds by "turning the earth inside out, making it hideous, and blighting every green thing, as it usually blights man's heart and soul." Bird frequently describes the landscape with long strings of participles or adjectives, depicting canyon walls, for example, as "castellated, embattled, rifted, skirted and crowned with pines," and Estes Park as a "grand, solitary, uplifted, sublime, remote, beast-haunted lair." Favorite metaphors appear again and again: she compares a lake to a mirror six times and the plains to the sea equally as often, and she dwells repeatedly on sunrises and sunsets. Only infrequently does she personify the mountains, but she does discuss the idea of a mountain having a personality: "It is one of the noblest mountains, but in one's imagination it grows to be much more than a mountain. It becomes invested with a personality." She personifies the Fountain River as "twinkling and laughing in the sunshine, or frowning in 'dowie dens' in the blue pine gloom." Occasionally, she lapses into cliché, as in a description of snow that "sparkled like diamonds," and she overuses a few words, such as "stately" and "rarified," which occur innumerable times.

Bird tells Hennie that, in Colorado, the "observing faculties are developed, and the reflective lie dormant." One might add that, in Bird's writing, certain senses are employed more than others. The air is vaguely "aromatic," but few specific smells are noted, other than the skunk's. While Bird frequently records the temperature and mentions her satisfaction at the taste of venison, she appeals most often to her reader's sight and hearing. She devotes much more attention to color than to shape, and although she notes the colors of wildflowers and strata of rock, color is most prominent in her repeated descriptions of sunrises and sunsets. In describing one sunset, she mentions indigo, Tyrian purple, rose-red, pink, and orange, a palette that expands to include grey, crimson, amethyst, violet, green, vermilion, scarlet, emerald, lemon, gold, blue, buff, chrysoprase, and aquamarine in subsequent sunrise and sunset descriptions. She reports both the sounds of the wilderness (the "cries of wild beasts and the roar of mountain torrents") and the sounds of man's incursion (the "slightly musical ring of the lumberer's axe"). She uses sound to draw attention to the virtual silence that surrounds her ("there were no sounds to be heard but the crackle of ice and snow, the pitiful howling of wolves, and the hoot of owls") and to help build a sense of danger ("I heard both wolves and the mountain lion as I crossed to my cabin last night").

The land often appears in Bird's work as an obstacle or threat, and she uses her encounters with it to define herself as adventurous, courageous, perseverant, and resilient. Her most sensational dramatization of nature as a personal challenge is the narrative of her climb up Long's Peak:

> Two thousand feet of solid rock towered above us, four thousand feet of broken rock shelved precipitously below; smooth granite ribs, with barely a foothold, stood out here and there; melted snow refrozen several times, presented a more serious obstacle; many of the rocks were loose, and tumbled down when touched. To me it was a time of extreme terror....[O]n the final, and, to my thinking, the worst part of the climb, one slip, and a breathing, thinking, human being would lie 3,000 feet below, a shapeless, bloody heap!

By reporting the real dangers and personal terrors of her ascent and then noting the confidence with which she greets the difficult descent ("I was no longer giddy, and faced the precipice of 3,500 feet without a shiver"), Bird constructs her climb as a triumph over both nature and her own fears. Bird also uses a snowstorm that freezes her eyelids shut as an opportunity to construct nature as a menacing antagonist and herself as a courageous, persistent "mountaineer" who overcomes passing fears. As she does in her Long's Peak narrative by introducing a depiction of a hypothetical fall, Bird heightens the suspense of this drama by mentioning the deaths of past travelers and imagining the possible consequences of prolonged exposure to the cold. When Bird reaches her destination, the reader readily acknowledges her as exactly the hero the author wishes to appear. Bird also designs her matter-of-fact description of three days snowbound at Estes Park not only to demonstrate that nature can threaten humanity on its own turf but also to show that she is equal to whatever challenge nature may dish out, even if it means standing in snow as she dresses inside her cabin. She again intensifies the drama of the situation, this time by implying that the reader's own vicarious experience of the adventure was almost lost when the storm wrenched Bird's writing book out of her hand, burying it in the snow.

On her journeys through Colorado, Bird also tackled dehydration, heat, snow blindness, altitude sickness, treacherous ice, and darkness so profound she could not see the ears of her horse. However, she does not always depict nature as a fearsome adversary; sometimes it is just a nuisance. She contends with various species of snake (including a rattlesnake, which she kills), black flies, and other "insect life, large and small, stinging, humming, buzzing, striking, rasping, devouring," and a skunk, which takes up residence under her cabin. Grasshoppers plague the Colorado farmers, she reports. Fierce gusts of wind rend her clothing into shreds as it dries on a clothesline, and the cold freezes any eggs, milk, butter, or preserves not stored on top of a heated stove.

Despite these annoyances, however, unmediated immersion in the wilderness exhilarated Bird:

> But, above all, it was exciting to lie there, with no better shelter than a bower of pines, on a mountain 11,000 feet high, in the very heart of the Rocky Range, under twelve degrees of frost, hearing sounds of wolves, with shivering stars looking through a fragrant canopy, with arrowy pines for bed-posts, and for a night lamp the red flames of a camp-fire.

The mountains shut out civilization, freeing Bird from restrictive social expectations. Bird also sought transcendence, which Lee Rozelle compares to Freud's "oceanic" feeling, in the solitary experience of nature. The scenery "satisfies my soul," she says, describing herself as "possessed" by the mountains. Nature inspired her to worship and offered an ideal sanctuary:

> To be alone in the park from the afternoon till the last glory of the afterglow has faded, with no books but a Bible and Prayer-book, is truly delightful. No worthier temple for a "Te Deum" or "Gloria in Excelsis" could be found than this "temple not made with hands."

She often describes particularly moving vistas as "unearthly" or "fantastic," calling one location "another world," another "fairyland," and another "dreamland." She relies heavily on words such as "entrancing" and "intoxicating" to convey the intense emotional impact of the landscape and exclaims at the beauty, glory, sublimity, majesty, magnificence, and grandeur of her surroundings. On several occasions, she remarks that the scene before her exceeds the power of language to describe.

Bird's depictions of nature as obstacle, threat, and sublime landscape certainly imply respect for the land, but her appropriation of nature as an antagonist in a drama focusing on herself and her construction of the landscape primarily as a catalyst for her own transcendence also suggest refusal to recognize nature as a separate subject that is not an object for human use. Bird appropriates nature for rather benign purposes—demonstrating her adventurousness and reaching spiritual satisfaction—but she nonetheless *uses* the landscape, treats it as an object. Bird believes nature belongs to the beholder. It is no surprise that Bird claims Estes Park is "mine by right of love, appropriation, and appreciation."

Bird describes not only the land itself and her relation to it but also the trees and plants that thrive in Colorado:

> Cotton-wood trees were green and bright, aspens shivered in gold tremulousness, wild grape-vines trailed their lemon-colored foliage along the ground, and the Virginia creeper hung its crimson sprays here and there, lightening up green and gold into glory.

What begins as a long list of wildflowers also grows into personification:

> Here are dandelions, buttercups, larkspurs, harebells, violets, roses, blue gentian, columbine, painter's brush, and fifty others, blue and yellow predominating; and though their blossoms are stiffened by the cold every morning, they are starring the grass and drooping over the brook long before noon, making the most of their brief lives in the sunshine.

She often uses one natural object as a metaphor for another, comparing the plains to the sea, scarlet poison oak to geraniums, and tufts of needles on fir trees to white chrysanthemums, for example. Scientific terminology appears only occasionally ("Of ferns, after many a long hunt, I have found only the *Cystoperis fragilis* and the *Blechnum spicant,* but I hear that the *Pteris aquiline* is also found") and clichés, such as "straight as an arrow" to describe a pine tree, are rare.

Whenever she reports at any length on an animal, Bird both describes it and assesses its relation to humankind. She notes the prevalence of bears in the woods and observes that they do not attack unless wounded or provoked. Her extended discussion of the "large villages...peopled" by prairie dogs betrays fascination, perhaps amusement, but she cannot help but see the creatures in terms of damage they will cause to the prairie, making travel difficult for settlers on their way west. She dwells on the marvelous engineering feats and careful providence of beavers but concludes with a remark about their coats as commodities. She celebrates the plentiful catch available to trout fishermen, and, though she questions the cruelty and "terrorism" involved in branding and slaughtering cattle, she clearly enjoys the exciting roundup in which she participates. Her most poetic depiction of wildlife forms a lengthy portion of her claim to possess Estes Park. In the passage, Bird appreciates the unique beauties of each creature, attributes moral qualities to some, and resents the threat humans pose to all 19 species she describes. Ultimately, however, her statement is still a claim of possession that objectifies nature.

Bird develops affectionate relationships with several domesticated animals in Colorado. She apparently prefers the companionship of her first horse to any human escort:

> I could have ridden him a hundred miles as easily as thirty. We have only been together two days, yet we are firm friends, and thoroughly understand each other. I should not require another companion on a long mountain tour.

She steps up as an advocate of more humane methods of training horses, but in a way that reveals that, despite her friendship with her horse, Bird still regards the species as properly at mankind's service. Bird appreciates the sagacity of her next horse, Birdie, who refuses to cross a bridge that Bird later learns is considered quite dangerous, once again valuing an animal for its service to humans. Bird's affection for Birdie and Ring, her guide's dog, seems to stem largely from services provided and the attention these animals lavish upon her.

A Lady's Life in the Rocky Mountains is a carefully crafted drama, designed to construct a specific idea of its author. Nature is recruited as the antagonist, against which the protagonist can define herself. Although filled with vivid descriptions of the land, its plants, and its animals, the book is not about the Rockies; they are relegated to a prepositional phrase that identifies the location of the book's main focus: Bird's life. Her personifications of mountains, flora, and fauna lend a poetic timbre to the work, but this figurative language is employed specifically for sentimental effect and does not represent recognition of nature as an independent entity in its own right.

Bird returned to Edinburgh in January 1874. Life at home soon brought her to the sick bed again, and a marriage proposal from doctor John Bishop made her uncomfortable. To escape both her illness and her doctor, Bird sailed for Japan in spring 1878. The ports of Japan mimicked the west, but as Bird traveled north, she found the people less civilized. In January 1879, Bird stopped in Malaya. She rode an elephant in a basket slung across the pachyderm's neck and was soaked when the elephant showered himself with muddy water. She delighted in a dinner party with two apes—Eblis (21 inches) and Mahmoud (4 feet)—at which all parties were served with crystal and porcelain. She accepted the domestication of both wild species.

In April 1880, after a battle with typhoid, her sister Hennie died. Hennie had been Bird's best friend and cherished audience, and Bird was devastated by her loss. That *Unbeaten Tracks in Japan* far outsold a competing book by Sir Edward Reid was little consolation. Needing a companion to lean on in her grief, Bird finally married John Bishop on March 8, 1881. She wore mourning black. Bishop assured Bird that she could travel whenever she pleased, but she strove to be a conventional Victorian wife. In 1882 the King of the Sandwich Islands awarded Bird the Hawaiian Literary Order of Merit for *Unbeaten Tracks*. John Murray threw her a large party, at which she held court dressed in Japanese attire. *The Golden Chersonese,* about Malaysia, appeared in April 1883 and was quite popular. Only Emily Innes's *The Golden Chersonese with the Gilding Off* criticized Bird's account, claiming that Bird was catered to wherever she went.

John Bishop died March 6, 1886, after several years' illness, and Bird felt free to fly. When Major Herbert Sawyer of the Intelligence Department of the Indian Army approached Bird about being his cover on a mission to Persia, she became a part of Britain's effort to gather the intelligence necessary to win the colonization race with France and Russia. At this point, Lila Harper notes, the thematic focus of Bird's writing underwent an important shift from "personal liberation" to the "success of British imperial expansion." Bird also altered her style, says Harper, to include more information about indigenous people, natural resources, and the shape of the land, in order to establish her scientific authority with professional groups, such as the Royal Geographic Society, and to convey the importance of her work to imperial security and progress.

In December 1891 *Journeys in Persia and Kurdistan* appeared in two 400-page volumes, with a picture of Bird astride her horse but without Bird's detailed maps of uncharted territory, which the Intelligence Department had classified. The successful book received over 90 reviews. In 1892 Bird turned down an invitation to speak to the all-male Royal Geographic Society. When the RGS decided to admit members of other geographic societies, they perforce admitted female members of those societies, including Bird, but then later refused further female members. Bird found this exclusion a "dastardly injustice to women."

In January 1894 Bird explored the Han River in Korea in a 28 foot by 5 foot boat. She professionally recorded the daily temperature, altitude, and barometric pressure and collected and dried numerous plants and flowers. Her long account of her six-week journey was published in its entirety in the RGS journal. To see China later in 1894, Bird traveled 1,300 miles west up the Yangtze River in an old houseboat, taking pictures

and developing them as she went. In Szechuan she adopted Chinese dress and hired a bamboo chair. The curiosity of the people turned to hostility as she went further inland. One local group almost hammered down her bedroom door; another crowd threw stones, knocking Bird unconscious. At China's border with Tibet she was able to see Mount Everest, a moment of triumph for Bird, as Evelyn Kaye notes. Bird spoke to the RGS on May 10, 1897, about her five months in the mountains of northwest China. Her talk included 45 slides and 200 photographs. She was the first woman to speak to the RGS. Her *Korea and Her Neighbors* (1898) sold 2,000 copies in two days and was reprinted five times in one year. In November 1899 *The Yangtze Valley and Beyond* appeared.

Bird was diagnosed with a fibroid tumor around her heart and lungs and died on October 7, 1904, at age 72. She was buried in Dean Cemetery in Edinburgh beside her parents, Hennie, and John Bishop. Notices of Bird's death appeared in the London *Times*, the *New York Times*, and the *Denver Post*, among many others. The RGS, although it never granted Bird an award while she lived, praised her work in its journal after her death.

Bird's work is valuable to students of American nature writing not only because *A Lady's Life in the Rocky Mountains* captures humankind's relation to nature in the nineteenth-century American West but also because it exemplifies nature writing as self-discovery and self-definition. Although Bird was not born in America and focused her later work on lands far from American shores, she represents an important moment in American nature writing. *A Lady's Life in the Rocky Mountains* shaped the way an entire generation of English speakers envisioned the American West. Her condemnation of the destruction of the land by commercial interests and her advocacy of the humane treatment of animals called her contemporaries to more responsible stewardship at a time when such was regularly discarded as romantic and impractical and anticipated

modern concern for sustainable interaction
with nature.

PRIMARY BIBLIOGRAPHY

Books

The Aspects of Religion in the United States of America,
anonymous (London: Sampson, Low, 1859; New
York: Arno, 1859).

The Englishwoman in America, anonymous (London:
Murray, 1856; New York: Arno, 1859).

Notes on Old Edinburgh, signed as I.L.B. (Edinburgh:
Edmunston & Douglas, 1869).

*The Hawaiian Archipelago: Six Months Among the
Palm Groves, Coral Reefs, & Volcanoes of the Sand-
wich Islands* (London: Murray, 1875; New York:
Putnam, 1882).

A Lady's Life in the Rocky Mountains (London: Murray, 1879; New York: Putnam, 1882).

*Unbeaten Tracks in Japan: An Account of Travels in the
Interior, Including Visits to the Aborigines of Yezo and
the Shrines of Nikkó and Isé* (2 vols., London: Mur-
ray, 1880; 1 vol., New York: Putnam, [1880?];
republished as *Unbeaten Tracks in Japan: An
Account of Travels on Horseback in the Interior,
Including Visits to the Aborigines of Yezo and the
Shrines of Nikkó and Isé*, 2 vols. (New York: Put-
nam, 1881); abridged as *Unbeaten Tracks in Japan*
(New York: Dutton, [1916]).

The Golden Chersonese and the Way Thither (London:
Murray, 1883; New York: Putnam, 1883).

*Journeys in Persia and Kurdistan, Including a Summer in
the Upper Karun Region and a Visit to the Nestorian
Rayahs*, 2 vols. (London: Murray, 1891; New York:
Putnam, 1891).

Heathen Claims and Christian Duty (London: Church
Missionary Society, 1893; New York: Board of Foreign Missions of the Presbyterian Church, 1893;
republished in *Heathen Claims and Christian Duty,
by Mrs. Bishop. Our Omnipotent Leader, by C.H.
Spurgeon* (London: Morgan & Scott, 1894; Boston:
Printed for American Board, 1898).

Among the Tibetans (London: Religious Tract Society, 1894; New York & Chicago: Revell, 1894).

*Korea and Her Neighbours: A Narrative of Travel, with
an Account of the Recent Viscissitudes and Present
Positions of the Country* (New York & Chicago:
Revell, 1897; 2 vols., London: Murray, 1898);
republished as *Korea and Her Neighbours: A Narrative of Travel, with an Account of the Vicissitudes and
Position of the Country*, 2 vols. (London: Murray,
1905).

*Japan and the Faith of Christendom: With Special Refer-
ence to the Work Supported by the Guild of St. Paul,
in the Diocese of South Tokyo* (London: Town-
shend, 1898).

*The Yangtze Valley and Beyond: An Account of
Journeys in China, Chiefly in the Province of Sze
Chuan and among the Man-Tze of the Somo Territory*
(London: Murray, 1899; New York: Putnam,
1900).

Chinese Pictures (London: Cassell, 1900; New York:
Bowman, [1900?]).

A Traveller's Testimony (London: C.M.S., 1905).

Other

Susan Ballard, trans., *Fairy Tales from Far Japan*,
preface by Isabella Bird (London: Religious Tract
Society, 1898).

Edward Bird, *The Revival in America by an English
Eye-Witness*, edited and introduced by Isabella
Bird (London: Seeley, 1858).

John Stuart Blackie, *Hymns and Poems of the Late
Henrietta A. Bird. With Biographical Sketch of the
Author*, ed. Isabella Bird (Edinburgh: James Tay-
lor, 1883).

"The Visitation of Mountain Jim," *Phantasms of the
Living*, eds. Edmund Gurney, Frederick Myers,
and Frank Podmore, 2 vols. (London: Rooms of
the Society for Physical Research, 1886), Vol. 1,
531–32.

Periodical Publications—Uncollected

"A Visit to Dr. Guthrie's Edinburgh Ragged
Schools," *The Leisure Hour* 10 (1861): 247–51.

"Australia Felix: Impressions of Victoria," *The
Leisure Hour* 26 (1877): 39–44; 87–92; 149–52;
183–86; 218–20; 249–51; 314–18; 413–16;
469–72.

"Letters from the Rocky Mountains," *The Leisure
Hour* 27 (1878): 24–28; 61–62; 72–76; 110–11;
136–41; 215–21; 280–85; 360–65; 471–75; 501–
8; 615–19; 634–37; 669–71; 693–96; 740–43;
781–84; 795–97.

"A Pilgrimage to Sinai," *The Leisure Hour* 35 (1886):
15–20; 94–98; 173–78; 233–38; 314–17.

"Under Chloroform," *Murray's Magazine* 3 (1887):
327–30.

"A Journey through Lesser Tibet," *The Scottish Geographical Magazine* (1892): 513–28.

"Among the Tibetans," *The Leisure Hour* 42 (1893):
238–44; 306–12; 380–86; 450–56.

"Notes on Morocco," *Monthly Review* 5 (1901):
89–102.

SECONDARY BIBLIOGRAPHY

References

Susan Armitage, "Another Lady's Life in the Rocky Mountains," in *Women and the Journey: The Female Travel Experience*, ed. Bonnie Frederick and Susan H. McLeod (Pullman: Washington State University Press, 1993), 25–35.

Pat Barr, *A Curious Life for a Lady: The Story of Isabella Bird* (London: Penguin, 1970).

Isabella Bird, *Isabella Lucy Bird's "A Lady's Life in the Rocky Mountains": An Annotated Text*, ed. Ernest S. Bernard (Norman: University of Oklahoma Press, 1999).

Kay Chubbuck, *Letters to Henrietta* (London: John Murray, 2002).

Lila Marz Harper, "Isabella Bird Bishop: An RGS Fellow," in *Solitary Travelers: Nineteenth-Century Women's Travel Narratives and the Scientific Vocation* (London: Fairleigh Dickinson University Press, 2001), 133–74.

Evelyn Kaye, *Amazing Traveler, Isabella Bird: The Biography of a Victorian Adventurer* (Boulder: Blue Panda, 1999).

Vera Norwood, "Heroines of Nature: Four Women Respond to the American Landscape," in *The Ecocriticism Reader: Landmarks in Literary Ecology*, ed. Cheryll Glotfelty and Harold Fromm (University of Georgia Press, 1996), 323–50.

Lee Rozelle, "Oceanic Terrain: Peristaltic and Ecological Sublimity in Poe's 'The Journal of Julius Rodman' and Isabella Bird's *A Lady's Life in the Rocky Mountains*" in *From Virgin Land to Disney World: Nature and Its Discontents in the USA of Yesterday and Today*, ed. Bernd Herzogenrath (Amsterdam and New York: Rodpi, 2001), 105–22.

Ulrike Stamm, "The Role of Nature in Two Women's Travel Accounts: Appropriation and Escape," in *Being/s in Transit: Travelling, Migration, Dislocation*, ed. Liselotte Glage (Amsterdam: Rodopi, 2000), 155–72.

Neltje Blanchan (Neltje Blanchan Doubleday) (October 23, 1865–February 21, 1918)

Gloria Shearin

Neltje Blanchan De Graff Doubleday's career as an author of nature books and magazine articles for the popular press was relatively short, with the bulk of her work completed over the course of less than 15 years—beginning in the late 1800s and ending around 1910. Only three of her books were published after that time, one posthumously; none contained much new information. Her topics—birds, wild flowers, and gardens—appealed to a wide audience, and her books sold well, no doubt partly because of Doubleday, Page & Company's willingness to advertise her works in publications such as *Atlantic Monthly* and *Harper's*, but also because the texts matched a national interest in nature. Apparently she preferred that readers not know her identity as publisher Frank N. Doubleday's wife, for all of her published work appeared under the pseudonym Neltje Blanchan. She was, according to her granddaughter "Neltje," a significant nature writer, one "who contributed much to Doubleday in its early days by writing the nature books that kept the presses rolling."

Today Doubleday's works remain significant to early theories of environmental preservation and the foundations of the conservation movement, particularly in her advocacy of legislation to protect bird populations. Not a trained scientist, she combined the science scholarship of others with her personal experience and a genuine love of her subjects. She argued for a harmony between humans and nature, depicting birds, insects, and plants in symbiotic relationships and humans marveling at their observations of nature. No doubt a careful researcher who drew on myriad sources (some not altogether accurate), Doubleday accentuated her aesthetic approach with a liberal inclusion of poetry from a wide range of authors and underscored the scientific basis of her information by equally numerous references to well-known individuals—Carl Linnaeus and Charles Darwin, for example. Likely her emphasis on bird songs stemmed from her musical training as a pianist.

Born October 23, 1865, in Chicago, Doubleday was the daughter of Liverius and Alice (Fair) De Graff. Both branches of her father's family—the Blanchans who had originated in French Flanders and the De Graffs—had settled in the Dutch-Huguenot colony at Esopus, New York, in the seventeenth century. Her father owned a men's clothing store and evidently prospered, as he educated his daughter in elite private schools, St. John's in New York City and Misses Masters' School in Dobbs Ferry, New York. Apparently, Doubleday received a good education in the fashion of her time, but it was not necessarily a scholarly one. In 1885, her family moved to Plainfield, New Jersey, and in 1886, when she was 20, she married Frank Nelson Doubleday, then editor of *Book Buyer*, subsequently manager of *Scribner's Magazine* (1887), and, eventually, owner of various Doubleday publishing firms. The Doubledays had three children. In 1892, when her first child was two, Doubleday launched her literary career when the Brooklyn Women's Indian Association published *The Piegan Indians*. Six books on birds and three on flowers and gardens followed, along with numerous magazine articles primarily for *Ladies' Home Journal* and *Country Life in America,* some book reviews and a biographical sketch, and at least one book chapter on Indian baskets. Doubleday also kept journals. The property of her granddaughter, these primarily chronicle her travels and are unpublished.

Except for her being a writer, Doubleday's adult life followed what was generally expected of women of her class—participation in philanthropic societies and travel. Writing in the *International Encyclopedia of Women Scientists,* Elizabeth Oakes characterizes Doubleday as possessing "charm, energy, and warmth" and as determined to make a name for herself. Certainly being so much a part of the publishing world probably led her to writing, but likely she was already inclined to research and study. Taking a moral stance, whether in relation to conservation or human behavior, may well have been second nature to her, for it is evident in her works, but it also figures in a story concerning Doubleday, Page & Company as a publishing firm. In 1900, while Doubleday and her husband were abroad, the publishing house accepted Theodore Dreiser's *Sister Carrie,* a novel many considered scandalous. When the couple returned and read the proofs, they were, by all accounts, horrified, and Frank Doubleday tried to void the contract. Unable to do so, he fulfilled it to the letter, printing only 1,008 copies, leaving many of these in storage, and refusing to publicize the work. A bitter Dreiser blamed Neltje Doubleday and repeated his version of the conflict as often as possible. Contemporary scholars believe that Neltje and Frank Doubleday may have been more concerned with the economic results of public reaction than with their personal beliefs.

Throughout her adult life, Doubleday undertook considerable charity work. In December 1917, she and her husband traveled to China on a mission for the American Red Cross. She died unexpectedly of unknown causes in Canton, China, on February 21, 1918. A memorial service was held at Matinecock Neighborhood House in New York, another of her charitable involvements.

Doubleday's first book, *The Piegan Indians,* a short volume of only ten pages, prefigured her later works devoted exclusively to nature. It followed, as Beverly Seaton notes in *American Women Writers,* the general thrust of nature writers whose eclectic interests included "Indian lore, birds, plants, and camping skills." Deborah Strom places the text and its emphasis on Native American education and handicrafts within the work of other female naturalists of that time, including Fannie Hardy Eckstrom and Cordelia Stanwood. Consisting of an anthropological and historical overview of the tribe coupled with an analysis of a report by Indian agent George Steel, her text urges the Brooklyn Women's Indian Association and the Bay Ridge Indian Association (Doubleday served as treasurer to this organization) to establish a mission on tribal grounds so that the Piegans "may have at least one efficient object lesson before them—that of a Christian home." Although, as Jerome A. Jackson states in *American National Biography,* the work was hardly "influential," it foreshadowed Doubleday's later concern with the damaging forces of modern civilization in its depictions of the natural environment and the primitive Indian life as destroyed by development, the locomotive, having "frightened away the moose, the deer, the fox and the bear from their hunting grounds."

Five years later in her first major work, *Bird Neighbors, An Introductory Acquaintance with One Hundred and Fifty Birds Commonly Found in the Gardens, Meadows, and Woods about Our Homes,* Doubleday adopted a successful format of combining scientific data with personal experience, all within the context of sheer joy in what she described. Unlike many of the other nature writers of her time, she generously supplemented her information with illustrations, often full color and full page. This approach assured Doubleday a niche in the popular literature of her day—translating scientific information, without the stale, impersonal tone of Latinate lists, into material ordinary individuals could understand to appreciate bird habitats and behavior. An assumption that readers want to know about birds, but do not necessarily want to know about them in scientific jargon, underlies her work. Although she objectifies birds—including scientific names and scientific terminology—the major portion of her text is personal, and her arrangement of content reflects not scientific categories but an ordinary, perhaps a poetic, approach to identification: color. After devoting a few pages to abbreviated scientific descriptions of bird families phrased in fragments, Doubleday identifies 19 habitats couched in nonscientific terminology. "Birds that choose conspicuous perches," "Birds of roadsides and fences," and "Birds that sing on the wing" are three. Her treatment of seasons and sizes involves lists only, but her treatment of the birds themselves is expansive and entrancing. Her mix of objective data with colorful and whimsical phrasing certainly was appealing since *Bird Neighbors* sold over 250,000 copies.

In presenting the various color categories, Doubleday refers to other bird watchers, but elevates herself to expert level and introduces her conservation agenda. She is frequently mindful of contradictory views of birds, describing, for example, the value for those with a "picturesque" eye of the "broad, strong dash of color...of crows flapping their course above a corn-field, against an October sky," but then acknowledging that the farmer with

his "practical eye" sees the same scene and, legitimately, reaches for his gun. A tension between these views appears throughout, and Doubleday seems to recognize its legitimacy from an economic standpoint, although sometimes she argues that some who condemn particular birds (not herself) are misguided and misinformed.

Doubleday cannot absolve some treatment of birds and frequently castigates "unthinking" humans (especially Southerners) for destroying countless wild birds to feed their desire for gourmet dinners and outlandish millinery decorations, and she often notes the effects of encroaching development on bird populations—disrupted migration paths, loss of natural habitat, and altered species behavior, including unsafe confidence in all humans. Yet she also shows an adversarial relationship between birds and other animals, particularly snakes, and between one kind of bird and another. She finds particularly offensive the cowbird that deposits eggs in the nests of other birds and the yellow-bellied sapsucker that has a "pernicious and most intemperate thirst for sap." Still, her sympathies clearly lie with the birds, despite damage some might cause, defending the downy woodpecker who in his "zeal" girds and thus kills a tree.

To engender a positive response to birds, she adopts an anthropomorphic view, labeling them "devoted mates," "wives," and "neighbors." However, even as she characterizes them in positive human terms, she emphasizes negative traits corresponding to human failings—the female who never learns her mate will "relapse into the savage and forget all his tender wiles," for example. She sprinkles her discussions with quotations from poetry, references to literary works, and personal stories of bird behavior to engage her readers, and she refers to acknowledged experts such as naturalist John Burroughs, who wrote the introduction to the book, and to respected scientific research facilities such as the Smithsonian Institution to lend credence to her content. Doubleday even correlates bird appreciation with patriotism. Some stories appear exaggerated. She maintains, for example, that she has been able to stroke "in the freest manner" wild birds sitting on their nest.

Birds That Hunt and Are Hunted, Life Histories of One Hundred and Seventy Birds of Prey, Game Birds and Waterfowls (also published later as *Game Birds*), Doubleday's second significant nature work, appeared in 1898, its format replicating that of *Bird Neighbors*: scientific data phrased in a lively manner, highlighted by personal observations and anecdotes. In this work, however, Doubleday adopts a stronger conservation stance from the outset, including an introduction written by G.O. Shields, president of the League of American Sportsmen and editor of *Recreation,* and, in later editions, a "note of appreciation" to the Audubon Societies, thereby situating her own book within national efforts to awaken the conservation conscience. Shields cites "alarming" statistics of declining bird populations and predicts the "total extermination of many birds" within 20 years if the current rate continues. While Doubleday in *Bird Neighbors* had referred to "unthinking" and "cruel" women who purchase hats decorated with bird feathers, Shields characterizes such behavior as having a "barbaric purpose" and calls for a "great crusade against bird slaughter." He maintains that both he and Doubleday hope for an increase in sportsmen who hunt "without guns."

Doubleday's own language is more subdued, more conciliatory. In her "Preface" she asserts that "Nature adjusts her balances so wisely that we cannot afford to tamper with them" from an economic standpoint; likewise, she notes the need for legislation and enforcement of laws to avert "wanton destruction of bird life." She condemns hunters for shooting inedible birds such as grebes and loons simply for sport and describes professional bird-egg hunters in emotional terms intended to sway her audience. She disdains women who wear hats ornamented with birds, for example terns, whole or in sections, but softens her condemnation with a reflection that chicken feathers are more often

being accepted as substitutes. In other instances, Doubleday romanticizes, appealing to her audience in a different manner—a jaeger, for example, is a "dusky pirate, strong of wing and marvelously skilful and alert in its flight." A corollary with Thoreau's affinity with nature appears in her reverence for birds. Her respect for Thoreau and his ideas emerges in more than one book.

Doubleday extends her appreciation of birds beyond the economics of agriculture to their clever behavior. Indeed, her portraits often add a touch of wry humor as illustrated in her description of auks, murres, and puffins as moving "with a shuffling motion, laboriously and with the underparts often dragging over the ground" and her portrait of grebes as "water-witches" ironically outsmarting hunters because of their ability to escape by diving deeply and swimming away, a trick practiced even by "fledglings." Again, she describes birds anthropomorphically as "devoted lovers and parents," a strategy likely intended to influence readers to accept her views. But, like humans, birds do not live together in harmony; some tyrannize smaller, weaker species. And some of the smaller, weaker species find ways to outsmart the larger ones.

Nature's Garden, an Aid to Knowledge of Our Wild Flowers and Their Insect Visitors, published in 1900, illustrated a logical expansion of Doubleday's interest in nature and reflected an appreciation for this subject, one apparently shared by an American public fascinated by all aspects of nature. It uses color to classify flowers since, according to Doubleday, novices with "no knowledge of botany...can most readily identify the specimen found afield by this method, which has the added advantage of being the simple one adopted by the higher insects ages before books were written." In her "Preface," Doubleday acknowledges a surfeit of similar texts, but distinguishes her work as different because it explores the relationship between wild flowers and the insects that gather nectar from them. She posits a flower as having "inner meaning, hopes and fears that inspire its brief existence, a scheme of salvation for its species in the struggle for survival that it has been slowly perfecting with some insect's help through the ages." As "sentient beings" flowers have evolved to assure their survival. The higher levels, without exception, no longer self-fertilize; instead they, like humans and animals, must mate with another flower, even though they require bees and other pollinators for this mating. Throughout the book, Doubleday refers to scientific issues, such as Sprengel's theory that orchids produce no nectar, and offers proof for or against these. Much of her discussion of wild flowers parallels her earlier discussion of birds. In a manner akin to her examination of bird migration patterns, usefulness of nonnative species, and threatened extinction, she considers the effects of plant dispersion across long distances and importation of species. She also warns of the dangers of overpicking specimens in the wild.

How to Attract the Birds and Other Talks about Bird Neighbors, published in 1902, differs in format from Doubleday's previous works and in audience, but not from her environmental and aesthetic stances. The text's language suggests it is directed toward a younger, less educated audience than the two previous books. However, as several of the chapters appeared in a series of articles for *Ladies' Home Journal,* beginning in March 1902—some under the same, some under slightly altered titles—Doubleday's audience may well have been adults. This book affirms Doubleday's belief that "the same primal motives govern the actions of plant, bird, beast and man alike,—that all sentient beings act intelligently through the same strong, animating desire, their powers differing only in degree, not in kind." It likewise affirms her ideas of symbiotic relationships, especially between plant and insect species. She attributes considerable intelligence to birds, showing them "learning" behaviors such as how to craft appropriate nests and describes their nests symbolically as representing a developed "aesthetic sense of the home-maker" and suggesting birds have an imagination. Scattered throughout the

chapters are first-person narratives, often experiences of epiphany. Her appreciation for bird songs and beauty appears in contrast to her dislike of domesticated birds, especially chickens, and she advances an explanation for bird migration, envisioning it as having begun as "roving excursions from home" that gradually lengthened and eventually became hereditary. She considers migration a subject that "stirs" the "imaginations as no other phase of bird life does" since, despite scientific inquiry, "the wonder and the mystery remain." Although her science is not consistently accurate, her enthusiasm for her subject is clear, and her representation of ecological relationships and mechanisms was much closer to the Darwinian view than she was probably aware.

Birds That Every Child Should Know, published in 1907 and identified as a children's book, is organized as conversational chapters, each examining a group of birds. Although certainly the book explains the value of bird study for children—it trains their eyes and ears, keeps children happily busy, and "exercises the sympathies"—it seems, as Jerome A. Jackson says, more directed toward teachers and members of the National Association of Audubon Societies, a newly formed environmental group. Doubleday again advocates enacting conservation laws on the order of those now in place in the North banning the confinement or sale of wild birds, questions why there is no law protecting the beautiful blue heron, and warns that Americans will "pay the penalty for ignorantly tampering with nature." She moderates her stance on hunting to sanction it for poor people who need the meat, but she has no "patience with the pampered epicures" who dine on song birds such as quail. Yet Doubleday is selective in terms of species that deserve protection. In the case of hawks, for example, she advocates the extermination of Cooper's hawk, the sharp-shinned hawk, and the goshawk because these eat poultry and song birds, but presents scientific proof—a report on the dissection of stomachs—to support her assertion that some hawks benefit humans by eating rodents that destroy crops. Often Doubleday includes statistics from scientific experiments or ornithologists. Sometimes when factual reports appear to be questionable—as in the case of a Professor Beal who contends that "tree sparrows alone destroy eight hundred and seventy-five tons of noxious weed seeds every winter"—she cautions that while she does not know how the figures were determined, they show "how incalculably great must be our debt to the entire sparrow tribe."

In 1909, Doubleday's writing took another turn, one at least partially deriving from her interest in wild flowers and their potential as garden flowers. Heralded in *The Nation* as a "satisfactory" book that "fills such a unique place in the literature of American gardening," *The American Flower Garden*, as lavishly illustrated as her other works had been, was based on her belief that humans must work in partnership with nature, "in harmony with her eternal laws," and should consult garden design experts even before building their homes. Chapters (some of which appear in *Country Life in America*) explore various garden styles (formal, old-fashioned, naturalistic, and wild), building materials (rock and water), and plants (trees and shrubs, perennials and annuals, bulbs, roses, and vines). Of particular value in this book are the detailed lists of plants suitable for each type of garden. Many of her admonitions—to buy good stock regardless of cost—are sensible, but an elitist attitude runs throughout the book as Doubleday criticizes popular taste—planting flowers in the shape of one's initials on an otherwise barren lawn, for example. She argues that ordinary people seldom understand design and that hired gardeners without direction may destroy the architect's attempts to connect a house with the landscape. Studying her book, she seems to suggest, would rectify many misunderstandings about color and the arrangement of plants.

To create gardens similar to those Doubleday described—particularly the formal water, rock, and rose gardens—would require acres, considerable capital, and a full-time staff. Although seemingly out of touch with

ordinary readers since none of the illustrations in the text picture gardens on a small scale, Doubleday may nonetheless have been aware of the incongruity between the "American" suggested by her title and illustrations and the American who could afford her gardens; frequently she argued that even those without large plots and financial resources could create beautiful spaces if they simply learned design principles and slowly implemented them. This argument seems similar to that made in contemporary popular periodicals. According to Doubleday, ever-multiplying perennials would result in an inexpensive but attractive garden for those willing to work and wait. She frequently advises trading plants with friends in order to have a garden "full of associations and of sentiment"; likewise, she suggests transplanting flowers, shrubs, and trees from the wild as another cost-saving measure, one that would create a naturalistic garden, the style she believes "is destined to become the dominant style of gardening" in the United States. What she does not recommend is falling prey to nursery catalogues. She contends the pictures in these publications beguile, and information regarding appropriate planting areas and zones are incomplete or inaccurate.

Birds Worth Knowing (1917), *Wild Flowers Worth Knowing* (1917), and the posthumously published *Birds; Selections from the Writings of Neltje Blanchan* (1926) drew from Doubleday's earlier works. *Birds Worth Knowing* and *Wild Flowers Worth Knowing*, adapted by Asa Don Dickinson, were published as part of Doubleday's *Little Nature Library* that included such works as *Garden Flowers Worth Knowing* (R. M. McCurdy), *Trees Worth Knowing* (Julia Ellen Rogers), and *Animals Worth Knowing* (Clarence M. Weed). A Canadian publication combining her earlier bird books was also published.

By standards of contemporary ecology and conservation, Doubleday's views fall short, even conflict. In advocating importation and exportation of plant and animal species while bemoaning the effects of one importation (the English sparrow), in not worrying about wild plants invading gardens and domesticated plants escaping into the wild, and in suggesting the extermination of certain bird species, Doubleday's stances are not those of today. According to Robert H. Welker, she was, however, "a vivid and fairly authoritative nature writer" with "a wide readership." Reading her books provides considerable insight into this country's early conservation movement. Her books contributed to the rise of this country's early conservation movement and participated in the rise of popular American nature writing along with those of her contemporaries, such as John Burroughs, Mabel Osgood Wright, and Susan Fenimore Cooper, all of whom advocated in their written work for the preservation of bird species and for a revaluation of the human relationship to the natural environment.

PRIMARY BIBLIOGRAPHY

Books

The Piegan Indians (New York: Brooklyn Women's Indian Association, 1892).

Bird Neighbors: An Introductory Acquaintance with One Hundred and Fifty Birds Commonly Found in the Gardens, Meadows, and Woods about Our Homes (New York: Doubleday & McClure, 1897; London: Sampson, Low & Marston, 1898; Toronto: G.N. Morang, 1900).

Birds that Hunt and Are Hunted, Life Histories of One Hundred and Seventy Birds of Prey, Game Birds and Waterfowls (New York: Doubleday & McClure, 1898).

Nature's Garden (New York: Doubleday, Page & Company, 1900; London: W. Heineman, 1901).

How to Attract the Birds (New York: Doubleday, Page & Company, 1902; London: Wm. Heinemann, 1903).

Birds That Every Child Should Know (New York: Doubleday, Page & Company, 1907).

The American Flower Garden (New York: Doubleday, Page & Company, 1909; Toronto: Mission Book, 1913).

Birds Worth Knowing (Garden City: Doubleday, Page & Company, 1917).

Canadian Birds Worth Knowing: Bird Neighbors, Birds That Hunt and Are Hunted (Game Birds), How to Attract the Birds, Birds Every Child Should Know (Toronto: Musson, 1917).

Wild Flowers Worth Knowing (Garden City: Doubleday, Page & Company, 1917).

Birds (Garden City: Doubleday, Page & Company, 1926).

Other

Maurus Jókai, *The Nameless Castle*, trans. S.E. Boggs, biographical sketch by Blanchan (New York: Doubleday, Page & Company, 1898).

"What the Basket Means to the Indian," in *How to Make Baskets* by Mary White (New York: Doubleday, Page & Company, 1901), 181–94.

Selected Periodical Publications— Uncollected

"Village Thrift," *Ladies' Home Journal* 18 (November 1901): 30.

"How to Encourage the Birds to Come," *Ladies' Home Journal* 19 (March 1902): 7.

"Why the Birds Come and Go," *Ladies' Home Journal* 19 (April 1902): 10.

"How Birds Built Their Nests," *Ladies' Home Journal* 19 (May 1902): 8.

"How Birds Care for Their Babies," *Ladies' Home Journal* 19 (June 1902): 3–4.

"How the Birds Protect Themselves," *Ladies' Home Journal* 19 (July 1902): 10.

"The Birds' Christmas Dinner," *Ladies' Home Journal* 20 (December 1902): 44.

"Lessons for Americans from the Art of Garden Design in Italy," *Country Life in America* 11 (March 1907): 533.

"Gardens Anyone May Have," *Ladies' Home Journal* 25 (April 1908): 44.

"Formal Gardens in America," *Country Life in America* 14 (July 1908): 271–74, 328, 330, 332.

"Naturalistic Gardens," *Country Life in America* 14 (September 1908): 443–45, 490, 492, 494, 496, 498.

"Perennials for a Thought-Out Garden," *Country Life in America* 15 (March 1909): 475–80.

"Joy of Gardening," *Country Life in America* 17 (March 1910): 541–44.

"Prussianizing the Campaign against Sparrows," *Country Life in America* 32 (January 1917): 82.

SECONDARY BIBLIOGRAPHY

References

W.M. Frohock, "Theodore Drieser," in *American Writers*, ed. Leonard Unger, vol. 1 (New York: Scribner's, 1974).

Jerome A. Jackson, "Doubleday, Neltje de Graff," in *American National Biography,* ed. John A. Garraty and Mark C. Carnes, vol. 6 (New York: Oxford University Press, 2000), 783–84.

"Neltje," personal interview (November 25, 2004).

Elizabeth H. Oakes, "Doubleday, Neltje Blanchan De Graff," in *International Encyclopedia of Women Scientists* (New York: Facts on File, 2000); *Science Online,* www.factsonfile.com

Beverly Seaton, "Nellie [sic] Blanchan De Graff," in *American Women Writers,* ed. Lina Mainiero (New York: Unger, 1970), 536–38.

Deborah Strom, ed., *Bird Watching with American Women: A Selection of Nature Writers* (New York: Norton, 1986).

Robert H. Welker, "Doubleday, Neltje Blanchan De Graff," in *Notable American Women 1607–1950,* ed. Edward T. James, vol. I (Cambridge: Belknap, 1971), 508–9.

John Bradbury
(August 20, 1768–March 16, 1823)

Alan C. Taylor

Though his name is virtually unknown to scientists and literary scholars alike, John Bradbury was the first professional naturalist to explore and describe the territory west of the Mississippi river. While his writings themselves remain largely unexplored terrain in the landscape of literary criticism, Bradbury's meticulous descriptions of the various native peoples and natural environments he encountered in his western travels are an important contribution to American letters. His only book, *Travels in the Interior of America* (1817), was published just three years after Nicholas Biddle's paraphrase of Lewis and Clark's journals and is therefore one of the earliest views of the vast, unexplored lands of the Louisiana Purchase.

John Bradbury was born on August 20, 1768, in the town of Stalybridge, England. At an early age Bradbury became captivated by the natural world and developed an interest in the natural sciences. Under the tutelage of his schoolmaster and mentor, John Taylor, Bradbury's inclinations toward the environment took firm root. Taylor seems to have bestowed a special interest on the precocious child, as he supplemented his curriculum of mathematics and natural history by allowing the young Bradbury to accompany him on frequent nature rambles and botanical explorations of the English countryside. Bradbury's interests were apparently so intense that his father bought him a copy of the works of Carl Linnaeus, which, according to one biographer, he "studied fervently." His father's gift must have been a significant gesture as Bradbury's family was large (seven persons in all) and of very slender means.

The family's constant financial troubles caused an end to the young Bradbury's formal education and resulted in his taking a position with one of the local cotton mills. However, Bradbury continued his education independently, teaching himself French and continuing his studies of the natural sciences in his spare time. At the age of 18, Bradbury followed in the steps of Taylor by creating a night school for young men and functioning as its teacher. Bradbury's teaching, like Taylor's, seems to have favored the natural sciences; despite his dire financial state, Bradbury somehow found the means to purchase a microscope and several other scientific devices for use in his classroom. And, like Taylor's, his teaching appears to have been excellent: one of his pupils was the celebrated Jethro Tinker (1788–1871), a botanist and entomologist whose contributions to those fields, while modest, were not insignificant.

In addition to his teaching and work at the cotton mill, Bradbury must have also been publishing—or at least circulating—some of his scientific writings to a wide audience.

Though the writings in question are currently unknown, they must have been significant because it is through them that Bradbury gained the attention of Sir Joseph Banks, a prominent member of the Linnaean Society of London. In 1792 Banks wrote to Bradbury, aged 24, requesting his audience at an upcoming congress of the Linnaean Society. Bradbury accepted the invitation and shortly thereafter became a member of the prestigious organization. Through the connections he forged in London, Bradbury began earning a living as a popular landscape designer, planning country seats and planting parks or gardens for wealthy patrons such as Sir John Parnell, Duke of Leinster. Though records of Bradbury's movements are incomplete during this period, it appears that Bradbury worked in this vein until his early thirties, living in both Manchester and Liverpool, and making frequent journeys to his various landscape commissions. Between jobs, he apparently took a walking tour of Ireland, where he is said to have discovered several new species of plants; evidence suggests that he may have also discovered his wife while on this tour. While there is no record of its date, Bradbury must have married during this period, as we discover in a letter dated March 15, 1809, that he was the father of eight children.

While in Liverpool, Bradbury made the acquaintance of William Roscoe, the president of the Liverpool Botanic Garden, and William Bullock, the wealthy proprietor of a Liverpool museum of natural history. Both men were also members of the Liverpool Philosophical Society, an organization with the goal of promoting the diffusion of scientific knowledge. However, the society seems to have held a particular interest in the science of cotton production, for among its most powerful patrons were the Earl of Derby and Colonel John Leigh Philips, prominent Liverpool mill owners. Because of the colonial conflicts over the West Indies, the mill owners' shipments of raw cotton were frequently interrupted; as a result, they set about procuring an additional, more consistent source of the material. The society conjectured that regions of the Louisiana territory might yield such a supply—they merely lacked a pair of expert eyes to investigate the territory's suitability for production. With his genuinely adventurous spirit and expertise in both cotton manufacture and the natural sciences, Bradbury must have seemed an ideal candidate for the job. He was soon possessed of a membership in the society and functioning as its secretary of correspondence. By 1809, Bradbury had been charged with the survey and exploration of the trans-Mississippi West from a base of operations in New Orleans. Within this enormous territory, Bradbury was to collect all the plants "not described throughout the whole range of Nat. History" for the Liverpool Botanic Garden, and to represent the interests of the mill owners by investigating the viability of the soil and climate for the production of cotton. Though he had originally planned to relocate his wife and eight children to the United States, his Liverpool sponsors were willing to pay him only £100 per year for his services—far too little to adequately provide for his large family in America. For this reason, Bradbury elected to travel there alone in late April 1809.

When Bradbury arrived in Charleston, South Carolina, he entered a country that had newly doubled in size. In December 1803, the United States had successfully negotiated the Louisiana Purchase, which transferred control of a massive territory measuring 827,000 square miles from France to the United States. Bradbury's Liverpool sponsors had shrewdly equipped him with letters of introduction to former president Thomas Jefferson, who was not only instrumental in the Louisiana Purchase but also perhaps America's most enthusiastic sponsor of the sciences. From Charleston, Bradbury immediately traveled to Monticello where he was Jefferson's guest for several weeks in August 1809. No doubt Bradbury benefited from the former president's knowledge of the newly acquired territory and gained important intelligence from Jefferson's firsthand knowledge of Lewis and Clark's report, which had yet to be published. At some point during their many conversations, Jefferson convinced Bradbury to change his base of operations from New Orleans to the frontier town of St. Louis, a decision that later frustrated his cotton patrons at home who were desirous of a report from the major port city. As Jefferson explained to Bradbury, the immediate vicinity of New Orleans had already been described by another botanist, Andre Michaux, in his *Flora Boreali-Americana*; Bradbury would be better served investigating the territory near the Missouri River, which, as Bradbury related to Roscoe, had "not as yet been explored by any naturalist." At the conclusion of his stay, Bradbury received a letter of introduction from Jefferson addressed to Meriwether Lewis, who was then serving in St. Louis as the governor of the Louisiana Territory. There Jefferson describes Bradbury as "a man of entire worth and correct conduct" and "a botanist of the first order." Indeed, Jefferson remarks in a letter to Benjamin Smith Barton that, during his stay at Monticello, Bradbury's indefatigable romps over the hills of the estate had already yielded several plants hitherto unknown to science.

After an arduous journey across the Appalachian mountains, Bradbury landed in St. Louis on December 31, 1809. Bradbury was not to meet Meriwether Lewis when he arrived as Lewis had died in Tennessee several months prior, an apparent suicide. However, by reason of a chance meeting in Philadelphia, Bradbury arrived in St. Louis with yet another English naturalist, Thomas Nuttall (1786–1859), who was destined to travel broadly and publish extensively on his botanical discoveries in the American outback. Bradbury spent the winter and early spring of 1809–1810 with Nuttall in St. Louis collecting bird, quadruped, and insect specimens—several of which he believed to be new discoveries. The pair also made several botanizing trips together during the late autumn and winter of 1810–1811. On one such trip, the duo visited the "Negro Fork" of the Merrimac River where a great deal of lead mining was underway. It was about this experience that Bradbury later wrote an article entitled "A Description of the Minerals and Plants Found at the Lead Mines in the Missouri Territory," which he published in 1817. In this article, Bradbury explains the scientific process of mining and refining lead ore and additionally describes the mineral composition of the soil in the immediate vicinity of the mines. At the conclusion of his article, Bradbury appended a matrix of plants encountered on his investigations among the "diggings," many of them flagged with the comment "(Sp. Nova.*)," or new species. Unfortunately, Bradbury was not to be credited with their discovery; before he could publish his findings with a complete scientific description, Nuttall had included them in his *Genera of North American Plants* (1818). Sadly, this would not to be the last time Bradbury would lose the recognition for his botanical findings.

In February 1811, Bradbury wrote Roscoe to inform him of a large shipment of plants then *en route* to Liverpool and that he would "set out in a few days along with a hunting party" who intended to follow the trail blazed by Lewis and Clark up the Missouri River. The leaders of this group, Wilson P. Hunt, Ramsey Crooks, and Donald McKenzie, were agents of the Pacific Fur Company—owned by John Jacob Astor—and would later be immortalized in Washington Irving's *Astoria* (1836). Irving's synthesis of these men's letters and journal observations provide a rare glimpse of Bradbury's personality and deportment. In Irving's representation, Bradbury appears as Nuttall's foil: while the rough-hewn Astorians were equally "puzzled" by the two botanists' "passion for collecting what they considered mere useless weeds," they frequently made "merry among themselves at [Nuttall's] expense, regarding him as some whimsical kind of madman." Bradbury, on the other hand, was "less exclusive in his tastes and habits and combined the hunter and sportsman with the naturalist." In contrast to Nuttall, Bradbury had a "strong relish for incident and adventure" and was possessed of a readiness "to join any hunting or other excursion." As Irving concludes,

Bradbury "conformed to the hardy and rugged habits of the men around him and of course gained favor in their eyes." Under the protection of the Astorians, Bradbury and Nuttall left St. Louis on March 13, 1811, on a 2,000-mile journey up the Missouri River to the site that would later become Bismarck, North Dakota.

It is with this momentous event that Bradbury begins his *Travels in the Interior of America* (1817). The account contains a wealth of observations from the long journey and is typical of the era's travel literature in its mixture of genres such as the adventure narrative, anthropological observation, and scientific description. Along the way, Bradbury relates his encounters with wilderness luminaries such as the mythical Daniel Boone (then in his eighties) and the legendary John Colter, miraculous survivor of a Blackfoot Indian running ritual and discoverer of the Yellowstone geysers. Bradbury also narrates his own narrow escapes from Sioux war parties intent on preventing the white traders' ascent up the Missouri River. Yet the journey was remarkably free of violence; Bradbury appears intent on only friendly cultural exchanges and is clearly fascinated by the social mores, material culture, and religious practices of the Mandan, Osage, Pawnee, and Sioux he encounters—frequently dedicating long passages to dispelling popular myths about America's native inhabitants. However interested he appears in indulging his "relish for incident" and in making anthropological observations, nothing seems to have attracted Bradbury's attentive eye more than the territory's flora and fauna: the text contains long descriptive passages of plants and animals such as the skunk, bear, elk, deer, and prairie dog—always careful to identify the species in question in the formal language of Linnaean taxonomy.

Many of Bradbury's natural observations on the American frontier are quite valuable. His relation of the feeding habits of the *columba migratoria*, or passenger pigeon, for example, provides a significant contribution to natural science: once the most populous bird species in North America, it is now extinct due to uncontrolled hunting during the nineteenth century. Bradbury writes that "this species of pigeon associates in prodigious flocks," frequently covering "an area of several acres in extent, and the birds are so close to each other that the ground can scarcely be seen." The flock moves "through the woods with considerable celerity, picking up, as it passes along, every thing that will serve for food." "It is evident," Bradbury writes, "that the foremost ranks must be the most successful, and nothing will remain for the hindermost. But that all may have an equal chance, the instant that any rank becomes the last, it rises, and flying over the whole flock, alights exactly ahead of the foremost." It was precisely this feeding strategy that made the passenger pigeon so vulnerable to the guns and nets of hunters; Bradbury's own claim to have killed "two hundred and seventy one" pigeons over a period of several hours with his "fowling piece" signals that he was himself the product of a time convinced of the inexhaustibility of the frontier. Bradbury's frequent and astonished descriptions of thundering herds of "innumerable" buffalo also testify to the ecological destruction that attended the settlement of the American West.

Bradbury is also capable of deploying a variety of conventions from eighteenth-century aesthetics such as the sublime, the picturesque, and the beautiful when describing landscapes. In his description of the company's encounter with "The Grand Saline," a gigantic salt plain first described by the explorer Zebulon Pike in 1803, Bradbury finds the geological formation "highly picturesque," possessing "the quality of looming, or magnifying objects, and this in a very striking degree, making...small billets of wood appear as formidable as trees." The area surrounding this lake of salt "is an assemblage of beautiful meadows, verdant ridges, and rude, misshapen piles of red clay, thrown together in the utmost apparent confusion, yet affording the most pleasant harmonies, and presenting us in every direction an endless variety of curious and interesting objects." In a particularly evocative passage, describing a vast plain rich in gypsum deposits, Bradbury invites the reader to

> imagine himself surrounded by the ruins of some ancient city, [where] the plain had sunk, by some convulsion of nature, more than one hundred feet below its former level; for some of the huge columns of red clay rise to the height of two hundred feet perpendicular, capped with rocks of gypsum, which the hand of time is ever crumbling off, and strewing in beautiful transparent flakes along the declivities of the hills, glittering, like so many mirrors, in the sun.

These moments, however, are few; Bradbury generally eschews metaphor and imaginative language in favor of the plain descriptive prose of the naturalist.

After reaching the terminus of the Missouri River portion of their trip, the Astorians were apparently so taken with Bradbury that they asked him to accompany them on their overland journey to the Pacific. Bradbury declined as he was unwilling to abandon his collected plant specimens (which had grown to "several thousands") and because he would have no guaranteed means of passage back to St. Louis from the western coast. Instead, he joined two traders, Manuel Lisa and Henry Marie Brackenridge (1786–1871), members of the Missouri Fur Company (Astor's main competitor), who were descending the Missouri to St. Louis with a load of Canadian furs. Brackenridge also published an account of this trip entitled *Views of Louisiana, Together with a Journal of a Voyage up the Missouri River in 1811* (1814), which, along with Bradbury's *Travels*, are the main source texts for Irving's *Astoria*. Bradbury said "painful" good-byes to the Astorians and to Nuttall, who elected to remain behind to botanize alone with the Mandan Indians. Bradford left with the fur traders for St. Louis on July 17; due to the swift current from hard rains that month, the party made the 1,800-mile journey in a mere 12 days, leaving little time for botanizing. Bradbury records that he was "mortified and chagrined" with Lisa

who repeatedly denied his attempts to collect July-growth plants on the return journey. When he arrived in St. Louis, Bradbury received the additional frustration of a letter from Liverpool explaining that his supporters had "determined to withhold" the stipend for his explorations. Though their reasons for doing so are unclear, it appears that Bradbury's financial backers had become irritated with his relocation to St. Louis and explorations of territories unrelated to the production of cotton. However, the letter also contained good news from a Mr. Shepard, manager of the Liverpool Botanic Garden, who informed Bradbury that his former shipment of plants had been received and were flourishing "in vast numbers."

After a lengthy and difficult illness while in St. Louis, Bradbury was asked by an acquaintance named H. W. Drinker to aid him in taking a barge of lead down the Missouri River to New Orleans, a distance of 1,350 miles. After having missed so many opportunities for collecting on his most recent journey, Bradbury enthusiastically accepted and the pair left for New Orleans on December 5, 1811. Bradbury writes that on December 10, he and Drinker were moored at New Madrid, Missouri. Bradbury found the place boring: with "only a few straggling houses" and "only two stores," the town hardly merited description. However, it was not to remain dull for long; in the early evening of that date, New Madrid experienced the largest earthquake in the history of North America. The quake was so violent that massive areas of land sank into the earth, new lakes formed, rivers ran backward, and even the mighty Mississippi dramatically altered its course. Newspaper reports state that the quake was so violent that it rang church bells in Boston, over 1,000 miles away. Scientists have calculated that the quake would have measured over 8.0 on the Richter scale, had it been invented. Bradbury remarks that he and his party survived only because they were on the water during the worst part of the event. Bradbury's account of the harrowing tremors in his *Travels* is considered by many to be the best eyewitness account of this devastating natural disaster.

After arriving safely in New Orleans, Bradbury dispatched his last collection of plants to Europe with the idea that he would soon follow them. Since his relationship with his Liverpool sponsors had dissolved, Bradbury sent his package to his son, John Leigh Bradbury, who mistakenly forwarded it to Liverpool. Unfortunately, before Bradbury could arrange passage home, the War of 1812 broke out, effectively ending all traffic across the Atlantic and stranding him in America until 1816. Bradbury appears to have waited out the war in New York, all the while anxiously waiting for the moment of his return to England and reunion with his family and the botanical findings that he planned to publish. Meanwhile, in Liverpool, William Roscoe was dividing Bradbury's plants among several members of the Linnaean Society. Through this process, Bradbury's discoveries came to the attention of another botanist, Frederick Pursh (1774–1820), perhaps the most unscrupulous naturalist of the era. When he returned to England, sometime during 1816, Bradbury discovered that Pursh had already published his plants in a book entitled *Flora Americae Septentrionalis* (1814). There Pursh writes he was "highly indebted to William Roscoe, Esq., who very obligingly communicated to me Mr. Bradbury's plants collected in upper Louisiana." Bradbury was heartbroken and writes that Pursh had described "almost the whole [of his collection], thereby depriving [him] both of the credit and profit of what was justly due to [him]." Bradbury's emotions were shared by Thomas Nuttall, whose discoveries were also pirated by Pursh. Though unable to publish a book on his plants, Bradbury did manage to publish his *Travels* in London during August 1817.

Perhaps because of the mistreatment suffered at the hands of his countrymen, Bradbury returned to America late in 1817, this time with his family, intending to make the new country his home. Bradbury discovered that America suited him; he writes that "In no part of the world is good neighbourship found in greater perfection than in the western territory, or in America generally." The historical record of what befell Bradbury after his return is slight; however, we know that Bradbury made stops in Philadelphia and St. Louis and that he finally settled in Middletown, Kentucky, near Louisville. Additionally, a recently discovered letter from Bradbury's friend and fellow naturalist, Constantine Samuel Rafinesque, indicates that by at least September 1822 Bradbury was "employed in a cotton manufactory." Bradbury's career had come full circle. A few months after Rafinesque's letter, in March 1823, Bradbury died after a brief illness. Only now, nearly 200 years after his death, have scholars begun to fully recognize and credit Bradbury for his invaluable contributions to the literatures of exploration and natural history.

PRIMARY BIBLIOGRAPHY

Books

Travels in the Interior of America, in the Years 1809, 1810, and 1811; Including a Description of Upper Louisiana, Together with the States of Ohio, Kentucky, Indiana, and Tennessee, with the Illinois and Western Territories, and Containing Remarks and Observations Useful to Persons Emigrating to Those Countries (London: Sherwood, Neeley, and Jones, 1817; 2nd ed., London: Sherwood, Neeley, and Jones, 1819; first American edition, ed. Reuben Gold Thwaites, vol. 5 of *Early Western Travels, 1748–1846* [Cleveland: A.H. Clark Company, 1904]).

Other

"A Description of the Minerals and Plants Found at the Lead Mines in the Missouri Territory," *Medical Repository* 18 (1816): 135–38.

SECONDARY BIBLIOGRAPHY

References

Charles Boewe, "Kentucky's Forgotten Naturalist," *Filson Club Quarterly* 74 (2000): 221–49.

John Bywater, Forward, *Travels in the Interior of America in the Years 1809, 1810, and 1811* (London: Sherwood, Neeley, and Jones, 1817; New York: Redex Microprint, 1966).

Washington Irving, *Astoria* (New York: Library of America, 2004).

H. W. Rickett, "John Bradbury's Explorations in Missouri Territory," *Proceedings of the American Philosophical Society* 94.1 (1950): 59–89.

Rodney H. True, "A Sketch of the Life of John Bradbury, Including His Unpublished Correspondence with Thomas Jefferson," *Proceedings of the American Philosophical Society* 68 (1929): 133–50.

William Byrd II
(March 28, 1674–August 26, 1744)

April D. Gentry

Because of extensive inventories of the natural world featured in his work, diarist William Byrd II deserves consideration as one of colonial America's nature writers. Little of Byrd's writing was published during his lifetime, as his body of work consists mostly of private diaries and letters that were not intended for wide circulation. Several of Byrd's works, however, offer rich depictions of both flora and fauna along what was then the Virginia/Carolina frontier. His descriptions of land and resources reflect not only his outstanding classical education and polished wit, but also what Pierre Marambaud calls Byrd's "land hunger," his perpetual desire to increase the holdings of his estates. Thus, though his language is often marked by literary techniques like analogy, metaphor, and biblical or classical allusion, Byrd's primary interest in the flowers, animals, or landscapes he encounters tends to be utilitarian rather than aesthetic. Overall, Byrd represents one of the early cataloguers of the rich natural world of colonial North America. His writing observes an abundance in nature that must have seemed both inexhaustible and readily available.

In some ways, Byrd's nature writing reflects the larger discourse of discovery and exploration prevalent during the seventeenth and eighteenth centuries. He frequently likens the members of his various traveling parties to knights, for example, suggesting that their expeditions are a form of quest or crusade into what he calls the "Terra Incognita" of the Virginia borderland. In some cases, his narratives clear up discrepancies about the actual names of, say, a river or a hill, but in many other cases Byrd simply renames what he sees, often humorously, as when he names two small mountains "Pimple" and "Wart." Byrd also makes references to Africa and Asia, other exotic locales about which travel narratives were being written, implicitly connecting those expeditions with his own.

Byrd, the first of four surviving children, was born in Virginia in 1674 to William and Mary Horsemanden Byrd. His father, the elder William Byrd, had received a substantial inheritance from an uncle and then further augmented the family fortune through planting and through the fur and slave trades. The elder Byrd also took an active role in Virginia politics, being appointed Auditor of the Public Accounts in 1687. The family's economic, social, and political wherewithal would provide both substantive training and a substantial patrimony for William Byrd II.

Byrd was sent to England in 1681, where he received an intensive classical education at Felsted Grammar School under Christopher Glascock and then, after a year of overseeing his father's business interests in the Netherlands, studied law at Middle Temple, being admitted to the bar in 1695. During his time at Middle Temple, Byrd counted future playwrights William Congreve and William Wycherly, historian John Oldmixon, and Chief Justice Benjamin Lynde among his friends. Byrd continued to circulate in the London intellectual community, and in 1696 he became a member of the Royal Society. In that same year Byrd returned to Virginia, but his developing political career sent him again to London in 1698 where he served as a colonial agent for Virginia until his father's death in 1704. According to Marambaud, upon his death the elder Byrd "was one of the richest men in Virginia and one of the most influential, both socially and politically"; upon his return to Virginia, the younger Byrd inherited his father's reputation and political power, along with the family estates, which totaled some 26,000 acres.

In 1706, Byrd married Lucy Parke, with whom he had four children, though only two lived beyond infancy. Lucy herself died in 1716 while she and Byrd were in London on both public and personal business. Throughout the marriage Byrd had worked to add to his estates, and when he wrote to present himself to the father of a prospective second wife only a few months after Lucy's death, Byrd listed 43,000 acres and 220 slaves among his assets. Byrd, ever an admirer of women and romantic intrigues, enjoyed his return to bachelorhood, and his socializing in search of a second wife is chronicled in his *London Diary*. Byrd stayed in London from 1715 to 1720, and again from 1721 to 1726. In 1724, the 50-year-old Byrd married Maria Taylor, age 25, a marriage that produced four children.

A year after his 1726 return to Virginia, Byrd was appointed as one of three commissioners for Virginia to survey the disputed borderline with Carolina. Controversy about the exact location of the boundary arose due to a discrepancy between Carolina's two charters: the 1663 charter gave the dividing line as 36° latitude, while the 1665 charter gave 36° 30', thereby drawing the line 30 miles farther north. A party composed of both Virginian and Carolinian commissioners as well as surveyors, workmen, and a chaplain was dispatched to establish the definitive border. The party surveyed the line for some 240 miles, from the coast to the foothills of the Appalachians, during the spring and fall of 1728, adjourning for the summer to avoid the threat of snakebites. The Virginia contingent bickered among themselves and with the Carolina contingent, supplies ran low, and the Carolinians left the party before the journey's completion. But the expedition did complete its task of plotting a mutually recognized boundary line and explored a good deal of frontier territory in the process, including the Dismal Swamp. Foreseeing imminent growth into these frontier areas, Byrd bought 20,000 acres of the Carolina territory along the dividing line, then another 6,000 Carolina acres that he named "The Land of Eden," then another 5,000, and then another 105,000 acres. The initial surveying expedition and subsequent explorations of the property he purchased gave rise to most of Byrd's writing about the natural world.

Byrd first recorded the progress of the survey expedition in journal form, which he titled *The Secret History of the Line,* and later modified and elaborated on those entries in *The History of the Dividing Line* with the intention of creating a more public document, probably for formal publication. The exact date of this second composition is not clear, but letters indicate that Byrd was at work on the *History* in 1736 and 1737, nearly ten years after the expedition was completed. Neither version was published during his lifetime; the pair of works was rejected for publication in the early 1800s by the American Philosophical Society, despite the recommendation of Thomas Jefferson. The *History* was first published in 1841 and the *Secret History* in 1929.

The *Secret History,* the first account written, pays far less attention to landscape than the later version, and spends a great deal more time on the personalities and habits of the survey party. Giving each member of the commission a false name fashioned by the conventions of Restoration drama (Byrd himself becomes "Steddy," for example, while other Virginia commissioners become "Meanwell" and "Firebrand"), Byrd records the progress of the party, their meals and health, and their quarrels. His tone is often sarcastic, especially when describing the conflicts among members of the party (the Carolina commissioners he renames "Judge Jumble," "Plausible," "Puzzlecause," and "Shoebrush"). These personal details and observations are largely absent from the *History*, certainly due to his intention to publish it. The *History*, by contrast, focuses its sarcasm not on individuals but on the inhabitants of Carolina more generally; Byrd describes them as ignorant, uncultured, and lazy, referring to the territory as "Lubberland." Other portions of the *Secret History*, such as transcriptions of formal correspondence among the parties involved in the expedition, were omitted from the later version as well. The *Secret History* also includes frequent mention of the sexual habits of the survey party, which were omitted almost entirely from the later version—and which were likely one reason the American Philosophical Society declined to publish the work. Byrd's richest nature writing lies within the *History*; there he expands on the notes in the *Secret History* to include lengthy descriptions of plant and animal life and the landscape of the borderland.

Byrd's frequent descriptions of plants are clearly shaped by his interest in medicine. Byrd had read a great deal in both classical and contemporary texts of medical science, and he actively used his knowledge. The *Secret History* records the major and minor ailments of the company and Byrd's diligent attempts to treat them; while these individual cases are omitted from the *History*, significant attention is paid to the identification and use of medicinal plants. For example, he mentions identifying and using ipocoacanna, which he also calls "Indian-Physic" and from which ipecac derives. He also extols the virtues of ginseng and dogwood bark. After the party reassembles in the fall of the year, and

after killing several rattlesnakes, Byrd carefully identifies a number of plants that are used as antidotes for snakebite: rattlesnake root or star-grass, St. Andrew's cross, and a variety of wild ginger. Other plants, such as penny-royal and dittany, he prescribes as insect repellants.

He also discusses plants with other, non-medicinal uses. He describes the "Spired Leaf Silk grass" plant, which he says is used by locals to make rope, for example, and he considers the value of water cane as a preventative of riverbank erosion. These descriptions are not always so specific as to be useful in identifying the plant (the spired leaf silk grass, he says, is "an evergreen, bearing on a lofty Stemm [sic] a large Cluster of Flowers of a Pale Yellow"), nor are they generally concerned with scientific classifications or Latinate names. As with the medicinal plants, the purpose of such descriptions seems to be to give a general impression of the territory and to inventory natural resources. Though he does occasionally speculate about the light, soil, and climate needs of some plants, he makes few suggestions for cultivating any of these wild species, believing that "it may pass for a Rule in Botanicks, that where any Vegetable is planted by the hand of Nature, it has more Vertue [sic] than in Places whereto it is transplanted by the Curiosity of Man."

Byrd reports sightings of numerous animal species and gives some remarks on their habits and habitats, though he most often discusses animals as food. He rates the tastiness of venison, bear, and various birds encountered on the expedition, as well as raccoons, possums, skunks, wildcats, and panthers. Perhaps surprising to a contemporary reader are his several descriptions of the party's encounters with buffalo. As with his descriptions of plants, his classifications of animals are more pragmatic than scientific; he writes that bears and raccoons are "Dog-kind," for example, while elk are "Deer-kind." He seems especially interested in bears and tells several stories about their eating, hunting, and parenting habits. He notes (with a pun) that they will not step onto branches too small to support their weight and "in these Instances, a Bear carries Instinct a great way, and Acts more reasonably than many of his Betters, who indiscreetly Venture upon frail Projects that wont bear them."

Byrd sees in the land its potential for development—or lack thereof. Whereas a botanist or naturalist might have been interested in the natural variety within a relatively unexplored environment like the Dismal Swamp, Byrd considers it a "filthy quagmire," asserting that "the Exhalations that continually rise from this vast Body of mire and Nastiness infect the Air for many Miles around, and render it very unwholesome." Byrd himself traveled only half a mile or so into the swamp itself with the surveyors, and then passed around it instead. He later published a treatise on the possibility of draining the swamp to make better use of the land, a project that he never brought to fruition.

Byrd also occasionally remarks on the beauty of the landscape and the pleasure of being outdoors. He mentions several times when the party declined invitations to board at houses they passed, for example, preferring the loveliness of sleeping under the open sky; he asserts that "at the foot of the Account Mankind are great Losers by the Luxury of Feather-Beds and warm apartments." Yet most often he simply states that a particular scene was beautiful rather than trying to render that beauty directly in language. When describing vines as "marry'd" to the trees around which they twine, he even begs leave to "be allowed to speak so Poetically." A hint at Byrd's reluctance to offer longer depictions of the scenic views might be found in the earlier *Secret History,* where he notes that one of his fellow commissioners found his report on the expedition "too Poetical." Perhaps this accounts for the generally empirical interest in nature throughout the narrative, anticipating the later, better-known natural catalogues of Georges-Louis Leclerc, comte de Buffon in France and Jefferson in America. Byrd's openness in his private diaries contrasts sharply with the relative impersonality

of the histories; this illustrates ways in which Byrd, a man of social and political stature, made careful distinctions between his public and private selves.

In addition to its fairly factual descriptions, however, the *History* also offers some questionable bits of woodlore, and Byrd's wry tone suggests that such sections are the work of a playful, rather than misinformed, author. He recounts one story, for example, that he claims to have heard about a man who, lost in the swamp, used a louse for a compass since "having no Eye-lids, [the louse] turned himself about till he found the Darkest Part of the Heavens, and so made the best of his way towards the North." Elsewhere, Byrd asserts that to catch prey, snakes "Ogle the poor little animal, till by force of the Charm he falls down Stupify'd and Senseless on the Ground" and then spit on them to make them slippery enough to swallow whole. He further claims that in order to more efficiently drag cows and other heavy prey to the river bottom, alligators "Swallow great stones" to increase their weight and then spit these stones back out before eating. Tales such as these seem intended to add enjoyable elements of wit and wordplay to the narrative.

Both of Byrd's other notable pieces of nature writing describe the same geographic area as the histories. In 1732 Byrd traveled through Virginia to investigate the feasibility of undertaking a mining operation, and he records that journey in *A Progress to the Mines.* Marambaud argues that here "Byrd reached the highest degree of detachment and objectivity possible to him," and *Progress* does indeed carry less of Byrd's trademark wit and sarcasm. Byrd describes the processes by which iron ore is extracted and melted down, and he records several long conversations on the costs of establishing and maintaining such an operation—costs that led him to abandon the endeavor. This work carries the utilitarianism of the histories to its further conclusion, and the natural world is present in the text only in terms of natural resources. Rocks are blown up, rivers are rerouted or harnessed for water power, and trees become charcoal. He does delight in finding a patch of ginseng, however, and "carried home this treasure, with as much joy, as if every root had been a graft of the tree of life." He also discusses the growing and preparation of a new kind of tobacco.

A year later, in 1733, Byrd made a surveying and planning trip through the 20,000 acres of Carolina territory he'd purchased, and his journal of that trip became *A Journey to the Land of Eden in the Year 1733. A Journey to the Land of Eden* shares many characteristics of tone, style, and content with the two histories. It features similar inventories of various plants and their uses, and similar accounts of animals and their relative desirability as food. It considers natural resources such as the location of streams and hills in relation to their impact on the land's dollar value, not surprising given that Byrd was traveling through land he had already purchased and hoped to make profitable.

Perhaps because it was not intended for wide publication, Byrd allows himself an especially elegant phrase or a sentimental description of some natural scene more often than he had in the *History*. After making several observations that the cane had died off in the area, for example, and explaining that this occurs every seven years as part of the plant's natural regenerative process, he alludes to the "late septennial slaughter of that vegetable." He also gives a picturesque second-person description of one site, putting the reader in the place of observer where

> there is scarce a shrub in sight to intercept your prospect, and grass as high as a man on horseback. Towards the woods there is a gentle ascent, till your sight is intercepted by an eminence, that overlooks the whole landscape.

He describes a river "rolling down its waters, as sweet as milk, and as clear as crystal." Yet these descriptions are set against the very businesslike matter of the visit, and Byrd makes frequent mention of the use to which particular plots of land will be devoted.

Throughout his life, Byrd remained an aristocrat, a planter, and a politician foremost; he wrote as a hobby rather than as a vocation. The primacy of these other roles, in addition to the increasingly independent spirit of his age, significantly shaped his perspective on the natural world as a source of potential resources and profits. The private format of most of his writing gave him a freedom to observe, record, and experiment, as well as the liberty to amuse himself and his self-selected readers with irony and caricature. His 4,700-acre plantation estate at Westover, with its vast and carefully planned gardens, reveals an ethos similar to that of his writing. Byrd established the largest library in the colonies, and was also a great collector of art. As William K. Boyd notes, Byrd "watched the turn of the seasons and marveled at the revelations of nature" at Westover, and he "experimented in fruit growing, studied wild herbs, and prescribed remedies for his sick friends." Upon his death in 1744, Byrd was buried in the garden at Westover.

PRIMARY BIBLIOGRAPHY

Books

Secret Diary of William Byrd of Westover, 1709–1712, ed. Louis B. Wright and Marion Tinling (Richmond: Dietz, 1941).

London Diary, 1717–1721, ed. Louis B. Wright and Marion Tinling (New York: Oxford University Press, 1958).

A Discourse Concerning the Plague, with Some Preservatives against It, by a Lover of Mankind (London: J. Roberts, 1721).

Commonplace Book of William Byrd II of Westover, ed. Kevin Berland, Jan Kirsen Gilliam, and Kenneth A. Lockridge (Chapel Hill: University of North Carolina Press, 2001).

Westover Manuscripts; containing A History of the Dividing Line betwixt Virginia and North Carolina, A Journey to the Land of Eden, A.D. 1733 *and* A Progress to the Mines, *Written from 1728 to 1736 and Now First Published*, ed. Edmund Ruffin (Petersburg, VA: E. and J.C. Ruffin, 1841; reprinted as *A Journey to the Land of Eden and Other Papers* with new introduction by Mark van Doren (New York: Macy-Masius, 1928).

Description of the Dismal Swamp and a proposal to drain the swamp (Metuchen, NJ: for C.F. Heartman, 1922; see also *Columbian Magazine*, April 1789, and *Farmers Register*, January 1, 1837).

Another Secret Diary of William Byrd of Westover, 1739–1741, ed. Maude H. Woodfin (Richmond: Dietz, 1942).

COLLECTIONS

History of the Dividing Line and Other Notes, from the Papers of William Byrd of Westover in Virginia, Esquire, ed. Thomas H. Wynne, 2 vols. (Richmond, 1866).

The Writings of Colonel William Byrd of Westover in Virginia, Esqr., ed. John Spencer Bassett (New York: Doubleday, Page & Co., 1901).

William Byrd's Histories of the Dividing Line betwixt Virginia and North Carolina, ed. William K. Boyd (Raleigh: North Carolina Historical Society, 1929; reprinted with new introduction by Percy A. Adams, New York: Dover, 1967).

Prose Works; Narratives of a Colonial Virginian, ed. Louis B. Wright (Cambridge, MA: Harvard University Press, 1966).

Letters

Letters of the Three William Byrds of Westover, Virginia, 1684–1776, ed. Marion Tinling (Charlottesville: University of Virginia Press for the Virginia Historical Society, 1977).

SECONDARY BIBLIOGRAPHY

Bibliographies

Rose Marie Cutting, *John and William Bartram, William Byrd II, and St. John de Crevecoeur: A Reference Guide* (Boston: G.K. Hall, 1976).

Biographies

Richmond C. Beatty, *William Byrd of Westover* (New York: Houghton Mifflin, 1932).

Pierre Marambaud, *William Byrd of Westover, 1674–1744* (Charlottesville: University Press of Virginia, 1971).

Randall Miller, *William Byrd II, 1674–1744* (Washington, D.C.: Beacham, 1988).

References

Philip A. Bruce, *The Virginia Plutarch* (Chapel Hill: University of North Carolina Press, 1929).

Carl L. Cannon, *William Byrd II of Westover* (New York, 1933).

Marshall William Fishwick, *Gentlemen of Virginia* (New York: Dodd, Mead, 1961).

Kevin J. Hayes, *The Library of William Byrd of Westover* (Madison: Madison House, 1997).

Jay B. Hubbell, *The South in American Literature, 1607–1900* (Durham: Duke University Press, 1954).

Kenneth A. Lockridge, *The Diary and Life of William Byrd II of Virginia, 1674–1744* (Chapel Hill: University of North Carolina Press for the Institute of Early American History and Culture, 1987).

Edd Winfield Parks, "William Byrd as a Man of Letters," *Georgia Review* 14 (Summer 1960): 172–76.

Margaret Beck Pritchard and Virginia Lascara Sites, *William Byrd II and His Lost History: Engravings of the Americas* (Williamsburg: Colonial Williamsburg Foundation, 1993).

Louis B. Wright, *The First Gentlemen of Virginia: Intellectual Qualities of the Early Ruling Class* (San Marino: Huntington Library, 1940).

Papers

The manuscripts and letters of William Byrd II are held variously at the Huntington Library, University of North Carolina, Virginia Historical Society Library, Colonial Williamsburg Foundation Library, and the College of William and Mary.

George Catlin
(July 26, 1796–December 22, 1872)

Angela Courtney

George Catlin is generally remembered for his artistic representations of the Native American tribes from the early 1800s. Before the advent of photography transformed the creation of such graphic chronicles, Catlin captured the life and customs of these tribal cultures with his own innate artistic abilities, making quick sketches and taking notes that he would enhance and augment later. Catlin is also famous for his exhibitions, precursors to the Wild West shows, in which he would tour and display his own art as well as members of various tribes for the education and entertainment of his audiences. His writing, often overshadowed by his other endeavors, cannot be separated from these projects. Catlin seemed to be captivated by the relationship that the human cultures he observed cultivated with their natural world. As he perceived these indigenous tribes, they held an intrinsic understanding of how to live in harmony with nature, as opposed to trying to dominate it, and as a result Catlin saw no divide between the people and the world in which they lived. To Catlin, his narrative observations of their lives are also observations of nature; the native tribes and nature were one and the same. The tribes had lived symbiotically with their natural world long before settlers threw them into chaos; thus his chronicles of the vanishing races were at the same time chronicles of nature.

In 1857 George Catlin published *Life among the Indians,* a repackaging of his earlier works about the Native Americans, this time written for children. Fearing that his life's work had been lost on older generations, he turned to the nation's youth. Borrowing liberally from his earlier works, he explains that his youthful interests—hunting and fishing—soon grew dormant, falling to the wayside while he attended law school and then practiced law. Appealing to the tendency of children to create their own worlds in classroom drawings, he explains that

> after having covered nearly every inch of the lawyers' table (and even encroached upon the judge's bench) with penknife, pen and ink, and pencil sketches of judges, juries, and culprits, I very deliberately resolved to convert my law library into paint-pots and brushes, and to pursue painting as my future, and apparently more agreeable, profession.

Developing a successful career as a portrait painter in Philadelphia, he soon turned his talent and passion to "the vanishing races of native man in America," and, with this new crusade, in 1832 began his most lasting and important endeavors. Catlin began a one-man campaign to redeem the reputation of the Indian tribal cultures, hoping to capitalize on the curiosity the American public had about these cultures that their ancestors had almost destroyed.

Born on July 26, 1796, in Wilkes-Barre, Pennsylvania, George Catlin was the fifth of 14 children born to Putnam and Polly Catlin. His father was a lawyer and a farmer, and soon after George's birth the family moved to southern New York. His interest in the life and plight of the Native American is often retrospectively connected to two incidents: the stories of short captivity of his mother and grandmother in 1778, and, more likely, his friendship with an Oneida Indian. Catlin recalls that he was nine or ten years old when he saw On-o-gong-way, the first real Native American he encountered, as both of them were stalking the same deer. A strong friendship developed between them, and Catlin learned much about the cultures that until then he had known only through stories. In a turn that ultimately colored young Catlin's perceptions, the Indian family left, and Catlin learned later that On-o-gong-way had been killed by white settlers. Although they tried, the Catlin family could never locate his wife and daughter.

It is these two events that would inform and influence Catlin's writing. During his youth, Indian tribes were generally looked upon as savages, something to be feared, a danger to the white settlers. Catlin's early life, however, allowed him a different worldview. His mother and grandmother were well cared for and even honored by their native captors, and his friendship with On-o-gong-way ultimately forced a young boy to see through the rhetoric of settlers who thought that the natives were a danger that was best removed or eliminated. He had the good fortune to experience a serendipitous friendship that led to the development of an artistic and educational avocation. He used his graphic and narrative talents to share his knowledge and respect for these vanishing races with the white settlers who regarded them with a combination of superiority and

fear. He became an early advocate for rehabilitating the history and reputation of the native tribes.

Putting aside his unsatisfying career in law, he moved to Philadelphia in 1823 where he worked as a portrait painter. In 1824 he was elected to the Philadelphia Academy of Art on the merit of some miniatures he sent the Academy. In 1826 he painted his first Native American portrait—Red Jacket, a Senecan orator. He married Clara Bartlett Gregory, a wealthy member of the social elite of Albany, New York, in May 1828. They would have four children, one boy and three girls. Clara wholeheartedly supported his belief in the importance of creating a visual record of the Native American tribes, although her family was skeptical of his ideas and abilities. With a wife and family, Catlin realized that he needed to earn a living, and he did little to hide the fact that money was also a priority; thus his crusade to document the dwindling tribes was not completely altruistic.

He met General William Clark in 1830 and traveled with him to see resettled tribes in Kansas and Wisconsin. Because Clark respected Catlin's plan to paint the Indian tribes, and his apparent natural ability to gain the trust of otherwise highly suspicious people, Catlin was able to paint portraits of the Native Americans who visited Clark to register complaints of treaty violations. Although ideally he wanted to have access to tribes that were yet untouched by the influx of the white settlers, Catlin was practical and went where he was able. His travels began in 1831 with visits to the plains tribes—the Kansa, Oto, Missouri, and Pawnee—along the Platte River in land that was to become the state of Nebraska. He visited the Mandan Sioux in 1832, only five years before the tribe was virtually destroyed by small pox. During this summer he traveled up the Missouri River on a steamboat. It was on this trip that he was contracted to the *New York Commercial Advisor* for a number of letters that were to become the first chapters of *Letters and Notes on the Manners, Customs, and Conditions of the North American Indians*. In 1834 he rode a steamboat up the Arkansas River to Fort Gibson to see the home of the Five Civilized Tribes, Cherokee, Choctaw, Chickasaw, Creek, and Seminole, relocated through the efforts of Andrew Jackson. In 1835 he and Clara went to Fort Snelling on the Mississippi River in what became Minnesota and stayed with the Ojibways.

In the summer of 1836, Catlin put together an exhibition of his paintings; the following year, 1837, saw the beginning of Catlin's Indian Gallery—a collection of 310 Indian portraits, 200 western paintings, and countless artifacts including headdresses, weapons, and drums. This time also represents a move away from life among the Indians to, instead, a lifestyle of self-promotion and sales. Most of Catlin's productions from this time onward—illustrations, publications, and exhibitions—were taken from the few years he spent among the tribes in the 1830s. He took the show to Boston, Philadelphia, and Washington, and although they were popular, soon the novelty wore off in America. The government refused to buy his collection and act on his idea to create a National Museum of the American Indian. As a result he toured the gallery in England, complete with a selection of members of the tribes. In England and other European countries his tours had varying degrees of success, from shows for royalty to shows with almost no audiences, but he would not return to America permanently for 30 years.

Inspired by the work of preparing an exhibition catalog of his paintings, Catlin decided a book of his collected letters illustrated with his pictures could garner some much needed money. He published descriptive catalogs in New York in 1837 and in London in 1840. His first book that was not a catalog of his gallery was published in 1841, *Letters and Notes on the Manners, Customs, and Conditions of the North American Indians*. The book was well received both critically and popularly, successfully targeting the curiosity of Americans for the mysteries of the native cultures. He captures with narrative and visual elements the tribes he observed from 1832 to 1839 and conveys an innate awareness that he was witnessing the destruction of these people. Catlin's attitude was always that of a helpless bystander; fully cognizant of the fact that the people he was painting were in a swift decline, he spoke in his introduction of setting out to capture images and stories of how they were living at the time. His goal was to capture the present, and he had little time for historical background or hypotheses for hope for the future. Seeing cultures disappearing, he felt the need to work quickly and make full use of the living resources that remained. It was this initial work that was to be the basis for most of the artistic and literary output for the rest of his life.

Catlin uses nature as the underlying structure for the compilation of his letters, organizing them along the rivers he traveled. Based mostly on his Missouri River trip of 1832 and Arkansas River trip of 1834, he also includes later visits to southeastern tribes undergoing imprisonment and relocation as a result of Andrew Jackson's Indian Removal Act of 1830 and to the Civilized Tribes as they were relocating to Oklahoma. His narrative letters convey in detail the country and the tribes he visited. His writing reflects a neoclassical style, orderly, simplistic, and relatively detached. The narrative is typically lacking in emotion, and often descends into a condescending tone that is surprising for a man who felt so passionately about the plight of the native tribes. Frequently he refers to them as "primitive" or "savages." Nevertheless, he always sees the beauty of the tribes, although sometimes primitive or terrifying, as being connected to their assumption that they were a part of the natural world. His descriptions of their wardrobes, makeup, dwellings, and rituals read as if he is writing about the rivers and trees—he approaches neither romantically, but rather with the distance of a scientist—a distance that is subtly tinged with an underlying sympathy and sorrow.

He devoted much time and space to the mysterious Mandan Sioux tribe, apparently one of his favorite tribes. He spent three weeks with this tribe that had long been shrouded in secrecy. They were wrongly thought to be the mythic tribe of Welsh-speaking Indians, the result of a Welsh expedition that never returned. They were a friendly tribe who accepted Catlin and allowed him to draw their pictures only after much convincing. He suggests that they feared him because his ability to capture the image of a person also gave him the power to take lives.

In 1848 he published *Catlin's Notes of Eight Years' Travel and Residence in Europe, with his North American Indian Collection, With Anecdotes and Incidents of the Travels and Adventures of Three Different Parties of American Indians whom he Introduced to the Courts of England, France, and Belgium*, and he again tried unsuccessfully to sell his collections to the U.S. Congress. The book was a failure critically and popularly, darker than his first book due in large part to the difficulties he had faced since leaving America in hopes of making money in Europe. His wife and son both died, and many members of his traveling exhibition had succumbed to small pox while in Europe. He offers a unique point of view in conveying combined impressions of Europe as seen through his eyes as well as through the eyes of his troupe. The poor sales of this book did little to help him; in 1852 he went bankrupt in London and had to sell some of his collection and mortgage his paintings to one of his creditors, never to redeem them. To end the decade, his wife's parents, who never believed in his vision, took custody of his daughters and brought them back to America.

The Breath of Life or Mal-Respiration and its Effects upon the Enjoyment & Life of Man, one of his more peculiar works, was published in 1862. This publication reads as part scientific treatise and part editorial, but in it he returns to the basic tenet that guided his earliest writings: the connection of the native tribal cultures to nature. Basing his premise upon the healthy conditions of the tribes he observed in their "primitive state," he asserts that their lifestyle—and their close bond with the natural world—made them a healthier and longer-lived race than the settlers. Although their mortality rates were higher, it was due to wars and accidents and not lifestyle. Much of his argument centers on the idea that they follow nature's law and nature's rhythms and sleep flat on their backs with closed mouths. This method, which starts with infants, allows for a natural sleep that allows the body a chance for recuperative repose that heals the damage of daily life.

Although dogged by financial difficulties and credibility issues, he was not one to give up easily. He went to Brazil in search of legendary gold mines in the Crystal Mountains. From this trip he published *Last Rambles Among the Indians of the Rocky Mountains and the Andes* in 1867. The veracity of his recollection of these travels is sometimes questioned since the facts do not always add up, and much of what he writes about could easily have come from a variety of other sources already in publication. The quality of his work shows signs of failing, lacking the earlier passionate dedication to a cause that likely faded as a result of years of disappointment and controversy.

In 1867 he wrote *O-Kee-Pa: A Religious Ceremony*, a defense of his 1841 description of this Mandan Sioux yearly religious ceremony that came under attack in Henry Rowe Schoolcraft's *Historical and Statistical Information Respecting the History, Condition, and Prospects of the Indian Tribes of the United States*. Ten years earlier, Catlin refused to work with Schoolcraft, and ill will remained between the two. Catlin returned again to the notes from his field work of the 1830s and described in detail the exhausting and torturous ceremony in which tribe members starve themselves and hang from spikes through punctured flesh. Nearing the end of his life, Catlin was unwilling to let his name and the veracity of his works be questioned without fighting back in one of the best ways he knew how—with his own writing and illustrations.

In 1870 Catlin finally moved back to the United States to live with his daughters. As he grew older and more feeble, Catlin began to lose his hearing. Yet, as late as 1871 he was constructing exhibits of his own work in New York and still trying to sell his collection to the Smithsonian. The American public was at best mildly interested in his exhibitions, and the Smithsonian granted him permission to mount an exhibit but was still not willing to buy the collection. With increasing bitterness and disappointment, he died in 1872 at the age of 76. It is only in recent decades, long after he watched his work go unappreciated, that Catlin's work is being revisited and he is again being given respect as an ethnologist, an artist, and a writer. His narratives and sketches are yet to be investigated for their potential usefulness to environmental historians.

PRIMARY BIBLIOGRAPHY

Books

Catalogue of Catlin's Indian Gallery of Portraits, Landscapes, Manners, Customs, Costumes, &c. (New York: Piercy & Reed, 1837).

A Descriptive Catalogue of Catlin's Indian Collection, Containing Portraits, Landscapes, Costumes, and Representations of the Manners and Customs of the North American Indians (London: C. Adlard, 1840).

Letters and Notes on the Manners, Customs, and Conditions of the North American Indians, 2 vols. (New York: Wiley & Putnam, 1841; London: Printed for the author by Tosswill and Myers, 1841); republished as *The Manners, Customs and Condition of the North American Indians* (London: Published by the author, 1841); republished as *Illustrations of the Manners, Customs, and Condition of the North American Indians*, 2 vols. (London: H.G. Bohn, 1845); republished as *North American Indians* (London: Chatto & Windus, 187?; Philadelphia: Leary, Stuart, 1913); republished as *Catlin's Indians* (Philadelphia: Hubbard Brothers, 1891).

Catlin's North American Indian Portfolio of Hunting Scenes and Amusements (London: Published by the author, 1844; New York: J. Ackerman, 1845).

Catlin's Notes of Eight Years' Travel and Residence in Europe, with his North American Indian Collection. With Anecdotes and Incidents of the Travels and Adventures of Three Different Parties of American Indians whom he Introduced to the Courts of England, France, and Belgium, 2 vols. (London: Author, 1848; New York: Burgess, Stringer and Company, 1848); republished as *Adventures of the Ojibbeway and Ioway Indians in England, France, and Belgium: Being Notes of Eight Years' Travels and Residence in Europe with his North American Indian Collection* (London: Published by the author, 1852).

Souvenir of the North American Indians as They Were in the Middle of the Nineteenth Century, 3 vols. (London: Published by the author, 1850; Chicago: C.W. Farrington, 1870).

Life Among the Indians: A Book for Youth (New York: D. Appleton, 1857; London: Sampson Low, 1861).

Prairie Scenes (New York: Currier & Ives, 1857).

The Breath of Life or Mal-Respiration: And its Effects upon the Enjoyment & Life of Man (London: Trübner, 1861; New York: J. Wiley, 1861); republished as *Shut Your Mouth* (New York: Wiley, 1864; London: Trübner, 1869).

An Account of an Annual Religious Ceremony Practised by the Mandan Tribe of North American Indians (London: Printed by Whittingham & Wilkins, 1863–1864).

Last Rambles Among the Indians of the Rocky Mountains and the Andes (New York: D. Appleton, 1867; London: Gall & Inglis, 1867); republished as *Rambles Among the Indians of the Rocky Mountains and the Andes* (London: Gall & Inglis, 1877).

O-Kee-Pa: A Religious Ceremony (London: Trübner, 1867; Philadelphia: Lippincott, 1967).

The Lifted and Subsided Rocks of America with Their Influences on the Oceanic, Atmospheric, and Land Currents and the Distribution of Races (London: Trübner, 1870).

North and South American Indians: Catalogue Descriptive and Instructive of Catlin's Indian Cartoons (New York: Baker & Godwin, 1871).

Other

Episodes from Life Among the Indians *and* Last Rambles, *With 152 Scenes and Portraits by the Artist*, ed. Marvin C. Ross (Norman: University of Oklahoma Press, 1959).

The Letters of George Catlin and His Family: A Chronicle of the American West, ed. Marjorie Catlin Roehm (Berkeley: University of California Press, 1966).

SECONDARY BIBLIOGRAPHY

Biographies

Brian W. Dippie, *Catlin and His Contemporaries: The Politics of Patronage* (Lincoln: University of Nebraska Press, 1990).

Loyd Haberly, *Pursuit of the Horizon: A Life of George Catlin, Painter & Recorder of the American Indian* (New York: Macmillan, 1948).

Harold McCracken, *George Catlin and the Old Frontier* (New York: Dial, 1959).

Robert Plate, *Palette and Tomahawk: The Story of George Catlin, July 27, 1796–December 23, 1872* (New York: McKay, 1962).

Marvin C. Ross, *George Catlin* (Norman: University of Oklahoma Press, 1959).

References

Thomas Donaldson, *The George Catlin Indian Gallery in the United States National Museum* (Washington, D.C.: Government Printing Office, 1886).

John C. Ewers, "George Catlin, Painter of Indians and the West," in *Annual Report of the Smithsonian Institution* (Washington, D.C.: Smithsonian Institution Report, 1956), 483–528.

John C. Ewers, *Artists of the Old West* (Garden City, NY: Doubleday, 1965).

John C. Ewers, *Indian Art in Pipestone: George Catlin's Portfolio in the British Museum* (Washington, D.C.: Smithsonian Institution Report, 1979).

James Gilreath, "George Catlin and Karl Bodmer: Artists Among the American Indians," in *Folklife Annual 1987*, ed. Alan Jabbour and James Hardin (Washington, D.C.: American Folklife Center at the Library of Congress, 1988), 34–45.

Marjorie Halpin, *Catlin's Indian Gallery: The George Catlin Paintings in the United States National Museum* (Washington, D.C.: Smithsonian Institution Press, 1965).

Royal B. Hassrick, *The George Catlin Book of American Indians* (New York: Watson Guptill Publications, 1977).

James Kipp, "On the Accuracy of Catlin's Account of the Mandan Ceremonies," in *Annual Report of the Smithsonian Institution* (Washington, D.C.: Smithsonian Institution Press, 1873), 436–38.

Edgardo Carlos Krebs, "George Catlin and South America: A Look at His 'Lost' Years and His Paintings of Northeastern Argentina," *American Art Journal* 22 (1990): 539.

Peter Matthiessen, "Introduction," in *North American Indians* (New York: Penguin, 1989), vii–xix.

Joseph R. Millichap, *George Catlin*, Western Writers Series, no. 27 (Boise, Idaho: Boise State University, 1977).

George I. Quimby, *Indians of the Western Frontier: Paintings of George Catlin* (Chicago: Natural History Museum, 1954).

Paul Reddin, *Wild West Shows* (Urbana: University of Illinois Press, 1999).

William H. Truettner, *The Natural Man Observed: A Study of Catlin's Indian Gallery* (Washington, D.C.: Smithsonian Institution Press, 1979).

Papers

The major holdings of Catlin's papers include the Bancroft Library, Berkeley, California; the Newberry Library, Evanston, Illinois; the California State Library, Sacramento; the Gilcrease Institute, Tulsa, Oklahoma; and the Amon Carter Museum, Fort Worth, Texas.

Susan Fenimore Cooper
(April 17, 1813–December 31, 1894)

Daniel Patterson

Susan Fenimore Cooper's literary career spans half a century, from the mid-1840s to her death on the last day of 1894. While she published in practically every genre of prose (including novel, short story, political polemic, history, biography, memoir, and scholarly introduction to another author's work), her cumulative contributions to nature writing comprise the most fully developed and coherent body of work in her career. During her lifetime, she was best known and universally praised as the author of *Rural Hours* (1850)—the first book of literary nature writing published by a woman in the United States, which appeared in nine editions before a final abridged edition in 1887—and as the author of important introductions to the novels of her father, James Fenimore Cooper. Scholars currently are studying the gamut of her literary production and clarifying Cooper's place in several genres; however, her significance as an early practitioner and theorist of nature writing is the focus of most studies of her work. Cooper's manner of representing nature is seen as a neglected and important alternative to the Thoreauvian tradition of American nature writing.

On April 17, 1813, Susan Cooper was born the second child of Susan Augusta De Lancey and James Fenimore Cooper in Mamaroneck, New York, at the luxurious home of her maternal grandparents. Shortly after her family of four moved to "Fenimore," their home in Cooperstown, in the summer of 1813, Cooper's older sister, Elizabeth, died. Two other sisters, Caroline Martha and Anne Charlotte, were born in 1815 and 1817, respectively. By her own account ("Small Family Memories"), Cooper enjoyed a secure, nurturing, and engaging childhood, including both her first four years at Fenimore and the subsequent years at various homes in West Chester County and New York City. Under her mother's tutelage, the author with her sisters learned to read and sew. Her affinity for her natural surroundings emerged and was reinforced early through frequent walks and rides through the local landscape. Cooper records that various family members encouraged her awareness of and familiarity with the nearby plant and animal species.

In June 1826, when Cooper was 13 and had completed two years of private French lessons, the Cooper family departed for England to begin a European stay that would last for over seven years. In July the Coopers began a two-year residence in Paris, where the author and her sisters attended a private boarding school for girls in the same building in which their parents rented an apartment. The European refinement of their daughters began here. In addition to the usual subjects of grammar, geography, history, and arithmetic, they studied music, drawing, and dancing. Susan Cooper proved especially adept at drawing. While in Paris, the Coopers moved in the highest social circles, including General Lafayette and Sir Walter Scott; the Cooper daughters, however, while frequently accompanying their parents to the balls and banquets, were kept within the conservative Episcopalian control of their pious mother.

Later travel took them to Switzerland and Italy, and the daughters added Italian to their languages, while continuing their drawing, music, and dancing. During a brief stay in Dresden, Cooper and her sisters received formal instruction in German; later she would also study Spanish and Latin.

Following the death of her father's copyist in 1831, Susan Cooper, her father's favorite daughter, became his amanuensis, remaining so until his death in 1851 (when she also became his literary executor). She was 18 then and attracting the attentions of several potential suitors, but her parents clearly intended to bring all their daughters home single, preferring that they be 20 or so before marrying and that they take American husbands. When she returned with her family to New York on November 5, 1833, Cooper was 20 and had attained the refinement of the highest standards of Victorian womanhood. Under the influence of her father, however, to the maintenance of whose reputation she devoted much of her later work, she never married. Apart from a few visits to Albany or Geneva in New York or to Washington, D.C., Cooper lived out the rest of her life in Cooperstown, which bore the name of her grandfather, William Cooper, a principal agent in the early development of the village. (See Kurth, especially 1–103, for a convenient overview of many of the known facts about Cooper's life.)

In Cooper's first period of literary productivity, she made a transition from fiction to nature writing. After first writing an unknown number of short stories in her late twenties and early thirties, Cooper completed a lengthy romance, *Elinor Wyllys* (1845), and her father arranged its publication. The

author's lifelong interest in landscape and, more specifically, in the theoretical discussion of American landscape, informs her novel as much as does the question of whom the heroine will marry. From this fictive world, Cooper then turned her literary labors to a representation of the physical environment of her rural village. From approximately two years of journal observations, and inspired by Gilbert White's *The Natural History of Selborne* (1788), she composed *Rural Hours*, her literary account of the natural history of Cooperstown. Much more forcefully than *Selborne*, however, and 14 years before George Perkins Marsh's *Man and Nature* (1864), *Rural Hours* comprises an argument for a wise restraint in the human treatment of the physical environment. What we now call "nature writing" became, for this new author, a tool of suasion, a genre by which she could present her vivid plea for a human presence in her landscape that would be sustainable indefinitely into the future.

In the wake of *Rural Hours*, Cooper was invited to contribute an essay on American landscape to a giftbook Putnam was promoting, *The Home Book of the Picturesque: Or American Scenery, Art, and Literature* (1852). The author of *Rural Hours* now shared the stage with Washington Irving, William Cullen Bryant, and her father, all of whom also contributed essays. At the center of Cooper's fanciful essay, "A Dissolving View," is an aesthetic and philosophical principle: "The hand of man generally improves a landscape"—except, that is, when the hubris of modern engineering is allowed to express its destructive potential.

Close on the heels of these two successful appearances as a new American nature writer, Cooper produced two works in which she expresses more of her emerging thought about how human culture should relate to the natural environment and about the great importance of representing that environment in literature. For the American edition of British naturalist John Leonard Knapp's *Journal of a Naturalist* (1829), Cooper prepared an introduction and an extensive set of natural history notes mostly devoted to clarifying the taxonomic differences between many European and North American plant and animal species that, to the confusion of many American readers, bear the same name. Her brief introduction argues that Americans should know their native species as inhabitants peculiar to their own country. Here Cooper also proposes that literary works that relate natural history are as satisfying and compelling for readers as the most popular forms of prose fiction. Thus, early in her career, she worked deliberately to broaden the popular audience for American nature writing and thereby to increase the likelihood that more such works would be written.

Her next project, *The Rhyme and Reason of Country Life* (1854), is a hefty anthology of nature poetry from around the world. Having argued that prose representations of nature should be more widely read, she now brings to her nation's parlors the world's poetic renderings of the natural. More so than any other single document, her introduction to this volume teems with insights into her thought and understanding of her purpose and place as a writer in her culture. For example, she theorizes about the motive behind nature writing. The ancient Greeks, she writes, did not write directly about their beautiful environment because they did not see themselves as independent of or as distinguishable from nature. Americans in her day, by contrast, are motivated to write about nature by a "fear that she should fail them." Cooper also suggests that rural nature writers hold one of the highest places in her culture. Whereas in past ages the most important writers worked from within cities because only there were people educated (with the result that the "tastes and habits" of the culture were "necessarily...more or less artificial"), in Cooper's young nation, the much wider dissemination of education and the other advantages of civilization free the "rustic population" from the urban perception that they are "only fit for ridicule and burlesque." Instead, the American intellectual or artist can work effectively from rural settings: "He may read and he may write there

with pleasure and with impunity. A wide horizon for observation opens about him today in the fields, as elsewhere." With general education "daily enlarging the public audience....No single literary class is likely...to usurp undue authority over others....Whatever is really natural and really worthy, may therefore hope in the end for a share of success." Education alone, however, is not sufficient; amid the divorce of science and religion that occurred in her century, Cooper does not waver from her conviction that only those authors affected by the revealed truth of Christianity will be able to write accounts of nature at all worthy of their subject. In the *Rhyme and Reason* introduction, she sets up her claim that Christian faith is essential to worthwhile nature writing in direct opposition to the purely secular views of Alexander von Humboldt, upon whose *Cosmos* (1845–1862) she relied heavily for much of her discussion of the world's nature poetry.

In Cooper's subsequent cultural analysis, America becomes the site of literature's full maturity, and the rural poet of nature becomes the culture's most important artist. The main distinguishing characteristic of American poetry, Cooper claims, is "a deeply-felt appreciation of the beauty of the natural world." This national affinity for the natural becomes for Americans a moral guide past the "follies of idle ostentation and extravagant expenditure" encouraged and cultivated by the cities, the centers of commerce and manufacture. By contrast, in America, "The influences which surround the countryman are essentially ennobling, elevating, civilizing, in fact." She concludes:

> It can scarcely, therefore, be an error of judgment to believe that while in past generations the country has received all its wisdom from the town, the moment has come when in American society many of the higher influences of civilization may rather be sought in the fields, when we may learn there many valuable lessons of life, and particularly all the happy lessons of simplicity.

Cooper's discussion in *Rural Hours* of the recent move to greater realism and accuracy in "descriptive writing, on natural objects" implies that literary representations of the natural can contribute to the "moral and intellectual progress" of the culture. Cooper's introduction to *The Rhyme and Reason of Country Life* provides a scholarly and philosophical analysis of her reasons for saying so.

In the history of American nature writing, no voice before Susan Cooper's of the early 1850s spoke so deliberately and argued so fully to advance the genre. However, her direct influence is difficult to gauge. While *Rural Hours* remained healthily present before American readers until Cooper's death—and while Thoreau mentions it in his *Walden* (1854) and it was widely reviewed and unanimously praised—the ideas she develops in the subsequent publications seem not to have engaged the minds of other editors and writers. Other than brief mentions as new publications, neither *Country Rambles* nor *Rhyme and Reason* was discussed in print.

Following the deaths of her father and mother (in 1851 and 1852, respectively) and the publications of *Country Rambles* and *Rhyme and Reason*, Cooper turned away from environmental projects to devote herself to maintaining her father's reputation, establishing herself as a magazine writer, and founding an orphanage and a hospital in her village. The major works through which the daughter shaped and sustained her father's fame were *Pages and Pictures, from the Writings of James Fenimore Cooper* (1861) and her introductions to Houghton Mifflin's 15-volume "Household Edition" of her father's novels (1876, 1881–1884). The "Household" introductions offered readers a more intimate knowledge of the novels by illuminating the history of their compositions, settings, and characterizations. When the last of these was published, Cooper was 71 years old and her father had been dead 31 years. Such a long-term commitment to these large and time-consuming introductions reflects the depth of her devotion to his memory.

During this period, however, Cooper also reemerged as a nature writer by producing a remarkable series of essays published (in *Appletons' Journal*) under the collective title of "Otsego Leaves." Since 1854, she had practically abandoned nature writing as a genre, but in 1878 she produced this rather nonchalant *tour de force* that recent readers have come to regard as her most mature and most fully realized contribution to American environmental writing. By conveying pertinent and complex ecological interdependencies in narrative prose that is vivid, fresh, and involving, the author seems to meet effectively the main challenge faced by all environmental writers: that is, how to catch and keep the interest of a reader in an essay about animals, plants, and the human relationship to the physical environment. While there is much that is remarkable about Cooper's "Otsego Leaves," two points in particular stand out in a consideration of her environmental thought: in the use she makes of information previously published in *Rural Hours*, Cooper transforms that work into a source of environmental history, which she argues was more important than most of her contemporaries suspected; and, in their treatment of birds and bird populations, these three essays become a work of literary ornithology, intended to guide others to the work of preserving bird species.

Susan Fenimore Cooper's work is valuable in part because in some of it she records the past environmental conditions of her region. More than this, however, her essays reveal what was in her day a rare insight: she wanted to teach her culture the value of knowing what a place was like in its original wild state before civilization brought its impact. Hers was an active, articulate voice, from her rural setting, suggesting a need for reliable sources of environmental history if her contemporaries wanted to take efficacious steps toward becoming a culture that was environmentally sustainable. Without accurate knowledge of earlier environmental conditions, "speculation" and "ambition" have their way, and the result is a culture shaped and driven by the short-term goals of profit and convenience, not by a desire to be good stewards of the land.

In various ways, "Otsego Leaves" strips Cooper of the mask she had donned earlier in *Rural Hours* as a "rustic bird-fancier" and presents her as an amateur ornithologist. When she explains her method of monitoring the number of bird nests in her village, she is describing the field work of an ornithologist. Similarly, when she analyzes the causes and consequences of declining bird populations, as she does in "Birds Then and Now," she is a naturalist working for the preservation of bird species by means of written accounts of her close observations. Indeed, her preservationist goals set her a generation ahead of other ornithologists.

A short essay published in *Harper's* just over a year before her death, "A Lament for the Birds," while not the last of her published writings, evokes for us Cooper's lifelong interest in environmental history. This essay makes rather emphatically the point that from the time when she conceived of her *Rural Hours* project in the late 1840s until her death half a century later, the mind of Susan Cooper was focused radically on the natural environment and on the human impact upon it. This closing lament literally echoes concerns expressed in "Otsego Leaves" and in *Rural Hours,* and in paraphrasing observations first published in the 1850 book, she transforms that book into a source of the environmental history she argues is needed if humans are to stop or even slow their destruction of plant and animal species. It is a beautiful, lyrical essay, but it sings no song of hope: "Alas for the vanished birds!"

Through her later decades, Cooper lived with her sister Charlotte in Byberry Cottage, a home built for them after the deaths of their parents. In addition to her writing, Cooper devoted much energy to family matters. Always interested in improving the quality of her village culture, in the winter of 1860 she began the "Christ Church Sewing School," which at one time instructed some 80 girls. To help meet increasing medical needs, she cofounded the Thanksgiving Hospital in 1868 and served on its board of directors. In 1871, she turned her charitable eyes on the orphans of her region and founded the Orphan House of the Holy Saviour, which by 1885 was housing and educating more than 100 orphaned children. When she died at 81 on December 31, 1894, her charitable works were widely known, and her literary reputation began to fade.

Susan Fenimore Cooper holds an interesting place in the history of American nature writing. Not only was she the first woman in the United States to publish a book-length work of nature writing, but she was also the first theorist and active promoter of literary environmental writing. In her manner of representing nature, although she often anthropomorphized the robins nesting in the eaves of her cottage home, she never reduced the natural realm to a system of symbols for the human soul, as the early Thoreau learned to do from Emerson. She felt that for nature writing to succeed in its cultural work of moving readers toward more sustainable relations to their physical environment, they must be moved by the pleasing conveyance of natural history and by the carefully drawn details of descriptive writing.

PRIMARY BIBLIOGRAPHY

Books

Elinor Wyllys. A Tale, anonymous, 3 vols., ed. J. Fenimore Cooper (London: Richard Bentley, 1845).

Elinor Wyllys: or, The Young Folk of Longbridge. A Tale, as Amabel Penfeather, 2 vols., ed. J. Fenimore Cooper (Philadelphia: Cary and Hart, 1846).

Rural Hours, anonymous (New York: Putnam, 1850; London: Bentley, 1850; enlarged edition, New York: Putnam, 1868; abridged edition, Boston: Houghton Mifflin, 1887; abridged edition, ed. David Jones, Syracuse: Syracuse University Press, 1968; an edition of the full 1850 text, ed. Rochelle Johnson and Daniel Patterson, University of Georgia Press, 1998).

Mount Vernon: A Letter to the Children of America (New York: D. Appleton and Co., 1859).

William West Skiles: A Sketch of Missionary Life at Valle Crucis in Western North Carolina, 1842–1862 (New York: James Pott and Co., 1890).

Other

"A Dissolving View," in *The Home Book of the Picturesque: Or American Scenery, Art, and Literature* (New York: Putnam, 1852; reprint, Gainesville, FL: Scholars' Facsimiles & Reprints, 1967), 79–94.

[John Leonard Knapp], *Country Rambles in England; or Journal of a Naturalist; with Notes and Additions, by the Author of "Rural Hours," Etc., Etc.,* ed. Susan Fenimore Cooper (Buffalo: Phinney & Co., 1853).

The Rhyme and Reason of Country Life: Or, Selections from Fields Old and New, ed. Susan Fenimore Cooper (New York: Putnam, 1854).

Appleton's Illustrated Almanac for 1870, ed. Susan Fenimore Cooper (New York: D. Appleton and Co., 1861).

Pages and Pictures, from the Writings of James Fenimore Cooper, with Notes by Susan Fenimore Cooper (New York: W.A. Townsend, 1861).

The Cooper Gallery; or, Pages and Pictures from the Writings of James Fenimore Cooper, with Notes by Susan Fenimore Cooper (New York: James Miller, 1865 [reprint of *Pages and Pictures* (1861)]).

Introductions to five volumes of the "Household Edition" of the *Works of James Fenimore Cooper: The Deerslayer,* xiii–xl; *The Last of the Mohicans,* ix–xxxviii; *The Pathfinder,* ix–xxxiv; *The Pioneers,* xi–xxxvi; *The Prairie,* ix–xxxii (Boston: Houghton Mifflin and Co., 1876).

"The Wonderful Cookie: A True Story," in *Wide Awake Pleasure Book* (Boston: D. Lothrop and Co., 1879), 348–53; reprint, *Wonder Stories of History* (Boston: D. Lothrop and Co., 1886).

"Small Family Memories," in *Correspondence of James Fenimore Cooper,* ed. James Fenimore Cooper, vol. 1 (New Haven: Yale University Press, 1922), 7–72. [Cooper dated this document "January 25, 1883."]

Introductions to ten volumes of the "Household Edition of the *Works of James Fenimore Cooper: Afloat and Ashore,* ix–xiv; *The Crater,* ix–xix; *Jack Tier,* vii–xiv; *Miles Wallingford,* vii–xvi; *The Pilot,* xiii–xxiii; *The Red Rover,* xi–xxi; *The Sea Lions,* xi–xxi; *The Two Admirals,* ix–xvii; *The Water-Witch,* ix–xxiii; *The Wing-and-Wing,* ix–xviii (Boston: Houghton Mifflin and Co., 1884).

Selected Periodical Publications— Uncollected

"The Lumley Autograph," *Graham's Magazine* 38 (January 1851): 31–36; 38 (February 1851): 97–101.

"Sally Lewis and Her Lovers," *Harper's New Monthly Magazine* 18 (April 1859): 644–53.

"Fragments from a Diary of James Fenimore Cooper," *Putnam's Magazine* 1 (February 1868): 167–72.

"Passages from a Diary by James Fenimore Cooper," *Putnam's Magazine* 1 (June 1868): 730–37.

"Bits," *Putnam's Magazine* 2 (August 1868): 145–48.

"The Battle of Plattsburgh Bay: An Unpublished Manuscript of J. Fenimore Cooper," *Putnam's Magasine* 3 (January 1869): 49–59.

"The Eclipse: From an Unpublished MS. of James Fenimore Cooper," *Putnam's Magazine* 4 (September 1869): 352–59.

"Village Improvement Societies," *Putnam's Magazine* 4 (September 1869): 359–66.

"The Magic Palace," *Putnam's Magazine* 5 (February 1870): 160–62.

"The Chanting Cherubs," *Putnam's Magazine* 5 (February 1870): 241–42.

"Insect-Life in Winter," *Putnam's Magazine* 5 (April 1870): 424–27.

"Madame Lafayette and Her Mother," *Putnam's Magazine* 6 (August 1870): 202–13.

"Female Suffrage: A Letter to the Christian Women of America," *Harper's New Monthly Magazine* 41 (August 1870): 438–46; 41 (September 1870): 594–600.

"Two of My Lady-Loves," *Harper's New Monthly Magazine* 45 (June 1872): 129–33.

"Rear-Admiral William Branford Shubrick," *Harper's New Monthly Magazine* 53 (August 1876): 400–407; reprint, *Rear-Admiral William Branford Shubrick. A Sketch* (New York: n.p., n.d.).

"Mrs. Philip Schuyler: A Sketch," *Worthy Women of Our First Century,* ed. Mrs. O.J. Wister and Miss Agnes Irwin (Philadelphia: J.B. Lippincott and Co., 1877), 71–111.

"Otsego Leaves I: Birds Then and Now," *Appletons' Journal* 4 (June 1878): 528–31.

"Otsego Leaves II: The Bird Mediæval," *Appletons' Journal* 5 (August 1878): 164–67.

"Otsego Leaves III: The Bird Primeval," *Appletons' Journal* 5 (September 1878): 273–77.

"Otsego Leaves IV: A Road-side Post-office," *Appletons' Journal* 5 (December 1878): 542–46.

"The Hudson River and Its Early Names," *Magazine of American History* 4 (June 1880): 401–18.

"The Adventures of Cocquelicot. (A True History)," *St. Nicholas: An Illustrated Magazine for Young Folks* 8, no. 12 (October 1881): 942–46.

"Missions to the Oneidas," *The Living Church* 8 (February 20, 1886): 709–10; 8 (February 27, 1886): 720–21; 8 (March 6, 1886): 736–37; 8 (March 13, 1886): 753; 8 (March 20, 1886): 768–69; 8

(March 27, 1886): 784; 9 (April 10, 1886): 28; 9 (April 24, 1886): 60–61; 9 (May 1, 1886): 75–76; 9 (May 15, 1886): 107–8; 9 (May 22, 1886): 123–24; 9 (May 29, 1886): 139; 9 (June 5, 1886): 155; "A Glance Backward," *Atlantic Monthly* 59 (February 1887): 199–206.

"A Second Glance Backward," *Atlantic Monthly* 60 (October 1887): 474–86.

"Financial Condition of New York in 1833," *Magazine of American History* 22 (October 1889): 328–30.

"The Life of Hattie Brant," *The Churchman: An Illustrated Weekly Newspaper Magazine* 60 (December 14, 1889): 748–50.

"The Childhood of Bishop Heber. I," *The Churchman: An Illustrated Weekly Newspaper Magazine* 62 (July 19, 1890): 81–83.

"College Life of Bishop Heber. II," *The Churchman: An Illustrated Weekly Newspaper Magazine* 62 (August 16, 1890): 205–6.

"College Life of Bishop Heber. III," *The Churchman: An Illustrated Weekly Newspaper Magazine* 62 (August 23, 1890): 232–33.

"Boyhood of Bishop Heber," *The Churchman: An Illustrated Weekly Newspaper Magazine* 62 (September 13, 1890): 319–22.

"The Talent of Reading Wisely," *The Ladies' Home Journal* 9 (February 1892): 18.

"A Lament for the Birds," *Harper's New Monthly Magazine* 87 (August 1893): 472–74.

"An Outing on Lake Otsego," *The Freeman's Journal* (Cooperstown, New York) April 12, 1894, p. 2.

"The Cherry-Colored Purse. (A True Story)," *St. Nicholas: An Illustrated Magazine for Young Folks* 22, no. 3 (January 1895): 245–48.

Selected Publications—Collected

Essays on Nature and Landscape, ed. Rochelle Johnson and Daniel Patterson (Athens: University of Georgia Press, 2002).

SECONDARY BIBLIOGRAPHY

References

Nina Baym, "Susan Fenimore Cooper and Ladies' Science," in *American Women of Letters and the Nineteenth-Century Sciences: Styles of Affiliation* (New Brunswick: Rutgers University Press, 2002), 73–90.

Lawrence Buell, *The Environmental Imagination: Thoreau, Nature Writing, and the Formation of American Culture* (Cambridge: Harvard University Press, 1995).

Rochelle Johnson, "Susan Fenimore Cooper's *Rural Hours* and the 'Natural' Refinement of American Culture," *ISLE: Interdisciplinary Studies in Literature and Environment* 7.1 (Winter 2000): 47–77.

Rochelle Johnson, "Placing *Rural Hours*," in *Reading Under the Sign of Nature*, ed. John Tallmadge and Henry Harrington (Salt Lake City: University of Utah Press, 2000), 64–84.

Rochelle Johnson, "*Walden, Rural Hours*, and the Dilemma of Representation," in *Thoreau's Sense of Place: Essays in American Environmental Writing*, ed. Richard J. Schneider (Iowa City: University of Iowa Press, 2000), 179–93.

Rochelle Johnson and Daniel Patterson, eds., *Susan Fenimore Cooper: New Essays on* Rural Hours *and Other Works* (Athens: University of Georgia Press, 2001).

Rosaly Torna Kurth, "Susan Fenimore Cooper: A Study of Her Life and Work" (dissertation, Fordham University, 1974).

Lucy Maddox, "Susan Fenimore Cooper and the Plain Daughters of America," *American Quarterly* 40.2 (1988): 131–46.

Vera Norwood, *Made from This Earth: American Women and Nature* (Chapel Hill: University of North Carolina Press, 1993).

Papers

The vast majority of Cooper's surviving letters are in private collections. For a list of letters and papers held in institutions, see Johnson and Patterson's *Susan Fenimore Cooper: New Essays on "Rural Hours" and Other Works*, pages 271–78. Significant collections are held at the Beinecke Rare Book and Manuscript Library of Yale University and at the Alderman Library of the University of Virginia.

J. Hector St. John de Crèvecoeur (January 31, 1735–November 12, 1813)

Thomas Patchell

Long before the term "ecology" was in standard usage, J. Hector St. John De Crèvecoeur was investigating the relationship between the European Settlers in the New World and the natural setting they were colonizing. Before the United States was a sovereign country, Crèvecoeur questioned and explored just what it meant to be an American, a category that was still in its nascent form. Crèvecoeur was not a native of the Americas, but he is considered to be one of the first truly American writers. He is the first to draw a connection between the various peoples in the new wilderness and the effects of that wilderness upon those peoples; he is also the first writer to define and exhibit the qualities of what would come to be known as the "American Dream." All of these feats were completed through the Revolutionary War era text, *Letters from an American Farmer*, a fanciful collection of epistolary essays Crèvecoeur wrote during his peaceful days as a farmer in Orange County, New York.

Crèvecoeur was born Michel-Guillaume Jean De Crèvecoeur in Normandy, France, in 1735 to a minor noble family with lands and an estate. He was raised in relative affluence and was well educated at a Jesuit college. Crèvecoeur studied Latin, mathematics, rhetoric, debating, surveying, and English, among other subjects, at the Jesuit College du Mont. He was an active student, and there is some proof of this in a flyer from the period advertising a debate the school was producing with Crèvecoeur listed as one of the principle participants, showing he was accomplished and probably well liked by his teachers and his peers. Though Crèvecoeur was not a practicing Catholic for the rest of his life, the Jesuits instilled a desire for knowledge in the young Crèvecoeur and the skill of careful observation and recording. Most notably, the Jesuits instilled the habit of writing on a daily basis, a habit Crèvecoeur would never lose.

In the year 1754, the 19-year-old Crèvecoeur moved to England and stayed at Salisbury with some relatives. This is a mysterious period in Crèvecoeur's life; little is known, but he must have honed his English speaking and writing skills during this time. He was engaged to marry while living in England, but his fiancée died before the marriage ever took place, and Crèvecoeur left for Canada. He arrived in the New World in 1755, enlisted in the French army, and fought in the French and Indian War. A skilled engineer, surveyor, and artilleryman, he was commissioned an officer at the battle of Quebec and subsequently commended in a communiqué to Louis XV for his mapmaking skill and his drawing of Fort George. (The map had assisted the French forces with their victory there.) In 1759, he was wounded in battle on the Plains of Abraham where the French General Louis Joseph Montcalm lost Canada to the British forces. For unclear reasons, Crèvecoeur decided to resign his commission while convalescing, and leave the army and Canada; some historians suspect Crèvecoeur may have made himself unpopular to his commanders by his pro-English sentiments. He received 240 pounds and passage to New York in the British Colonies in return for his resignation.

On December 16, 1759, Crèvecoeur arrived in New York; he had changed his name to James Hector St. John, presumably to sound less French and more English. In the following years, Crèvecoeur became a surveyor and something of a traveling salesman; his routes carried him from Nova Scotia and Vermont all the way to the southern region of Virginia. He may have even traveled to Bermuda and Jamaica during these years, and there was probably no man better acquainted with the American frontier and wilderness than Crèvecoeur. He became a naturalized subject of King George and resident of New York in 1765.

In the spring and summer of 1767, Crèvecoeur was part of an expedition that let him experience the majesty of the American wilderness deeper than ever before in his travels. This trip took the French wanderer over the Appalachian Mountains and down the Ohio River to St. Louis and up the Mississippi River to the Great Lakes and to the location of what is now the city of Chicago. Crèvecoeur returned to New York by passing through Fort Dearborn, Fort Niagara, and the Mohawk Valley (where he visited with the Oneida Indians), finally passing through Albany. Returning to New York, Crèvecoeur bought a tract of 250 acres of land in Orange County. In 1769 he married Mehetable Tippett, of a wealthy Tory family, and started a farm, which he named Pine Hill. These years of Crèvecoeur's life seem to be the most content and happy, and he and his wife produced three children, America-Frances (Fanny), born on December 14, 1770, Guillaume-Alexandre (Ally), born on August 5, 1772,

and Philippe-Louis, born on October 22, 1774.

During this period, he began to write a series of fanciful epistle-like essays that would eventually become his most famous work, *Letters from an American Farmer*. The peaceful years at Pine Hill allowed Crèvecoeur to observe and record the animals, plants, and habits and customs of the various inhabitants of New England; he also wrote of the land itself, with a fanciful subjectivity, while also describing the newly forming American identity. Many critics and writers believe Crèvecoeur to be the genesis of the idea of the American Dream, and the relationship between industriousness on the part of the free individual, and the success resulting from that industry. During this time period Crèvecoeur develops one of his most memorable ideas, that people are like plants: plant them in fertile and prosperous soil, and they will become fertile and prosperous.

During the 1770s, increasing discontent among the colonies disrupted Crèvecoeur's peaceful idyll, and he decided to return to Europe, presumably to claim his ancestral lands. Being a loyalist, he was coming under growing suspicion from his patriotic neighbors, which was another possible reason for his return to Europe. He arrived in New York City at the end of the decade with his son Ally, and ironically he was imprisoned by the British forces occupying the city as they believed him to be a spy for the colonists. With the help of letters from friends on his behalf, Crèvecoeur was finally released from prison and sailed for England some time around 1780 with his son. Crèvecoeur's ship was wrecked off the Irish coast where he managed to save himself, his son, and a manuscript he had been carrying with him. When he arrived in London in 1781, he turned the manuscript for *Letters from an American Farmer* over to a publisher named Davies and Davis (Samuel Johnson's publisher), and left for France; 27 years had passed since he had left the land of his birth. *Letters* was published in 1782 (nine years before Franklin's autobiography) and was an overnight success. Crèvecoeur was not immediately aware of the book's popularity until he was invited to Paris by a family friend, discovered by the literary circles, and lionized in the Paris salons.

The reader of *Letters* may easily forget that the text's narrator is not Crèvecoeur the Anglicized Frenchman of Orange County, New York, but rather his persona James, the English-American of Carlisle, Pennsylvania. The *Letters* are not purely historical, nor are they purely literary, but something of a mixture of both genres in an epistolary framework. Crèvecoeur is something of a product of the enlightenment and a prelude to romanticism. The premise of *Letters* involves a self-reported simple country farmer who is talked into writing letters to a learned Englishman who has studied at Oxford in England. The letters are to be an innocent exposition of life in the New World around New England and the frontiers of the colonies still under the English crown through the eyes of a farmer in a voice that is at once exuberant and somewhat naïve.

Crèvecoeur opens *Letters* with a simple dedication to the Abbé Raynal, an apparent inspiration for the work and another Frenchman writing in and about the New World in his *Philosophical History of the Indies*. In this dedication, Crèvecoeur commends Raynal for his work and claims that it caused him to reflect on the state of nations and the commerce between them, which in his view should be a uniting force, but had become only disruptive. Here, Crèvecoeur also makes the first known reference to North America as being an "asylum of freedom" for the rest of the world. The letters create for the reader a New World that is an idyllic pastoral that ends in a state of peril.

The opening letter serves as a strangely presented introduction to the project. Creating the persona of James, the letter drifts from epistolary prose to a dramatic play-like structure of dialogue between the farmer, his bucolic wife, and their minister. The minister and wife convince the modest farmer he can write such letters to a learned man, a minister in Oxford, England. The farmer is soon

convinced that the exotic nature of his subject, and the newness of the flora and fauna and way of life he would be discussing, would overcome any weakness in his own editorial or intellectual abilities. The narrator denies twice that he is any kind of naturalist or scientist, even though describing nature quickly becomes one of the primary objectives of *Letters*.

Crèvecoeur's descriptions of the creatures, plants, and pastimes around his farm begin in "Letter II: On the Situation, Feelings, and Pleasures of an American Farmer." Focusing primarily on bees, wasps, hornets, and birds, the letter is a catalog rich in fanciful writing on flying creatures. The narrator discusses bees at some length, exclaiming they "above any other creature attract my attention and respect." Bee hunting is discussed at length, including the chopping down of trees with hives in their hollows for removal to the narrator's farm. Stories of aggression between bees and birds and wrens and swallows demonstrate Crèvecoeur's powers of observation and his tendency toward fanciful interpretations of his observations. For example, bees are revived after being rescued from the craw of a bird killed by the narrator, and he tells of living in harmony with a hornets' nest in his house for the purpose of controlling the fly population. The idea of natural abundance is asserted with examples of huge flocks of pigeons that are frequently killed and eaten by the colonists. The chapter also extends the thesis that all that is good in America is a product of the rich soil.

The celebrated "Letter III: What is an American?" is the most famous and anthologized of all of the letters. Here, the focus is on people and the effects of the new and rich soil upon those people. James compares people to plants, the premise being that if the soil is rich the person living off of it will be prosperous as well. Therefore, while a melting-pot ideology is proposed and celebrated in Letter III, it is ultimately successful farming that makes Americans people of any worth. Thus, Indians and hunters do not prosper, since they do not connect with the land through husbandry, and the Irish fail to prosper because they are quarrelsome and lazy drunkards who have been weakened by growing easy crops like potatoes. The closer Americans are to the frontier and the Indians, the more animalistic and savage they become. The formula for happiness in the New World is personal industry and rich soil. The letter ends with a story that predates *Horatio Alger* about an industrious Scots immigrant, Honest Andrew, who has found the good life in America through earnestness, hard work, and the abundance of natural resources.

"The Nantucket Letters," Letters IV, V, VII, and VIII, are all descriptions of the Island of Nantucket and its inhabitants who do not farm, but "plough the rougher ocean." These letters tend to be more concrete collections of data cataloguing everything on the island from people to animals, ponds, and swamps; they portray a new, fairly naïve, industrious people, interacting with the wilderness that quickly recedes from them. The geographical location and physical measurements of the island are recorded in Letter IV, but they are now known to be incorrect as reported. Nantucket is described as a utopia where the European Americans, Indians, and nonhuman nature live in peace and harmony. James describes this island in minute detail and gives its history and a summary of its commerce. Of particular interest is his recording of Indian tribes that had died out since the arrival of Europeans in the New World and some of the causes of their demises.

The second of the Nantucket letters, "Letter V: Customary Education and Employment of the Inhabitants of Nantucket," is a methodical examination of the Quakers' industry on the Island of Nantucket, from their children's educations to how they retire from their labors later in life. The letter contains a detailed history of the whaling fishery started by the Society of Friends on Nantucket, who (in a rare break from Crèvecoeur's major theme) were forced to industry by the poor quality of their soil. According to the farmer James, the narrator of *Letters*,

the people of Nantucket started as master fishers of cod around their island, and then began to hunt the abundant whales that were once frequently sighted off of their shores; as the whales receded, the Quakers followed and the fishery grew until it spread all around the globe. (In many ways, other peoples learned whaling from these intrepid Americans.) The Society of Friends soon had commerce with lumber, whalebone, and whale oil, which they traded throughout the Indies, the Americas, and Europe for other commodities, which they would often sell for profit and reinvest in their conglomerate operation. Letter V seems to foreshadow the famous American novel *Moby Dick*.

The Society of Friends are the major subject of "Letter VII: Manners and Customs at Nantucket." James discusses the problematic growth of the Society on Nantucket and then remarks on the resulting Quaker communities on the mainland in places like New Garden and on the river Kennebec. Crèvecoeur proposes one of his favorite themes in this section, that harsh climates and environments produce moral and industrious men while temperate climates produce men who are effeminate and lazy. The pleasant lack of ministers and lawyers on Nantucket is praised and followed by a diatribe against lawyers, likening them to plants that "grow in soil cultivated by others" and are deadly to all of the "vegetables" around their place of growth. The Quakers are described as physically and socially healthy people who worship the "Parent of Nature"; they prosper from taking advantage of the abundant resources of the New World, are progressively antislavery and simplistic even in their funeral rights, and succeed by "Clearing forests, making the face of Nature smile."

The Society of Friends and their relationship to their environment are also the subject of "Letter VIII: Peculiar Customs At Nantucket." James mentions the Quakers' "ungrammatical" speech, and he then goes on to describe their abhorrence of idleness and their ways of entertaining each other. Crèvecoeur's narrator finds them to be so intermarried that they address each other and anyone on the island by such familial titles as "Cousin, uncle, or aunt." The Quakers' primary entertainment is listening to stories of whaling voyages by young Friends recently returned. As a testament to the Quakers' industry, it is noted that even while talking they keep their hands busy with knives carving wood into useful items. The letter ends with the narrator's visit to a house on the remote part of the island that seems to be the most peaceful passage of all the Nantucket letters. James reflects on the meditative and destructive qualities of the ocean, and returns to one of his major themes: that Americans lack the history and culture of Europe but actually have much more here in this new and free world of superabundance. Incidentally, a clear narrator-author distinction surfaces in Letter VIII, as James the American farmer claims to have never been to Europe or seen the "beauties" it contains —an unambiguous reminder that we are reading the words of a fictitious narrator.

The Nantucket letters are interrupted by "Letter VI: Description of the Island of Martha's Vineyard and of the Whale Fishery." The letter begins with measurements of the island and then explains that most of the men, European and Indian, go to Nantucket to become whalemen. A careful description of the whaling industry follows. Crèvecoeur records the use of Nattic (Indian) expressions as being common to all on whaling boats and explains that it is no wonder, since the Indians were allies from early on in what he describes as "this new warfare." The letter includes Crèvecoeur's map of Martha's Vineyard, and more details about killing whales and a register of the various types of whales known to humans. Once again, the ocean's effect upon humans is explored, and the poor quality of the soil is given as reason for the men of Martha's Vineyard to turn to whaling. In spite of this, the narrator reports that the men kill whales with the "Indifference...a landman takes to clear a piece of swamp."

The transition from Letter VIII to Letter IX forms a drastically critical shift in the narrator's subject matter and tone. The subject turns from the industrious Quakers of Nantucket to physical evil in the form of slavery. The letter is entitled "Description of Charles Town; Thoughts on Slavery; On Physical Evil; A Melancholy Scene." And like the structure of the title, the letter moves like a carefully crafted series of mental steps in an argument. The letter begins with a summary description of Charles Town and the destructive effects of the temperate climate on the health and minds of the men of the town; the climate is too ideal for growing crops, and the men become decadent and waste their health. Here Crèvecoeur draws together some of his themes and puts them into a moral condemnation of slavery. The description of Charles Town is uncharacteristically brief; it seems as if Crèvecoeur sets up a framework for the letter and then abandons it, turning to the plague of lawyers in Charles Town, and the idea that law is the new religion, and attorneys its priests.

With an abrupt transition, the letter moves to slavery; the destructiveness of slavery is exposed in the detailed sufferings of familial and physical losses of the black slaves. The narrator seems desperate at this point and appeals to Nature, wondering where this equalizing force can be in the face of such human evil. The letter rails against the hypocrisy of humankind, its pretense of civilization and higher values such as art and religion in the light of the misery and cracking whips of slavery. The narrator pleads the case of blacks being just as human as whites based on their similar desires, emotions, and natures. The farmer James claims that black slaves are treated much better in the North, but regardless calls for the emancipation of all slaves. The story of a clergyman who tried to convince his congregation to treat their slaves with more dignity and being censured relates the hardheartedness of the South and its peculiar institution.

Crèvecoeur now returns to his great theme of nature affecting human behavior and builds the argument that slavery flourishes where natural conditions are temperate and fertile. Just as in previous letters the narrator proposes the idea that easy conditions of planting and growing causes people in the Americas to become decadent, he here argues that such conditions have caused entire civilizations to fall into wickedness and ruin. Again, it is only when fertile soil is combined with personal industry that healthy and moral people are produced. The problem of slavery comes in an oddly natural and vicious circle: temperate climates and fertile soil bring easy crops and money, slaves follow, and the owners decay as a result of the relief from their physical labors.

The narrator's sociopolitical theories are blended with a look at a Nature that is not always beneficent, but destructive and dangerous to humans all over the globe in the form of volcanoes, plagues, and other natural disasters. The letter ends with a return from the general to the specific and the most graphic image in all of the letters. The farmer walks through the woods and comes across an African slave hanging in a cage and being literally eaten alive by insects and birds. The farmer, horrified, gives the slave water but is unable to fulfill the suffering man's wish for death. Upon arriving at his destination, the farmer finds that the slave has killed an overseer. The narrator seems unsatisfied with his host's tired arguments for such drastic measures with slaves, and the letter ends with a weary "Adieu."

Perhaps the last return to the original tone of *Letters* occurs in letter "X: On Snakes; And On The Humming-Bird." This fanciful naturalism is reminiscent of the second letter, as it takes the same tone and subject matter and departs from the serious and dismal outlook of Letter IX. The letter discusses varieties of snakes in detail, and specifics are given about the Indians cooking rattlesnakes and eating them as Europeans eat eels. The letter verges on the preposterous as the narrator describes a tame rattlesnake that returned from swimming when called by the boys who own it, and that wriggled on its back like a cat when they stroked its belly. Another rattlesnake story involves a farmer surviving a snake attack and then dying upon removing his leather boots; his son inherits the boots and

also dies upon their removal. A physician declares the two dead men to have been bewitched. A neighbor soon inherits the boots and almost dies upon removing them, but he is treated for snake venom and lives; upon inspection, the boots still have the snake's fangs in their leather from the original attack. This strange story is probably the best example in *Letters* of Crèvecoeur's Enlightenment thinking and his proto-Romanticism, in which he uses a strange blend of pseudo-empirical data and a fable-like lesson.

In "Letter XI: From Mr. Iw-n Al-z, A Russian Gentleman, Describing the Visit He Paid At My Request To Mr. John Bertram, The Celebrated Pennsylvanian Botanist" Crèvecoeur makes use of a historical figure to render an Enlightenment model of the ideal relation between human culture and Nature. The letter is not narrated by the farmer James, but by a Russian immigrant named Iwan who visits the historical John Bartram (whose name Crèvecoeur spells "Bertram"). The letter is presumably written by Iwan to James, and then sent to James's correspondent. The reasons for this new narrator are unclear and may have historical origins, but the Russian narrator seems indistinguishable from James and is also a farmer. Bertram is more of an agricultural engineer than a botanist, and his methods of fertilization and irrigation are principle subjects of the letter. His construction of "banks," or earthen enclosures, for water are of great interest to the Russian, as are his draining of swampland to prepare the land for cultivation (another recurring theme). Bertram has controlled the Schuylkill River to his advantage, and purchased a small spring, which he directs to irrigate and fertilize his crops. Crèvecoeur's fascination with the Quakers as an ideal people also resurfaces in Letter XI. Bertram, a Quaker, lives a modest, rational, industrious, and progressive life. He is hospitable, he solves farming problems with scientific precision, he uses the natural resources around himself to great benefit, and he treats blacks with fairness and dignity. The letter ends with another rendering of the respect with which Crèvecoeur regards Quakers and their relationship with the natural world.

Letters from an American Farmer ends with a letter that is something of a return to the preoccupation with human evil from the Charles Town letter and the closest look at Native Americans that *Letters* offers. The letter reads with a tone of frustrated desperation, and the narrator lacks the exuberance of many of the former letters. "Letter XII: Distresses of a Frontier Man" seems to be the gaff for the outrageous idealism and promise of many of the earlier letters. The letter makes reference to the coming calamity of war and characterizes the farmer as the little man caught between forces of aggression beyond his control. This is the only letter that contains anti-British sentiment. The passages are sarcastic and somewhat ambiguous, but a certain frustration with the British Colonial forces is evident. James compares the king to Nature, saying both should create, spare, and protect rather than destroy (contrary to Crèvecoeur's view of nature in the Charles Town letter). Much of the letter is devoted to the American Indians and the prospect of the endangered farmer fleeing the European colonies and living with the natives. The letter captures the colonial-European view of Native Americans better than any other source. While the Indians are "the immediate children of Nature," "Superior in many instances," "marked by the very hands of Nature," and "undefiled offspring" of Nature, James fears that his children may become too "Indianized" and not retain any vestiges of their former civilized state. He writes that the Indians are not warlike or vengeful, but he also argues against European-Indian union in marriage "on natural grounds." Crèvecoeur lauds the Indians for many reasons for which he formerly praised America itself: lack of temples or priests, lack of too many laws, freedom from care or concern other than their own subsistence, and freedom from the "fictitious society" of the Europeans, yet he admits a "keen regret" about leaving his house and farm to go and live with them. He contends that

there must be something better about the Indians because thousands of Europeans have become Indians, but not one Indian has chosen to become a European.

The debate continues on the biographical or historical value of *Letters from an American Farmer,* but the value of the book proceeds from its formulation of the American Dream and American character, and from its combination of Enlightenment ideas with pre-Romantic sentiments. The book looks forward to a host of American writers and their themes—James Fenimore Cooper, Herman Melville, Edgar Allan Poe, Henry David Thoreau, Harriet Beecher Stowe, John Greenleaf Whittier, Robert Frost—and a host of others in some ways descend from Crèvecoeur and his ideas. Even though many of the book's descriptions of plants and animals are fanciful, Crèvecoeur was the first naturalist writer to render several of them and show concern for their status in the wilderness. Crèvecoeur makes the observation that Europeans went to the wilderness as spectators, a strangely evocative statement about European viewpoints of the New World and its inhabitants.

Crèvecoeur's publications are relatively few. *Letters* is his undisputed masterpiece, but his other works merit some notice. *Sketches of Eighteenth-Century America: More "Letters from an American Farmer"* follows in the tradition of the original, but the book is more episodic and not as structurally cohesive as its predecessor. *Sketches* was not published or constructed by Crèvecoeur, but was edited and put together by three scholars in 1923. The book is a collection of leftover essays from the English and French versions of *Letters;* like its predecessor it has an emotional tone and records the early days of a nascent republic. Of most note are the sketches "On the Susquehanna: The Wyoming Massacre," and the piece "Landscapes," the latter written in the format of a play.

Crèvecoeur's final work about America was written while he was in his sixties and surviving the terrors of yet another revolutionary war, the French Revolution.

La Voyage dans la Haute Pensylvanie et dans l'etat de New York (1801) represents the last literary writing of Crèvecoeur in French or English. The book's subject is the same as all of Crèvecoeur's works: the land and people of the early American republic. The book poses as a French translation of a work in English, and Crèvecoeur's style and themes are typical. Of particular interest and pleasure is the sketch of a Native American myth of dubious origin about the barbarity of humans and the creation of beavers. The book shows Crèvecoeur's optimism for the new American Republic and praises its leaders for avoiding tyranny and bloodshed after the victory over the British. Like the other sequels to *Letters*, the book does not reach the greatness achieved by Crèvecoeur's first book, but it demonstrates that its author was still captivated by and hopeful for the future of a new land that he once called his own.

During Crèvecoeur's two years in Paris following his 1781 return, he was a favorite at the famed salons of that period, particularly at those of his family friend, the Countess d'Houdetot, and, during the summers, at her brother's estate at Versailles, Le Marais. The former farmer was revered for his stories and knowledge about the wilderness, peoples, and happenings in the Americas and his agricultural expertise. He even constructed a lightning rod using Benjamin Franklin's guidelines during one of these gatherings. During this time he kept an irregular correspondence with Franklin, though the two never actually met in this period.

Crèvecoeur's remaining years in France did not see the end of his writing. Most of these later writings were pamphlets or agricultural tracts, like his treatise on the growth and use of the potato. In these years he lived an increasingly reclusive existence, and during the time of the French Revolution his popularity waned as the French were not interested in reading about an imperial colony removed from them in time and space and now ideology. He died at his daughter's house in Sarcelles, France. The cause of death was stated as being a heart attack and health problems blamed on his time in the English jails; he was 78 years old.

Since the publication of *Letters*, there has been much controversy about the book's authenticity. During the decade in which it was published, after its initial warm welcome it was attacked in American papers as a fraud. Allegations were made that Crèvecoeur was neither American nor a farmer, and it was also added that he was a Catholic. The book was derided as a "hoax to lure English farmers to America" where they were no longer so welcome. The book was defended by intellectuals of the time such as Benjamin Franklin as being authentic, and its author as being an observant and intellectual man. Though there are obviously fanciful entries and descriptions, much remains unclear about what is actual autobiography, and what is not; the book remains in a hazy realm of Enlightenment historical fiction.

Regardless of whether the book is completely false or factual, the fact does remain that Crèvecoeur became a compelling voice for this new wild land, and inspired many of America's greatest nature writers. And although Crèvecoeur's major fame arises from his description of the character of a newly created people, it is in his descriptions of their relationship with the natural world of plants and animals that he establishes himself as the proto-ecologist of the new American land.

PRIMARY BIBLIOGRAPHY

BOOKS

Letters From an American Farmer (London: Davies and Davies, 1782; Philadelphia, Matthew Carey, 1793).

Lettres d'un cultivateur Americain, ecrites a W.S. Ecuyer, depuis l'anee 1770, jusqu'a 1781, 2 vols. (Paris: Cuchet, 1784); enlarged edition, 3 vols. (Paris: Cuchet, 1787).

Voyage dans la haute Pensylvanie et dans l'Etat de New York, par un Membre adoptif de la Nation Oneida (Paris: De l'imprimerie de Crapelet, Chez Maradan, 1801).

Sketches of Eighteenth-Century America: More "Letters From an American Farmer," ed. Henri L. Bourdin et al. (New Haven: Yale University Press, 1925).

Journey Into Northern Pennsylvania and the State of New York, trans. Clarissa S. Bostelmann (Ann Arbor: University of Michigan Press, 1964).

Letters from an American Farmer and Sketches of Eighteenth-Century America, ed. A. Stone (New York: Penguin, 1981).

More Letters from an American Farmer: An Edition of the Essays in English Left Unpublished by Crèvecoeur, ed. Dennis D. Moore (Athens: University of Georgia Press, 1995).

SECONDARY BIBLIOGRAPHY

Biographies

Gay Wilson Allen and Roger Asselineau. *St. John de Crèvecoeur* (New York: Viking Penguin Inc., 1987).

Robert de Crèvecoeur, *St. John de Crèvecoeur: sa vie et ses oeuvres* (Paris: Librairie Des Bibliophiles, 1883).

Julia Post Mitchell, *St. Jean de Crèvecoeur* (New York: Columbia University Press, 1916).

References

Philip Beidler, "Franklin and Crèvecoeur's 'Literary' Americans," *Early American Literature* 13 (Spring 1978): 50–63.

Marcus Cunliffe, "St. John de Crèvecoeur Revisited," *Journal of American Studies* 2 (August 1975): 129–144.

Myra Jehlin, "J. Hector St. John Crèvecoeur: A Monarcho-Anarchist in Revolutionary America," *American Quarterly* 31 (Summer 1979): 204–22.

D.H. Lawrence, "The Symbolic Meaning: The Uncollected Versions of *Studies in Classic American Literature*" (Arundel, England: Centaur Press, 1962), 53–70.

Leo Marx, *The Machine in the Garden: Technology and the Pastoral Ideal in America* (New York: Oxford University Press, 1968).

John B. Moore, "The Rehabilitation of Crèvecoeur," *Sewanee Review* 35 (April 1927): 216–30.

Thomas Philbrick, *St. John de Crèvecoeur* (New York: Twayne Publishers, 1970).

Mary E. Rucker, "Crèvecoeur's *Letters* and Enlightenment Doctrine," *Early American Literature* 13 (Fall 1978): 193–212.

Papers

An important collection of Crèvecoeur's manuscripts is housed in the Manuscript Division of the Library of Congress, Washington, D.C. Other manuscripts are kept in England at the Library of the Town of Salisbury, the Salisbury Cathedral Library, The Wiltshire County Archives, and in France at the Municipal Library of Mantes-la-Jolie, the Bibliotheque Nationale, the Bibliotheque de L'Arsenal, the Archives de L'Armee, the Archives Nationales, and the Archives of the Department du Calvados. M. Jean de Crèvecoeur still owns pencil and gouache portraits and maps drawn by Crèvecoeur while a soldier in Canada.

Elizabeth Fries Lummis Ellet
(October 1818?–June 3, 1877)

Kandi Tayebi

Elizabeth Fries Lummis Ellet's work as a poet and historian began at age 17 and continued throughout her life. Although she is best known for her accounts of women in the Revolutionary War, her earliest efforts were poetry published in various journals. Throughout her career, she wrote prolifically and showed great versatility, writing in a variety of genres—poetry, essay, criticism, tragedy, biography, fiction, history, and children's stories. Her history *The Women of the American Revolution* solidified her reputation and is still considered her most important contribution. As a lover of nature, she wrote travel writings that explored not only the regions but the people as well. During her time, critics praised her poetry and prose writing, citing her as one of the best native writers, but currently, critics have focused on her relationship to Edgar Allan Poe and his negative assessment of her, ignoring her poetry but acknowledging her contribution to historical writing.

In October 1818, Elizabeth Fries Lummis was born in Sodus Point, New York, on Lake Ontario, to William Nixon Lummis, a well-to-do physician, and Sarah Maxwell Lummis, his second wife. Elizabeth was named after her father's first wife, Elizabeth Fries. There is some question as to her date of birth, which was reported as 1818 during her lifetime, but based on her New York death certificate that

recorded her death at the age of 64, at least one scholar has argued that 1812 is her real date of birth. An abstract from the "Record of Descendants of Edward Lummis of Ipswich, Mass." records her birth as October 31, 1809. Lummis also states that she published her first book of poetry at 16 and that she married at 17, yet neither age matches her recorded dates of birth. However, her first book was published under her married name, and thus it appears that her own comments are not a reliable source of information on her age.

Lummis's childhood was filled with information about the heroic acts of family and friends during the Revolutionary War. The house in which she grew up at Sodus Point had been rebuilt after the original building was burned by a British raiding party during the War of 1812. Her mother was the daughter of a renowned military officer, General Maxwell, who fought in the Revolution, perhaps fueling Elizabeth's love of military history.

Lummis attended school in Geneva and completed her education at Friend's Female Seminary in Aurora, New York. Her first foray into publishing was a translation of *Euphemia of Messina: A Tragedy* (1834), one of Silvio Pelico's most admired plays. While still in her teens, she began writing poetry and soon published her first book, *Poems,*

Translated and Original (1835). This work combined her own poems, many of which had already been published in periodicals, and poems she had translated from French, Italian, German, and Spanish. She wished to make Continental texts available to women not trained in foreign languages. Included in the book was an original five-act tragedy, *Teresa Contarini,* which enjoyed a successful showing in New York and also some Western cities. This tragedy was the only play she wrote. A very prolific writer, she turned her experiences into published poems and essays and eventually collected them into books. Most of her later works went into multiple editions, and she contributed more than 100 poems, stories, or sketches to gift books and periodicals, including *American Monthly, Godey's Lady's Book, Southern Literary Messenger, Democratic Review, Southern Quarterly Review,* and others. Her works were collected in different variations and sold as gift books for the holiday seasons.

At the age of 17, approximately, Lummis married William Henry Ellet, a chemist who immediately accepted an academic appointment at South Carolina College in Columbia, South Carolina. Shortly after marrying her husband, Ellet moved to the South where she remained until 1849 when she returned to New York. Most of her literary career was spent in South Carolina.

Ellet attempted to acquaint her audience with aspects of German literature by publishing *The Characters of Schiller* (1839), an analysis and criticism of the principal characters in Schiller's plays, as well as essays on Schiller's creative genius, and *Evenings at Woodlawn* (1850), a collection of German legends and traditions. Showing her versatility, she also published a historical novel about a fourteenth-century queen, *Scenes in the Life of Joanna of Sicily* (1840). In the same year, she published *Rambles about the Country* (1840), which further demonstrated her ability to describe the scenery of the American landscape. This travelogue related interesting scenes and people from all over the United States and was used in the Massachusetts public school system for a short time. Although written for children, the book was the only work in which she wrote extensively on the African Americans. In this book, Ellet describes Southern society and the relationship between whites and African Americans. She asserts that poor whites had a much worse situation than slaves because of the laws restricting the treatment of slaves by the slave masters. She argues that the slaves had to be treated humanely. Her conservative ideas about race are evident also in her later descriptions of Indians and their "savage" behavior toward white women settlers. These early works drew on her ability to take secondary sources often in another language and make them entertaining for an American audience that had no experience with Continental texts or thoughts. She was able to popularize difficult material and bring places and historical events to life.

During her lifetime, she was associated with the New York Southern group of antebellum writers and often feuded with the New England group of writers, including her infamous arguments with Rufus W. Griswold, Frances Osgood, and Edgar Allan Poe. Poe and Osgood began a flirtation with each other although both were married to other people. Ellet told Osgood that Poe's wife had shown Ellet letters from Osgood to Poe that were incriminating. She claimed to be saying this in the best interest of Osgood. Later, her account was corroborated by Anne Lynch and Margaret Fuller who visited Poe's house to retrieve the letters for Osgood. The letters, according to John Walsh, suggested that Osgood's daughter Fanny was really the child of Poe. Since Anne Lynch was the hostess of New York's best known literary salon, the scandal became very public, and Poe was banished from the literary scene of the New York literati. Poe in response excluded Ellet from his "Literati" series for *Godey's Lady's Book* despite his earlier publication of and praise for her work.

Ellet also fought with Griswold over her failing to provide enough acknowledgment of his help on her projects. After she published *The Women of the American Revolution* (1848–1850), Griswold felt that he was not recognized even though he had introduced her to the officials at the New York Historical Society where she located some of her materials for the text. Similar to Poe, Griswold at first praised Ellet's work but then became critical of her writing after personal issues arose. Although he admits that her book was a "valuable and interesting work," he gives the credit for the research to a "few gentlemen more familiar than herself with our public and domestic experience" (199). Ellet further enraged Griswold when, during his divorce, she testified on behalf of his wife and wrote letters to his mistress informing her that he was involved with another woman also. William Gilmore Simms also accused Ellet of not acknowledging his contribution to her research. Simms claimed to have given her the idea for *The Women of the American Revolution*. Ellet, in an article in *Godey's Lady's Book*, singles out Simms for suggesting the project, yet still Simms states in a letter that she "has shown no grateful feeling in return" (148). For Simms, Griswold, and Poe, Ellet's concern for the treatment of women, her conservative values that imposed her morality on others, and her refusal to show enough gratitude and submission when confronted with important literary men were seen as meddling gossip and the actions of a jealous woman. Recently, critics have begun to reassess her works by first understanding that earlier accounts of her contribution to literature were tainted by the statements of her male rivals, Poe and Griswold.

An excellent researcher, Ellet brought her resourceful research strategies, her entertaining writing style, and her penchant for detail to the role of women in the Revolutionary War. She is acclaimed as the first, scholarly female historian of American women. Her unique combination of scholarly, historical research with a domestic viewpoint, sentimental feeling, and scholarly standards changed the dominant male understanding of history, especially of war. Her most famous

work, *The Women of the American Revolution* (1848–1850) in three volumes, chronicles the contributions of women across the United States to the fight for independence. The work consisted of sketches of over 150 women from almost every state, including the frontier of Kentucky, although much of her work was concentrated in the southern and middle states that endured the longest British occupation. Since she was living in South Carolina and therefore had access to the materials of the region and the families of the historical figures, women from that state represented a larger proportion of the entries. She also ensured that the women ranged from well-known figures to relatively unknown women, from nationally prominent women like Abigail Adams or Martha Washington to regionally recognized patriots. Her reputation grew as she published the sketches separately in popular periodicals.

Using anecdotes, diaries, letters, and other primary sources, Ellet narrates a story of the Revolutionary War in which women play an essential role. In an anecdotal style, she preserves the history of a nation's women and the family stories. She describes the hardships that women endured while portraying the women's heroic deeds that helped to overthrow the British oppression. Ellet's women contribute to the war effort intellectually and physically by providing advice to the leaders, intelligence from the enemy, and materials for the soldiers, and even by taking up arms against the British.

Her approach to history became even more unique as she used materials collected but not used in *The Women of the American Revolution* to prepare her book *Domestic History of the American Revolution* (1850), which combined a narrative of the successive events of the war with details and anecdotes from the domestic lives of Americans at the time. In this way, she provided a viewpoint of the war from the ordinary American, not the military leaders or their families. This technique would form the basis for much of her later work.

Using a similar technique, Ellet wrote *Pioneer Women of the West* (1852), which explores the lives of women involved in the westward expansion. Though the work is epi-sodic and Ellet found meager correspondence and documents for the time, she succeeds in describing the landscape of a developing country and the people who dared to settle the wild countryside. She reported on the practical information, such as the food and furnishings, as well as the mental obstacles faced by the new inhabitants. Her people struggle with the oppressive silence and vast-ness of the open space. They are influenced by the solitude that is a part of their everyday existence. The landscape, as dangerous as it is beautiful, encourages listening to the wild birds sing as well as human industriousness. Nature and the people interact in powerful, if not always comforting, ways.

Her lifelong love of nature, especially Sodus Point, became the basis of much of her early poetry. She loved not only the natu-ral environment of the lake but also the local people. In her book *Summer Rambles in the West* (1853), she describes the beautiful land-scape of the area and then introduces the reader to the town itself. Most of the second half of the first chapter focuses on the activ-ities of the locals and their interaction with the environment, ending with a description of a fireworks display.

The book also covers her travels up the Mississippi. Ellet explores not only the natu-ral world around her as she rides in a steam-boat up the river, but also the people, legends, and towns around the area. She dis-cusses captivity narratives, stories of lost chil-dren, historical figures from the area, and even the domestic activities of the inhabi-tants, both white settlers and Indians. Ellet traveled up the St. Croix in the comfort of a steamboat to view the frontier, and this trip resulted in Chapters IX and X. Using pic-turesque terminology, she eloquently describes the scenery of the Dalles and the Lower St. Croix Valley. Her view of the Dalles is an example of the Romantic sublime nature, one that consists of "craggy summits," roaring caverns, and "sheer and awful pre-cipices." Ellet leads the reader from the edge of the river up the hills, describing the

contrasting colors of the landscape like a painter. As she journeys into Illinois, Ellet describes the prairie and the people who live on the wide open expanse. These settlers feel the encroachment of the growing cities, which to Ellet's eyes are a long distance away. She provides for the reader the juxtaposition of the wild prairie life, the city furnishings in the house, and the well-cultivated garden. Each description complicates the life and views of the settlers of the area. She shows the complexity of the interactions between newly settled immigrants from Philadelphia and the locals. The history of the area is mixed with Ellet's own family history and anecdotes. Among the descriptions of nature, Ellet intersperses firsthand accounts of impor-tant local events, historical information, and customs. She illustrates the importance of the day-to-day existence of average people in shaping the history of a place.

Using a combination of anecdotal experi-ences drawn from letters, diaries, journals, and even interviews with historical figures, Ellet succeeds in developing a style that marks her as one of the first writers to docu-ment the lives of women and their contribu-tions to the establishment of America. Ellet recovers the voices of women in at least three more of her books: *Women Artists in All Ages and Countries* (1859), *The Queens of American Society* (1867), and *The Court Circles of the Republic* (1869). Her chronicle of the woman artist traces female art from ancient times of weaving and spinning to the nineteenth cen-tury, which Ellet believed was full of promise. She credits the increase in women artists in her time to the growing popularity of art among the general public and an increase in collecting by wealthy patrons. Although not a woman who supported emancipation for women, she did believe that educational opportunities were important for the female artist. Ellet fills her work with sketches of many women artists, ending the book with a lengthy section on Harriet Hosmer, an American sculptor. Ellet describes her as a Romantic artist, one whose picturesque life and perseverance had allowed her genius to shine through and display her artistic excellence.

The Queens of American Society celebrates women throughout American history who were known for their beauty, social leadership, and family. Looking at this narrow segment of society, Ellet followed the same anecdotal style of her earlier historical works to explore and document the manners, fashions, and customs of the socially dominant families of the time. While her other works had looked at people in society who were relatively unknown but had performed important services to the nation, this book focused on the influence of the elite. Together with *The Court Circles of the Republic*, which looked at society in the nation's capital under 18 different presidents, these two books helped write the history of the women who had shared the lives of the most important men in the republic.

Ironically, even though Ellet celebrated and recovered the experiences and achievements of the women who were Revolutionaries, pioneers, and leaders of the new society in America, Ellet's work has not been lauded by most feminist critics. Her heroines were often conservative and carried forward the objectives of the male-dominated society, which perhaps explains part of the neglect of her works by critics and historians. Yet she was able to acknowledge the role women played in establishing the new nation, and she validated their voices and the media through which they chose to express themselves: diaries, letters, and personal remembrances. Students of nineteenth-century America can still receive information from her work that has not been chronicled in such an effective way ever again. Her books provide information about the manners and personalities of the American people and the landscapes of the new country that are left out of most conventional histories.

In 1849, the Ellets returned to New York where William began working at the Manhattan Gas Company. After her husband's death in 1859, the same year in which she published *Women Artists in All Ages and Countries*, Ellet continued to write,

completing two more books while living in the city. She died June 3, 1877, after converting to Catholicism.

Ellet had an impressive publication record that crossed various genres. Although her verse generally is written in traditional metrical forms, it is often thought-provoking and provides the reader with a unique and detailed view of the landscape and people of America in the nineteenth century. Her subjects range from spirituality to biography and nature. She also was widely recognized for her linguistic abilities, as demonstrated in her numerous translations and reviews. In addition, her versatility allowed her to write sketches, essays, novels, drama, help books, and travel literature.

Ellet refused to play the role of self-effacing woman writer, and she insisted on the credit she was due. Her assertive behavior and her early arguments with major literary figures probably created much of the negative assessment of her work right up to the present time. Critics have described her writing as "gossipy" and "superficial," but a closer look at her work clearly shows that she was a prose writer with excellent critical and research skills. Her contribution to our understanding of the history and development of our nation has kept the memories of our female ancestors and their relationship to the natural environment alive.

PRIMARY BIBLIOGRAPHY

Books

Poems, Translated and Original (Philadelphia: Key & Biddle, 1835).

The Parlour Scrap Book: Comprising Sixteen Engravings, with Poetical and Other Illustrations, by Ellet and Willis Gaylord Clark (Philadelphia: Carey, Lea and Blanchard, 1836).

The Characters of Schiller (Boston: Otis, Broaders, 1839).

Rambles about the Country (Boston: Marsh, Capen, Lyon & Webb, 1840).

Scenes in the Life of Joanna of Sicily (Boston: Marsh, Capen, Lyon & Webb, 1840; London: W. Smith & Co., 1840).

The Charm: A Series of Elegant Colored Groups with Descriptive Illustrations (Philadelphia: Carey & Hart, 1847).

The Women of the American Revolution, 3 vols. (New York: Baker & Scribner, 1848–1850); revised as *The Eminent and Heroic Women of America* (New York: Arno Press, 1974); revised as *Revolutionary Women in the War for American Independence: a One-Volume Revised Edition of Elizabeth Ellet's Landmark 1848 Series* (Westport, CT: Praeger, 1998).

Evenings at Woodlawn (New York: Baker & Scribner, 1849).

Family Pictures from the Bible (New York: Putnam's/ London: Putnam's American Agency, 1849).

Domestic History of the American Revolution (New York: Baker & Scribner, 1850).

Nouvelettes of the Musicians (New York: Cornish, Lamport, 1851); republished as *The Cecilian Gift* (New York: Leavitt, 1859); republished as *The Philopoena: A Gift for all Seasons* (New York: Leavitt & Allen, n.d.).

Watching Spirits (New York: C. Scribner, 1851).

Pioneer Women of the West (New York: C. Scribner, 1852).

Summer Rambles in the West (New York: J.C. Riker, 1853).

The Practical Housekeeper; a Cyclopedia of Domestic Economy…Comprising Five Thousand Practical Receipts and Maxims (New York: Stringer & Townsend, 1857); revised as *The New Cyclopedia of Domestic Economy…* (Norwich, CT: H. Bill, 1872).

Women Artists in All Ages and Countries (New York: Harper, 1859).

Love in a Maze, or, the Debutante's Disenchantment (New York: Beadle and Adams, 1865).

The Queens of American Society (New York: C. Scribner, 1867).

The Court Circles of the Republic, or, The Beauties and Celebrities of the Nation Illustrating Life and Society under Eighteen Presidents, Describing the Social Features of the Successive Administrations from Washington to Grant, by Ellet and R.E. Mack (Hartford, CT: Hartford Publishing Company, 1869).

Translations

Silvio Pellico, *Euphemio of Messina: A Tragedy* (New York: M. Bancroft, 1834).

SECONDARY BIBLIOGRAPHY

References

Scott E. Casper, "An Uneasy Marriage of Sentiment and Scholarship," *Journal of Women's History* 4.2 (1992): 10–35.

Susan Phinney Conrad, *Perish the Thought: Intellectual Women in Romantic America, 1830–1860* (New York: Oxford University Press, 1976), 116–22.

John S. Hart, "Elizabeth F. Ellet," in *The Female Prose Writers of America* (Philadelphia: E.H. Butler & Co., 1855), 177–88.

Alma Lutz, "Elizabeth Fries Lummis Ellet," in *Notable American Women, 1707–1950*, ed. Edward T. James (Cambridge: Harvard University Press, 1971), 569–70.

Carol Mattingly, "Legacy Profile: Elizabeth Fries Lummis Ellet (1818–1877)," *Legacy* 18.1 (2001): 101–7.

Elizabeth Phillips, "Elizabeth Fries Lummis Ellet," in *American Women Writers*, ed. Lina Mainiero (New York: Frederick Unger Publishing Company, 1979), 581–83.

William Gilmore Simms, *The Letters of William Gilmore Simms*, vol. 4, four vols., ed. Mary C. Simms, Alfred Taylor Odell, and T.C. Duncan Eaves (Columbia: University of South Carolina Press, 1952–56).

Nicole Tonkovich, "Elizabeth Ellet," in *The Oxford Companion to Women's Writing in the United States*, ed. Cathy N. Davidson and Linda Wagner-Martin (Oxford: Oxford University Press, 1995), 274–75.

John Evangelist Walsh, *Plumes in the Dust* (Chicago: Nelson-Hall, 1980).

Papers

Elizabeth Fries Lummis Ellet's extant letters and papers are in the following locations: New York Public Library (Duyckinck, Ford, and Stauffer Collections); Yale University (Beinecke Library —Ellet papers); Harvard University (Houghton Library—Ellet letters and Sparks manuscripts); Boston Public Library (Griswold manuscripts); Library of Congress (Lewis Reeves Gibbes Collection); Connecticut Historical Society (Hoadley Collection).

Ralph Waldo Emerson
(May 25, 1803–April 27, 1882)

Elizabeth Addison

Ralph Waldo Emerson's central work, universally regarded as containing seeds of all his other work, is a little book called *Nature*, published in 1836. It marked Emerson's arrival as a literary presence who would come to dominate American literature in the nineteenth century and beyond. In this first little book, he announced the basic themes of his lectures, essays, poems, and books of the next 50 years. Defining nature both as the bedrock of existence and as the counterpart of the mind, he asserted the animation of nature by spirit, and therefore its ability to signify spiritual facts in a universal language. Thus it is essential to any original writer, and in a sense almost all of Emerson's writing might be called "nature writing."

Two stances characterize Emerson's writing about nature. One is an ecstatic experience in nature, an exalted feeling of nature's influence and a oneness with it; the other is a naturalist's apprehension of its patterns and laws, an experience of nature as infinitely variable but unified. The first is fluid, creative, and evanescent; the latter works as a kind of fate or necessity undergirding the way things are. Thus, although certainly his journals and poems are studded with exquisite descriptive passages, Emerson's nature writing does not so much describe and explore the surface of material nature as assert its relation to other aspects of human existence—nature and the imagination, nature and spirit, nature and art.

The fourth child of a minister descended from early Puritans, Emerson was born May 25, 1803, in Boston, Massachusetts. His father, William, died just short of Emerson's eighth birthday; he and his four surviving brothers were raised by their mother, Ruth Haskins Emerson. Their aunt, Mary Moody Emerson, a self-taught Calvinist and nature mystic, helped shape the intellectual development of the brothers, particularly Charles, Edward, and Waldo (as Emerson was called). After graduating from Harvard in 1821, Waldo taught in his brother William's school for young ladies in Boston and, following family tradition and his Aunt Mary's wishes, he began divinity studies in 1825. Before he was out of his teens, Emerson like his aunt had experiences of nature's spiritual power: on June 9, 1822, he wrote in his journal that a "mountain-solitude" could open the individual to "a sensible exaltation and a better claim to his rights in the universe." He took long walks and spoke often in his journals of inspiration derived from his time in the woods or on the road.

Emerson wrote his first sermon in 1826 but shortly thereafter traveled to Charleston, South Carolina, and St. Augustine, Florida, for his health. In 1827 he returned to

Cambridge and preached in the First Church of Boston. He met Ellen Tucker of New Hampshire, whom he married in 1829, the same year he was ordained junior pastor of Boston's Second Church. Their brief marriage was shadowed by her tuberculosis, but lightened by her spirit, her jokes, and her literary efforts. When she died at age 19 on February 8, 1831, he went into a deep grief from which he emerged only after opening her coffin in March 1832. Biographers and scholars have speculated on his purpose in this action, but certainly he saw and accepted, without comment, the natural state of her body. The following summer he revisited Crawford Notch, one of the most inspiring natural spots in New Hampshire, a place he had visited with Ellen; in this spectacular setting he decided to leave the ministry. Uncertain of his future when he resigned in September, he traveled to Europe and England, a mind-expanding experience of Alps and cathedrals, art and science. Meeting the Romantics William Wordsworth and Samuel Coleridge near the end of his journey, he found those elderly nature poets less stimulating in person than he had expected from their writing.

What he found especially stimulating he found in Paris. On July 13, 1833, Emerson recorded in a famous journal passage his visit to the Cabinet of Natural History in the Jardin des Plantes (Garden of Plants). Here was an attempt to lay out specimens of all living forms in a classified system that to Emerson revealed not only their relations to each other but also their relation to himself. He felt like a "bridegroom" in the exhibit of birds and found himself "moved by strange sympathies" even with scorpions and geological specimens. The passage concludes with his vow, "I will be a naturalist." In its bounty and variety, both as an exhibit and as a research center, the Jardin des Plantes provided Emerson with an external enactment of nature's unity and order. In his own feeling, he found an internal enactment of its correspondence with himself. On his return journey on September 6, 1833, he confirmed his intention to write his "book about nature."

At this point, however, Emerson was still suspended between his life as a preacher and his life as a lecturer and writer. He continued to preach at various churches until 1839, but he began his career as a lecturer in the winter of 1833–1834 with four talks on natural history in Boston. These contain many early statements of ideas and even passages that would form part of *Nature*. In the first lecture, "The Uses of Natural History," delivered November 5, 1833, he recounted his experience of the Jardin des Plantes as a "natural alphabet." Nature, he said, is so fitted to the five senses that its beauty invites contemplation and study; its patterns satisfy the mind. Furthermore, it corresponds to the mind. It is a living language, one that lends itself to the writer's self-expression. In the January 6, 1834, lecture, "The Relation of Man to the Globe," he pointed out that any weather at any time of the day or night can express a state of feeling; the earth is like an onion whose many layers represent past ages and former species, and, on the other hand, it is a "moveable observatory" that enables the astronomer to expand his or her observations. It lends itself to scientific discovery and delight because "It is all design. It is beauty. It is all astonishment." Another January 1834 lecture explored the symbolic possibilities and practical uses of water, from its "eternal circulation through nature" to its provision of force by mechanical power. In "The Naturalist," presented in May 1834, Emerson called for "a perfect Theory of Animated Nature" and for integration as well as accuracy in the findings of natural science. He was well on the way to his little book *Nature*, to be published anonymously almost three years later.

They were an eventful three years. In 1834, he received an inheritance from Ellen's estate and learned of his brother Edward's death in Puerto Rico, where he had gone in an attempt to recover from mental illness and tuberculosis. This year Emerson wrote or drafted several of his best nature poems, "The Rhodora," "Each and All," and "The Snow-Storm." These poems succeed in showing the correspondence of the poet's inward feelings with the outward appearance of nature, and, furthermore, the outward appearance they show succeeds in piquancy of expression. Here are embodied, in particular natural things, some of the ideas that would appear in more abstract form in *Nature*. In "The Rhodora," an isolated pool in the May woods is the specific setting that gives rise to two ideas—that "Beauty is its own excuse for being" and that a single "Power" rules flower and poet—and two clear images: the "purple petals" are complemented by the "black water," and the redbird's hot, garish plumes contrast with the cool water and flower. In "Each and All," the many natural appearances cited in the poem are placed in the larger context that makes them what they are and gives them their beauty. The "red-cloaked" peasant, the heifer, the bird "on the alder bough" in sight of the river and sky, the seashells washed by "the latest wave"—all these disappoint when separated from "the perfect whole," yet beauty persists and renews itself in further natural images, such as the curling ground pine, the "violet's breath," the acorns and pinecones, the trees, and "the eternal sky." The poet, of course, discovers and makes this new artistic arrangement of these natural things, and in "The Snow-Storm" the "frolic architecture" of the snow becomes an image of artistic creation.

During the winter of 1834–1835 Emerson gave his first full course of lectures in Boston. His topic was biography. He had determined, however, that he would find what he himself had to say, no longer trying to fit into preconceived expectations for these lectures as he had, to some extent, done for the ones on natural science. In the excitement of preparing that series on biography, he wrote to a former pupil a letter that anticipated the conjunction of nature, language, and spirit that would appear in *Nature*. Writing on January 23, 1835, to this young man, Benjamin Peter Hunt, he asked whether Hunt had been reading in natural science and been taken by its "laws of terrible beauty which took the soul of Newton & Laplace & Humboldt"; whereas

these laws are amazing, Emerson explained, for himself their "best charm" is "their correspondence with Spiritual laws of which they seem but symbol & prophecies." The following day he wrote a letter of proposal to Lydia Jackson, and she agreed to marry him. On February 1, he expressed to her what he had hinted to Hunt; he called himself

> a poet in the sense of a perceiver & dear lover of the harmonies that are in the soul & in matter, & specially of the correspondences between these & those. A sunset, a forest, a snow storm, a certain river-view, are more to me than many friends.

Yet this year also brought two important new friends, Bronson Alcott and Margaret Fuller.

The following summer, August 1835, he bought a house in Concord, not far from the ancestral home where his father and aunt had been raised and where he had boarded with his stepgrandfather, the Reverend Ezra Ripley. In September he married Miss Jackson, whom he began to call Lidian. That winter he gave another series of lectures in Boston, this one on English literature. In May 1836 his youngest brother, Charles, whom he regarded as a kind of soul mate, died suddenly, again of tuberculosis. In his journal, Emerson said, on May 16, "The eye is closed that was to see Nature for me, & give me leave to see." Later he spoke of Charles's detailed knowledge of birds and plants. In June Emerson wrote that "Power is one great lesson which Nature teaches Man. The secret that he can...harmonize all the outward occurrences with the states of mind, that must he learn." When *Nature* was published anonymously in Boston in September 1836, Emerson and Lidian were anticipating the birth of their first child.

As Merton Sealts and others have shown, the ideas in *Nature* emerged from many journal entries and passages in the early lectures. Emerson had contemplated and developed this material for a long time. Its center is that attempt to harmonize the outward signs of nature with the mind, the parallel of natural facts and spiritual facts, "the correspondences between these & those"—indeed, as he had told Lidian, "the harmonies that are in the soul & in matter." The five senses draw these analogies or harmonies with the creative co-operation of the mind; originality results when perceivers encounter the universe for themselves. The book, actually a long essay, has received considerable study of its sources and meaning. Antecedents for the ideas have been traced in sources from ancient philosophy to Kant and Coleridge or even Emerson's contemporaries. The structure can be compared to an ornate baroque cathedral or to a Puritan sermon with its explication of the text, its implications, amplifications, and applications. The movement is toward greater abstraction, but Emerson concluded *Nature* by directly urging the reader to make the world in his or her own mind's image: "Build, therefore, your own world."

In the first edition, Emerson like a good minister offered as a motto a classical text for explication. It is from Plotinus, defining nature as an imitation of the mind's wisdom, something that "doth only do, but not know." When he republished the essay as part of *Nature, Addresses, and Lectures* in 1849, he replaced that epigraph or motto with a short poem of his own. This change is significant because his own poem emphasizes not the split between nature and the mind but the parallels; furthermore, its transcending movement from the "worm" to the human predicts the movement of the essay from nature as "commodity" to nature as "spirit."

Emerson began *Nature* with a call for "an original relation to the universe" inspired by the powerful flow of life we find in nature. He defined nature not only in its usual sense ("space, the air, the river, the leaf") but also as "all which Philosophy distinguishes as the NOT ME, that is, both nature and art, all other men and my own body." Emerson thus implied that the "me" was nonphysical; that is, the self was a spiritual entity. Finding a way to bring the "me" into relationship with the physical being was the task, or finding a way to make the physical being transparent, revealing the spirit in both the individual

and universal senses. Asking the end or purpose of nature, he called for a true theory that would explain all phenomena, even such mysterious ones as "language, sleep, dreams, beasts, sex."

The best-known passage in *Nature* is the first chapter's "transparent eyeball" image. Christopher Pearse Cranch, a poet associated with Emerson and his friends, caricatured Emerson in this passage in a famous cartoon. Cranch pictured the eyeball as a head on a tall, long-legged figure with bare feet, but the passage is usually interpreted as an image for the power of creative perception or even as a mystical union with nature. The essay's speaker, feeling the "perfect exhilaration" of nature even on a messy field of melting snow, loses the sensation of his individual self: "all mean egotism vanishes. I become a transparent eyeball. I am nothing. I see all. The currents of the Universal Being circulate through me; I am part or particle of God." Emerson said, however, that the power to produce this feeling is not in nature alone, but in the human, or in the harmony between the natural and the human.

The chapters of *Nature* move from particular natural things to more and more abstract powers, with nature as the medium for each. "Commodity" treats nature as apprehended through the senses. In "Beauty," nature harmoniously delights not only the senses but also the spirit and the mind; it is even an end in itself, as the rhodora's beauty is "its own excuse for being." In "Language," nature is not only delightful to the mind but also the vehicle of thought. Because words have their roots in the physical world, each word originally stood for an observable thing; writing is good in proportion to its connection with these natural roots. Thus the "Language" chapter is important for everything Emerson later said about poetry and good writing. In "Discipline," nature is not only the vehicle for thought but also a "school" for both the "Understanding" and the "Reason." Following Immanuel Kant and Samuel Taylor Coleridge, Emerson understood the Understanding to be the mind as it apprehended sense impressions (as in "Commodity" above, and as in Lockean philosophy) and the Reason to be the higher mind that apprehended nature's laws or general principles. Thus nature teaches, in her "school," the interaction of these intellectual faculties.

Finally, in the chapter called "Idealism," Emerson took on the question of whether nature actually exists or is insubstantial, "only in an apocalypse of the mind." Asking this question, he determined that the "spirit, that is, the Supreme Being" puts nature forth through the human, who "rests upon the bosom of God; he is nourished by unfailing fountains, and draws, at his need, inexhaustible power." Thus the transparency with which the essay began has become a creative power, a vehicle for God's creation of nature. According to Richard Lee Francis, the essay is "a blueprint, an architectonic, for the construction of the self out of the world's body, of the *me* out of the *not me*." In the final chapter, "Prospects," Emerson applied these assertions to scientists, who may not be asking the right questions if they are not asking about the "occult relations" of nature to the human, and rounded the essay by promising that "the influx of the spirit" will be accompanied by the departure of temporary annoyances such as "swine, spiders, snakes, pests, mad-houses, prisons, enemies."

When his son Waldo was born, shortly after the publication of *Nature*, Emerson was fascinated by this new creature. On October 31, 1835, he recorded in his journal Lidian's remark that a child presents a new aspect daily as the sky changes every hour, and he added that the father is the one near enough to see the infinite beauty of the child: "He looks with microscope." He lectured that winter on the philosophy of history. The following year he was invited to substitute for a previously scheduled speaker to give the annual oration before the Phi Beta Kappa Society at Harvard.

In that oration, called "The American Scholar" and delivered August 31, 1837, Emerson set forth the original or ideal scholar, whom he called "Man Thinking,"

never a "mere thinker" or "parrot of other men's thinking." Nature is this scholar's first and most important teacher. It is a "web of God" continuously circling the scholar, endless and boundless like the individual spirit. The mind, he said, begins to see systems and relations radiating throughout all of nature, like lines in a spider's web, and scientific "laws" tie facts together in those systems. Furthermore, these laws apply to the soul, so that nature corresponds to the soul, part for part. Knowing nature is knowing one's own mind. Books can be the scholar's second teachers because they embody the act of creation. Each is properly a transcript of life into truth and may be read for inspiration. The third teacher is action in the world, which provides the scholar with language and material. In fact, even the common and "low"—such things as "the meal in the firkin; the milk in the pan"—are the "suburbs and extremities of nature" and alike share its eternal laws. This celebration of the common, Emerson said, is one of the "auspicious signs" of the times.

In the spring of 1838 Emerson wrote to President Martin Van Buren an eloquent letter of protest at the treatment of the Cherokees. In his journal for April 23, he called the letter "merely a Scream but sometimes a scream is better than a thesis." A few days later he wrote of gladness in hearing a bird or a piping frog, or seeing a star, to enliven his solitude and imagined nature's saying, "Well do not these suffice?" Through the coming months he wrote frequent observations of the beauty of nature on the one hand, frequent complaints about the Unitarian clergy on the other. He began walking in the woods with Henry David Thoreau, whom he had met in 1837. On July 15 he went at the invitation of the Harvard Divinity School seniors to give a formal address, and he so outraged the Unitarian stalwarts that he was not invited back for more than two decades.

Considering the musings in his journal, it is not surprising that in the Divinity School address Emerson essentially told the students to turn and look out the window if they wanted to be inspired. There they would see summer, see the grass and meadow flowers blooming, hear the birds, smell the pine and new hay. At night they would feel the coolness through which stars "pour their almost spiritual rays." Emerson went on to praise nature as a source of continuous miracles, asserted the unity of its laws with the religious sentiment and the laws of the soul, indeed with the "active mind" working "in each ray of the star, in each wavelet of the pool," always moving and growing. He contrasted these manifestations of natural laws with the deadness of traditional Christianity, which resisted new miracles, new revelations. In another example, he described a snowstorm falling outside the church and drew a contrast between the "beautiful meteor of the snow" and this "spectral" preacher, who has not been able "to convert life into truth." Only if people can see God in themselves can they see a reason for their existence, he said, and that is particularly true of ministers, so they would be well advised to seek solitude in nature. A miracle is not a miracle if it is unnatural, if it is not "one with the blowing clover and the falling rain."

On July 24, less than ten days after the Divinity School address, Emerson delivered an address called "Literary Ethics" at Dartmouth College. Again, more emphatically, he asserted the necessity of nature for originality in language. Nature admonishes the speaker that the "world is new, untried." Furthermore, it is "undescribed": much nature poetry has but a superficial acquaintance with its objects, and here Emerson gives a catalogue of sights and especially sounds foreshadowing Whitman's. As in *Nature*, in this address Emerson moved from the "not me" to the "me"; he expressed the "pain of an alien world; a world not yet subdued by the thought," but then the "me" experienced the "moist, warm, glittering, budding, melodious hour" of the daybreak and opened his soul "to become as large as nature." A further passage celebrates the American woodland, with its ancient trees and tiny flowers, its crow and eagle, with its ever-changing and

unsung loveliness—and, again, the connection between this beauty and the speaker's soul. Even a small fact of nature will open up a new view that incorporates all theories. As before, Emerson concluded this address with a return to Nature, the source of all good in the soul.

In the three years between "Literary Ethics" and the publication of his first series of essays in 1841, Emerson gave two winter lecture series, one on human life and another on "The Present Age"; he preached his last sermon in January 1839 and fathered a daughter, Ellen, born a month later; he helped conceive and launch the Transcendental journal, *The Dial*, edited by Margaret Fuller from 1840 until Emerson took it over in 1842; and he welcomed Thoreau into his household that spring of 1841. He worked closely with Fuller on the journal and spent considerable time helping with the American publication of Thomas Carlyle's work. All of these activities delayed a long-cherished project: Emerson had admired Montaigne's essays and had intended since 1835 to produce a book of his own using the lectures as seed material. These series of formal lectures were carefully researched and written, but to produce the essays Emerson modified them extensively using fresh material from new invention or from his journals.

Emerson considered calling this book "Forest Essays." Although he ended up calling it simply *Essays*, and later *Essays, First Series* to distinguish it from the second series published in 1844, natural images permeate the language throughout. The comments on nature itself, too, are spread throughout the essays. Originally an essay called "Nature" was intended to make a pair with "Art," the last in the volume as published, but Emerson had to send the book to press without that essay. A statement at the conclusion of "Art" may come closest to Emerson's view. He says there that nature is superior to art because it "transcends all our moods of thought"; that is, we cannot fully understand "its secret." Nature is both useful and beautiful, and its beauty comes from its vitality; "it is alive, moving, reproductive." Even the most useful inventions of the industrial revolution, when used "in love" are like extensions of nature's flowing. As that concluding essay looks forward, so the first essay in this volume, "History," looks backward, but only to say that history and its achievements can be the province of every individual because every individual shares in the nature of every other. Thus history is real and alive—not past but present—for each person. Furthermore, neither science nor history as "old chronology" leads us into nature as well as the "idiot, the Indian, the child, and unschooled farmer's boy."

The universal laws that govern nature and infuse human life with spirit are, in a sense, the real subject of every essay, whether the title is "History," "Self-Reliance," "Compensation," "Spiritual Laws," "Love," "Friendship," "Heroism," "The Over-Soul," "Circles," "Intellect," or "Art." As Emerson took up these familiar topics, one after the other, he transformed familiar views by setting each topic in the context of nature's laws, which reflect the spirit's laws. Yet Emerson infused this form of idealism, asserting the value of universal laws or ideas about the nature of things, with natural images. It was his habit to do so; for example, in a journal entry on September 21, 1841, he recorded the death of his stepgrandfather, the Reverend Ezra Ripley, calling him "this oak of ninety years" whose falling "makes some sensation in the forest old & doomed as it was." He rooted his language in real things that appealed to the senses—particularly the sight—of the reader. As a gardener and fruit-tree planter, he was particularly disposed to use images of seed sowing and the growth of trees, vegetables, and fruits. Nature's law is growth, he said in "Compensation." In "Spiritual Laws," he called it a "lesson from nature, which always works by short ways," that the spirit works effortlessly by falling like ripe fruit. Even "Friendship" follows the laws of nature; friends too must ripen. In the essay "Intellect," which begins with images of natural dissolutions, he said that the intellect is a "menstruum" or solvent

that dissolves "fire, gravity, laws, method, and the subtlest unnamed relations of nature." Although intellect abstracts facts from personal reference, Emerson said, the most abstract philosophies only restore their readers to "a simple, natural, common state."

Certain other observations about nature unify these essays. Nature is self-reliant; in nature, all things are able to help themselves. Nature flows from pure Being, so there is a "sublime family likeness throughout her works." On the other hand, nature is "always and never the same." The law is the same, but the "troops of forms" are always new, because "all things renew, germinate, and spring." Thus it is essential to respect nature, know its sciences, and be true to the senses. Although it may look stable, nature is "not fixed, but sliding." It is a moving energy. All of nature and its power are present in each particle of nature; there is "one type under every metamorphosis." Finally, nature's law is the law of cause and effect. Violations and distortions of nature lead to the evils of society; thus heroes and reformers are necessary. Fruit is an effect of growth, punishment a fruit of crime.

Later in August 1841, some months after his first group of essays was published, Emerson gave a commencement oration for Waterville (later Colby) College, in Maine. His Aunt Mary Moody Emerson, then a resident of Maine, was present. This oration revealed to the astute listener, as certainly his aunt was, a shift from the emphasis of *Nature*. In the previous three years, Emerson had been reading extensively in Pythagorean, Zoroastrian, and Neoplatonic writers. Robert Spiller, in a headnote to the oration in the *Collected Works*, suggests that this piece marks Emerson's transition from idealism to pragmatism. In his biography of Emerson, Robert Richardson, Jr., credits these sources with moving Emerson from the Germanic idealism apparent in *Nature* to a dynamic pantheism, similar to that in his poem of 1841, "Woodnotes II," where a pine tree speaks for life in nature as a flowing metamorphosis, not solid but a dream. Hints of these newer emphases were evident in the essays.

The expected presence of Aunt Mary may have led Emerson to his emphasis on ecstasy as the end of nature.

In this talk, "The Method of Nature," Emerson used the idea from his reading that the physical world flows—or emanates—from pure spirit. Thus he placed nature as subordinate to intellect in the divine order; it is the body of what was once an idea, or "pure law." Using a chemical metaphor, he said that nature has precipitated from the "solution" of the mind, and so it is "the bright sediment of the world." It therefore "testifies to truth." As an emanation constantly moving, however, it is an effect, not a cause, and its wholeness is only a result of perception. Its particulars, though each tells of its universal origin, get lost in the proliferation of nature, which is in "rapid metamorphosis." When applied to the human, Emerson said, this "redundancy or excess of life" is called ecstasy. The genius carries out the work of nature by contacting this flow of nature and delivering "the thought of his heart from the universe to the universe." In the conclusion to this address, Emerson eloquently tied nature to self-reliance, character, action, the "Supreme Presence," and the American landscape. The stars and the "yet untouched continent of hope glittering with its mountains in the vast West" are assurances, Emerson said, of continuing possibilities for his hearers. The soul is divine and its qualities "penetrate the ocean and land, space and time, form and essence, and hold the key to universal nature." Nature is the soul's native element, which is "wider than space, older than time, wide as hope, rich as love." The method of nature, then, is flowing and changing constantly, and in the human being this flowing produces ecstasy.

Between the birth of his second daughter, Edith, in November 1841, and the death of his first son, Waldo, in late January 1842, Emerson gave a series of lectures on "The Times," which, Spiller says in a headnote, were the first to be written for both the platform and the printed page at the same time. Unlike the syntheses of those in *Essays: First Series*, these essays did not require Emerson to piece together material from journals and lectures written at various times. One lecture not published by Emerson, on poetry, was reviewed by Walter Whitman. Another of these, "The Transcendentalist," which he did publish in *Nature, Addresses, and Lectures*, clarifies Emerson's emphasis on consciousness in relation to nature and sensory impressions. Transcendentalism, he said, is actually "Idealism as it appears in 1842." He explained that the term comes from Immanuel Kant, who asserted that the mind acquires experience, or sense impressions, through ideas or intuitions that are already in the mind itself. Kant's philosophy was a response to that of John Locke, who thought that everything in the mind was first in the senses, that the mind was a "tabula rasa" or "clean slate" until the senses drew pictures upon it. The ideas or intuitions of Kant's conception transcend sense experience and give it meaning. This perspective "transfers every object in nature from an independent and anomalous position without there, into the consciousness." In one's own consciousness is an "invisible, unsounded center" from which the world's "procession of facts" flows. Although a pure idealist or "Transcendentalist," Emerson said, does not exist, and although he poked a little fun at the exaggeration, he still said the times are colored by this "tendency to respect the intuitions, and to give them, at least in our creed, all authority over our experience." Nature again is subordinate to the intellect, to the conscious and unconscious mind, but paradoxically it is the law of the mind as well.

In February 1842, only a month or two after this lecture, Emerson's young son Waldo died of scarlet fever, an illness of only a few days. He had been an apparently gifted and certainly charming child. Nature had again taken what might well have been Emerson's most prized natural fact. The poem "Threnody," apparently begun not long after the death but not completed until later, enlists both nature and fate into the grieving process. Nature—here in particular the

South-wind and the Day—cannot remake her creation, though she "finds young pines and budding birches," and Fate cannot retake the boy she has let fall. That nature goes on as usual, with April bringing new life and blooms, adds to the agony. In fact, the death may be a failure of nature, "nature's costly lie." But at the turning point of the poem, the "deep Heart" answers with assurance that the only way past grief is into, not away from, nature. The flowing of love through nature is also the flowing of spirit and a reassurance of blessing and renewal.

In 1844, Emerson bought 14 acres at Walden Pond. He considered building a cabin there to get closer to nature's beauties, but his friend Henry Thoreau was the one who did, the following year. In February he read a lecture in Boston on "The Young American"; amid concerns for the industrializing indicated by the growth of cities, railroads, and commerce, Emerson concluded that the land would benefit as people grew disgusted with city life and moved out to use their arts on the "native but hidden graces of the landscape." The last issue of *The Dial* was published in April under Emerson's editorship, and a new son, Edward, was born in July. In August he gave his first antislavery speech. And in October his *Essays: Second Series* was published. For this volume, generally considered more worldly and accessible than the first, he had considered the title "The Poet and Other Essays." "The Poet" is one of several essays in the collection that extend and elaborate his treatment of nature; others are "Experience," "Character," "Nature," and "Nominalist and Realist." Unlike the epigraphs to essays in the first collection, here Emerson's own poems provided most of the epigraphs, and most of them explicitly include nature as a central presence.

Following the dialectical pattern so often seen in his collections, where one view is followed by a contrary view so that the opposites and contradictions balance each other, Emerson began the volume with two essays that show contrary responses to nature. In the first, "The Poet," Emerson celebrated the "fugacity" of nature, its fleeting quality,

as a source of symbols for the poet, who fastens them to meaning. In the second, "Experience," he explored nature's fugacity as a problem. It makes nature a moving surface so that people cannot see nature clearly. Nature confuses, clouds, baffles human perception. But, as the epigraph made clear, it is also the "dear nature" who takes the baffled and alienated child by the hand to express relationship: "these are thy race."

In "The Poet," the universal laws of nature become "rhymes." Nature is full of patterns that repeat in various forms, and Emerson imagined these as the rhymes of things. He also imagined them as a dance, a creation of Beauty, an invention. Every "thing," or "sensuous fact," can be material for the poet, who sees the spirit even in the ordinary, such as a desolate stretch of pine forest, and who can take anything in nature to express that spiritual infusion. The poet approaches nature with expectancy, receiving its flow and imparting its meanings. This process Emerson called "naming"; nature names herself, he said, and the poet's naming is a second nature. By taking the flow of nature and naming things in it, the poet gives them meaning. Instinct is important in this process, and so is a willingness to abandon oneself to the flow. The resulting poem renovates nature, makes it new to the eye that sees it through the poem, and thus pleases like "the iterated nodes of a sea-shell."

In "Experience," by contrast, nature does not seem so generous; she has given too little spirit for creation. In fact, nature is a kind of trickster, loving secrecy, making fools of people. Human temperament or mood limits one's perception of nature, as looking through glass beads colors the vision. The flow of nature, so inspiring to the poet, now seems to create illusion. As the essay proceeds, the experience of nature gradually becomes less deceptive. The movement (succession) is necessary to vigor and circulation. Human perception is limited to the surfaces of nature, the physical life and meeting of physical needs, but one is to accept this condition and "skate well on the surfaces." Nature is just as present in the midst of human life as in the world of woodland animals such as the fox and woodchuck; it can be seen daily in sunrises and sunsets and has no real secrets. Furthermore, nature "is no saint" but loves the pleasures of the body; nature lives in the moment, in "the strong present tense." Natural geniuses are artless, creating what they can by "the grace of God," not by calculation. With this acceptance of reality, Emerson said, one finds that a new world opens, an ideal world that he imagined as "this new yet unapproachable America I have found in the West," where one sees mountains with "the tranquil eternal meadows spread at their base." Though one sees through subjective lenses, yet "it is the eye that makes the horizon"; self-trust is the only possibility when everything one sees is colored by the self. The deceptions of time are just that—deceptive—and moments of solitude can redeem by giving hope and sanity.

For the essay on nature in this volume, Emerson took a different tack from *Nature* or from "The Method of Nature"; in fact, the subject of the essay "Nature"—originally intended as a companion to "Art" in the first series of essays—was the natural world itself. Emerson still emphasized the beholder, the experience, but he was less concerned with natural law than with simple enjoyment, sensory delight. In an October afternoon when "the world reaches its perfection," he suggested, his reader might enter the forest and find at once there sanctity and reality. The beauties of nature are entrancing and stimulating. Furthermore, they are healing. Nature made human beings as well as mountains and cities, however, so "rural influences" may be overrated. What is really exciting is behind the beauty—the living movement of nature, the "quick cause" that brings all of nature's variety through transformation and growth. Here Emerson returned to geology, chemistry, and biology to demonstrate the relationships of natural things. The human brain contains these sciences and natural histories, yet there is more to take in. Nature overdoes it in producing more seeds, more sense

impressions, more excess of inspiration for prophets, but the poet always feels the best of nature is farther off, like the sunset. This seeming deceptiveness can cause uneasiness or helplessness, but it only proves that nature still keeps its secrets; it is more than we can fully fathom. Its embodied laws—the relationships of all natural things and their workings—indicate a kind of "sanity" to teach us wisdom. Nature and thought are interchangeable, like water and ice and vapor. As solids precipitate from solutions, so the "world is mind precipitated." The human mind, then, is of the same substance as nature.

In November of the following year, 1845, Emerson purchased as a woodlot another 41 acres at Walden Pond, this across the water from the smaller parcel, where Thoreau had already taken up residence in his cabin. That winter, Emerson lectured on "Representative Men," the series that would give rise to his next book of essays. In 1846 he saw the publication of *Poems,* a collection including many of his best. Here the reader finds the particulars that vivify the ideas in the essays. In "Nominalist and Realist," one of the essays in the previous volume, Emerson had made clear that nature must be taken as a whole to get truth, as a color wheel must rotate quite fast to make a whole. Nature "resists generalizing," he said. In "The Sphinx," the first poem in this volume, he showed nature as a metamorphosis through the image of the riddling and unitary sphinx whose answer to the idealistic "poet" is to melt, spire, flower, silver, stand, and flow into the "thousand natures" of nature. This poem was first published in *The Dial* in 1841, and in a note to the Centenary edition Edward Emerson reported his father's explanation, in 1859, that the mind should be able to see the whole—not just the differences—in each form of nature. The second poem, "Each and All," written in 1834 and discussed above, made the complementary point that the mind needs the whole to apprehend nature's beauty. In this volume also appeared the other two fine poems of that year, "The Rhodora" and "The Snow-Storm."

Although *Poems* did not, perhaps, reveal all of the "thousand natures" of which the sphinx spoke, it did include nature as experienced in blackberry picking, in farming and harvesting the land's riches, in the bumble-bee's peaceful joy at taking the sweet nectars of summer. Emerson gave several poems natural speakers, as the poplar in "To Rhea," published in *The Dial* in 1843. In others, the poet directly addressed a natural object, as in "The Humble-Bee," where the bee itself is a kind of poet. In a journal entry May 9, 1837, a year of economic collapse that affected his family and friends and indeed the nation, Emerson said, "The humble-bee and pine-warbler seem to me the proper objects of attention in these disastrous times." The long poems "Woodnotes I" and "Woodnotes II" covered both the tiny details—such as the subtle tints of violets and the prevalence of natural forms with five parts—and the "fatal song" that all things "rhyme" with other things, or in other words that nature is infused throughout with one essence. In the latter poem, the speaker—or poet—is a pine tree; its poem concludes with a vibrant image of Pan as a symbol of nature who, like the sphinx, takes not one form but many, as do waves or flames.

Emerson followed this sweeping poem in his volume with "Monadnoc," the mountain-top view that all the atoms in nature "march in tune" to the human mind that knows its "secret," and "Fable," a small squirrel's view of its own unique talents: even the mountain cannot "crack a nut." More particulars—leaf, bark, acorn, raindrop, rainbow, spider web, wine drop, stars, lily bell—are the forms through which glides Beauty in "Ode to Beauty." All these natural particulars, and the ecstatic life that pulses through them, are the materials of the poet, a concept more fully delineated in "Saadi" and the two "Merlin" poems. Another poet-speaker in "The Apology" goes to "grove and glen" to bring home the thoughts and secret mysteries of nature.

But other poems in the volume expressed an opposing view, one closer to the one Emerson expressed in the essay "Experience," that nature had become monotonous and meager. In "The Day's Ration," the cup in which one can gather the nectar or wine of experience is so small that it easily overflows; in "Blight" the nectar is withheld so that nothing in nature can thrive and life itself is "a dupe." Again, Emerson included a list of natural particulars, but now they are not so much inspirations as "herbs and simples" or medicinal plants that might help if only one knew how to use them. But this attitude is itself curative: "Musketaquid" expressed Emerson's sense that such humility could reward the poet with healing in his "woodland walk," his hearing of the thrush, his finding of wild grapes or flowers. Dated 1838, "Dirge" portrayed the loneliness of a landscape where he and his now-deceased brothers had once played and enjoyed nature. And "Threnody," as discussed above, engaged this question more deeply: the answer to grief has to be love's "tidal flow" in nature, carrying the finite to the infinite. The volume closes with "Concord Hymn" and its prayer that the memorial stone be gently spared by Time and Nature, which have redeemed the battlefield where the "rude bridge" has been washed away by the stream.

Emerson sailed for England in October 1847, returning the following summer after time in Paris and a June lecture series in London. In 1849, accordingly, he lectured on "English Traits." He also published a volume that collected his early essays and addresses, all of which are discussed above: *Nature*, "The American Scholar," the Divinity School address, "Literary Ethics," "The Method of Nature," "Man the Reformer," the lectures on "Times," and "The Young American." Then in 1850 he produced, from his lecture series of five years earlier, *Representative Men*. The introduction and two of the "representative" portraits supported and enlarged Emerson's commentary on nature. In the introductory essay, "Uses of Great Men," Emerson explicitly said that each person takes the raw material of nature and makes it usable; each person is intuitively connected to a particular category of natural things and acts to interpret it for others. Each person is a center for nature, a point from which and through which "threads of relation" connect to every natural object. Natural objects then hold truths that wait for the "brain"—the human brain—that can see them and "humanize" them, making of them not just scientific truth but art, architecture, "conversation, character and politics." The geniuses who spend their lives with these objects can interpret them because they actually participate in them, becoming one with what they observe. And all this interpretation is possible because there is an underlying unity of all things, both the "me" and the "not-me," a concept the Jardin des Plantes experience had crystallized for Emerson back in 1832. Although all things and all people are connected by these threads of relation, still all are unique; "great men" have the two special functions of helping people see beyond themselves and helping prevent people from aggregating into undifferentiated lumps. Nature abhors such lumps, Emerson concluded, and wants each individual thing to remain itself.

In the essay on the first representative man, "Plato, or the Philosopher," Emerson articulated his idea of the One and the Many, explaining Plato's ideas in Krishna's Hindu terms: the world is a manifestation of Vishnu, the Hindu god who is identical with all things and all people. Krishna is considered an incarnation, or human embodiment, of Vishnu; in the *Bhagavad Gita*, Krishna as a character explains how this eternal, abiding unity is related to the temporary embodiments of nature. "Nature is the manifold," Emerson summarized in this essay. The mind tends to unity, but action tends to diversity; creation diversifies the primordial unity. "Nature opens and creates." Getting this understanding, however, does not master nature; Plato's idealism may have done away with the reality of nature in theory, but nature was still there all the same. In "Plato: New Readings," a short essay occasioned by a new translation, Emerson added the comment that Plato marked an epoch in the growth and evolution of Nature.

What in "The Poet" and "Merlin" he had called the "rhymes" of nature—the repeated forms and parallels in natural objects—is Emerson's emphasis in his discussion of his second representative man, the strange thinker "Swedenborg, or the Mystic." Many biographers and critics have traced Swedenborg's influence on Emerson, which came to him through secondary sources. In this essay, Emerson made clear what he found exciting and what he found mistaken. Swedenborg saw that nature was "self-similar," namely in repeating key forms over and over on different planes; he saw the correspondences of soul and science and the flowing of one nature through all its forms. But, Emerson said, Swedenborg applied this idea too widely. He carried it to extremes and overgeneralized. Emerson called this "pedantry" and said nature would take revenge on the limitation it imposed. If there is a keynote of nature, it must "tally" with nature's best beauties and strengths, the rainbow, the mountain, the flowers, the tides, and the stars. People want to know, Emerson said, each particular animal and plant and seashell, the wonders of each natural form, more than general truths—especially when those truths are clumsily expressed.

The essays on Napoleon and Goethe both emphasize nature's need to be valued, but for different purposes. These representative men are two halves of one whole. In "Napoleon, or the Man of the World," Emerson depicted the soldier-statesman as a splendid creature of nature, one of those great men nature creates because she wants them. His strength as a leader was that he respected the power of nature and did not fight it, Emerson said. His was the strength of the external life. Goethe's was the strength of the internal life, the mind. In "Goethe, or the Writer," Emerson presented him as the philosopher and writer who could master nature's multiplicity. He could report nature truly because he could see the connections between natural facts, all of which can speak to the intelligent. Goethe could write about them in such a way as to give them humanity and poetry. Whether fossils or limestone formations, natural facts as Goethe saw them could seem alive. Emerson especially praised Goethe's idea—one that would find its way into Thoreau's *Walden*—that a leaf is the basic component of every plant, all parts of which are leaves in various forms. Similarly, he said, Goethe considered animal skeletons as various forms of vertebrae. Such poetic unity is a secret of Goethe's strength as a writer. When Emerson said that all of Goethe's words stand for things, he affirmed Goethe's ability to connect his language to living things; therefore, Goethe's is a living language.

Margaret Fuller's translations of Goethe had helped disperse these ideas among the Transcendentalists and others. In 1850, the same year that *Representative Men* was published, Emerson lectured westward as far as Cleveland and Cincinnati. But in July, less than a month after his return from this Midwestern speaking tour, his colleague and friend Margaret Fuller Ossoli was returning from Italy with her new husband and son when their ship foundered just offshore near Long Island. The whole family drowned. With their mutual friends William Henry Channing and James Freeman Clarke, Emerson did what he could to gather her papers and produce a two-volume collection of recollections and writings. This work, called *Memoirs of Margaret Fuller Ossoli*, was published in 1852. At the national level, the Compromise of 1850 with its Fugitive Slave Law accelerated Emerson's speaking against slavery.

Emerson's winter lecture series for 1851–1852 was on "The Conduct of Life," a series in which he returned to his philosophical themes, though with a more practical slant. He lectured widely this year as far as St. Louis, Montreal, Waterville, Maine, and Philadelphia, and for several years he continued this pattern of long lecture tours. His mother, Ruth Haskins Emerson, died in 1853. The following year, Emerson lectured on "Topics of Modern Times" in Philadelphia. These many activities delayed the appearance of the book *The Conduct of Life*, based on the lecture series, until 1860.

Walt Whitman sent Emerson a copy of his new self-published book of poems, *Leaves of Grass*, in 1855. Emerson's letter of thanks, written July 21, 1855, has become one of the most famous letters—if not the most famous—in American literature. In Whitman's poems he saw that transcendental sense of nature, that "large perception" he had been writing about since his first book. Whitman saw the divine—the hand of God, the spirit of God—infusing all natural objects, from the ant to the ocean, from pokeweed to clouds. Furthermore, he declared the correspondence of this divinity with his own nature, both mind and body. Emerson recognized their kinship, and he let Whitman know it. Whitman let the public know it by publishing the letter in the *New York Tribune* and printing a phrase from it on the spine of his second edition, in gold.

In the late 1850s, Emerson tended to speak of nature with a new, down-to-earth quality. When Sleepy Hollow Cemetery was dedicated September 29, 1855, his short speech pointed out that cultivated parks and gardens bring out "natural advantages" in the landscape through art, a function especially valuable for "anxious, over-driven Americans." Sleepy Hollow was part of the rural cemetery movement, which fostered more natural surroundings for the dead, and Emerson suggested people could "sleep well" in this place, "as in the palm of Nature's hand." An arboretum of varied trees would bring varied and colorful birds, of which Emerson named ten.

English Traits, based on his trip to England in 1847–1848, was published in 1856. It is Emerson's only book of travel writing. Nature was only incidental to his subject, but he did explore the genetic heritage of Britain as well as its geographic situation as an island. Its religion, he said, was not transcendental; he deplored its prayers for wealth rather than right. And its landscape he called "over-cultivated," quite in contrast with America's "great sloven continent" where primordial wildness dwarfs humankind. It is interesting, therefore, that in 1857 he moved the remains of his mother and his son Waldo to Sleepy Hollow, the newly cultivated cemetery of

Concord. Curiously, he opened their coffins as he had his first wife Ellen's.

In December 1857 Emerson gave a lecture on "Country Life" before the Concord Lyceum. Sometimes called "Walking" by Emerson scholars, the newly edited *Later Lectures* differentiate it from a longer lecture with some of the same material, given the following spring. Ronald A. Bosco and Joel Myerson, editors of these volumes, call the former "Country Life (Concord) 2 December 1857" and the latter "Country Life," Lecture I in the *Natural Method of Mental Philosophy* series, first given March 1, 1858, and revised for numerous other deliveries up until 1867. Both lectures appear to have been inspired by an experience Emerson recorded in his journal May 2, 1857. A day earlier, he and Thoreau had walked to nearby Goose Pond, and talked of making a "book on walking." Walking, Emerson said in the first and much shorter of these lectures, was a way to find unexpected treasures in the farm, the garden, the woodlot; birds and sunsets, landscapes and lanes for walking were included free. As in the dedication for Sleepy Hollow, he asserted the value of an arboretum and of a personal calendar for the year's natural events. He said that two companions were best: an artist, who has an eye for beauty, and a naturalist, who can explain the scientific aspects of what the walker might see. Such a pursuit has in it a hint of immortality because life is always beginning. Deciphering nature's particular "hieroglyphic," however, may not explain its more universal truth.

In the longer lecture of 1858, Emerson went into a great deal more detail about natural particulars such as types of apples and trees, forests and seasons. The forest, he said, gives older people the same feeling it did when they were young, so it is comforting as a "dodge" for aging, especially because old trees are the most grand and beautiful. Here Emerson enumerated many Native American uses for natural objects. Here he recalls a sight at the seashore, the wind blowing back the waves like women's hair, a picture of grace and freedom. Here too he drew a

beautiful portrait of the natural year: in June a person feels alive with the flowing of sap like the trees, and October is a tranquil portrait of color and light. Though farmers wear their powers "meekly," they are "metamorphoses" of sun, moon, rainbow, and flood. Thus nature is a cure for egotism, yet at the same time it fosters the "peculiar genius" of each person. It draws human interest because it is made of the human, just as the human is made of nature. It is "vast and strong," but people who become its interpreter are its master, as the Sphinx said.

Emerson returned to an old idea, but with a twist, in the fourth lecture of this series. Called, like the series, "The Natural Method of Mental Philosophy," and delivered March 24, 1858, this lecture emphasized the analogies of nature to the processes of the mind. Emerson credited Plato with this concept of analogy, again a seeming return to his early thought. But here, instead of asserting the mind's power to understand the laws of nature, Emerson suggested that the laws of nature can be a path to understanding things that "skulk and hide in the caverns of human consciousness." In other words, he reversed the poet's process to show that the path of things can travel in both directions, from things to the mind, as well as from the mind to things.

In November 1857 Emerson contributed four poems to the first issue of the *Atlantic Monthly*. "Brahma" and "Days" would become two of his most studied and admired poems. Both have a cryptic quality. "Brahma" recalled the riddling of "The Sphinx" in the 1847 *Poems*. Its paradoxical Hindu perspective emphasized the illusions of nature and of human life, with an identity hidden behind multiplicity; Brahma represented a universal spirit present in everything and everybody. "Days" presented both the enthusiastic, transcendental view of nature as promised each morning, and the realistic possibility that, in the distraction of the moment, such promise may yield only "a few herbs and apples." In this painful imagery, Emerson expressed his disappointing sense that the days of nature are often silent and hide their messages from the poet's creating vision.

In the first "Country Life" lecture, Emerson had said that the ideal way to learn science was to accompany Louis Agassiz wherever he wanted to go. In 1858, Emerson bought a gun and went with Agassiz, Oliver Wendell Holmes, and others on a camping and specimen-gathering trip to the Adirondacks. The trip resulted in a long narrative poem, "The Adirondacs: A Journal," written in blank verse, which would appear as the second poem in his second volume of poetry. Emerson was now 55 years old.

Amid rumbles that preceded the Civil War —and Emerson took positions not only on antislavery and abolition but also on the John Brown case—he published his 1860 volume *The Conduct of Life*. As the title indicates, this work was more concerned with societal than artistic issues, but Emerson the artist still had things to say about nature. Both in the opening essay, "Fate," and in the closing essay, "Illusions," he wrote of nature as problematic. In the former, he wrote that nature essentially is fate, or necessity, or the laws of the world. In what may be a reference to the drowning of his friend Margaret, he said that nature does not mind "drowning a man or a woman, but swallows your ship like a grain of dust." It does not pamper but will freeze a person "like an apple." Nature is tyrannical, predatory, and fierce; it is most emphatically not a "divinity student." Rather, it provides the limits within which people live their lives: "Nature is what you may do. There is much that you may not." The pages of nature's book are layered like the earth's geology and evolving life forms. Law rules what might otherwise seem casual, and our attempts to decorate or "whitewash" are futile: "We cannot trifle with this reality, this cropping-out in our planted gardens of the core of the world."

Yet Emerson still asserted human power, intellectual power, and necessary freedom. Because they are related both to the lower forms of life and to the lightning's power to create new planets, human beings still may compose and decompose nature by a process of spirit or thought. It is more practical, Emerson said, to avoid contemplating nature's limits too much; their right use, he said, is to bring human conduct up to the "loftiness" of nature: "A man ought to compare advantageously with a river, an oak, or a mountain. He shall have not less the flow, the expansion, and the resistance of these." Thought is the vehicle for this transcendence; it "dissolves the material universe by carrying the mind up into a sphere where all is plastic." Thus a person who penetrates the causes of nature can learn to swim, not drown; a person who learns to skate can use the cold to become graceful rather than to freeze. All natural things are in a web of relation, where fate slides into freedom and freedom into fate. History results from the interaction of thought and nature. Nature is the Blessed Unity, the Beautiful Necessity, and finally, Emerson said, the embodiment of philosophy and theology.

Emerson opened the final essay in *The Conduct of Life*, "Illusions," with a description of Kentucky's Mammoth Cave. This detailed a description of a specific occasion and a real place is extremely rare in his published essays. Although similar passages appear in the journals and letters, Emerson tended, as he incorporated such material into his more formal work, to remove the more personal references. He wanted to find the larger generalizations. The point of this unusually detailed passage, however, was that the best beauty of the place was an illusion, the apparent sight of stars shining in the night sky. It was not real. In this essay, Emerson explored ideas—many of them drawn from his reading in Hindu and other Asian religious and philosophical texts—of nature as illusion. The concerns here recall those in "Experience," where reality was seen as hiding behind surfaces. Illusions surround human life, he said in this later essay, and even time and space are only "forms of thought." Yet people want nature to back them in what they do, and this sense of illusion serves to stimulate the will.

As this book was being published and the nation was preparing to enter the Civil War,

Emerson's lecturing and writing continued. In 1862 he lectured at the Smithsonian in Washington and met President Lincoln. That summer Thoreau died; Emerson preached the funeral oration, and in it he drew some implied comparisons between his own and Thoreau's interest in nature. Thoreau was interested in every natural fact, Emerson said, and had an extraordinarily sensitive ability to observe, hear, and measure them; in fact, he carried spyglass, microscope, knife, and notebook where he kept a careful calendar of returning birds, plants, and flowerings. He was an excellent guide for a walk and "knew the country like a fox or a bird." Yet he did not like to separate his observations from the connections they made in his mind, Emerson said approvingly.

In 1863—the year his Aunt Mary Moody Emerson died and he himself turned 60—Emerson lectured throughout the Midwest; in 1865 he gave 77 lectures. The peak of his lecturing career came in 1867, when he gave 80 lectures and went to both Minnesota and Iowa twice. That year he also gave another Phi Beta Kappa oration at Harvard and published, in April, his second volume of poetry, *May Day and Other Pieces*. The title poem was a long celebration of nature in springtime, the second a narrative in blank verse of the 1858 trip to the Adirondacks. That poem concluded with the idea that, at the close of the trip, "Nature, the inscrutable and mute" had allowed something like a smile after all, "As if one riddle of the Sphinx were guessed." According to Hyatt Waggoner, the best poems in this volume—"Brahma," "The Titmouse," "Terminus," "Days," and "The Boston Hymn"—do compare with the best of the earlier collection.

As nature writing, and as a contrast with the spring poems, "The Titmouse" is the most interesting of these. Here Emerson described an experience of being caught in "the snow-choked wood" during a January storm of "arctic cold." Tempted to give up and lie down to sleep in the snow, still "three dangerous miles" from home, the poem's speaker hears the cheery cry of a titmouse or

chickadee and is inspired by its tiny and defiant playfulness. He imagines it reminding him that the cold, blowing air is of the same substance as the bird himself, for the bird is a "poet" and tells the secret of nature. The soul, "stout within," can protect him from fear. Furthermore, its black and gray colors "outshine" all other hues. Robert Richardson, Jr., in his biography of Emerson, calls attention to two other of these poems, "Waldeinsamkeit" and "Two Rivers." Of the former, though it was written at the John Murray Forbes estate on Naushon Island, Edward Emerson said the title suggested both Walden and its woods in which Emerson found solitude.

Hyatt Waggoner, in his book *Emerson as Poet*, emphasizes Emerson's use of observations and propositions that aim at shocking readers into fresh perceptions. His interest in nature, Waggoner says, is really an interest in the nature of reality and how people perceive and imagine a "meaningful cosmos." When Emerson wrote, "the majority of his readers could be depended upon to identify Revelation with the Bible," so to assert that nature could be read as scripture—and read in the spirit in which it was written, that is, in the spirit of its creator—would have surprised, if not startled. That this assertion permeates the poetry as well as the prose (or, as Waggoner calls them, prose-poems) and that Emerson found so many ways and contexts in which to express it—these are the achievements that declare Emerson the poet he wanted to be.

Emerson's last 15 years were a slow decline first of expressive powers and then of memory, though he continued to reap honors and to lecture. In 1870 he published the last book he put together by himself, *Society and Solitude*. Here nature appears most obviously in "Farming," from Emerson's oration called "The Man with the Hoe," given at a Middlesex cattle show in 1858. In 1870 he also lectured at Harvard on the "Natural History of Intellect," his still-developing concept of unity between mind and nature. In 1871 he took his last long Western trip. Richardson gives some touching details. He traveled to the West Coast in a private Pullman car provided by his son-in-law, William Forbes. He watched the Western landscapes unroll from the back of the train. He stopped in Utah to meet Brigham Young. In California he named a tree in the Mariposa Grove of redwoods, choosing the name Samoset after the Native American who had befriended the Plymouth colonists. He visited Yosemite, not yet a national park, and met John Muir, then 33, in effect passing a baton for nature writing to a new generation. Muir taught Emerson to distinguish among three evergreens and watched him wave goodbye from horseback as his party left Muir's valley.

After a house fire in 1872, during its repair, Emerson traveled in Europe and Egypt with his daughter Ellen. Increasingly he refused invitations to speak or even to visit except for special occasions. His memory was failing with a type of aphasia that was especially embarrassing to a writer and speaker such as he. With Edith's help, in 1874 he produced an eccentric anthology of the family's favorite poems, *Parnassus*. With Ellen's help and that of James Elliot Cabot, he published *Selected Poems* in 1876. After several years of happy work at home, he was caught in rain on a walk and contracted pneumonia. He died eight days later, on April 27, 1882. He was buried in Sleepy Hollow Cemetery, the natural retreat he had helped dedicate, where he too could now sleep with the others "as in the palm of Nature's hand."

For Emerson, then, nature was not just nature as commonly interpreted. Among his poems, especially, those usually identified as the best, are often the ones that are specific as to time and place—the ground pine or river in Concord, the rhodora on a windy May day, the titmouse in the snow. In Emerson's lectures and essays, too, nature's particularities and examples tend to come as images from science and from his life as a householder and walker in the woods around his home in Concord. But nature is more than its manifestations. It is a flaming metamorphosis of seen and unseen, phenomenon and noumenon, natural object and eternal law. At times in his work this law is scarcely distinguishable from scientific principle, and at others it is scarcely distinguishable from God. At all times, however, whether open to the poet's vision or opaque, whether resistant to human shaping or not, it matters. It rules. It is the true fabric of life, of mind, of literature, and of all human endeavor. It is the ground from which transcendence begins and to which it returns.

PRIMARY BIBLIOGRAPHY

Books

Nature (Boston: Munroe, 1836).

Essays [First Series] (Boston: Munroe, 1841; London: Fraser, 1841; expanded, Boston: Munroe, 1847).

Nature; An Essay, and Lectures on the Times (London: Clarke, 1844).

Orations, Lectures, and Addresses (London: Clarke, 1844).

Essays: Second Series (Boston: Munroe, 1844; London: Chapman, 1844).

Poems (London: Chapman, 1847; Boston: Munroe, 1847); revised and enlarged as *Selected Poems* (Boston: Osgood, 1876); revised and enlarged again as *Poems* (Boston & New York: Houghton Mifflin, 1884 [volume 9, Riverside Edition]; London: Routledge, 1884; revised, Boston & New York: Houghton Mifflin, 1904 [volume 9, Centenary Edition]).

Nature; Addresses, and Lectures (Boston & Cambridge: Munroe, 1849); republished as *Miscellanies; Embracing Nature, Addresses, and Lectures* (Boston: Phillips, Sampson, 1856); republished as *Miscellanies* (London: Macmillan, 1884).

Representative Men: Seven Lectures (Boston: Phillips, Sampson, 1850; London: Chapman, 1850).

English Traits (Boston: Phillips, Sampson, 1856; London: Routledge, 1856).

The Conduct of Life (Boston: Ticknor & Fields, 1860; London: Smith, Elder, 1860).

May-Day and Other Pieces (Boston: Ticknor & Fields, 1867; London: Routledge, 1867).

Society and Solitude. Twelve Chapters (Boston: Fields, Osgood, 1870; London: Sampson, Low, Son & Marston, 1870).

Letters and Social Aims (Boston: Osgood, 1876; London: Chatto & Windus, 1876).

The Works of Ralph Waldo Emerson, 3 vols. (London: Bell, 1883).

Lectures and Biographical Sketches (Boston & New York: Houghton Mifflin, 1884; London: Routledge, 1884).

Miscellanies (Boston: Houghton Mifflin, 1884 [vol. 11, Riverside Edition]; London: Routledge, 1884).

Natural History of Intellect and Other Papers (Boston & New York: Houghton Mifflin, 1893 [vol. 12, Riverside Edition]; London: Routledge, 1894).

Two Unpublished Essays: The Character of Socrates; The Present State of Ethical Philosophy (Boston & New York: Lamson, Wolffe, 1896).

The Journals of Ralph Waldo Emerson, 10 vols., ed. Edward Waldo Emerson and Waldo Emerson Forbes (Boston & New York: Houghton Mifflin, 1909–1914).

Uncollected Writings: Essays, Addresses, Poems, Reviews and Letters (New York: Lamb, 1912).

Young Emerson Speaks: Unpublished Discourses on Many Subjects, ed. Arthur Cushman McGiffert, Jr. (Boston: Houghton Mifflin, 1938).

The Early Lectures of Ralph Waldo Emerson, vol. 1, ed. Stephen E. Whicher and Robert E. Spiller (Cambridge, MA: Harvard University Press, 1959); vol. 2, ed. Stephen E. Whicher, Robert E. Spiller, and Wallace E. Williams (Cambridge, MA: Harvard University Press, 1964); vol. 3, ed. Robert E. Spiller, and Wallace E. Williams (Cambridge, MA: Harvard University Press, 1972).

The Journals and Miscellaneous Notebooks of Ralph Waldo Emerson, 16 vols., ed. William H. Gilman and others (Cambridge, MA: Harvard University Press, 1960–1983).

The Poetry Notebooks of Ralph Waldo Emerson, ed. Ralph H. Orth and others (Columbia, MO: University of Missouri Press, 1986).

The Topical Notebooks of Ralph Waldo Emerson, vol. 1, ed. Susan Sutton Smith (Columbia & London: University of Missouri Press, 1990).

The Topical Notebooks of Ralph Waldo Emerson, vol. 2, ed. Ronald A. Bosco (Columbia & London: University of Missouri Press, 1993).

Emerson's Antislavery Writings, ed. Len Gougeon and Joel Myerson (New Haven & London: Yale University Press, 1995).

The Later Lectures of Ralph Waldo Emerson, 1843–1871, 2 vols., ed. Ronald A. Bosco and Joel Myerson (Athens, GA: The University of Georgia Press, 2001).

Collections

Emerson's Complete Works, 12 vols. (Boston & New York: Houghton Mifflin, 1883–1893 [Riverside Edition]; London: Routledge, 1883–1894).

Complete Works of Ralph Waldo Emerson, 12 vols. (Boston & New York: Houghton Mifflin, 1903–1904 [Centenary Edition]).

The Collected Works of Ralph Waldo Emerson, 5 vols. to date (Cambridge, MA: Harvard University Press, 1971–).

Essays & Lectures, ed. Joel Porte (New York: Literary Classics of the United States, 1983).

Other

Thomas Carlyle, *Sartor Resartus*, edited, with a preface, by Emerson (Boston: Munroe, 1836).

Memoirs of Margaret Fuller Ossoli, 2 vols., written and edited by Emerson, William Henry Channing, and James Freeman Clarke (Boston: Phillips, Sampson, 1852); 3 vols. (London: Bentley, 1852).

Parnassus, ed. Emerson (Boston: Osgood, 1875).

Letters

The Letters of Ralph Waldo Emerson, vols. 1–6 ed. Ralph L. Rusk, vols. 7–10 ed. Eleanor M. Tilton (New York: Columbia University Press, 1939–1995).

The Correspondence of Emerson and Carlyle, ed. Joseph Slater (New York & London: Columbia University Press, 1964).

The Selected Letters of Ralph Waldo Emerson, ed. Joel Myerson (New York: Columbia University Press, 1997).

SECONDARY BIBLIOGRAPHY

Bibliographies

Robert E. Burkholder and Joel Myerson, *Emerson: An Annotated Secondary Bibliography* (Pittsburgh: University of Pittsburgh Press, 1985).

Walter Harding, *Emerson's Library* (Charlottesville: University Press of Virginia, 1967).

Joel Myerson, *Ralph Waldo Emerson: A Descriptive Bibliography* (Pittsburgh: University of Pittsburgh Press, 1982).

Manfred Putz, *Ralph Waldo Emerson: A Bibliography of Twentieth-Century Criticism* (New York: Peter Lang, 1986).

Concordances

George S. Hubbell, *A Concordance to the Poems of Ralph Waldo Emerson* (New York: H.W. Wilson, 1932).

Mary Alice Ihrig, *Emerson's Transcendental Vocabulary: A Concordance* (New York: Garland, 1982).

Eugene F. Irey, *A Concordance to Five Essays of Ralph Waldo Emerson* (New York: Garland, 1981).

Biographies

Gay Wilson Allen, *Waldo Emerson* (New York: Viking, 1981).

John McAleer, *Ralph Waldo Emerson: Days of Encounter* (Boston: Little, Brown, 1984).

Robert D. Richardson, Jr., *Emerson: The Mind on Fire* (Berkeley: University of California Press, 1995).

Ralph L. Rusk, *The Life of Ralph Waldo Emerson* (New York: Scribners, 1949).

References

Gordon V. Boudreau, *The Roots of Walden and the Tree of Life* (Nashville, TN: Vanderbilt University Press, 1990).

Michael P. Branch, "'Angel Guiding Gently': The Yosemite Meeting of Ralph Waldo Emerson and John Muir, 1871," *Western American Literature* 32 (1997): 127–49.

Lee Rust Brown, *The Emerson Museum: Practical Romanticism and the Pursuit of the Whole* (Cambridge & London: Harvard University Press, 1997).

Eduardo Cadava, *Emerson and the Climates of History* (Stanford, CA: Stanford University Press, 1997).

Phyllis Cole, *Mary Moody Emerson and the Origins of Transcendentalism: A Family History* (New York and Oxford: Oxford University Press, 1998).

Denis Donoghue, "Emerson at First: A Commentary on *Nature*," *Emerson and His Legacy: Essays in Honor of Quentin Anderson*, ed. Stephen Donadio, Stephen Railton, and Ormond Seavey (Carbondale and Edwardsville: Southern Illinois University Press, 1986), 23–47.

Richard Lee Francis, "The Architectonics of Emerson's *Nature*," *American Quarterly* 19 (Spring, 1967): 39–53;, reprinted in Sealts and Ferguson, *Emerson's Nature—Origin, Growth, Meaning*, 164–74.

Alan D. Hodder, *Emerson's Rhetoric of Revelation: Nature, the Reader, and the Apocalypse Within* (University Park, PA: The Pennsylvania State University Press, 1989).

F. DeWolfe Miller, *Christopher Pearse Cranch and His Caricatures of New England Transcendentalism* (Cambridge, MA: Harvard University Press, 1951).

B.L. Packer, *Emerson's Fall: A New Interpretation of the Major Essays* (New York: Continuum, 1982).

Sherman Paul, *Emerson's Angle of Vision: Man and Nature in American Experience* (Cambridge, MA: Harvard University Press, 1966).

Joel Porte, *Emerson and Thoreau: Transcendentalists in Conflict* (Middletown, CT: Wesleyan University Press, 1966).

Robert D. Richardson, Jr., "Emerson and Nature," in *The Cambridge Companion to Ralph Waldo Emerson*, ed. Joel Porte and Saundra Morris (Cambridge: Cambridge University Press, 1999), 97–105.

David Robinson, "Emerson's Natural Theology and the Paris Naturalists: Toward a Theory of Animated Nature," *Journal of the History of Ideas* 41 (January–March 1980): 69–88.

David Robinson, "Fields of Investigation: Emerson and Natural History," in *American Literature and Science*, ed. Robert J. Scholnick (Lexington: University of Kentucky Press, 1992), 94–109.

William Rossi, "Emerson, Nature, and Natural Science," in *A Historical Guide to Ralph Waldo Emerson*, ed. Joel Myerson (New York & Oxford: Oxford University Press, 2000), 101–150.

Merton M. Sealts, Jr., and Alfred R. Ferguson, eds., *Emerson's* Nature—*Origin, Growth, Meaning* (New York & Toronto, 1969).

David Van Leer, *Emerson's Epistemology: The Argument of the Major Essays* (New York: Cambridge University Press, 1986).

Albert J. von Frank, "The Composition of *Nature*: Writing and the Self in the Launching of a Career," in *Biographies of Books: The Compositional Histories of Notable American Writings*, ed. James Barbour and Tom Quirk (Columbia: University of Missouri Press, 1996), 11–40.

Albert J. von Frank, "*Essays: First Series* (1841)," in *The Cambridge Companion to Ralph Waldo Emerson*, ed. Joel Porte and Saundra Morris (Cambridge: Cambridge University Press, 1999), 106–20.

Hyatt H. Waggoner, *Emerson as Poet* (Princeton: Princeton University Press, 1974).

R.A. Yoder, *Emerson and the Orphic Poet in America* (Berkeley: University of California Press, 1978).

R.A. Yoder, "Toward the 'Titmouse Dimension': The Development of Emerson's Poetic Style," *PMLA* 87 (1972): 255–70.

Papers

The majority of Emerson's papers are deposited in the Ralph Waldo Emerson Memorial Association collection at the Houghton Library at Harvard University.

Eliza W. Farnham
(November 17, 1815–
December 15, 1864)

Nancy McKinney

liza W. Farnham was well known during her lifetime as a philanthropist, social reformer, and author. Until recently she has been best known to modern scholars for her work in prison reform, serving a controversial term as women's matron at Sing Sing prison in New York state and editing a book on phrenology and criminology. Farnham has been rediscovered by feminist literary scholars interested in her travel narrative, *Life in Prairie Land* (1846), and her memoir and cultural study, *California, In-Doors and Out* (1856). It is in the context of her travel writing that Eliza Farnham merits attention as a nature writer.

Eliza Woodson Burhans was born on November 17, 1815, to Cornelius and Mary Wood Burhans at Rensselaerville, New York. When their mother died in 1820, the children were taken in by various relatives; Burhans lived with her grandfather for two years, then with an aunt and uncle in Maple Springs, New York. Her father died during the time she resided there. Her autobiography, *My Early Days* (1859), details the emotional deprivation she experienced under the care of her domineering, atheistic aunt. Although denied schooling, the girl read extensively, including works of Paine,

Volney, and Voltaire, and found solace in nature. The Burhans children were reunited at Palmyra, New York, in 1831. With the help of a brother, Burhans received some formal education, attending The Albany Female Academy and teaching school.

After the family's reunion in 1831, Burhans's sister, Mary, married John M. Roberts, a teacher and abolitionist, and moved with his family to Groveland, Illinois, near Pekin in Tazewell County. Burhans traveled to Illinois in 1835 to live with the Robertses at their homestead, Prairie Lodge. She remained in the state four and one-half years. On July 12, 1836, Burhans married Thomas Jefferson Farnham, a young attorney whom she had met while studying in Albany. They lived in Tremont, Illinois, the county seat where Thomas Farnham practiced law, and the couple had a son. Several times in 1837 and 1838 Eliza Farnham returned to Prairie Lodge to nurse her sister Mary, whose health was failing. In the summer of 1838, Mary died of consumption; Farnham's young son died two weeks later, during an epidemic.

In 1839 the Farnhams were living in Peoria, Illinois. Thomas Farnham organized an exploratory expedition to Oregon; Eliza Farnham remained at Peoria, but traveled throughout the state. In *Life in Prairie Land,* she describes traveling to Alton in southern Illinois and Springfield in central Illinois, and visiting friends in the Rock River country in northwestern Illinois. In the fall of 1840, upon Thomas Farnham's return from Oregon, the couple left Illinois to settle near Poughkeepsie, New York.

Life in Prairie Land chronicles Farnham's experience in Illinois from 1835 to 1840. It is a collection of sketches that reads like a novel; a travel narrative written in the romantic style of the day, but foreshadowing the development of local color writing and realism; a humorous book with a purpose beyond entertainment or diversion; a personal and subjective account that employs techniques of fiction; and an autobiography that only partially reveals its subject. Farnham is a transitional writer whose book bridges gaps between travel literature, romantic iconography, and local color realism.

It is Farnham's transitional role that places her among literary naturists. Her keen observation and vivid description place her in the company of early nineteenth-century women writing in the local sketchbook tradition, which culminated, as Lawrence Buell notes, in regional realism. In Farnham's chapter-length account of attending a traveling menagerie and circus, she focuses on the crowd, which she terms "my menagerie," and captures the celebratory atmosphere of the day along with the exotic nature of both the entertainment and the Westerners themselves:

> At this moment [the principal street] is lined with a crowd of all ages and sexes, dressed in a great variety of styles. We descend the slope, cross the bridge, and are at once in the midst of them....There are three [ladies] walking along together. One of them has on a pair of paper shoes, and is obliged, as she wishes to keep her feet in them, to tread rather daintily; the others, more prudent, have walked in their substantial leather shoes and carry the finer ones wrapped in their pocket handkerchiefs.

Later, at home ten miles distant from the site of the circus, Farnham and her family are awakened during the night by the sound of the menagerie passing by on its way to its next performance. She reports:

> The following morning the elephant was found to have left the print of his foot in the soft turf beyond the house. It was about fifteen inches deep, and large enough to allow a child of six or seven years to sit down in it. It was not obliterated for many weeks.

With her succinct prose, Farnham conveys the scene and its implication that the welcome diversion was remembered and enjoyed for many weeks, and that, on the prairie, the exotic and the mundane comfortably coexist.

A Transcendentalist influence upon Farnham is apparent from the organic and inchoate structure of *Life in Prairie Land,* and from Farnham's use of a cycle of seasons as an organizing pattern; however, she employs a counterpointed narrative that contradicts the chronological chapter arrangement and creates a unifying series of thematic motifs. Farnham interjects throughout the text single incidents that occur outside the chronology of her own story; the incidents interrupt the narrative and provide a dark element, revealing the dystopic aspect of the region. In one example, a Quaker family who moved into Farnham's village prospered, then suffered tragedy when the husband failed to return from a winter's day of hunting. After the spring thaw, his body was discovered in a stream near his home. In part one, chapter 22, Farnham introduces the family and foreshadows the tragedy; in part two, chapter 24, she recounts the family's story, focusing on the wife's grief and suggesting how arbitrarily events change the lives of Westerners. In another instance, Farnham tells "the story of the dark man's griefs." In part one, chapter 6, she hints at a melancholy story; in part one, chapter 9, she promises to tell the story; and in part one, chapter 10, she finally recounts the tale of a couple who arrive in the spring, start a farm and family, then, in their second year during a two-month period of unusual spring storms, fall ill in an epidemic. The wife and child die, leaving the man to work the farm alone, hopeless and dejected. The tale is embedded in a larger discussion of the abundance of fresh water and reliable rainfall, the return of spring to the prairie, and the social and physical freedom enjoyed by the residents. Farnham's counterpointed narrative provides an alternative, somewhat sentimental portrait of frontier life, which, taken along with her personal chronological narrative, presents a composite, more complete picture of the frontier experience, encompassing both the ideal and the disastrous.

Farnham writes in the American pastoral tradition, with her Western sojourn and return to the east as the archetypal retreat from society, renewal in nature, and return to society with the hope of improvement. She uses the machine in the garden theme, as described by Leo Marx, to express ambivalence toward the inevitable development of the West. A powerful description of a steamboat shattering the silence of the natural world is followed by a reflection upon the spiritual effect of traveling the vast and beautiful system of Western waterways. The juxtaposition of man and nature in opposition and man and nature in harmony reflects the author's ambivalence. Though Farnham questions the likely future effect of civilization on the region's land, animal life, and waterways, she ultimately favors prudent development. She expounds on the tendency of the freedom-loving residents to move on when civilization encroaches. In considering westward migration and the development of the region, which she regards as a natural process of new groups displacing resident groups, Farnham exhibits true sympathy for the Native Americans who had been reduced from their former position of strength and dominance over the area. She faults the whites for the "indecent, the fraudulent" means that were used to precipitate the displacement of the Native Americans. *Life in Prairie Land*, the account of Farnham's experience, represents a means to improve the society she left, then returned to, renewed.

Farnham uses mannerisms of the picturesque, a genre of nature writing popular at mid-century, to describe the landscape, notably in the account of her first view of the prairie, an obligatory scene in travel narratives about the Western frontier. She highlights the immensity and grandeur of the plain, using sea imagery and an artist's vocabulary:

> [T]he country opened before [us] , and swept away to the eastern horizon, a distance of many miles—a smooth, open plain, undotted by a tree or other familiar object....I see it now, its soft outline swelling against the clear eastern sky, its heaving surface penciled with black and brown lines, its borders fringed with the naked trees!

Describing the "deep joy" of a spring morning on the prairie, Farnham again employs the picturesque:

> We are within the borders of a little grove. Before us stretches a prairie; boundless on the south and east, and fringed on the north by a line of forest, the green top of which is just visible in a dark waving line between the tender hue of the growing grass and the golden sky. South and east as far as the eye can stretch, the plain is unbroken save by one "lone tree," which, from time immemorial, has been the compass of the red man and his white brother.

Whether or not Farnham read about landscape aesthetics, her use of the picturesque reveals that she was familiar with it as a literary trend.

Additionally, Farnham's work shares the roots of literary bioregionalism, as described by Buell. Within the context of her journey to the frontier, Farnham details her local travels in Illinois and includes natural history as a significant means to describe and explain the region. Farnham's local travels include visits to nearby neighbors and trips farther afield to southern, central, and northwestern Illinois. Local excursions provided opportunities for Farnham to describe the homes, practices, and attitudes of her neighbors. One such visit describes the lady of the house preparing tea for the visitors. It took all day at the hearth for the preparation of pumpkin, gingerbread, wheat biscuits, pie, and a pot of tea. With the addition of dried beef, pickles, and plums, the meal was ready and the company sat down to eat at seven o'clock. Farnham asserts that she is not exaggerating but allows that "such extreme slowness is not characteristic." More distant trips gave Farnham the experience to consider Western hospitality to strangers and the degree to which women were willing to be inconvenienced for visitors' sake. It was a necessity for homesteaders to lodge travelers, feeding them and their animals, and making room in limited quarters for their shelter. Some were more generous than others in the reception of travelers, and sometimes illness made it impossible for families to accommodate such guests. In part two, chapters 19 through 21, Farnham describes traveling with her brother and a driver in extreme weather through the night, past four houses where the inhabitants either would not or, in one case, could not admit them for the night.

Excursions provided Farnham the material for discussions of natural history. Her description of animals and plants varies in character from fanciful to precise and realistic. The quail, mentioned as Farnham's favorite bird, is the subject of an imaginative passage in which the quail's "Bob White" call becomes the call and response of two quarrelsome birds hiding from and seeking each other until interrupted by Mrs. Bob White, who insists upon her husband's help to establish order among her "rebelling" nestlings. Farnham's realistic description of the grouse reveals a familiarity with the bird and a habit of observing wildlife:

> He is a large, mottled grey bird, with a heavy ruff of feathers running over his head, which adds much to the watchfulness and timidity of his appearance. Their nests are built on the open prairie in some thick knot of grass. This bird has no proper song, and is in general a very silent inhabitant of these vast plains. When hunted or overtaken by the traveler, they rise suddenly with a whirr, somewhat similar to, but not so distinct as that of the pheasant, and fly very rapidly.

Farnham goes on to detail the flight of the grouse, and characterize the "peculiar noise" of the bird as "between the whistle of the quail and the hoarse blowing of the nighthawk, but louder than either." Farnham interjects humor with a lengthy account of the gopher, "a passionate devotee of subterranean architecture" who, "[i]f he is ejected from premises which he has improved, he never mourns his loss, nor institutes legal proceedings to recover damages, but, with unabated energy, seeks another site and commences anew." Within the comic account, Farnham includes a precise, less satirical observation of the animal's size, coat, and appearance, as well as her memory of sharing a joke with a local boy upon their coming across one of the gopher's "little towns, which must have contained near three hundred little dark mounds on the space of an acre." Following Farnham's description of the gopher is a shorter and more serious account of the fox, which characterizes the animal as "very much such a fox [on the prairie] as elsewhere, . . . making unscrupulous sallies against grouse, quails, and other featured neighbors," presumably including the gopher. Farnham's fanciful descriptions entertain but, combined with her astute realistic observations, provide factual information about the region's natural history.

In a wide-ranging, chapter-length discussion of weather, Farnham begins with conditions in late autumn, compares Western winters with Eastern, describes the phenomena of extreme weather changes characteristic of the region, and finishes with the late-January thawing of streams and waterways. Farnham reports that rain in November follows "[h]eavy winds from the west and north sweep[ing] over the immense plains" and that snowfalls begin "in the latitude of 41°" in mid-December, but "they rarely whiten the ground till much later in the season." Farnham observes that Western winters are "much shorter and less severe than those in the same latitudes in the eastern states." Commenting on the short duration of severe weather, she states that a few cold days are "followed by fair, sunny days often mild as those of June." She explains that such mild days are a feature of the region's weather, though they are irregular in occurrence. Farnham discusses "sudden and extreme changes" in weather by relating an instance in 1837 when the temperature dropped suddenly, within a span of about ten minutes, from mild to frigid, killing many unprotected people and animals. Farnham notes that winter suspends navigation on streams and the upper Mississippi River until late January. She illustrates the inconvenience and danger using the example of a party of young people who plunged through the unstable ice while trying to cross a frozen stream. Farnham's discussion of the climate is punctuated with details of winter pioneer life: sleds for transportation, a diet of game birds, the cruel slaughter of weakened deer, a settler's typical first winter, and fireside activities of both men and women. She places equal importance on the accurate description of the Western climate and of the challenges facing the humans living there.

Life in Prairie Land incorporates both an immediate record of people and places and a thoughtfully recollected memoir. Diaries that Farnham kept while living in Illinois seem likely to have provided details and impressions otherwise easily forgotten over time. She wrote her book five to six years later while living in New York, where her concerns about social reform matured under the influence of New England Transcendentalism.

During the period between 1840 and 1848 Farnham wrote, worked for prison reform, and met the New York literati. She became acquainted with poet William Cullen Bryant and attended the literary salon of writer Anne Charlotte Lynch. In 1843 Farnham contributed articles on women's place in society to the magazine *Brother Jonathan*. She wrote *Life in Prairie Land* between 1844 and 1846.

In 1844 Farnham became matron of the women's division of Mount Pleasant State Prison (now called Sing Sing), where she instituted reforms. She had the support of prominent prison board member John

Bigelow, a friend of William Cullen Bryant. Georgiana Bruce (later Georgiana Bruce Kirby) was one of Farnham's assistants. Bruce, as a student, had been a worker and resident at the experimental, utopian community Brook Farm from 1841 to 1844. There, Bruce met the Transcendentalist luminaries, including Margaret Fuller. Fuller visited the prison and addressed the inmates during Farnham's tenure there. Because her prison reform measures were controversial, Farnham was forced to resign her position as matron in 1848. She then worked at the Perkins Institute for the Blind in Boston.

Following her husband's death while traveling in California in 1848, Farnham sailed to California in the spring of 1849 to settle his estate, traveling with her were two sons, Charles and Edward, born after the couple had relocated in New York from Illinois. At the same time, she also initiated a plan for female emigration to California, though that plan ultimately failed. Farnham's experiences in California were varied during the years 1850 to 1856. She operated a farm, El Rancho de Libertad, in Santa Cruz county for several years. On March 23, 1852, Farnham married William Fitzpatrick and they had a daughter, Mary. The marriage ended in divorce, and in 1854 the girl died; Farnham's son Edward died the next year. While living in California, Farnham taught school, recommended reforms for San Quentin prison, and lectured.

In 1856 Farnham returned to New York City. Her book *California, In-Doors and Out* was published in the same year. From 1859 to 1862 Farnham was back in California, lecturing and working at the Stockton Insane Asylum. Her autobiography *My Early Days* was published in 1859; it was retitled *Eliza Woodson* and republished in 1864. Returning to the East in 1862, Farnham worked for abolition and the women's movement. In 1863 Farnham volunteered as a nurse at Gettysburg and contracted tuberculosis. Her two-volume treatise *Woman and Her Era* was published in 1864. In New York on December 15, 1864, Eliza Farnham died of consumption. Her last book, *The Ideal Attained,* written in the 1860s, was posthumously published in 1865.

Farnham's travel book, *Life in Prairie Land,* is an important early example of nature writing. It embodies and presents a distinctive female voice and view of the Illinois prairie frontier and of mid-nineteenth-century American society. John Hallwas considers the importance of Farnham's book to lie in her "sensitivity to the landscape and to man's interaction with [the landscape]"; Robert Bray credits Farnham as "one of the most important social thinkers ever to discuss emigration to Illinois." *Life in Prairie Land,* a transitional book embodying characteristics of a number of genres, presents a strong case for inclusion as an example of literary naturism. Farnham, a young woman when she experienced the prairie, brought with her a sensitivity to, and a deep love for, nature. She wrote within the American pastoral tradition because she was living its premise: to retire from society, experience spiritual renewal in nature, and return to society with the hope of improving it. *Life in Prairie Land* can be seen as one of the first of a lifetime's worth of efforts toward societal reform, but its literary representation of the American prairies looms as one of Farnham's greatest achievements as a writer.

PRIMARY BIBLIOGRAPHY

Books

Life in Prairie Land (New York: Harper, 1846).

California, In-Doors and Out (New York: Dix & Edwards, 1856).

My Early Days (New York: Thatcher & Hutchinson, 1859).

A Lecture on the Philosophy of Spiritual Growth (San Francisco: Valentine, 1862).

Woman and Her Era, 2 vols. (New York: Davis, 1864).

The Ideal Attained (New York: Plumb, 1865).

Editions

My Early Days (New York: Thatcher & Hutchinson, 1859); published as *Eliza Woodson; or, The Early Days of One of the World's Workers. A Story of American Life* (New York: Davis, 1864).

California In-Doors and Out, facsimile, introduction by Madeleine B. Stern (Nieuwkoop: Netherlands: B. De Graaf, 1972).

Life in Prairie Land, facsimile, introduction by Madeleine B. Stern (Nieuwkoop: Netherlands: B. De Graaf, 1972).

Life in Prairie Land, introduction by John Hallwas (Urbana & Chicago: University of Illinois Press, 1988).

Other

Marmaduke B. Sampson, *Rationale of Crime and Its Appropriate Treatment,* edited and preface, notes and illustrations by Farnham (New York: Appleton, 1846); reprinted, *Rationale of Crime,* introduction by W. David Lewis (Montclair, NJ: Patterson Smith, 1973).

Selected Periodical Publications— Uncollected

"Rights of Women: Reply to Mr. Neal's Lecture," *Brother Jonathan,* 5 (1843): 236–38, 266–68, 363–67.

SECONDARY BIBLIOGRAPHY

References

Robert C. Bray, *Rediscoveries: Literature and Place in Illinois* (Urbana: University of Illinois Press, 1982).

Lawrence Buell, *The Environmental Imagination: Thoreau, Nature Writing, and the Formation of American Culture* (Cambridge: Harvard University Press, 1995).

John E. Hallwas, "Eliza Farnham's *Life in Prairie Land,*" *Old Northwest* 7 (1981–1982): 295–324.

John E. Hallwas, "Introduction," in Eliza W. Farnham's *Life in Prairie Land* (Urbana: University of Illinois Press, 1988).

James Hurt, *Writing Illinois: The Prairie, Lincoln, and Chicago* (Urbana: University of Illinois Press, 1992).

Annette Kolodny, "Mary Austin Holley and Eliza Farnham: Promoting the Prairies," in her *The Land Before Her: Fantasy and Experience of the American Frontier 1630–1860* (Chapel Hill: University of North Carolina Press, 1984), 93–111.

W. David Lewis, *From Newgate to Dannemora: The Rise of the Penitentiary in New York, 1796–1848* (Ithaca: Cornell University Press, 1965).

W. David Lewis, "Eliza Wood Burhans Farnham," in *Notable American Women 1607–1950,* edited by Edward T. James, vol. 1 (Cambridge: Harvard University Press, 1971), 598–600.

Leo Marx, *The Machine in the Garden: Technology and the Pastoral Ideal in America* (Oxford: Oxford University Press, 1964).

Nancy McKinney, *"Life in Prairie Land*: Eliza Farnham's Transcendentalist Text," *MidAmerica* 25 (1998): 13–24.

Helen Beal Woodward, "Biology Triumphant: Eliza Woodson Farnham," in her *The Bold Women* (New York: Farrar, Straus & Young, 1953), 337–356.

Papers

Eliza W. Farnham's correspondence is collected at the Harvard College Library, the California State Library, the Boston Public Library, and the New York State Library.

[Thomas] Wilson Flagg
(November 5, 1805–May 6, 1884)

Patricia Kennedy Bostian

To the reader of natural history, the name Wilson Flagg often means very little. One of the earliest contributors to the genre of the nature essay, he is often overshadowed by Henry David Thoreau and John Burroughs, his contemporaries. Flagg freely confesses to being influenced by both authors; however, he clearly goes his own way, his rambles through the New England countryside with its natural phenomena and inhabitants faithfully recorded. He was an early contributor of nature essays to *The Atlantic Monthly*, he found a broad readership because of his compelling prose style, and he awoke many general readers to the world of nature they regularly took for granted.

Born Thomas Wilson Flagg to Isaac Flagg and Elizabeth Frances Wilson in Beverly, Massachusetts, he dropped the "Thomas" early in his career. After graduating from Phillips Andover Academy in 1821, he studied medicine at various locations, including Harvard, but never practiced as a physician. Many of his essays, however, refer to the medicinal properties of plants and reflect his continuing interest in the subject of medicine. In one rather lengthy article, for example, he praises the newly maligned services of the village housewife who grew plants of limited medicinal value that were the early precursors to modern medicine. He married Caroline Eveleth in 1840; they had two sons,

Isaac and Bernard Whitman Flagg, and Flagg settled into the quiet life of observation and writing that marked his later works.

An early interest in politics led him to contribute political articles to *The Boston Weekly Magazine* and several newspapers and to pen an unsuccessful satire, *The Tailor's Shop* (1844). Although modern readers may find many of Flagg's early essays published in *The Boston Weekly Magazine*, such as "Nobility of Families and Races" (1840) and "Nature of Hereditary Honors" (1841), offensive with their views of the superiority of Anglo-Saxons, his nature writing is still largely free of overt racism. He was employed by the Boston Custom House from 1844 to 1848 before turning his full attention to a love for nature that had been awakened in him as a child of eight. An interest in natural history began on a trip through lower New Hampshire's "Dark Plains" in what he described as almost a religious conversion. Flagg focused his explorations close to home. The most extensive traveling he did was through Tennessee, Virginia, and the pine barrens of North Carolina.

Much of what we know about Flagg's approach to nature writing comes from prefaces he wrote for his collected works. In *Studies in the Field and Forest* (1857), he writes, "The object of this work is to foster in the public mind a taste for the observation of

natural objects and to cultivate that sentiment which is usually designated as the love
of nature." In his "Dedicatory Epistle" of
The Woods and By-Ways of New England, he
admits that he has no scientific training, that
his observations of nature are merely interpretations of the "oracle" of nature. *The
Atlantic Monthly* published "Botanizing" in
1871. In the introduction to the essay, Flagg
suggests that the study of botany is more
appropriate for females than other branches
of the natural sciences since they generally
"cannot without some eccentricity of conduct follow birds and quadrupeds to the
woods." His own interest in botany began
when, as a child, he was sent to collect flowers for his sisters. He expounds upon the joy
and excitement that finding new species can
bring, taking the reader on an imaginary tour
of the countryside and pointing out the vegetation that botanists enjoy on their rambles.
Flagg's sometimes whimsical writing style is
revealed in the essay's conclusion:

> Evening calls [the botanist] out from his re-
> treat, to pursue another varied journey among
> the fairy realms of vegetation, and ere she
> parts with him curtains the heavens with
> splendor and prompts her choir of sylvan war-
> blers to salute him with their vespers.

Flagg's style combines occasional poetic passages, strongly influenced by the British neoclassical tradition, and minute descriptions
of the observable details of the plant and
animal species and ecological processes he
studies.

It is also in these introductions that one
learns of Flagg's relatively isolated, yet happy,
life with his family. In his introduction to *The
Birds and Seasons of New England* (1875),
Flagg characterizes his representations of
nature and sets his work in the context of
his domestic life:

> My book differs from learned works…as a
> lover's description of a lover's hand would dif-
> fer from [an] anatomical description of it….I
> have pursued my tasks alone, except as I have
> read and conversed with my wife and children.
> She and they have been the only companions

> of my studies and recreations during all the
> prime of my life. But, perhaps from this cause
> alone, I have been very happy. The study of
> nature and my domestic avocations have
> yielded me a full harvest of pleasures, though
> it was barren of honors.

The public persona he carefully shaped had
wide appeal since it paired a life of nature
study to the attainment of a happy family life.

A frequent contributor of his oracular
interpretations to *The Atlantic Monthly*, Flagg
also published many of his early essays on scenery and landscape in Charles M. Hovey's
two gardening journals, *The American Gardener's Magazine* and *The Magazine of Horticulture*, as well as in *The Boston Magazine*.
Two early essays, "The Plumage and Songs
of Birds" (*The Boston Pearl*, 1835) and "Seasons of the Wild Flowers of New England"
(*The Boston Weekly Magazine*, 1838) show-
case Flagg's writing style. A strong attention
to details is accompanied by a deeply
thoughtful exploration of any topic on which
he is writing. In "The Plumage and Songs of
Birds," Flagg describes the colorful plumage
of some New England bird species and delves
into the possible reasons for their gaudy colors. He is never abstract and keeps his reader
in mind, using vocabulary that is plain and
accessible to his readers. Flagg seldom departs
far from this plain style, which he does
decorate with occasional poetic or fanciful
passages.

Flagg's early works were praised in an 1855
North American Review editorial, which
argued that attention needed to be brought
to Flagg and to Hovey's journals—both of
which were undervalued. This comment
seems to be a constant in the reviews of
Flagg's work throughout his career. Reviewers
were regularly quick to point out Flagg's merits: his deep and thoughtful observation of
the New England countryside, his elegant
descriptions, and his clear philosophy. Some
considered his books indispensable. They
often conclude with censuring readers for
not acknowledging Flagg's worth.

A thorough assessment of Flagg's development as a naturalist and as a writer is

hampered by the vast number of his essays, some of which were reprinted in other journals. Many of these essays were later collected in book form and then rearranged in subsequent volumes. His shorter essays on natural subjects are scattered in Hovey's two journals (1835–1855), and sometimes reprinted in *The New England Farmer*, to which he contributed articles in the late 1850s and early 1860s. These shorter pieces are often portraits of birds that are particular to New England farms. In 1856 he published several essays entitled "Portraits from the Field and Farm Yard," in which he describes the chickadee, the crow, the owl, the blue jay, and the wood thrush. Other writings are more technical in nature and discuss trees: "On the Relation of Trees to the Atmosphere and Climate" (1856), "The Electric Agency of Plants and Trees" (1857), and "Relation of Trees to the Soil" (1857). All show evidence of a writer whose earlier medical training predisposes him to a scientific approach to farming.

Although he is best known for his nature essays, Flagg also published poetry. Most of his poetry chooses birds and the natural world for its subject as well. Many of these poems were published in *The Boston Weekly Magazine*. Later efforts appeared in *The New England Farmer*. An often-reprinted piece, "The Bobolink" (1862), is representative of his poetic efforts:

Up flies Bobolincon, perching on an apple-tree,
Startled by his rival's song, quickened by his raillery.
Soon he spies the rogue afloat, curveting in the air,
And merrily he turns about, and warns him to beware!

In Flagg's poetry, as in his prose, he endeavors to recreate the natural experience for the reader with an array of details. Still-life illustrations are not for Flagg—his poetry depicts animals, birds, and even farmers in action. All of his poems project motion and activity; from the darkening clouds scudding in "The Storm" to a summer walk in "'Twas on a

Summer's Afternoon," Flagg represents nature as a dynamic realm of relationships among plant and animal species.

Studies in the Field and Forest, published in 1857, is Flagg's first collection of his nature writings and is composed of 40 essays that date back as early as 1839. The essays are arranged as a diary of the New England year. It is in the introduction to *Studies in the Field and Forest* that Flagg's theories of the pleasures of nature are first consolidated. Nature is there to be enjoyed by all, but it is only the cultivated observer who will be able to look below her superficial beauties to "perceive an infinite world of wonders and stores of happiness." To this work were added several more essays, along with beautiful photographs, and then it was published as two volumes: *The Woods and By-Ways of New England* (1872) and *The Birds and Seasons of New England* (1875). These essays underwent a final production as *Halcyon Days* (1881), a collection of brief general descriptions of nature "as revealed under New England skies through a New England atmosphere, interspersed with essays on the sentiments awakened by natural scenes and aspects." Flagg's preface to *Halcyon Days* outlines the organizational scheme of the books and their respective themes:

> *Halcyon Days* contains the greater part of my general descriptions of nature, and on our sentiments as awakened by her scenes and aspects. The second volume contains descriptions of trees and forests, and essays on their special relations to climate, salubrity, and the general prosperity of the country. The third volume treats of birds, chiefly as songsters, and of their services to agriculture.

Along with these three, often-reconfigured titles, Flagg edited *Mount Auburn: Its Scenes, Its Beauties, and Its Lessons*, a volume celebrating the Mount Auburn cemetery, in 1861. This collection of essays on "death, sepulture, sorrow, immortality, and kindred themes" is given scant notice by the reviewers, although the *North American Review* reviewer takes the opportunity to criticize the lack of credit Flagg receives as a writer. *Putnam's Monthly's* 1857 review of *Studies in the Field and Forest* reveals another common theme in Flagg reviews. Flagg is almost universally praised as "quiet and delightful," a "sympathetic observ[er] of nature."

Henry David Thoreau, Flagg's contemporary, objects to the "quiet and delightful" qualities that others praised. In an 1857 letter to Daniel Ricketson, he says,

> Your Wilson Flagg seems a serious person, and it is encouraging to hear of a contemporary who recognizes nature so squarely [...]. But he is not alert enough. He wants stirring up with a pole. He should practice turning a series of somersets rapidly or jump up and see how many times he can strike his feet together before coming down. His style, as I remember, is singularly vague (I refer to the book) and before I got to the end of the sentences I was off the track.

To Thoreau's criticism that he ought to be more passionate about his subject, Flagg replies that he enjoys living a "retired" life that is lacking in "enthusiasm." A "Dedicatory Epistle" to Ricketson opens his 1872 *The Woods and By-Ways of New England*. In it Flagg outlines the pleasures of his simple, retired life with his wife and children, and his belief that his life's simplicity is what has led to his time spent observing nature and his happiness in doing so. He writes that he has employed his time in firsthand observation of "her aspects and interpreting her problems" instead of hearing or reading about them through secondary sources. By doing so, he explains, he has spent the prime years of his life in the company of his wife and children, wanting no other company.

To date, W.G. Barton has written the only lengthy assessment of Flagg's writing. In "Thoreau, Flagg, and Burroughs," he addresses the three naturalists' approaches to their subjects and writing styles. Although Barton does admit some of Flagg's defects, Flagg often comes out on top in this assessment of the three. In the following passage, Barton sums up what is often concluded by Flagg's critics:

Flagg is in the habit of theorizing about and analyzing the effect of scenes upon the human mind in general. His style is finished and orderly, very unvarying. He seldom digresses, makes few classical allusions, and has not many short striking passages. He is never obscure, as Thoreau often is. He is careful not to overstate or understate. Thoreau and Burroughs purposely overstate. Flagg is perfectly self-possessed. In his books [...] his strong assurance [is] accompanied by gentleness of nature.

An 1885 *Scribner's Magazine* review also compares Flagg with Thoreau, and, again, Flagg is assessed as the superior. Praising Thoreau's "alertness and penetration," the reviewer admits that though Flagg could use more of this trait, readers would then have to cope with the accompanying traits of "intellectual somersaults" and "interminable preaching" associated with Thoreau. Flagg may not belong to the same school of nature writers as Thoreau, but he does not aspire to. Commenting on Flagg's essay about Thoreau in *The Woods and By-Ways*, Lawrence Buell suggests that Flagg, an avowed antitranscendentalist, can nevertheless feel and convey the power such a sacred place as Walden Pond can exert on the observer of nature. Flagg admits that Thoreau's habitation of Walden Pond inspires one to feel the power of place, but he relegates his contemporary to the status of poet, not philosopher. A *Harper's* reviewer in 1859 compared Flagg to Izaak Walton and Asa Gray, other noted nature writers, but one critic of *The Woods and By-Ways of New England* objected to the catalogue-like style of some of the book's essays. And this is a fair assessment. His "tree" essays from that work, which are collected in *A Year Among the Trees*, are examples of the cataloguing that is often seen in nature field books: "The Chestnut is ranked among the largest of our forest trees"; "the leaves are long, lengthened to a tapering point"; "they are clustered in stars, containing five to seven leaves." Many of the essays in *The Woods and By-Ways of New England* are devoted to specific trees and their descriptions.

The *North American Review* (1857) argues that his descriptions possess a charm unknown to those of the mere naturalist or the casual observer, because "they are not a dry enumeration of particulars, nor a collection of vague, indefinite impressions, but pictures from life, whose originals anyone may see for himself." Flagg "philosophizes with a clearness of conception and a simplicity of expression not very like the inexplicable utterances that characterize much of what passes under the name of philosophy at the present time." An 1873 review of *The Woods and By-Ways of New England* (*Harper's Monthly*) makes a comparison to a contemporaneous title by Mme. Michelet, *Nature, or the Poetry of Earth and Sea*, where it seems that Flagg's "American" style is preferable to the "exaggerations, paradoxes, and [the] too striking anti-theses" of the French writing style. "The Frenchman describes the effect which nature has produced upon him; the American describes nature itself." Once again he is admired for his quiet yet intimate detachment and his sympathetic observation of the often unnoticed details of the natural world. This review quotes, somewhat freely, Flagg's statement that "My book differs from learned works as a lover's description of his lady's hand differs from Bell's anatomical description of it."

If all of Flagg's essays were written in the style of field books, he would still be an invaluable companion to the amateur botanist and naturalist tramping through eastern New England's forests, fields, and along her sea shores. But Flagg does more than just describe the colors of the trees' leaves. His opening essay in *The Woods and By-Ways of New England*, "On the Domestic Scenery of New England," described as photographic by a *Literary World* reviewer, bemoans the loss of aspects of nature due to progress. Flagg is not against progress, as the essay insists, but he rather believes that "the great fallacy of the present age is that of mistaking the increase of the national wealth for the advancement of civilization."

The essay "The Primitive Forest" is a contemplation of the history of North America's primitive forests and their plants and animals. It introduces another subject of concern to Flagg—the conservation of species and the damage humans can do to nature. But not every essay in *The Woods and By-Ways of New England* dwells on conservation. "Rural Life in New England" focuses on the pleasures of the farming life. An essay on Thoreau, in which he explains his reasons for categorizing him as poet rather than philosopher, is included as well. Flagg's subjects are far-ranging yet do not stray far from observation of nature.

Thomas Wentworth Higginson published an article in *The Atlantic Monthly* (1862) in which he praises Flagg's essays on birds ("The Singing Birds and Their Songs," "The Birds of the Garden and Orchard," "The Birds of the Pasture and Forest," all published in 1858 and collected in *Birds and Seasons of New England* in 1875) as being some of the few significant contributions to the study of ornithology. In his introduction to the book, Flagg writes, "My essays are not biographies of the Birds. I treat of them chiefly as songsters, and speak only of those habits which render them useful, interesting, or picturesque." He also remarks that he is "much indebted to Mr. John Burroughs, whose essays on Birds and kindred spirits in 'The Atlantic Monthly' I formerly read with great pleasure." In an 1876 *Harper's* article on American literature, Edwin P. Whipple also praises Flagg's descriptions as being of the same quality as Audubon's—high praise indeed for an amateur bird watcher. Serious birders still list Flagg's books as being essential field guides to New England's birds.

While Flagg's books are often seen as valuable companions on one's walks through the woods and fields, they are also marvelous records of life in rural New England—the people as well as the flora and fauna. *Halcyon Days* collects many of his more philosophical works. In essays such as "Rural Architecture," "Simples and Simplers," and "Rural Life in New England," we see that Flagg's respect for life extends beyond the naturalist's expected purview. In an 1873 review of *The Woods and By-Ways*, the writer admits that, although the scenic passages are notable, he enjoys Flagg's descriptions of humans and their occupations even more. Flagg tends to romanticize the simple life of the farmer and the village dweller. "The Field and the Garden," originally published in *The Atlantic Monthly* in 1871, praises a cottager's garden with its medicinal plants, simple flowers, and weeds. He then dismisses a florist's garden filled with wonderful varieties of cutting flowers as being artificial and unworthy of a true plant lover.

In *Halcyon Days,* Flagg gathers his widely scattered essays that reflect his particular picturesque ideals. In works entitled "The Dreary and the Desolate," "The Pastoral and the Romantic," "Ruins," and "Flight of the Wood-nymphs," he betrays his lack of tolerance for those uncultivated souls who cannot find appreciation in the simple details of natural life. In his essay "The Picturesque," among others, Flagg is seemingly at odds with the Romantic tendency toward the sublime. The idea that the beauty of nature is evident only in craggy hills, the "wavy line," or a stormy sea strikes Flagg as nonsensical. To him, the picturesque landscape requires the presence of humanity to make it so. To a "boor," as Flagg refers to those who do not share his opinion, "scenes that would suggest a thousand delightful images to a cultivated man," are lost. "If [a] rock does not reach to the clouds, if [a] tree does not rear itself stupendously into the air, or if [a] house is not magnificent in size or embellishments, they are nothing to him, because they excite no admiration." He takes great pains to distinguish the picturesque from the sublime. Rudeness without a human focus is not sympathetic, but neither are panoramic heights. He likes the quaintness of cottagers tilling a field in a mountain valley; the pastoral is poetic and should remain so. As evidence of his preference for the crooked road to the straight, with its suggestions of things not seen, Flagg gives the example of the great rock jutting from a stormy sea. The promontory surrounded by perilous waters means nothing without a lighthouse containing a

single family, occupying themselves in some simple way constantly on the verge of death.

Flagg disdained artificiality in landscaping. L. A. Millington, in an article comparing Thoreau and Flagg, takes note of the latter's disgust for manicured lawns, garden statuary, and perfect hedge rows. Flagg devoted many essays to the discussion of the types of architecture that are appropriate to a country landscape and will add to rather than detract from the natural surroundings. From "Country Houses" published in 1854 to "Rural Architecture" (1876), Flagg pursued the study of rural dwellings and their place in the landscape. Flagg argues that in these essays his object is to demonstrate that the Romantic sublime can be found in scenes more common than "nature's monstrosities."

> We may sail round the globe in quest of scenes of grandeur and beauty; but we shall seek in vain for anything more beautiful than the rainbow, or more sublime than the sun emerging, as it were, from the ocean at sunrise, enshrouded in the dappled hues of morning.

That Flagg cherished nature is evident in all of his writings, but his philosophical musings are tempered by his New England practicality. It grieved him to describe those places where the trees and the forest inhabitants were gone, destroyed by human beings. In Flagg's later years (1879 to 1880), he contacted T. W. Higginson proposing that sites in Middlesex Fells be named a nature conservancy, and this remains in a preserved state today just outside Boston.

We see more of his conservationist tendencies in his volume *Birds and Seasons of New England.* This passage from "Plea for the Birds" shows Flagg at this most heated:

> Although birds are great favorites with man, there are no animals, if we except the vermin that infest our dwellings, that suffer such unremitted persecution. They are everywhere destroyed, either for the table or for the pleasure of the chase. As soon as a boy can shoulder a gun, he goes out, day after day, in his warfare of extermination against the feathered race.

He spares the birds at no season and in no situation. While thus employed, he is encouraged by older persons, as if he were ridding the earth of a pest. Thus do men promote the destruction of one of the blessed gifts of Nature.

Such highly inflamed rhetoric, cultivating the metaphorical language of warfare, is common in Flagg's conservation writings. Even early in his career he wrote several articles asking the general public to care for familiar bird species ("Spare the Birds" [1855] and "Plea for the Robin" [1858]).

In "Songs and Eccentricities of Birds," originally published in 1879, Flagg shows that he was also stirred to ire by the thoughtlessness of the general populace for its love affair with a particular creature—the English sparrow. Brought to the United States even though it is viewed as a pest in Europe, the bird was embraced by the public, and millions of bird boxes were built to accommodate them, while domestic species such as bluebirds, wrens, and martins were diminishing in numbers. Flagg becomes quite heated as he rails against a bird that he perceives to have little value for the American landscape. He complains about the proliferation of the English sparrow and predicts, in a letter to the *Boston Transcript* in 1892, that they will oust many other species. He submits a plea to the public to devise a way to rid Boston and its environs of the "evil," as he calls the sparrow.

Wilson Flagg writes that his object is to inspire his readers to a love of nature. He argues that the inroads of progress in creating a national wealth should not be confused with a subsequent increase of civilization. In his essay, W.G. Barton quotes Flagg as believing that happiness is oftener acquired "by habits of contentment and simplicity than by feverish ambition and ostentatious display." Often overshadowed by writers like Thoreau and Burroughs, Flagg's simple, quiet style and deep love of nature produced thoughtful essays on the plants, animals, and people of New England. Although his writing style relegates him to minor status, his

constant presence before and warm welcome by the reading public continued to nurture and broaden a readership for nature writing in America.

PRIMARY BIBLIOGRAPHY

Books

Analysis of Female Beauty (Boston: Marsh, Capen & Lyon; New York: B.F. Griffin, 1834).

Tailor's Shop, or, Crowns of Thorns and Coats of Thistles Designed to Tickle Some and Nettle Others: Intended Chiefly for Politicians (Boston: W.B. Kimball, 1844).

Studies in the Field and Forest (Boston: Little, Brown, 1857).

Prize Essay on Agricultural Education (Boston: J.H. Eastburn's Press, 1858).

Mount Auburn: Its Scenes, Its Beauties, and Its Lessons (Boston and Cambridge: J. Monroe and Co., 1861).

The Woods and By-Ways of New England (Boston: J.R. Osgood and Co., 1872).

The Birds and Seasons of New England (Boston: J.R. Osgood and Co., 1875; published as *A Year with the Birds; or, The Birds and Seasons of New England* [Boston: Estes and Lauriat, 1881]; published as *A Year with the Birds* [Boston: Educational Publishing Co., 1890]).

Halcyon Days (Boston: Estes and Lauriat, 1881).

A Year among the Trees; or, The Woods and By-Ways of New England (Boston: Estes and Lauriat, 1881; Boston: Educational Publishing Co., 1890).

Selected Periodical Publications— Uncollected

"The Art of Political Lying," *The Boston Pearl* 5.7 (October 31, 1835): 50–52.

"Journalism," *The Boston Pearl*, 5.9 (November 14, 1835): 65–67.

"The Plumage and Songs of Birds," *The Boston Magazine* 5.12 (December 5, 1835): 90–92.

"Season of the Wild Flowers of New England," *The Boston Weekly Magazine* 1.3 (September 22, 1838): 17.

"Immortality," *The Boston Weekly Magazine* 1.3 (September 22, 1838): 18.

"An Essay on the Law of Honor," *The Boston Weekly Magazine* 1.5 (October 6, 1838): 37–39.

"Essay on Political Honesty," *The Boston Weekly Magazine* 1.30 (March 30, 1839): 238.

[Thomas] Wilson Flagg

"Essay on Political Cant," *The Boston Weekly Magazine* 2.1 (September 7, 1839): 5.

"Oaths and Interjections," *The Boston Weekly Magazine* 2.19 (January 11, 1840): 146–47.

"Anatomy of Politics," *The Boston Weekly Magazine* 2.40 (June 20, 1840): 214–15.

"Distinctions Founded on Wealth," *The Boston Weekly Magazine* 2.46 (August 1, 1840): 361–62.

"Nobility of Families and Races," *The Boston Weekly Magazine* 3.2 (September 26, 1840): 13–14.

"On the Divisions of the Spoils," *The Boston Weekly Magazine* 3.8 (November 7, 1840): 60–61.

"On Prejudices Respecting Pedigrees among Americans," *The Boston Weekly Magazine* 3.13 (December 12, 1840): 100–101.

"Nature of Hereditary Honors," *The Boston Weekly Magazine* 3.42 (July 3, 1841): 333.

"Country Houses," *The United States Magazine of Science, Art, Manufactures, Agriculture, Commerce and Trade* 1.18 (May 15, 1854): 18–19.

"Spare the Birds," *Friends' Intelligencer* 11.50 (March 3, 1855): 800.

"Portraits from the Field and Farm-Yard: The Chickadee, or Black Cap Titmouse," *The New England Farmer* 8.1 (January 1856): 37.

"Portraits from the Field and Farm Yard: The Crow," *The New England Farmer* 8.2 (February 1856): 103–4.

"Portraits from the Field and Farm Yard: The Blue Jay," *The New England Farmer* 8.4 (April 1856): 192.

"On Certain Birds That Might Be Domesticated," *The New England Farmer* 8.6 (June 1856): 283–84.

"On the Relation of Trees to the Atmosphere and Climate," *The New England Farmer* 8.7 (July 1856): 299.

"Portraits from the Field and Farm Yard: The Owl," *The New England Farmer* 8.8 (August 1856): 374–75.

"Portraits from the Field and Farm Yard: The Wood-Thrush," *The New England Farmer* 8.12 (December 1856): 545–46.

"On The Relation of Trees to the Soil and the Atmosphere," *The New England Farmer* 9.4 (April 1857): 190–92.

"Clearing and Draining: Their Effect on the Atmosphere," *The New England Farmer* 9.6 (June 1857): 287–88.

"Electric Agency of Trees and Plants," *The New England Farmer* 9.7 (July 1857): 325–27.

"On the Planting of Trees," *The New England Farmer* 9.9 (September 1857): 436–37.

"Relation of Trees to the Soil," *The New England Farmer* 9.11 (November 1857): 503–5.

"Temperance and Cheerfulness," *The New England Farmer* 9.12 (December 1857): 565–66.

"On the Reality of the Science of Medicine," *The New England Farmer* 10.1 (January 1858): 47–48.

"Dr. Loring's Report—Science and Experience," *The New England Farmer* 10.3 (March 1858): 147–48.

"Plea for the Robin," *The New England Farmer* 10.5 (May 1858): 205–6.

"Is Farming Profitable?" *The New England Farmer* 10.7 (July 1858): 316–18.

"Another Plea for the Robin," *The New England Farmer* 10.12 (December 1858): 567–68.

"Agricultural Progress," *The New England Farmer* 11.1 (January 1859): 52–54.

"Agricultural Progress—Mammoth Farm Company," *The New England Farmer* 11.2 (February 1859): 87.

"Female Education," *The New England Farmer* 11.3 (March 1859): 126–28.

"Agricultural Market Fairs," *The New England Farmer* 11.8 (August 1859): 377–79.

"A Few Notes on Dwelling-Houses," *The New England Farmer* 11.9 (September 1859): 412–14.

"Notes on Popular Fallacies," *The New England Farmer* 11.11 (November 1859): 503–4.

"Tuberous Roots: Or the Most Important Tuberous Roots Used by Different People for Food," *The New England Farmer* 13.1 (January 1861): 29.

"Tuberous Roots: Or the Most Important Tuberous Roots Used by Different People for Food," *The New England Farmer* 13.2 (February 1861): 61–62.

"Mr. J.W. Mannings Nursery," *The New England Farmer* 13.7 (July 1861): 302–3.

"On the Keeping Properties of Eggs," *The New England Farmer* 14.8 (August 1862): 347–48.

SECONDARY BIBLIOGRAPHY

References

Kingsbury Badger, "Bradford Torrey: New England Nature Writer," *The New England Quarterly* 18.2 (June 1945): 234–46.

W.G. Barton, "Thoreau, Flagg, and Burroughs," *Essex Institute Historical Collections* (January–March 1885): 53–80.

Stanley W. Bromley, "The Original Forest Types of Southern New England," *Ecological Monographs* 5.1 (January 1935): 61–89.

Paul Brooks, *Speaking for Nature: How Literary Naturalists from Henry Thoreau to Rachel Carson Have Shaped America* (San Francisco: Sierra Club Books, 1980).

Lawrence Buell, "The Thoreauvian Pilgrimage: The Structure of an American Cult," *American Literature* 61.2 (May 1989): 175–99.

Wilson Flagg, "Letter to Mr. Higginson Concerning Preservation of Buttonwood Knoll in Middlesex Fells," 1880, Harvard Loeb Library.

Wilson Flagg. "Middlesex Fells Proposed as a Site for a Forest Conservatory, in a Letter Addressed to Colonel T.W. Higginson," 1879, Harvard Loeb Library.

T.W. Higginson, "The Life of Birds," *The Atlantic Monthly* 10.59 (1862): 368–77.

L.A. Millington, "Thoreau and Flagg," *Old and New* 11.4 (April 1975): 460–65.

Henry David Thoreau, *The Correspondence of Henry David Thoreau*, ed. Walter Harding and Carl Bode (Westport, CT: Greenwood Press, 1974).

Edwin P. Whipple, "American Literature," *Harpers* 52.310 (March 1876): 514–33.

Papers

The Frances Loeb Library at Harvard University houses a few of Flagg's letters.

John Charles Frémont
(January 21, 1813–July 13, 1890)
Jessie Benton Frémont
(May 31, 1824–December 27, 1902)

Kim Leeder

John Charles Frémont ("Frémont") and Jessie Benton Frémont ("Benton") were one of the most controversial and renowned literary pairs of the nineteenth century. Benton has never been formally acknowledged as a coauthor of Frémont's exploration reports, but their collaboration is now generally accepted as fact. The opening to Donald Jackson and Mary Lee Spence's collection of Frémont's work, for instance, notes that Benton had "an ability to write which would provide young Frémont with a lifelong amanuensis and ghost-writer." Together, Frémont and Benton crafted a number of books and reports, the most significant of which is the *Report of the Exploring Expedition to the Rocky Mountains in the Year 1842, and to Oregon and North California in the Years 1843–'44* (1845).

The *Report of the Exploring Expedition*, which captures the details of Frémont's first and second surveying expeditions in then-unmapped areas of the American West, is an engaging blend of science and drama that nineteenth-century American readers devoured as a travel guide, adventure story, and invitation to emigrate to the West. It is

more fluidly written than the journals of Lewis and Clark, was more popular in its time than Washington Irving's *Adventures of Captain Bonneville*, and has more factual value than James Fenimore Cooper's Leatherstocking novels. From an ecocritical perspective, the *Report of the Exploring Expedition* reflects an aesthetic appreciation of the American landscape that is exceptional for its genre. While the typical exploration narrative focuses upon the "useful" qualities of a new region (fertile soil for farming, hardwood forests for logging, etc.), the Frémonts expressed an early admiration for the sublime beauty of nature.

John Charles Frémont was born in Savannah, Georgia, on January 21, 1813. His parents were Charles Frémon (Frémont added the "t" in 1840), a French emigré and teacher, and Anne Beverly Whiting Pryor, wife of a distinguished Revolutionary War veteran. The two met in Richmond, Virginia, and eloped in 1811. As his family was a subject of scandal, much of Frémont's youth was spent moving from town to town in the southern states. Although he was a bright student, he proved to be an undisciplined one: he was expelled from the College of Charleston in 1830.

In his late teenage years, Frémont had the good fortune to befriend a well-known diplomat and politician, Joel Roberts Poinsett. In 1833 Poinsett aided Frémont in obtaining a commission as a math teacher on the sloop of war *Natchez,* which sailed throughout South America and gave the 20-year-old his first taste of military travel. Meanwhile, Poinsett was appointed Secretary of War in 1836 by President Martin Van Buren. This position put Poinsett at the head of the U.S. Army's Bureau of Topographical Engineers, the agency most involved in exploring the young nation's territories. A year later, Poinsett used his new powers to secure Frémont a position on a railroad survey from Charleston to Cincinnatti. Frémont greatly enjoyed the job, which he described in his *Memoirs* as "cheery, wholesome work. The summer weather in the mountains was fine, the cool water abundant, and the streams lined with azaleas.[. . .] The survey was a kind of picnic with work enough to give it zest." The next year, the leader of this survey invited Frémont on another survey, a military reconnaissance of Cherokee Indian lands in Tennessee, North Carolina, and Georgia. These two Appalachian surveys whetted Frémont's appetite for outdoor government survey work and set him on what he called "the path he was destined to walk."

Frémont's next appointments in 1838 and 1839 were two mapmaking surveys of the Upper Mississippi and Upper Missouri basins as an assistant to French surveyor and cartographer Joseph N. Nicollet. The young surveyor's first taste of true frontier life was yet more evidence that the young man had found his true calling. By the time Nicollet and Frémont completed the two surveys and returned to Washington, D.C., Frémont had gained a thorough education not only in surveying, astronomy, geography, and other scientific skills, but in practical matters such as how to foster diplomatic relationships with Indian groups, and how to organize and run a survey.

In 1841, Frémont met Jessie Ann Benton, daughter of senator Thomas Hart Benton and Elizabeth McDowell Benton. Jessie Benton was born on May 31, 1824, and unlike Frémont, her childhood had been one of privilege and affluence. During her youth, Benton's family lived chiefly in Washington, but spent their time between sessions of Congress visiting their estate in Cherry Grove, Virginia, and their third home in the frontier town of St. Louis. As she grew up, she often accompanied her father to Congress and the White House, and became acquainted early with the intricacies of politics. Along with her sisters, Benton received a liberal education in history, geography, writing, languages, and other subjects.

By 1838, Benton had already received marriage proposals, so her parents sent her to a prominent Georgetown boarding school. When romance flared between Frémont and Benton, her parents (who disapproved of the match) quickly acted to have Frémont sent out of Washington. To his surprise and pleasure, Frémont was commissioned to lead a minor survey of the Des Moines River in Iowa. The parents' plan, however, was not successful: once Frémont completed the survey, he and Benton eloped and married on October 19, 1841. Soon after their marriage, Frémont—with some help from Benton—published his report of the Des Moines River survey, *Northern Boundary of Missouri* (1842). Concise and unadorned, this report lacked the color and drama that the later reports would possess, and it attracted none of the attention. In her biography *Jessie Benton Frémont*, Pamela Herr reads this report as an indicator of things to come:

> Brief and factual in tone, it nonetheless had flashes of charm and interest unusual in a government document, qualities that foreshadowed the Frémonts' later collaborations. Amid data on vegetation, rock structure, and river depth was a fleeting picture of a road "fragrant with white elder" and a vivid glimpse of an Indian encampment by a river.

With his connection in Washington now firmly established, Frémont was commissioned in 1842 to lead his first of five major expeditions in the West. His orders were to survey a well-used but uncharted emigrant road from the Missouri River across parts of Kansas, Nebraska, and Wyoming, and as far west as South Pass in the Rockies. Once he had reached South Pass and the Continental Divide, however, Frémont could not resist the lure of the mountains. He veered from his orders and directed his group northwest along the Wind River Range's western slope and into the higher elevations. Climbing what Frémont mistakenly believed to be the Rockies' highest mountain, he led a small party on a difficult, rocky trek to the top of a peak which they measured at 13,500 feet. Most historians believe that the mountain they climbed is today's Frémont Peak in Wyoming, but like the exact course of any of Frémont's expeditions, this is only conjecture.

Late in 1841, Frémont returned to Washington, where he and Benton were reunited. In October 1842, Benton gave birth to their first child, Elizabeth "Lily" Benton. Frémont and Benton then set to work on the report of his travels: Frémont relating his stories aloud and Benton taking dictation, asking questions, and shaping the report. A highly educated and creative woman, Benton considered writing with Frémont as her "most happy life work." She had long listened avidly to tales from other travelers in the Western territories, and had a resulting familiarity with the content that, in combination with her natural literary skills, made her an ideal coauthor. The two completed the report in 1843, at which time it was presented to Congress and promptly printed as *A Report on an Exploration of the Country Lying between the Missouri River and the Rocky Mountains on the Line of the Kansas and Great Platte Rivers.*

Upon its publication, the report was an instant best seller. Frémont's factual experiences and Benton's dramatic flair created an irresistible combination of science and adventure that captured readers' imaginations. Complete with maps, sketches, illustrations, and scientific data about formerly unknown areas, the report replaced mythology with facts about the Western landscape. It began to make the West a real place, accessible to average Americans. And, especially in concert with the report of the Second Expedition, it served as a major spark in the conflagration of westward emigration.

Frémont's Second Expedition, which began in the spring of 1843, was intended to determine a more southern route across the Rockies, to explore parts of Oregon, and to determine the nature of the area between the Rockies and California. For most of its passage to the Pacific, this survey followed what is now known as the Oregon Trail, with a detour to the Great Salt Lake in Utah. At the Pacific coast, Frémont's party abandoned the emigrant road and headed south through rougher terrain, crossed the snowy Sierra Nevada mountains with difficulty at Carson Pass (in the first recorded winter crossing of this range), and journeyed south nearly to Los Angeles before returning across the Great Basin in a northeasterly direction. The expedition was eventful and replete with challenges and difficulties that Frémont and Benton would detail in the next report. Most significant was the discovery that the famed San Buenaventura River, which was widely believed to cross the continent and provide a water route between the eastern states and the Pacific Ocean, was truly a myth. It was also during this expedition that Frémont coined the term "Great Basin" to describe the region lying between the Rocky and Sierra Nevada mountain ranges.

After the 15-month expedition, Frémont and Benton set to work on the report, which was presented to Congress in March 1845. Pleased with the results, the U.S. Senate ordered the reports of Frémont's First and Second Expeditions combined in a printing that was released later that year as *Report of the Exploring Expedition to the Rocky Mountains in the Year 1842, and to Oregon and North California in the Years 1843–'44.* The volume was reviewed with enthusiasm, reprinted in newspapers throughout the country, and sold out in multiple printings. In his definitive biography of Frémont, *Pathfinder*, Tom Chaffin explains,

> What was new in Frémont's reports was their scientific maps and measurements, and their literary voice, transcending the prosaic flatness of previous Western tour books. In their eloquence, their geographic breadth, their attention to the sublime, and their reimagining of the American landscape, his narratives offered a fresh voice in American literature.

Indeed, the *Report of the Exploring Expedition* would influence such writers as Henry David Thoreau (*Walden*), Walt Whitman ("Passage to India"), and Henry Wadsworth Longfellow (journals, and *Evangeline*).

In this report, as in the previous one, Frémont and Benton's complementary mix of science and drama gives life to the expeditions without sacrificing information. The famous "bee scene" on the summit of the highest peak in the Rockies attained by Frémont is a perfect example of Frémont and Benton's literary collaboration:

> Here, on the summit, where the stillness was absolute, unbroken by any sound, and the solitude complete, we thought ourselves beyond the region of animated life; but while we were sitting on the rock, a solitary bee (*bromus, the humble bee*) came winging his flight from the eastern valley, and lit on the knee of one of the men. It was a strange place, the icy rock and the highest peak of the Rocky mountains, for a lover of warm sunshine and flowers; and we pleased ourselves with the idea that he was the first of his species to cross the mountain barrier—a solitary pioneer to foretell the advance of civilization.

As Chaffin points out, Frémont and Benton were very likely drawing on previous literature in their use of the bee as a pioneering symbol. The same device had been used in William Cullen Bryant's "The Prairies," as well as in Washington Irving's *Tour on the Prairies*.

Frémont's Third Expedition began in the summer of 1845, and brought the explorer across the continent yet again to California, this time via Colorado, Utah, and Nevada. His party crossed the Rockies west of present-day Denver, pausing at the Great Salt Lake, and crossed through Utah, through Nevada, and into California on a route that roughly equates to today's Interstate 80. The expedition crossed the Sierra Nevada mountains at the pass that would later be named for the ill-fated Donner Party.

Frémont determined to spend the winter in California before returning east. However, California was still a Mexican territory, and hostilities toward the U.S. presence in the area were rising. Frémont became embroiled in revolts among the American settlers and, when California was taken by the United States in 1846, was absorbed into the military. It was at this point that Frémont made a grave mistake by aligning himself with Commodore Robert Stockton, one of two military leaders who competed for power in the new territory. Commodore Stockton and Brigadier General Stephen Watts Kearny both believed themselves to have orders from Washington that gave them authority in California. Stockton appointed Frémont governor of California, and the explorer accepted the position despite warnings from Kearny. In 1847, formal orders finally arrived from Washington giving Kearny full authority in California. Frémont was ordered back to Washington and charged in a federal court-martial under the counts of mutiny, refusing a lawful command from a superior officer, and conduct prejudicial to military discipline. Frémont was declared guilty on all charges and dismissed from the army.

Despite the verdict, the U.S. Senate still asked Frémont to complete an account of his Third Expedition. He and Benton resumed their normal collaboration, but a difficult pregnancy and resulting sickly child forced Benton to abandon the project and concentrate on the health of herself and their young son, named Benton. Left alone in his work, and lacking any real talent for or interest in writing, Frémont was unable to capture the vivid, evocative style that his wife had brought to their previous books. The final report of the Third Expedition was published as *Geographical Memoir upon Upper California, in Illustration of His Map of Oregon and California* (1848).

In October 1848, Frémont embarked on yet another survey, this time privately funded by a group of St, Louis businessmen who were eager to have a stake in the building of a continental railroad. Frémont's goal was to find a pass at the 38th parallel through the Rocky Mountains that could be crossed at any time of year. Reaching the mountain range in December, Frémont's party persisted, suffered, and eventually fell apart and retreated from the bitter cold and snow. Ten members of the 32 member party died in the attempt. Finally abandoning the mountain crossing, Frémont took the remnants of his party south through present-day New Mexico and Arizona to California. Hearing news that gold had been discovered, he hurried to a 70-acre tract in the Central Valley that he had bought a few years earlier.

In the winter of 1848–1849, Benton traveled by steamship and met Frémont in San Francisco. Renting a wing of a house in Monterey, they settled for the first time into a domestic life together. Gold was discovered on their property, dubbed *Las Mariposas,* and they set to work collecting the bounty that would make them wealthy for a time. Frémont became involved in the creation of the California constitution and was elected senator for a brief stint in the U.S. Congress in 1850, just as California became a state. He and Benton had their second and third children, John Charles II and Anne Beverly, in 1851 and 1853.

The explorer organized his fifth and last expedition largely because he was determined to redeem the failed Fourth Expedition. During the winter of 1853–1854, the grim Frémont and a small band of men managed to cross the San Juan Mountains in central Colorado. He achieved his goal of proving that the snowy mountains at the 38th parallel were crossable year-round, but his achievement had no impact upon westward development.

Frémont and Benton wandered between the East coast, West coast, and Europe during the 1850s. The year 1854 saw the birth of their fifth and last child, Francis Preston. In 1856 Frémont ran for U.S. President as the first candidate for the newly formed Republican Party, but lost to James Buchanan. In 1861, when the Civil War broke out, Frémont was appointed to a high-ranking position as commander of the U.S. Army Department of the West, but was dismissed when he issued an emancipation order that President Abraham Lincoln had not approved. Assigned next to a lesser position in Virginia, Frémont led an untrained group of soldiers against the infamous Thomas J. "Stonewall" Jackson. Beaten, outwitted, and frustrated by the situation, Frémont resigned from the army in 1862.

For the next few years, Frémont became involved in railroad speculation. His association with the Memphis, El Paso, and Pacific line and related investments in France led to his conviction on the charge of fraud in the French courts. The railroad line slid into bankruptcy, and the fortune the Frémonts had made from the gold mining on their California property dwindled away. As Frémont's career plummeted, Benton's began to rise: in 1863, she made the leap to publish her first independently written book, *The Story of the Guard: A Chronicle of the War*. The book is a collage of reflections, letters from Frémont and other players, and commentary on the Civil War. Meandering and simple in language, it is the first of several of Benton's writings whose main purpose was to defend her husband's character—in this case, his actions during the war.

The Story of the Guard was somewhat stilted and apologetic as Benton sought to navigate the newly opened road of female authorship. Meeting with reasonable success in her first effort, however, Benton began to pursue writing as a creative outlet for herself and as a means of supporting her family. In 1873, she arranged to publish a series of character sketches for the *New York Ledger* under the column title "Distinguished Persons I Have Known." Her weekly column described high-profile individuals of the time, including Andrew Jackson, Kit Carson, and Hans Christian Anderson.

In subsequent years, Benton wrote extensively about her experiences and travels in the United States and abroad. A collection of her writing was printed as a three-part series in *Harper's* magazine in 1877–1878 under the title "A Year of American Travel," and was followed up in book format under the same title in 1878. Benton's third book, essentially an early guide to colleges, was published in 1884 as *How to Learn and Earn.* In 1885, Frémont and Benton found a publisher interested in financing the production of Frémont's memoirs. The couple rallied and set to work, piecing together remnants of their earlier texts and filling in the details. The first volume of *Memoirs of My Life* was published in three parts in 1886, but received little enough attention that Belford, Clarke & Company cancelled plans for a second volume. Not allowing herself to be discouraged, Benton continued to actively write and publish independently authored magazine articles in *Harper's* and *Century,* as well as in the short-lived *Wide Awake* and *Land of Sunshine* magazines (the latter was retitled *Out West* and *Overland Journal*). A fourth book of Benton's stories, *Souvenirs of My Time,* was published in 1887.

Frémont—sometimes with his family, sometimes without them—continued to wander from coast to coast, and from business venture to business venture. He served as governor of the Arizona Territory from 1878 to 1881, but met with little success in the position. His investments tended toward failure, and his family's finances suffered. During a trip to New York City, in July 1890, he fell ill and died.

Shortly after Frémont's death, Benton completed and published an article that he had begun writing for *Century Magazine,* "The Origin of the Frémont Explorations." Benton continued to write articles and published two more collections of her work: *Far-West Sketches* (1890), which gathered together some of Benton's colorful stories about life in frontier California that had previously been published in *Wide Awake* between 1888 and 1889, and *The Will and the Way Stories* (1891).

Benton remained in Los Angeles until her death in 1902. *Mother Lode Narratives,* which included stories from *Far-West Sketches* and added a number of Benton's previously unpublished letters from California, was published posthumously in 1970.

To date, the legacy of the Frémont exploration narratives has been largely overlooked in literary studies. This may be due in part to the fact that Frémont's expeditions were not "first contact" forays, since he often followed established emigrant trails instead of plunging into unknown wildernesses. The journals of Lewis and Clark, which preceded the first Frémont report by about 30 years, have been read and studied far more widely than the *Report of the Exploring Expedition to the Rocky Mountains in the Year 1842, and to Oregon and North California in the Years 1843–'44.* Yet the latter is more lucidly written and more scientifically detailed, meriting attention as a literary and historical document. Benton's articles and books have been equally disregarded, fading into the bustle of nineteenth-century settlers' stories. Though recognized in the field of history, the writings of John Charles and Jessie Benton Frémont deserve and will reward further study from a literary and ecocritical perspective. For in the realm of literature, the Frémonts' texts remain uncharted territory.

PRIMARY BIBLIOGRAPHY

Books

John Charles Frémont
Northern Boundary of Missouri, 27th Congress, 3rd session, serial 420, House document 38 (Washington: Printed by order of the U.S. Congress, 1842).
A *Report on an Exploration of the Country Lying between the Missouri River and the Rocky Mountains on the Line of the Kansas and Great Platte Rivers,* 27th Congress, 3rd session, serial 416, Senate document 243 (Washington: Printed by order of the U.S. Senate, 1843).

Report of the Exploring Expedition to the Rocky Mountains in the Year 1842, and to Oregon and North California in the Years 1843–'44, 28th Congress, 2nd session, serial 461, Senate executive document 174 (Washington: Gales & Seaton, 1845); 28th Congress, House executive document 106 (Washington: Blair & Rives, 1845).

Geographical Memoir upon Upper California, in Illustration of His Map of Oregon and California, 30th Congress, 1st session, serial 511, Senate miscellaneous document 148 (Washington: Wendell & Van Benthuysen, 1848); 30th Congress, 2nd session, House miscellaneous document 5 (Washington: Tippin & Streeper, 1849).

Memoirs of My Life (Chicago and New York: Belford, Clarke, 1886).

Jessie Benton Frémont

The Story of the Guard: A Chronicle of the War (Boston: Ticknor & Fields, 1863).

A Year of American Travel (New York: Harper, 1878).

How to Learn and Earn; or, Half Hours in Some Helpful Schools, by Benton Frémont, Ella Farman Pratt, Mrs. John Lillie, E.E. Brown, et al. (Boston: D. Lothrop, 1884).

Souvenirs of My Time (Boston: D. Lothrop, 1887).

Far-West Sketches (Boston: D. Lothrop, 1890).

The Will and the Way Stories (Boston: D. Lothrop, 1891).

Mother Lode Narratives, ed. Shirley Sargent (Ashland, OR: L. Osborne, 1970).

Collections

John Charles Frémont

The Expeditions of John Charles Frémont, 3 vols., ed. Donald Jackson and Mary Lee Spence (Urbana, Chicago, and London: University of Illinois Press, 1970, 1973, 1984).

Jessie Benton Frémont

The Letters of Jessie Benton Frémont, ed. Pamela Herr and Mary Lee Spence (Urbana and Chicago: University of Illinois Press, 1993).

Other

John Charles Frémont

"In Command in Missouri," in *Battles and Leaders of the Civil War*, vol. 1, ed. Robert U. Johnson and Clarence C. Buel (New York: Century, 1887).

"Proclamation on Slaves," in *Essential Documents in American History 1492–Present* (Great Neck, NY: Great Neck Publishing, 1997).

Jessie Benton Frémont

"Biographical Sketch of Senator Benton in Connection with Western Expansion," in *Memoirs of My Life*, by John Charles Frémont (Chicago and New York: Belford, Clarke, 1886), 1–17.

Selected Periodical Publications— Uncollected

John Charles Frémont

"The Conquest of California," *Century Magazine* 41 (April 1891): 917–928.

Jessie Benton Frémont

"Distinguished Persons I Have Known," *New York Ledger*, January 2, 9, 16, 23, 30, 1875; February 6, 13, 20, 1875; March 6, 27, 1875; April 3, 17, 1875.

"A Year of American Travel," parts 1–3, *Harper's New Monthly Magazine* 55 (November 1877): 905–916; 56 (December 1877): 84–96; 57 (January 1878): 272–284.

"The Origin of the Frémont Explorations," *Century Magazine* 41 (March 1891): 766–771.

SECONDARY BIBLIOGRAPHY

Biographies

John Charles Frémont

John Bigelow, *Memoir of the Life and Public Services of John Charles Frémont* (New York: Derby & Jackson, 1856).

Tom Chaffin, *Pathfinder: John Charles Frémont and the Course of American Empire* (New York: Hill and Wang, 2002).

Frederick S. Dellenbaugh, *Frémont and '49, The Story of a Remarkable Career and its Relation to the Exploration and Development of our Western Territory, Especially of California* (New York and London: G.P. Putnam's Sons, 1914).

Ferol Egan, *Frémont, Explorer for a Restless Nation* (Garden City: Doubleday, 1977).

Cardinal Goodwin, *John Charles Frémont: An Explanation of His Career* (Palo Alto, CA: Stanford University Press, 1930).

Allan Nevins, *Frémont, The West's Greatest Adventurer*, 2 vols. (New York and London: Harper & Brothers, 1928).

Allan Nevins, *Frémont, Pathmarker of the West* (New York: Appleton Century, 1939).

Andrew Rolle, *John Charles Frémont: Character as Destiny* (Norman: University of Oklahoma Press, 1991).

Samuel M. Smucker, *The Life of Col. John Charles Frémont and His Narrative of Explorations and Adventures in Kansas, Nebraska, Oregon and California* (New York and Auburn: Miller, Orton & Mulligan, 1856).

Charles W. Upham, *Life, Explorations and Public Service of John C. Frémont* (Boston: Ticknor & Fields, 1856).

Jessie Benton Frémont

Pamela Herr, *Jessie Benton Frémont* (New York: Franklin Watts, 1987).

Catherine Coffin Phillips, *Jessie Benton Frémont: A Woman Who Made History* (San Francisco: John Henry Nash, 1935).

Ruth Painter Randall, *I, Jessie: A Biography of the Girl Who Married John Charles Frémont, Famous Explorer of the West* (Boston and Toronto: Little, Brown and Company, 1963).

Papers

Collections of John Charles Frémont and Jessie Benton Frémont's manuscripts and correspondence are in the Huntington Library; the James S. Copley Library (La Jolla, California); the Missouri Botanical Garden Library (St. Louis); the New York Historical Society; the New York Public Library; the Southwest Museum (Los Angeles); the University of California, Berkeley, Bancroft Library; and the William R. Perkins Library, Duke University.

William Hamilton Gibson
(October 5, 1850–July 16, 1896)

Daniel Patterson

In the last quarter of the nineteenth century, in a period of only some 20 years, William Hamilton Gibson produced a significant and large body of illustrated nature essays that have received surprisingly little attention in the century that has passed since. At the end of his life, Gibson was praised for his ability to render his scientific knowledge of the natural world in beautiful illustrations and essays. His contemporaries ranked him in importance and excellence with Henry David Thoreau and John Burroughs.

William Hamilton Gibson was born among the lower Berkshire hills of western Connecticut in the village of Sandy Hook to Elizabeth Charlotte (Sanford) Gibson and Edmund Trowbridge Hastings Gibson on October 5, 1850. His mother was from Brooklyn; his father, from Boston. Gibson was a descendant of Francis Dana (1743–1811), a former chief justice of the Massachusetts Supreme Court, and Richard Henry Dana, Sr. (1787–1879), whose son would achieve fame as the author of *Two Years before the Mast* (1840). Gibson was also descended from John Gibson (1601–circa 1694), who was born in England but came to Cambridge, Massachusetts, before 1634. Through the Hastings line of his family, he counted the famous John Cotton of Boston among his ancestors. The artist-naturalist was thus of New England "blue blood," or, as he wrote about himself, "I am a way-back Puritan." He was prouder of the Danas and the Trowbridges and their more patrician culture.

His father worked as a stockbroker in New York, and Gibson was able to attend the private boarding school known as "the Gunnery" in nearby Washington, Connecticut. He later attended the Brooklyn Polytechnic Institute. He did not distinguish himself as a student, but his passion for nature study and drawing were evident very early. When he was 17, while recovering from an illness, he wrote a letter to a friend that reveals his interest in nature and shows a clear affinity for a Thoreau-like ability to focus on the other-than-human:

> You ask me what I do all day. This question is very easily answered. It is the same thing over and over again day after day. The great part of the time I spend in the woods alone. I start off about ten o'clock in the morning and ramble through the woods and thickets....Oh, I do not believe I could be happy if this pleasure were taken away from me. I am always happy alone in the woods. I dare say I am destined to spend half my life in just such places. This is the daily program of the way I spend my time. Silly isn't it? But I can't help it. It is my nature to enjoy nature, and I mean to do it at every opportunity.

Nevertheless, he was known throughout his life for his gregarious and affable personality.

Despite his father's hopes that his son would become a stockbroker like himself, Gibson found a way to develop his talent for drawing and to satisfy his desire to study nature. When his father died in 1868, Gibson had to earn a living. Without much enthusiasm, he became an insurance agent in Brooklyn, but soon his passion for drawing led him to run the risk of setting himself up as an artist. He apparently did not lack for self-confidence, and his success was not long in the making. Some of his earliest professional drawings appeared in *Frank Leslie's Boys' and Girls' Weekly* and *Frank Leslie's Chimney Corner*. He sold botanical sketches to the *American Agriculturist* and to Appletons' *American Cyclopaedia*. In addition to early illustrations published in *Hearth and Home,* he picked up odd jobs from several lithographers doing a variety of graphic work. A major development for Gibson's career occurred between 1872 and 1874 while the installments of D. Appletons' *Picturesque America* were being published and 15 of Gibson's engraved illustrations were included. When this two-volume work was completed, it was hailed as "the most magnificent illustrated work ever published," cost Appleton $250,000 to produce, and sold almost a million copies. It contained hundreds of illustrations and placed Gibson's name among those of the leading illustrators of the day. William Cullen Bryant was the volume editor. Thus, by the mid-1870s, Gibson's reputation as a professional artist was established, as was his studio in Brooklyn with views of city, park, bays, and distant highlands in New Jersey. During this time he also married. On October 29, 1873, Emma Ludlow Blanchard of Brooklyn, daughter of Charles A.S. Blanchard, married Gibson. Henry Ward Beecher conducted the ceremony. The Gibsons began a pattern of living through the winters in Brooklyn while Gibson developed material he had gathered and begun to work on during the milder seasons in their home on a hill near Washington, Connecticut, as well as in other scenic New England settings. Their Connecticut home was known as "The Sumacs."

Gibson's first book, *The Complete American Trapper; or, the Tricks of Trapping and Trap Making* (1876), and its later expansion as *Camp Life in the Woods and the Tricks of Trapping and Trap Making* (1881) are designed as practical volumes of well-illustrated instructions for "American boys" in how to trap animals of all sorts and how to camp out in the woods. The prose style matches the practical intent of the volume, but Gibson does hope to impress his American boy readers with the idea that

> Trapping does not consist merely in the manufacture and setting of the various traps. The study of the habits and peculiarities of the different game here becomes a matter of great importance; and the study of natural history under these circumstances affords a continual source of pleasure and profit.

He expresses a wish that he could omit a discussion of steel traps altogether because of their cruelty, but because he wants his book to be complete and because steel traps are so widely used, he does include them. Nevertheless, in his first books, Gibson positioned himself to become a popularizer of nature study, which was his own boyhood passion. Already he had moved beyond an identity as mere illustrator.

In the fall of 1878 his reputation as an illustrator received a significant boost from a particularly masterful drawing of peacock feathers entitled "The Peerless Plume," which adorned and framed the opening page for "Birds and Plumage," an article conceived and suggested by Gibson but written by Helen S. Conant (*Harper's New Monthly Magazine* 57 [August 1878]: 385–403). "The Peerless Plume" received extravagant praise and brought Gibson to the very front rank of American illustrators. Charles Eliot Norton, the highly influential cultural critic and professor of Fine Art at Harvard, was moved by the plume to write Gibson a personal letter of praise and gratitude:

> It is not merely subtle and refined execution which is shown in the piece, but a poetic

feeling for the quality and charm of the feather itself and for its value in composition. Your feather ought to be as well known as Rembrandt's shell or Hollar's furs.

Between August 1879 and November 1880, Gibson published a remarkable series of illustrated narratives of the four New England seasons in *Harper's New Monthly Magazine*. Shortly thereafter they were published as *Pastoral Days; or, Memories of a New England Year*. Gibson had not intended to become an author in addition to being an artist and a naturalist; in fact, when he had proposed to write the article that became "Birds and Plumage," he was turned down. In a letter to a friend, Gibson describes the rather accidental manner by which he began to write:

> I had never yet had the remotest idea of becoming a writer. The way in which I happened to take up more serious writing was through a suggestion of Mr. Henry M. Alden, the editor of Harper's Magazine. I returned one summer from a vacation spent in Washington, Connecticut, and was describing to him my school-life, telling him little episodes which had been recalled by my visit to Mr. Gunn. Mr. Alden seemed interested, and when I was done, said to me, "I want you to write that out for the magazine."

The essay he wrote and illustrated was published as "Snug Hamlet," but later became the "Summer" section of *Pastoral Days*. When it was favorably received,

> Mr. Alden suggested that I prepare an article to go with it, which, as this had to do with summer, should treat of winter. This, too, was written, "The Winter Idyl." Then followed others upon spring and autumn. With these four sketches I had enough for a book; and "Pastoral Days" was the result, which proved a great success.

His success as a writer surprised both him and his friends.

Pastoral Days is a large-format, expensive gift book published for "the holidays" in 1881. (The 1880 Chatto and Windus London edition probably appeared at approximately the same time as the first American edition.) Gibson was well known as an illustrator by this time, and he was developing as a writer. The pains taken to design and the expense of publishing this volume show that Harper and Brothers had reason to expect upper-middle-class readers to purchase it. The gilt-edged pages measure 9 inches by 11-5/8 inches; the spine is embossed in gold, and the front cover bears an elaborate embossed title and floral illustration in green, red, and gold. On 153 pages there are 76 illustrations, the title and engraver of each one of which Gibson gives in a list of illustrations in the front matter. One of the engravers was Henry Marsh, whose engravings had inspired Gibson in his youth.

With *Pastoral Days*, Gibson's development from illustrator-for-hire to literary naturalist-illustrator is practically complete. The major innovation of this volume is the degree to which text and illustration are integrated. The illustrations do not simply help tell the story; they are not subordinate to the prose. Gibson's engraved drawings are inextricable from the prose—sometimes even graphically, that is, literally so. For example, in the spring section of *Pastoral Days*, the next-to-last page bears a full-page engraving of blue flags (a kind of wild iris) growing beside water on which a few lily pads are visible; standing amidst the blue flags is a graphic page on which a few lines of Gibson's text are printed. Thus, this page of Gibson's book contains an illustration of irises growing around a page of text. It is a display of draftsman's wit, perhaps, but it shows the extent to which Gibson wanted to integrate his visual art with his verbal art. In the history of American nature writing before 1900, this stylistic mannerism is uniquely his.

The four essays comprising *Pastoral Days* describe the sequence of natural phenomena that mark the passing of the seasons in New England. This sequence of phenomena Gibson shapes into a procession of nostalgic tableaux of New England rural life set amongst the native flora and fauna. Several autobiographical episodes are included as well. While the seasonal changes in dozens of species are woven into a pastoral landscape, there is little natural history and even less encouragement to nature study. These developments in Gibson's writings would come along shortly after *Pastoral Days*, about which one reviewer wrote with justice: "The grace and sweetness of the pictures and the pensive gentleness of the text cloy the palate a little, but there are too many attractions in the book to let it be easily laid aside" (*Atlantic Monthly* 47 [February 1881]: 301). With less reserve, Gibson's biographer writes of the engravings in *Pastoral Days*,

> The simple truth about it is that it really touched the high-water mark in the history of nature-illustration by means of wood-engraving. It was everywhere hailed as exhibiting the very best work of its kind ever achieved.

With *Highways and Byways; or, Saunterings in New England* (1882), Gibson fully assumes his role of literary naturalist and writes to encourage nature study and to teach his readers how to see wonders in the familiar and local, and his artist's eye gives his writing a clear distinctiveness. Not even Audubon wrote about nature from so painterly a perspective. Among the many phenomena observable to New England saunterers that Gibson treats in this collection of four essays is the role that the New England fences play in the lives of, not only humans, but also of many species of plants, animals, and lichens. He brings out the picturesque beauty of the typical "Yankeeland" fences, but by including in his accounts the interactions of many mammals, birds, flowers, and insects with the fences, Gibson's picturesque is not static but dynamic. One might think of it as an ecological picturesque.

In coaching his readers to pay closer attention to their local environment, Gibson demonstrates that even the fences themselves reward closer investigation, as this characteristically visual description of the New England zigzag rail fence shows:

The careless abandon of its lines—a repetition of form in which absolute repetition is continually defied by the capricious convolution of the woody grain, for there are not two rails made in the same mould—and their gray, satiny sheen, their weather-beaten stains of moss and lichen, and the ever-changing play of lights and shadows from their waving weeds and vines, make the old rail-fence truly an object of beauty in our landscape. Often have I lingered in its angles, and a hundred times have I thought of the host of pictures and reminiscences which might fill a book to the glory of a fence corner.

He continually distinguishes himself from other nature writers by teaching his readers to see the phenomena of their physical environment as a painter sees them.

In the final essay of this volume, "Among Our Footprints," he opens by agreeing with Thoreau's experience of "having met with but one or two persons in the course of my life who understood the art of walking." Gibson notes that even among many who claim to love nature and "taking walks," many of them do so in a frame of mind that keeps them from a just appreciation of the environment they walk through: "It would almost seem as though some folks carry their eyes in their pockets whenever brought face to face with Nature." A heightened awareness of ecological relationships can lead the trained eye from one easily observed phenomenon to another more difficult to observe. As one example, Gibson narrates a walk during which a large beetle "almost tipped my ear with his buzzing wings, and finally alighted near a clump of yarrow close by." He then cites the common question, "What becomes of all the dead birds?" and cryptically offers the buzz of the beetle's wings as the answer. He follows the easily observed beetle to the yarrow: "Beneath that clump of yarrow I found just what I had expected—a small dead bird—and the grave-diggers were in the midst of their work." He explains that several beetles were consuming the bird's body and thereby facilitating the natural process of returning flesh to soil. Gibson includes a drawing of a dead bird on its back, its two delicate feet curling upward from its feathers, and several beetles probing into the feathers from various angles while two beetles on the wing in the background are flying in to join the group in the foreground consuming the bird. This illustration would have run counter to his mollifying, nostalgic purposes in *Pastoral Days*, but with *Highways and Byways* Gibson assumes his role as insightful naturalist with greater confidence and, with a barb or two borrowed from the contrarian Thoreau, teaches his readers what he thinks they need to know.

Gibson's career was brief, but its development continued unabated. His first child, a son named Hamilton, was born in May 1883. A second son, Dana Gibson, was born in 1888. Throughout, Gibson continued his nature study and drawing as well as his practice of publishing illustrated essays in magazines and later gathering them into some of the most handsome books being published in this country in the 1880s and 1890s. In rapid succession he produced *Happy Hunting-Grounds; A Tribute to the Woods and Fields* (1886), *Strolls by Starlight and Sunshine* (1891), and *Sharp Eyes; A Rambler's Calendar of Fifty-two Weeks among Insects, Birds, and Flowers* (1891). The discernible development in his work in the 1890s is his deepening interest in representing ecological relationships. The human presence in his work steadily decreases as his knowledge of ecology increases over the years. All of his later books reflect this new focus of his work as a literary naturalist: *Our Edible Toadstools and Mushrooms and How to Distinguish Them* (1895), *Eye Spy; Afield with Nature among Flowers and Animate Things* (1897), *My Studio Neighbors* (1898), and *Blossom Hosts and Insect Guests* (1897).

In an interview conducted a year before his death and reported by Barnet Phillips, Gibson recounts some important childhood experiences, perceptions, and influences. From his earliest days, he perceived an interdependent relationship between flowers and insects: "From my baby days I was curious about flowers and insects. The two were always united in my mind." Gibson attributed his fascination with the natural world to a childhood experience of finding a chrysalis in a forest: "There was nothing remarkable in that, for I knew what it was. But, wonderful to relate—providentially I deem it—as I held the object in my hand a butterfly slowly emerged, then fluttered in my fingers." Gibson also recalls that even as a child he linked natural phenomena to spiritual insights:

> suddenly the spiritual view of a new or of another life struck me. I saw in this jewel born from an unadorned casket some inkling of immortality. Yes, that butterfly breaking from its chrysalis in my hand shaped my future career.

His eye and hand as an illustrator were trained by his "most methodical" grandmother, who required him to sew patchwork for quilts: "Sewing must have helped me, for it was eye-training, and when I went to work with a pencil and a paint-brush I really had no trouble." As influential childhood reading, he names the novels of James Fenimore Cooper and Jacob Abbott's Rollo books, but he was especially influenced by "Harris on Insects," that is, *A Treatise on Some of the Insects Injurious to Vegetation*, by Thaddeus William Harris (1862):

> I studied that over and over again. It was the illustrations of Marsh which fascinated me. I never found a bug, caterpillar, or butterfly that I did not compare my specimens with the Marsh pictures. I learned this way much which I have never forgotten.

Henry Marsh was a zoological illustrator whose white-line engravings of drawings were extremely detailed and became very influential in the United States.

Aware of the importance of nature study to even the youngest readers, he often adopted a style solicitous of the attention of child readers and spun the life history of an insect into a narrative of travel and adventure with encouragement to further original nature study. In *Eye Spy*, for example, he relates an encounter with a little girl he met on a country road who described the beetle that is the subject of the essay ("The Story of the Floundering Beetle"):

> "I've got a funny blue bug at home in a box that I want to show you," said she; "he's blue and awful fat, and hasn't got any wings, but when you touch him, he just turns over on his back, and trembles his toes and leaks big yellow drops out of his elbows."

In the middle of this page, Gibson has incorporated a drawing of three views of this beetle that help narrate the girls' story: the beetle is shown walking normally, rolled onto its side, and lying on its back exuding the oily yellow substance from its leg joints. This illustration also shows his distinctive stylistic manner of composing pages as a blend of prose and drawings that work together to tell a single narrative of natural history.

By relating in detail the life histories of plant species and that of their insect pollinators, Gibson hoped to teach the lesson that the lives of the most common "weeds," "which we meet every day in our walks, and which we claim to 'know' so well," can be seen as "beautiful mysteries." One of his purposes as a popularizer of natural history was to cultivate a broader readership for environmental essays about the lifeways of plant and animal species. One of his strategies was to narrate and illustrate the "beauty of the commonplace." By teaching readers to see that the life histories of common flowers and wasps yield compelling narrative plots, he hoped to kindle in his readers a desire to investigate their own local, familiar environments. In his narrative ecology, he often stressed recent findings about the symbiotic relationships existing among various blossoms and the insects selected to pollinate them. In an essay entitled "A Homely Weed with Interesting Flowers" (in *Eye Spy*), for example, he narrates the plot of the pollination of the figwort by a wasp and leads the reader to the following insight:

> in light of the "new botany," which recognizes the insect as the important affinity of the flower—the key to its various puzzling features

of color, form, and fragrance—every commonest blossom which we thought we had "known" all our lives, and every homely weed scarce worth our knowing, now becomes a rebuke, and offers us a field of investigation as fresh and promising as is offered by the veriest rare exotic of the conservatory.

Similarly, Gibson worked to teach and fascinate his readers with explanations of adaptive blossom structures and insect behavior first explained by Darwin. In "Riddles in Flowers," Gibson explains in prose and picture the process of cross-pollination, opening the essay with an illustration of stamens and petals that vary greatly from one another and are intended to puzzle the reader. In summarizing the history of how it was discovered that the shape of a stamen and a petal are adaptations to facilitate cross-pollination, Gibson hopes to complicate his readers' conception of the world of plants and insects by teaching them to see a network of interdependent relationships:

> It was not until the flowers were studied in connection with the insects which visit them that the true secret of these puzzling features became suspected.

"Take almost any flower we chance to meet," he writes, "and it will show us a mystery of form which the insect alone can explain." Botany thus conducted in this more ecological light Gibson refers to as "the new botany." The "old botany" was conducted by "mere botanists," taxonomists who were satisfied with the study of structure for the purpose of classification. The new botany is informed by Darwin's theory of natural selection and its emphasis on adaptation, but for Gibson it is still, to some extent, a religious pursuit:

> It was not until they [i.e., the new botanists] had become philosophers and true seers, not until they sought the divine significance, the reason, which lay behind or beneath these facts, that the flowers disclosed their mysteries to them.

Gibson avoids the intractable, metaphysical position of Louis Agassiz that all existing species are thoughts in the mind of God and that all were created at the same time and given physical features by God that figure in relationships among species, but he also avoids the godlessness of the Darwinian view of natural adaptation as completely determined by environmental conditions. Gibson carried the natural theologians' belief in the theory of design forward into the age of evolutionary biology, and no doubt at least partially because of that sustained a broad readership among America's middle class.

The extreme accuracy (even amid a romantic rendering) of his illustrations of plants, animals, and fungi reflects his conviction that in nature there is nothing of minor interest. The least dramatic phenomenon and the least noticeable object reward the closest investigation. His biographer writes: "He taught by his art the greatness of the little, the divinity of the familiar." Thoreau promulgated this viewpoint, and Gibson had a deep affinity for the Concord saunterer. In 1888, he reported to a friend that

> There are few authors whom I love more than Thoreau...I have read him with love and reverence, and have visited his haunts as sacred ground, and have pictured those haunts in projected compositions, and yet hope to see them realized.

Another aspect of Gibson's affinity for the worldview of Thoreau appears in a plan, consisting of extensive notes and an outline, Gibson left behind to write and illustrate a book that, as his biographer characterizes it, "should describe the history of the endless movement of water, from cloud to mountain-top, from the heights to the valleys, from the valleys to the sea, and back to the clouds again." Just as Thoreau, toward the end of his life, was designing a "Kalendar," within which he could record his observations of natural phenomena and thereby create a representation of nature's comprehensiveness, so too did Gibson come to aspire to design a framework that would enable him to express a more comprehensive conception of natural systems.

Following the publication of *Sharp Eyes* late in 1891, the work he was doing for an illustrated botany (which he did not complete) led him to accept an invitation to offer a series of lectures, or as Gibson characterized them, "familiar talks on Nature, covering botany, entomology, and ornithology." Over the next four years, he continued delivering such lectures, most of which he illustrated with charts, before clubs, schools, colleges, and popular audiences. A series of six lectures he delivered in Hardman Hall in New York City was so successful that he earned $850 and caused the manager of the hall to write: "The news of your success in Hardman Hall is phenomenal. I can assure you that you are the only man in the United States who could have done such a business." Invitations poured in from all over the country, and Gibson turned much of his energy to this new development in his career. In 1894, he presented his nature lectures 64 times before audiences of scientists, lay people, and children. No one since Agassiz had had such success as a naturalist-lecturer.

Even amid such a demanding schedule, he managed to prepare a volume on mycology, publishing *Our Edible Toadstools and Mushrooms* in 1895. His health was damaged, however. For several months before his death, he experienced dizziness and fainting spells, occasionally even while lecturing. The separate previously published pieces of his last three books were not yet all gathered when Gibson suffered a stroke and died on July 16, 1896. Posthumously published were *Eye Spy* (1897), *My Studio Neighbors* (1898), and *Blossom Hosts and Insect Guests* (1897). His biographer notes that the last entry in Gibson's journal, dated four days before his death, reads: "Lecture, Holiday House."

At the beginning of the twentieth century, there was a great forgetting of nineteenth-century American nature writers. Many factors brought this about, among which no doubt would be counted the rise of the automobile and suburban lifestyles, World War

I, the Depression, the rise of modernism in literature, and the ever-accelerating growth of industrialization and the transfer of populations from the country to the city. The work of recovering this rich, complex, and deep tradition of the earlier writers is underway, and Gibson's work will undoubtedly soon begin to receive the critical and scholarly attention it deserves. His body of work is quite distinctive because it is so well illustrated and because the author himself created these illustrations. Art historians and historians of book illustrations will have as much to say about Gibson as will the scholars of literature. Among the first questions that will be addressed is whether the assessment of John Coleman Adams, who was Gibson's friend as well as his biographer, is accurate:

> Thoreau has a more philosophic sweep, Burroughs the nicer literary touch, but Gibson has the livelier imagination, the more exuberant wit, the keener sense of the human aspects of life among the lowly bugs and blossoms.

PRIMARY BIBLIOGRAPHY

Books

The Complete American Trapper; or, the Tricks of Trapping and Trap Making (New York: J. Miller, 1876; Philadelphia: Bradley, Garretson, 1879).

Camp Life in the Woods and the Tricks of Trapping and Trap Making; Containing Comprehensive Hints on Camp Shelter, Log Huts, Bark Shanties, Woodland Beds, and Bedding, Boat, and Canoe Building, and Valuable Suggestions on Trappers' Food, etc. (New York: Harper and Brothers, 1881; 1883; 1905; 1909; Guilford, Connecticut: Lyons Press, 2002).

Highways and Byways; or, Saunterings in New England (New York: Harper and Brothers, 1882; 1883; and 1903).

Happy Hunting-Grounds; A Tribute to the Woods and Fields (New York: Harper and Brothers, 1886; 1887).

Sharp Eyes; A Rambler's Calendar of Fifty-two Weeks among Insects, Birds, and Flowers (New York: Harper and Brothers, 1891; 1892; 1893; 1896; 1897; 1898; 1904; 1919).

Strolls by Starlight and Sunshine (New York: Harper and Brothers, 1891).

Our Edible Toadstools and Mushrooms and How to Distinguish Them; A Selection of Thirty Native Food Varieties, Easily Recognizable by Their Marked Individualities, with Simple Rules for the Identification of Poisonous Species (New York: Harper and Brothers, 1895; 1899; and 1903).

Blossom Hosts and Insect Guests; How the Heath Family, the Bluets, the Figworts, the Orchids and Similar Wild Flowers Welcome the Bee, the Fly, the Wasp, the Moth and Other Faithful Insects (New York: Newson and Company, 1897; 1901).

Eye Spy; Afield with Nature among Flowers and Animate Things (New York: Harper and Brothers, 1897; 1898).

My Studio Neighbors (New York and London: Harper and Brothers, 1898; 1900; 1904).

Our Native Orchids; A Series of Drawings from Nature of All the Species Found in the Northeastern United States (New York: Doubleday, Page, and Company, 1905).

Collections

Pastoral Days; or, Memories of a New England Year (London: Chatto and Windus, 1880; New York: Harper and Brothers, 1881; New York: Harper and Brothers, 1882; 1886; and 1908).

Secrets Out of Doors; Told and Illustrated by William Hamilton Gibson (New York and London: Harper and Brothers, 1913).

Other

The Master of the Gunnery; A Memorial of Frederick William Gunn, ed. W. Hamilton Gibson (New York: The Gunn Memorial Association, 1887).

Catalogue of American Water Colors, Original Drawings, Studies in Black and White and Monotint, Artists' and Remarque Proofs, etc., etc., the Works of W. Hamilton Gibson [sold…by order of the artist…March 19th, 20th, and 21st…at the American Art Galleries] (New York: American Art Association, 1888).

Selected Periodical Publications—Uncollected

"Foreground and Vista at the Fair," *Scribner's Magazine* 14 (July 1893): 29–37.

Letters

The Allison-Shelley Manuscript Collection in Rare Books and Manuscripts, University Libraries, Pennsylvania State University, University Park, Pennsylvania, houses two letters from Gibson to E.C. Stedman (dated December 11, 1888 and

April 2, 1889) in which Gibson discusses his work. The Buffalo and Erie County Historical Society Archives houses "Letters from artist William Hamilton Gibson and sculptor J. Massey Rhind" to Augusta C. Graves, 1894–1896. The Ohio Historical Society, Columbus, Ohio, houses five letters from Gibson to Edward F. Webster concerning speaking engagements in Wellington, Ohio. Many letters to and from Gibson are printed in John Coleman Adams's biography, which is noted below.

SECONDARY BIBLIOGRAPHY

Biographies

John Coleman Adams, *William Hamilton Gibson: Artist—Naturalist—Author* (New York: G.P. Putnam's Sons, 1901).

References

Ann Shelby Blum, *Picturing Nature: American Nineteenth-Century Zoological Illustration* (Princeton: Princeton University Press, 1993).

H. Daniel Peck, *Thoreau's Morning Work: Memory and Perception in* A Week on the Concord and Merrimack Rivers, *the Journal, and* Walden (New Haven: Yale University Press, 1990).

Barnet Phillips, "A Naturalist's Boyhood," in William Hamilton Gibson's *Eye Spy: Afield with Nature among Flowers and Animate Things* (New York: Harper and Brothers Publishers, 1903), xi–xvi.

Chandler Robbins Gilman
(September 6, 1802–
September 26, 1865)

David Visser

The work of Chandler Robbins Gilman was published for more than two decades in the mid-nineteenth century. He was a well-regarded physician and professor, and the majority of his published writing, speaking, translating, and editing endeavors concern the medical field. Before he took his professorial chair, however, Gilman worked in other genres, though his work outside his professional field has been virtually ignored until the present. His *Legends of a Log Cabin* (1835) is set in the American West but speaks nonetheless to the diverse population of a young nation. In *Life on the Lakes* (1836), Gilman's persona blossoms from a rather pedestrian doctor in the Michigan wilderness into a burgeoning nature writer. This account of his experiences on the Great Lakes frontier establishes him as an early American nature writer at work before the publishing careers of Susan Fenimore Cooper and Henry David Thoreau began.

Chandler Robbins Gilman was born on September 6, 1802, in Marietta, Ohio, to Benjamin Ives Gilman and Hannah Robbins Gilman. His father was a versatile and successful businessman. After starting out as a profitable fur merchant in Ohio, he served an active role as a delegate to the convention responsible for forming the Constitution of the State of Ohio. Next, he pursued the business of shipbuilding, the first man to do so on the Ohio River. The embargo of 1807 prompted the elder Gilman to move his family to Philadelphia, where he was profitable as a member of the business house of Gilman & Ammidon. While in Philadelphia with his mother, young Chandler Robbins Gilman began his formal education at Phillips Academy before moving on to Andover and then Harvard. Gilman earned his MD at the University of Philadelphia in 1824. Shortly thereafter, Gilman moved to New York City to begin his professional career.

On November 3, 1825, Gilman married Serena Hoffman, daughter of the distinguished merchant Martin Hoffman, Sr. Shortly thereafter, Gilman, who would earn a reputation as a man of character in the medical field, turned down a professorship at a Virginia university because he refused to rear and raise children in the slave-owning South. The early endeavors, however, of Gilman and his wife to start their family were met with heartbreak. Their first son, Benjamin Ives Gilman, died before his first birthday. Their first daughter, Mary Hoffman Gilman, survived just over two months. Eventually they faired better. In all, they had eight children together.

His initial foray into the literary world came in assisting his relative, Charles Fenno Hoffman, with the overseeing of the *American Monthly Magazine*. The effect of Hoffman on Gilman cannot be overstated. In 1835, Hoffman published his *Winter in the West*, an account of an excursion made by the author into the American West. Gilman's earliest published work, *Legends of a Log Cabin*, appeared later that year. Hoffman, who submitted his manuscript as written "By a New-Yorker," is echoed in Gilman's "Anonymous" submission. Furthermore, Gilman dedicates his work, in friendship, to Hoffman. In it, the narrator, George (who is undeniably Gilman), is compelled to leave Philadelphia and travel to the Ohio wilderness on "urgent business." After barely surviving a fierce snowstorm, George at last finds the log cabin of his old acquaintance Balt Williams, who is every bit the prototypical rugged frontiersman.

Within the small cabin George encounters a host of characters taking refuge from the storm, among them a Methodist preacher, an Englishman, a Frenchman, a Yankee, a Wyandot Indian, an enslaved negro, the aforementioned Balt, and his wife. The group elects to pass the time by telling stories, and the book's subsequent chapters are composed of the different characters' separate tales. Although each character relieves George of the narrative during the chapters their respective stories occupy, the voice throughout is noticeably that of Gilman.

As the proprietor of the cabin, Balt Williams offers his story first. Entitled "The Hunter's Vow," the tale is one of revenge. After being unable to stop the murder of his father at the hands of an Indian, young Hamilton Cass vows to gain vengeance. The story vilifies the "savages" as murderers of not only men but also women and children, but later draws an interesting parallel when the confession is made that white settlers also slaughter women and children. In the end, the story affirms the values of frontier justice over those of peaceful coexistence and forgiveness. The story climaxes and concludes when Hamilton returns to his village carrying the severed head of the Indian responsible for his father's death.

Next, Mr. Stone, the Methodist preacher, is encouraged to tell a story. His account, "The Heiress of Brandsby," is the story of a wealthy, godless, young girl who falls for and marries a penniless yet noble Methodist preacher (though this is not Stone himself). Issues of racial tension are again presented in this account, as the slave-owning heiress is taught equalitarian values by the abolitionist preacher.

The Frenchman's story is set in Paris during the Reign of Terror. The story, which smacks of a cautionary tale warning against the mentality of mob justice, includes an intensely powerful scene depicting the beheading of a man, his daughter, and her son all in succession. While acknowledging the atrocities that took place and claimed the lives of family members, the Frenchman nevertheless remains patriotic and supportive of the original tenets of the revolution. This prompts George to engage in an honorific discussion of Napoleon, a theme repeated in his next book.

In an effort to stem an argument that develops between the Frenchman and the Englishman, George prompts the latter to tell a story of his own. "George Grey: A Tale of the English Law," is the title of the Englishman's story, an account that the narrator describes as being preceded by a lengthy diatribe on the merits of the English legal system. When the actual voice of the Englishman is finally provided to the reader and his account ensues, a more contradictory example to these merits could hardly be offered. The tale is of the unfortunate death of a child and the distressing manner in which the law not only protects those responsible for his death, but also condemns his father for his understandable reaction to the heart-wrenching events.

The Yankee's story, "The Sleigh Ride," is included next. Set in Maine, the tale is primarily concerned with the power structure and courting practices of a small New

England town. The New England dialect in which the Yankee tells his tale is the most convincing dialect offered amongst the characters, presumably due to Gilman's familiarity with it.

The Wyandot's story, told next, presents a poignant moment in this early Gilman text. The story begins with the murder of Winteheh, a Wyandot chief, by white settlers even though a truce had been called between the two groups. Unlike Balt's initial story in which the son of the murdered settler sought blood, the chief's son, lashed during his father's murder, returns home but wastes away and dies shortly thereafter. Even after the murder of their chief, the Wyandots have faith in the promise of the whites to police their own. In a gesture of sham justice, the white settlers arrest the guilty parties—and release them after only four days in prison. Upon hearing of this, another one of the chief's sons, Mecami, finally does take matters into his own hands, killing and scalping the white man responsible for his father's death. Nevertheless, Mecami complies when summoned by a white jury, is found guilty by an all-white jury, and is hanged the very next day. With her husband and two of her sons dead, Winteheh's widow drowns herself in the Ohio River. Winteheh's remaining children, daughter Outesie and son and storyteller Chargha, flee from the area with hopes of settling with their cousin on the Muskingum River. No sooner do they arrive than they are attacked by whites and Outesie is captured. She is shot by one of the men even as she pleads for her life and entreats him for mercy by calling him "brother." Gilman draws added attention to this account by claiming, in an asterisked remark, that this story is absolutely true, as he has knowledge of a man living on the Mississippi who killed an Indian girl in the aforementioned manner, including the detail of her calling him "brother." The aftermath of the story is, in many ways, just as important as the story itself. Following the murders of his father, two brothers, and sister, and the suicide of his mother, Chargha is the last of his line left to relate the history of his family, only he must do so to a collection of white men.

Finally, George provides his own story, entitled "The Minute Men: A Tale of '75," a patriotic and rather idealistic account of the mishmash of groups that composed the Continental Army in America's battle for independence. Featured specifically in the story is the Battle of Bunker Hill.

The cabin's inhabitants retire for the evening after George's story and, finding the weather has cleared the next morning, depart in their separate directions.

The inclusion of the particular characters in this book cannot be dismissed as coincidental. The individual characters are portrayed as the representatives of their respective nationalities and races, and this portrayal contributes to a view of America as a melting pot of different cultures. Sharing a single cabin are the Englishman and Frenchman, the ancestries of each being heavily responsible for the identity of the young United States. The Yankee represents the newer generation of what used to be the colonists. The preacher speaks to the emphasis placed on religion by the fledgling country. Balt Williams, of course, is the frontiersman continually pushing westward, at the expense, of course, of Chargha, the native whose people used to dwell on the land that the white men now own. The character of Balt, however, may have been inspired by more than just the prototypical frontiersman image. Gilman's father, while an early settler of the Marietta, Ohio, area in which *Legends of a Log Cabin* is set, evidently experienced (and narrowly escaped) many attacks from angry natives. The inclusion of Balt as the host of this collection of storytellers may, therefore, serve as a sort of tribute to Gilman's father, who passed away just two years before the publication of *Legends of a Log Cabin*.

Power, in *Legends of a Log Cabin*, is conferred upon whoever the storyteller is at the time; after all, that character has the floor. So it is interesting to note not only who does speak but also who is not afforded the opportunity to speak. In a move quite characteristic of the country in the 1830s, the woman, Mrs. Williams, and the negro, Sip, are the only two in the cabin not given a chance to tell their tales. The other characters relay stories of their backgrounds and the things important to them. Mrs. Williams and Sip, by being denied this opportunity to speak, are effectively posited as powerless beings.

If Gilman's *Legends of a Log Cabin* does not accurately reflect many of the complexities of American history, it does display the issues deemed salient and interesting by the citizens of an America not yet half a century old. Furthermore, the book raises questions of voice in early American fiction; that is, the stories told are all, in the end, determined by those given the chance to speak. The issues raised are issues important to white men. Even when the native, Chargha, is granted the floor, his story is neither discussed by the men nor addressed by the narrator.

Chandler Robbins Gilman's inclusion among the ranks of American nature writers, however, is based not on the societal observations ingrained in *Legends of a Log Cabin*. The categorization of Gilman as a nature writer is due to the startling transformation undergone by his persona in his 1836 work, *Life on the Lakes*.

In 1835, an attack of neuralgic rheumatism severely threatened Gilman's health. *Life on the Lakes* is the result of a successful attempt by Gilman, along with his brother-in-law Martin Hoffman, to bolster his condition. The text of Gilman's two-volume, narrative *Life on the Lakes* is delivered in an almost entirely epistolary format, as Gilman relays the events of a trek to the Great Lakes from his home in New York. Gilman's journey takes him through Lakes Ontario, Erie, Huron, and Superior, climaxing with Gilman's visit to the Pictured Rocks of what would soon thereafter become Michigan's Upper Peninsula. Gilman, Hoffman, and their co-travelers then proceed south through Lake Michigan to Chicago, and eventually to the Mississippi River, where the travelogue concludes.

Life on the Lakes is far from a traditional Thoreauvian observation, study, and appreciation of nature, what Lawrence Buell describes

as a "meticulous daily extrospection." At the outset, Gilman emphasizes his need to escape from the city and seek out the tranquility of nature, immediately characterizing the work as a pastoral account (though he does not relay his weakened condition). Even though Gilman's group traverses a frontier teeming with wildness, Gilman's focus is far from being strictly environmental. In fact, Gilman begins the narrative by professing, and exemplifying, ignorance to matters of nature. Throughout the first volume, Gilman's sporadic natural descriptions are decidedly more scenic and subjective than empirical or scientific. As he heads north, Gilman's prose accurately reflects the viewpoint of the metropolitan doctor unaccustomed to life in the wilderness.

Gilman's pastoral natural descriptions occur rarely in the narrative's first volume, but what the travelogue lacks in its representation and rendering of nature is repaid in its historical and sociological value. Gilman utilizes the urban stops made during the trip's first week or so to provide background to cities such as Niagara, Buffalo, Erie, Cleveland, and Detroit. It is quickly apparent that Gilman considers no subject out of bounds. He brazenly conveys his mostly negative opinions of the many ethnicities populating these cities:

> A French gentleman is too French for me; a German gentleman almost always smokes tobacco, and that you know I can't abide. An Italian knows too much about music; a Spaniard or Portuguese is black-looking, and wears mustaches; but an English gentleman is almost always a fine, noble fellow, with a heart (as they say in Connecticut) as big as a meeting house. Now for the other side of the picture. It is my devout belief that a vulgar Englishman is vulgar to a degree utterly unapproached by any other kindred, nation, or tongue under heaven. But breakfast waits, let us away.

In the midst of Gilman's clearly biased views, however, early American urban history is being written. Gilman is an astute observer of the architecture of the cities he visits, as well as of the manner in which they have been planned and laid out, as he comments about their respective road systems and building placements.

As he observes these growing cities, Gilman's focus is continually on the future, and while he confesses to not being a very "american American," his tone is nonetheless consistently optimistic. He describes the excitement with which the people of Erie, Pennsylvania, are looking forward to the building of the canal. He mentions the anticipation of Clevelanders for the railroad to come to their city. In this manner, Gilman postpones nature writing, as he catalogues the mentality of a growing American nation. *Life on the Lakes* is a composite work of several genres.

The historical content of *Life on the Lakes* is most relevant to Michigan history. Gilman relates the tension between Michigan and his native Ohio, which preceded the Battle of Toledo and Michigan's subsequent statehood. Pressing north through Lake St. Claire, into Lake Huron, and up to Mackinac Island, Gilman encounters numerous Chippewa tribesmen, and these encounters increase exponentially as he continues farther north. Gilman even includes several Chippewa legends in his narrative. As he observes the Great Lakes natives, Gilman describes their architectural methods and living practices yet often passes on the opportunity to relay descriptions of anything that may display his own ignorance; at one point he refuses to describe a Chippewa canoe, instead referring his readers to a museum wherein they may see the sight for themselves. Despite these occasional evasions, at this point in his journey Gilman's persona begins to turn his focus more regularly to the natural rather than the human. As he progresses more deeply into the northern reaches of the Great Lakes, he begins to provide descriptive accounts of several rivers, islands, lakes, and other landscape features of both the lower and upper peninsulas of the soon-to-be state.

Gradually, however, as the expedition continues north and farther away from civilization, Gilman begins to amend his pampered expectations. A desire for comfort is replaced by a need for survival: "We had little time, however, and, to tell the truth, little inclination, to look for the picturesque—the eatable had more charms for us." Whereas earlier Gilman whined over the type of beef served at suppertime, he now craves a simple crust of bread. While he formerly pined for the luxuriousness of a hotel bed, Gilman comes to experience happiness in a rustic, floorless cabin on Lake Superior. He even professes a love for his canoe.

As the voyage continues, Gilman's interests begin to favor the scientific over the scenic. He not only hypothesizes about the nature of the water's color, but precedes Thoreau's interests in the depths of Walden Pond as he begins noting depth readings of Lake Superior. Soon thereafter, Gilman ponders the problems of a cedar bush while directly addressing the shrub. He procures his first scientific specimen, a sample of peat, and even takes interest in witnessing that a horse will, indeed, eat fish. By the end of the text, Gilman actually regrets his lack of training in the natural sciences.

Nevertheless, it should not be assumed that Gilman's behavior is hereafter that of an ardent conservationist. Gilman's hypocrisy is exhibited in no place more poignantly than in a disturbing episode in which Gilman, seeking to prove his newfound ruggedness, engages in the felling and burning of trees purely for entertainment, during which he compares himself to and even quotes the conquering Napoleon. While the subject of his writing takes on a much more natural focus, Gilman's persona does not come to resemble a frontiersman himself. Throughout the account, he is carried from the canoe to the shore and back again on the shoulders of the men in his hired traveling party in an effort to keep his feet warm and dry.

An important phenomenon that occurs in Gilman's *Life on the Lakes* is the transformation undergone by the author's persona on this journey. While Gilman's writing lacks the environmental fervor of Thoreau, the intellectual aspirations of Emerson, the philosophy of Fuller, and the experimentation of Whitman, his travelogue provides something that none of the aforementioned writers can match: an unfeigned and endearing naiveté. One may be able to trace the progression of, say, Thoreau's philosophy over a period of 20 years by noticing the gradual rejection of Emersonian transcendentalism in his journal and other published works. Gilman's transformation, on the other hand, occurs completely within the two volumes of *Life on the Lakes*. Although educated, he is a gentleman doctor, not a natural scientist or environmentalist. Because of this, the lay reader can identify with Gilman. And it certainly does not hurt that Gilman's writing is exceptionally engaging. The following review of *Life on the Lakes*, taken from an early twentieth-century history of the Mackinac country, formidably characterizes the work:

> There is a freshness about these volumes, like a breeze off the lakes. They are full of the joy of abounding energy, and the author had a keen sense of humour. There is not a dry line between their covers.

Gilman begins the piece as both completely ignorant and completely indifferent to the ways of nature. Gradually, however, his immersion in the Michigan wilderness spawns new questions, questions about nature and her systems: about the Lakes and their tides, the bays and their coastlines, the forests and the nature of their formations. It is in the asking and answering of these questions that Gilman's writing transcends mere travelogue and becomes nature writing. Between the introductory pages in New York and the trip's conclusion in the old Northwest, Gilman becomes an American nature writer before his readers' eyes.

In the end, a healthy Gilman seems to echo *carpe diem* themes, hardly surprising given the illness that gripped him at the trip's beginning. Gilman also predates the Thoreauvian emphasis on constant awareness, as he contends that by facing death on the often treacherous Great Lakes, he has learned that the key to life is avid consciousness, as he advises his readership to continually "stop and think."

The majority of Gilman's published writing is medical in nature, including some lectures that he delivered at the College of Physicians and Surgeons of the University of the State of New York. The first of these lectures to be published was his Introductory Address of November 6, 1840, delivered shortly after being elected Professor of Obstetrics and the Diseases of Women and Children earlier that year. Gilman's lecture focuses on his own field, obstetrics. He catalogues the difficulties that will present themselves to students during their studies and afterwards in their practice. The greatest part of the lecture, however, is devoted to extolling the virtue of aiding women. Gilman proclaims, "It is our happy lot to repay in part the incalculable debt which man owes to woman—to woman, too often the sport of his wayward passions, by his licentiousness made a plaything, by his brutality a slave." Although Gilman is quite complimentary of women (especially considering the time in which he is writing), this feminist tone quickly abates, as he soon thereafter refers to women as "a help mate for man." Gilman emphasizes the high degree to which women should be cherished for the noble duty that they perform as mothers, and continues by explaining both the mental and physical attributes of women that enable them to bear and raise children. The address is primarily positive, as Gilman only briefly acknowledges the pain of confronting death in the daily life of a physician. As he concludes, Gilman challenges his students with a choice. Through dedication, labor, and perseverance, Gilman asserts, any doctor can be remembered as "God's minister for good." The ill-prepared physician, on the other hand, Gilman describes as "God's minister for evil, God's scourge." Gilman encourages the students to make the wise choice. His lecture was well received, as his students took the initiative of publishing it.

Gilman's successful entrance into the medical community, however, was followed shortly thereafter by a season of intense tragedy. His youngest daughter, three-year-old Elizabeth Hale Gilman, perished on February 17, 1842. Eight days later, five-year-old Annie Wotherspoon Gilman followed her sister in death. And three days afterward, on her 39th birthday, Gilman's wife, Selena, perished as well. Gilman was now a widower, and a father of four. Although his friends and family were concerned for his sanity after enduring such a catastrophic ordeal, Gilman's strong constitution and concern for the well-being of his remaining children sustained his strength through the misfortune. His fortunes did improve, for over the next couple of decades he lost only one more of his children with Selena. He married the 22-year-old Hannah Hawkhurst Marshall on September 19, 1844, and the new couple started having children of their own. They would have three, all of whom survived to adulthood.

In 1845, Gilman lent his services to Dr. Henry Maunsell, as the editor for the American edition of *The Dublin Practice of Midwifery*. Gilman, holding the work in great esteem, professes in his preface that he has made alterations only with great care and caution. He attributes his involvement in the project to his desire to help produce this highly useful reference tool for the benefit of his students, a sentiment consistent with the passionate manner in which Gilman served his students and institution. He was a popular instructor whose engaging (and often humorous and sarcastic) lectures extolled the morality of the medical profession. When, later in life, his health faltered, no loss saddened the ever-social Gilman more than his resignation from his professorial chair.

Gilman was, like his mother, an intelligent conversationalist who enjoyed the intellect of others. He was also an avid reader, a pastime that, until 1847, claimed most of his leisure time. It was in this year that his interests were captivated by the microscopic investigations being performed by Louis Agassiz. His ignorance of German, however, hindered Gilman's attainment of the familiarity he desired. He studied the language fervently, and after a period of only two weeks possessed

a reading knowledge that enabled him to, in 1847, engage in another reissuing project, translating *Tracts on Generation* from the German with Theodore Tellkampf. Gilman's interest in embryology was noted by Agassiz, then at Harvard, who encouraged Gilman to undertake the project in a letter included in the front matter of the published translation. In Gilman's response, he states his goal as the introduction of the "*German Sciences*" (his italics) of ovology and embryology into the field of American Medicine. Gilman's patriotic sentiments were never lost—even in the scientific realm. Although his first microscope was one of Chevalier's (one of the first imported from Paris to America), he soon abandoned it when his countryman Spencer concocted his own. Gilman even prepared a patriotic account for the *American Journal of Science and Arts*.

While Agassiz, therefore, definitely affected the career of Gilman, Gilman may have affected Agassiz's as well. Roughly seven months after the aforementioned correspondence and 13 years after the trip that inspired *Life on the Lakes*, Agassiz traveled to Lake Superior himself, later publishing *Lake Superior: Its Physical Character, Vegetation and Animals, Compared with those of Other and Similar Regions* in March 1850.

A substantial portion of Gilman's medical writing is tied to the brothers Theodric Romeyn Beck and John Broadhead Beck. In 1851, shortly after the death of John B. Beck, Gilman published his short "Sketch of the Life and Character of John Broadhead Beck, M.D., Late Professor of Materia Medica and Medical Jurisprudence in the College of Physicians and Surgeons, New-York," in which he extols the values and accomplishments of Beck as a doctor, teacher, and man. Following Beck's death, Gilman became the College's Professor of Medical Jurisprudence.

Beginning in 1856, Gilman edited and contributed to all three editions of the *Lectures on Materia and Medicine* compiled by his late friend, Dr. John B. Beck. In his initial preface, Gilman describes his editing duties as "merely ministerial," as he professes his goal of devotedly preserving Beck's original messages. This does not stop him, however, from occasionally injecting his own bracketed comments into the text of Beck's lectures for the purpose of relaying his own preferences regarding the subject under discussion. The lectures generally follow a similar format: they address the history and properties of myriad medicines, along with their effects in battling disease. In an effort to make the collection more useful to students, Gilman himself pens a section on the "new and fashionable" agent cod liver oil, as well as an entire chapter on the promising anesthetics of the time. There are few changes made from the first to third editions, published six years apart. In Gilman's second edition preface, he underscores the need for revision given the progressive nature of medicine as a science. In his third edition preface, Gilman acknowledges the honor of having been chosen to edit what has become, as Gilman writes, "*the* text book of Materia Medica."

Also in 1856, Gilman delivered the introductory address to his own College of Physicians and Surgeons of New York. His speech was later published at the request of the students to whom it was given. The purpose of the speech is to acknowledge the tension present between those in the legal and medical fields, and to urge those of the latter field to alter their behavior to better facilitate relations with those of the former. His tone in accepting, on behalf of his profession, the majority of the blame for the problems that have arisen between the two vocations borders on apologetic—though this attitude toward the legal system would gain considerable rancor in about a year's time. Gilman focuses particularly on the issue of moral insanity in criminal trials; a year later, his opinions on this matter were actually heard in a criminal trial.

Gilman had testified in many trials, and he was somewhat of a favorite for the manner with which he provided clear and to-the-point evidence. In 1857, Gilman testified in the criminal trial of Charles B. Huntington

for forgery. Gilman's role in the trial pertained to Huntington's principle defense of moral insanity. Gilman testified on behalf of Huntington, attesting that unlike sanity, insanity presents itself in multiple forms, one of which is moral insanity. Moral insanity, Gilman contended, is caused by an abnormality in the brain resulting in the desire of an otherwise rationale individual to commit crimes. Although Gilman's testimony was not contradicted in the trial, Huntington was eventually found guilty, largely due to the judge's ruling that "the opinions of the medical witnesses were formed on a 'principle not recognized in our law.'" The debated principle was the issue of whether or not the defendant knew he was committing a crime. Gilman testified that although he believed Huntington was aware of his unlawful acts, he was still insane. Gilman, eager to substantiate his opinions rendered mute in court, contributes an appendix to the published proceedings of the trial, entitled "A Medico-Legal Examination of the Case of Charles B. Huntington, with Remarks on Moral Insanity and on the Legal Test of Sanity." In this essay, Gilman provides the details of several cases from around the world in which the symptoms of moral insanity have been exhibited and acknowledged. He challenges the legal profession to cease shunning the existence of moral insanity due to the problem it presents with regards to the law and instead rework the law so that it is consistent with the findings of the medical field. Furthermore, Gilman harangues the logic upon which the legal field dismissed moral insanity: that is, the concept that merely being aware that one is breaking the law eliminates any possibility of being deemed insane in a court of law, a policy that Gilman believed to be "vain and futile." Gilman relays the history of inconsistencies characteristic of the legal profession's fluctuating regard for the insanity defense. His criticism is scathing; he goes so far as to designate those wrongly executed as being victims of "judicial murder." This account is, at the very least, a marked departure from his somewhat repentant introductory address delivered only a year earlier.

Gilman took on another project involving the interrelations of the medical and legal fields in 1860, editing, preparing a preface for, and contributing to the 11th edition of Beck's *Elements of Medical Jurisprudence*. Gilman's preface is quite comparable to the preface he prepared for the first edition of the *Lectures on Materia and Medicine* following the 1851 death of John B. Beck. In *Medical Jurisprudence*, however, Gilman writes to honor the life of John's eldest brother, Theodric Romeyn Beck, who died in 1855. Again, Gilman is effusively respectful to the memory of the most recently departed Beck brother, professing his own "inability to do justice to such a trust" without the aid of many friends. The two-volume text concerns, as Beck explains in his introduction, "that science which applies the principles and practices of the different branches of medicine to the elucidation of doubtful questions in courts of justice." Gilman contributes the final chapter of the text, entitled "Medical Evidence." In it, Gilman focuses primarily on the role of physicians as witnesses in court cases.

Chandler Robbins Gilman was, first and foremost, a doctor. The majority of his published work pertains to the medical field. However, his 1836 travelogue *Life on the Lakes*, though virtually ignored in literary history, is an important text in the canon of American nature writing. Published a year before Thoreau began keeping his journal, Gilman's account provides natural description of the Great Lakes region prior to Michigan statehood along with early metropolitan and social history of the Midwest. Even though Gilman's position as a professor and doctor dictated his inclusion among society's elite, *Life on the Lakes* is really the story of an everyman in nature. Gilman's classification as an American nature writer, then, is by no means as an environmental specialist or masterful poet. Instead, Chandler Robbins Gilman's contribution to the genre is in his perspective. His text is both pastoral and representative: while he finds beauty, relaxation, and challenge in the wilderness, his text consistently lacks the idealism capable of alienating readers.

In 1864, troubled by heart and kidney disease, Gilman and his family left New York for a quiet residence in Connecticut. Just as the Great Lakes had done nearly 30 years prior, the country reinvigorated Gilman—though only briefly. He passed away on September 26, 1865, in Middletown, Connecticut. He was 63 years old. In accordance with his wishes, his body was not brought back to New York City for interment, but was rather laid to rest in the more natural country of Middletown.

PRIMARY BIBLIOGRAPHY

Books

Legends of a Log Cabin, anonymous (New York: George Dearborn, 1835; republished in Upper Saddle River, New Jersey: Literature House, 1970).

Life on the Lakes, 2 vols. (New York: George Dearborn, 1836).

Other

"Introductory Address to the Students in Medicine of the College of Physicians and Surgeons of the University of the State of New-York," introductory address, College of Physicians and Surgeons of the University of the State of New-York, November 6, 1840.

The Dublin Practice of Midwifery, by Henry Maunsell, MD, ed. Chandler R. Gilman, MD (New York: W.E. Dean, 1845).

Tracts on Generation, translated from the German by C.R. Gilman, MD, and Theodore Tellkampf, MD (New York: Samuel S. & William Wood, 1847).

"Sketch of the Life and Character of John Broadhead Beck, MD, Late Professor of Materia Medica and Medical Jurisprudence in the College of Physicians and Surgeons, New-York," *The New-York Journal of Medicine, and the Collateral Sciences* 7.2 (1851): 145–53; reprinted New York: John F. Trow, 1851.

Lectures on Materia Medica and Therapeutics, Delivered in The College of Physicians and Surgeons of the University of the State of New York, by John B. Beck, MD, ed. C.R. Gilman, MD (New York: Samuel S. & William Wood, 1856; 3rd edition, New York: Samuel S. & William Wood, 1861).

"The Relations of the Medical to the Legal Profession: Being the Introductory Address Delivered at the Opening of the Fifty-First Session of the College of Physicians and Surgeons, of New York, October 20, 1856" (New York: Baker & Godwin, 1856).

"A Medico-Legal Examination of the Case of Charles B. Huntington, with Remarks on Moral Insanity and on the Legal Test of Sanity," in *Trial of Charles B. Huntington for Forgery* (New York: John S. Voorhies, 1857).

Elements of Medical Jurisprudence, by Theodric Romeyn Beck and John B. Beck, ed. C.R. Gilman (Philadelphia: J.B. Lippincott & Co., 1860).

"Medical Evidence," in *Elements of Medical Jurisprudence,* by Theodric Romeyn Beck and John B. Beck (Philadelphia: J.B. Lippincott & Co., 1860).

Preface to the 11th Edition of *Elements of Medical Jurisprudence,* by Theodric Romeyn Beck and John

B. Beck (Philadelphia: J.B. Lippincott & Co., 1860).

SECONDARY BIBLIOGRAPHY

References

Lawrence Buell, *The Environmental Imagination: Thoreau, Nature Writing, and the Formation of American Culture* (Cambridge: Harvard University Press, 1995).

Arthur Gilman, *The Gilman Family: Traced in the Line of Hon. John Gilman, of Exeter, N.H., with an Account of Many Other Gilmans in England and America* (Albany: Joel Munsell, 1869).

Charles Fenno Hoffman, *Winter in the West* (New York: Harper & Brothers, 1835).

"Gilman, Chandler Robbins," in *Appleton's Cyclopaedia of American Biography,* vol. 2 (New York: D. Appleton and Company, 1888–1889).

John D. Godman, MD
(December 20, 1794–April 17, 1830)

Susan A.C. Rosen

John Davidson Godman's literary career, though only modestly discussed by modern scholars, established new standards and pathways for the study of natural history in the nineteenth century. Godman's earliest interests were simultaneously human anatomy and the natural sciences. In 1823 he began the ambitious project of scientifically and systematically characterizing and cataloguing American mammalians, and by 1826 he published the first two volumes of *American Natural History: Part I. Mastology*. The third volume of the series was published in 1828. Late in 1828, Godman became ill with tuberculosis and, forced to retire from the practice and teaching of medicine, he began working on the sketches later titled *Rambles of a Naturalist*. About this time, Godman writes,

> Until the last three weeks past, I was exceedingly low, unable to sit up, eat, or perform any function advantageously. Since then I have greatly recovered in all respects.[. . .] Not withstanding all these drawbacks, I have had my family to support, and have done so merely by my pen.

Thomas Lyon suggests Godman "may have been the first American to attempt to make a living by writing about nature." Godman was dedicated to the role of observation in both his study and teaching of anatomy as well as in his nature studies. One of Godman's most important contributions to the field of nature writing is the high standard of analytical observation he applied to his fieldwork in the natural sciences. In the first essay of *The Rambles of a Naturalist*, Godman writes, "[. . .] conjectures are forbidden, where nothing but observation is requisite[. . .]." Dr. Sewall's memoir suggests that had Godman lived, he "might have shone as the poet of nature, not less than her historian, had circumstances awakened his powers."

John Davidson Godman was born in Annapolis, Maryland, on December 20, 1794, one of eight children of Samuel and Anna (Henderson) Godman. Godman's mother died before he was two years old, and his father died soon afterward. Orphaned in 1805, Godman first lived with an aunt in Wilmington, Delaware, who appears to have instilled in her ward a great desire to learn. After Godman's aunt died, it was determined that his grandmother was unable to care for him, and, because Godman's father lost most of his estate before his death, Godman moved to Baltimore where a married sister, Mrs. Stella Miller, lived. At the age of 17, John Davidson Godman became indentured as an apprentice to a newspaper printer in Baltimore. Through letters to his friend and eventual mentor Dr. William N. Luckey, Godman expressed his disinterest in pursuing a career as a printer and his desire to study medicine. Dr. Luckey recalled the young John Godman as an intelligent and eager reader.

In 1814, Godman left his printing apprenticeship to become a sailor under Commander Joshua Barney, then stationed in the Chesapeake Bay, and he participated in the bombardment of Fort McHenry in the Baltimore Harbor. On April 10, 1815, at the invitation of Dr. Luckey, Godman arrived at the Luckey home in Elizabethtown, Pennsylvania, to begin his medical studies. After his initial study of medicine with Dr. Luckey, Godman moved to Baltimore to further his studies at the University of Maryland Medical School. Primarily because of the patronage of Professor John B. Davidge, Godman began attending lectures in medicine at the Baltimore school in autumn 1816 and continued through autumn 1817. One of Godman's professors fractured a limb prohibiting him from finishing out the semester's coursework. Godman, considered an exceptional student, was asked to fill in the chair of anatomy at the University of Maryland. This moment appears to have sparked his lifelong career as a medical professor at a number of institutions. Godman passed his graduation exams on February 7, 1818.

After Dr. Godman's graduation, he first practiced medicine in New Holland, Maryland, but soon returned to Anne Arundel County in Maryland to begin his medical practice. From his *The Rambles of a Naturalist*, it is clear that Godman was drawn to the environment. He noted:

> My only compensation was this, the house was pleasantly situated on the bank of Curtis Creek, a considerable arm of the Patapsco, which extended for a mile or two beyond us, and immediately in front of the door expanded so as to form a beautiful little bay. Of books I possessed very few, and those exclusively professional; but in this beautiful expanse of sparkling water, I had a book opened before me, which a life-time would scarcely suffice me to read through.

According to one of his biographers, it was during his time in Anne Arundel County that he began to seriously study natural history.

Dr. Godman returned to Baltimore, then moved to Philadelphia to begin teaching in the Philadelphia Anatomical Rooms. In Philadelphia, on October 6, 1821, Godman married Angelica Kaufman Peale, daughter of Rembrandt Peale and granddaughter of C.W. Peale. Soon after, they moved to Cincinnati, Ohio, for Godman to accept a professorship of anatomy in the Medical College of Ohio. The fledgling school failed, so after one year, but while in Cincinnati, Dr. Daniel Drake introduced Godman to medical journalism, and Godman along with John P. Foote, a Cincinnati bookseller, issued the first series of the *Western Quarterly Reporter of Medical, Surgical and Natural Science*. Godman wrote approximately half of the journal's 600 pages during the journal's two-year existence.

Dr. Godman returned to Philadelphia in the autumn of 1822 where he began writing what would become *American Natural History*. Godman carefully standardized his text using George Cuvier's dental system and Carl Linnaeus' *Systema Naturae*. The three volumes examine North American mammalians through class, order, genus, and varieties. Godman also includes studies of indigenous peoples and common animals such as raccoons, bears, the domestic dog, and so on. A contemporary review of *American Natural History* in *The North American Review* (24.55, [April 1827]: 467–68) noted, "Dr. Godman has undertaken the important task of giving to the public a natural history of our country adapted to the mass of readers." However, Godman was not the first to publish a text detailing North American mammals. In 1825, Richard Harlan published *Fauna Americana: Being a Description of the Mammiferous Animals Inhabiting North America*, a work that Godman and his colleagues knew to be plagiarized significantly from A.G. Desmarest's *Mammalogie* (1820). In a letter addressed to Dr. Thomas P. Jones, the editor of the *Franklin Journal*, Godman carefully supports his assertions of Harlan's plagiarism while at the same time defending his own work in the field of American natural history. The two authors carried on a bitter and public dispute, but Godman's would emerge as the more original work.

During his time in Philadelphia, Godman expanded his professional career in the natural sciences. Godman became a member of the Academy of Natural Sciences of Philadelphia, serving on a committee to review papers about natural history, primarily to prevent publication of errors. In 1824, he was elected to the Franklin Institute where he offered to lecture on natural history to the Institute members. In 1825 the board of the Franklin Institute appointed Godman to a chair of natural history, and in the same year Godman was elected to a membership in the American Philosophical Society.

After the publication of the first two volumes of *American Natural History*, Dr. Godman accepted a professorship at Rutgers Medical College in New York. There he continued work on the third volume of *American Natural History*, which he published in 1828. In the third volume, Godman devotes a significant portion of the text to "Whale-Fishery," a clear departure from the species-specific entries that precede the final section of the book. In this portion of the text, Godman uses first-person narrative to describe his own experiences whaling when he writes, "When fish have been struck by myself, I have on different occasions estimated their rate of descent." In "Whale-Fishery" Godman also departs from the careful scientific structure of the first two volumes by including lively narratives by several sea captains of whaling expeditions, which relate to the readers thrilling tales of whaling while confronting stormy seas or facing other adverse conditions. Godman published this section of the third volume independently as *American Whale Fishery* in 1828; thus it might be considered an early entry to the emerging genre of American maritime literature. Published after Owen Chase's narrative about the Essex of Nantucket (1821) and James

Fenimore Cooper's *The Pilot: A Tale of the Sea* (1823), and predating major works by well-known American maritime writers such as Richard Henry Dana and Herman Melville, *American Whale Fishery* is a nonfiction hybrid that anticipates the work of later maritime naturalists in its integration of science and narrative.

Because of a serious lung infection, Dr. Godman was forced to retire from teaching and move to a more temperate climate. He moved his family to the West Indies for the winter and spring of 1829, but when he returned to the United States, he was still seriously ill with tuberculosis. He settled in Germantown, Pennsylvania, with his wife and three children, where he spent the rest of his life. While in Germantown, Godman wrote articles on natural history for the *Encyclopaedia Americana*, finishing up through the letter C. During the last few months of his life, Godman wrote the essays that were later collected under the title of *The Rambles of a Naturalist* but which first appeared in *The Friend*, a Quaker religious and literary journal. *The Rambles of a Naturalist* is a collection of 12 essays. In the first essay, Godman educates his readers about the proper way to study nature and then demonstrates his observational technique through the remaining essays. Godman walks, and in his walks he stops for long periods of time to take notice of his environment, looking carefully for evidence of various species. He returns to the same places over and over again, visiting at different times of the day and during different seasons, calling this behavior his "repeated excursions." He refuses to fall into hasty generalization; thus, in these essays he does not write about any aspect of a species or place that he cannot observe for himself or for which he cannot find corroborative evidence. Most notable are the Anne Arundel County essays discussing his walks along the Magothy River, Curtis Creek, and the Chesapeake Bay. These essays integrate nature studies with social commentary. He writes of the life of a resident physician and of the "blight of slavery," while discussing muskrats, crows, and crabs. His studies of the Chesapeake Bay blue crab precede William Warner's 1976 Pulitzer Prize winning text *Beautiful Swimmers* by almost 150 years but remain as fresh and accurate as modern accounts of the Chesapeake Bay. In Godman's essays, the reader sees the naturalist's fascination with different species of crabs. In addition to the Chesapeake Bay blue crab, *callinectes sapidus*, he writes about Long Island's fiddler crabs, *gecarcinus*, and the *cypoda pugilator* crabs he discovers while in the West Indies. Godman's rambles and observations, not limited to animal studies, take him to consider forest communities as well. Godman, moved by his walks in the forests, comments, "But wherever nature is, and under whatever form she may present herself, enough is always proffered to fix attention and produce pleasure, if we will condescend to observe with carefulness." John Davidson Godman, MD, died in Germantown, Pennsylvania, on April 17, 1830.

At Godman's passing, his career as physician, naturalist, and author were widely commemorated, and his most significant contribution to the history of American nature writing, *Rambles of a Naturalist*, remained marginally available for two or three decades after its initial publication. Thereafter, however, he faded from view—as did most of America's literary environmental writers because of Thoreau's rising reputation. Godman's *Rambles* have yet to receive the analysis and recognition they deserve. To date only one of these essays has been anthologized. When the full history of American nature writing is written, however, it will be clear that Godman was, as Lawrence Buell writes, the "first American to produce a nonspecialized book of environmental essays."

PRIMARY BIBLIOGRAPHY

Books

Analytic Anatomy: A Lecture Introductory to a Course Delivered in the Philadelphia Anatomical Rooms, Session of 1823–24 (Philadelphia: William Brown, Printer, 1824).

Anatomical Investigations, Comprising Descriptions of Various Fasciae of the Human Body (Philadelphia: H.C. Carey & I. Lea, 1824).

Contributions to Physiological and Pathological Anatomy Containing the Observations Made at the Philadelphia Anatomical Rooms during the Session of 1824–5 (Philadelphia: H.C. Carey & I. Lea, 1825).

Monitions to the Students of Medicine, A Lecture Introductory to the Course Delivered in the Philadelphia Anatomical Rooms, Session of 1824–4 (Philadelphia: J.R.A. Skerret, Printer 1825).

American Natural History, Volume I, Part I—Mastology (Philadelphia: H.C. Carey & I. Lea, 1826).

American Natural History, Volume II, Part I—Mastology (Philadelphia: H.C. Carey & I. Lea, 1826).

Anatomy Taught by Analysis: A Lecture Introductory to a Course Delivered in the Philadelphia Anatomical Rooms, Fifth Session of 1825–6 (Philadelphia: William Fry, Printer, 1826).

A Letter to Dr. Thomas P. Jones, Editor of the Franklin Journal (Philadelphia: printed for the author, 1826).

Professional Reputation; an Oration Delivered before the Philadelphia Medical Society, Pursuant to Appointment, Feb. 8, 1826 (Philadelphia: Benjamin & Thomas Kite, 1826).

Lecture Introductory to the Course of Anatomy and Physiology in Rutgers Medical College, Delivered on Friday, Nov. 2, 1827 (New York: William A. Mercein, Printer, 1827).

American Natural History, Volume III, Part I—Mastology (Philadelphia: Carey, Lea & Carey, 1828).

American Whale Fishery (Philadelphia: Stoddart & Atherton, 1828).

Addresses Delivered On Various Public Occasions with an Appendix Containing A Brief Explanation of the Injurious Effects of Tight Lacing Upon the Organs (Philadelphia: P.A. Carey, Lea, & Carey, 1829).

American Natural History, 2nd ed., 3 vols. (Philadelphia: Stoddart & Atherton, 1831).

Rambles of a Naturalist (Philadelphia: Thomas T. Ash—Key and Biddle, 1833), originally published in *The Friend: A Religious and Literary Journal* (3:14 [1830]: 105–6; 15: 116–17; 16: 121–23; 17: 129–30; 18: 139–40; 19: 147–48; 20: 153–54; 21: 161–62; 22: 170–71; 23: 177–78; 24: 186–87; 26: 202–3.

Rambles of a Naturalist: With a Memoir of the Author (Philadelphia: Association of Friends for the Diffusion of Religious and Useful Knowledge, 1859).

American Natural History: Part I: Mastology and Rambles of a Naturalist, reprint ed. (New York: Arno Press, 1974).

Other

The Philadelphia Journal of the Medical and Physical Sciences, vols. 1–14, ed. N. Chapman, MD, W.P. Dewees, MD, and John D. Godman, MD (Philadelphia: H.C. Carey & Lea, 1820–27).

Western Quarterly Reporter of Medical, Surgical and Natural Science, ed. John D. Godman, MD (Cincinnati: J.P. Foote; New York: E. Bliss & E. White, 1822–1823), vol. 1, no. 1 (January/March 1822) through vol. 2, no. 2 (April/June 1823).

The Journal of Foreign Medical Science and Literature, ed. John D. Godman, MD (Philadelphia: E. Littell, 1824), new series, vol. 4.

Ode: Suggested by Rembrandt Peale's National Portrait of Washington (Philadelphia: Printed by Jesper Harding, 1824).

Manual of Surgical Operations; Containing the New Methods of Operating Devised by Lefranc, by J. Couter; translations and notes by John D. Godman (Philadelphia: H.C. Carey & I. Lea, 1825).

Anatomy and Physiology, by J. Bell and C. Bell, ed. John D. Godman, 2 vols. (New York: Collins and Co., 1827).

Lafayette in America in 1824 and 1825; or, Journal of a Voyage to the United States, by A. Levasseur; trans. John D. Godman (Philadelphia: Carey and Lea, 1829; New York: Research Reprints, 1970).

Godman contributed several articles to the *Encyclopaedia Americana* 13 vols. (Philadelphia: Carey, Lea, and Carey, 1829–1833) to the end of the letter C.

Selected Periodical Publications— Uncollected

"On the Actions of the Animal Economy: Some observations on the Propriety of Explaining the Actions of the Animal Economy by the Assistance of the Physical Sciences," *Philadelphia Journal of the Medical and Physical Sciences*, vol. III, no. 5 (1821): 46–45; reprinted *Western Quarterly Reporter of Medical, Surgical and Natural Science*, vol. 1 (1822): 60–67.

SECONDARY BIBLIOGRAPHY

References

Lawrence Buell, *The Environmental Imagination: Thoreau, Nature Writing, and the Formation of American Culture* (Cambridge: Harvard University Press, 1995).

Thomas Lyon, *This Incomperable Lande: A Book of American Nature Writing* (New York: Penguin Books, 1989).

Stephanie Morris, "John Davidson Godman (1794–1830): Physician and Naturalist," *Transactions and Studies of the College of Physicians of Philadelphia* (4th ser., Vol. 41, No. 4, April 1974).

Thomas Sewall, *Memoir of Dr. Godman, Being an Introductory Lecture, Delivered November 1, 1830* (New York: Published for the Tract Society of the Methodist Episcopal Church by B. Waugh and T. Mason, 1832).

A Sketch of the Life and Character of Dr. John D. Godman (Philadelphia: Published by the Tract Association of Friends, 1830).

Papers

John D. Godman's letters and papers are held in the following collections: The College of Physicians, Philadelphia; Gratz Collection; Ferdinand J. Dreer Collection, Physicians, Surgeons and Chemists, vol. II, Historical Society of Pennsylvania; Maria Dickinson Logan Collection, Historical Society of Pennsylvania; Townsend-La Maistre Collection; The Franklin Institute Archives.

Louis Hennepin
(1640–ca. 1701)

Winter Elliott

Louis Hennepin's life and career exhibit many of the same contradictions and incongruities as does the robust and assertive personality that so clearly inhabits the pages of his books. A Recollect priest as well as an explorer and restless adventurer, Hennepin authored three volumes of American discoveries—the *Description de la louisiane* (1683, translated as *A Description of Louisiana*, 1880), the *Nouvelle découverte* (1697, translated as *A New Discovery*, 1698), the *Nouveau voyage* (*New Journey*, 1698)—and one volume of religious invective, the *La morale pratique du jansénisme* (*Practical Morals of Jansenism*, 1698). While ostensibly travel narratives, Hennepin's first three books also present some of the earliest and most detailed descriptions of the American panorama. Equally interested in its inhabitants and its natural environment, and undaunted by myriad dangers and difficulties, Hennepin offers a vision of a vast new country, filled with such profuse life—plant, animal, and human—that its plentitude is at once both divine blessing and human temptation.

Throughout his life, Hennepin never quite reconciled two strong, conflicting impulses; he describes himself as

> from my infancy very fond of travelling; and my natural curiosity induc'd me to visit many parts of Europe one after another…and in gratifying this natural itch, was I led to this discovery of a vast and large country, where no European ever was before myself.

However, only a few pages later in the *Nouvelle découverte*, Hennepin describes a "strong inclination to retire from the world, and regulate my life according to the rules of pure and severe virtue." With difficulty, Hennepin tries to resolve the apparent problem of satisfying that itch of his and, yet, living apart from the world, noting that he was "overjoyed" when he discovered that he had entered into a long and notable tradition of religious exploration and mission. Hennepin's solution to this problem suggests a fundamental problem of all of his works, an unhesitating willingness to interpret—and reinterpret—events as they best suit his own desires and self-image. Never an uncertain narrator, Hennepin confidently manipulates both the language and the reality of his texts. Indeed, much of what is known of Hennepin's life is drawn only from his own writings and is seldom verifiable by outside sources. Moreover, the autobiographical information given in his books is often contradicted by both logic and contemporary observers.

Hennepin was baptized Jean Hennepin on April 7, 1640, in Belgium, at Ath in the province of Hainaut, although an earlier date and a different place of birth have both been alternately proposed. Some biographers argue that Louis Hennepin was actually born Antoine Hennepin on May 12, 1626, and, although Hennepin himself states that he was born in Ath, one biographer, Pierre Margry, suggests that Hennepin was actually born at Roy, in the province of Luxembourg. Though the rest of Hennepin's life, including his death, is equally characterized by uncertainty, one persistent and certain theme emerges: travel.

Hennepin entered the order of Saint Francis around the age of 17, beginning his novitiate in the Recollect Convent at Béthune in the province of Artois. Later, while in Ghent, one of his sisters earnestly sought to dissuade Hennepin from his growing obsession with travel and exploration, but, as Hennepin remarks, "this inclination to travel did so much the more fix it self in my mind." Hennepin set out to visit the great churches and convents of Italy and Germany, but, upon returning to the Netherlands, found his wanderlust stymied by the interference of his superior, Father William Herinx (Guillaume Herincx), who settled him in a convent in Hainaut, giving him the duties of a preacher. After a year, Hennepin was allowed to go to Artois, and then to Calais, where he describes himself as "skulking" behind the doors of inn houses, listening to sailors telling of their adventures. In his account of the sailors' stories, Hennepin appears attracted, not only to the idea of discovery, but also to the significant dangers and perils that the sailors faced.

Hennepin then acted as a missionary in Holland, spending eight months in 1673 in Maastreicht in the Netherlands, tending to the wounded of the war begun by Louis XIV in 1672. Although suffering for a time of an illness he describes as a fever, and nearly losing his life, Hennepin claims to have been present at the battle of Seneffe on August 11, 1674. Finally, in 1675, Hennepin was permitted to realize his dreams and journey beyond his native European shores. In order to balance the power of the Jesuits, Frontenac, Governor General of Canada, had asked Louis XIV of France to send additional Recollect missionaries to the country, and Louis had granted his request. Father Louis Hennepin was among the five Recollect priests chosen, and in Canada Hennepin began his most significant work. In his travels around Canada, too, as well as in his journeys along the Mississippi, Hennepin gathered the material that later formed the substance of his immensely popular—and controversial—narratives.

Of his three volumes dealing with journeys in America, Hennepin's second book of exploration, the *Nouvelle découverte*, published in 1697 in Utrecht, offers the most detailed information about his experiences as a missionary—and as an explorer. Published 14 years after the 1683 volume *Description de la Louisiane*, the *Nouvelle découverte* adds to the sparser descriptions of the Louisiana volume and makes the incredible claim that Hennepin journeyed from Fort Crèvecœur to the mouth of the Mississippi between February 29 and March 25 and returned by April 10. Beginning much earlier than the *Description de la Louisiane*, which commences with the start of La Salle and Hennepin's journey, the *Nouvelle découverte* also gives substantially more information about Hennepin's early life and motivations. Significantly, too, it generally includes much more detailed descriptions of the new landscape and peoples initially encountered by Hennepin in Canada and within the vast territory of Louisiana.

From the time of his arrival in Quebec, Hennepin displayed his characteristic restlessness, roaming the countryside by foot and in canoes. At first Hennepin remained mostly in and around Quebec, preaching during Advent and Lent at the Cloister of Saint Augustine. For a trial mission he was sent about 120 leagues beyond Quebec, where Hennepin established a mission house and traveled amongst the Iroquois villages, advancing his knowledge of that people and their language. Despite his almost incessant movement, though, Hennepin comments that all of his travel had "no other effect than to augment the itching I had to discover remoter countries."

Hennepin views the ample natural splendor of those new countries with a utilitarian and ruthlessly practical eye. Given frequent and highly successful raids by Iroquois warriors, Hennepin evaluates any new setting based upon its potential for defense; he praises Fort Frontenac, for example, for its advantageous location. Hennepin is also persistently aware of the possibilities for European settlement, noticing that the ground along Lake Ontario is very fertile, offering possibilities for the cultivation of "Indian and European corn, pulse, pot-herbs, gourds, and water-melons" as well as for the breeding of poultry and "horned beasts." Indeed, Hennepin concludes his description of the Great Lakes by suggesting that

> it were easie to build on the sides of these great Lakes, an infinite number of considerable towns, which might have communication one with another by navigation for five hundred leagues together, and by an inconceivable commerce which would establish it self among 'em.

Notably, Hennepin also maintains many of the native names for places and things, a habit that sometimes lends his rather prosaic description an almost poetic imagery. In his description of the Great Lakes, for example, Hennepin notes that Lake Ontario "is likewise call'd in the Iroquese [sic] language, Skanadario; that is to say, a very pretty Lake." The remainder of Hennepin's description of the lake reveals his practical concerns:

> This Lake Ontario is of an oval figure, and extends it self from east to west. Its water is fresh and sweet, and very pleasant to drink; the lands which border upon it being likewise very fertile. It is very navigable, and can receive large vessels: Only in winter is it more difficult, because of the outrageous winds which are frequent there. From this lake one may go by barques, or by greater vessels to the foot of a great rock that is about two leagues off the fall of the river Niagara....

Almost the entirety of Hennepin's description is focused upon the lake's usefulness, either as water to drink, land to cultivate, or a passage to navigate.

Hennepin's descriptions also often revolve around the sheer enormity of the land into which he ventured; he often remarks upon the sheer *size* of his surroundings, from forests to lakes, from prairies to rivers. It is this fascination with the dimensions of the world around him, especially when compared to the settled and tame European countries of his birth, that emanates from his description of the Niagara Falls. Hennepin's is the earliest written European impression of the Falls, and his narrative conveys both wonder and a sense of terrible destructive potential. Hennepin describes the falls with a tone of dreadful awe, observing that

> betwixt the Lake Ontario and Erié, there is a vast and prodigious cadence of water which falls down after a surprizing and astonishing manner, insomuch that the universe does not afford its parallel....At the foot of this horrible precipice, we meet with the river Niagara, which is not above half a quarter of a League broad, but is wonderfully deep in some places. It is so rapid above this descent, that it violently hurries down the wild beasts while endeavoring to pas [sic] it to fed [sic] on the other side, they not being able to withstand the force of its current, which inevitably casts them down headlong above six hundred foot.

Although Hennepin accurately portrays the power of the Falls, that raw, devastating energy does not repel him. Instead, the danger and natural hazards implicit to the Falls —and, indeed, to the unknown lands Hennepin had only begun to explore—fascinate Hennepin, magnetizing his interest and attention.

Hennepin's first years in Niagara, though spent in a continual blur of activity, did not afford him the opportunity he most desired: true exploration beyond the established and relatively safe boundaries of French civilization in the New World. In 1678, though, Hennepin joined La Salle on his journey to the mouth of the Mississippi. At this point in his life, Hennepin's *Description de la louisiane* begins, with his later *Nouvelle découverte* also reiterating the events of that voyage. The two narratives do not again diverge until early in 1680.

Hennepin's voyage with La Salle is characterized by extremes; the natural world around Hennepin and the other adventurers is one of either great, abundant plenty or stark deprivation. The voyagers succeed in ascending the Niagara River, and Hennepin's early impression of the world around him is one of beauty and profuse wildlife. In the *Description de la louisiane*, he depicts a landscape teeming with stags, hinds, roebucks, wild turkeys, bears, and swans—all of which could be eaten. He also notes that the forests contain various fruit trees, including walnut, chestnut, plum, and apple trees; the land also offers grapes to make wine and timber to build.

However, the voyage also presents the explorers with extreme difficulty; the abundant opportunities for food and shelter sometimes offered by the natural world are more frequently entirely absent. Hennepin notes that the travelers often fell short of provisions, and accordingly ate little. The land itself, Hennepin suggests, was at fault for the men's sufferings; the voyagers paddle relentlessly in search of better lands, fortified by only a handful of corn cooked under ashes or boiled in water. Several even ate berries and wild fruit, and subsequently feared that their foraging had poisoned them. Hennepin often views the countryside as a hostile environment, in which only active and timely divine interference and aid—occasionally in the rather mundane form of a dead but edible animal—saves the travelers. Indeed, Hennepin notes several times that the deficiencies of the natural landscape only increase his veneration for God, an unsurprising tendency given his vocation and commitment as a Recollect missionary. For example, after his capture by a Sioux tribe in 1680, Hennepin observes in the *Description de la louisiane* that

> We had never more greatly admired the providence of God than during this voyage, because we did not always find, and finding, did not always kill, deer; but eagles, which are

common on these vast stretches, sometimes let fall from their claws bream or large carp which they were carrying to their nests.

Despite their hardships, however, the travelers persisted, and in early 1680, Hennepin, along with Michel Accault and Antoine Auguel (called by Hennepin Aco or Ako and Le Picard), left Fort Crèvecœur on La Salle's orders and set off toward the upper Mississippi.

In *Description de la louisiane*, Hennepin recounts his eventual capture by Sioux Indians in April 1680, but in the *Nouvelle découverte*, Hennepin claims to have made it to the mouth of the Mississippi and back between the end of February and his capture in April. Hennepin effectively maintains to have preceded La Salle's journey to the mouth of the Mississippi by two years, and he contends that he did it in only a month. Even Hennepin's contemporaries viewed this statement with justifiable incredulity, and modern scholars overwhelmingly discredit this story, as well as Hennepin's justification that he only waited until after La Salle's death to advance his claim of priority for fear of reprisal by La Salle.

Hennepin's prolonged captivity amongst the Sioux Indians, though, gave him much opportunity both to observe their customs and to gain additional acquaintance with the environment. Hennepin tends to equate the natural world with its native occupants, giving the Native Americans many of the same characteristics he associates with their surroundings. Where advantageous for the European settlers he envisions colonizing the new world, Hennepin eulogizes the new world; but when faced with difficulty, Hennepin merges a nature insensible to the suffering of Hennepin and his companions with natives often indifferent to missionary goals and teachings. Hennepin also assigns similar goals to the colonization of the new land and the conversion of the Native Americans to Christianity. Just as it is Hennepin's objective to "open the hard hearts of that barbarous people," the European intent, unsurprisingly, is to civilize and control the wilderness, cutting down or burning passable ways across the landscape.

The *Description de la louisiane* contains a section on "manners and customs of the Indians" that Hennepin's later volumes lack. Hennepin observes that

> Before discussing Indian manners, it would be well to speak briefly about the fertility of the Indian country. This will show one how easily rich colonies could be established there. There is, I admit, much forest to be cleared, but the uncultivated tracts are none the less valuable. Few places in the world are more fruitful. None of the necessities of life are lacking; there is an abundance of everything. The soil is very suitable for sowing. In the vast region of Louisiana beautiful prairies are to be seen stretching to the horizon.

Admiring the resilience and physical strength of the Native Americans in much the same expansive language as he uses to describe their lands, Hennepin comments that

> The fact that Indians are without bodily defects leads one to believe that, given training and association with Frenchmen, their mental development would equal their physical development.

But Hennepin's hopes for French and European modification and control of the new country, both of its lands and its native peoples, are not always so glowingly reinforced. Indeed, Hennepin concludes that

> Until Christians are the absolute masters of the Indians, missionaries will have scant success without a very special grace of God, a miracle which He does not perform for every people.

Hennepin portrays the Native Americans he encountered as indifferent to European beliefs, superstitious, and migratory—all qualities that hinder his conversion attempts. Hennepin imbues the natural landscape with this same indifference to the welfare of the would-be European settlers, and for both the land and its native peoples he offers the same solution: absolute European domination.

Hennepin was eventually rescued from the Sioux by the intervention of Daniel Greysolon Dulhut (or Du Luth or Lhut) and made his way to Quebec by Easter week of 1681. On the way, Hennepin found a warm reception with Count Frontenac, who housed him and cared for him for 12 days, listening eagerly to Hennepin's tales of the dangers and hazards of his journeys. Returning to the monastery at Quebec, Hennepin found that he had been considered dead and that a mass of requiem had, indeed, been said for him two years prior to his rescue. Soon after his arrival in Quebec, Hennepin returned to Europe, where he retired, albeit briefly, to the convent at St. Germain-en-Laye, and wrote his first account of his travels.

Hennepin's *Description de la louisiane* appeared in Paris very early in 1683. It was a huge and immediate success, with new editions appearing in 1684 and 1688 and translations made into Italian, Dutch, and German. Ironically, those very qualities of the work that rendered it distasteful to critics made it immensely popular to a general public hungry for the tales of adventure, peril, and deprivation that Hennepin was quite ready to provide. However, other ecclesiastics were not quite so tolerant of Hennepin's sometimes very tall tales, and La Salle had prefaced Hennepin's reception in Europe by sending home a letter commenting that the priest was much prone to an exaggerated, and conceited, version of reality.

Indeed, Hennepin eventually fell into such disfavor with his superiors that he was forced to curry favor with the king of England, eventually journeying to Holland to publish his later books. Hennepin had also begun to long for the adventurous life of an explorer, and actively sought support and assistance for returning to America. But Hennepin's conflicts with his superiors continued to grow, and in 1696 he was even barred from preaching in Utrecht. Nevertheless, Hennepin, failing to find a willing publisher in Amsterdam, succeeded in publishing the *Nouvelle découverte* in Utrecht in 1697, followed by the *Nouveau voyage* in 1698. These latter works Hennepin dedicated to William III of England, just as he had directed his first volume to Louis XIV, and he also sought William III's support in returning to America as a missionary. Hennepin continued to remain popular with the public if not with his peers, and the *Nouvelle découverte* and the *Nouveau voyage*, like the *Description de la louisiane*, were published in several editions and variously translated. Unfortunately for Hennepin's credibility and reputation, the *Nouvelle découverte* also introduces his claim to have preceded La Salle's exploration along the Mississippi, an assertion that was received with disbelief and some animosity. More hastily written than the *Nouvelle découverte*, the *Nouveau voyage* sought to capitalize on Hennepin's indisputable success with his first two books.

Hennepin's final volume, *La morale pratique du Jansénisme*, develops an undercurrent established in the *Nouveau voyage*, outright criticism of and warfare with his superiors and fellow ecclesiastics. In the *Nouveau voyage* Hennepin had attacked the vicar apostolic, and in *La moral pratique* Hennepin condemned Dutch jansenism and aired a variety of complaints. Almost immediately after the publication of this volume, Hennepin was expelled from Utrecht.

Hennepin continued to entreat both William III and Louis XIV to return him to the Americas, but Louis XIV frankly stated that he would have the troublesome priest arrested if he set foot in Canada. Leaving Utrecht, Hennepin journeyed to Rome, where he continued to campaign for his return to missionary work. He spent some time in the convent of Aracœli in Rome. A penultimate historical notice of Hennepin occurs in March 1701, when a letter observes that he had managed to convince Cardinal Spada to provide funds for a new mission in the Mississippi country. However, in July 1701, Hennepin asked for and was denied permission to tend to the "apostate religious" in Holland. Ultimately, then, the end of Hennepin's life is indefinite. Almost until

the very last notice of him in a historical document, Hennepin continued to attempt a return to the Americas; whether or not he eventually succeeded is unknown.

Nor is it entirely certain to what degree Hennepin exaggerated, embellished, plagiarized, or consciously fabricated his tales of exploration and adventure. Despite that weighty degree of uncertainty, though, in his day Hennepin was undeniably one of the most popular narrators of the American landscape. Moreover, it was that very exaggeration, that tendency to romanticize both the countryside and his own sufferings, that made him so very popular. As Pierre Berthiaume observes, Hennepin's genre is almost more novel than travel narrative; and it is certainly Hennepin's immediate willingness to supply a multitude of details about the setting of the new world, its peoples, and his own difficulties that makes his books so appealing to the reader's imagination. Although Hennepin freely plagiarized a number of sources, including Le Clercq's *Établissement de la Foi*, he imprints his works with his own distinct personality. That assured, extravagant character dominates his pages, giving his narratives an imaginative vision that both sets him apart from other contemporary travel writers and wrecks his reputation as a truthful chronicler of real events. Like his own temperament, his vision of the world partakes of extremes, either wholly positive or totally negative, completely active in the world and yet removed from it.

Although as an autobiographer Hennepin cannot be trusted, his depictions of the early, wild, dangerous American territories are striking and sometimes exhaustively detailed. Over several hundred years of consistent critical interest, inquiry, rancor, and, finally, condescension, Hennepin has been called both an outright liar and a shameless plagiarist. Yet, his work was overwhelmingly popular in its own time and remains significant today. As Jean-Roch Rioux comments, "Let us at least leave to this enigmatic personage the glory which is his due: that of having shared in the discoveries made in New France and of having succeeded in making them known to Europe." Indeed, whether plagiarist or not—and scholars generally agree that Hennepin stole much, if not all, of his writings from the diaries and books of other explorers, even if those same scholars seldom agree on the particulars of Hennepin's sources—Hennepin's works remain important and noteworthy sources of information about the early American landscape. Ultimately, he colors his description of America's natural resources and native inhabitants with the ink of his own personality, creating a vision of an expansive, vibrant, plentiful, and sometimes savage new world limited, like Hennepin himself, by human ambition, arrogance, pride, and deceit.

PRIMARY BIBLIOGRAPHY

Books

Description de la louisiane, nouvellement découverte au sud-ouest de la Nouvelle-France par ordre du Roy. Avec la carte du pays; les mœurs et la manière de vivre des sauvages (Paris 1683); translated as *A Description of Louisiana* (New York: John G. Shea, 1880); translated by Marion E. Cross as *Father Louis Hennepin's Description of Louisiana, Newly Discovered to the Southwest of New France by Order of the King* (Minnesota: University of Minnesota Press, 1938).

Nouvelle découverte d'un très grand pays situé dans l'Amérique entre Le Nouveau Mexique et la mer glaciale. Avec les cartes et les figures nécessaires et de plus l'histoire naturelle et morale et les avantages qu'on en peust tirer par l'établissement des colonies. Le tout dédié à sa majesté Britannique Guillaume III (Utrecht, 1697); translated as *A New Discovery of a Vast Country in America, Extending above Four Thousand Miles, between New France and New Mexico* (London: Printed for M. Bentley, J. Tonfon, H. Bonwick, T. Goodwin, and S. Manship, 1698); Reprinted as *A New Discovery of A Vast Country in America*, 2 vols., ed. Reuben Gold Thwaites (Honolulu: University Press of the Pacific, 1903; reprinted 2003).

Nouveau voyage d'un païs plus grand que l'Europe. Ave les réflections des enterprises du Sieur de la Salle sur les mines de Ste Barbe etc. Enrichi de la carte, de figures expressives, des mœurs et manière de vivre des sauvages du nord et du sud, de la prise de Québec, ville capitalle de la Nouvelle-France, par les Anglois, et avantages qu'on peut retirer du chemin racourci de la Chine et du Japon, par le moien de tant de vastes contrées et de nouvelles colonies. Avec approbation et dédié à sa majesté Guillaume III Roy de la Grande Bretagne (Utrecht, 1698).

La morale pratique du jansénisme (Utrecht, 1698).

SECONDARY BIBLIOGRAPHY

References

Pierre Berthiaume, *L'Aventure américaine au XVIIIième siècle: Du voyage à l'écriture* (Ottawa: Les Presses de l'Université d'Ottawa, 1990).

Jean Delanglez, *Hennepin's Description of Louisiana: A Critical Essay* (Chicago: Institute of Jesuit History, 1941).

Bernard DeVoto, *The Course of Empire* (Boston: Houghton Mifflin, 1952).

Raymond F. Dolle, "Hennepin's Story of La Salle in Indiana," *Indiana English* 12.1 (Fall 1988): 4–7.

Jean-Roch Rioux, "Louis Hennepin," *Dictionary of Canadian Biography*, vol. 2, 1701–1740 (Canada: University of Toronto Press, 1969), 277–82.

Gordon M. Sayre, *Les Sauvages Americains: Representations of Native Americans in French and English Colonial Literature* (Chapel Hill, NC: University of North Carolina Press, 1997).

Justin Winsor, *Narrative and Critical History of America*, vol. 4 (Boston: Houghton Mifflin and Company, 1884).

Francis Higginson (ca. 1586–1630)

Anne-Marie Libério

Francis Higginson's literary production amounts to a single narrative, his *New-Englands Plantation. Or, a Short and True Description of the Commodities and Discommodities of that Countrey*. From a literary point of view, Higginson's account of New England can be considered as an exploration narrative, written in nonfictional prose. Higginson's relation does not display the usual creative features of fiction, but his erudition helped him create a text stylistically close to what Nina Baym calls "historical narratives" or "origins narratives," and Higginson might be labeled a "literary historian." Interestingly, Josephine Piercy characterizes these early accounts as "pamphlets of newes," "published for the benefit of prospective residents." Although there has been some debate among literary critics on whether Higginson's and a few of his contemporaries' writings really belong to American literature, Charles F. Richardson observes that

> American literature in the colonial period was in its day of small things, promising indeed, but without great achievement.[...] Those faithful records of sight and experience were the index fingers pointing to future achievements.

Although Higginson's records of sight and experience were primarily promotional in purpose, they became in effect one of the first literary representations of New England's flora, fauna, and climate and thus hold a place in the earliest moments of American nature writing.

The most exhaustive piece of information on Francis Higginson's life will be found in one of his descendants' work: *Life of Francis Higginson* (1891), by Thomas Wentworth Higginson. The earliest records of Francis Higginson's family in England date back to his paternal grandmother, Joanne Higginson, who was a pious, charitable, and well-off widow in late sixteenth-century England. Of her three sons, Thomas, Nicholas, and John, the latter received a Master of Art degree from Jesus College, Cambridge, in 1568. Three years later, John Higginson was appointed to the vicarage of Claybrooke, Leicester. Thomas W. Higginson reports that Mr. [Magister: ecclesiastical status] John Higginson "lived[...]till the age of one hundred and four." The vicar had five sons, John, Francis, Nathaniel, Nicholas and William, and four daughters. His exact birth date is unknown but can be estimated between 1586 and 1588. As the Reverend Cotton Mather puts it in the passage of his *Magnalia Christi Americana* (1702) about Francis Higginson: "I hope it will be accounted no defect in our history of this worthy man, if neither the day, nor the place of his birth can be recovered."

Francis Higginson obtained an MA in 1613 in Cambridge, either from Emanuel College, according to Cotton Mather, or from Jesus College, according to Thomas W. Higginson; other sources mention St. John's College. In 1615, Higginson settled in Claybrooke, Leicester, and married Anne Herbert, who bore him nine children—John and Theophilus (twins, born in 1616), Francis, Timothy, Samuel, Mary, Anne, Charles, and Neophytus (presumably born in 1630). From 1615 to 1627, Higginson acted as minister of the conformist, Anglican Church in Claybrooke. There he became acquainted with nonconformist ministers Arthur Hildersham and Thomas Hooke. Because of his skills as a preacher and the exemplarity of his upright and pious life, the Reverend Higginson was admired by his congregation and placed under the supervision of Bishop Williams of Lincoln. Nonetheless, his strictness soon proved incompatible with the Anglicans' intemperance, which he could observe as well in the church leaders' indulgence of various forms of corruption, as in the perverted teachings offered by the Church of England ministers. Consequently, Higginson shifted to religious nonconformism. He did not, at least initially, endeavor to create a religious community distinct from Anglicanism, as the Separatists had done, for his case was against the ministers, not the Church of England. Rather, his goal was to preach a gospel purified from the distortions introduced by Anglican pastors. The concepts of truth and purity punctuate and recur throughout Higginson's life and writings.

Progressively, Higginson was more clearly threatened by the London bishopric, headed by the Reverend Laud, who, unlike Bishop Williams of Lincoln, demonstrated his fierce determination to eradicate puritan representatives. By 1627, Higginson was forced to resign from the Anglican ministry, and was expecting trial before the High Commission Court for religious nonconformism.

However, he then was offered an invitation by the Massachusetts Bay Company authorities to join new settlers in their 1629 voyage to New England. This is described in Higginson's writings as a providential solution God granted him in order to escape the Anglican judges, and to enable him to advance his theological views. When he writes of his purposes for leaving England, Higginson places first this divine duty. Encouraged by the Reverend Hildersham, Higginson signed an "Agreement" with the Bay Company: "A true note on the allowance that the New England Company gave by common consent and order of their court and counsell unto Mr. Francis Higginson, minister, for his maintenance in New England," on April 8, 1629. The Company appointed John Endicott governor, and the Reverends Francis Higginson, Samuel Skelton, and Francis Bright ministers. The council of the Massachusetts Bay Plantation was composed of nine more members. With the local board formed, and King Charles I's charter granted on March 4, 1629, for the establishment of the new colony in America, Higginson, his wife, his nine children, and some "two hundred Passengers" left the Isle of Wight aboard the *Talbot* and the *Lyon's Whelpe* on May 4, 1629. Two more ships, the *Four Sisters* and the famous *Mayflower*, would join them in Massachusetts in June 1629.

In his account of the sea passage, Higginson asserts that the trip was under God's care, for it was exceptionally quick and safe, as they were at sea only about 50 days before landing in New England, compared to previous longer sea crossings from England to America. Moreover, very few passengers died—three only, from a smallpox epidemic that broke out on the ship. Although among the deceased was one of Higginson's youngest daughters, Mary, the Reverend considered that her death was favorable since she was divinely exempted from further earthly pains. In a rallied mood of thanksgiving to God, the *Talbot* reached Nehum kek [Salem] on June 24, 1629.

Once in America, the geographical distance from England and its Anglican plaintiffs, the opportunities of religious freedom offered by the New World together with the influence of earlier puritan settlers in New Plymouth under Governor Bradford swayed Higginson and the new colonists to move from Anglican nonconformism to Congregationalism. Therefore, the puritan group stepped further toward ecclesiastical independence from the Church of England. Higginson was approached by the board of the colony on August 6, 1629, to put in writing a "confession of [new] faith," on the occasion of which the Reverend Skelton was ordained as first pastor of the Salem Congregation. Higginson was selected as first teacher of the colony because of his broad knowledge of the liberal arts and his talent as a speaker. However, although the whole of Salem's settlers approved of the creation of the Congregation in August, a dissident faction led by Samuel and John Brown emerged shortly after. They claimed their opposition to separatism from the Church of England since in their coming to America they intended to set themselves apart from England's social perversions, not from its Church. Higginson's voice was a prominent one in the discussions of this matter. Governor Endicott solved this religious dissent by sending both brothers back to England. The influential participation of Higginson in this episode shows the power churchmen assumed in Puritan communities, in both religious and secular matters.

Both as a temporal and a spiritual guide and as a writer, Francis Higginson is noted for the unambiguousness of his prose. The text entitled "Generall considerations for the Plantation in New England, with an answer to several objections," which he produced before his going to New England, echoes his methodical mind, in the present case to demonstrate in eight points the advantages the English had in departing to America, and in seven points, the counteranalysis to the suspicions his compatriots nurtured against migration. The first goal of the New England settlement was the propagation of the gospel, a Christian duty that concerned the entire English nation. As for the nonconformists, America provided them

a free shelter for the expansion of their reformed faith. The New World is referred to as a "virgin land," where moral corruption had not yet penetrated, a land unlike England in this regard. The American wilderness is depicted as a vast area waiting for the English to cultivate and improve it. Regarding wealthier Englishmen, leaving their mother country would enable them to purify their souls and also to become models for less well-off prospective settlers.

Answering opponents to migration, Higginson puts forward first that the universality of Christianity renders its practice as significant in England as in any other part of the world, and second, especially in the case of nonconformists, they should not risk being destroyed by Anglican authorities to carry out their duty of Church purification. Concerning the difficulty of appropriating New England lands, Higginson argues that since Indians are nomadic peoples with neither legal land titles to present nor delimited territories, the English could easily and justifiably allot to themselves all the lands they needed. Furthermore, in Higginson's words, a large number of natives were opportunely decimated by "a miraculous plague whereby the greater part of the country is left voide of inhabitants." The Reverend was convinced that migration for religious motives, like his own, was bound to succeed, contrary to the migration of other Englishmen who migrated for economic profit. An unwavering confidence in God's favorable views of puritan migration is mentioned throughout Higginson's literary production.

The narrative entitled "A True Relation of the Last Voyage to New England" is divided into two parts. The author first gives details of the crew's daily progress at sea. He reports the climatic changes from their departure on the Thames at Gravesend on April 27, 1629, until their arrival at Salem on June 30, 1629. The relation includes a description of Higginson's daughter's sickness and death from smallpox at four years old on April 19, 1629. In the second part of the sea journal, Francis Higginson describes in five points the piety and harmony among the passengers, and the comfort and quickness of the voyage thanks to God's blessing.

The same confidence is found in Higginson's masterpiece: *New-Englands Plantation*. The manuscript was sent to England on the return voyage of the *Mayflower*. After the manuscript reached England in November 1629, Michael Sparke printed it three times in London. In the first edition, only "a Reuerend Divine now there resident" helps identify Francis Higginson as author. The second and third editions were enlarged with a letter by "Master Graves, Engynere now there resident." In the second edition was also enclosed a "Catalogue of such needfull things as euery Planter doth or ought to provide to go to New-England; as namely for one man, which being doubled, may serve for as many as you please[. . .]for a whole yeere." The five sections of the "catalogue" refer to the "Apparell" or clothing, "Armes," "Tools" for house building, fishing, hunting, and farming, "Household implements," and "Spices," including sugar and fruit. Higginson did not forget to remind newcomers that they should not expect to find books, nets, lines, bacon, and goats available in America. Finally, the Reverend cites "the names of the most remarkable places in New-England," which consists of transcriptions of the spoken Native American place names.

New-Englands Plantation, the author's position as a clergyman notwithstanding, is mainly concerned with pragmatic rather than theological matters. Higginson's main goal is to convey practical knowledge about an unknown land to his countrymen in England. Along with its informative feature, *New-Englands Plantation* can be defined as a didactic catalogue directed at prospective English settlers. From the epilogue one can determine that the text is chiefly directed at newcomers, or "them that are to goe [to New England]." Besides, the migration of nonconformists is especially encouraged, since America offers them a retreat. Higginson's intent to involve his readers in the adventure of settling America is evident in the way he directly

addresses the reader from the start: "Reader, do not disdaine to read this relation."

In its outward aspect the text has a catalog-like structure, presenting a double list of benefits on the one hand, and of disadvantages on the other. The text is divided into seven sections. The first exposes the migrants' principal intent, being the free propagation of a purified—that is, Reformed—gospel doctrine, and the "commodities" the author sees in the fauna and flora indigenous to the Bay Colony. Higginson afterward describes succinctly the other three elements: "Waters [. . .]with the things belonging to the same," "the Aire[. . .]with the Temper and Creatures in it," and "the Fire," which Higginson relates to wood. Quite disproportionately, the "discommodities" are limited to four points in one page out of 18: the flies, the frost—the only aspect the Reverend portrays as worse in America than in England—the snakes, and various shortages, such as the scarcity of horses. The sixth section, where Higginson introduces the reader to the Natives, is particularly typical of the author's care to reassure his compatriots who remained in England. He cleverly depicts Native Americans in ways Englishmen could understand: local leaders are, for example, equated to "Kings." Amerindians are pictured in a few words and in a down-to-earth manner. The author indicates native population figures, which are low; their physical appearance; their weapons, which seem poorly sophisticated; and their way of life. Paradoxically, Higginson does not put forward the conversion, nor the civilizing of Indian peoples by the English. On the contrary, Higginson insists upon the harmony between English settlers and Native Americans regardless of their divergent cultures. *New-Englands Plantation* goes on and ends in a positive tone. In the last section entitled "Of the present conditions of the Plantation and what it is," the reader is told that concord also regulates the relations between earlier and more recent settlers in New England. The final lines of the narrative emphasize the religious freedom non-Anglicans are given in America.

Higginson uses a simple style to portray the newly discovered American landscape and to praise New England's countryside, comparing it to that of England in order to fight a representation, common in England at the time, according to which New England's lands were inhospitable and barren. His intent to convince and to be understood is perceptible in the smoothness of his prose and the clear division of the narrative into simple, discrete chapters. *New-Englands Plantation* was intended to be as fluid as the pioneers' experience in settling the country was supposed to be easy. Higginson achieves the fluidity of movement in his narrative partly by means of linking and transitional phrases such as "we will now begin" or "now I will tell you of [. . .]. " His stylistic goals of simplicity and comprehensibility are also apparent in the profusion of connective terms the author uses, such as "therefore," "also," "thus," "besides," and "neither [. . .] nor." "First," "secondly," "thirdly," and "fourthly" are other connective devices relied upon in the text.

Higginson's purpose of attracting new settlers in order to increase the colony's inhabitants and make the colony prosper is evident in his promotional prose. The Reverend's enthusiasm, which is a major characteristic of *New-Englands Plantation*, is conveyed throughout his narrative by repeated enumerations of the land's advantages: "The fertilitie of the Soyle is to be admired at, as appeareth in the aboundance of Grasse that groweth euerie where both verie thicke, verie long, and verie high in diuers places [...]." On the subject of the English settlers' dealings with the Natives, Higginson is one of the very few optimistic Englishmen declaring that Indians "doe generally professe to like well of our comming and planting here." Higginson's eulogies to New England are also expressed by the repetition of the term "aboundance" and the recurrence of adjectives presenting the country as a cornucopia: "aboundance of Sea Fish," "Excellent Vines," "plentifull of all wood," "plenty of Candles."

The cataloging strategy of the text and the use of nouns in the plural appear as so many literary techniques used to point out the fertility of the land and the profusion of its resources.

The zealous Reverend also insists on producing accurate descriptions of New England throughout his account. Significantly, Higginson presents his narrative as a "True Description," and in his opening dedication "To the Reader," he invites him to "here reade the truth, [. . .] thou shalt find without any [. . .] bumbasted words, or any quaint [. . .] additions [. . .]." He further asserts, "I will indeavour to shew you what *New-England* is [. . .] and truly endeavour by Gods helpe to report nothing but the naked truth [. . .]." He uses two additional strategies to differentiate his writing from other comparable descriptions:

> *Travellers may lye by authoritie,* and so may take too much sinfull libertie that way. Yet I may say of my selfe as once *Nehemiah* did in another case: *Shall such a Man as I lye?* No verily: It becommeth not a Preacher of Truth to bee a Writer of Falshod in any degree [. . .].

Higginson, using his position as a clergyman as a badge of honesty, clearly distinguishes his description from those produced by whimsical "travelers."

Within the body of the text the author creates the impression of truthfulness by elaborating the material details of the land's physical attributes—the fauna, the flora, the four elements—but the attributes he thus depicts are all selected to reinforce his theme of natural abundance; he is not interested in providing the reader with a more general knowledge of the region. He relies upon the concreteness of his descriptions to authenticate his narration. Furthermore, the Reverend's empirical use of direct observation gives an almost scientific turn to his narrative:

> I have beene carefull to report nothing of *New-England* but what I have partly seene with mine owne Eyes, and partly heard and

inquired from the mouths of verie honest and religious persons, who by liuing in the Countrey a good space of time haue had experience and knowledge of the state thereof, & whose testimonies I doe beleeue as my selfe.

Consequently, *New-Englands Plantation*, one of the earliest literary representations of territory that would in time be part of the United States, renders the new land as a vivid catalog of natural abundance that can easily be commodified. And its style will make the account useful to any newcomer regardless of his educational attainments.

Like *New-Englands Plantation*, Higginson's "Letter [. . .] sent to his Friends at Leicester," in July 1629, is aimed at migrants from England. The author first announces the impending arrival of new settlers from different English cities. He warns forthcoming migrants to hasten their departure before English authorities oppose any further nonconformists' migrations. Higginson also recommends bringing over carpenters and cattle. This letter stands as an exception in Higginson's writings, for it is less optimistic and more pragmatic in tone about the sea passage and daily life in America for new settlers. To conclude, the author emphasizes the necessity to bring enough food, medicine, and raw material, as iron and glass, for the first year ashore.

In the author's last text, the "Confession of Faith [and] Covenant of Grace," no complex theological notions prevent the full understanding of its points of doctrine. The founding manuscript of the new Congregation had to be clear enough to unite the whole community. And unity was crucial to build a society far removed from traditional British social structures and Anglican ecclesiology.

The ingenuity with which he describes early American religious affairs and nature makes Higginson's writings stand out from other Puritan texts of his time. The three printings within a single year (1630) of *New-Englands Plantation* indicate how successful the Reverend's narrative was at the time, and since so many Europeans formed their first impressions of America's flora,

fauna, climate, and landscape from this document, Higginson must be considered as an early contributor to the history of American nature writing. Morerover, as one of the earliest accounts of an English settlement in America, Higginson's narrative takes on a central place in early American literature as it allows today's readers to recreate the seventeenth-century New England landscape. Furthermore, while Francis Higginson's group failed to permanently establish the colony of Salem because of the harshness of the 1629 winter, their experience paved the way for the "Great [puritan] Migration" of 1630 aboard the *Arbella*, led by John Winthrop. With other Congregationalist leaders, Winthrop took advantage of the 1629 emigrants' errors, and ensured the perpetuation of his community by carefully preparing for the migration before sailing for American shores.

Nonetheless, probably because he was too optimistic about New England's being a perfect refuge, and made overly enthusiastic by the looming threats from Anglican authorities, Higginson did not mention as part of the "discommodities" of his *New-Englands Plantation* the danger of epidemics, one of which actually caused his death 15 months after he set foot on American soil in June 1629. Governor John Winthrop thus recorded Francis Higginson's demise in September 1630, as having occurred on August 6, 1630 "of a fever."

PRIMARY BIBLIOGRAPHY

Books

New-Englands Plantation. Or, a Short and True Description of the Commodities and Discommodities of that Countrey. Written by a reverend Divine now there resident (London: Printed by T.C. and R.C. for Michael Sparke, 1630; Washington, D.C.: P. Force, 1835; vol. 1, no. 12 of *Transactions of the American Historical Society*: 1–14; Amsterdam: Theatrum Orbis Terrarum & New York: Da Capo Press, 1970).

New-Englands Plantation. Or, a Short and True Description of the Commodities and Discommodities of that Countrey. Written by Mr. Higgeson

[Higginson], a reverend Divine now there resident. Whereunto is added a Letter, by Mr. Graves an Enginere, out of New England, the second edition enlarged (London: Printed by T. & R. Cotes, for Michael Sparke, 1630; New York: New England Society in the City of New York, 1930; New York: Lenox Hill Pub. & Dist. Co., Burt Franklin, 1971).

New-Englands Plantation. Or, a Short and True Description of the Commodities and Discommodities of that Countrey. Written by Mr. Higgeson [Higginson], a reverend Divine now there resident. Whereunto is added a Letter, by Mr. Graves an Enginere, out of New England, the third edition enlarged (London: Printed by T. & R. Cotes, for Michael Sparke, 1630).

New-Englands Plantation: with the Sea Journal and Other Writings, edited by Bruce Rogers (Salem, MA: Essex Book and Print Club & Cambridge, MA: Riverside Press, 1908) [including: a facsimile of the 3rd edition of *New-Englands plantation*].

Other

"Generall considerations for the Plantation in New England, with an answer to Several Objections," in *Collection of Original Papers Relative to the History of the Colony of Massachusetts Bay*, ed. Thomas Hutchinson (Boston: Printed by Thomas and John Fleet, 1769), 27–31; in *Life of Francis Higginson*, ed. Thomas Wentworth Higginson (New York: Dood, Mead, and Company Publishers, 1891), 40–51.

"Confession of Faith [and] Covenant of Grace; Whereof Thirty Copies [were taken for the] Thirty Persons [which were to] Begin the Working of Gathering the Church," in *Life of Francis Higginson*, ed. Thomas Wentworth Higginson (New York: Dood, Mead, and Company Publishers, 1891), 80–81.

"Some Brief Collections of a letter that Mr. Higginson Sent to His Friends at Leicester [July 1629]," in *Collection of Original Papers Relative to the History of the Colony of Massachusetts Bay*, ed. Thomas Hutchinson (Boston: Printed by Thomas and John Fleet, 1769), 47–50; in *Life of Francis Higginson*, ed. Thomas Wentworth Higginson (New York: Dood, Mead, and Company Publishers, 1891), 72–75.

"A True Relation of the Last Voyage to New England, Declaring All Circumstances with the Manner of the Passage We Had by Sea, and What Manner of Country and Inhabitants We Found When We Came to Land: and What Is the Present State and Condition of the English People that Are There Already. Faithfully Recorded According to the Truth, for the Satisfaction of Very Many of my Loving Friends, Who Have Earnestly Requested to be Truly Notifyed in These Things, Written from New England, July 24, 1629," in *Life of Francis Higginson*, ed. Thomas Wentworth Higginson (New York: Dood, Mead, and Company Publishers, 1891), 48–68.

SECONDARY BIBLIOGRAPHY

Biographies

Thomas Wentworth Higginson, *Life of Francis Higginson, First Minister in the Massachusetts-Bay Colony, and Author of "New England's Plantation" (1630)* (New York: Dood, Mead, and Company Publishers, 1891).

Cotton Mather, "Janus Nov-Anglicanus; the Life of Mr. Francis Higginson, *Magnalia Christi Americana; or, the Ecclesiastical History of New-England, from its First Planting, in the Year 1620, unto the Year of Our Lord 1698, in Seven Books*, 1702, vol. 1, book 3, ed. the Reverend Thomas Robbins, with translations of the Hebrew, Greek, and Latin quotations by Lucius Franklin Robinson (Hartford: Silas Andrus & Son, 1853), 354–366.

John William T. Youngs, *The Congregationalists* (New York: Greenwood Press, 1990).

References

Nina Baym, "Early Histories of American Literature: A Chapter in the Institution of New England," *American Literary History* 1.3 (Fall 1989): 459–88.

Stephen Fender, *Sea Changes: British Emigration and American Literature* (Cambridge, G.B.: Cambridge University Press, 1992).

Thomas Wentworth Higginson, *Descendants of the Reverend Francis Higginson, First "Teacher" in the Massachusetts Bay Colony of Salem, Massachusetts and Author "New-Englands Plantation" (1630)* (Cambridge?, MA: Private printing, 1910).

Sidney Perley, *The History of Salem*, 3 vols., vol. 1: 1626–1637 (Salem, MA: S. Perley, 1924): 89–184.

Josephine K. Piercy, *Studies in Literary Types in Seventeenth Century America (1607–1710), in Two Parts*, part 1 (New Haven: Yale University Press; London: Oxford University Press, 1939).

Charles F. Richardson, *American Literature, 1607–1885*, vol. 1 (New York; London: G.P. Putnam's Sons, 1888).

David S. Shields, "Exploratory Narratives and the Development of the New England Passage Journal," *Essex Institute Historical Collections* 120, no. 1 (1984): 38–57.

John Edwards Holbrook
(December 30, 1796– September 8, 1871)

Daniel Patterson

In the preface to his monumental *North American Herpetology* (1842), John Edwards Holbrook observes, "In no department of American Zoology is there so much confusion as in Herpetology." Holbrook's five-volume natural history of his young nation's amphibian and reptile species brought the needed order to this branch of the natural sciences, and it was widely praised for doing so. Upon Holbrook's death, Louis Agassiz wrote, "Holbrook's elaborate history of American Herpetology was far above any previous work on the same subject. In that branch of investigation Europe had at that time nothing which could compare with it." As early as 1851, however, Charles Girard, another accomplished zoologist, had referred to Holbrook as the "Father of American Herpetology," a distinction that is still universally acknowledged. In an age of tremendous advances in American natural history, Holbrook's scientific contributions were very significant, comparing easily with John James Audubon's contributions to ornithology and Thomas Nuttall's contributions to botany. Like those other, better-known naturalists, Holbrook's accomplishment extends beyond the natural sciences, for the scientist's prose accounts of 147 species of amphibians and reptiles often are evocative enough to be considered as contributions to American nature writing as well.

On December 30, 1796, Holbrook was born to Silas and Mary (Edwards) Holbrook at his mother's family home in Beaufort, South Carolina. Shortly after his birth, the decision was made to move the family to his father's family home in Wrentham, Massachusetts, where Holbrook spent his childhood and attended school. Little is known about these early years, but at the time Wrentham was developing cotton mills and a straw goods manufactory; it was also dominated by a Congregational church, which several Holbrooks attended. The future herpetologist began his higher education at nearby Brown University, from which he received his AB degree in 1815. He then went to Philadelphia to study medicine at the University of Pennsylvania, from which he received the MD in 1818. Immediately after earning his medical degree, Holbrook began to practice medicine in Boston, but he wanted to continue his training and studies, which he did by spending the next four years in the prestigious institutions of Paris and Edinburgh. In his later medical practice, Holbrook was known to avoid performing surgery whenever possible because of his aversion to the suffering of patients. Whether this understandable aversion or his childhood experience of his natural environment in eastern Massachusetts might have predisposed the young physician to seek out new directions of research is uncertain, but it is certain that when he arrived in Paris, he was quickly attracted to the Jardin des Plantes, one of Europe's most influential natural history institutions, and the site of Georges-Louis Leclerc, comte de Buffon's work between 1739 and 1788. Whether Holbrook's specific interest in herpetology was already in place is also unclear, but he quickly began to work and study with the Jardin's two zoologists who were most interested in herpetology: André Duméril and Gabriel Bibron. He also studied with Georges Cuvier and Achille Valenciennes, both of whom produced significant work in ichthyology, which no doubt influenced Holbrook's later work in that field. These eminent French zoologists (with the exception of Cuvier) remained Holbrook's friends throughout their lives, and he cited their published work frequently in his own.

With significant new knowledge of zoology acquired in Paris and of medicine acquired in Edinburgh, Holbrook returned to his own country in 1822 and decided to make his home in Charleston, South Carolina, near his birthplace and his mother's extended family. There he began to practice medicine and study herpetology. He succeeded quickly and joined with a group of Charleston's leading physicians to found, in December 1823, the Medical College of South Carolina. When it opened in 1824, Holbrook was one of the seven physicians chosen to form the faculty of the college and train the 30 students. Holbrook held his position as professor of anatomy, lecturing one day a week, for more than 30 years. As a lecturer, he is said to have inspired his students with a profound regard for the high seriousness of their future careers as physicians. There was a certain homiletic tone in his lectures, which were popular with the students. The surviving accounts suggest that he was also

highly regarded as a physician in his medical practice. His partner in that practice, Thomas Louis Ogier, has written that Holbrook was highly skilled in his manner of winning the trust of patients and comforting them, by whom he was quite well liked. His only limitation as a physician seems to have been his deliberate avoidance, when possible, of obstetrics and major surgical procedures. Ogier characterized this behavior:

> He would advise the operation to be performed, speak of all the details, and often assist, until the operation was under way, and then quietly withdraw himself until it was over, when he would again appear, say something cheerful to the patient, and attend him afterwards with the greatest kindness and efficiency.

Despite being known as somewhat careless in matters outside medicine or natural history, he was seen as a genial, reliable, and important presence in Charleston society.

In 1827, Holbrook married a descendant of two of South Carolina's most important families, Harriott Pinckney Rutledge. Signatures of her ancestors appear on both the Declaration of Independence and the Constitution. Holbrook's success and high visibility in Charleston together with his mother's connections to the city no doubt made so prominent a match possible. Harriott Holbrook's engaging personality, her impressively broad knowledge, her deftness as a manager of a household, and her genuine affection for her husband have been attested to by such prominent visitors to the Holbrook home as Frederika Bremer and Louis and Elizabeth Agassiz. Harvard's world-famous zoologist noted that the Holbrooks' lives seemed "so closely knit together that it is difficult to speak on one without the other," while his wife, Elizabeth Agassiz, remarked at Mrs. Holbrook's ability to engage Harvard's leading naturalist in informed conversations about her husband's herpetological work and about the origins of humankind. There is no doubt that Harriott Holbrook contributed significantly to her husband's ability to devote so much of his time, resources, and concentration to carrying out his ambitious scientific work.

The Holbrooks also owned 33 slaves, who were no doubt also helpful to Holbrook's work. They certainly would have been employed in capturing, keeping alive in various enclosures, and generally maintaining the living animals he needed for his study. Throughout the *North American Herpetology*, Holbrook regularly cites the common, local names for amphibian and reptile species used by slaves.

Sometime after his move to Charleston, Holbrook, with the encouragement of the French naturalists, with whom he continued to correspond, decided to prepare a monograph on American herpetology. In his 1842 Preface to *North American Herpetology*, Holbrook remarks on some of the difficulties a project of such scope faced. While his goals were to produce a comprehensive account of America's amphibian and reptile species and to describe as "new" only those species that had not been previously described in the scientific literature, he worried that his distance from libraries with good natural history holdings and from museums with other specimens for comparison would result in his "describing animals as new that have long been known to European Naturalists." He goes on to acknowledge in gratitude the assistance he received from many of the nation's leading naturalists, including the few publishing herpetologists, as well as from interested friends and neighbors. He faced some difficulties, but he was well connected and actively cultivated a network of professional and amateur naturalists.

It is worth noting that through roughly the same years that Holbrook was developing his *Herpetology*, Audubon was at work on his *Birds of America* (1827–1838) and *Ornithological Biographies* (1831–1839). Holbrook was certainly aware of Audubon's gigantic project no later than October 1831 when Audubon arrived in Charleston and stayed several weeks with the Reverend John Bachman, who became a lifelong friend of Audubon and his Charleston agent for soliciting subscriptions to *Birds of America*. Holbrook knew Bachman well; in his Preface Holbrook acknowledges a debt to Bachman "for many interesting remarks on the habits of our Reptiles, particularly those of the Alligator." The contemporaneous development of America's first great ornithology and herpetology is interesting from a historical perspective since it is generally thought that a nation's ornithology would emerge earlier than its herpetology. As Holbrook explains in his 1842 Introduction, herpetology "has been more neglected than all other branches of Zoology." He might have had the growing popularity of Audubon and his ornithology in mind when he elaborated the reasons for this cultural neglect:

> for the study of Reptiles offers difficulties more numerous and insurmountable than those presented by any other class of vertebrated animals. Inhabiting, for the most part, deep and extensive swamps, infected with malaria, and abounding with diseases during the summer months, when Reptiles are most numerous, time is wanting to observe their modes of life with any prospect of success. Regarded, moreover, by most persons as objects of detestation, represented as venomous, and possessed of the most noxious properties, few have been hardy enough to study their character and habits.

Sensing thus the general public aversion to crawling creatures, and apparently lacking Audubon's promotional flare, Holbrook quietly made his case for the importance of herpetology:

> Reptiles offer many striking points of interest to the student of nature. To one who would trace the chain of organized bodies, their connexion, their relation with each other, and with the great whole, the study of Herpetology is highly interesting and important. The Reptiles occupy a prominent place in the scale of creation. Neither the highest, nor yet the lowest of vertebrated animals, they fill a space between the Birds and Fishes, and without them a vast link in the chain of animated beings would be wanting.

Audubon did not have such cultural biases to overcome to establish the public interest in his *Birds*.

Holbrook engaged an Italian-born artist, J. Sera, to create the illustrations for his *Herpetology*. Little is known about Sera, but he had some small reputation as a painter of landscapes and theater scenery; he also advertised himself locally as a musician. He is said to have prided himself on giving the animals he drew for Holbrook a distinctive physical expressiveness, often through their eyes. The earliest of Sera's drawings for Holbrook is dated 1831; when the artist died in 1836, only about half of the illustrations had been completed. Holbrook then employed John H. Richard, who, in his illustrations, rather emphasized the close details of surface features. By the time the entire work was published in 1842, Holbrook had used drawings from 17 different artists, among whom was Maria Martin, Bachman's sister-in-law, who also drew some background landscapes, flowers, trees, and branches for Audubon's *Birds of America*. This is an interesting moment in the history of the development of natural history illustrations: Audubon's *Birds* is the last significant work of natural history to use copperplate engravings, and Holbrook's *Herpetology* is one of the first whose illustrations are lithographs. Seen in this context, Richard's notation on two of his lithographs, those of the alligator and the collared lizard, becomes a graphic celebration by a scientific illustrator: "From Life on Stone."

To increase the likelihood that the hand-colored lithographs would faithfully represent the colors and color patterns of the living animals, Holbrook saw to it that the artists drew from living specimens: "almost every one was done from life." Coloring from live animals is especially important in a work of herpetology since many reptile and amphibian species lose coloration upon death and alter coloration when preserved in alcohol. For each of the several illustrations that were prepared from a nonliving specimen, Holbrook includes a note to inform the reader of the fact. Holbrook originally issued a first

volume in 1836 and then three more by 1840, but new species continued to come to his attention, and he soon realized that new genera would have to be established and his original organization modified accordingly. He gathered as many copies of this "first edition" as he could and burned them. The full five-volume work printed in 1842 is therefore the second edition.

Holbrook adheres to the same general structure for each of his natural history accounts of reptile and amphibian species: the opening taxonomy is followed by a description of physical features, after which the colors and dimensions are described; the species' behavior and geographic distribution follow, and the account concludes with a consideration of how the species has been identified in previously published works of natural history. (He announced his intention to publish an accompanying study of the anatomy of these same species, but he never produced this work.) Within this recurring structure, however, and even while maintaining a prose style that could not be charged with unscientific excess or literary affectation, Holbrook achieves a natural history that evokes a vivid world alive with all manner of crawling creatures, and he conveys this world through the quiet voice of his persona, a Southern gentleman herpetologist deeply engaged in knowing this world.

Holbrook's prose evokes a vivid presence of the animals he represents. When he writes of the eastern box turtle (*Terrapene carolina*), for example, he conjures a surprisingly varied and impressively large assemblage of them: "In no other tortoise is there such a great variety in the color and markings of the shell. I have seen more than one hundred living specimens together, and could not select two precisely alike." He gives the great populations of the southern water snake (*Nerodia fasciata*) a vivacious omnipresence: "It swims with great rapidity, and hundreds at a time may be seen darting through the water in all directions, constantly protruding their tongues, as if to feel the objects before them." When he writes of the "eel-shaped, though robust" siren (*Siren lacertina*), the fact that the herpetologist's human slaves lived in very different relationships with many of the animals he studied rises vividly from the page:

> [the siren] is abundant in our rice-fields, and are often thrown out in great numbers, at certain seasons, when the ditches are cleaned; being regarded, however, as venomous by the slaves, they are instantly killed or dreadfully mangled, and left to serve as food for raccoons or for turkey-buzzards ever on the watch.

The relationships conveyed here among siren, enslaved human, raccoon, and vulture make this passage especially dynamic, approaching even an ecological perception. There are so many references to the presence of snakes and lizards in houses and outhouses that they become a refrain. The anole (*Anolis carolinensis*), for example, "is a bold and daring animal, haunting outhouses and garden fences; and in new settlements it even enters the houses, walking over the tables and other articles of furniture in search of flies." The yellow rat snake (*Elaphe obsoleta quadrivittata*), along with several other species of reptiles, is represented as "frequenting the vicinity of houses, and sometimes making its way into the cabins of the negroes." Holbrook thus implies that the "houses" were to some degree less open to reptiles than were the "cabins."

Through the five volumes of *North American Herpetology*, Holbrook's persona emerges gradually but clearly as a gentleman naturalist whose domestic life and scientific vocation were seamlessly unified. He reveals, for example, that he kept numerous animals captive in and about his home. No doubt reminding many of his readers of Gilbert White's famous tortoise, Timothy, Holbrook reveals that he had a long association with the gopher tortoise (*Gopherus polyphemus*): "In the wild state they are represented as nocturnal animals, or as seeking their food by night: when domesticated, and I have kept many of them for years, they may be seen grazing at all hours of the day." He kept in confinement specimens of many other species, even the water moccasin, "the terror of

the negroes that labour about rice plantations, where they are more dreaded than the Rattlesnake." The fact that Holbrook's persona gives even so common a creature as the southern toad (*Bufo terrestris*) a space in his own house reflects the perfect union of herpetologist and *homo domesticus* in this persona's identity:

> during the summer months he would retire to a corner of the room, into a habitation he had prepared for himself, in a small quantity of earth, placed there for his convenience. Towards evening he would wander about the room in search of food, seizing greedily whatever insect came in his way. Some water having been squeezed from a sponge upon his head one hot day in July, he returned the next to the same spot, and seemed very well pleased with the repetition; nor did he fail during the extreme heat of the summer to repair to it frequently, in search of his shower-bath.

Holbrook's use of the passive voice ("Some water having been squeezed") removes his persona from the foreground to adjust the reader's focus on the toad's behavior, but it also serves as a thin veil that fails to obscure the hand that held the sponge—the hand of a physician, naturalist, plantation owner, husband, and leading citizen of a vibrant port city sustained on the backs of enslaved Africans, a human hand providing a gentle "shower-bath" for a common toad.

This hand nonetheless signifies the deep involvement in the lives of his subjects that Holbrook's persona enacts. The reader comes to see this herpetologist habitually looking into and under objects most people would ignore or avoid. One sees him looking for the squirrel tree frog (*Hyla squirella*), for example, "under the bark" of decaying trees; he found this species "[o]ften...about old houses, and under logs and boards." That he regularly peered into wells becomes apparent when he reports about the bullfrog's aquatic nature: "I have known them to live in wells for years." He also looked into much smaller holes and over time improved his understanding of which species were associated with which holes; about the eastern spadefoot (*Scaphiopus holbrooki*), he writes, "it lives in small holes about six inches deep, excavated by itself in the earth, which for a long time I mistook for holes of insects." Much of his knowledge of the behavior of reptiles and amphibians came from various kinds of experimentation, often conducted over long periods of time. He determined that the southern hognose snake (*Heterodon platyrhinos*) will not bite by prodding many of them "many times" with the end of his "walking-stick or cane." He concluded that the same species deliberately feigns death when threatened by coming upon "many instances" of the behavior and apparently waiting there until the snake began to move again. He could report that the gopher tortoise is "remarkably strong" as a result of having placed "a weight of two hundred pounds or more" on the back of one he had domesticated. An unfortunate eastern box turtle helped Holbrook determine that that species "is entirely a land animal; indeed, it is so bad a swimmer, that it will drown at the end of a few days if thrown into water."

Despite causing the deaths of numerous animals, Holbrook's persona evinces a delight in, and even affection for, many of the species he has observed and studied. The southern cricket frog (*Acris gryllus*), for example, "is a merry little frog"; he reveals his delight in their presence in his home: "I have kept several for months in a glass globe on a few sprigs of purslain...feeding them occasionally with flies." In his discussion of the American toad (*Bufo americanus*), he represents this species as a maligned and misunderstood victim. It is "very mild and timid," dwelling in "dark and lonely corners" until evening when it "issues from its place of concealment in search of insects," where it often "falls a prey to snakes and owls." The herpetologist explains to his readers that the long-standing human aversion to the toad results from its "unhandsome exterior"; he assures them, however, that it is nevertheless "perfectly harmless, destroying only the insects that nature has apportioned for its food." In his account of the green sea turtle (*Chelonia mydas*), he expresses profound regret that

humans slaughter so many of them and take their eggs. He creates a pitiable image of the many that are captured on a beach when they come to lay their eggs:

> these are turned on their backs, nor can they resume their natural position, in consequence of the shortness of their necks, and peculiar arrangement of their fins, and thus they remain until they can be leisurely collected the next day.

His disdain for the "eggers" is clear:

> [they] do not confine their depredations to the nests of the Green Turtles, but they seize upon those of all other species, as well as upon the eggs of thousands of sea birds that seek the same localities during their breeding season.

His sympathy for the green turtle is enhanced by his contrasting expression of admiration for its ability to navigate the oceans:

> it is not a little singular, that animals so low in the scale of creation, should have the instinct to return to these haunts from great distances, hundreds and even thousands of miles.

The herpetologist's delight and affection for his subjects manifests itself further in his response to the beauty of many species, which he frequently notes. One of the most closely detailed and fully developed descriptions is of one of the smallest animals in the entire work, the ornate chorus frog (*Pseudacris ornate*). Holbrook's fascination with the "great beauty of this little animal" moves him to describe it so intricately that the description of this inch-long frog is more than half as long as his description of the thirteen-foot alligator. Holbrook's persona enacts a scientist performing a labor of love when he records details that, as a reader would fairly infer, he must have used a magnifying lens to see:

> on the anterior part of the thigh are several small yellow spots; on the posterior surface these spots are so numerous and so closely approximated, as to resemble at first view a yellow waving line.

For the sake of accuracy and precision, Holbrook rarely employs figurative language, but on the rare occasions when he does, it is something beautiful, such as the singing of the green treefrogs (*Hyla cinerea*), that moves him to metaphor:

> Their noise proceeds from a single note, which, at a little distance, is not unlike the sound of a small bell; and there seems in general to be one leader of their orchestra, and when he raises his note, hundreds take it up from all parts of the cornfield, and when he stops, the concert is at an end, until he again begins.

Holbrook believed that no American species of amphibian or reptile was identical to any European species. Whether this shows a trace of nationalism or not, the belief could certainly provide a motive and inspiration for involving oneself in the work of identifying and describing these unique species. The uniqueness of America's frogs, turtles, and snakes would also inform the herpetologist's imaginative look westward, which occurs in the very brief conclusion to *North American Herpetology*. There he anticipates the many species that are yet to be discovered in the "vast country west of the Mississippi." In Holbrook's view, it was a country alive with crawling creatures with the power to fascinate. And if his persona is not strictly "scientific," it is because of his susceptibility to this power.

After *North American Herpetology* was published, Holbrook and his wife (they never had any children) traveled to Europe, where he returned to the Jardin des Plantes and visited his friends and colleagues there, where Holbrook's work received high praise. Possibly influenced by the work of ichthyology published by Cuvier and Valenciennes, Holbrook turned to that branch of the natural sciences when he returned home. His original intent was to cover all the species across a large part of the Southeast. The only part of this known to have been published was titled *Southern Ichthyology: or, a Description of the Fishes Inhabiting the Waters of South Carolina, Georgia, and Florida* (1847). It consists of just 32 pages. Holbrook decided then that the scope of this project was too large, and he focused on the fish of his home state only. In 1855 he published what was to have been only the first volume of *Ichthyology of South Carolina*. When a fire, according to Holbrook's preface to the 1860 second edition, destroyed "all the plates, stones, and original drawings" for his work, Holbrook revised the text and had all the plates redrawn. Once again, he found himself recalling issued copies of a first edition and replacing them with a second edition. In 1860, the first volume was published, but no more were published before the Civil War began, during which Holbrook's materials for this project were apparently destroyed.

When the war came, Holbrook served in the Confederate army as a medical officer; he was also appointed to chair the examining board of surgeons for South Carolina. During the war, he was often among the soldiers and had to endure the difficult conditions of that war. In 1863, his wife of 36 years died in Columbia, South Carolina. When the war ended, Holbrook was alone and had lost most of his wealth and material possessions, including his books and papers. He began spending time with friends and relatives in Massachusetts. His northern colleagues honored him in 1868 by electing him to the National Academy of Sciences despite his involvement with the Confederate army. He died of a stroke at his sister's home in Norfolk, Massachusetts, on September 8, 1871. His body was returned to Charleston, where he was buried in the Magnolia Cemetery.

Holbrook undoubtedly saw himself as writing primarily for a scientific audience, and as primarily a writer of objective accounts of reptiles and amphibians. His *North American Herpetology*, however, is not merely a storehouse of knowledge; it is also a window enabling views of a cryptic but fascinating world. Holbrook's persona is consistently reserved, yet the caring patience evident in the detailed descriptions and the subtle affective responses to a world enlivened by such a variety of life-forms make that persona compelling, persuasive, and authentic. *North American Herpetology* is an expressive verbal and graphic representation of nature viewed through the eyes of someone who habitually looked under logs and beneath the bark. And the expressive voice of this work should be considered in the context of other distinctive naturalist voices of Holbrook's day, such as those of John D. Godman, Thomas Nuttall, and John James Audubon. It is the voice of a naturalist unable to confine himself strictly to the ways of science.

PRIMARY BIBLIOGRAPHY

Books

American Herpetology; or, a Description of the Reptiles Inhabiting the United States (Charleston, SC: E.J. van Brunt, 1835).

North American Herpetology; or a Description of the Reptiles Inhabiting the United States [first edition], 4 vols. (Philadelphia: J. Dobson, 1836–1840).

North American Herpetology; or a Description of the Reptiles Inhabiting the United States [second edition], 5 vols. (Philadelphia: J. Dobson, 1842).

Southern Ichthyology: or, a Description of the Fishes Inhabiting the Waters of South Carolina, Georgia, and Florida, No. II (New York & London: Wiley & Putnam, 1847).

Ichthyology of South Carolina (Charleston, SC: John Russell, 1855; second edition, Charleston, SC: Russell and Jones, 1860).

Edition

North American Herpetology, ed. Kraig Adler (n.p.: Society for the Study of Amphibians and Reptiles, 1976).

Letters

A number of Holbrook's letters are held at the Academy of Natural Sciences, Philadelphia. Louis Agassiz possessed 106 of the original herpetological drawings prepared for Holbrook (dated 1831–1852); those are now in the Museum of Comparative Zoology at Harvard University. Many of Holbrook's papers were probably destroyed or scattered when Charleston was ransacked by Sherman's army during the Civil War.

SECONDARY BIBLIOGRAPHY

References

Kraig Adler, "New Genera and Species Described in Holbrook's 'North American Herpetology,'" in *North American Herpetology*, ed. Kraig Adler (n.p.: Society for the Study of Amphibians and Reptiles, 1976), xxix–xliii.

Elizabeth Cabot Cary Agassiz, *Louis Agassiz, His Life and Correspondence*, 2 vols., ed. Elizabeth Agassiz (Boston: Houghton Mifflin and Co., 1885).

Louis Agassiz, "Dr. John E. Holbrook of Charleston, S.C.," *Proceedings of the Boston Society of Natural History, 1870–71* (1872): 347–51.

Ann Shelby Blum, *Picturing Nature: American Nineteenth-century Zoological Illustration* (Princeton: Princeton University Press, 1993).

Frederika Bremer, *The Homes of the New World; Impressions of America*, 3 vols., trans. Mary Howitt (London: A. Hall, Virtue, and Co., 1853).

Hubert Lyman Clark, "John Edwards Holbrook," in *Dictionary of American Biography*, vol. 9, ed. Dumas Malone (New York: Charles Scribner's Sons, 1932), 129–30.

Theodore Gill, "Biographical Memoir of John Edwards Holbrook," *National Academy of Sciences Biographical Memoirs*, vol. 5 (Washington: National Academy of Sciences, 1905), 47–77.

Charles Girard, "On a New American Saurian Reptile," *Proceedings of the American Association for the Advancement of Science* 4 (1851): 200–202.

Wayne Hanley, *Natural History in America: From Mark Catesby to Rachel Carson* (New York: Quadrangle, 1977).

Christoph Irmscher, *The Poetics of Natural History: from John Bartram to William James* (New Brunswick, NJ: Rutgers University Press, 1999).

Thomas Louis Ogier, *A Memoir of Dr. John Edwards Holbrook, Read before the Medical Society of South Carolina...November 1st, 1871* (Charleston, SC: Walker, Evans and Cogswell, 1871).

Richard D. Worthington and Patricia H. Worthington, "John Edwards Holbrook, Father of American Herpetology," in *North American Herpetology*, ed. Kraig Adler (n.p.: Society for the Study of Amphibians and Reptiles, 1976), xiii–xxvii.

Papers

Holbrook's surviving letters, manuscripts, and journals are held at the South Caroliniana Library of the University of South Carolina, Columbia, South Carolina.

Thomas Jefferson
(April 13, 1743–July 4, 1826)

Patrick M. Erben

On March 2, 1809, two days before retiring from his second term as President of the United States, Thomas Jefferson expressed to a friend his elation over returning to Monticello, his estate in rural Virginia:

> Never did a prisoner, released from his chains, feel such relief as I shall on shaking off the shackles of power. Nature intended me for the tranquil pursuits of science, by rendering them my supreme delight. But the enormities of the times in which I have lived, have forced me to take a part in resisting them, and to commit myself on the boisterous ocean of political passions.

Indeed, Jefferson frequently yearned to leave behind his public obligations and dedicate himself to the study of natural history and the management of his plantation. Yet most of his writings display no fundamental rift between his interests in "science" and politics. A proponent of Enlightenment thought, Jefferson applied the discourse of nature to a wide range of subjects, including politics, philosophy, religion, and art. As Charles A. Miller notes, "Nature was Jefferson's myth for all purposes, a flexible idea that gathered together his deepest beliefs." Far from treating nature exclusively in the abstract, however, he followed late seventeenth-century philosopher John Locke in insisting that all knowledge derives from unmediated sensory experience. In his writings, Jefferson joined the concrete, physical nature he encountered in his studies of natural history, during his travels in Europe and on his plantation at Monticello, with the quasi-divine nature of Enlightenment philosophy and religion.

The third child of Peter Jefferson and Jane Randolph, Jefferson was born on the family's estate Shadwell in the Virginia Piedmont. Peter Jefferson had quickly added to his inherited estate by patenting a large tract of land in an unsettled area that later became Albemarle County. In his "Autobiography," Jefferson notes that his father "was the 3d or 4th settler" in this area. A self-taught surveyor and mapmaker, Peter Jefferson joined Joshua Fry in surveying the border between Virginia and North Carolina, producing the first reliable map of their home state. When his father died in 1757, Thomas was only 14 years old, but with about 7,500 acres of land now belonging to the estate, his future income was secure.

In 1760, he entered William and Mary College in Williamsburg, where his instruction relied almost exclusively on Dr. William Small, a Scottish professor of mathematics. Small inculcated in his student the secular and scientific patterns of Enlightenment thought. In spite of his passion for science, philosophy, and classical languages, Jefferson decided to enter a career in law, a profession that would grant him a respectable income, pave his way to public service, and allow him to manage his plantation. At age 21, while still enrolled as a student, Jefferson inherited about 5,000 acres and commenced running the estate.

Residing at the Shadwell estate, Jefferson began to document the cycles of cultivation in gardening and farming, and he continued these records throughout his life. In 1766, he made the first entries in his *Garden-Book*, noting the blooming of various spring flowers. Along with his *Farm-Book*, begun in 1774, Jefferson's *Garden-Book* forms the principal repository for information regarding the management, planning, and supervision of his various plantations. The listing of many domestic and foreign plants reflects Jefferson's horticultural experiments and his attempts to introduce the cultivation of European wine grapes to America. The *Garden-Book* provided Jefferson with his first opportunity to perform the primary task of natural history: the recording of specific details derived from observation of the natural environment and the tracing of changes and patterns in nature over time. Jefferson's interest in natural history agreed with his preference for the collection of concrete data and the study of particular nature in a well-defined geographical area. In comparison, Benjamin Franklin's experiments with electricity investigated into the laws of universal nature, belonging to a brand of science known as natural philosophy.

Jefferson began preparations for building Monticello in 1767, and he moved in three years later. The little mountain (hence the Italianate name "Monticello") where the house and gardens were to be located was part of his father's original land grant in Albemarle County. The elevation provided a view of the Rivanna River nearby, the forests and hills of the Virginia Piedmont, and the Blue Ridge Mountains to the west. Jefferson's choices for the house and its location were influenced by the writings of sixteenth-century Italian architect Andrea Palladio, who recommended building country estates

on a hill or mountain. Jefferson was admitted to the bar in 1767, and through this law practice he quickly gained entrance into politics, allowing him to become a member of the Virginia House of Burgesses two years later. In 1772, Jefferson married Martha Wayles Skelton, daughter of wealthy landowner John Wayles. Jefferson was extremely private about his domestic life, and very little is known about his wife and their marriage. At the death of Martha's father in 1773, 11,000 acres and 135 slaves passed into Jefferson's estate. Though he had to sell half of the land to cover Wayles's debts, the inheritance doubled Jefferson's possessions.

In 1774, Jefferson wrote his first tract on politics, a set of instructions for the Virginia delegates to the First Continental Congress, published as *A Summary View of the Rights of British America*. Jefferson for the first time articulates his views on civil government based on natural law and natural rights. Throughout the tract, he enumerates reasons for shaking off the rule of the British Parliament over the American colonies instead of merely limiting its authority. Not until the end, however, does he forcefully insist on natural law as the basis of the colonists' rights. Jefferson announces that the grievances of the Americans have been laid out before the king "with that freedom of language and sentiment which becomes a free people, claiming their rights as derived from the laws of nature, and not as the gift of their chief magistrate."

Jefferson placed the insistence on natural rights in the very beginning of his draft of the *Declaration of Independence* for the Second Continental Congress in 1776. He announces that the right of the American colonies to assume a "separate and equal station" among other nations does not rest on constitutional or historical precedent but on the "laws of nature and of nature's God." In the next paragraph, Jefferson defines the "self-evident" rights or "truths" derived from the "laws of nature." He replaces "nature's God" with "Creator," a term satisfying the Christian faith of most eighteenth-century Americans but also evoking the deistic identification of God and the creation. This "Creator" (or nature itself), Jefferson claims, endowed "all men" with "inherent and inalienable rights." Congress revised his draft to read "certain inalienable rights," thus diminishing the insistence on natural rights and limiting them to a "certain," specifiable number.

While in Philadelphia for the Second Continental Congress, Jefferson began his first meteorological records in the back of his "Memorandum Books." Starting July 1, 1776, the entries initiated a contiguous record of daily weather conditions until Jefferson's death. Initially, he only recorded the temperature at various times of the day. The entry for July 4, 1776, shows a low temperature of 68°F at 6 a.m. and a high temperature of 76°F at 1 p.m. Jefferson's meteorological observations became more complex in 1784. In addition to the temperatures, he also noted conditions such as precipitation, cloud cover, and winds, as well as the appearance of birds and the blooming of trees.

In 1777, Jefferson wrote the "Virginia Statute for Religious Freedom." Adopted in 1786, the statute translates the principle of natural law to the question of religious freedom. Nature, Jefferson states, endowed human beings with innate morality. While this natural sense of ethics is present in everyone, people possess free will to choose a specific religion based on the "evidence proposed to their minds." Since human beings can be deceived by their senses, it is reprehensible that "legislators and rulers, civil as well as ecclesiastical, who, being themselves but fallible and uninspired men, have assumed dominion over the faith of others." The "Virginia Statute for Religious Freedom" finally emphasizes that "the rights hereby asserted are of the natural rights of mankind." Any civil legislation trying to curb such freedom would "be an infringement of natural right." Jefferson was particularly proud of this act because it established the separation between church and state in Virginia and served as a model for the new nation.

In 1779, during a difficult period of the Revolutionary War, the Virginia House of Delegates elected Jefferson governor. Late in 1780, British troops invaded Virginia and eventually drove Jefferson from his home at Monticello. During this time, he wrote *Notes on the State of Virginia*, his longest and most complex work. Jefferson's book evolved from a survey distributed in the fall of 1780 by François Marbois, secretary of the French legation in Philadelphia. Marbois solicited information about the 13 American states for a report to his superiors in the French government, who were evaluating their aid for the American republic during the Revolutionary War. Jefferson was the obvious choice for answering the questions because of his political position and his reputation in the learned community. In January 1780, he had been elected as a member of the American Philosophical Society, the premier association of scientists in the new nation. In December 1781, he finished a draft of his answers and sent the manuscript to Marbois, but he continued to gather information in order to expand and improve his work.

Notes on the State of Virginia represents Jefferson's attempt to synthesize the manifold meanings of nature occupying his thought—the natural environment, natural beauty, human nature, natural rights, and the natural economy—and to understand their impact on society. His rearrangement of Marbois's questions leads the reader through a description of Virginia's environmental features, its borders, and its indigenous population, to a discussion of the society, laws, and culture established by its European settlers. The powerful imagery and the dramatic tone of many parts of *Notes on the State of Virginia* have ranked Jefferson's work among the classics of early American literature. The book advertises the promise and grandeur of Jefferson's home state and of the entire country, thus establishing an essential link between American nature and the new American nation.

Divided into 23 "queries," the book begins with a description of Virginia's boundaries in

Query I. The chapter introduces the scientific character of the work with one of its many lists of facts derived from natural history. The exact coordinates for Virginia's boundaries impress on the reader an image of the state's size and visualize the promise for future settlement. Jefferson proudly proclaims that Virginia alone is "one third larger than the islands of Great Britain and Ireland." Query II, entitled "Rivers and Navigation," catalogues the main bodies of water in Virginia and assesses their use for shipping. The abundance of waterways in Jefferson's account advertises the state's suitability for commerce, not only in the eastern parts of Virginia but also in its western territories such as the Ohio valley.

In Query IV, "Mountains," Jefferson imbues American nature with a sense of national pride and aesthetic appeal. His description of the passage of the Potomac River through the Blue Ridge Mountains promotes a natural spectacle that is "worth a voyage across the Atlantic." Similar to a landscape painter, Jefferson creates a "scene" or "picture" that transforms the reader into an onlooker. His composition is influenced by two central terms of eighteenth-century aesthetic theory—the sublime and the beautiful. Following British philosopher Edmund Burke, Jefferson understood the sublime as a wild, grand, or elevated scene that inspires a feeling of awe or terror. The beautiful was defined as a calm scene that existed on a human scale. Jefferson juxtaposes both elements in his description of the passage of the Potomac to portray "perhaps one of the most stupendous scenes in nature." Simultaneously advancing a scientific theory of the development of this formation, he assembles a dramatic plot in which the Shenandoah River and the Potomac River "rush together against the mountain, rend it asunder, and pass off to the sea." While this scene "hurries your senses," the

> distant finishing which nature has given to the picture is of a very different character. It is a true contrast to the fore-ground. It is as placid and delightful, as that is wild and tremendous.

> For the mountain being cloven asunder, she presents to your eye, through the cleft, a small catch of smooth horizon...inviting you, as it were, from the riot and tumult roaring around, to pass through the breach and participate in the calm below.

In Query V, Jefferson's discussion of several caves in the Virginia limestone country reveals his scientific skepticism. In his description of the "Blowing Cave," a cavern that expels a constant flow of air, Jefferson evaluates various hypotheses in explanation of this phenomenon but dismisses all previous theories as inadequate in light of concrete evidence: "But a constant issue of air, only varying in its force as the weather is drier or damper, will require a new hypothesis." His description of Virginia's Natural Bridge joins literary and scientific categories and simultaneously promotes nature as the most remarkable feature of the United States. While measuring its height, Jefferson praises the Natural Bridge as "the most sublime of Nature's works." He again transforms the reader into a spectator, moved by the aesthetic grandeur of nature:

> It is impossible for the emotions arising from the sublime, to be felt beyond what they are here: so beautiful an arch, so elevated, so light, and springing as it were up to heaven, the rapture of the spectator is really indescribable!

The land surrounding the Natural Bridge was later purchased by Jefferson, who maintained and promoted it as a public trust.

Query VI, the longest chapter of the book, joins a larger eighteenth-century discussion known as "the dispute of the new world." European scientists and philosophers had established a theory of the degeneration of nature in America. They argued that the American "wilderness" was evidence of the land's ongoing decline. Only cultivation could maintain a standard of fertility and health. The most well-respected proponent of this theory was Georges Louis Leclerc, Comte de Buffon, director of the *Jardin Roi* in Paris and author of the monumental *Histoir Naturelle, Gènèrale et Particuliére*. The

French naturalist had advanced the specific argument that fewer species of quadrupeds existed in America, that New World animals were without exception smaller than their Old World counterparts, and that domestic animals introduced to America declined in size and weight because of the continent's supposedly cold and humid climate. These adverse environmental conditions, according to Buffon, affected human beings and animals alike.

Jefferson uses the methods of natural history to refute Buffon in his own discipline and to celebrate nature as the greatest endowment of the American nation. He begins with a discussion of the mammoth, whose existence would defy all of Buffon's claims. Several findings of mammoth skeletons in North America proved that such an animal had at least existed in the past and that it was larger than the Old World elephant. Jefferson explains that the frequency of such mammoth fossils increases farther north, which refutes Buffon's assumption that colder climates produce smaller animals. The existence of fossils alone did not satisfy Jefferson, and he provides anecdotal evidence gathered from Native Americans that the mammoth still existed in the western and northern reaches of America. For Jefferson, extinction was implausible because it violated the eighteenth-century theory of the "Great Chain of Being," which maintained that the loss of a single species would upset the entire system.

Jefferson, not resting on the single example of the mammoth, assembled three tables containing data on the number and weight of quadrupeds in North America and Europe. As Jefferson scholar Frank Shuffleton explains, these tables and charts undermine the very "methodological and philosophical underpinnings of Buffon's argument." The French naturalist lacked data in support of his claims, and this deficiency discredited his entire work. Jefferson, in contrast, flaunted long lists of specific measurements. Shuffleton notes that Jefferson relied on three different sources—his own observations, information from a circle of friends, and books by naturalists such as Peter Kalm and Mark Catesby, who, unlike Buffon, actually had firsthand experience of nature in the New World.

Jefferson also takes issue with Buffon's polemic that nature in America reduces its native people to little more than animals and subdues the faculties of European settlers. Buffon associated a supposedly weak libido among American Indians with their ostensible lack of social and cultural achievements. Jefferson argues that any lack of fertility among native tribes stems from food shortages or physical exertion during times of war. After defending the physical characteristics of American Indians, Jefferson refutes the implication of an underdeveloped moral sensibility. He quotes the Mingo Chief Logan, whose speech about the murder of his entire family won much praise throughout the colonies for its eloquence and sentiment. Moving on to the transplanted European population, Jefferson cites Benjamin Franklin, George Washington, and David Rittenhouse as examples for the genius emerging from the New World.

Query VII, "Climate," turns to the influence of culture on nature. Jefferson asserts that a "change in our climate...is taking place very sensibly. Both heats and colds are become much more moderate within the memory of even the middle-aged." He ascribes this development to human activity such as deforestation and agriculture. Jefferson's approach emphasizes historical change, a quality that Buffon's natural history lacked. Shuffleton argues that this notion of environmental change also allowed Jefferson to "present the Indian disappearance as a natural and inevitable phenomenon and thus obscure the role of the European invasion in their demise." Jefferson's lists of the number of surviving members of various tribes in North America clearly insert Native Americans into the system of natural history. He laments that Indian languages are disappearing, but his concern seems more scientific than humanitarian. The study of the linguistic correspondences between Native American languages could have furnished clues of their geographical origin.

Both contemporary and modern readers have been disturbed by Jefferson's discussion of the racial differences between blacks and whites in the query on "Laws." His description of blacks indeed undermines the credibility of his own proposal for the abolition of slavery in *Notes on the State of Virginia*. In fact, Jefferson adopts Buffon's logic by arguing for a connection between what he deemed the negligible intellectual achievements of blacks, their underdeveloped morality, and their inferior beauty. All differences between races, Jefferson asserts, are founded in nature:

> Whether the black of the negro resides in the reticular membrane between the skin and scarf-skin, or in the scarf-skin itself; whether it proceeds from the colour of the blood, the colour of the bile, or from that of some other secretion, the difference is fixed in nature, and is as real as if its seat and cause were better known to us. And is this difference of no importance?...Are not the fine mixtures of red and white, the expressions of every passion by greater or less suffusions of colour in the one, preferable to that eternal monotony, which reigns in the countenances, that immoveable veil of black which covers all the emotions of the other race?

After the abolition of slavery, Jefferson concludes, blacks have to be colonized outside of the United States to avoid racial conflict.

In Query XIX, "Manufactures," Jefferson delivers his famous paean on the virtues of an agricultural society. He believes that the expansiveness of the continent would for many generations afford sufficient land to base the economy of the United States entirely on agriculture. The independent farmer embodies the ideal of the republican citizen and guarantees the moral health of the nation. Jefferson endows agriculture with a religious significance reminiscent of pagan societies:

> Those who labour in the earth are the chosen people of God, if ever he had a chosen people, whose breasts he has made his peculiar deposit for substantial and genuine virtue. It is the focus in which he keeps alive that sacred fire, which otherwise might escape from the face of the earth.

Jefferson believes that manufacturing corrupted society, and he hopes to ban it from the new nation.

Jefferson's term as governor of Virginia ended with the turmoil of British occupation in 1781, and the following year brought another blow with the death of his wife Martha. This personal tragedy left Jefferson severely depressed. Nevertheless, he reentered politics as a Virginia congressional delegate in 1783. He drafted the "Plan of Government for the Western Territory" (March 1, 1784), adopted as the Ordinance of 1784. Jefferson's plan laid the foundation for the territorial policy of the United States. All land already in possession of the United States or to be acquired in the future was to be divided into republican states and incorporated into the Union with a status equal to the original states. In April, Jefferson wrote the "Report of a Committee to Establish a Land Office" for the regulation of all land sales and the geographical division of the Western territories. Jefferson's report created the characteristic grid that has determined the linear borders of Western states.

Later in 1784, Jefferson was appointed to join John Adams and Benjamin Franklin in Paris to negotiate trade agreements with France and other European nations. Before his return to America in 1789, Jefferson made several trips through England, France, Italy, Holland, and Germany. The travel journals and numerous letters he wrote during this period testify to his interest in the agriculture of other countries and the possibility of introducing new plants, animals, and farming techniques to the United States. Other points of interest included the different landscaping styles he encountered. Jefferson disliked the formality of French gardens, particularly the contrived fountains at

Versailles. He championed the "natural" style of English gardens, advanced in Thomas Whateley's *Observations on Modern Gardening*. According to Jefferson biographer Merrill D. Peterson, "the object of landscape, as distinguished from gardens in the French mode, was to reproduce artfully the beauties of nature in country estates." Jefferson and Adams saw a number of estates that had realized this ideal when they visited England in the spring of 1786.

In the summer of 1786, Jefferson had a brief romance with Maria Cosway, a married painter of landscapes and miniatures. Jefferson and Cosway shared an appreciation of art, music, and landscape gardening, and they spent much time together visiting royal gardens near Paris. In late September, Maria and her estranged husband left together for England, and the relationship between Jefferson and Cosway cooled considerably. On October 12, 1786, however, Jefferson sent Maria a long letter known as "A Dialogue between my Head and my Heart." The voice of the "Heart" exults Maria's virtues and his affections for her, while the "Head" cautions against a romantic involvement. In his letter, Jefferson returns to the theme of advertising the natural beauty of America. He declares that "The Falling spring, the Cascade of Niagara, the Passage of the Potowmac thro the Blue mountains, the Natural bridge" are all "worth a voiage across the Atlantic." The letter became famous for Jefferson's description of the natural setting of his Virginia estate:

> And our own dear Monticello, where has nature spread so rich a mantle under the eye? mountains, forests, rocks, rivers. With what majesty do we there ride above the storms! How sublime to look down into the workhouse of nature, to see her clouds, hail, snow, rain, thunder, all fabricated at our feet! And the glorious Sun, when rising as if out of a distant water, just gliding the tops of the mountains, and giving life to all nature!

Jefferson's next travel journal, entitled "Memoranda taken on a journey from Paris into the southern parts of France, and northern Italy, in the year 1787," also demonstrates his interest in the agricultural traditions of the regions he visited. Jefferson alleges that most farmers in France "are less happy and less virtuous in villages, than they would be insulated with their families on the grounds they cultivate." While noting the oppression of the people through local authorities, he was fascinated by the mixed cultivation of wine, wheat, and fruit trees, and he hoped to apply such methods at Monticello. Jefferson collected cuttings from various types of vines, but he was never successful at cultivating them in Virginia. Other agricultural marvels Jefferson encountered on this journey were the olive tree and Piedmont rice, and he hoped to introduce both to South Carolina. During his stay in northern Italy, Jefferson even smuggled seed rice out of the country. On his way to Bordeaux, he shipped on the Canal de Languedoc, an important engineering feat of the late seventeenth century. Jefferson's journal entries bespeak his interest in the utility of nature, particularly in agriculture and transportation.

In 1788, Jefferson went on his last journey while staying in Europe. His journal, entitled "Memorandums on a Tour from Paris to Amsterdam, Strasburg, and back to Paris," mainly concerns his observations on Germany. Jefferson followed the rich wine culture along the Rhine, and he collected numerous clippings to be transported to Virginia. He collected ideas for the improved plow he designed later, and he enjoyed the character of the people he encountered along the way. Jefferson recognized the similarity between the cultural landscape German immigrants had shaped in many parts of North America and the Palatinate region along the Rhine, where most of these immigrants had originated.

Much of Jefferson's term in Paris was taken up with negotiating political and economic treaties. In order to break down French import restrictions on American whale products, Jefferson wrote *Observations on the Whale-Fishery* in late 1788. The treatise demonstrates his acumen for employing scientific facts in arguments on trade and the economy. He provides a survey of the commercial uses of whale oil, the history of whaling, and the different whale species and quality of oil they produce. Of particular interest to readers of Herman Melville's *Moby Dick* is Jefferson's description of the Sperm whale, which

> begins now to be best found in the latitude of the cape of good hope, and even of cape Horn. He is an active, fierce animal and requires vast address and boldness in the fisherman...he is rare, and shy, soon abandoning the grounds where he is hunted.

Jefferson had a few copies of his tract printed and distributed to several French officials, who eventually lifted the prohibitions.

Jefferson returned to the United States in November 1789. Upon his arrival, he learned of his nomination as Secretary of State. He took on the position reluctantly and returned to farming at Monticello in 1794. Jefferson spent the period until his election for vice president in November 1796 remodeling Monticello and adding to his gardens. In March 1797, he was installed both as vice president of the United States and as president of the American Philosophical Society. In the latter capacity, Jefferson delivered the paper "A Memoir on the Discovery of Certain Bones of a Quadruped of the Clawed Kind in the Western Parts of Virginia" on March 10, 1797. Based on recent fossil discoveries, Jefferson developed a theory of the existence of a huge, lion-like creature he named "megalonyx" or "great-claw." As in his work on the mammoth, Jefferson's description of the megalonyx infuses science with national pride. He argues that the animal still exists and cites Native American tales of "terrible roarings." Eventually, Jefferson's fossils were identified as belonging to the "megatherium" or "great-sloth," which had been discovered in Paraguay. His Federalist enemies claimed that Jefferson's scientific explorations were irreconcilable with the conduct of state affairs. Luther Martin, attorney general of

Maryland, disputed Jefferson's incrimination of Colonel Cresap for the murder of Logan's family in *Notes on the State of Virginia*. In 1800, Jefferson published an appendix that absolved Cresap from the actual murders but proved his ultimate responsibility for the massacre.

Jefferson's election for President in 1800 revived his interest in the exploration of the West. After the Louisiana Purchase of 1803 had doubled the territory of the United States, Jefferson appointed Meriwether Lewis and William Clark as the leaders of an exploratory expedition to the Pacific Ocean. Jefferson had never been more than 50 miles west of Monticello, but the purchase sparked his enthusiasm about the commercial and scientific possibilities of the western country. On June 20, 1803, Jefferson sent Lewis a set of specific "Instructions" for the expedition. Jefferson hoped that Lewis and Clark would discover a "north-west passage" as a route of transcontinental trade. They also were to chart precisely the geographical location of all rivers, mountains, and other landmarks and, thus, map a territory that had so far existed only in the imagination of most Anglo-Americans.

The majority of Jefferson's "Instructions" reflect his interest in natural history. He specifies the study of native American tribes, their customs, languages, economy, and political relations. "Other objects worthy of notice" are soil and topography, animals, fossils, minerals, traces of volcanic activities, and climate. Jefferson further asks Lewis to seek out scientific novelties such as plants and animals "not known in the U.S." and "the remains or accounts of any which may be deemed rare or extinct." Lewis should assess the climate according to temperatures, "the portion of rainy, cloudy, & clear days, by lightning, hail, snow, ice, by the access & recess of frost, by the winds prevailing at different seasons, the dates at which particular plants put forth or lose their flower, or leaf, times of appearance of particular birds, reptiles or insects." Though Lewis and Clark found about 300 miles of mountainous terrain separating the headwaters of the

Missouri and Columbia, they also brought back knowledge of hitherto unknown animal and plant species, and they made contact with numerous Native American nations.

During his second presidency, Jefferson began to express his desire to retire from public office, return to his estate, and rededicate himself to agriculture and horticulture. His *Garden-Book* contains various plans for additions and alterations to the Monticello gardens. He regularly corresponded with William Hamilton in Philadelphia, whose estate "The Woodlands" was considered the finest example of landscape gardening. They exchanged plant specimens and ideas about landscaping. In a letter of July 1806, Jefferson expresses his plans for modeling his grounds at Monticello after English gardens. The British climate, he explains, is perfectly suited for the combination of open ground and clusters of trees "distributed with taste." In order to attain the same effects in Virginia, more shade is necessary. Jefferson envisions a high layer of shade trees, which provide a canopy and create the "appearance" of open ground. With respect to its views, he finds Monticello unequalled:

> Of prospect I have a rich profusion and offering itself at every point of the compass. Mountains distant & near, smooth & shaggy, single & in ridges, a little river hiding itself among the hills so as to shew in lagoons only, cultivated grounds under the eye and two small villages.

The landscape surrounding Monticello offered what Jefferson believed was the perfect "middle state" between wilderness and cultivation.

Jefferson returned to Monticello after retiring from office on March 4, 1809. While spending much time in improving his grounds, Jefferson increasingly contributed to the cause of public education. In 1817, he completed his architectural plans for the "academical village" that would become the University of Virginia. Jefferson presided over the commission for planning the university, which met at Rockfish Gap in the Blue Ridge Mountains in the summer of 1818. In the report, Jefferson proposes the creation of six professorships pertaining to nature: "physico-mathematics" (including astronomy and geography), "physics or Natural Philosophy," "Chemistry" (including agriculture), "Mineralogy" (including geology), "Botany," and "Zoology." Jefferson's horticultural metaphor in favor of education demonstrates his lifelong faith in the inextricable connection between nature and human life:

> We should be far...from the discouraging persuasion that man is fixed, by the law of his nature....As well might it be urged that the wild and uncultivated tree, hitherto yielding sour and bitter fruit only, can never be made to yield better; yet we know that the grafting art implants a new tree on the savage stock, producing what is most estimable both in kind and degree. Education, in like manner, engrafts a new man on the native stock, and improves what in his nature was vicious and perverse into qualities of virtue and social worth.

PRIMARY BIBLIOGRAPHY

Books

A Summary View of the Rights of British America. Set forth in some resolutions intended for the inspection of the present delegates of the people of Virginia. Now in convention. By a native, and member of the House of Burgesses (Williamsburg, VA: Printed for Clementia Rind, 1774; London: Printed for G. Kearsly, 1774).

Notes on the State of Virginia (Paris: Privately printed, 1785; London: J. Stockdale, 1787; Philadelphia: Pritchard & Hall, 1788).

A Manual of Parliamentary Practice For Use in the Senate of the United States (Washington, D.C.: Printed by Samuel Harrison Smith, 1801; enlarged edition, Washington, D.C.: Published by William Cooper/Georgetown: Published by Joseph Milligan, 1812).

The Autobiography of Thomas Jefferson, in vol. 1 of *Memoirs, Correspondences and Miscellanies from the Papers of Thomas Jefferson*, 4 vols., ed. Thomas Jefferson Randolph (Charlottesville, VA: F. Carr, 1829); republished as *Memoirs, Correspondences and Private Papers of Thomas Jefferson* (London: Colburn & Bentley, 1829).

An Essay Towards Facilitating Instruction in the Anglo Saxon and Modern Dialects of the English Language (New York: Printed by J.F. Trow for the Trustees of the University of Virginia, 1851).

The Life and Morals of Jesus of Nazareth [English text only] (St. Louis, Chicago, & New York: N.D. Thompson, 1902); [Greek, Latin, French, and English texts] (Washington, D.C.: U.S. Government Printing Office, 1904).

The Commonplace Book of Thomas Jefferson, ed. Gilbert Chinard (Baltimore, MD: Johns Hopkins University Press/Paris: Les Presses Universitaires de France, 1926).

The Literary Bible of Thomas Jefferson: His Commonplace Book of Philosophers and Poets, ed. Gilbert Chinard (Baltimore, MD: Johns Hopkins University Press/Paris: Les Presses Universitaires de France, 1928).

Thomas Jefferson's Garden Book, 1766–1824, ed. Edwin Morris Betts (Philadelphia, PA: American Philosophical Society, 1944).

Thomas Jefferson's Farm Book, ed. Betts (Princeton, NJ: Princeton University Press, 1953).

Editions and Collections

The Writings of Thomas Jefferson, ed. Henry A. Washington, 9 vols. (Washington, D.C.: Taylor & Maury, 1853–1854).

The Writings of Thomas Jefferson, ed. Andrew A. Lipscomb and Albert Ellery Bergh, 20 vols. (Washington, D.C.: Thomas Jefferson Memorial Association, 1903–1904).

The Complete Jefferson, ed. Saul K. Padover (Freeport, NY: Books for Libraries Press, 1943).

The Declaration of Independence, ed. J.P. Boyd, revised edition (Princeton, NJ: Princeton University Press, 1945).

The Papers of Thomas Jefferson, first series, ed. Julian P. Boyd and others, 29 vols. to date (Princeton, NJ: Princeton University Press, 1950–); second series, edited by Charles T. Cullen and others, 1 vol. to date (Princeton, NJ: Princeton University Press, 1983–).

Notes on the State of Virginia, ed. William Peden (Chapel Hill: University of North Carolina Press, 1954).

Thomas Jefferson: Writings, ed. Merrill D. Peterson (New York: Library of America, 1984).

Jefferson's Literary Commonplace Book, ed. Douglas L. Wilson (Princeton, NJ: Princeton University Press, 1989).

Jefferson's Memorandum Books, 1767–1826, ed. James A. Bear, Jr., and Lucia C. Stanton, 2 vols. (Princeton, NJ: Princeton University Press, 1997).

Notes on the State of Virginia, ed. Frank Shuffelton (New York: Penguin Books, 1999).

Letters

Gilbert Chinard, *Jefferson et les Ideologues, d'après s correspondance inedité avec Destutt de Tracy Cabanis J.-B. Say et Auguste Comte* (Baltimore, MD: Johns Hopkins University Press/Paris: Les Presses Universitaires de France, 1925).

The Letters of Lafayette and Jefferson, ed. Gilbert Chinard (Baltimore, MD: Johns Hopkins University Press/Paris: "Les Belles Lettres," 1929).

The Correspondence of Jefferson and Du Pont de Nemours, ed. Gilbert Chinard (Baltimore, MD: Johns Hopkins University Press/Paris: "Les Belles Lettres," 1931).

The Adams-Jefferson Letters, 2 vol., ed. Lester J. Cappon (Chapel Hill: University of North Carolina Press, 1959).

The Family Letters of Thomas Jefferson, ed. Edwin Morris Betts and James Adams Bear, Jr. (Columbia: University of Missouri Press, 1966).

The Republic of Letters: The Correspondence between Thomas Jefferson and James Madison, 1776–1826, ed. James Morton Smith, 3 vols. (New York: Norton, 1995).

SECONDARY BIBLIOGRAPHY

Bibliographies

Frank Shuffleton, *Thomas Jefferson: A Comprehensive Annotated Bibliography of Writings About Him, 1826–1980* (New York: Garland, 1983).

Frank Shuffleton, *Thomas Jefferson: An Annotated Bibliography, 1981–1990* (New York: Garland, 1992).

E. Millicent Sowerby, *A Catalogue of the Library of Thomas Jefferson*, 5 vols. (Washington, D.C.: Library of Congress, 1952–1959).

Biographies

George Tucker, *The Life of Thomas Jefferson*, 2 vols. (Philadelphia: Carey, Lea & Blanchard, 1837).

Dumas Malone, *Jefferson and His Times*, 6 vols. (Boston: Little, Brown, 1948–1981).

Merrill D. Peterson, *Thomas Jefferson and the New Nation: A Biography* (New York: Oxford University Press, 1970).

Joseph E. Ellis, *American Sphinx: The Character of Thomas Jefferson* (New York: Knopf, 1997).

References

I. Bernhard Cohen, *Science and the Founding Fathers: Science in the Political Thought of Jefferson, Franklin, Adams, and Madison* (New York: Norton, 1995).

Antonello Gerbi, *The Dispute of the New World: The History of a Polemic, 1750–1900*, trans. Jeremy Moyle (Pittsburgh, PA: University of Pittsburgh Press, 1973).

John C. Greene, *American Science in the Age of Jefferson* (Ames: Iowa State University Press, 1984).

Donald Jackson, *Thomas Jefferson & the Stony Mountains: Exploring the West from Monticello* (Urbana: University of Illinois Press, 1981).

Myra Jehlen, *American Incarnation: The Individual, the Nation, and the Continent* (Cambridge, MA: Harvard University Press, 1986).

Barbara McEwan, *Thomas Jefferson: Farmer* (Jefferson, NC: McFarland, 1991).

Charles A. Miller, *Jefferson and Nature: An Interpretation* (Baltimore, MD: Johns Hopkins University Press, 1988).

Frederick Doveton Nichols and Ralph E. Griswold, *Thomas Jefferson, Landscape Architect* (Charlottesville: University of Virginia Press, 1978),

Pamela Regis, *Describing Early America: Bartram, Jefferson, Crèvecoeur, and the Rhetoric of Natural History* (DeKalb: Northern Illinois University Press, 1992).

George Green Shackleford, *Thomas Jefferson's Travels in Europe, 1784–1789* (Baltimore, MD: Johns Hopkins University Press, 1995).

Frank Shuffelton, foreword to *Notes on the State of Virginia*, by Thomas Jefferson (New York: Penguin, 1999).

Papers

Major collections of Jefferson's papers can be found at the Library of Congress, the Massachusetts Historical Society, the University of Virginia, the Missouri Historical Society, and the Henry E. Huntington Library.

Peter (Pehr) Kalm
(March 6, 1716–November 16, 1779)

Katrina Neckuty

One of the most important figures to observe the North American colonies in the eighteenth century was Finnish/Swedish botanist Pehr (Peter) Kalm. An avid natural scientist and protégé to Carl Linnaeus, he was sent to North America by the Swedish Academy of Science in order to supply Sweden and Finland with foreign plants that would benefit their economies. Kalm meticulously recorded all plants he observed and gave particular attention to those he believed could be transplanted in his native country. He also observed the social, political, and environmental conditions of New England and Canada.

Kalm is best known for his *Travels into North America* (1770–1771): a two-volume work that describes only part of his expedition for the Swedish Academy of Science. Originally published in Swedish as *En Resa Til Norra America* (1753, 1756, 1761) in three volumes, it was instantly well received by the European community. Unfortunately, his published accounts reflect only the first 14 of the 31 months Kalm spent in North America. Although Kalm had completed another volume of his travels, it remained unpublished, and most of his notes were later destroyed in the 1827 fire at the Turku Library. Only six of his notebooks are still intact, as they were on loan to another professor at that time.

Kalm dedicated his entire professional life to nurturing his "foreign" plants in the interest of Sweden's and Finland's economies. His work as a natural scientist was valuable to the field of botany, as his findings revealed previously unnamed plants. However, Kalm's observations are also important historically for tracking ecological change in North America. Kalm has also earned a place in travel and nature writing since his diary brought others to both North American plants and society.

Kalm was born in Ångermanland, Sweden, March 6, 1716, to Finnish parents Gabriel and Katarina (Ross) Kalm, who fled their native country during the Russian occupation of Finland. His father, a minister in the parish of Närpiö, died six weeks after Peter was born. Kalm and his mother returned to Finland in 1721, after Russian forces withdrew, and settled near Vassa. He and his mother struggled, rebuilding their lives and home after the war, relying on nearby relatives for support. Kalm's cousin Johannes Gezelius proved most reliable in helping the widow and her son. Later, in a letter to Baron Sten Carl Bielke, Kalm would say that Gezelius was like a father to him during his childhood.

In 1735, Kalm attended the University of Åbo to study theology. Here, he befriended Bishop Johannes Browallius, a naturalist, who introduced Kalm to Baron Sten Carl Bielke. With their encouragement, he took a more rigorous interest in the natural sciences, mineralogy, meteorology, and philosophy. Kalm proved to be an ambitious student and notetaker in all of his coursework, and gained the respect of many different professors. Most importantly, his attention to detail and studies in climate and meteorology proved useful when he was making observations of North America.

As a student of theology and a clergyman's son, Kalm was expected to finish his degree and then pursue either teaching or a church position. This course of action would alleviate financial worry; however, Bielke had a different idea in mind for Kalm. Shortly after their introduction in 1740, Bielke became his benefactor and funded his education thereafter. This gave Kalm the financial freedom he needed to focus solely on natural science. Bielke was seeking someone like Kalm who was both ambitious and educated in the natural sciences to look after his own gardens and land. Bielke also was interested in sending Kalm to other countries, hoping that he would find a way to enhance Sweden's and Finland's economies.

Kalm started at the university in Uppsala on December 5, 1740. He was immediately advised to pursue scholarship under Carl Linnaeus, who had become famous at this time in the field of botany. Kalm wrote letters of introduction and impressed Linnaeus with his knowledge and desire to pursue natural science. He had expressed "great desire" to become his student, and Linnaeus was mutually pleased to have a student who was committed and well-versed in the natural sciences. The following fall, Kalm began his tutelage under Linnaeus.

In 1742, Kalm made a journey to Bohuslän in western Sweden, funded by Bielke, in order to catalogue and observe plants. Kalm prepared for this journey by reading travel literature and natural history accounts, taking notes on what others had observed on expeditions. His notes on Bohuslän, *Wästgötha och Bohusländska resa*, were published in

1745 and marked his first scientific expedition. Shortly after this trip, in 1743 he was appointed to travel to South Africa, which was never fulfilled. However, in 1744, he traveled with Bielke to St. Petersburg and Moscow in search of new plants. The results of this trip encouraged Bielke to present the possibility of foreign travel for the benefit of the Swedish and Finnish economies to the Swedish Royal Academy of Science. He believed that bringing "useful" plants into the countries would enable independent production of goods and less dependency on foreign markets. Bielke had long thought of Kalm as a potential candidate for such missions, and hoped to do more research in Siberia, since their climate was similar to that of the Scandinavian countries.

Although the Swedish Royal Academy of Science was enthusiastic about Bielke's plans to introduce foreign plants to their landscape, they felt that Linnaeus should be consulted. Linnaeus agreed that collecting seeds and plants from similar latitudes to Sweden and Finland would benefit the country financially; however, he did not endorse the exploration of Siberia. Linnaeus thought a trip to North America would be more useful and important to their cause; it would also be less expensive. According to Linnaeus, a trip to Siberia would require a military escort and additional costs for living and travel.

Linnaeus had a personal interest in learning more about the natural history of North America; he also knew botanists in the region who could provide information and seeds for their cause. Linnaeus corresponded with John Bartram, Cadwallader Colden, and J. Mitchel—all of whom were able natural scientists. Despite Linnaeus's decision, Bielke was still focused on Siberia. The question of destination was in flux until the summer of 1745, when it was finally decided that the expedition to North America could yield more plants of potential use than those in Siberia.

Throughout all the changes regarding the trip, Kalm remained the only constant: he would be the one to undertake this journey because he had both experience and "youth" in his favor. Of Kalm, Linnaeus once said:

> He has all the requirements one could wish for in one person for carrying out of such a task, for he is strong in health, was brought up in poverty, is equally satisfied with bad as with good food, and has thus grown up able to stand whatever may befall; his keenness on plants, animals and stones is so great that he will run miles to get a single moss.

Both Bielke and Linnaeus came to the decision that the most "profitable" direction would be north to Hudson Bay and Canada because the climate was similar to their own. According to other botanists, there were many unidentified plants in this area that could be useful to their country. Even though the Academy had a destination in mind, Kalm unfortunately would be unable to leave Sweden for the expedition until 1747 due to lengthy trip preparations.

Some natural products that were believed to have the potential to bring financial stability to Sweden and Finland were the following: rice, pines, spruce, mulberry, and the "wild oxen," which provided both milk and meat. These could potentially provide food staples, clothing, and lumber, which were in short supply. However, the most important of these was the mulberry, used for silk production. The English were very successful with using the mulberry in this area of trade, and the Swedish believed that they too might be successful in creating a lucrative business. Although the aforementioned plants were ones of greatest interest, the Academy made it clear that Kalm should be attentive to others that might prove equally useful.

To aid Kalm on his journey, the Academy created a memorandum outlining the duties required of him while in North America. Thus, economic utility became the impetus of planning the expedition to North America, with furthering the field of natural science or international relations as secondary concerns to the country. Essentially, the memorandum described both the "economic significance and botanical practi-

cability" of introducing foreign crops into Sweden and Finland. Included were lists of tree and plant varieties that held their "interest," such as several varieties of oak. In the "directive" that was laid out for Kalm, he was also encouraged to find plants of medicinal value, in addition to those of purely commercial value.

In 1747, Kalm was appointed chair of economics at the University of Åbo, a position that had been newly created for him upon his return. As *professor oeconomiae*, he had two tasks: to bring the country new sources of unlimited wealth in the form of plants, and to lay the foundation for a wealthy future for Finland and Sweden through his academic instruction. However, aside from his expected duties, Kalm also had a more personal vested interest in this exploration: to make his name immortal so that those in future generations would know his work. Finally, after his university appointment was ensured, the money for the expedition in hand, and passports were collected for travel, Kalm was ready to depart. He left on October 16, 1747, with Lars Jungström—a professional gardener and Bielke's faithful servant —for England, and eventually to North America, and began what would become a four-year journey.

In February 1748, Kalm arrived in London and befriended Abraham Spalding, a Swedish merchant who had settled in London. Kalm's visit to England was integral to the success of his expedition because he needed to make additional contacts with other natural scientists and receive letters of introduction to natural scientists in North America. Spalding later introduced Kalm to Peter Collinson, who took Kalm to a meeting of England's Royal Society. Here, Kalm made other important acquaintances with Marcus Catesby and Cromwell Mortimer. He also met Phillip Miller, author of the *Gardener's Dictionary*, which proved to be invaluable to Kalm when observing plants in North America. Although Kalm's main goal was to procure and cultivate plants from North America, he could not help observing the plants and lifestyles of the English.

Because of difficulty in arranging a means of travel to North America, Kalm spent a total of six months in England. At this time, he continuously took note of the architecture, social and rural life, as well as methods of agriculture used around London. In his opinion, England was further advanced in agriculture than any other country, and he continued to emphasize this years later in his future lectures at Åbo.

In August 1748, Kalm was finally able to leave England for North America. On the *Mary Gally*, he was surrounded by emigrants who had hopes of starting a new life in North America. Thus, Kalm was able to witness firsthand American immigration. His crossing went relatively quickly; having been blessed with mild weather, he arrived in Philadelphia six weeks later.

Upon his arrival in Philadelphia, Kalm was astounded by the variety of trees and plants that he saw and became immediately aware of the magnitude of his research. Indeed, he felt a huge burden lie before him, and developed an acute sense that it was necessary to begin immediately. With letters of introduction from Collinson in hand, he set out to find Benjamin Franklin, who had himself already gained status in the international world of science. Franklin immediately took a liking to Kalm and introduced him to Swedish countrymen around the city.

Because of his late arrival to New England, he would be unable to make accurate observations further north because most trees had lost their leaves, and most plants, their blossoms. Hence, he decided to winter in Philadelphia. Although this set him back in terms of the time outlined by the Swedish Academy, Kalm looked forward to observing the few plants that still were green in Philadelphia.

During his stay in Philadelphia, he met John Bartram, who was a self-taught naturalist and fieldworker. According to Kalm, Bartram "[was] everything, farmer, joiner, turner, shoemaker, bricklayer, gardener, minister, carpenter, and I don't know what else, a

brilliant fellow." In *Travels*, Kalm also made note of Bartram's skills in observation:

> He has shown great judgment and an attention which lets nothing escape unnoticed. Yet with all these qualities he is to be blamed for his negligence, for he did not care to write down his numerous and useful observations.

This insight is one illustration of the degree of importance Kalm gave to close attention to detail and to accurately recording observations.

That winter, Kalm also traveled to New York to visit Cadwallader Colden, an acquaintance of Linnaeus. Colden, a member of the Governor's Council and an amateur natural scientist, had promised Linnaeus that he would do his best to assist Kalm on his journey. Colden was well-apprised of the conditions within Canada that might affect Kalm, that is, the strained political situation between the French and English colonies along the border. He gave Kalm advice on a route through Canada and provided him with a few maps to aid him through the Hudson Bay area.

After securing plans and maps for Canada, Kalm returned to Philadelphia and to the neighboring community of Raccoon, which was largely Swedish. Here, Kalm settled in until the following spring when he would begin observations farther north. One of Kalm's acquaintances from Sweden, Johan Sandin, was a minister in Raccoon, but unfortunately died before they were reunited. During Kalm's time in North America, he continuously returned to Raccoon and occasionally filled in as a preacher. He eventually married Sandin's widow, Anna Margaretha.

While he wintered in Raccoon, he learned much of the "economic" value and medicinal use of plants. Kalm writes: "Several people peeled the roots of the *Cornus florida*, or Dogwood, and gave this peel to patients; and even some people who could not be cured by the jesuit's bark, have recovered by the help of this." Other medicinal remedies were revealed to Kalm, regarding teas and various plant parts. However, because he was unable to physically see the plants, he decided to remain until "nature was green again" in order to match the proposed use with his informants' descriptions. Because the usefulness of the plants would not be known for years after the journey, it was necessary to see how the plants adapted to the climate. Kalm had to make sure that his observations were not based solely on the impressions of others, but on his own observations. He investigated the conditions of plant growth, such as the quality of soil, temperature, and surrounding plants. Kalm also noted when the plant bore leaves, fruits, or flowers. Because most of these plants had already been described, it was not as critical for him to note specific botanical information.

Also during this time, Kalm wrote detailed descriptions of Philadelphia in his diary, noting its straight, broad streets, and buildings. In *Travels*, Kalm writes:

> But in most of the streets is a pavement of flags, a fathom or more broad, laid before the house, and four-foot posts put on the outside three or four fathoms apart. Those who walk on foot use the flat stones, but riders and teams use the middle of the street.

Kalm also took detailed notes on the population, commerce, and lifestyles of this multicultural city. He recognized the achievement of those who came with nothing, like Franklin, yet built grand houses and successful businesses. He also commented on slavery, different fauna, such as beaver and mink, and the use of lumber. Of slavery, Kalm wrote:

> Formerly the negroes were brought over from Africa, and bought by almost everyone who could afford it, the Quakers alone being the exception.[...] However, many people cannot conquer the idea of its being contrary to the laws of Christianity to keep slaves.

This exemplifies Kalm's interest in writing his observations on human society as well as those about the natural world.

Kalm was greatly impressed by the multiple churches and sects, as well as the general wealth of the colonies. Kalm also observed a strong sense of pride and freedom amongst the colonists. He noted that everyone in the community, as well as their property, "was protected by the law" and "enjoy[ed] such freedom that one can say he is a king in his own house." His diary makes it clear that Kalm was greatly impressed by the attitude and ability to make free choices within the colonies without answering overmuch to a sovereign.

When the weather suited him the following spring, Kalm made his journey to the interior of French Canada. It was here that the majority of plants were thought to be adaptable to the climate and temperatures of Sweden and Finland. Kalm continued to record detailed accounts of plants and trees in his diary, yet also gave equal attention to political and societal details. He witnessed many problems within colonies and between the colonies and their "parent" countries.

In essence, Kalm was able to provide a thorough account of the cultural relationships that emerged in North America, as well as those formed in the natural environment. Kalm wrote:

> The goods, with which the province of *New York* trades, are not very numerous. They chiefly export the skins of animals, which are bought of the *Indians*, great quantities of boards coming for the most part from *Albany*; timber and ready-made lumber, from that part of the country which lies about the river *Hudson*...

Thus, Kalm illustrated the great increase of trade amongst the North American colonies, as well as trade that was increased internationally. Conversely, an increase of trade meant an increase of extraction of natural resources that Kalm duly noted.

In July 1749, Kalm arrived at Crown Point (St. Frédéric), where, as Martti Kerkkonen notes, he "gained a most favorable impression of the French." He was treated hospitably by the French and had become well known because of his expedition. Kalm was impressed with the French colonies' understanding of natural sciences and felt that they had a "higher" appreciation than the English colonies whose "main interest was in getting rich quickly and any other sort of knowledge was laughed at." He met several French officers who were attuned to the workings of natural science, and collected information on plants and the environment daily. This attention to detail was without a doubt admired by Kalm, as he continuously recorded notes on the culture, society, and natural environment of French Canada.

Kalm benefited much from the French government because of his nationality and his area of expertise. The relations between the Swedish and French governments were very strong at the time, and because Sweden had funded French scientists in the past (with research in Scandinavia) the French insisted on covering all of Kalm's expenses accrued in French Canada. Kalm continued on to Montreal, where he met the Marquis de la Galissonniere, who was well-versed in natural science. At Kalm's request, the Marquis was invited to become a member of the Swedish Academy of Science.

Much to Kalm's dismay, the areas around Montreal proved to have fewer "useful" plants than imagined, and most were not ready to be collected at the time he was there. Kalm had no other choice but to pay others in Canada to collect seeds and plants for him and ship them to him after he returned to Philadelphia. However, upon returning to Quebec, Kalm was told about several useful plants that he might find around the Great Lakes region and Niagara.

Before leaving for this portion of Canada, Kalm immediately wrote to the Swedish Academy, asking for an extension to collect plants that he thought would be exceptionally "advantageous" for Sweden. He also assured them that all plants were gathered at above 40 degrees latitude north since there was some concern he might be collecting too far south. This letter helped to restore the Academy's confidence in Kalm, which was declining after his initial setbacks. The letter contained Kalm's primary reason for not going farther north: very few plants grew north of Hudson's Bay, and the ones that did were not essential to their cause.

While traveling in Canada, in August 1750, Kalm visited Niagara Falls, and is credited with being the first to write an account of the Falls in English. Shortly after witnessing its magnificence in August 1750, he wrote a letter to Franklin, sending him a detailed record of his observations. Franklin published Kalm's account in the *Pennsylvania Gazette*, and it was later republished in Bartram's *Travels in Pensilvania and Canada* (1751). His account of the Falls also brought him international recognition upon its publication in London.

However, in his own *Travels*, Kalm offers more analysis of the Falls and his reaction. He writes:

> It is enough to make the hair stand on end of any observer who may be sitting or standing close by, and who attentively watches such a large amount of water falling vertically over a ledge from such a height. The effect is awful, tremendous!

He also comments that Niagara Falls was undoubtedly the largest in the world and could be heard from afar:

> The falling waters cause a loud roar...[and] can sometimes be heard at Riviere a la Boeuf, which is located fifteen French miles to the south; and at Fort Niagara, which is six French miles away.

Kalm returned to Pennsylvania in September 1750 and stayed again through the winter. He continued to collect information and seeds and paid several visits to Bartram and Franklin. Kalm eventually left North America for London in February 1751, much to his distress because he believed there were more plants to discover and observe. Finally, in August 1751, he reached his "native soil" and returned to the University of Åbo. Here, he immediately began to condense and sort through his findings, and gauge the level of economic improvement his research would provide to Sweden and Finland.

The information that Kalm compiled on his journey proved to be extremely extensive. He hoped its publication would consist of a three-volume work; however, only two volumes were published due to the complications with locating a publisher. Kalm also intended to publish a unified work on the flora of Canada, entitled *Flora Canadensis* using his observations recorded while in French Canada. Because of this plan, he chose not to include these passages in *En Resa Til Norra America* (1752); however, his notes on Canada eventually disappeared, leaving much unknown about his observations there.

After returning to Åbo, Kalm was given time to prepare the account of his expedition for the public. In the autumn of 1752, he gave an address on his journey and its relevance to raising the Finnish economy. Because the topic was so new, many students were eager for this event, and he quickly became a popular professor among economic students. Once his travels were published in Europe, the interest in Kalm's research surged since it was the most in-depth scientific report on North American flora and social conditions to date. In 1753, he wrote a letter to Linnaeus, requesting the possibility of return since he found "scarcely a single plant that I hadn't seen earlier in Sweden." He also missed the landscape and the freedom that was associated with North America. However, Kalm's request was denied, and he eventually found solace in gardening, teaching, and writing.

Although few American plants thrived in and proved to be of economic use in Kalm's native climate, the thought of trying to acclimatize both native and foreign plants to the area remained enticing. Years after his journey, more plants were brought from Central Europe and Russia, which proved to be better adapted than the plants from North America. Despite this, Kalm spent 15 years cultivating his American varieties with limited success; most plants that did survive bore fruit or vegetables, but none produced a great enough quantity to prove useful to the country.

In 1757, Kalm was ordained a Lutheran clergyman, while maintaining his post at the University of Åbo. Between the years of 1757 and his death in 1779, Kalm was the recipient of a doctor's degree in theology from the University of Lund, the Order of the Star of Vassa in 1772, and an array of memberships in various national and international societies. Aside from his work on *Travels to North America*, over 85 of his letters to his colleague Carl Fredrik Mennannder have been published. Kalm also directed over 147 students with theses concerning issues of economy, American flora, and the admittance of foreign plants into the Scandinavian landscape.

Although Kalm did not bring financial success to Sweden and Finland through his research on North American flora, he succeeded in producing one of the finest natural history accounts of the region in the eighteenth century. In a letter to his colleague, C.C. Gjorwell in April 1764, Kalm wrote: "Natural history alone without consideration of its use in human life is pure balderdash and not a jot better than a lot of metaphysical ravings." Always the natural scientist, Kalm tried to remain objective but believed in adding breadth to his accounts. He did not merely comment on a single plant or animal but was determined to cite its function and use to society. However, despite his utilitarian beliefs, his enthusiasm for the natural world and his discoveries therein cannot be overlooked.

The number of known species particular to North America rose from 250 to 700 because of Kalm's work, and he is credited (by Linnaeus) with discovering 90 of these. Linnaeus named the American mountain laurel, *Kalmia latifolia*, after him, as well as the genera *Kalmia*, which now has five species to its credit; a small and separate genus of *Kalmiella*; three species: *Hypercium*, *Lobelia*, and *Pachylepis Kalmii*; and one insect, *Hygus* or *Cimex Kalmii*. Thus, it is that through Linnaeus Kalm was granted the immortality he sought.

Because of its nature, Kalm's expedition was conducted in the spirit of utilitarianism;

however, his account provides historical background we need today for gauging both social and environmental change in America. Although his primary concern was to find useful flora for his own economy, Kalm repeatedly notes the drastic consumption of resources by the colonists. He writes:

> ...from their gross mistakes and carelessness for futurity, one finds opportunities every day of making all sorts of observations, and of growing wise at the expence of other people. In a word, the corn-fields, the meadows, the forests, the cattle, &c. are treated with great carelessness....

Kalm offers a detailed account that cannot be rivaled in the age when most natural history accounts were as much fiction as fact. Although generally regarded as natural history, Kalm's work serves as both travel and nature writing, culminating in both a social and an environmental commentary on a society that did not foresee the consequences of its actions.

PRIMARY BIBLIOGRAPHY

Books

En Resa til Norra America (Stockholm: Lars Salvii, 1753–1761).

Des Herren Peter Kalms Beschreibung der Reise die er nac dem Nordlichen America unternommen hat I, II, III (Gottingen: Wittwe A. Vanderhoek, 1754, 1757, 1764).

Travels into North America by Peter Kalm, translated into English by John Reinhold Forster (Warrington: William Eyres, 1770; London: T. Downdes, 1771).

Peter Kalm's Travels in North America: The English Version of 1770, revised from the original Swedish, 2 vols., ed. Adolph B. Benson (New York: Dover Public, 1937).

Travels into North America. Translated by John Reinhold Forster (Barre, MA: The Imprint Society, 1972).

Other

Articles published by Peter Kalm, concerning his North American Journey

"Beskrifning huru socker göres uti Norra America af åtskilliga slags trän" (1751; English translation in *Agricultural History* 13 [1939]).

"Beskrifning om mays, huru den planteras och skötes I Norra America, samt om denna sädes artens mångfaldiga nytta" (1751; English translation in *Agricultural History* 9 [1935]).

"Beskrifning på de vilda dufvor, som somliga år I så otrolig stor myckenhet komma til de södra engelska nybyggen I Norra America" (1759; English translation in *Annual Report of Smithsonian Institute* [1911]).

"Rön om den americanska så kallade tuppsporre hagtorns nytta til lefvande häcker" (1773; English translation in *Agricultural History* 24 [1949]).

"Beskrifning på norr-americanske mulbärsträdt, Morus rubra kalladt" (1776; English translation in *Agricultural History* 24 [1950]).

"Om egenskaperne och nyttan af det americanska valnöt-trädet, som kalas hiccory" (1778; English translation in *Agricultural History* 19 [1945]).

SECONDARY BIBLIOGRAPHY

References

Sven Ahman, "Plants for Scandinavia," *Garden Journal of the New York Botanical Garden* 2 (1952): 139–41.

John Bartram, *Observations on the Inhabitants, climate, soil, rivers, productions, animals and other matters worthy of notice. Made by Mr. John Bartram, in his travels from Pensilvania to Onondago, Oswego and the Lake Ontario, in Canada. To which is annex'd, a curious account of the cataracts at Niagara. By Mr. Peter Kalm, a Swedish gentleman who traveled there* (London: printed for J. Winston and B. White, 1751).

John Bartram, *Travels in Pensilvania and Canada* (Ann Arbor, MI: University Microfilms, 1966), 79–94.

Adolph Benson and Naboth Hedin, eds., *Swedes in America: 1638–1938* (New Haven, CT: Yale, 1938).

William Bingley, *Biographical Conversations, On Celebrated Travellers* (London: J. Sharpe, 1819).

Georg Borgstrom, "Pehr Kalm: Some Retrospective Remarks," *American Swedish Historical Foundation Yearbook* (Philadelphia: A.S.H. Foundation, 1966), 37–44.

Michael P. Branch, ed. *Reading the Roots: American Nature Writing before Walden* (Athens: University of Georgia Press, 2004).

Gunnar Broberg, "Pehr Kalm," *Biographical Dictionary of American and Canadian Naturalists and Environmentalists*, ed. Keir B. Sterling et al. (Westport, CT: Greenwood, 1997), 421–23.

William Cronon, *Changes in the Land: Indians, Colonists, and the Ecology of New England* (New York: Hill & Wang, 1983).

Robert Elman, *First in the Field: America's Pioneering Naturalists* (New York: Mason & Charter, 1977).

Howard Ensign Evans, *Pioneer Naturalists: The Discovery and Naming of North American Plants and Animals* (New York: Holt, 1993).

Wayne Grady, *Bright Stars, Dark Trees, Clear Water: Nature Writing from North of the Border* (Boston: Nonpareil, 1992), 1–7.

Charles Coulston Gillispie, ed., *Dictionary of Scientific Biography* (New York: Charles Scribner's Sons, 1970–1976), 7: 210–11.

Francess G. Halpenny, ed., *Dictionary of Canadian Biography* (Toronto: University of Toronto Press, 1979), 4: 406–7.

Wayne Hanley, *Natural History in America: From Mark Catesby to Rachel Carson* (New York: Quadrangle, 1977).

Albert Bushnell Hart and Blanche E. Hazard, *Colonial Children* (New York: Macmillan Co., 1914).

Norma Olin Ireland, *Index to Scientists of the World from Ancient to Modern Times: Biographies and Portraits* (Boston: F.W. Faxon, 1962).

Terry G. Jordan and Matti Kaups, *The American Backwoods Frontier: An Ethnic and Ecological Interpretation* (Baltimore, MD: Johns Hopkins University, 1989).

H.O. Juel, "New Light on the Collection of North American Plants Made by Peter Kalm," *Proceedings of the Academy of Natural Sciences of Philadelphia* 81 (1929): 297–303.

Joseph Kastner, *A Species of Eternity* (New York: Alfred A. Knopf, 1977).

Martti Kerkkonen, *Peter Kalm's North American Journey: Its Ideological Background and Results* (Helsinki: University of Finland, 1959).

Esther Louise Larsen, *Papers on Pehr Kalm* (Cambridge, MA: Harvard Botanical Library, 1955).

Jack L. Lindsey, *Worldly Goods: The Arts of Early Pennsylvania* (Philadelphia: Philadelphia Museum, 1999).

J. Lucas, "Kalm's Account of his Visit to England on His Way to America," *Spectator* (April 29, 1893), 544–45.

Peter C. Mancall, *Land of Rivers* (Ithaca, NY: Cornell University Press, 1996).

Carolyn Merchant, *Ecological Revolutions: Nature, Gender, and Science in New England* (Chapel Hill: University of North Carolina Press, 1989).

E.J. Moyne, "Two Finnish Scholars in America," *Delaware Notes*, Vol. 24 (Newark: University of Delaware, 1951), 113–28.

Peninah Neimark and Peter Rhoades Mott, *The Environmental Debate: A Documentary of History* (Westport, CT: Greenwood Press, 1999).

Donald Culross Peattie, *A Gathering of Birds: An Anthology of the Best Ornithological Prose* (New York: Dodd & Mead, 1939), 97–109.

Henry Savage, Jr., *Lost Heritage* (New York: William Morrow, 1970).

Carl Skottsberg, *Pehr Kalm: Minnesteckning* (Stockholm: Almqvist & Wiksells, 1951).

James Grant Wilson and John Fiske, eds., *Appleton's Cyclopaedia of American Biography* (New York: D. Appleton & Co., 1888–1889; Detroit: Gale Research, 1968).

Papers

The manuscript of Kalm's diary is held at the Helsinki University Library, in Helsinki, Finland. Account records from his journey can also be found in Helsinki at the National Archives. Kalm's lecture notes and letters to the Baron Sten Carl Bielke are housed at the Uppsala University Library (Uppsala Universitets Bibliotek), and various other letters composed by him are held at the National Archives in Stockholm, as well as at the Kaolinksa Institute (also in Stockholm). Of other notable interest are the Minutes and Accounts of the Academy, which can be found at the Library of the Swedish Academy of Sciences.

Clarence King
(January 6, 1842–December 24, 1901)

David Finney

Clarence King's literary output was limited, but his single book-length work aimed at a broad audience—*Mountaineering in the Sierra Nevada* (1872)—was instantly popular and remains a significant contribution to mountaineering literature and the literature of California and the American West, as well as to nature writing in general. His other published writings comprise several articles (ranging in subject from the landscape and people of the American West to contemporary literature, the education system, architectural theory, and Cuban politics) and a fictional vignette titled "The Helmet of Mambrino." King was arguably the most influential American geologist of his generation, and his contributions to that field lie mainly in his work on the Geological Survey of the 40th Parallel—whose seven-volume report is today considered not only a monumental scientific achievement for its time but an artistic one as well—and in his role as first director of the U.S. Geological Survey. He published two works of scientific theory that were intended for a popular audience and were published in the mainstream press, "Catastrophism and Evolution" (1877) and "The Age of the Earth" (1893). Both were highly controversial at the time of their publication, and "Catastrophism and Evolution" continues to be examined by historians of science and scholars of nature writing. Today, King is best remembered as the tragic figure of his friend Henry Adams's *The Education of Henry Adams* (1918) and the rumored author of Adams's anonymous novel, *Democracy* (1880); however, his representation of the American West—in particular California's Yosemite Valley—is viewed by scholars as an important point of contrast to those of other writers of the time (especially John Muir). His writing is also beginning to be explored in the context of his membership, as a young man in the 1860s, in a group of avant-garde New York critics known as the American Pre-Raphaelites.

Clarence Rivers King was born on January 6, 1842, in Newport, Rhode Island, the first child of Caroline Florence Little and James Rivers King, in the dormered house on Church Street in which the King family had lived for generations. The Little family were strict Moravians, a sect whose numbers were dwindling in Newport. King's widowed maternal grandmother, Sophia Little, the daughter of a U.S. Senator from Rhode Island, was an outspoken abolitionist who published several works of poetry, drama, and fiction in the 1840s and 1850s. King's paternal great-grandfather had painted portraits of Ezra Stiles and George Washington. For decades, the Kings had been engaged as merchants in the China trade and, during his wife's pregnancy, James King was called away for the six-month sea passage to East Asia. He returned in 1845 to see his son for the first time, but soon heard from Hong Kong that his oldest brother had died during the return trip to the United States.

The 18 months King spent with his father were marred by another tragedy. His mother became pregnant again, but his first sister, also named Florence, soon died. When James King reluctantly departed again for China, his wife was pregnant with their third child, Grace Vernon King.

In 1848, news reached Newport that King's father had perished, like his uncle, at sea. The news arrived almost simultaneously with the death of Grace. This string of catastrophic losses would affect Clarence King's emotional life and would color his literary and scientific work. In the short term it caused him and his mother to forge a close and protective relationship. In subsequent years, another of King's two remaining paternal uncles lost his life at sea in Asia, and the fourth King brother steered the family business—upon which the livelihoods of Clarence and Florence King depended—to bankruptcy by 1857.

Because of the uncertain financial picture and a need to find Clarence proper schooling, his mother moved them from Newport, first to Pomfret, Connecticut, then to New Haven, Connecticut, where King's maternal uncle was studying at Yale. An episode from Pomfret, relayed in a letter by King's mother after his death in 1901, illustrates in her mind his inherent interest in the natural world: One winter day the seven-year-old King took his mother across frozen fields to where he had uncovered a fossilized fern in one of the many stone walls that crisscross that part of the New England countryside. When he asked her what it was and she could not answer, she sent to her brother in New Haven for a geology text; "from that time," she writes, "my rooms became a veritable museum where all kinds of specimens were studied with enthusiasm." After New Haven, the pair settled in Hartford, where King attended secondary school. There he met James Gardiner (the spelling was changed in

middle age from "Gardner") and Daniel Dewey. The boys trekked the woodlands around Hartford, camping, fishing, sketching wildlife, and hatching a plan to live on three farms in a row, across which a brook would run, full of trout. When school was through, the two other boys immediately headed to university while King took a job in New York City. At that time, his mother remarried. King shortly grew dissatisfied with the city and, reaffirming his lifelong passion for natural science, enrolled in the Sheffield Scientific School at Yale. He coaxed Gardiner into joining him there in 1862.

At Sheffield, King was immersed in a burgeoning community of professional scientists. But the Sheffield community was at odds with Yale's highly classical educational system. As King puts it in his article "Artium Magister," at Yale "an American professor of a classical subject felt entitled...to look down upon a teacher of natural science." In spite of the condescension from the rest of the university, Sheffield afforded King the opportunity to study with some of the leading chemists, physicists, and geologists in America.

In 1861, the Civil War began at Fort Sumter. Southern students fled Yale's campus. After graduation, King, Gardiner, Dewey, and another friend took a cruise on Lake Champlain, where they were required to carry papers proving they did not intend to evade the draft by their foray to Canada. Soon after, Dewey volunteered for the Union Army. Gardiner, too, had aimed to enlist, but was forbidden for medical reasons by a doctor. King avoided service altogether; there is no record he registered for conscription. The reasons may include the pacifism of his Moravian upbringing, or the wishes of a mother who had already suffered unimaginable loss. In letters to Gardiner from the time, King expresses squeamishness at the notion of "pushing the bayonet." The letters show he felt passion for the Northern cause—particularly the call for slavery's abolition by radicals like his grandmother—but lacked the wherewithal to fight for them in the army.

Before transferring from Rensselaer Polytechnic Institute in Troy, New York, to join King at Yale, Gardiner had been studying the writings and art of John Ruskin. He and King carried out a lively discussion of Ruskin's work by mail, continuing it in person after their reunion. Ruskin's spiritual relationship with landscape resonated with both their Christian faith and their enthusiasm for the natural sciences. For the two young men, the two need not be at odds. When they moved to New York City together, their enthusiasm for Ruskin led them to a group of young intellectuals who dubbed themselves "The Association for the Advancement of Truth in Art," or the American Pre-Raphaelites after the British Pre-Raphaelite Brotherhood, which included Ruskin and Dante Gabriel Rossetti. Their meetings produced a magazine, *New Path*, whose stated purpose was to create a new kind of American art that would "observe and record truth, whether of the visible universe or of emotion." Its prescription for artists was a monkish regimen of study and, for art, a painstaking fidelity to details of the visible world. *New Path* became a vehicle for ruthless criticism of popular American artists like Robert Bierstadt. But against the backdrop of the Civil War, the American Pre-Raphaelites' aesthetic crusade gained only minor attention. For King and Gardiner, the war exacted a personal cost as well; Dewey was killed in a minor battle in Louisiana.

The loss of Dewey convinced King and Gardiner to quit New York. With letters of introduction from professors at Yale, the two headed west in 1863 intending to seek work with the California State Geological Survey under Josiah Whitney (the brother of King's German professor). On a boat bound for Sacramento, they met by chance Professor William Brewer of Yale, Whitney's assistant. Upon arrival, Brewer helped them find work.

King's years on the California State Geological Survey are the subject of the bulk of *Mountaineering in the Sierra Nevada*. Eight of the book's chapters originally appeared as a series of seven articles in the *Atlantic Monthly*, the first of which, "The Range," was published in May 1871. Before that, King published two other articles based on his travels that would not be included: "The Falls of the Shoshone" (1870) and "Active Glaciers Within the United States" (1871), a popularized version of an essay published in the *American Journal of Science* documenting his discovery of active glaciers around Mount Shasta, a discovery that provided King, still in his twenties, a moment of national celebrity.

The public's appetite for colorful stories about California seemed insatiable; Bret Harte's poems in dialect had made him famous and earned him a wide following; King, a natural raconteur, aimed to please the same audience. The excitement "Active Glaciers Within the United States" generated led King to agree to write more popular pieces for the *Atlantic Monthly*. He also contracted with the publisher J.R. Osgood to publish a book that included them. King and Gardiner had long spoken of writing an account of their experiences in California that embodied the principles of the American Pre-Raphaelitism, and this was a perfect opportunity. "The Range" (1871), the first article that would go on to become a chapter in *Mountaineering in the Sierra Nevada*, shows the American Pre-Raphaelite ambition side by side with colorful storytelling in the vein of Bret Harte. As one early critic pointed out, the article is divided into two sections. The first is a broad description of the physical constitution and natural history of the Sierra Nevada, in which attention is paid not only to geologic details but also artistic ones like color and shape. The second is a humorous and embellished vignette of King's first approach of the Sierra Nevada from the desert with Gardiner. The contrast between King the scientist and aesthete and King the raconteur creates a narrative tension that runs through all of King's work.

Mountaineering in the Sierra Nevada (1872) quickly became a critical and popular success, even as some reviewers pointed to King's penchant for exaggeration. The book remains one of the most important works of American frontier literature, documenting a new age of scientific exploration, as well as a classic of mountaineering literature. In supplementing his published articles with new material, King has the book's narrative arc follow his quest to climb the highest peak in the Sierra—which would be, at the time, the highest peak in the United States. In the first edition, the book concludes with an account of King's scaling of Mount Whitney and, he believes, reaching the ceiling of the country.

In *The Literary History of the United States*, Wallace Stegner deems *Mountaineering in the Sierra Nevada* "in many ways the most delightful book of its decade." As an example of nature writing, the book's significance is complex. King increasingly felt, in the 1860s, that the careful study of nature his American Pre-Raphaelites endorsed failed to yield the transcendental experience they expected. Throughout the California State Geological Survey, King found the moments of experience that ought to have been sublime (per the Ruskinian model), such as the summiting of Mts. Tyndall and Whitney, instead bewildering or even horrifying. David Wyatt, a contemporary critic, calls it King's "career in the mirage of geology." Along with several of the American Pre-Raphaelite painters, in practice King came to find the group's philosophy fundamentally flawed, and *Mountaineering in the Sierra Nevada* records that conclusion. John Muir, meanwhile, scoffed at King's tall tales.

In a famously embarrassing episode, a young geologist published an article in 1873 proving King had not, in fact, reached the true peak of Mount Whitney as he claimed. Within a month, King had climbed Mount Whitney again and acknowledged his mistake; the peak, he said, had been shrouded in fog on his first attempt and he had failed to see it altogether. The 1874 edition of *Mountaineering in the Sierra Nevada* contains additional pages on the controversy as well as a new final chapter, "The People," which shifts the conclusion from the obvious failure of nature to yield transcendence (he had not even achieved the penultimate summit he believed he had) to the notion of "fraternity." This seems fitting, as the sections of the book that exude the most pathos and narrative power, and are also, incidentally, most often anthologized, are the harrowing, if embellished, mountaineering episodes.

The revised 1874 edition of *Mountaineering in the Sierra Nevada* effectively ended King's career as an author of popular literature. As Henry Adams laments in *The Education of Henry Adams*, the remainder of King's life may have contained professional successes like his appointment as the U.S. Geological Survey's first director, but it was generally characterized by more psychological and financial catastrophes. His relationship with his beloved friend James Gardiner grew strained. His mother and stepsiblings became a financial burden. Repeated business ventures ended in ruin and debt, and he was committed for several months to an asylum. The woman he married in 1888 was an African American; he hid the relationship from everyone and lied to her and his children about his true identity until the week of his death.

In Washington, D.C., during his tenure as director of the U.S. Geological Survey, King became a member of the "Five of Hearts," an exclusive social clique comprising King, the Henry Adamses, and the John Hays. Adams was the grandson and great-grandson of John Quincy Adams and John Adams, respectively, historian, editor of the *North American Review*, and a former professor at Harvard. Hay had been Abraham Lincoln's personal secretary, achieved fame as the author of *Castilian Days* and *The Breadwinners*, and worked in the diplomatic service (he would later serve as secretary of state in the McKinley and Theodore Roosevelt administrations). King, the fifth "Heart," was long considered one of America's most prominent *bons vivants* and bachelors.

After 1874, King published sporadically on various subjects in the mainstream press. "Catastrophism and Evolution" (1877), in particular, is an important contribution to his idiosyncratic body of nature writing. In the article, which was originally delivered as a commencement address at Sheffield Scientific School, then published in the *New York Tribune* and *American Naturalist,* King lays out a theory of the earth's geologic history that is punctuated by episodes of sudden geological change. This theory stood in stark contrast to the prevailing "uniformitarian" theory proposed by Charles Darwin and Charles Lyell and championed by John Wesley Powell, King's successor at the U.S. Geological Survey. Critics ridiculed King's theory, which he termed "modified catastrophism," as a throwback to pre-Darwinian creationist conceptions of natural history. And certainly it is tempting to question the theory as a manifestation of King's catastrophic personal history. But King adamantly defended "modified catastrophism" as a product of his extensive fieldwork (arguably he was the most active field geologist of his generation); gradualism, he said, failed to explain phenomena he observed in nature. Recently, scholars have begun to reevaluate "Catastrophism and Evolution" in light of new research suggesting the earth has, in fact, been subjected to periods of accelerated geologic change. As a work of nature writing, the article is boldly progressive. With it, King attempted to take a case formed by his decades in the field directly to the people, to change a prevailing scientific viewpoint about the earth's history. But he failed to find a sympathetic audience until late in the twentieth century.

In his later years, King worked feverishly, if fruitlessly, as a mining engineer and promoter of various mining ventures. He made a tour of Europe in 1882 and 1883, where he added to a prodigious collection of art and bric-a-brac and met the hero of his youth, John Ruskin. In the final decades of his life, he supported himself, his mother, and his secret family with loans from Hay. When he died in 1901 in Phoenix, Arizona, of tuberculosis, King's estate, which contained little more than a storeroom full of artwork, was auctioned to repay his debts. Hay and Gardiner established a trust to support King's mother and, as the

truth became known to them, quietly offered another to his wife and children living in Queens, New York.

In 1904, the members of the Century Association in New York, of which King and many of his friends were members, published a memorial volume to commemorate his life. *Clarence King Memoirs—The Helmet of Mambrino* was edited by King's colleague since the California State Geological Survey, James D. Hague. It reprinted, along with essays by friends like Adams, Hay, and William Dean Howells, "The Helmet of Mambrino" (1886), King's only other work of fictional (or highly embellished nonfictional) narrative apart from sections of *Mountaineering in the Sierra Nevada.* It recounts a trip King makes to Spain in search of the barber's basin Don Quixote wore on his head for a helmet. But *Mountaineering in the Sierra Nevada* remains King's overwhelming literary achievement and an important piece of American nature writing. King did not see himself as a nature writer, *per se,* rather as a scientist who sought to make his work available to a wide audience, and as a natural raconteur whose tall tales sometimes found their way into print. Later in life, King dismissed his book as "a slight book of travel" and even purchased the original plates and had them destroyed to prevent further printings. But his book gave Americans their most vivid and compelling picture of California since John Frémont's *Report of the Exploring Expedition to the Rocky Mountains and to Oregon and North California* (1845). Its mountaineering passages, with their harrowing moments of *l'esprit de corps* and derring-do, inspired generations of climbers. And, on the heels of the Civil War, its failed American Pre-Raphaelite ambitions document the close of an age of romanticism in much of American letters.

PRIMARY BIBLIOGRAPHY

Books

Mountaineering in the Sierra Nevada (Boston: J.R. Osgood, 1872; with new foreword, maps, and 17 new pages in the chapter on Mount Whitney and "The People" [Boston: J.R. Osgood, 1874]; edited with an introduction by Francis P. Farquhar [New York: W.W. Norton, 1935]).

Systematic Geology, in *Report of the U.S. Geological Exploration of the Fortieth Parallel,* ed. Clarence King et al., vol. 1 (Washington, D.C.: Government Printing Office, 1878).

Clarence King Memoirs—The Helmet of Mambrino, ed. James D. Hague (New York: Printed by G.P. Putnam's Sons for the Clarence King Memorial Committee of the Century Association, 1904).

Selected Periodical Publications— Uncollected

"The Falls of the Shoshone," *Overland Monthly* 5 (October 1870): 379–85.

"Active Glaciers Within the United States," *Atlantic Monthly* 27 (March 1871): 371–77.

"The Range," *Atlantic Monthly* 27 (May 1871): 602–13.

"Through the Forest," *Atlantic Monthly* 27 (June 1871): 704–14.

"The Ascent of Mount Tyndall," *Atlantic Monthly* 28 (July 1871): 64–76.

"The Descent of Mount Tyndall," *Atlantic Monthly* 28 (August 1871): 207–15.

"Kaweah's Run," *Atlantic Monthly* 28 (October 1871): 396–405.

"Wayside Pikes," *Atlantic Monthly* 28 (November 1871): 564–76.

"Shasta," *Atlantic Monthly* 28 (December 1871): 710–20.

"John Hay," anonymous, *Scribner's Monthly* 7 (April 1874): 736–39.

"Bancroft's Native Races of the Pacific States," *Atlantic Monthly* 35 (February 1875): 163–73.

"Catastrophism and Evolution," *American Naturalist* 11 (1877): 449–70.

"Style and the Monument," anonymous, *North American Review* 141 (November 1885): 443–53.

"The Helmet of Mambrino," *Century Magazine* 32 (May 1886): 154–59.

"The Biographers of Lincoln," *Century Magazine* 32 (October 1886): 861–69.

"Artium Magister," *North American Review* 147 (October 1888): 369–84.

"The Education of the Future," *Forum* 13 (March 1892): 20–33.

"The Age of the Earth," *American Journal of Science* 45 (January 1893): 1–20.

"Shall Cuba Be Free?" *Forum* 20 (September 1895): 50–65.

"Fire and Sword in Cuba," *Forum* 22 (September 1896): 31–52.

SECONDARY BIBLIOGRAPHY

References

Henry Adams, *Democracy,* anonymous (New York: Henry Holt, 1880).

Henry Adams, *The Education of Henry Adams* (Boston: Massachusetts Historical Society, 1918).

Linda S. Ferber and William H. Gerdtz, *The New Path: Ruskin and the American Pre-Raphaelites* (Brooklyn, NY: The Brooklyn Museum, 1985).

Patricia O'Toole, *The Five of Hearts: An Intimate Portrait of Henry Adams and His Friends, 1880–1918* (New York: Clarkson Potter, 1990).

Wallace Stegner, "Western Record and Romance," in *Literary History of the United States,* ed. Robert Spiller et al., vol. 2 (New York: Macmillan, 1946).

David Wyatt, *The Fall into Eden: Landscape and Imagination in California* (Cambridge: Cambridge University Press, 1986).

Papers

The Clarence King Papers, which includes letters, diaries, photographs, and letterbooks assembled by James D. Hague, are held at the Huntington Library in San Marino, California. A small collection is also held at the library of the American Philosophical Society in Philadelphia, Pennsylvania. Records associated with the Geological Survey of the 40th Parallel are located in the National Archives. The James Terry Gardiner Papers are held at the New York State Archives in Albany, New York, and the minutes of the Association for the Advancement of Truth in Art are a part of the Peter B. Wight Papers at the Ryerson and Burnham Libraries at the Art Institute of Chicago.

Thomas Starr King
(December 17, 1824–March 4, 1864)

Daniel Patterson

Starr King's contributions to American nature writing grew out of his experiences among and affinity for mountains, specifically two mountain ranges: the White Mountains of New Hampshire and the Sierras of California. His career was a quick one since he was only 39 years old when he died, but it was intense. Early in the 1850s he quickly rose to national fame as a preacher and lecturer; during the same period he was also making numerous trips into the White Mountains and writing about them. Although Thoreau was exploring and writing about mountains in Maine by the mid and late 1850s, King did not have literary models for his own representation of his White Hills. The work he published in 1859 was original and was recognized and praised as such at the time. One contemporary characterized King's *The White Hills* as "a volume of aesthetic teaching, thus far without a rival." King finished out his career with even greater intensity in California, where he was drawn to explore and render in prose the much vaster Sierras. At his death, he was famed for his preaching, lecturing, and patriotism. Today it is his nature writing that has taken on a renewed significance.

Thomas Starr King was born December 17, 1824, in New York City to Susan Starr (King) and the Reverend Thomas Farrington King, a Universalist minister of British ancestry. Susan Starr's grandfather and grandmother had emigrated to the United States from Germany's Rhineland with their son (and her father) Thomas near the end of the eighteenth century. After becoming a businessman in New York City, Thomas married a woman of French descent, Mary Lavinus. Susan Starr, their second daughter, was visiting her parents in New York City when Starr King was born; his father was then living and preaching in Norwalk, Connecticut. From his father, Starr King is said to have inherited his affability and humor; from his mother, his intellectual abilities. After a brief time in Hudson, New York, the Reverend Thomas King moved his family, in 1828, to the picturesque seaport town of Portsmouth, New Hampshire, where he ministered at the Universalist church and where Starr King spent some seven years of his youth. In 1835, the Reverend King assumed the pastorship of a Universalist church in Charlestown, Massachusetts, where Starr King continued his education in close proximity to Boston and Cambridge, as well as to the sites of the beginnings of the American War of Independence. Starr King excelled in his formal schooling, impressing everyone with his writing and speaking talents and with his vivacious personality. One teacher wrote that he was "uncommonly mirthful, he was as fond of books as he was of fun." When he was 15, his father's death brought an end to his formal schooling by requiring him to earn money to support his mother and five younger siblings. After a brief stint as clerk and bookkeeper in a dry-goods store, Starr King, having just turned 16, became assistant teacher at the Bunker Hill Grammar School in Charlestown. After two years, he was appointed principal of the West Grammar School in Medford, but because of a larger salary offered by the Charlestown Navy Yard, he became a bookkeeper there in 1843.

While he had hoped to attend a university, he did not cease to educate himself through a variety of means. He was drawn particularly to readings in philosophy and to the acquisition of languages. He regularly attended public lectures and formed a club of sorts devoted to the improvement of the minds of the young men who attended its meetings. During this time, Starr King established friendships that would last throughout his life with the Reverend Edwin H. Chapin, the Reverend Hosea Ballou (Medford's Universalist minister who would later become the first president of Tufts College), and Theodore Parker. In his diary on April 13, 1843, Parker recorded the following early impression of King:

> Saw schoolmaster Thomas Starr King,— capital fellow, only nineteen. Taught school three years. Supports his mother. He went into Walker's three courses of lectures, and took good notes. Reads French, Spanish, Latin, Italian, a little Greek, and begins German. He is a good listener.

King's regular discussions with Ballou influenced his intellectual and religious development; he would later refer to Ballou as his "theological father." Even without formal theological training, King seems to have been destined for the ministry. By the time he was 20, Chapin and Parker were encouraging him to preach and finding opportunities for him to do so locally. When he was 22, the Charlestown Universalist church, which his father had once pastored, selected King as their new minister. After two years, he made a move to the Hollis Street Unitarian Church in Boston, where he would minister for 11 years.

King married Julia Wiggin, of an East Boston family, on his 24th birthday, December 17, 1848, and thus began a very successful tenure in Boston. He quickly became known as one of Boston's best preachers and developed with remarkable rapidity into one of the most popular lyceum speakers in the country. He was much sought after socially as well. He nevertheless saw himself as a social reformer. Believing as he did that the elevation of the individual is a means to the elevation of society, he wrote sermons and delivered lectures with reform in mind. In a letter to a friend in June 1849 he reports his view that ministers have "the right and duty" "to act as reformers, to speak in Anti-Slavery meetings, and temperance and peace meetings, if they have the power of popular address," a power that all accounts attest he wielded very effectively. He was also motivated to lecture by a need for money with which to support his mother and invalid brother, to whom he gave one-third of his Hollis Street salary. He is said to have been ranked as one of the four most popular lyceum lecturers, along with Chapin, Wendell Phillips, and Henry Ward Beecher. King characterizes the attendance at one of his lectures in January 1849 as both abundant and approving:

> It was jammed and crammed, the largest of the season, except when Webster spoke. Every seat was filled, two hundred extra ones were provided, and then at least a hundred people stood around the doors. It took with critics and people, the audience were amazingly still, except when they applauded, which was not seldom.

Part of King's appeal came from his quick humor; he was, as one person has described him, "constitutionally hilarious."

Shortly after assuming the Hollis Street pastorate, King began taking his summer vacations in New Hampshire's White Mountains. Other than occasional sermons and orations, the only book that King published grew out of his decade of extended summer explorations of the rugged regions surrounding Mount Washington. Physically, aesthetically, intellectually, and theologically, King flourished as a mountain traveler. He so took to mountains that his conception of heaven changed, at least figuratively speaking; in a letter to a friend in July 1850, he joked significantly, "There must be grand mountain scenery in Heaven." He was moved to write about his experiences and perceptions in his "White Hills," and his series of lengthy letters to the *Boston Evening Transcript* were popular enough to encourage him to develop them into an unusually literate guidebook. He might also have been encouraged by the publication of Thoreau's *Walden* (1854). In a letter to the Reverend William Rounseville Alger dated August 1, 1854, shortly after his return from the mountains, King reveals that he was one of the first people to read *Walden* as well as one of the few to have read Thoreau's first book, *A Week on the Concord and Merrimack Rivers* (1849):

> On the way I read Thoreau's "Walden" in an advance copy. The first half disappointed me as being poorer than "Concord and Merrimac." But the latter half is wonderful; the chapter on "Spring," "Winter Animals," with a description of squirrels, the "Conclusion" being more weird and winding farther into the awful vitalities of nature than any writing I have yet seen.

King also has the distinction of being probably the first person to have lost a copy of *Walden*; after assuring Alger that he will experience "rapture" when he reads *Walden*, King laments: "Alas, I left my copy in the cars."

King's *The White Hills: Their Legends, Landscape, and Poetry* (1859) is one of the earliest descriptive guidebooks written for a place other than popular seashore destinations. It is arranged by regions and not, as he would have preferred, by geographic subjects such as "rivers, passes, ridges, peaks, &c.," as he explains in his preface. While the arrangement by regions would be more helpful for a guidebook, it might, he feared, result in

repetitiousness in the descriptive passages. The romantic poetry of nature was at the height of cultural fashion at this time, so King interweaves "with his own inadequate prose passages from Bryant, Emerson, Longfellow, Whittier, Lowell, and Percival, that interpret the scenery of our highlands." Since the tourist "cannot carry a poetic library on a journey among the hills," he has also culled passages from "Wordsworth, Scott, Tennyson, Goethe, Shelley, and Byron." This was the age of the romantic picturesque; accordingly King's announced purpose is to "introduce the poetic selections, that instead of being mere additions and ornaments, they shall continue and complete the description attempted, or embody the predominant sentiment of the landscape." It is clear that he was advised to pander to popular taste and forego his preferred design that would have foregrounded the realities of terrain.

This is a large book (over 400 pages) and truly lavishly illustrated, containing a map and 62 illustrations, depicting all the major sights that sightseers should look for. Since it is a guidebook, much of the prose is pedestrian, merely moving the reader from one place to another, for example:

> There are four avenues of approach to the two highest ranges of the New Hampshire mountains,—the valleys of the Saco, the Merrimac, the Androscoggin, and the tributaries of the Connecticut. Railroads connect with every one of these natural paths, except the Saco.

Nevertheless, King's voice as a tourist guide is often wryly animated; he assumes, for instance, that he can omit any accounts of places of lodging on the premise that

> travellers are moved to spend their money and time, not primarily to study the gastronomy of Coös County in New Hampshire, or to criticize the comparative upholstery of the largest houses there.

And his most accomplished landscape descriptions embody his intent to introduce his readers to the richest feasts of loveliness and grandeur that are spread by the Summer around the valleys, and to be refreshed by the draperies of verdure, shadow, cloud, and color, that are hung by the Creator around and above the hills.

This goal lies behind the evocativeness of his best descriptions; his aesthetic might usefully be called the religious picturesque.

His instructions to his readers on how to view a mountain could come directly from the essays of Thomas Cole, the leading theorist of the Hudson River Valley school of landscape painters. "Going close to a great mountain," King warns, "is like going close to a powerfully painted picture; you see only the roughnesses, the blotches of paint, the coarsely contrasted hues, which at the proper distance alone are grouped into grandeur and mellowed into beauty." King goes on to explain that to view a great mountain, such as Mount Washington, to greatest effect,

> it is only at a distance of some miles that the effect of foreshortening is corrected, and it stands out in full royalty. And from such a point of view alone, by the added effect of atmosphere and shadows, is its real sublimity discerned. The majesty of a mountain is determined by the outlines of its bulk; its expression depends on the distance, and the states of the air through which it is seen.

Furthermore, he instructs his readers to learn to view landscape features in the light and particular climatic conditions best suited to bring out their particular qualities:

> Some hills need rain, or a thick air, to tone down the raggedness of their foreground, and reveal the beauty of their lines. Others show best under the noon-light; others demand the sunset glow.

Whereas many American writers became nature writers out of a desire to blend science and literature, Starr King did so by bringing his understanding of the theory of landscape painting to bear on his guidebook prose. As a tour guide, he was also a teacher of art theory.

King wants to improve the "mind and taste" of his readers by means of his landscape descriptions; he explains that a visit to the White Mountains should lift a visitor

> above mere appetite for wildness, ruggedness, and the feeling of mass and precipitous elevation, into a perception and love of the refined grandeur, the chaste sublimity, the airy majesty overlaid with tender and polished bloom, in which the landscape splendor of a noble mountain lies.

Like Susan Fenimore Cooper, Henry David Thoreau, Elizabeth C. Wright, and other nature writers, King believed that a proper appreciation for the American landscape can improve the morality and intellect of Americans and thereby improve the cultural generally.

One of the chief means by which King overcame what he considered the disadvantages of arranging his book by region was to render many scenes in terms of a landscape painting. Also by weaving into his accounts legends, Indian traditions, folklore, and recent history associated with the various places, he creates an interesting and varied tapestry that accounts for the whole history of the human inhabitation of each tableau.

But the processes of nature do not always result in mere aesthetic scenery, however; the natural world that King renders also contains drama, even tragedy, for humans who live amid its wilder locales and in close proximity to its forces. As part of the human history of Crawford Notch, a high pass south of Mount Washington, King includes the story, long well known and reported in popular sources, of the Willey family destroyed by avalanche and floods of rainwater and swollen streams. Mister Samuel Willey, Jr., and his family were making their living by providing lodging, food, and conveniences for travelers along the new road through the Notch, but their home stood at the base of a mountain that rose swiftly 2,000 feet above them. The Willey's witnessed an avalanche that barely missed their home in June 1826, but they did not move their home. In August, under drought conditions, the entire area "was dried to powder." A severe storm of several days' duration flooded the streams and washed the house and family members away; several were found and buried, but others were never recovered. King's descriptions of some of the actions and effects of flood waters are clearly designed to convey the dramatic and tragic implications for humans of natural processes beyond their control. For this, he moves beyond the picturesque to create an almost realistic sublime. The entire Mount Washington range

> was devastated by landslides. Great grooves could be distinctly seen where the torrents had torn out all the loose earth and stones, and left the solid ledge of the mountain bare. Wherever there was a brook, stones from two to five feet in diameter were rolled down by thousands, in tracks from ten to twenty rods wide, dashing huge hemlocks before them, and leaving no tree nor root of a tree in their path.

It is noteworthy that a nature writer so immersed in the conventions of the picturesque and the sublime of this period could turn out passages amid a tale of human tragedy so realistic that they remind us today more of John McPhee than of John Muir, with whom King's philosophy of nature agreed much more closely. King was learning—and subsequently teaching readers—that the bare facts of nature themselves unadorned with an anthropomorphic rhetoric of pathos can communicate dramatically, that is, that the processes of ecology can be transformed into the suspense and drama of narrative plots. This particular strain of American nature writing was not fully developed until Rachel Carson wrote *The Edge of the Sea* (1955), published almost a century later.

Starr King was famous when *The White Hills* appeared, and liberal churches in cities across the country tried to lure him away from Hollis Street. After 11 years there, King appears to have been ready for a change. The prospect of helping a new Unitarian Church in San Francisco through its difficulties

appealed to him, and he seems to have felt a need to exercise his abilities in a larger field of action. At this time he wrote to a friend in New York:

> I do think we are unfaithful in huddling so closely around the cosy stove of civilization in this blessed Boston, and I, for one, am ready to go out into the cold and see if I am good for anything.

On March 25, 1860, King preached his farewell sermon to the Hollis Street congregation (published as "Words at Parting"), and on April 5 the King family, including now a young daughter Edith, started on the steamship *Northern Light* for San Francisco by way of the Isthmus of Panama. Julia was frequently ill, but Starr King's buoyant spirits seem to have remained strong throughout the journey. He was not without moments of introspection, however. After boarding the ship in the Bay of Panama that would take them to their destination, King observes upon watching pelicans feeding in the sea: "I watched them a long while on the hot morning, and came to the conclusion that it is hard work to get a living on this globe." On April 28, they arrived in San Francisco. The next morning, King delivered his first sermon in California and began to establish his reputation as an orator. Soon people were traveling by river boat from Sacramento on Saturday nights in order to hear him preach on Sunday mornings. The reputation and financial health of the church were also secured by King's dynamic presence. After managing to clear away the congregation's $20,000 debt, King raised some $80,000 to build the larger and finer church the congregation needed. King donated $5,000 himself from lecture fees. Julia despised San Francisco and being so far from her family and friends, but her husband's success was irresistible. Besides, in this new place, he was no longer disparaged as a "graduate of the Boston Navy Yard."

This writer of mountains, however, was quickly drawn into the surrounding landscape. He wrote on May 11, 1860, to a friend who was also an editor of the *Boston Evening Transcript:*

> I have been some fifty miles into the country already and have seen some scenery that could not be surpassed for color. I shall enjoy my work here, and the country will be a perpetual resource and delight.

The country would also become the subject of some 20 descriptive essays he would publish in the *Transcript,* intending eventually to produce a book about California's mountains. These essays comprise King's second major contribution to American nature writing. Only eight of them have been republished, as *A Vacation among the Sierras; Yosemite in 1860* (1962).

King's letters to "friend *Transcript*" are lively, jocular, and vividly descriptive. He writes as an Easterner for his familiar Eastern readers. His enthusiasm is evident in the fact that he made his first trip into the Sierras within three months of his arrival in San Francisco, leaving wife, child, and parishioners behind for two weeks. His first letters describe the modes of transportation and lodging that were still developing that travelers in the Sierras had to rely upon. He describes the lower gold mining operations extensively and with praise for the ingenuity of those who were devising ways to extract wealth from the earth. As he and his unnamed companions rise higher into the Sierras, however, there are ever fewer people to account for, and his attention turns increasingly to the wonders of a landscape that will stretch the limits of his ability to help Bostonians conceive of Western mountains and valleys.

King's account of their first encounters with the sugar pines is telling in this regard:

> I suppose that in three hours we saw ten thousand which were more than two hundred feet high. In the mountain districts of New Hampshire it is very rare to find a hemlock or fir more than three feet in diameter. Time and again we dismounted and put our measuring line around columns, fit to uphold an entablature of Phidias, that were twenty-eight and thirty feet in girth, supporting their topmost spray nearly three hundred feet above us. Trees of eighteen and twenty feet circumference could have been counted by hundreds.

King is mindful of his readers' need of help in conceiving the scale of the "Big Trees," the giant sequoias, so he adopts a very deliberate pedagogy as he leads his Eastern readers up to his first representation of them:

> Was it possible that, before sunset, I was to stand by a living tree more than ninety feet in circuit, and over three hundred feet high? Think what these figures mean, my hasty reader, when transformed into solid bark and fibre. Take a ball of cord, measure off a hundred feet from it, cut it and tie the ends, and then by the aid of four or five companions, stretch it into a circle, (if you have a parlor spacious enough to permit the experiment), and imagine that space filled with the column of a vigorous cedar. Now conceive this tree rooted on the Common near the Park street entrance. What do you say to the idea of looking up its smooth trunk to a point higher than the topmost leaf of any elm on the Tremont street mall, and of seeing there a bough thicker than the largest of those elms shooting out from it? What do you say to the fact that its plume would nod a hundred feet above the vane of Park street spire? What do you say to the possibility, if it lay hollowed on the ground, of driving a barouche and four through it, without their being able to touch the highest point of its curved ceiling "with a ten foot pole?"

His oratorical finesse is evident in the phrasing and cadences of this passage, and one of the most gifted preachers of the nineteenth century thus creates the uniqueness of his style in the history of American nature writing.

Starr King also distinguishes himself as a nature writer by the rhetorically subtle expression of sophisticated insights. In an account of his encounter with a sequoia named "Mother of the Forest," for example, which with a circumference of 56 feet was "little more than half the size of the monarchs in Mariposa," King manages to suggest a vastness that is more profound than mere physical vastness:

> There were a hundred trees in the Mariposa grove larger than this, and all of them together did not make half the impression on me that this one stamped into the brain at the first sight. We need to see the "Mother of the Forest" towering near Trinity Church in New York, and over-topping its spire with a column whose life is older than the doctrine of the Trinity, to appreciate its vastness.

People feel small when they stand among these trees, but so should Western Civilization, this Bostonian nature writer suggests.

Despite his occasional claim to be unable to describe an object or phenomenon, and despite his being no more than a "graduate of the Boston Navy Yard," King consistently sent back to the *Boston Evening Transcript* some of the most carefully crafted descriptive prose written in the nineteenth century. As he approaches Bridal Veil Falls in his account of the Yosemite Valley, for example, he begins by surrendering: "I am not going to describe it. The ponderous and the sentimental adjectives shall be undisturbed in my Worcester's Dictionary." He nevertheless continues thus:

> The wall is here about a thousand feet high, for a distance of an eighth of a mile. It sags in the centre, and there, eight hundred feet over my head, was the curve of the cataract, as it pours from the level stream for its unbroken descent of a sixth of a mile. Not a single projection from the wall, or bulge in it, is there to fret or mar the majesty and freedom of the current. It was probably fifteen feet wide where it started its descent; it kept its curve and a concentrated life for some three hundred feet; and then gravitation got hold of it, shook it apart, and made it tumble headlong through the air for five hundred feet more, scattering millions of pearls, and whole sheets of filmy mist, to be smitten with splendor by the sun.

In 1805, when Meriwether Lewis found fault with his description of the Great Falls of the Missouri River in central Montana, he was

right. However, when Starr King feigned a similar incompetence, he knew that his readers knew that he was up to the task. His desire for accuracy would reduce the "ponderous and the sentimental adjectives" to irrelevance, and his oratorical ear would aid the precision of his eye by coherently rendering the processes of a natural phenomenon in grammatical constructions that roll fluidly off the tongue.

During the last phase of King's life, he threw himself into the cause of saving California for the Union amid the extreme divisiveness of the Civil War. At the beginning of the Civil War, some 40 percent of Californians of European descent were Southerners, and together with many others in the state, they had largely controlled the state government for the preceding decade. Therefore, California was deeply divided on the issue of whether to back the Union or the Confederacy. Starr King's reputation as a "Patriot" emerges during this time because of his incessant and extensive preaching and lecturing devoted to keeping California in the Union. He raised extraordinary amounts of money for the United States Sanitary Commission, the agency charged to care for the Union soldiers. His health deteriorated as a consequence of his exertions for the Union, and on March 4, 1864, he died of diphtheria and pneumonia. At the time of his death, no man in California was better known or more broadly beloved, and he had been in the state not quite four years. There are statues of him in San Francisco's Golden Gate Park and in Washington, D.C. Mountains are named for him both in the Sierras and in his White Hills.

In his insightful introduction to King's eight Yosemite letters, *A Vacation among the Sierras; Yosemite in 1860*, John A. Hussey remarks: "It would be ironic if, in the long run, King should be remembered principally as a nature writer." What seemed ironic in 1962, however, seems rather inevitable some 40 years later. In 1962, significantly the year in which Rachel Carson published *Silent Spring*, the extent of the planet's environmental degradation was only beginning to be known, and over the next several decades it would worsen. As the threats to both environmental and human health increased, the cultural response brought about a renaissance of environmental writing in the United States, and contemporary authors such as Wendell Berry, Annie Dillard, Edward Abbey, Josephine Johnson, Barry Lopez, and Edward Hoagland found their voices and their audiences. Swayed by similar concerns, scholars began to turn to the study and cultural analysis of nature writing, both recent and past. The recovery, republication, and reinterpretation of early American nature writing is part of this work. Starr King was indeed both "Patriot and Preacher," as his friend Charles Wendte eulogized him, but he was also a nature writer whose potential for the representation of the physical environment was brought into full expression by his experiences of mountain landscapes, both east and west. And his audience seems ready for him now.

PRIMARY BIBLIOGRAPHY

Books

Discourse Delivered before the Ancient and Honorable Artillery Company on their CCXIII Anniversary (Boston: A. Tompkins, 1851).

The Railroad Jubilee: Two Discourses Delivered in Hollis-Street Meeting-House, Sunday, Sept. 21, 1851 (Boston: Benjamin H. Greene, 1851).

The Death of Mr. Webster: A Sermon Preached in Hollis Street Meeting-House, on Sunday, October 31, 1852 (Boston: B.H. Greene, 1852).

The Losses and Gains of a Church: A Sermon Preached in Hollis-Street Meeting-House, Sunday, September 19, 1852, on Occasion of the Death of Mr. Daniel Weld (Boston: J. Wilson, 1852).

A Short Review of Dr. Edward Beecher's Work on "The Conflict of Ages" (Boston: Abel Tompkins, 1854).

An Oration Delivered by Rev. T. Starr King, of Boston, Mass., at Fulton, Oswego County, July Fourth, 1855 (Fulton, New York: T.S. Brigham, 1855).

A Sermon Preached at the Installation of Adams Ayer as Associate Pastor of the Unitarian Society in Charleston, N.H. June 7, 1855, co-authored with Henry W. Bellows et al. (Brattleboro, VT: O.H. Platt, 1855).

A Sermon Preached at the Installation of Caleb D. Bradlee, as Pastor of the Allen-Street Church in Cambridge, Dec. 11, 1854; with the Charge, Right Hand of Fellowship, and Address to the People (Boston: B.H. Greene, 1855).

A Lecture on Hildebrand: Delivered before the Young Men's Christian Union, in Boston (Boston: A. Tompkins, 1857).

The Doctrine of Endless Punishment for the Sins of This Life, Unchristian and Unreasonable: Two Discourses Delivered in Hollis Street Church (Boston: Crosby, Nichols, 1858).

The White Hills: Their Legends, Landscape, and Poetry (Boston: I.N. Andrews, 1859; Boston: Crosby, Nichols and Company, 1860, 1862, 1863, and 1864; Boston: Crosby and Ainsworth, 1866 and 1868; Boston: Woolworth, Ainsworth, and Company, 1869; New York: Hurd and Houghton, 1870; Boston: Chick and Andrews, 1871; Boston: William F. Gill and Company, 1876; Boston: Estes and Lauriat, 1887; Bowie, Maryland: Heritage Books, 1991 [facsimile of Chick and Andrews, 1871]).

Address in Memory of Miss Sarah Paul: Preached in Hollis Street Church, June 26, 1859 (Boston: George C. Rand and Avery, 1860).

Trinitarianism Not the Doctrine of the New Testament: Two Lectures Delivered Partly in Review of the Rev. Dr. Huntington's Discourse on the Trinity, in the Hollis Street Church, January 7 & 14, 1860 (Boston: Crosby, Nichols, 1860).

Words at Parting: A Sermon Preached in Hollis Street Church, Sunday Morning, March 25, 1860, At the Close of a Ministry of Eleven Years (Boston: Walker, Wise, 1860).

Fourth of July Oration (San Francisco: J.G. Coggins, 1862).

"He Was a Good Man": A Discourse in Memory of Frederick William Macondray, Preached in the First Unitarian Church, San Francisco, Sunday Morning, August 31, 1862 (San Francisco: Towne and Bacon, 1862).

American Nationality; An Oration (San Francisco: R.C. Moore, 1863).

Oration Delivered before the Grand Lodge of Free and Accepted Masons of California (San Francisco: E. Eastman, 1863).

Patriotism, and Other Papers (Boston, Tompkins, 1864).

Spiritual Christianity (Boston: American Unitarian Association, 1880–1889?).

The Organization of Liberty on the Western Continent: An Oration Delivered before the Municipal Authorities of the City of Boston, at the Celebration of the Seventy-sixth Anniversary of the Declaration of American Independence, July 5, 1852 (Boston: Rockwell and Churchill, 1892).

Socrates; an Oration, ed. Ernest Carroll Moore (San Francisco: H. Wagner, 1924).

Collections

A Vacation among the Sierras; Yosemite in 1860, ed. John A. Hussey (San Francisco: Book Club of California, 1962). [A collection of eight Yosemite letters originally published in the *Boston Evening Transcript* on December 1, 15, and 31, 1860; January 12, 19, 26, and February 2 and 9, 1861].

Christianity and Humanity: A Series of Sermons, ed. Edwin P. Whipple (Boston: J.R. Osgood, 1877 and 1878; Boston: Houghton, Osgood, and Company, 1880; Boston: Houghton, Mifflin, and Company, 1882, 1887, 1888, and 1897).

Substance and Show, and Other Lectures, ed. Edwin P. Whipple (Boston: J.R. Osgood, 1877 and 1878; Boston: Houghton, Osgood and Company, 1879; Boston: Houghton, Mifflin, and Company, 1884, 1887, 1890, and 1894).

Other

A Scripture Catechism for Sabbath Schools (Boston: William A. Hall, 1856; San Francisco: Agnew and Deffenbach, 1861).

The Relation of This Life to the Next (Albany, NY: Ladies' Religious Publication Society, 1859).

The New Discussion of the Trinity; Containing Notices of Professor Huntington's Recent Defense of That Doctrine, Reprinted from "The Christian Examiner," "The Monthly Religious Magazine," "The Monthly Journal of the Unitarian Association," and "The Christian Register," co-authored with F.D. Huntington and Orville Dewey, includes sermons by Starr King (Boston: Walker, Wise, and Company for the American Unitarian Association, 1860).

"Peace: What It Would Cost Us: Address Delivered in Platt's Music Hall, San Francisco," broadside printed "For the benefit of New York and Massachusetts volunteers" (San Francisco, 1861; reprinted as Peace: What It Would Cost Us. Starr King's Best Sermon, Delivered August 29, 1861, at Platt's Hall (San Francisco: Francis Valentine and Company, 1861 and 1891).

Letters

The United States Mint in San Francisco holds several letters from King; letters are also held by the Massachusetts Historical Society.

SECONDARY BIBLIOGRAPHY

Biographies

Arnold Crompton, *Apostle of Liberty: Starr King in California* (Boston: Beacon Press, 1950).

Richard Frothingham, *A Tribute to Thomas Starr King* (Boston: Ticknor and Fields, 1865).

William Day Simonds, *Starr King in California* (San Francisco: Paul Elder and Company, 1917).

Charles W. Wendte, *Thomas Starr King: Patriot and Preacher* (Boston: Beacon Press, 1921).

References

Paul Brooks, *Speaking for Nature: How Literary Naturalists from Henry Thoreau to Rachel Carson Have Shaped America* (San Francisco: Sierra Club Books, 1980).

John A. Hussey, "Introduction," in *A Vacation among the Sierras; Yosemite in 1860,* ed. John A. Hussey (San Francisco: Book Club of California, 1962).

Papers

The "Thomas Starr King Papers, 1839–1863" are housed at the Bancroft Library of the University of California, Berkeley; the Boston Public Library holds various manuscripts as well.

Caroline Kirkland
(Mrs. Mary Clavers)
(April 17, 1813–December 31, 1894)

Mary DeJong Obuchowski

By 1850, Caroline Kirkland was well known for her books on the Michigan frontier including *A New Home—Who'll Follow?* (1839), *Forest Life* (1842), and *Western Clearings* (1845). As editor of and contributor to respected periodicals, she became an established literary figure in the 1840s and 1850s. As an early realist and satirist, she used her work not only to generate an appreciative audience in search of entertainment but also to promote issues for which she was an advocate. Among her causes were rehabilitation of women prisoners, the anti-slavery movement, women as writers, and the environment. For the latter she was particularly well equipped, having spent the years from 1837 to 1843 in Michigan just as it was being settled. There, she and her husband founded the town of Pinckney and watched the clear-cutting of the forests, wildcat speculation in land, and gradual development of the community. In reporting her observations, she combines a lively appreciation of natural phenomena with a spirited defense of the woodlands, which she saw the homesteaders removing without concern for either their beauty or their functions as windbreaks, shade, or ecological value.

Born in New York City into a family with literary interests, Caroline Matilda Stansbury was the first of the 11 children of Samuel and Eliza Alexander Stansbury. Her grandfather, Joseph Stansbury, had published loyalist satiric verses in Rivington's *Royal Gazette*. At the time of Caroline's birth, her father, Samuel, worked for an insurance company. Her mother read and wrote sentimental romances. Bright and intellectual as a child, at eight Caroline entered a Quaker school run by her father's sister, Lydia Mott. While teaching in another of her aunt's schools, in New Hartford, New York, she met William Kirkland, who was then a tutor in classics at Hamilton College.

After Caroline and William married on January 10, 1828, they opened a girls' school in Geneva, New York. In 1835, they decided to move to the frontier. In order to earn money to take advantage of the land boom, William Kirkland took an offer to become principal of the Detroit Female Seminary, at which Caroline both helped her husband with administrative work and taught. Of their seven children, four survived.

During their time in Detroit, William began to accumulate land in Livingston County. On this area of wooded and marsh land, the Kirklands proposed to found a town, which they called Pinckney. They started their trip west in 1839. In the opening chapters of *A New Home—Who'll Follow*, she recounts their mishaps with a mixture of tears and humor, as well as their residence in a one-room log cabin, after which their more permanent house, a small frame structure, seemed like a palace.

The motives for the Kirklands' trip to and residence in rural Michigan seem to have been primarily financial, although a sense of adventure and an idealistic concept that they could create a model community may have impelled them as well. On the other hand, her disillusion caused by land speculation scams, ignorant and rough settlers, corrupt politicians, and a lack of facilities for health and medicine permeates Caroline's articles and books. So, too, does her bemusement with the manners and practices of her new neighbors and their varying attitudes toward work, other people's property, social caste, and cleanliness. However, her enthusiasm for the landscape, clear air, fresh water, vivid changing seasons, and potential abundance of the soil more than balances her disgust.

Kirkland's letters from Michigan to friends in New York so delighted them that she put her observations into a book. *A New Home* consists of sketches, sometimes linked by events, of characters, events, and places she encountered on the frontier. She asserts that there will be no plot, and that her readers should anticipate no romantic descriptions such as those by James Hall in his *Legends of the West* (1833) or those by Charles Fenno Hoffman. Those writers had misled her about the realities of a journey by wagon to the barely settled wilderness. In addition, they failed to note poor roads and widely separated primitive facilities for travelers in need of food and shelter, the intense labor necessary for survival on the frontier, and the hardships of housekeeping where the facilities that an Easterner takes for granted simply do not exist. She adopts a satirical tone to describe the difference between dream and actuality in the village she calls "Montacute," noting that swamps may only appear to be meadows, and that domestic life in a "loggery" lacks Eastern comforts.

Using the pen name "Mrs. Mary Clavers" and changing the names of the villages and villagers, Kirkland describes, usually with apparent relish, the crude manners and antieducational attitudes of her neighbors, not forgetting to poke fun at her own ignorance in bringing out city furniture to a wilderness setting, expecting servants among pioneers who assert a determined equality of status, and wearing paper-soled slippers on a trek through a marsh. She records dialect, such as pronunciations of "marsh" as "mash" and of "massasauga," a rattlesnake, as "massisanga." Such customs as the settlers' habit of indiscriminate borrowing of anything to which they feel entitled, with or without the owners' permission, also come under her scrutiny. On the other hand, she also portrays the generosity of spirit, fierce independence, stoicism, and individualism of the people whom she encounters.

Critical response to *A New Home* was almost universally enthusiastic. In one of a series of articles called "The Literati of New York City," Edgar Allan Poe wrote,

> With a fidelity and vigor that prove her pictures to be taken from the very life, she has represented "scenes" that could have occurred only *as* and *where* she has described them. She has placed before us the veritable settlers of the forest, with all their peculiarities, national and individual; their free and fearless spirit....

When her neighbors heard about the book, however, they were not so happy. Although few read the book, they were ready to take offense at the ridicule to which they felt she had subjected them.

Her most significant work has been placed among that of the early literary realists because of her fidelity to detail and her revolt against the sentimentalism with which the West had previously been described. The focus of critical response has been on her portrayal of character and situation, that is, on human interactions, rather than on the outdoors, and, indeed, she has an eye for the quirky character and an ear for the droll and outrageous in dialect. However, not a great

deal of attention has yet been paid to her attitude toward nature, one of the factors that
drew her to Michigan. In *A New Home*, she
repeatedly expresses pleasure in the odors
and views of the abundant wild flowers along
the routes that she travels. Rides and trips to
the surrounding country were treats. She
writes, for example, "The drive was a charming one....In a tour of ten miles, we saw
three lovely lakes, each a lonely gem set deep
in masses of emerald green...," and notes
that the children "were in raptures with the
beautiful flowers, and the lake...."

The wilderness had its drawbacks as well as
its beauties for Kirkland. Regarding the trip
from Detroit to "Montacute," she warns readers to beware of "mudholes," into one of
which their carriage slipped. In the early days
of their stay, during the absence of "Mr.
Clavers" on business, she decided to move
from the close quarters of lodgings into a log
hut. Alone with three children in a one-
room cabin overheated by the fire, she found
the night so hot that she had to leave both
doors open. Thus exposed to the wilderness,
she was terrified. She says,

> the fear of being devoured by wild beasts, or
> poisoned by rattlesnakes, caused me to start
> up after every nap with sensations of horror
> and alarm .... At length sleep fairly overcame
> fear, and we were awakened only by a wild
> storm of wind and rain which drove in upon
> us and completely wetted every thing within
> reach.

Kirkland never overcame her fear of rattlesnakes or toads. She records an incident in
which a visitor killed a massasauga as if it
were the equivalent of a cougar, and reveals
that she fainted after stepping on a toad, saying, "I did not repent my fainting though it
was not a snake, for if there is anything
besides a snake that curdles the blood in my
veins it is a toad."

Nevertheless, in *A New Home*, Kirkland's
first hint of environmentalism appears.
Shortly after their arrival, she and her husband look over the site of the village and discuss with the speculator the plans for
developing the public square. She writes that

she "particularly requested that the fine oaks
which now graced it might be spared when
the clearing process commenced." Although
the "land-shark" agreed effusively, she sadly
adds, "I believe these very trees were the first
'Banquos' of Montacute."

Kirkland develops the nature themes she
established in *A New Home* in more detail
in *Forest Life*, a further book of sketches of
frontier life. Stung by the hostile reactions
of her neighbors to *A New Home*, she promises that in this volume, she will give "only
...a general outline of truth, with a saving
veil of acknowledged fiction" (2: 233); that
is, she will not ridicule foibles of specific settlers, but explain the way of life there in
broader terms, illustrated with her own personal experiences rather than those of others.
The narratives in these volumes tend to be
either typical sentimental fiction of the
period, particularized by the region, or devastating tales of greed, laziness, self-deception,
and other negative characteristics of human
nature magnified by the isolation and hardships of pioneer life. They supplement and
illustrate discussion of wilderness development, customs, and manners.

As much as she deplores the lack of culture
and refinement in rural Michigan, she does
not, however, endorse wholeheartedly the
attitude that the wilderness there must be
totally subdued in the pursuit of "civilization." She portrays the settlers as clear-
cutting the land and then abandoning it for
further conquests. The pioneers girdled trees
by cutting out a strip of bark, circling the
trunk and thus killing the tree. Kirkland
refers to this process repeatedly, as she grieves
the clear-cutting of the great forests.
Although she understands the settlers' need
to remove trees for farmland, she regrets their
impulse to do away with every tree in sight,
saying:

> Would I could hope that the fine remnants of
> the original forest that still remain to us, were
> to be allowed foothold on this roomy earth.
> They too must fall ere long before the "irre-
> sistible influence of public opinion." The
> Western settler looks upon these earth-born

columns and the verdant roofs and towers which they support, as "heavy timber," nothing more. He sees in them only obstacles which must be removed, at whatever sacrifice, to make way for mills, stores, blacksmiths' shops,—perhaps churches,—certainly taverns. "Clearing" is his daily thought and nightly dream; and so literally does he act upon this guiding idea, that not one tree, not so much as a bush, of natural growth, must be suffered to cumber the ground, or he fancies his work incomplete. The very notion of advancement, of civilization, of prosperity, seems inseparably connected with the total extirpation of the forest.

She particularly bemoans the loss of a shade tree that new neighbors cut down when the Clavers loaned them the piece of property on which it grew.

Similarly, she objects to the apparent need to make roads straight, regardless of the variations in or beauties of the landscape. On the family outing when she feels impelled to vent her irritation at this, however, she describes the children as delighting in the antics of a chipmunk and three fawns. This leads her to exclaim, regarding Michigan,

> I know of no feature of rural beauty in which our green peninsula is found wanting. If the richest meadow-land shut in by gently swelling hills and fringed with every variety of foliage—if streams innumerable, not wild and dashing it is true, but rapid enough to insure purity—if lakes in unparalleled variety of size and figure, studded with islands and tenanted by multitudes of wild fowl—if these be elements of beauty, we may justly boast of our fair domain, and invoke the eye of the painter and the pen of the poet. No spot on earth possesses a more transparent atmosphere.

In the same rich chapter, she describes the famous "oak-openings," the meadow-like spaces between clusters of oak trees that characterized pre-twentieth-century southern Michigan. She theorizes that variations in the soil and in its depth lead to differences in the kinds of vegetation that the land can support. Pointing out further evidence of

Michigan's unique landscape, Kirkland comments on its marshes, saying,

> The other "feature" to which I alluded—a very wide and flat one—the prodigious amount of wet prairie or "marsh"—the produce of millions of springs which percolate in every direction this diluvial mass—is said to promise magnificent resources for—our great-Grandchildren.

The technique of slipping a blade of understatement into an otherwise glowing commentary illustrates both her humor and her realism. On a more positive note, she shows how nature can operate as a healing influence on a trip the family takes as a palliative to "ague." Even the plagues of flies, mosquitoes, and midges have a favorable aspect to Kirkland. In a later chapter, she lays out their characteristics in all their annoying detail, saying, "One may observe, *en passant*, that ours is a rare region for the study of entomology."

The Kirklands returned to New York in 1843, burned by speculation, appalled by corruption, and resented by the citizens of Pinckney. William turned to editing the New York *Mirror* and Caroline, having already begun to contribute to such magazines as *Graham's* and the *Knickerbocker*, wrote for the *Mirror* and other publications. In addition, she opened a girls' school and entertained her friends, including Edgar Allan Poe, Lydia Maria Child, Lydia Sigourney, Nathaniel P. Willis, William Cullen Bryant, Evert Duyckinck, and many other literary figures. Among her other projects was a final book of sketches from Michigan life, *Western Clearings*. William took on the editorship of a Unitarian publication, the *Christian Inquirer*. In the midst of this period of productivity, in 1846 William died suddenly by drowning as he was boarding a ferry at night, probably having missed his footing because of his poor sight.

Caroline and William had been close, not only as man and wife, but as partners in their various enterprises, and Caroline, emotionally and economically bereft, felt the loss deeply. Caroline took over William's position at the *Christian Inquirer* briefly, and in 1847 became editor of the *Union Magazine of Literature and Art*.

Many of the editorials and book reviews she wrote for the magazine at this time reflect her love of the outdoors and her sensitivity to weather, fresh air, and living things. For example, in almost every issue, her column "Editorial Miscellany" begins with a reference to the season or the weather or natural phenomena of the month, as in one for April 1848. Here she contrasts the gentle, gradual awakening of the European countryside to "an overflowing vitality, a vigorous and exulting bound into full maturity" of spring in her parts of North America. Among the books she chooses to mention in Books of the Month, she frequently points out the descriptions of natural phenomena as assets, as in Longfellow's *Evangeline*, which she praises for its

> series of delicious pictures—dissolving views —melting one into the other with such exquisite gradation, that at the end we seem to have had unrolled before us a length of silken tissue, painted with a succession of scenes both Italian and Flemish, all lighted from sun-set skies, and rich with golden haze.

She comments on books not only of literary merit, but also on history, art, and natural science. She also solicited articles, fiction, poetry, art, and music from prominent figures of the time, including many of her friends, and published Henry David Thoreau's "Ktaadn, and the Maine Woods" serially in 1848.

In 1848 the publisher of the *Union* paid Kirkland to travel to Europe on the condition that she send back reports on her journeys there. Several of them appeared in the magazine, and she expanded and included them with others in *Holidays Abroad*, which appeared in 1849. Of special interest to her were the views of landscape peculiar to each region. For instance, on approaching Lucca, she exclaims, "Range beyond range of distant hills lay basking, or misty, as the rays fell upon them directly or aslant." She compares the prospects that she sees in reality to those depicted in paintings, contrasts European waterfalls unfavorably to those in North America, and ridicules guides who exaggerate the virtues of the scenes they advertise, especially well-known ones. But she looks at them with a devouring eye, appreciative of landscapes with or without human figures.

On her return to New York, Kirkland found that John Sartain had bought the magazine, naming it *Sartain's Union Magazine*, with John S. Hart as her co-editor, essentially displacing her. She continued, however, to write articles for *Sartain's* and for other magazines.

In much of her prose during this period, Kirkland's affinity for nature still comes through clearly. In *Western Clearings*, she incorporates descriptions of weather and landscape into brief stories and sketches of frontier activities, such as seasonal parties. Short essays such as "Harvest Musings," which contrasts city and country activities during late-summer heat, and "Idle People," a humorous depiction of supposedly lazy people gathering the wild bounty of the countryside—wild plums and grapes, honey, and nuts —serve as links between tales by providing a setting or atmosphere for the stories that follow. Many of Kirkland's periodical articles, including a series of "Western Sketches" in the *Union* during 1847 and 1848, found their way into *Western Clearings* and also into some of her later books, *The Evening Book* (1852), *A Book for the Home Circle* (1853), and *Autumn Hours* (1854). Some of these exhibit her delight in landscape and the outdoors in every season, as do her description of Bryant's home in *Homes of American Authors* (1853) and the biography *Personal Memoirs of Washington* (1857).

Besides defending American forests, Kirkland was involved in other social issues, with prefaces to books on behalf of Native Americans (*Dahcotah*, by Mary H. Eastman, 1849) and women's rights (*Woman, Her Education and Influence*, by Marion Reid, 1854), a book that promoted rehabilitation of women prisoners (*The Helping Hand*, 1853), as well as antislavery activism. In spite of pacifistic beliefs, she was working on a project for Civil War soldiers at the time of her death.

As Kirkland's reputation as an early realist grows, so too does the recognition that she was among the first to see the destructive relationship between urban progress and environmental decline. Although the voice in Kirkland's writing is often satirical, and she chooses the comical, ridiculous, pathetic, and outrageous in human activities, her articles and books subtly but clearly express the positive influences of the outdoors on the human body and spirit, and she deplored the failure of the people on the frontier to recognize their responsibility for nurturing the environment that nourishes them.

PRIMARY BIBLIOGRAPHY
Books

A New Home—Who'll Follow? Or, Glimpses of Western Life, as Mrs. Mary Clavers (New York: C.S. Francis/Boston: J.H. Francis, 1839); republished as *Montacute; or, A New Home—Who'll Follow?* 2 vols. (London: E. Churton, 1840); republished as *The Settler's Home, or, Glimpses of Western Life* (London: Allman, 1845); republished as *Our New Home in the West; or, Glimpses of Life among Early Settlers* (New York: James Miller, 1872).

Forest Life, as the author of "A New Home," 2 vols. (New York: C.S. Francis/Boston: J.H. Francis, 1842; London: Longman, 1842).

Western Clearings, as Mrs. Mary Clavers (New York: Wiley & Putnam, 1845; London: Wiley & Putnam, 1846).

Holidays Abroad: or, Europe from the West, 2 vols. (New York: Baker & Scribner, 1849).

The Book of Home Beauty (New York: Putnam, 1852).

The Evening Book; or, Fireside Talk on Morals and Manners, with Sketches of Western Life (New York: Scribner, 1852).

A Book for the Home Circle, or, Familiar Thoughts on Various Topics, Literary, Moral, and Social. A Companion for the Evening Book (New York: Scribner, 1853).

The Helping Hand, Comprising an Account of the Home for Discharged Female Convicts and an Appeal in Behalf of That Institution (New York: Scribner, 1853).

Autumn Hours, and Fireside Reading (New York: Scribner, 1854).

Personal Memoirs of Washington (New York: Appleton, 1857).

Other

Jonathan Dymond, *The Principles of Morality and the Private and Political Rights and Obligations of Mankind: Abridged and Provided with Questions, for the Use of Schools and for Young Persons Generally*, adapted by Kirkland (New York: C.S. Francis/Boston: J.H. Francis, 1842).

Marion Reid, *A Plea for Women*, ed. Kirkland (New York: Farmer & Daggers, 1845); republished as *Woman, Her Education and Influence*, introduction by Kirkland (New York: Fowlers & Wells, 1848).

Spencer and the Faërie Queen, edited, with an introduction, by Kirkland (New York: Wiley & Putnam, 1847; London: Wiley & Putnam, 1847).

Mary H. Eastman, *Dahcotah, or, Life and Legends of the Sioux around Fort Snelling*, preface by Kirkland (New York: John Wiley, 1849).

Garden Walks with the Poets, ed. Kirkland (New York: Putnam, 1852).

"Bryant," in *Homes of American Authors; Comprising Anecdotical, Personal, and Descriptive Sketches, by Various Writers* (New York: Putnam, 1853).

A Few Words in Behalf of the Loyal Women of the United States, by One of Themselves (New York: W. Bryant, 1863).

The School-Girl's Garland, A Selection of Poetry, in Four Parts, edited by Kirkland (New York: Scribner, 1864); republished as *The Garland of Poetry for the Young: A Selection in Four Parts*, 2 vols. (New York: Scribner, 1866).

Patriotic Eloquence: Being Selections from One Hundred Years of National Literature, edited by Kirkland (New York: Scribner; Cleveland: Ingham & Bragg, 1866).

Poetry of the Flowers, edited, with an introduction, by Kirkland (New York: Crowell, n.d.).

Selected Periodical Publications— Uncollected

"Harvest Musings," *The Knickerbocker* 20 (November 1842), 419–25.

"Western Sketches," *Union Magazine of Literature and Art*, 1 (July 1847): 45–48; 1 (August 1847): 89–91; 1 (September 1847): 114–16; 1 (October 1847), 179–81; 1 (November 1847): 229–31; 1 (December 1847): 282–83; 2 (January 1848): 43; 2 (March 1848): 137–38; 2 (April 1848): 166–67; 2 (May 1848): 211–12; 2 (June 1848): 274–75.

"Editorial Miscellany," *Union Magazine of Literature and Art,* 1 (August 1847): 95–96; 1 (September 1847): 143–44; 1 (October 1847): 192; 1 (November 1847), 239–40; 2 (March 1848): 139; 2 (April 1848): 190–91; 2 (June 1848): 286; 3 (July 1848): 46.

"Books of the Month," *Union Magazine of Literature and Art,* 1 (September 1847): 142–43; 2 (January 1848): 46–48; 2 (April 1848): 191–92.

"Sight-Seeing in Europe," *Union Magazine of Literature and Art,* 3 (July 1848): 1–5; 3 (August 1848): 49–54; 3 (October 1848): 145–51; 3 (November 1848): 193–99; 3 (December 1848): 241–46; *Sartain's Union Magazine of Literature and Art,* 4 (January 1849): 57–62; 4 (March 1849): 181–85; 4 (April 1849): 232–35.

"Odds and Ends of Travel," *Sartain's Union Magazine of Literature and Art,* 5 (September 1849): 139–42.

"Bush-Life," *Sartain's Union Magazine of Literature and Art,* 6 (January 1850): 70–74.

"The Log School-House," *Sartain's Union Magazine of Literature and Art,* 6 (April 1850): 251–56.

"Summer Recreation," *Sartain's Union Magazine of Literature and Art,* 7 (October 1850): 243–47; 7 (November 1850): 261–66; 7 (December 1850): 370–72.

SECONDARY BIBLIOGRAPHY

References

Lorraine Anderson and Thomas S. Edwards, eds., *At Home on This Earth: Two Centuries of Women's Nature Writing* (Hanover, NH: University Press of New England, 2002).

Jennifer A. Dawes, "Women Writers and the American Wilderness: Responses to the Frontier in Caroline Kirkland's *A New Home—Who'll Follow?* and Eliza Farnham's *Life in Prairie Land*" (MA thesis, University of Houston, 1997).

James Hall, *Legends of the West* (Philadelphia: Key and Biddle, 1833).

Charles Fenno Hoffman, *A Winter in the West,* 2 vols. (New York: Harper and Brothers, 1835).

Langley Carleton Keyes, *Caroline Matilda Kirkland, A Pioneer in American Realism* (Dissertation, Harvard University, 1935).

Annette Kolodny, *The Land Before Her: Fantasy and Experience of the American Frontiers, 1630–1860* (Chapel Hill: University of North Carolina Press, 1984).

William S. Osborne, *Caroline M. Kirkland* (New York: Twayne, 1972).

Scott Peeples, "'The Servant Is As His Master': Western Exceptionalism in Caroline Kirkland's Short Fiction," *American Transcendental Quarterly* 13 (December 1999): 305–16.

Edgar Allan Poe, "The Literati of New York City.— No. IV," *Godey's Magazine and Lady's Book,* 4 (August 1846): 75–76.

Audrey J. Roberts, "The Letters of Caroline Kirkland" (Dissertation, University of Wisconsin, 1976).

Nancy Walker, "Caroline Kirkland," in *Nineteenth-Century American Women Writers: A Bio-Bibliographical Critical Sourcebook,* ed. Denise D. Knight (Westport, CT: Greenwood, 1997), 286–92.

Sandra A. Zagarell, "Introduction," to *A New Home —Who'll Follow? or, Glimpses of Western Life,* by Mrs. Mary Clavers, an actual settler [Caroline Kirkland] (New Brunswick: Rutgers University Press, 1990), xi–l.

Papers

Caroline M. Kirkland's manuscripts are held by the Cincinnati Historical Society; the Harry Ransom Humanities Research Center, University of Texas at Austin; and the Newberry Library, Chicago. Collections of her letters are in the Alderman Library, University of Virginia; the John M. Olin Library, Cornell University; the Bentley Historical Library, University of Michigan; the Historical Society of Pennsylvania; the Massachusetts Historical Society; the Houghton Library, Harvard University; the Newberry Library, Chicago; and the Milton S. Eisenhower Library, Johns Hopkins University.

John Lawson
(?–September [?] 1711)

Stuart Noble-Goodman

Although he wrote only one book—*A New Voyage to Carolina*—John Lawson remains a noteworthy figure in early American nature literature. He remains so for a number of reasons, including the thoroughness and priority of his survey of the Carolinas, his stylistic skill, and his sympathetic portrait of the indigenous people of the Piedmont plateau. U.P. Hedrick termed *Voyage* "the most accurate and detached of the early natural histories of North Carolina," and Richard Davis found it the "only great book on the Indians" from the colonial Carolinas. Among Lawson's other achievements are his appointment as Surveyor-General of North Carolina, his completion of the earliest survey of the Piedmont plateau, and his participation in the planning and founding of Bath and New Bern, North Carolina's oldest European-founded towns.

There are no confirmed records of Lawson's life before 1700. Historians speculated for many years that he was from Yorkshire, but, perhaps based on the strength and extent of his relationships in London, more recent scholarship has led scholars to believe that he was from London and had some training in chemistry. In any case, he was a man with many skills as a writer, adventurer, natural historian, and surveyor.

Lawson appears in the historical record in 1700, when he, in his words, "accidentally met with a gentleman" who told him that "Carolina was the best country I could go to." Scholars have speculated that this "gentleman" was James Petiver, an Englishman and great collector of botanical specimens. Petiver had numerous contacts in the Colonies and was eager to expand his collection. It is entirely possible that Lawson's trip was not, as his glib comment implies, an impulsive adventure, but rather a paid expedition to gather botanical specimens. Whatever the precise nature of his expedition, Lawson was in the port city of Charleston in 1700 and was commissioned to conduct a survey of the interior of North Carolina. He conducted this survey between December 1700 and February 1701. Both Lawson's courage and his curiosity were on full display in this first survey; prior to his expedition, the interior of North Carolina—both the land and its inhabitants—were essentially unknown.

He was accompanied by a small group of white men as well as Native American guides. There was great possibility of danger, sickness, and conflict with the native people of the area. Avoiding insects may, in fact, have played a role in the timing of the survey, which was conducted during the dead of winter. This survey deepened Lawson's interest in and attachment to North Carolina, and, following it, he acquired significant land holdings in the state. His connections to North Carolina grew when he helped plan and found Bath—North Carolina's oldest white township—in 1706. He also helped found New Bern near some of his other land holdings. His continuing engagement in and connection to North Carolina led to his appointment as Surveyor-General of North Carolina. Although, like many aspects of the Lawson chronology, the precise date is uncertain, he was appointed sometime before 1709.

In January 1709 Lawson traveled to England to oversee the separate publication of his book, which had been in print since December 1708 as part of John Stevens's multivolume *A New Collection of Voyages and Travels* (1708–1710). While there, he was retained by the Lords Proprietors of Carolina to prepare a map of that colony. He was separately appointed to help resolve a boundary dispute between North Carolina and Virginia, which he settled successfully. Lawson's *New Voyage* did appear in 1709 as its own work, published by J. Knapton, Stevens's publisher in London. Subsequent printings, however (and for reasons that are not clear), were misleadingly titled *The History of Carolina; Containing the Exact Description and Natural History of That Country*. Editions appearing in London in 1714 and 1718 bore that title, as did later editions of 1860, 1903, and 1937. It is no wonder, of course, that the German editions of 1712 and 1722 replicated the mistake. It was not until University Microfilms published a new edition, as part of their *March of America Facsimile Series*, that the error was corrected, and the original title page restored.

In the Preface to *Voyage*, Lawson notes that most of the travelers to America are "persons of the meaner sort, and generally of a very slender education," and that it is his intention to provide "a faithful account... laid down with impartiality, and Truth...." Despite Lawson's disclaimer, the book, like many of the travel accounts of the day, is a mixture of natural history, sociology, speculation, and propaganda.

The book is divided into five main parts: "A Journal of a Thousand Miles Travel among the Indians from South to North Carolina," "A Description of North Carolina," "An Account of the Indians of North Carolina," "The Second Charter Granted by King Charles II to the Proprietors of North Carolina," and "An Abstract of the Constitution of North Carolina." The final two sections are historically significant, but as they refer to legal arrangements recorded elsewhere, they are much less informative than the first three. Certainly they lack the color, wit, and humor of the other three parts.

"A Journal of a Thousand Miles Travel..." is the account of the original 1700–1701 trip. Homer Kemp has noted that the survey trip was actually only about 550 miles, which is still remarkable "for having taken place over 59 days in winter." But the title does give us insight into the sense of grandeur that Lawson carried with him on these expeditions. He seems keenly aware that these narratives are his opportunity to secure a place in history, for he is working with what is essentially a blank slate; his journey is one of discovery, but not just as a survey. Not only is the land unmapped, but also the natural history—the botany, biology, geology—is uncharted. There is no recorded prior contact with the native people of the area, and the entire scope of human activity—social, economic, spiritual—lay untold before him. There was reason, then, for him to feel the significance of this journey.

Although he claims in his Preface to have, "...in the following Sheets, given you a faithful Account thereof, wherein I have laid down every thing with Impartiality, and Truth, which is indeed, the Duty of every Author, and preferable to a smooth Stile, accompany'd with Falsities and Hyperboles," Lawson's "Stile" is robust and competent, and he is, like many eighteenth-century environmental writers and discoverers, not entirely averse to "Hyperbole." He begins, for example, by describing a "pleasant and healthful Country...inhabited by none but

Savages, who covet a Christian Neighbour-hood, for the Advantages of Trade, and enjoy all the Comforts of Life free from Care and Want."

The five-page Introduction to the "Journal" is overtly promotional, a cornucopia of natural wealth, filled with game, fertile lands, "pleasant and navigable rivers," covered over with improvements, and functioning in peaceful lassitude under the monarchy. All of the comforts of civilization are available, "fair parsonage house[s]...considerable Trade with both Europe, and the West Indies, whereby [the inhabitants] become rich, and are supply'd with all Things necessary for Trade, and genteel Living...." They even fight the Spaniards. This verdant, productive, peaceful colony was no doubt attractive to the "Lords-Proprietors of the Province of North Carolina" who are so abjectly and protractedly praised in the "Dedication." Lawson depicts the colony as particularly inviting to investment: "The Merchants of *Carolina*, are fair, frank Traders. The Gentlemen seated in the Country, are very courteous, live very nobly in their Houses, and give very genteel Entertainment to all Strangers and others, that come to visit them." Having set the stage for his adventure, Lawson offers the "Journal" itself.

It begins on December 26, 1700, in Charlestown, with a party of ten. There are frequent encounters with Indians, and Lawson is notable in his almost unilaterally favorable impression of them. These "Christian Natives" he finds to be "a straight, clean-limb'd People." In particular, his impression of the native women is that they are "very fair, and generally as well featur'd, as you shall see any where, and have very brisk charming Eyes, which sets them off to Advantage." He presses on, even suggesting that "our European daughters of Thunder" might do well to emulate the obedient, demure Indian brides. He is also an early chronicler of the often tragic contact between Europeans and indigenous people, who are "afflicted withal" by "any Distemper" passed on by Europeans. Lawson made it a habit to study closely the native peoples he met, and he is both judgmental and sympathetic in his treatment.

On one hand, Lawson could observe sympathetically that

> These *Sewees* have been formerly a large Nation, though now very much decreas'd, since the *English* hath seated their Land, and all other Nations of *Indians* are observ'd to partake of the same Fate, where the Europeans come....

But in meeting the Tuscarora—ironically the tribe that would eventually kill him—he found them lazy and obtuse. He frowned on the "whorish" traditions of young Indians having numerous sexual partners through adolescence until they chose a mate.

The "Journal" is happily concluded, with Lawson and his party swinging back through the Piedmont to what is now Pamlico Sound, meeting the Tuscarora Indians on the banks of the Eno River, following it to the Neuse and thence back to the seaboard. Certainly, the "Journal" made for engaging reading, and demystified Carolina as a savage and wild place. Potential settlers and investors could only have been encouraged by this tale of a small band of white people making their way safely and easily through this land of plenty in mid-winter, fed and entertained at almost every stop by friendly natives. As a promotional writer, Lawson never missed an opportunity to praise the weather, land, or inhabitants of the territory.

From the "Journal" Lawson moves to "A Description of North Carolina," which begins with an outstanding and thorough topographical survey of the entire coast, from Cape Fear north to the Outer Banks and south to the border. There are descriptions of the various crops grown and the mild climate, as well as the herbs and edible native plants available. The cattle, swine, and crops all flourish, and Lawson emphasizes the high likelihood that one would subsist, and even prosper, with very little effort. There follows a fairly short section, "The Present State of Carolina," in which Lawson describes the economic and cultural matrix of the area, leading up to Lawson's assertion that the time is propitious for "purchasing the Lords Land at the most easy and moderate Rate of any Lands in *America*," especially compared (pointedly) to Virginia and Maryland. Lawson includes here descriptions of markets, economies, even the geology of the region; this section is consistent with the promotional tract language of fecundity and ease of living—Carolina is safely distant from the frontier, its natives are friendly, its slaves are healthy and plentiful, and its land is cheap and enormously productive.

The fourth part, "The Natural History of North Carolina," is perhaps the most useful and enduring of the sections. It contains a remarkably thorough catalog of the flora and fauna, extending from the birds of the air to the types of whales found off the coast, from the merest shrub to the mightiest oak and pine. It is a delightful catalog, with many lyrical passages, such as the following:

> Therefore we can entertain but small hopes of the Improvement of the Vine, till some skilful in dressing Vines shall appear amongst us, and go about it, with a Resolution, that Ordering the Vineyard shall be one half of their Employment. If this be begun and carried on, with that Assiduity and Resolution which it requires, then we may reasonably hope to see this a Wine-Country; for then, when it becomes a general Undertaking, every one will be capable to add something to the common Stock, of that which he has gain'd by his own Experience. This way would soon make the Burden light, and a great many shorter and exacter Curiosities, and real Truths would be found out in a short time.

There are also occurrences of subtle Southern levity: "Cinkapin is a sort of Chestnut, whole Nuts are most commonly very plentiful; insomuch as the Hogs get fat with them." The catalog is filled with knowledge of natural history and exhaustive taxonomies, especially botanical. The narrative is a trove of early eighteenth-century customs, practices, and technological processes. Furthermore, as Homer D. Kemp notes, Lawson's list of birds is one of the most complete from the early period of North Carolina's settlement.

The fifth section is a 70-page treatise on Indian affairs, "An Account of the Indians of North Carolina." As noted above, Lawson's treatment is both sympathetic and severe—not surprising, of course, in an early eighteenth-century Englishman. There are several noteworthy sections, especially a comparative section on English and Indian vocabulary and dialects, as well as a wealth of information about Indian medical practices. Ultimately, Lawson makes a very progressive suggestion at the conclusion of the treatise: that Europeans marry Indians as the surest way to Christianize them. This certainly would have seemed a radical concept to the "Lords-Proprietors" back in England. The final two sections—"A Second Charter of North Carolina" and "An Abstract of the Constitution of North Carolina"—are straightforward transcriptions and technical discussions of the machinery of government.

Lawson had gone back to England to tend to his publishing affairs, but he had also during that period spent considerable time as a member of the Temple Coffee House Botany Club, headed by James Petiver. He and Petiver apparently made plans for an extensive collection of botanical specimens, as complete as Lawson could gather when he returned to North Carolina. Also, before he returned, he was engaged by a Baron Graffenried to assist in the settling of a group of Palatines in North Carolina. In the year or so before his death, he fulfilled this obligation, helping plan and found with the Palatines the town of New Bern in 1710.

Ironically, Lawson's death came at the hands of the Indians he had so ardently supported in his writings. In September 1711, while he and Baron von Graffenried were on a surveying expedition, they were captured by a Tuscarora tribe. This tribe, with many others, had become desperate over European encroachments on their land. The Cary Rebellion (named after the governor at the time) left the colony divided and dispirited, which probably encouraged the tribes to strike back. Emboldened by the troubles in the settlements and anxious to stop their spread, it has been suggested that the natives might have interpreted Lawson's surveying activities as part of the expansion of white settlement. In any case, they tortured and killed Lawson, but set Baron von Graffenried free. Von Graffenried was later to claim that Lawson's death was a result of his mistreatment of the Indians, but such an account does not seem congruent with Lawson's long-standing commitment to Indian welfare and emancipation.

Lawson's legacy, though limited by his untimely death, is as a close chronicler of native customs and culture, and as a wonderfully keen and thorough natural historian and travel writer. His account is useful to the student of early colonial literature as well as to the anthropologist and biologist. His defense of the native people of the Carolinas still rings as an early liberal voice, and his natural history catalogs impress readers as particularly thorough accounts of North Carolina's flora and fauna.

PRIMARY BIBLIOGRAPHY

Books

A New Voyage to Carolina; Containing the Exact Description and Natural History of That County, in *A New Collection of Voyages and Travels*, ed. John Stevens, vol. 1 (London: J. Knapton, 1708; republished separately, London: J. Knapton, 1709).

The History of Carolina; Containing the Exact Description and Natural History of That Country (London: W. Taylor and J. Baker, 1714).

The History of Carolina; Containing the Exact Description and Natural History of That Country (Raleigh, NC: Strother & Marcom, 1860).

A New Voyage to Carolina; Containing the Exact Description and Natural History of That County: Together with the Present State thero., in *March of*

America Facsimile Series, No. 35 (Ann Arbor, MI: University Microfilms, Inc., 1966).

SECONDARY BIBLIOGRAPHY

References

Percy G. Adams, "John Lawson's Alter Ego—Dr. John Brickell," *North Carolina Historical Review*, 34 (July 1957): 313–26.

Matt H. Allen, "John Lawson, Gentlemen [sic]," Address to the North Carolina Society of Colonial Dames of America, 1900–1926 (Wilmington, n.d.), 170–79.

Richard Beale Davis, *Intellectual Life in the Colonial South, 1585–1763* (Knoxville: University of Tennessee Press, 1978).

Frances Harriss, ed., Introduction to Lawson's *History of North Carolina* (Richmond, VA: Garrett and Massie, 1937), ix–xvii.

U.P. Hedrick, *A History of Horticulture in America to 1860* (New York: Oxford University Press, 1950), 122–24.

Homer D. Kemp, "John Lawson," in *Dictionary of Literary Biography, Volume 24: American Colonial Writers, 1606–1734*, ed. Emory Elliot (New York: Bruccoli Clark Layman, 1984), 189–92.

Hugh T. Lefler, ed., Introduction to *A New Voyage to Carolina by John Lawson* (Chapel Hill: University of North Carolina Press, 1967), xi–liv.

Raymond P. Stearns, "James Petiver, Promoter of Natural Science, c. 1663–1718," *Proceedings of the American Antiquarian Society* 62 (April 16, 1952–October 15, 1952), 243–365.

Vincent H. Todd, ed., *Christoph Von Graffenried's Account of the Founding of New Bern, with an Historical Introduction and an English Translation* (Raleigh, NC: North Carolina Historical Commission, 1920).

Stephen Weeks, "John Lawson," in *Biographical History of North Carolina from Colonial Times to the Present*, ed. S.A. Ashe (Greensboro, NC: C.L. Van Noppen, 1905–1917), II, 212–18.

Joseph LeConte
(February 26, 1823–July 6, 1901)

Bernie Quetchenbach

Joseph LeConte was a scientist, a university professor, a charter member of the Sierra Club, and a science writer whose range extended to include philosophical and nature writing. Appealing to both popular and professional audiences, he addressed a wide variety of subjects ranging from geology to physiology and from evolution to religion. His *A Journal of Ramblings Through the High Sierra of California with the "University Excursion Party"* is an eloquent record of camping and exploring in the Sierra Nevada in the nineteenth century.

Joseph LeConte was born in 1823 at Woodmanston in Liberty County, Georgia. His father, Lewis (sometimes spelled Louis) LeConte, was a rice planter and an amateur naturalist known for his gardens of flowering shrubs and botanical specimens from South Africa. Joseph's mother, Anne Quarterman LeConte, died three years after his birth. The sixth of seven children, Joseph had little early formal education. According to William Blair, however, he was tutored by Alexander Stephens, who eventually became Vice President of the Confederacy.

During the 1840s and early 1850s, LeConte alternated between domestic life in the South and higher education, mostly in the North. Despite his lack of formal preparation, Joseph attended the University of Georgia, graduating in 1841, and the College of Physicians and Surgeons in New York City, where he completed medical school in 1845. During the summer of 1844, he traveled with his cousin John L. LeConte to the Great Lakes, visiting Niagara Falls and the area around Lake Superior. In 1846, LeConte married Caroline Elizabeth Nisbet, with whom he eventually had five children: Emma, known for her Civil War diary; Sallie; Josephine, who died at the age of two; Caroline; and Joseph, Jr., who was born soon after the LeContes emigrated to California.

After graduating from the College of Physicians and Surgeons, LeConte practiced medicine in Macon, Georgia, until 1850, when he enrolled at Harvard, where he met members of the New England intelligencia such as Ralph Waldo Emerson and James Russell Lowell and studied with the leading scientists Louis Agassiz and Asa Gray. Agassiz, particularly, had a lasting influence on LeConte, though LeConte would eventually break from his mentor's position by accepting the theory of evolution.

Upon completion of his studies at Harvard, LeConte returned to the South, where he held professorial positions at Oglethorpe University (1852–1853), the University of Georgia (1853–1857), and South Carolina College (1857–1862), while maintaining control over an inherited plantation in Liberty County and the 60 slaves who worked it.

During a family camping trip in the summer of 1858, he climbed Mount Mitchell in North Carolina, the highest Appalachian peak.

LeConte's early publications, concerning disparate subjects including medicine, education, and geology, reflect the breadth of his professional interests. His examination of landform geology would lead to some of his most significant accomplishments. A student research trip with Agassiz resulted in "On the Agency of the Gulf Stream in the Formation of the Peninsula of Florida," which appeared in the *Proceedings of the American Association for the Advancement of Science* in 1857. Biographer Lester Stephens characterizes LeConte as one of the last of the scientific generalists. Though his lack of a particular specialization fueled criticism that his knowledge in a given subject was often incomplete, LeConte's versatility, a reflection of his holistic conception of intellectual life, led him to become one of his era's foremost synthesizers and popularizers of scientific research and ideas.

During the Civil War, LeConte continued at South Carolina College until the institution suspended operations in 1862. He served the Confederacy by facilitating the purchase of caves where saltpetre was harvested and, as a chemist, by preparing medicines. In 1864, he joined the Confederate Nitre and Mining Bureau, claiming in his *Autobiography* that he was hired "with the rank and pay of major." Stephens notes that, though this claim seems to rest on pay equivalency rather than on a military commission, because of the direct bearing of his work on the war effort, LeConte would have been considered a prisoner of war had he been captured.

LeConte's war experiences are reflected in *Instructions for the Production of Saltpetre*, published by the State of South Carolina in 1862, and in *'Ware Sherman*, published posthumously in 1937, describing his journey from his home in Columbia, South Carolina, into Georgia to rescue his daughter Sallie and other relatives endangered by the advancing Union Army. This journal, consisting of dated entries and illustrated with sketches

by the author, includes landscape descriptions of swamps and woodlots where LeConte hid to avoid Union soldiers. *'Ware Sherman* exhibits a Romantic sense of connection between the landscape and the observer's state of mind. On his tense rail journey into familiar yet threatening country, for example, LeConte "looked out a moment into the dark and solemn pine woods and, huddling down again, fell asleep." Although lamenting that "The task I had undertaken was no light one to a man of my student habits of life," LeConte presents himself in scenes of outdoor adventure, for which he was prepared by "my duck-hunts in boyhood in the swamps of Liberty." In attempting to protect Confederate Nitre and Mining Bureau property from Union troops near the end of the war, LeConte lost not only mining supplies but personal manuscripts as well.

After the war, LeConte operated a flatboat delivering goods to Columbia until 1866, when the college was reopened as the University of South Carolina. Never a believer in racial equality, LeConte found conditions in the Reconstruction South not to his liking, especially since, as his daughter Caroline notes in her "Introductory Reminiscence" to *'Ware Sherman*, the legislature was discussing opening the university to African American students. Moreover, the personal and professional connections that LeConte had secured with northern scientists were compromised or suspended as a result of the war. Discouraged, LeConte joined his older brother John in applying at the new University of California, where both brothers were offered positions in 1869. John, the first faculty member hired by the university, eventually advanced to the institution's presidency. Accepting the university's chair in chemistry and geology, Joseph, whose journey to California made him one of the first passengers on the newly completed transcontinental railroad, remained a University of California professor until his retirement and death in 1901. Writers including Caroline LeConte have recorded LeConte's enthusiastic prediction, made soon after his arrival on the West

Coast, that the University of California would grow into a major center of learning.

LeConte continued to write and publish articles and papers, gradually finding his opportunities increasing as the war receded in time. His first-published major book, *Religion and Science*, based on "Sunday lectures" he had begun in South Carolina, was printed in 1873 by Appleton, which remained his primary publisher for the rest of his life. The book concerns a subject that LeConte would treat repeatedly, most notably in *Evolution: Its Relation to Religious Thought* (1888), one of his most widely read works. Typical of LeConte is the attempt to reconcile science and religion, at odds because of evolutionary theory and mechanistic explanations of natural phenomena, by revealing underlying connections between modes of understanding.

Although he occasionally considered returning to the South, LeConte, who was 46 years old when he arrived in California, adapted to his new home both personally and professionally. In 1874, he rejected a geology position offered by the state of Georgia, in part because of salary concerns but also, according to Stephens, because he was satisfied with the University of California. He and his brother John also turned down teaching appointments at the University of Georgia. Stephens relates that the University of Texas considered offering LeConte a faculty position as late as 1883, but by that time "he was too much rooted in California to entertain serious thoughts of moving."

The Western landscape provided much material for LeConte's papers on glaciation, mountain building, and other aspects of geology and became important to him as a source of recreation and spiritual renewal. In July 1870, he embarked on the first of a series of summer explorations of Yosemite and the Sierra Nevada (he would eventually expand his travels to include Crater Lake and other destinations in the Pacific Northwest). His initial trip is the subject of *A Journal of Ramblings in the High Sierra of California by the "University Excursion Party,"* which was published for distribution to student participants in 1875, republished in limited edition

printings, and later published by the Sierra Club, most recently in 1960. In a 2000 *Sierra* magazine retrospective, editor Joan Hamilton characterized the book as an account of "the geologist's exuberant horseback ride across California to explore the scientific and aesthetic wonders of the Yosemite Valley."

In *Ramblings*, LeConte's fascination with and spiritual response to the Sierra wilds is clear. The book features Sunday meditations such as one at Lake Tahoe in which he reaches an Emersonian conclusion that "Natural beauty is but the type of spiritual beauty." Always a scientist, he includes the full text of several lectures on glaciation, the formation of alkaline lakes, and similar subjects, which he delivered "by request" at the campfire. As in his other writings, LeConte employs literary, classical, and biblical allusions in *Ramblings*. For example, describing clothes washing in camp, LeConte suggests that if the gender of the participants were changed, the scene would resemble "the exquisite washing scene of Princess Nausicaa and her damsels, or of Pharaoh's daughter and her maids."

Camping in Yosemite valley, LeConte first met John Muir. Already locally well known among LeConte's associates, Muir accompanied the party for a portion of their trip. In *Ramblings*, LeConte recounts discussions with Muir concerning glacial geology, a subject of mutual interest and occasional disagreement. Examining a pair of concentric volcanic cones at Mono Lake, LeConte offers his interpretation of the cones as "a beautiful example of cone-and-rampart structure" before adding that "Mr. Muir is disposed to explain it differently." Despite their differing interpretations of some geological features, each respected the other's opinions. Stephens notes that Muir responded to LeConte's first publication on mountain building by "commending him for his original ideas"; Stephens also establishes that Muir visited LeConte at his home in addition to encountering him in the Sierras.

Observing birds at Mono Lake, LeConte suggests in *Ramblings* that phalaropes, swimming shorebirds, would "undergo a

Darwinian change into web-footers," adding in a note in the 1900 edition that they already had developed partial webs. LeConte's emerging Neo-Lamarckian understanding of evolution is apparent. The phalaropes would develop webbed feet because webs would be useful to them; thus, there is a direct relationship between function and evolutionary change, passed through the generations as what he would come to call a "residuum" of experience. Though inclined against mechanistic science and trained by the leading proponent of the special creation of species, LeConte was, according to Stephens, "virtually convinced" of the validity of evolutionary theory by the time Agassiz died in 1873.

LeConte's prolific writings and reputation as a scientist and teacher earned him increasing professional recognition during the 1870s, when he was admitted to the American Philosophical Society, the National Academy of Sciences, the American Academy of Arts and Sciences, and the New York Academy of Arts and Sciences. Stephens points to these professional honors as evidence "that Joseph LeConte's reputation had finally exceeded that of his brother" and fellow scientist John.

LeConte's *Elements of Geology*, published in 1877, became a standard academic text, going through multiple editions during LeConte's life and still in service until the 1920s. Stephens endorses Ernest Hilgard's assertion that the book became "probably the most widely used text-book of geology in the English language," though the evolutionary framework, more obvious in the third and subsequent editions, may have made it less popular in the South than it would have been otherwise. Geology was the closest thing to a professional specialization in LeConte's career. In addition to *Elements of Geology* and *A Compend of Geology* (1884), Stephens credits him with "nearly sixty articles on geological topics" composed "in the face of a heavy teaching load and a commitment to other scholarly endeavors." Along with Richard Henry Dana, LeConte was a major

proponent of the contractionalist theory, which posited that mountains were formed as a result of the cooling of the earth's interior. He remained a central figure in American geology even when the theory itself began to lose credence.

Sight: An Exposition of the Principles of Monocular and Binocular Vision, published in 1881, received generally good reviews, including one by William James, who, according to Stephens, found the book very admirable. Like other reviewers, however, James critiqued the author's failure to familiarize himself with all of the available work in the field, particularly by German researchers, and his neglect of psychological factors involved in vision. The book's mixed reception is evidence of the increasing specialization of science, as the growing body of scientific work made it difficult for a generalist such as LeConte to keep current in multiple and mostly unrelated fields. Still, LeConte felt confident enough about his work on vision to say, in the *Autobiography* he wrote near the end of his life, that "my researches on the phenomena of vision, I am sure did clear up the thought in this field."

In 1888, LeConte published *Evolution and Its Relation to Religious Thought*. Written for a general audience, the book is the culmination of his long-term consideration of evolution and of the relationship between scientific inquiry and religious faith. After attempting to recast his early mentor Agassiz, who consistently rejected evolutionary theory, as a forerunner of Darwin, LeConte offers a thorough, methodical account of the evidence for evolution. Once the case for Darwin's theory has been established, LeConte attempts to reconcile evolution and religion by revealing that evolution applies not only to biology, but has analogs in other sciences such as geology, and, beyond science, in civilization and religion as well. He concludes that "the doctrine concerns alike every department of science—yea, every department of human thought." His approach to reconciling differences is not through compromise; instead, he seeks a level of insight so penetrating and encompassing as to make the apparent disagreements disappear. Noting praiseful reviews in American and European scientific periodicals, Stephens proclaims the book "a huge success," concluding that "it quickly became a leading work on the subject."

Despite his association with the Neo-Lamarckian school of thought, LeConte accepted Darwinian selection as an important, even paramount, mechanism of evolution. According to Peter J. Bowler, LeConte differed from other Neo-Lamarckians because he "showed a far greater willingness to compromise with Darwinism." But LeConte maintained that the Lamarckian factor, inheritance through use, was also significant. Neo-Lamarckism offered a form of evolution amenable to teleological interpretations of human destiny, with all creation aspiring through the action of "vital force" toward humanity as its topmost evolutionary branch. Characteristically, LeConte saw an analogous relationship between the natural process of biological evolution and the human process of conscious cultural change.

LeConte never abandoned his belief in the superiority of the white male, concluding in "The Race Problem in the South," an address included in *Man and the State*, published by the Brooklyn Ethical Association in 1892, that people of African descent are "generalized" compared to whites. Stephens notes that LeConte's interpretation of evolution provided a scientific rationale as he "enunciated the racial and sexual stereotypes of his generation." LeConte recognized that racial mixing could ameliorate racial differences, but he found this concept personally distasteful and hazardous to the well-being of the "higher race." His Lamarckian perspective, however, led him to acknowledge the value of education and societal change in benefiting all races. Bowler says that, of all the American Neo-Lamarckians, "It was LeConte...who most clearly exploited the American school's philosophy of evolution to defend the claim that reformed social conditions might improve the human race." Accordingly, in "The Race Problem in the

South," LeConte notes that association with the "higher race" had already led African Americans to "race-evolution," making slavery obsolete as an appropriate system of race relations. While LeConte's version of evolution helped him justify the prejudices of his upbringing, it also precluded belief in absolute and permanent racial hierarchies.

As one of America's most prominent scientists and scientific philosophers, LeConte continued to contribute to intellectual and civic life during his last decade. In 1891, he became president of the American Association for the Advancement of Science. Also in 1891, as First Vice President of the American Committee of the Geological Congress, he addressed a major convention of international geologists. In addition to his involvement in professional scientific organizations, LeConte was a charter member of the Sierra Club. In his foreword to a Sierra Club edition of *Ramblings*, Francis P. Farquahar claims that, although LeConte, traveling in Europe in 1892, was unable to participate in the club's initial organization, "The memory of Joseph LeConte is such a rich heritage that it should be familiar to all who love the Sierra, especially to members of the Sierra Club." The Sierra Club's online history lists LeConte as a board member from 1892 to 1898 and observes that LeConte's son Joseph, Jr., also served on the board. Farquahar notes, and William Dallam Ames agrees, that LeConte was planning to join the Club's first large-scale excursion into the Sierras in 1901, when he died at a campsite in the Yosemite Valley on July 6.

At the time of LeConte's death, his *Autobiography*, begun in 1900 at the request of his daughter, had been drafted. William Dallam Ames revised and edited the *Autobiography*, which was published in 1903. The book pays particular attention to LeConte's early life, covering in rich detail his trip to the Great Lakes in 1844 and the Native American settlements he visited near Lake Superior. LeConte also reiterates his belief in the significance of Agassiz and remarks that "it was left to the American thinkers," such as LeConte himself, to establish that evolution and religious principles were not contradictory.

The scope and prolific output of Joseph LeConte's writings and publications is almost inconceivable today. The LeConte-Woodmanston Foundation estimates that he authored 175 papers and articles, in addition to his books, several of which, including *Ramblings, Evolution and Its Relation to Religious Thought*, and *'Ware Sherman*, are currently in print. Peaks in the Great Smoky Mountains and the Sierra Nevada are named in his honor, as is a lodge in Yosemite National Park. Joseph LeConte is remembered as a pioneer California intellectual, a leading scientific popularizer, and an outdoors enthusiast whose *Ramblings* serves as a prominent example of an early literary response to the Sierra landscape.

PRIMARY BIBLIOGRAPHY

Books

Instructions for the Manufacture of Saltpetre (Columbia, South Carolina: C.P. Pelham, State Printer, 1862).

Religion and Science (New York: D. Appleton, 1873).

A Journal of Ramblings Through the High Sierras of California by the "University Excursion Party" (San Francisco: Francis and Valentine, 1875; San Francisco: Sierra Club, 1930, 1960).

Elements of Geology (New York: D. Appleton, 1877).

Sight: An Exposition of the Principles of Monocular and Binocular Vision (New York: D. Appleton, 1881).

A Compend of Geology (New York: D. Appleton, 1884; New York: American Book Company, 1898).

Evolution and Its Relation to Religious Thought (New York: D. Appleton, 1888; London: Chapman and Hall, 1888).

Outlines of the Comparative Physiology and Morphology of Animals (New York: D. Appleton, 1900).

The Autobiography of Joseph LeConte, edited by William Dallam Ames (New York: D. Appleton, 1903).

'Ware Sherman: A Journal of Three Months' Personal Experience in the Last Days of the Confederacy (Berkeley: University of California Press, 1937; Baton Rouge: Louisiana State University Press, 1999).

Other

"The Race Problem in the South," in *Man and the State: Studies in Applied Sociology. Popular Lectures and Discussions Before the Brooklyn Ethical Association* (New York: D. Appleton, 1892), 349–82.

Selected Periodical Publications— Uncollected

"On the Science of Medicine and the Causes Which Have Retarded Its Progress," *Southern Medical and Surgical Journal*, New Series, VI (August 1850): 456–74.

"On the Agency of the Gulf Stream in the Formation of the Peninsula of Florida," *Proceedings of the American Association for the Advancement of Science* X, part 2 (May 1857): 46–60.

"The Principles of a Liberal Education," *Southern Presbyterian Review* XII (July 1859): 310–35.

"On Some of the Ancient Glaciers of the Sierras," *American Journal of Science*, Third Series, V (June 1873): 448–53.

"Flight of Birds," *Nature* IX (November 6, 1873): 5.

"On the Structure and Origin of Mountains, with Special Reference to the 'Contractional Theory,'" *American Journal of Science*, Third Series, XVI (August 1878): 95–112.

"Evolution in Relation to Materialism," *Princeton Review*, Fourth Series, VII (March 1881): 149–74.

"Science and Literature," *Overland Monthly*, Second Series, I (February 1883), supplement: 8–10.

"What is Evolution?" *Popular Science Monthly* XXXI (November 1887): 721–35.

"The South Revisited," *Overland Monthly*, Second Series, XIV (July 1889): 22–31.

"Memoir of John LeConte, 1818–1891," *National Academy of Sciences Biographical Memoirs* III (1895): 369–93.

SECONDARY BIBLIOGRAPHY

Biography

Lester D. Stephens, *Joseph LeConte: Gentle Prophet of Evolution* (Baton Rouge and London: Louisiana State University, 1982).

References

William Dallam Ames, "Preface," in *The Autobiography of Joseph LeConte*, ed. William Dallam Ames (New York: D. Appleton, 1903), v–xiii.

William Blair, "Introduction to the 1999 Edition," in *'Ware Sherman: A Journal of Three Months'*

Personal Experience in the Last Days of the Confederacy, by Joseph LeConte (Baton Rouge: Louisiana State University Press, 1999), vii–xvii.

Peter J. Bowler, *The Eclipse of Darwinism: Anti-Darwinian Evolution Theories in the Years Around 1900* (Baltimore: Johns Hopkins University Press, 1983).

Francis R. Farquhar, "Foreword," in *A Journal of Ramblings in the High Sierra of California with the "University Excursion Party,"* by Joseph LeConte (San Francisco: Sierra Club, 1960), v–x.

Joan Hamilton, "Inside Sierra: The Green Millennium," *Sierra* (January/February 2000): 12.

Carolyn LeConte, "An Introductory Reminiscence," in *'Ware Sherman: A Journal of Three Months Personal Experience in the Last Days of the Confederacy,* by Joseph LeConte (Baton Rouge: Louisiana State University Press, 1999), xix–xxxv.

"Joseph LeConte," LeConte-Woodmanston Foundation, http://www.hist.armstrong.edu/publichist/LeConte/leconte-home.htm

"Joseph LeConte: Scientist and Savant," Sierra Club, *Sierra Club History,* http://www.sierraclub.org/history/key_figures/leconte/index.asp

Graceanna Lewis
(August 3, 1821–February 25, 1912)

Patricia Kennedy Bostian

Graceanna Lewis was inspired to study nature by her Quaker beliefs, becoming one of the best-educated female naturalists of her day. Often overshadowed by female scientists of the day, such as astronomer Maria Mitchell, and her male counterparts who received the academic positions she so desired, Lewis pursued a life-long study of the natural world. Beginning with ornithology, the field she is best known for, she extended her interests to include sea creatures and the plant kingdom as well. Lewis devoted the majority of her life to a study of the wonders of the natural world and teaching others, especially girls, to love and appreciate nature as a gift from a divine creator.

Born the second of four daughters to John and Esther Fussell Lewis in Chester County, Pennsylvania, Lewis was educated at home by her mother until she was old enough to attend the Kimber Boarding School for Girls. Lewis was influenced by Abigail Kimber's pursuit of botanical studies. Kimber, along with Esther Lewis and her friend Mary Townsend, sister to ornithologist John Townsend, are credited with influencing her to become a naturalist.

Her early energies, shaped by her Uncle Bartholomew Fussell and the Quaker stance on abolition of the slave trade, were devoted to working with the Underground Railroad and teaching in a "colored school." Her home was a station on the Railroad line, and the family helped hundreds of slaves to freedom. Lewis's first publication was *An Appeal to Those Members of the Society of Friends Who, Knowing the Principles of the Abolitionists, Stand Aloof from the Anti-Slavery Enterprise.*

By the end of the Civil War, though, she was on her way to becoming a scientist. Her love of birds developed into a serious study, beginning with Thomas Nuttall's 1832 *Manual of Ornithology of the United States and Canada* and *The Birds of North America* (1858) written by Spencer F. Baird and John Cassin, men who were to become her mentors. Lewis became part of the growing community of amateur naturalists who were working to chart the thousands of unknown plant and animal species of North America. Since women were still often denied access to formal scientific training, Lewis, like many others, relied on male friends and family members for access to materials for her study.

Upon her move to Philadelphia in the early 1860s to be closer to the Academy of Natural Sciences, Lewis met Spencer Baird, an expert on ornithology, and John Cassin, curator of birds at the Academy of Natural Sciences. She spent seven years studying under their tutelage, emerging as one of the country's most knowledgeable female naturalists. By 1865, her confidence in her abilities prompted her to offer her services as lecturer on scientific subjects. Although Lewis was praised by the West Chester, Pennsylvania, *American Republican* for her "thoroughness and earnestness," her interests and speaking styles ran counter to the public's desire for entertaining lecturers, and Lewis did not draw great audiences. Finding scientific jobs was also difficult. Unable to obtain a professorship at Vassar, the newly established college for women, she taught at preparatory schools and continued her research on her own.

In the 1860s, Lewis was attracted to the ideas of Louis Agassiz. Agassiz disputed Darwin's theory of natural selection, arguing that speciation was not random, but that every species developed as a part of God's unfolding plan. His adherence to the ideals of Lorenz Oken's *Naturphilosophie*, the belief system that held that everything springs from a primary source, usually seen as God, influenced Lewis. The belief in a teleological explanation for the universe strengthened Lewis's findings and led her to see the natural world as a series of symmetrical systems, a stance that was rejected by many of her contemporaries.

Also following in Agassiz's steps, she developed (as his work had suggested) a classification scheme based on embryology. For Lewis, it was not enough to provide descriptions of birds, their physical attributes, habits, and songs; she needed to forge a chain of teleological argument that would link each species of bird to the laws of nature and to their creator. In 1868 she published the first installment of *Natural History of Birds: Lectures on Ornithology*, which she envisioned extending to ten parts. Deborah Warner, Lewis's biographer, notes that although there were catalogs of the bird specimens held by various museums, there were few books for the layperson that treated American birds as living creatures. Lewis's *Natural History* was an attempt to fill this void.

The first part of the proposed series provides an overview of ornithology. Additional parts were to explore plumage, nesting habits, songs, and a variety of other topics. Lewis begins her study with a discussion of the egg. Her constant theme is that of the connectedness of life to the creator—every aspect of this first lecture on ornithology is devoted not just to an exploration of the topic at hand, but to strengthening her argument of a divine life force that informs all creation. She speaks about the formation of a bird out of its yolk and albumen as a gathering of cells, marching obediently to their designated spots, in a "divine, unvarying order" according to the "exact plan laid down for the species."

After her discussion of egg formation, Lewis moves on to explain the system of classification of birds, frequently citing Thomas Henry Huxley's system. In a diagram of the animal kingdom as she understood it in the 1860s, Lewis shows *homo sapiens* at the top of the chart, as a separate class from mammals: "[A]nd supreme above all, distinguished by intellect and the possession of the religious faculties, is Man." The species of bird are situated between the reptiles and humankind—some leaning toward reptiles in their habits and inclinations, some toward humans. The majority of the book's contents is concerned with the subcategories of birds; Lewis supplies a brief overview of each "tribe," providing information about their habitats and habits.

Another tenet of *Naturphilosophie* held that natural systems can be profitably subjected to mathematical analysis. According to Warner, Lewis posited that "there can be no doubt that both animal and vegetable life do group according to some law of numbers." Other diagrams illustrate her burgeoning interest in phyllotaxis, the study of the arrangement of the leaves of plants in mathematical formations. One shows the various species of birds as being ordered in a spiral as flower petals are. Lewis observes that "it appears that the progress from Radiate to Man does not occur in any direct line, but rather in a spiral." She illustrates this observation with a conical arrangement of species from plant to man, and adds that "the progress within the classes themselves, occurs in a spiral from the point of origination of the class, outward towards the circumference, as trees branch in spirals around the main stem." She finds in this arrangement proof of an ordered force behind the formation of the universe.

A later section of the book finds Lewis grappling with Newtonian mathematical conceptions of the cone and how that shape is reflected in the animal kingdom. She theorizes that the shapes that could be given to the organization of the animal species rely on the nature of the "ebb and flow" of the life-force pulsing between the creator and his work, the cone representing the flow of life-forces "upward and laterally"—"to its Giver." The last section returns to a discussion of the eggs of birds, using them to comment on the order of species from which they derive. The brief discussion of eggs leads to Lewis's final analysis: "Who would have supposed that even in the form, the quality and color of the eggs of birds, the majestic flow of the tidal forces of life could be expressed." That God was behind the intricacies inherent in an ordered system was indisputable to Lewis.

In the 1890s, as the evidence for evolution accumulated, Lewis came to embrace it, but she rejected Darwin's theory that random variation is a mechanism in natural selection. For her, evolution was an example of the wonders of the creator and justification of one's study of nature and worship of the divine life force. She took great offense at one Reverend Tallmadge's 1893 sermon denouncing evolutionists as infidels and atheists. Her last article on evolution, "Truth and the Teachers of Truth," appeared in 1896 and argued that divinely directed progress was at the heart of evolution—the unfolding of God's plan for the perfection of his creation is legible in the record of the emergence of new species on Earth.

Lewis's goal with *Natural History of Birds* was to provide a book equaling her friend Mary Townsend's work on insects, *Life in the Insect World,* published in 1844. Townsend produced the volume to encourage children to appreciate and understand nature as the work of a divine creator. As an early subscriber to *Natural History of Birds,* Spencer Baird was supportive of Lewis's work, but the speculative nature of the book may have kept him from pushing for the publication of the additional installments. As with her lectures, Lewis's ideas were too complex for the lay audience, and yet not sophisticated enough for the scientific community. Failing to obtain enough subscribers, the remaining nine parts of her *Natural History of Birds* never appeared in print.

In 1870, "The Lyre Bird" appeared in *The American Naturalist.* A meticulously detailed study of this Australian bird, the article argues that the lyre birds should not be included in their present suborder of *Passeres,* which includes thrushes and wrens. Citing Thomas Henry Huxley's studies of the bird, she posits that the lyre bird is in a classification of its own. The article shows Lewis's wide range of reading. Along with Huxley, she cites British naturalists John Gould and Thomas B. Wilson, whose collections of specimens were available to Lewis at the Academy of Natural Sciences in Philadelphia.

The lengthy article describes in extensive detail the habits of the lyre bird and its Australian habitat. Having never traveled to Australia, Lewis relied on Gould's writings. She is much impressed by the bird's brilliantly plumed tail, and devotes several pages to minute observation of the structure and arrangement of the lyre bird's tail feathers. She bemoans the practice of hunters donning hats made of these very tail feathers to trick the lyre bird into revealing its hiding place. The feathers of the killed bird are then used to adorn ladies' hats, a practice Lewis deplores in other writings as well.

Along with her discussion of the lyre bird in its native environment, she offers an account of its life in captivity, again based on the work of another ornithologist, George Bennett of Australia. The final section of the article examines the various arguments made for the bird's inclusion in several different genera. She notes the reasoning behind the ornithologist's assignments, and then provides her own analysis. As is typical in all of Lewis's work, she credits others for their efforts and carefully considers their expertise; however, she never shies away from offering her own opinion, whether it deviates from standard consensus or not.

Deborah Warner notes that Lewis's illustration of the lyre bird, which accompanied the article, was reproduced in one of the period's most important bird guides, Elliott Coues's *Key to North American Birds*, with no mention of its source. In 1870 Lewis was refused membership in the Academy of Natural Sciences of Philadelphia. She had also twice failed to obtain positions at Vassar. These disappointments led Lewis to question her abilities as a naturalist, and in 1871 Lewis experienced a mental collapse.

Although Baird credited her with being a well-respected naturalist, at the age of 50 she was unable to land any scientific jobs, and she was tired of her teaching duties. After selling her home, she returned to her studies, continuing to seek a classification scheme that would describe the order of relationships between the animal and vegetable kingdoms. The publication of Lewis's article on the crystalline structures of bird feathers, *Symmetrical Figures in Birds' Feathers*, in *The American Naturalist* in 1871, again set her energetic spirit in motion.

As in many of her writings, Lewis combines lyrical passages with scientific vocabulary to describe what she observes. In this study, her observations are of slides of cut bird feathers viewed under the lens of her new possession—a microscope. Examining the feather capsules of a nestling dove, she delights in the symmetrical structures that appear. In a whimsical passage, Lewis says,

> At the same moment the little granules moved to order, there before the astonished gaze were diamonds such as Aladdin might have envied, in form as varied, but far more symmetrical than the frost work on a window pane of a winter's morning.

Such whimsy is often overshadowed by the inclusion of technical language such as this passage in which Lewis contributes the formation of the structures to "polarizing forces whose operation is co-extensive with the universe."

She developed more fully her idea that phyllotaxis could be used to chart the animal kingdom as well as the arrangement of leaves and flower petals. Again, the ideas to which Lewis was drawn were outmoded and criticized by the scientific community. A major hindrance to her research and studies was her lack of formal education. Not trained as other early naturalists were by mentors and by field observations of their subjects, Lewis missed out on the continued advances made by the scientific community to which she had no access. The physical limitations of encroaching age were also hindrances to her studies.

She continued doing the work she loved, however, and in 1875 she was asked to deliver a paper to the Third Congress of Women held in Syracuse, New York. Lewis spoke on "Science and Women." Her paper shows the influence of both the Quaker belief in the equality of the sexes and the increasing efforts of the suffragist movement. She begins by praising the scientific community for opening its doors, and minds, and accepting women's contributions to scientific knowledge. Although her work was never rewarded with a scientific appointment, she acknowledges the unstinting assistance and tutelage she received over the years from those established within the community. After bestowing accolades on various scientific institutions and affirming their continued importance, Lewis moves on to list the achievements of women in various scientific endeavors: Rachel L. Bodley in chemistry, Mary Treat in botany, and Annette Buckle in embryology.

The paper, although exhibiting her approval of the advances women have made in the scientific world, notes that there is much more to be done. Her own 1870 bid for membership in the Academy of Natural Sciences of Philadelphia was rebuffed; however, the

Academy later reversed its decision and allowed Lewis and two other women to become members. Lewis objected to her culture's low expectations for women's involvement in science and to the barriers women faced when attempting to gain a formal scientific education. In "Science and Women" she says, "If nothing else, we should ask for Women everywhere the highest scientific culture attainable, for the sake of the happiness it would afford her." Lewis continues her argument for equal scientific training by claiming that "The presence of Woman in Science is as needful as that of Man; the harmonious development of human thought depends on it." In a rejoinder to Edward Drinker Cope's assessment of woman's "infantile traits," she asserts that "the enjoyment of women should not be infantile; they should grow with her growth." She concludes her paper by countering the lingering popular arguments of Darwin (that women are evolutionarily inferior to men) and Edward Clarke (women are intellectually unsuited for serious study) by arguing that with the proper opportunities and support, women "will move forward in the ever ascending road of progress, fulfilling her womanly destiny; inseparable from the destiny of man—the destiny of the human race."

In 1909, at the age of 88, Lewis delivered the paper "Some Remarkable Fishes" to the Delaware County Institute of Science, later publishing it in that Institute's proceedings. Although never losing interest in her feathered friends, Lewis began a study of sea creatures, particularly sea algae and jellyfish. Her study of the lives and habits of jellyfish at the Longport beaches of New Jersey, "At Longport, New Jersey, in September," was published by the Delaware County Institute of Science in 1909. In the article, Lewis exhibited what Warner calls poetic tendencies. Warner quotes from a passage on ocean waves, foam "caught and woven into sheets of lace-like spray." Her later works do appear to be more aesthetic in nature, with increasing attention paid to enjoying the natural world and conveying the beauty of it, rather than to minutely described observations coupled with complex analyses of how the observed events fit her natural theories. What began as a study of birds more than 40 years earlier, extended to include the aquatic world, and the world of plant cultivation as well. Lewis was active for all of her 91 years.

In the early 1890s she was commissioned to draw a series of watercolor paintings of Pennsylvania trees and their leaves. She also created tree leaf charts for schools and supplied instructive pamphlets to accompany them. The more frequent publication of works about nature for the lay audience encouraged writers to produce books and articles promoting the appreciation and enjoyment of nature. Lewis responded to this trend by painting hundreds of pictures of flowers for mere pleasure, and her writings became more relaxed and contemplative. Two works, "Birds and Their Friends" (1896) and "Longport after the Season" (1909), were especially accessible.

Lewis did not appear to be involved in either the Audubon Association, which established bird-watching clubs on college campuses such as Vassar, or its organ, *Bird-Lore*, begun in 1899. That she upheld their causes is evident, though, in her comments on at least one occasion, on the "barbarism which would destroy these lovely creatures [pea-fowl and other birds sporting plumes or crests of feathers] for purposes of personal adornment" in "Birds and Their Friends." The article, published in the *Friends Intelligencer and Journal*, traces Lewis's development as a naturalist.

Lewis notes several times in the article that she did not have access to plates and specimens in her early years of ornithological study. The scientific tone of her other works is missing in "Birds and Their Friends." The article devotes itself to expounding upon the joys of bird watching. She recounts personal relationships that she has developed with certain birds and their families over the years, narrating the misadventures of robins falling from their nests and the banding together of catbird, robin, and sparrow to chase away invading cats. A particularly delightful account of a wood thrush entering the open door of her parlor in search of a nesting place shows Lewis at her most relaxed.

Instances supporting her belief that birds thrive in conditions where human kindness abounds punctuate the article. One gentleman waits to roof his house until a nest full of robins has fledged; a group of workers on her farm are careful not to disturb the nest of a robin on their work site. Lewis firmly espouses humankind's duty to all living creatures, and suggests that the pecuniary remuneration provided by one's devoted care to the bird life on his property is considerable. The sheer number of harmful insects kept in check by hungry birds, determines Lewis, should be enough to convert anyone to a love for and devotion to birds.

Lewis exhibits an understanding of the darker side of nature as well, however. She relates an incident wherein a nesting pair of robins was attacked by wrens who wanted the spot for their own nest, destroying the eggs and flying at the robins. Lewis does not wax poetic over the "tragedy," but coolly describes what she has observed and places the occasion in terms of naturally unfolding events in which she declines to interfere.

"Birds and Their Friends" concludes with a passage extolling the virtues of the microscope for truly appreciating the glories of birds' plumage. Lewis's own microscope was obtained in 1869 and became an indispensable tool for her in identifying species and drawing detailed illustrations for various projects over the succeeding decades.

In 1900 Lewis published a series of articles about Media, Pennsylvania, describing the natural history of the area: "Urbanista in Spring" was followed by an article on each season. The tone and purpose of the essay is very different from that of her detailed studies of the habits of birds. She takes the reader on a beautifully described journey of the area surrounding her home, her detailed descriptions of the trees and their inhabitants heavily laden with poetic imagery. That Lewis knows every plant and animal species in the environs of Media is clear—she names

dozens of trees, and she describes the songs of every bird.

Her poetic nature shines in such passages as this one: "The dark tree trunks lift their branches in Arabesque tracery against the brown hillside." This lyrical mode combines with her religious beliefs shining throughout the four essays as in this passage from "Urbanista in Spring":

> The sunset gilds the world to our mental vision as it transmutes the tree tops to gold, and the moon in her radiant pathway bears us upward to the Eternal Source of Light and Love and Being. The earth lies fresh and pure beneath our gaze and the "Morning and the evening are the first day."

Few passages from her later writings are free from the reverent tone that places her enjoyment of nature and its beauties squarely in the hands of her creator.

Many of the publications in Lewis's later years appeared in the *Friends' Intelligencer and Journal*, a Quaker organ. Along with her nature studies, she contributed reminiscences of friends and others active in the abolitionist cause or in the local scientific community. Her later years also saw Lewis doing work with the suffragist movement in Media, Pennsylvania. Although she made few inroads into the professional scientific community because of her status as a woman, her lack of formal education, and her belief that nature was the result of a divine hand, Graceanna Lewis left her mark on the scientific world as a highly respected amateur naturalist. Her delicately written contributions to the genre of the nature essay are imbued with the joyous faith of one who sees the hand of her creator in all that is around her.

PRIMARY BIBLIOGRAPHY

Books

Natural History of Birds: Lectures on Ornithology, in Ten Parts. Part I (Philadelphia: J. A. Bancroft & Co., 1868).

The Development of the Animal Kingdom: A Paper Read at the Fourth Meeting of the Association for the Advancement of Women (Nantucket: Hussey & Robinson, 1877).

Other

An Appeal to Those Members of the Society of Friends Who, Knowing the Principles of the Abolitionists, Stand Aloof from the Anti-Slavery Enterprise (N.p., n.d.).

Selected Periodical Publications— Uncollected

"The Lyre Bird," *The American Naturalist* 4.6 (August 1870): 321–31.

"Symmetrical Figures in Birds' Feathers," *The American Naturalist* 5.11 (November 1871): 675–78.

"Science for Women," *Papers Read at the Third Congress of Women, Syracuse, N. Y., October 13–15, 1875* (Chicago: Fergus Printing Company, 1875): 63–66.

"Miss Lewis' Chart of the Animal Kingdom," *The New Century for Women* (November 4, 1876): 197.

"Chester Springs Soldiers' Orphans' School," *The Woman's Journal* 8 (August 11, 1877): 252.

"On the Genus Hyliota," *Proceedings, Academy of Natural Sciences of Philadelphia* (1883): 128–30.

"The Late John M. Broomall," *Friends Intelligencer and Journal* 52 (1894): 724.

"Birds and Their Friends," *Friends' Intelligencer and Journal* 53 (1896): 762–63; 779–80.

"Anti-Slavery Reminiscences: The Mobbing of Frederick Douglass in 1843," *Friends' Intelligencer and Journal* 54 (1896): 398–400.

"Recollections of Anti-Slavery Times, Dr. Bartholomew Fussell," *Friends' Intelligencer and Journal* 54 (1896): 220–21, 235–36.

"Truth and the Teachers of Truth," *Friends' Intelligencer and Journal* 54 (1896): 282–84.

"Ada Fussell: A Noble Life," *Friends' Intelligencer and Journal* 57 (1900): 464–65.

"Urbanista in Spring Time," *Friends' Intelligencer and Journal* 57 (1900): 523–24.

"Urbanista in Summer," *Friends' Intelligencer and Journal* 57 (1900): 724–25, 741–42.

"Urbanista in Autumn," *Friends' Intelligencer and Journal* 57 (1900): 849–50.

"Urbanista in Winter," *Friends' Intelligencer and Journal* 58 (1901): 193–94, 210–11.

SECONDARY BIBLIOGRAPHY

Biography

Deborah Jean Warner, *Graceanna Lewis: Scientist and Humanitarian* (Washington, D.C.: Smithsonian Institution Press, 1979).

References

Marcia Myers Bonta, "Graceanna Lewis: Portrait of a Quaker Naturalist," *Quaker History* 74.1 (1985): 27–40.

Marcia Myers Bonta, *Women in the Field* (College Station, TX: Texas A&M University Press, 1991).

Deborah Strom Gibbons, "Modern Birdwatching Literature," in *American Nature Writers*, ed. John Elder, vol. 2 (New York: Charles Scribner's Sons, 1996), 1079–1098.

"Graceanna Lewis: Naturalist, Philanthropist, Reformer," *Woman's Progress in Literature, Science, Art, Education & Politics* 3 (1894): 6.

Robert J. O'Hara, "Representations of the Natural System in the Nineteenth Century," *Biology and Philosophy* 6.2 (1991): 255–74.

Papers

The Fussell-Lewis Family Papers are held at Swarthmore College, Friends Historical Museum. The Spencer Baird Correspondence is held by the Smithsonian Institution Archives.

Meriwether Lewis
(August 18, 1774–October 11, 1809)

Peter T. Koper

The Lewis and Clark Expedition was the first party of Americans to cross the continent and return to report on the interior geography of the West. Thomas Jefferson planned the expedition even before the Louisiana Purchase in 1803 because accurate information was essential to his desire for national expansion. The Corps of Northwestern Discovery was a military expedition authorized by Congress at Jefferson's request with scientific, economic, and political purposes. The expedition described and mapped the route, described new species of plants and animals, inventoried some resources on the route, and described the indigenous people of the upper Missouri and Columbia regions. It discovered that the Rockies were far larger and their terrain more difficult to pass through than expected, laying to rest for good the centuries-old hope for an easy water route across the continent. Even so, the expedition drew Americans to the Louisiana Purchase and the Columbia River, thus furthering the migrations that outweighed the colonial ambitions of France, Spain, and Britain and made the United States a continental nation.

One major program of the expedition was literary, and Donald Jackson has called Lewis and Clark "the writingest explorers." Meriwether Lewis announced a three-volume account of the expedition immediately after

they returned, began the work, delayed for various reasons, and died prematurely. Clark then contracted with Nicholas Biddle, who completed a narrative of the expedition, which combined and rephrased entries by both Lewis and Clark, in 1814. Biddle omitted most of the scientific and technical material in the journals, which was thus not generally available until Elliott Coues published it in 1894. The edition of the journals by Reuben Gold Thwaites in 1904–1905 presented the explorers' separate entries in eight volumes. Thus the full range of Meriwether Lewis's writing was not available to the public for a century after he wrote it. Continued recoveries and publication of material written during the expedition, all of it recently brought together in Gary Moulton's *The Definitive Journals of Lewis and Clark*, have meant that it and its authors are a larger part of the American imagination now than they were in most of the nineteenth century. Although Meriwether Lewis wrote a major portion of the approximately one and a half million words in the surviving journals, he himself never published a book. His reputation as a writer rests on the later editors who have made him part of the American mainstream.

Meriwether Lewis was born on August 18, 1774, in Albemarle County, Virginia, at Locust Hill, the family holding seven miles west of Charlottesville and within sight of Thomas Jefferson's home at Monticello. His father, William Lewis, and his mother, Lucy Meriwether Lewis, were cousins, both from prominent families of the slave-holding gentry of the area. His father's death and the remarriage of his mother in 1780 took Lewis to Georgia, whose remote frontier made woodcraft natural to him. As the oldest son, Lewis returned to Virginia in his early teens to supervise the family property while studying with a series of tutors. In 1790, when his mother was widowed for a second time, Lewis brought the entire family back to Locust Hill, and his schooling was cut short by his duties as a planter.

In 1795, after militia service against the Whiskey Rebellion, he accepted a commission in the regular army, serving for six months at one point under William Clark. Lewis was hardworking, honest, and good at logistics. Duties as a paymaster sent him throughout the old Northwest. He gained experience with Native American tribes and achieved the rank of captain in 1800.

When Jefferson became president of the United States on February 23, 1801, he offered his young neighbor a position as private secretary, telling him that "your knoledge of the Western country, of the army and all it's interests & relations has rendered it desirable for public as well as private purposes that you should be engaged in that office." Scholars disagree about whether the president had already decided that the young captain should lead an expedition to the Pacific. Three times in the previous decades Jefferson had promoted such expeditions. In 1792, after Robert Gray found the mouth of the Columbia River, Jefferson had raised a subscription in the American Philosophical Society to send a solo traveler across to the Columbia. Lewis had asked Jefferson to let him make the trip, even though he was then only 18 years old. Jefferson refused, but it is possible that Lewis's request was still on the president's mind when he appointed him secretary in 1801. In any case, Lewis eagerly accepted the appointment, and his chance to go west was not long in coming.

In the spring of 1801, Louisiana was ceded to France by Spain. In the same year, Alexander Mackenzie published his account of his crossing of the continent, and hence of Britain's claim on the Pacific Northwest. The book was in Jefferson's hands in 1802 and spurred him to counter British claims by organizing an exploration of the Missouri, nominally French, and a crossing of the mountains to the Pacific, via the territory now nominally British. Sometime in 1802, he asked Lewis to lead such an expedition, and on January 18, 1803, Jefferson sent his plan to Congress in a "confidential" message. Jefferson suggested that "an intelligent officer with ten or twelve chosen men, fit for the enterprize and willing to undertake it... might explore the whole line," establish relations with the Native tribes on the route, and open up trade. Commerce—what some recent scholars have called imperialism, others nationalism—and curiosity were Jefferson's motives. These coincided with Lewis's abilities and his desire for adventure.

With Congressional approval on the record, although still private, Jefferson wrote the physician Benjamin Rush on February 28, 1803, to recommend his commander:

> Capt. Lewis is brave, prudent, habituated to the woods, & familiar with Indian manners & character. He is not regularly educated, but he possesses a great mass of accurate observation on all the subjects of nature which present themselves here, & will therefore readily select those only in his new route which shall be new.

Lewis's intense preparations involved both the logistics of the expedition and also tutorials with some of the best-educated men in the country. Traveling between Monticello, Washington, Harpers Ferry, Lancaster, and Philadelphia, Lewis worked on cartography with Albert Gallatin, celestial observations with the astronomer Andrew Ellicott, medical matters with Rush, and botany with Benjamin Smith Barton, who taught Lewis how to describe, label, and preserve specimens. Lewis was busy, and he exhibited one of his most important qualities, the remarkable liveliness of mind that was to make him a great naturalist.

Final arrangements in mid-June 1803 included a letter of credit to cover additional expenses, authorization from the war department to requisition army personnel for the crew, and a decision that a reliable second in command was necessary. His old comrade William Clark accepted Lewis's offer to be co-commander of the expedition. The final draft of Jefferson's instructions to Lewis, dated June 20, 1803, gave him a broad mandate to look for a water route to the Pacific, establish relations with and study the native tribes, and undertake a program of scientific study. Jefferson was careful to advise that several copies of all notes should be made "& put into the care of the most trust-worthy of your attendants, to guard, by multiplying them, against the accidental losses to which they will be exposed." He also asks that Lewis send back "a copy of your journal, notes, & observations, of every kind" as opportunity presented itself. The records of what they saw would make the work of the expedition science instead of folklore.

Lewis left Washington for Pittsburgh on July 5, 1803; news of the Louisiana Purchase had changed the expedition into exploration of new American territory. At Pittsburgh, he collected supplies forwarded from Philadelphia and Harpers Ferry as well as recruits and headed downstream. He picked up Clark at Clarkesville in Indiana Territory and recruited additional men as they moved. They reached the Mississippi River on November 14, already too late to start upstream on the Missouri River that fall, and made a winter camp, Fort Dubois, on the east side of the Mississippi a few miles upstream from St. Louis.

Lewis began his journal when he left Pittsburgh; visible immediately is one feature of his writing. No entries between September 19 and November 11, 1803, survive. Similar gaps in his records appear later. Relatively little material survives from May 14, 1804, when he left St. Louis on his journey up the Missouri until he left the Mandan villages

on April 7, 1805, when daily entries resume. Another gap appears in August 1805 after the party crossed the Lemhi Pass and lasts until January 1, 1806, when he resumed entries while wintering at Fort Clatsop. The last hiatus can be explained with some certainty. On August 11, 1806, he was wounded in a hunting accident and ceased writing.

The other gaps are harder to explain and have been discussed at length by Thwaites (1.xxiv–lx), Paul Russell Cutright (1976), Donald Jackson (1987.55–75), and Moulton (2.1–48), among others. Moulton notes that Lewis left 39 pages in the Ohio River journal blank, suggesting that he saved space for writing he intended to do later. That Lewis was simply "lax" in his writing is thus one possibility. Donald Jackson cites the account on May 14, 1805, of the swamping of the white pirogue—"the articles which floated out was *nearly all* caught by the Squar" [emphasis added]—as evidence that some of the papers were surely lost on the expedition.

The captains seemed to have worked on a daily basis, making rough notes that were later transcribed into longer documents, whether red leather journals or the reports composed in the comparative leisure of Fort Mandan and Fort Clatsop. Lewis's report to Jefferson from Fort Mandan, April 7, 1805, says that he has shipped "a part of Capt. Clark's private journal, the other part you will find inclosed in a separate tin box." This suggests that the extensive journal entries by Clark for the upstream voyage are copies done underway or at Fort Mandan. The journal's final entry, made in St. Louis on September 26, 1806, reports "a fine morning we commenced wrighting &c." But Cutright is certain that this entry could not refer to the recopying of the journals from rough notes. They were not in St. Louis long enough to do that.

So much other material by Lewis survives from the period when they were en route from St. Charles to Fort Mandan that Moulton believes Lewis was probably not keeping a daily journal. On July 14, 1804, after a sudden squall scattered his papers, Clark had to consult with the sergeants and think a bit to reconstruct the events of the preceding day. He did not, apparently, have an entry by Lewis that he could consult. What Moulton suggests, in effect, is that they had divided the labor of writing, with Clark doing the daily record. That Lewis was writing during this period is clear from the orders that he drew up and from the detailed geographical, botanical, and mineralogical reports that he sent back to Jefferson in the spring of 1805.

Depression is a topic important in recent biographical studies of Lewis, and some scholars think it affected the journals. The shorter length of entries made on the return trip might reflect their passage over country already described rather than depression at not having found a water route to the Pacific. The hiatus that most nearly fits a psychological explanation is the sudden cessation of entries when Lewis crossed the Lemhi Pass in August 1805, possibly because of a complex of intense emotion based on the challenge ahead in the Bitterroots.

The journals of Lewis and Clark have grown in importance as new editions and studies make the story available to larger audiences. They provide an adventure tale with similarities to epic, heroes doing great deeds in a setting of national importance, but they are not epic. They seize the imagination because, in Patricia Waters's words, they are a "pragmatic, functional, empirical account of an adventure that can only have happened once." Only one expedition can be the first American expedition to cross the continent. The journals encompass the full range of Jefferson's Enlightenment mind, as absorbed and mirrored by the minds of his captains. Upstream from St. Louis much was new; after the Mandan villages, everything was new. Leaving these native villages on April 7, 1808, Lewis invoked Columbus and Cook as they entered country "on which the foot of civilized man had never trodden...." The Native tribes whose deserted villages he noted along the river, already decimated by disease, were in Lewis's vision a part of nature that he had come to civilize. The landscape of the great plains, seen for the first time

and before white settlement had made it an agricultural ecology, evoked the language of Edenic plenty. On May 7, 1805, their route passes, as it does repeatedly, "one of the most beautifull plains we have yet seen." Huge herds of buffalo, elk, and antelope made hunting easy. Fish, birds, plants, rivers and creeks, and landmarks of various kinds were new. Lewis and Clark responded to dangers, conflicts, the cultures and rituals of Native tribes, diplomacy, trade, and sexual encounters, mixing gripping personal narrative with such scientific data as weather records, biological descriptions, and notes from celestial observations. The mix of data about the land and records of personal encounters with wilderness places the journals at the threshold of a new genre.

Clark's prose is interesting in its own right, his flexible spelling being only a detail, soon a charming one, of a prose style that is laconic, precise, and informative. Lewis had much more formal education than Clark and his writing shows it. He is always more fluent and, with regard to spelling and grammar, more correct. He shows the range of purposes in the expedition in the range of topics he discusses: trade, diplomacy, geography, defense, ethnography, and natural history. Cutright notes that the amount of technical information in Lewis's work exceeds that "found in all of the other journals combined." One demand on their writing was shared by both captains. Few have had to name as many new things as they did. Lewis and Clark encountered, according to Cutright, 178 plants and 122 animals that were new to science. Many of their names for plants, animals, rivers, and other features have remained in use.

Lewis's failure to publish limited the impact of their scientific work because Biddle omitted most of it and deprived the expedition of credit for many of its scientific discoveries. Biddle's elisions had another effect as well. Gunther Barth comments that Biddle stripped Lewis "of his mercurial temper, his despair as well as his emphasis, and excised most of the words Lewis used to express his sense of mission." One feature of Lewis's style that differentiates him from Clark and that Biddle obscures is his infrequent but interesting efforts to be literary.

These passages—the most discussed of which are his description of the White Cliffs along the Missouri, his responses to the Great Falls, and his birthday soliloquy on August 18, 1805—show Lewis's exposure, in ways that cannot be fully recovered but that certainly include his experience in Jefferson's household, to tropes of romantic sensibility. The shift in sentiment about landscape that is part of American Romanticism, and Lewis's participation in it, has been traced by Albert Furtwangler. Lewis's descriptions of the White Cliffs, May 31, 1805, are stylized gothic, but Lewis's self-consciously literary mode is most in evidence at the Great Falls, June 14 and 15, 1805, where he uses language whose origin is in European aesthetics. The Falls, he says, are the "grandest sight I ever beheld." He wrote a description but "was so much disgusted with the imperfect idea which it conveyed of the scene" that he "wished for the pencil of Salvator Rosa or the pen of Thompson" so he could do justice to this "sublimely grand object." The next day, when he describes one of the cataracts as "pleasingly beautiful" while another is "sublimely grand," he echoes the distinction from Burke's aesthetics that had by then become a commonplace of the romantic response to landscapes. Patricia Waters, among others, notes that these are the least typical passages in the journals. At the Great Falls, he is looking at a great natural spectacle far more impressive than the scenes in Virginia that had moved Jefferson to romantic rhapsody. His effort to rise to the occasion stylistically seems to Waters "as much an external requirement—this is the way one ought to feel—as it is a genuinely evoked expression of one's relation to natural phenomena, to what is incommensurate with the self."

The typical Lewis was on a scientific expedition whose goal was factual information. Then the core of his prose style is Baconian; he is transmitting data. One of the most

intense impulses of the British Enlightenment was Bacon's empiricism, which was linguistic as well as experimental and inductive. When the Royal Society was founded in 1662, Thomas Sprat reported its resolve "to reject all the amplifications, digressions, and swellings of style: to return back to the primitive purity, and shortness, when men deliver'd so many *things*, almost in an equal number of *words*" [emphasis his]. This passage, directly descended from Bacon's attack on rhetoric, and the attitude toward language it represents are the ancestors of Lewis's typical writing.

He was on an incredible adventure, and the quintessentially American one; his language did not have to make the land magnificent. The land was already magnificent; all he had to do was describe it in clear and direct language. Most of the time, he thought of himself as a scientist recording for Jefferson and the American Philosophical Society. This, and perhaps the sheer pressure of time while on the trail, meant that most of his descriptions do not take the time to develop the schemes and tropes of sentimentality. Lewis offers dozens of passages where his scene setting, arising from a style called for two centuries before him, reads as if it were written two centuries after him.

On May 26, 1805, coming out of the Missouri Breaks, he climbed the hills at the edge of the river, "beheld the rocky Mountains for the first time," took compass bearings, and then observes

...these points of the Rocky Mountains were covered with snow and the sun shone on it in such manner as to give me the most plain and satisfactory view. while I viewed these mountains I felt a secret pleasure in finding myself so near the head of the heretofore conceived boundless Missouri; but when I reflected on the difficulties which this snowey barrier would most probably throw in my way to the Pacific, and the sufferings and hardships of myself and party in them, it in some measure counterballanced the joy I had felt in the first moments in which I gazed on them; but as I have always held it a crime to anticipate evils I will believe it a good comfortable road until I am compelled to believe differently.

There is both beauty and danger in this scene but no talk of the beautiful or the sublime. Lewis's voice here is that of an American encountering the land, in his case in literally unique circumstances, but in ways that are paradigmatic of the American experience. He describes it and what it means for him, within a narrow and highly personal framework that, because he is the leading edge of American expansion, also has enormous implications for modern history and especially the modern history of the Native American tribes.

This simple and honest passage—the mountains are beautiful, or Lewis is proud, a little scared, but catches himself and returns to resolution—or the dozens of equally interesting ones, long and short, illustrate the qualities that must have made Jefferson call on him in the first place. Lewis's bear stories are not tall tales but understated accounts of how many balls were fired and what the bear did and what the men did. His best sentences are laconic, as on May 11, 1805: "these bear being so hard to die reather intimedates us all." He makes the work, the danger, the delight, the anger, and the novelty real by means of a prose style that is immanently referential. Virtually every scholar agrees that Lewis was a good writer, though comparatively few work directly with his prose style.

The last years of Lewis's life contrast sharply with the heroic success of the expedition. On his return, he was a celebrity in St. Louis, Washington, and Philadelphia, but Jefferson, whose selection of Lewis as captain had been a stroke of genius, in what most scholars agree was a mistake, made him Governor of Louisiana Territory on March 3, 1807. Readers were eager for his journals, and Lewis was eager for the money he would make by publishing them, but he embroiled himself in conflict over the rights to publish, first with a private named Frazier, and then with Patrick Gass, who went ahead with

the publication of his own journal in 1807. Lewis contracted with John Conrad of Philadelphia, who issued a prospectus promising the first volume in 1808. Lewis was deflected from his editorial work by his political obligations in St. Louis and by the social scene in the East. At the same time, problems were developing in St. Louis because of his effort to administer Louisiana by mail, while remaining in the East to attend to the journals.

Lewis apparently dithered. He had given no copy to Conrad when he finally left for St. Louis, arriving there on March 8, 1808. The year's delay had given the Territorial Secretary in St. Louis, Frederick Bates, time to become, by various accounts, either a duplicitous enemy or bureaucratic problem whose superior had been out of town. Once in St. Louis, Lewis was busy negotiating with the tribes and traders of Louisiana, with some success. But in the summer of 1809, the Secretary of War, William Eustis, refused to honor a $500.00 bill submitted by Lewis. Stung and endangered financially, Lewis set out for Washington in September, intending to settle the matter. He died en route at Grinder's Stand, a cabin 72 miles from Nashville on the Natchez Trace. James Neelly, an Indian agent from Fort Pickering who was accompanying Lewis, relayed the report that Lewis had committed suicide.

Biographers divide on the question, some arguing that murder and robbery are more likely explanations. A number of witnesses report that Lewis was drinking heavily. Jefferson, who had written Lewis on August 16, 1809, to wonder "when your work will begin to appear," believed that his friend had committed suicide and, in the short biography written to accompany the Biddle edition of 1814, commented that "Governor Lewis had from early in life been subject to hypocondriac affections," depression seeming to run in the family. Most recent opinion accepts Jefferson's judgment, whose implication is that, once Lewis was finished with the great enterprise that had summoned his powers, he was unable to withstand the humiliations of his weaknesses, including his failure to edit the journals that exhibit so clearly his genius as a writer.

PRIMARY BIBLIOGRAPHY

Editions

History of the Expedition Under the Command of Captains Lewis and Clark, to the Sources of the Missouri: Thence Across the Rocky Mountains and Down the River Columbia to the Pacific Ocean: Performed during the Years 1804-5-6, by Order of the Government of the United States, 2 vols., edited by Nicholas Biddle with revisions by Paul Allen (Philadelphia: Bradford and Innskeep, 1814).

Travels to the Source of the Missouri River and Across the American Continent to the Pacific Ocean Performed by Order of the Government of the United states, in the Years 1804, 1805, and 1806. By Captains Lewis and Clarke. Published from the Official Report, and Illustrated by a Map of the Route, and Other Maps, edited by Nicholas Biddle with revisions by Paul Allen (London: Longman, Hurst, Rees, Orme, and Brown, 1814).

History of the Expedition Under the Command of Lewis and Clark to the Sources of the Missouri River, Thence Across the Rocky Mountains and Down the Columbia River to the Pacific Ocean, Performed During the Years 1804-5-6, by Order of the Government of the United States. A New Edition Faithfully Reprinted from the Only Authorized Edition of 1814, With Copious Critical Commentary, Prepared Upon Examination of Unpublished Official Archives and Many Other Sources of Information, Including a Diligent Study of the Original Manuscript Journals and Field Notebooks of the Explorers Together With a New Biographical and Bibliographical Introduction, New Maps and Other Illustrations, and a Complete Index, 4 vols., edited by Elliot Coues (New York: Francis Harper, 1893–1894).

Original Journals of the Lewis and Clark Expedition 1804–1806 Printed from the Original Manuscripts in the Library of the American Philosophical Society and by Direction of Its committee on Historical Documents Together With Manuscript Material of Lewis and Clark from Other Sources, Including Note-Books, Letters, Maps, Etc., and the Journals of Charles Floyd and Joseph Whitehorse Now for the First Time Published in Full and Exactly as Written, 8 vols., edited with an introduction, notes, and index by Reuben Gold Thwaites (New York: Dodd, Mead & Co., 1904–1905).

The Journals of Captain Meriwether Lewis and Sergeant John Ordway Kept on the Expedition of Western Exploration, 1903–1806, edited with an introduction and notes by Milo M. Quaife (Madison: Publications of the State Historical Society of Wisconsin Collections, 1916).

The Journals of Lewis and Clark, edited by Bernard DeVoto (Boston: Houghton Mifflin, 1953).

The Lewis and Clark Expedition, edited with an introduction by Archibald Hanna (Philadelphia and New York: J.B. Lipincott, 1961), reprint of the 1814 Biddle-Allen edition.

The Journals of the Lewis and Clark Expedition, 13 vols., edited by Gary E. Moulton (Lincoln: University of Nebraska Press, 1983–2001); vols. 2–13 reprinted in paper 2002.

The Lewis and Clark Journals: An American Epic of Discovery: The Abridgement of the Definitive Nebraska Edition; Meriwether Lewis, William Clark, and Members of the Corps of Discovery, edited with an introduction by Gary E. Moulton (Lincoln and London: University of Nebraska Press, 2003).

Letters

Donald Jackson, ed., *Letters of the Lewis and Clark Expedition, with Related Documents: 1783–1854*, 2nd ed., 3 vols. (Urbana: University of Illinois Press, 1978).

SECONDARY BIBLIOGRAPHY

Bibliography

Stephan Dow Beckham, Doug Erickson, Jeremy Skinner, and Paul Merchant, *The Literature of the Lewis and Clark Expedition: A Bibliography and Essays* (Portland: Lewis and Clark College, 2003).

Biographies

Stephen E. Ambrose, *Undaunted Courage: Meriwether Lewis, Thomas Jefferson, and the Opening of the American West* (New York: Touchstone, 1996).

John Bakeless, *Lewis and Clark: Partners in Discovery* (New York: William Morrow, 1947).

Richard Dillon, *Meriwether Lewis: A Biography* (New York: Coward McCann, 1965).

David Lavender, *The Way to the Western Sea: Lewis and Clark Across the Continent* (New York: Harper & Row, 1988).

References

Gunther Barth, "Timeless Journals: Reading Lewis and Clark with Nicholas Biddle's Help,"

Pacific Historical Review 53.4 (November 1994): 499–514.

Paul Russell Cutright, *A History of the Lewis and Clark Journals* (Norman: University of Oklahoma Press, 1976).

Paul Russell Cutright, *Lewis and Clark: Pioneering Naturalists* (Urbana: University of Illinois Press, 1986).

Albert Furtwangler, *Acts of Discovery: Visions of America in the Lewis and Clark Journals* (Urbana and Chicago: University of Illinois Press, 1993).

Donald Jackson, *Among the Sleeping Giants* (Urbana and Chicago: University of Illinois Press, 1987).

Thomas Sprat, *History of the Royal Society*, edited with a critical apparatus by Jackson I.. Cope and Harold Whitmore Jones (St. Louis and London: Washington University Press and Routledge & Kegan Paul, 1958).

Patricia Waters, Mr. *Jefferson's Literary Pursuit of the West* (PhD dissertation, University of Tennessee, 1998).

Papers

The papers of the Lewis and Clark Expedition are scattered among the following: American Philosophical Society, Philadelphia; Eleanor Glasgow Voorhis Memorial Collection, Missouri Historical Society; Meriwether Lewis Anderson Papers, Missouri State Historical Society; William Clark Papers, Missouri State Historical Society; Meriwether Lewis Papers, Missouri State Historical Society; Grace Lewis Miller Papers, National Park Service, Jefferson National Expansion Memorial Archives, St. Louis.

Olive Thorne Miller
(June 25, 1834–December 26, 1918)

Linda Elizabeth Peterson

Olive Thorne Miller discovered birds and her passion for them in 1880 when she was nearly 50 years of age. Despite coming to ornithology this late in life, she combined intense observation with considerable expressive skill to emerge—in the company of Mabel Osgood Wright, Neltje Blanchan, and Florence Merriam Bailey, all her junior by a generation—as one of the most highly regarded popular bird writers in the last years of the nineteenth century. Miller's career as a nature writer—and as an activist, lecturer, and educator—dominated her life for the 30 years prior to her death in 1918; this prolific period yielded hundreds of articles, most of which were collected into her 19 books, 11 of them about birds. An early biographer in *A Woman of the Century* notes that when Miller turned to writing about birds for children, "her field was practically unoccupied." Today, as Paul Brooks suggests, she stands as "a pioneer in a field that she made her own: the fine art of fostering a love of nature in the young." Miller was already a productive if unremarkable children's writer when she began to focus on nature; putting all of her experience to work in the service of her new love of birds was a relatively simple matter. This natural shift unveiled a readership hungry for accessible, literary material about birds, a readership that soon came to include adults. Eschewing

scientific discourse and thus ornithology journals, Miller published articles regularly in children's magazines, namely *Youth's Companion* and *St. Nicholas,* and in those for adults, most especially *The Atlantic Monthly, Scribner's Monthly, Harper's Bazaar,* and *Harper's Magazine.* Brooks's assessment of her career is therefore too limited: while she may have begun her nature writing career with pieces for children, by the end of that highly successful career she had also written a great deal for adults.

Tied to the domestic expectations of her age and having little direct relationship to academe and formal research, Miller was repulsed by the killing of birds, especially songbirds, for study (as she was also by the wholesale slaughter for women's hats and by male hunting customs). She took those in her field to task first and forcefully separated herself from the standard ornithological practice of the era. She is especially eloquent in *In Nesting Time* about what she rejected: "Our predecessors," she insists, "have dissected and weighed and measured every little part of their bodies;...they have pulled to pieces the nests...and mounted and labeled and set up in cases the whole external of the little creatures. All that can be learned by violence, all the characteristics evolved by fear and distress are duly set down in books." Quick to say in the same passage that such work was initially necessary, she asserts her hope that it is finished. Instead, "what is needed," she writes in the preface to *The First Book of Birds*, "is not the science of ornithology—however diluted—but some account of the life and habits, to arouse sympathy and interest in the living bird." Her dedication to the "living bird" never wavered. From her first essay on birds to her final book, Miller used conventional language to charm and inform her readers with bird behavior and what she imagined to be the birds' motivations and emotions. Nor did Miller's concern for her readers waver. In "The Study of Birds —Another Way," she writes, "I regard it as one of the most important uses of the study to lead the student to Nature herself;...to acquaint him with...the benefit to mind and heart, as well as to body, of close friendship with the Great Mother." Her central commitment, then, was twofold: to render living birds so sympathetically that readers would, first, identify with them and thereby protect them and, second, follow them into nature's curative sanctuary.

Olive Thorne Miller, christened Harriet Mann, was born to Mary Holbrook and Seth Hunt Mann on June 25, 1831, in Auburn, New York. Since her father was a banker unable to settle in one position, her childhood was spent "all along the road," as she later put it to Laura Holloway. Her first move with her family came when she was 11 years old. During their five-year stay in a small college town in Ohio, Miller began her education in a private school (a practice that her parents would continue for the whole of her somewhat erratic schooling). Before she finally settled in Chicago for 20 years following her marriage to Watts Todd Miller in 1854, she also lived in Wisconsin, Illinois, and Missouri. The eldest of four and the only girl, she was lost in a family that did not share her zeal for books and writing. It is likely that the frequent uprooting also exacerbated her struggles with shyness and self-consciousness about her appearance, evident even in early childhood. As her close friend Florence Merriam Bailey notes in a memorial, Miller's

insecurities became so painful as she grew into adulthood that people were a "terror" to her. Miller turned to books and writing: "To shut myself up where no one could see me, and speak with my pen, was my greatest happiness."

Miller's years in Chicago were conventional. She bore four children (between 1856 and 1868) and, putting aside her writing, fulfilled the role of conscientious wife and mother, later noting sardonically to her biographer in *A Woman of the Century* that in her husband's prosperous family "the dish-cloth was mightier than the pen." In a more reflective moment with her friend Bailey, she later acknowledged, "I denied myself the joy of my life—the use of my pen...and it was not until my children were well out of the nursery that I grew wise enough to return to it."

Her return to the pen at first yielded opinion pieces that were routinely rejected; finally, at the suggestion of a friend, she turned to facts and produced what she called "sugar-coated pills of knowledge" for young readers. In 1870 a religious weekly with a children's column accepted her first piece. Some 375 articles and stories and five books followed in the next 12 years, most of them for children and published under the pseudonym Olive Thorne. Among these largely forgettable pieces, however, were a number of engaging nature sketches, which appeared under the name Harriet M. Miller. By 1879 she had blended these names and adopted Olive Thorne Miller, the pseudonym she used for the rest of her career.

A five-year span beginning around 1875 brought significant personal and professional change. Early in this period, Miller moved to Brooklyn, New York, and brought out her first book of children's nature writing, *Little Folks in Feathers and Fur and Others in Neither* (1875). Relying heavily on previous nature pieces, she compiled a collection of 89 brief sketches of an astonishing range of creatures from the common mouse to squirrels in Sumatra. Since the book depends on secondary research rather than direct observation, the meticulously detailed narratives of animal behavior that were to become her hallmark are not evident. What is noteworthy in this first full-length work, however, is the position she takes in relation both to formal science and to her readership. "This book makes no pretensions to be a scientific work. Indeed, it is scrupulously otherwise," she declares in the preface. In order to engage and educate "little people," her goal, she continues, is not to "intrude upon the field of the scientific naturalist," but rather to "take his discoveries, and translate them into the vulgar tongue that every-one may enjoy the delightful results of his work." As she spells out her purpose for this book, she gives notice of what is to come in all of her subsequent writing about birds: an informal, lively style that seeks to engage and move a broad, general audience.

Near the end of this transitional period, Miller was ushered into the world of birds. In 1880 Miller's friend Sara A. Hubbard visited, and Miller took her to observe the birds in Brooklyn's Prospect Park. In so doing, Miller accidentally transformed her work and her life. Hubbard's enthusiasm being "contagious," Miller continued to observe; two years later the *Atlantic Monthly* accepted her first article on birds. Now fully captivated, she "cared for no other study," she told Bailey. Seeking a fuller connection to her subjects, Miller transformed the library of her home in Brooklyn into an aviary so that she could observe captive birds in the winter. In the summer she sought out their natural haunts, traveling increasingly longer distances until by the end of her fieldwork around the age of 71, she had visited and written about New York's countryside, Maine, Massachusetts, Vermont, New Hampshire, Ohio, North Carolina, Michigan, Colorado, Utah, and California.

Most commentators consider *A Bird-Watcher in the West* (1894) to be Miller's finest book. More reflective and personal than her usual work, it is also more thematically unified and stylistically mature than her first three bird books, *Bird-Ways* (1885), *In Nesting Time* (1888), and *Little Brothers of the Air*

(1892). These three books reveal a parallel evolution in the quality of her fieldwork and the complexity of her composition: as her field range widened and her observational methods improved, so too did her grasp of her authorial purpose and her sense of essayistic forms.

Bird-Ways emerged primarily out of her early observations in her aviary and around her home. Miller entitled the last essay of the book "These Are Your Brothers," a phrase she borrowed from Jules Michelet's *The Bird* (1895) and used frequently throughout her writing and teaching, eventually highlighting its significance with two book titles, *Little Brothers of the Air* and *The Bird Our Brother* (1908), her last original work. While this concept of a human fraternity with the wild, this figuring of birds as persons, today sounds overly romantic and perhaps patronizing, it was a common locution of the day and one that harkened back to Alexander Wilson, America's first ornithologist, and his *American Ornithology* (9 vols.; 1808–1814), in which he espoused the view that birds have habits and feelings similar to humans. Indeed, Miller's language is anthropomorphic—bird pairs are spouses who tend solicitously to each other's needs, and captive birds yearn for freedom's happiness. So carefully rendered, however, are the details of bird activity and the notes of songs that the essays are never overburdened with sentimentality. In fact, an anonymous contemporary reviewer in the *Overland Monthly* (February 1886) links Miller's book to work by John Burroughs and Bradford Torrey, applauds the "delicate recognition of the kinship between the bird and humanity," and recommends the book to "every lover of warm thinking in good English."

Miller's next book, *In Nesting Time*, is an uneven collection. Like its predecessor *Bird-Ways*, it lacks coherence because the essays generally stand as separate pieces. This problem is highlighted in the book's final essay, a piece on the exotic birds of paradise after 14 essays devoted to common American birds, birds that Miller knew intimately from experience. Furthermore, her trips to North

Carolina brought her into contact with "the negro" and now leave current readers with an acrid taste of the racism of the day. The unfortunate remarks about idleness and stealth are, however, at least brief and appear largely in only one essay. Setting them aside and focusing on individual essays reveal the book's strengths, most of which can probably be attributed to her venturing into the countryside for many of them. In so doing, she forced herself to narrate her own activity, describe the birds' native environments, and reflect on how humans treated them. The sequence of essays that captures her search for the mockingbird in North Carolina is especially rich; part travel narrative and part quest, they resonate with the excitement of discovery and the frustration of seeing mockingbirds' nests destroyed and the birds killed or caged. This wider engagement with the wild also mutes some of the anthropomorphic flights of *Bird-Ways*.

The third book of this early period, *Little Brothers of the Air*, is a fitting prelude to *A Bird-Watcher in the West*. First, gone is the aviary. In turning exclusively to outdoor settings, Miller finds a simple but effective organizational strategy for her book: one section of essays describes her findings on the shore of the Great South Bay of Long Island while the second set covers her work in the Black River Country of northern New York. Second, in situating all of her essays in the natural world, she also fastens upon the aspect of bird behavior that she found most important to her work—nesting birds with their emerging young. In the opening paragraph of the first essay, she asserts that a student unfamiliar with nesting time "has almost everything to learn, for into those few weeks is crowded a whole lifetime of emotions and experiences which fully bring out the individuality of the bird." Her language, of course, retains some of the sentimentality of her earlier books, but the long hours of observation under the duress of a hot sun and humming mosquitoes can only engage and inspire readers of any era. An *Overland Monthly* (October 1888) reviewer

finds readers to be "blessed" by "so tireless a student" and declares Miller to be "one of the best writers for the non-scientific public on bird life."

In the early spring of 1891, Miller set out for the West, specifically Camp Harding, a tourist camp at the base of the Cheyenne Mountains outside Colorado Springs where she would live for a couple of months and observe the birds of the Front Range. In the spring of 1893, she returned to the West, this time to Utah. Living in the only boarding house in the "village" of Salt Lake City, she spent the spring and summer tramping the shores of the Great Salt Lake and the foothills of the Wasatch Range with Florence Merriam Bailey. The groups of essays that grew out of these Western excursions begin and end *A Bird-Lover in the West*. The middle section, entitled "The Middle Country," is devoted to the birds of southern Ohio. Since this book is explicitly for readers from the East Coast, she simply asserts in the preface that even Ohio is west for them and therefore appropriate to her title. This coordinating of structure and location, a strategy she devised for *Little Brothers*, and the clearly defined audience presage the command she holds over her material. She now balances her narratives of travel and discovery with fully sustained ruminations on the necessity of "a really re-creative recreation" in nature, the spiritual vacuity of the typical tourist, and the degradation of landscape that she finds all too frequently. There is, too, a fresh ebullience in her descriptions of birds and the stunning places in which she finds them. *A Bird-Lover in the West*, then, is the culmination of her development as an artist; the mountains especially called for her finest work, and she had cultivated the capacities to answer.

After *Four-Handed Folk* (1896), a children's book about animals, Miller returned to birds with *Upon the Tree-Tops* in 1897. While a few individual essays retain the vitality and specificity of *A Bird-Lover in the West*, this volume as a whole gives the impression of a collection of leftovers rushed into print.

She returns to material from the aviary for the last section and to Colorado in a single essay in the book's main section. Most disconcerting are the failures to specify the location for many of the essays and to relate the essays to one another. More than once the reader is left wondering whether Miller herself had read her finished project, so disjointed is the organization.

After this creative lull, Miller crossed into the new century with a renewed sense of commitment. Since "The Study of Birds—Another Way," published in *Bird-Lore* (1900), presents a carefully considered curriculum, it is clear that Miller had vanquished the painful shyness of her youth and had for some time been teaching school groups and speaking publicly. Furthermore, with a significant popular following and memberships in the Linnaean Society, the American Ornithologists' Union (AOU), and the newly formed National Association of Audubon Societies, she extended her devotion to the living bird into direct advocacy, joining the AOU's Committee on the Protection of North American Birds and speaking out for the education of children about birds to her professional colleagues.

Given her commitment to education, it is not surprising that most of Miller's writing of this period was expressly for children. Adapting her lessons and talks, she offered a primer on bird morphology, behavior, and observational techniques in *The First Book of Birds* (1899) and then followed with an elementary discussion of the Linnaean classification of birds in *The Second Book of Birds: Bird Families* (1901). She completed this unofficial trilogy for children with *True Bird Stories from my Note-Books* (1903), a set of essays in which birds are given human names and their behavior is illustrated through story. That Louis Agassiz Fuertes, a young bird artist who was fast rising to justified fame, provided color illustrations for the last two of these books is a clear sign of the high regard she garnered from the worlds of ornithology and literature.

Miller undertook a second major transition in her early seventies, moving in 1904 with her daughter to the outskirts of Los Angeles after her husband's death. *With the Birds in Maine* also came out in this year. Considered by many readers to be equal to *A Bird-Lover in the West*, it was her last book for adults and the last from field notes she had collected over the previous ten summers. She would put out two more books on birds—*The Bird Our Brother: A Contribution to the Study of the Bird as He Is In Life* (1908) and *The Children's Book of Birds* (1915), a reissue of the *First* and *Second Book of Birds* under one cover—and at least four more books of children's stories before her death at 87 on December 26, 1918.

While it contains no fresh fieldwork, *The Bird Our Brother* is nevertheless a fitting denouement to an important career. In it Miller affirms her deepest convictions: the bird is "our brother" and should be studied "in life"; the book, she insists in the preface, "is simply an earnest attempt...to present him as an individual, a fellow pilgrim in this fair world of ours." What follows are essays that incorporate an extensive range of birds, her many years in the field, and the best of the ornithological scholarship (amateur and professional) of her time in order to capture a general sense of birds' "individuality," "intelligence," "language," and so on. In *Birds and Men* (1955), Robert Henry Welker suggests that Miller's neglect by literary scholarship is appropriate because she "bestowed the gift of sight rather than insight." Current scholars, however, can look at all that Miller in fact *saw*, both in the birds themselves and in humanity's connection to them, and find there a considerable contribution to American nature writing.

PRIMARY BIBLIOGRAPHY

Books

Little Folks in Feather and Fur, and Others in Neither (New York: E.P. Dutton, 1875).

Bird-Ways (Boston: Houghton Mifflin, 1885).

In Nesting-Time (Boston: Houghton Mifflin, 1888).

Little Brothers of the Air (Boston: Houghton Mifflin, 1892).

A Bird-Lover in the West (Boston: Houghton Mifflin, 1894).

Four-Handed Folk (Boston: Houghton Mifflin, 1896).

Upon the Tree-Tops (Boston: Houghton Mifflin, 1897).

The First Book of Birds (Boston: Houghton Mifflin, 1899).

The Second Book of Birds: Bird Families (Boston: Houghton Mifflin, 1901).

With the Birds in Maine (Boston: Houghton Mifflin, 1904).

The Bird Our Brother: A Contribution to the Study of the Bird As He Is In Life (Boston: Houghton Mifflin, 1908).

The Children's Book of Birds (Boston & New York: Houghton Mifflin, 1915; report of *The First Book of Birds*, 1899, and *The Second Book of Birds*, 1901).

Selected Periodical Publications— Uncollected

"Popular vs. Scientific Ornithology," letter, *The Auk: A Quarterly Journal of Ornithology* 11 (January 1894): 85–86.

"The Study of Birds—Another Way," *Bird-Lore* 2 (October 1900): 151–53.

Selected Publications—Collected

"The Mockingbird's Nest" (from *In Nesting Time*) and "On the Coast of Maine" (from *With the Birds in Maine*), in *American Fields and Forests: Henry D. Thoreau, John Burroughs, Bradford Torrey, Dallas Lore Sharp, and Olive Thorne Miller* (Boston: Houghton Mifflin, 1909).

SECONDARY BIBLIOGRAPHY

Biographies

"Harriet Mann Miller," *American Women Writers: A Critical Reference Guide from Colonial Times to the Present*, ed. Lina Mainiero (New York: Frederick Unger, 1981).

"Miller, Mrs. Olive Thorne," *A Woman of the Century: Fourteen Hundred-Seventy Biographical Sketches Accompanied by Portraits of Leading American Women*, ed. Frances E. Willard and Mary A. Livermore (Buffalo: Charles Wells Moulton, 1883; report. Detroit: Gale Research Company, 1967).

Robert H. Welker, "Miller, Olive Thorne," *Notable American Women 1607–1950: A Biographical Dictionary*, vol. 2, ed. Edward T. Jones (Cambridge: Harvard University Press, 1971).

References

Florence Merriam Bailey, "Mrs. Olive Thorne Miller," *The Auk: A Quarterly Journal Of Ornithology* 36.1 (April 1919): 163–69.

Paul Brooks, *Speaking for Nature: How Literary Naturalists from Henry Thoreau to Rachael Carson Have Shaped America* (Boston: Houghton Mifflin, 1980).

Felton Gibbons and Deborah Strom, *Neighbors to the Birds: A History of Birdwatching in America* (New York: Norton, 1988).

Laura C. Holloway, *The Woman's Story as Told by Twenty American Women* (New York: John B. Alden, 1889).

Hans Huth, *Nature and the American: Three Centuries of Changing Attitudes* (Berkeley: University of California Press, 1957).

Joseph Kastner, *A World of Watchers* (New York: Knopf, 1986).

Harriet Kofalk, *No Woman Tenderfoot: Florence Merriam Bailey, Pioneer Naturalist* (College Station: Texas A&M University Press, 1989).

Vera Norwood, *Made From This Earth: American Women and Nature* (Chapel Hill: University of North Carolina Press, 1993).

Robert Henry Welker, *Birds and Men: American Birds in Science, Art, Literature, and Conservation, 1800–1900* (Cambridge: Harvard University Press, 1955).

Papers

A collection of Olive Thorne Miller's papers is housed in the Library of Congress.

Thomas Nuttall
(January 5, 1786–September 10, 1859)

Michael Ziser

Despite the fact that Thomas Nuttall entered and left the world in England, retained his English citizenship to the end, and passed more time in his native country than anywhere else, there is no doubt that his life was really lived in America. The 28 years he spent in the United States (1808–1811; 1815–1823; 1825–1841; and briefly in 1847–1848) were by far the happiest and most productive of his existence. During his time in Philadelphia, Boston, and various outposts on the western frontier, Nuttall made important contributions to several branches of science, including mineralogy, entomology, zoology, and ornithology. His greatest passion, however, was for botany, and his achievements in discovering, describing, and publishing previously unknown American plant species earned him a high reputation among his peers that has only grown with the passage of time. Less conspicuously but no less importantly, Nuttall played a vital role in the establishment or invigoration of many of the first institutions and journals of science to endure in America.

Thomas was the firstborn son of Margaret and James Nuttall, a struggling middle-class couple in the small village of Long Preston. Situated in a dale amid the windswept Pennine moors of western Yorkshire, Long Preston's primary industries were sheepherding and limestone quarrying. It was a relatively wild place, offering caves, fossils, and rock outcroppings to engage the curious Thomas, who was encouraged by his mother to explore the surrounding territory.

At the age of 14, Thomas was enlisted as an apprentice in the thriving Liverpool printing shop of his Uncle Jonas. Known as the Caxton Press, the shop produced a wide variety of published materials, including affordable periodicals on religion, biography, and travel, as well as more prestigious books such as the *Foedera* of Thomas Rymer and the *Bibliographical Dictionary* of Adam Clarke. Like Benjamin Franklin across the Atlantic, Nuttall learned a great deal about language and style from the works whose type he set. Remaining gaps in his education he filled through voracious courses of self-study conducted nights and Sundays.

The desire for scientific exploration that would eventually consume Nuttall was first enflamed during a series of naturalizing trips taken in his late teens around the Pennines with friend John Windsor. En route to various summits, the two young men examined striking local geological formations—broken and faulted limestone strata, sinkholes, and caves filled with stalactites—and the equally interesting plant communities that changed with the altitude and soil conditions. Back in Liverpool, Thomas began to frequent the private botanical garden of William Roscoe and John Shepherd as well as the natural artifacts on display at the new Liverpool Museum. An education in natural history was put in reach by the subscription libraries, through which Nuttall had access to accounts of naturalist-explorers like André Michaux and Alexander von Humboldt, and was supplemented by periodic public lectures given by English naturalists. Perhaps Thomas's most intensive introduction to scientific natural history, however, came when he helped set the type for a descriptive guide, organized according to the Linnaean system, to the Liverpool Museum's collection of specimens from Captain Cook's South Sea voyages.

By the time the term of his apprenticeship was up, Nuttall had resolved to explore America's vast floral and faunal riches, the great majority of which had yet to be described scientifically. Jonas Nuttall, who hoped his nephew would take over his publishing house, at first refused to help pay the fare to America, and Thomas was forced to spend a desperate year in London looking for biological employment and struggling—not for the last time—to keep body and soul together. In the end he obtained enough for the journey, and in the spring of 1808 he sailed for Philadelphia.

Nuttall started botanizing as soon as his feet touched American soil, and before long the novelty of the flora required him to seek guidance in one of the few college textbooks on the subject, Benjamin Smith Barton's *Elements of Botany*. Unable to locate a copy in bookstores, he sought out its author. Barton, a medical doctor and professor at the University of Pennsylvania, harbored ambitious plans to publish a comprehensive and systematic American flora, and he was delighted to meet an "innocent" enthusiast like Nuttall, who might help him reach his goal. Through Barton, Nuttall was introduced to eminent naturalist William Bartram, the Linnaean exhibits at Peale's Museum, and the commercial nurseries and seed houses of Bernard M'Mahon and David Landreth. Nuttall also

undertook two long collecting expeditions for Barton, one around Delaware and the other over the Poconos to Wilkes-Barre, Pennsylvania, and Niagara, New York. These were the first of many perilous forays into the interior that the young botanist would make over the next 30 years.

Satisfied that Nuttall was a competent and reliable assistant, Barton then proposed that he hazard a much longer and more ambitious trip to the Great Plains, which had been officially explored by Lewis and Clark only a few years before. To Nuttall this was a dream come true, and in 1810 with few supplies and even fewer apprehensions he set out. The untenable itinerary laid out by Barton soon yielded to geographical and political realities, and at Michilimackinac, Nuttall fell in with one of John Jacob Astor's fur-trading parties, naturalizing alongside the trappers. It was on this stretch of the journey that Nuttall first earned literary notice, showing up in two accounts of the trip, Henry Breckinridge's *Journal* and John Bradbury's *Travels*, both of which served as sources to Washington Irving's *Astoria*, a later popular account of the Astorian expedition. With varying degrees of mockery, each writer remarked Nuttall's absorption in his collecting activities, which sometimes led him astray from the more pressing requirements of the journey through a hostile wilderness. Accounts of Nuttall getting lost or using his rifle as a shovel or as storage for seeds contributed to literary caricatures of the absent-minded professor, including Obed Bat of James Fenimore Cooper's *The Prairie*, although there were an ample number of other early American models for the type.

Nuttall traveled with his collections down the Missouri and Mississippi Rivers to New Orleans in the winter of 1811. Because of inadequate funds, an impractical route, and the looming war between America and Britain, Nuttall decided not to follow Barton's original plans, which called for him to travel overland via Indiana, Kentucky, and Virginia. Instead, he sent his specimens (minerals, fossils, plants, insects, birds, and mammals) and notes off to Philadelphia and boarded a ship for Liverpool. There he remained for the next three years, dispersing his seeds and specimens to London nurserymen, publishing a nursery catalog of his American plants, establishing a garden on the grounds of his uncle's estate, exploring the countryside, and taking part in the meetings of the Linnaean Society.

When Nuttall returned to Philadelphia in 1815, he promptly embarked on two long expeditions to the South. The first took him into the Blue Ridge Mountains, down the Potomac, south by boat to Savannah, then by foot through Georgia, South Carolina, and North Carolina before coming to a stop in Wilmington (North Carolina). In addition to collecting many new specimens, Nuttall made the acquaintance of William Baldwin, a physician and skilled botanist in Savannah. On the second trip, of 1816–1817, Nuttall traveled west to Pittsburgh and Cincinnati before turning south through Kentucky and the Cumberland Gap to Charleston. In Lexington he established relations with another accomplished doctor-botanist, Charles Wilkins Short.

Back in Philadelphia, Nuttall began to reap the harvest of his prolonged field excursions. Now a scientist of recognized merit, he was elected to the American Philosophical Society and the Academy of Natural Sciences. Along with the young entomologist Thomas Say, with whom he had a long and warm friendship, Nuttall was instrumental in launching the Academy's *Journal,* for which he solicited and refereed articles and even set much of the type on the first few issues. Most of his time, however, was spent composing his first major publication, *The Genera of North American Plants,* which superseded Frederick Pursh's *Flora Americae Septentrionalis.* Less expensive and of far higher quality than Pursh's work, the *Genera* surpassed even Michaux's *Flora Boreali-Americana,* then the summit of American botany, for accuracy and comprehensiveness. Both Caleb Cushing and Constantine Rafinesque gave it largely laudatory reviews. Although he would have preferred to

organize the work according to Jussieu's natural systematics, which categorized plants according to their overall similarities, Nuttall ultimately decided to use the more artificial sexual taxonomy of Linnaeus for the sake of compatibility with existing Linnaean floras. Nuttall compensated for this act of expedience, however, by detailing the evidence of natural relatedness in his descriptions, effectively supplying the information upon which a natural system could be based. These descriptions, which also included information on distribution and ecological affinities, were written in English rather than the traditional Latin. All of these innovations were in keeping with Nuttall's assertion in his introduction that advances in botany were best effected through broad participation and cooperation rather than the individual ambition of specialists alone.

Anxious to resume his field studies, Nuttall raised money from his Philadelphia acquaintances to fund an 18-month-long excursion to the Arkansas Territory. The trip took him down the Ohio River to Cincinnati and Louisville before turning east toward the Rockies. Outside of Fort Smith, illness prevented Nuttall from reaching the mountains, and he floated down river through Natchez to New Orleans. The ill-fated journey yielded many new specimens and a great deal of ethnographic information on the native inhabitants of Arkansas. It also produced the naturalist's only substantial nonscientific work, *Journal of Travels into the Arkansa Territory*, which is distinguished less by its prose style than by its wealth of historical and ethnographic information about the near Southwest in the years following the Louisiana Purchase.

When Nuttall returned to Philadelphia in 1820, he had plenty of scientific work to keep him busy. In addition to composing the account of his Arkansas travels described above, he was distributing specimens from the trip to the appropriate experts and publishing many scientific papers in the newly reinvigorated *Journal of the Academy of Natural Sciences*. Geology and mineralogy in particular absorbed his attention during this time period, and he contributed several significant papers on these subjects during his stay in Philadelphia. One of these, "Observations on the Geological Structure of the Valley of the Mississippi," noted similarities between geologic strata in the American South and Yorkshire, anticipating the general method of comparative stratigraphic analysis that would eventually become central to geology. Nuttall also gave an extremely well-received public lecture course on botany at the Academy's hall.

In 1823 Nuttall was appointed instructor in natural history at Harvard and curator of the college's dilapidated botanical garden. Cambridge society agreed with Nuttall, and except for a few short visits to England and a tour of the Southeast in 1830, he spent the next ten years lecturing to appreciative students at Harvard and slowly building up the botanical garden with the meager funds allotted to him. Dissatisfied with the antiquated botanical textbooks then available to his students, Nuttall wrote a much-improved replacement, *Introduction to Systematic and Physiological Botany*. Deliberately minimizing the technical vocabularies that discouraged nonspecialists, Nuttall modeled his engaging approach on Rousseau's *Letters on the Elements of Botany*.

In the late 1820s Nuttall began work on a new publication, the *Manual of Ornithology of the United States and Canada*. Conceived as a field guide to birds, Nuttall's book put the ornithological researches of forerunners like Alexander Wilson and contemporaries like John James Audubon within the reach of middle-class nonspecialists, giving popular bird-watching its first appreciable boost in prose much suppler than the stilted performance of his earliest writings. Nuttall's own direct experience with living birds and their habitats comes across in the *Manual*, whose detailed but nontechnical observations and memorable anecdotes are suffused with his personal enthusiasm. At every opportunity Nuttall remarks the interconnection of human and bird life, and the end of his introduction includes a plea for the moral and

legal protection of the latter. In the midst of composing the work Nuttall struck up a friendship with Audubon, from whose *Ornithological Biographies* he borrowed accounts to supplement Wilson's writings and his own notes, and to whom he provided a considerable number of his own bird specimens for reproduction in the *Birds of America*. The *Manual* was reissued through the end of the century, and an influential association, The Nuttall Ornithological Society, was formed in Nuttall's honor in 1873.

In 1834 Nuttall finally got the opportunity to take a long-dreamed-of voyage through the Rockies. Traveling with the visionary explorer and trader Nathaniel Wyeth on an expedition to establish American rights to the Oregon Territory, Nuttall was joined by the young ornithologist John Kirk Townsend, whose published journal of the trip became a classic of frontier writing. The trip was all Nuttall could have hoped for, and he collected a wide array of new and interesting plants. Once the party had made it to Fort Vancouver on the Pacific, Nuttall made two trips to Hawaii, where he was presented with a flora so novel it baffled his immediate understanding. From Hawaii, Nuttall continued to Monterey, Santa Barbara, San Pedro, and San Diego in California, becoming the first American naturalist to visit the region. There he once again entered into the American literary record, this time wandering along a San Diego beach picking up shells in *Two Years Before the Mast*, the account of former Harvard student Richard Henry Dana, Jr. Nuttall caught a ride on Dana's ship, the *Alert*, around the cape back to America, having made an unsuccessful plea to the captain to drop him off at the southernmost tip of Patagonia.

Back in the United States, Nuttall traveled between Philadelphia, New York, and Boston. Much of his time was spent in describing the new specimens culled from the Wyeth expedition, which he had agreed to publish in Torrey and Gray's projected *North American Flora*, and in updating his ornithological manual with new discoveries. The infighting that was becoming common among ambitious American naturalists during this period finally caught up with Nuttall, who had a falling out with the members of the Philadelphia Academy of Natural Sciences over his use of the Academy Hall and with Torrey and Gray over their treatment of his contributions to their aborted *North American Flora*. Nuttall turned his attention to the publication of plants discovered during his Arkansas voyage almost 20 years before. Also absorbing his attention was a systematic treatment of the *Compositae* (sunflower or aster family), one of the largest and most complex families of flowering plants. He also set about a comprehensive updating of François-André Michaux's beautifully illustrated study of North American trees, the *Histoire des arbres forestiers de l'Amérique septentrionale*. The resulting edition, *The North American Sylva*, is a masterful contribution to American botany prefaced with a personal recounting of Nuttall's journeys in the American interior.

The *Sylva* was the last of Nuttall's American productions. In 1842 he returned to England to take possession of his Uncle Jonas's estate. The bequest stipulated that Nuttall remain in residence at least nine months out of the year, and this effectively precluded his remaining in America any longer. Nuttall suffered greatly from his confinement to Nutgrove Manor, but in time he again took up some of his old botanical pursuits, tending his own garden, visiting the Royal Garden at Kew, corresponding with botanical explorers on the Indian subcontinent, and raising plants (particularly rhododendrons) from Asia. His period of great discovery and influence was over, however, and in 1859 he died of bronchitis.

Thomas Nuttall's characteristic disregard for material comfort and his exacting intellectual standards made him a great field botanist and judicious scientist. Now perhaps obscured by some of the more abrasive and ambitious naturalists who succeeded him, Nuttall nevertheless holds his place as the most important field botanist in early America. His writings, geared primarily toward a scientific or lay-scientific audience, reveal a deep love of natural exploration that drove him repeatedly to abandon his home and risk his safety in the service of science.

PRIMARY BIBLIOGRAPHY

Books

A Catalogue of New and Interesting Plants, Collected in Upper Louisiana, and Principally on the River Missourie (London: J. Williams, 1813).

The Genera of North American Plants (Philadelphia: printed for the author by D. Heartt, 1818).

A Journal of Travels into the Arkansa Territory, during the year 1819, with Occasional Observations on the Manners of the Aborigines (Philadelphia: Thomas H. Palmer, 1821).

Introduction to Systematic and Physiological Botany (Boston: Hilliard, Gray, Little, and Wilkins; Richardson and Lord, 1827; Cambridge, MA: Hilliard and Brown, 1827; revised, Cambridge, MA: Hilliard and Brown, 1830).

A Manual of the Ornithology of the United States and of Canada: The Land Birds (Cambridge, MA: Hilliard and Brown, 1832; revised and enlarged edition, Boston: Hilliard, Gray, & Co., 1840).

A Manual of the Ornithology of the United States and of Canada: The Water Birds (Cambridge, MA: Hilliard and Brown, 1834; revised and enlarged edition, Boston: Hilliard, Gray, & Co., 1840).

The North American Sylva (Philadelphia: J. Dobson, 1842–1849; revised edition, Philadelphia: D. Rice and A.N. Hart, 1857).

Selected Periodical Publications—Uncollected

"Observations on the Geological Structure of the Valley of the Mississippi," *Journal of the Academy of Natural Sciences of Philadelphia* 2 (1821): 14-52.

"A Catalogue of a Collection of Plants Made Chiefly in the Valleys of the Rocky Mountains or Northern Andes, Towards the Sources of the Columbia River, by Mr. Nathaniel B. Wyeth," *Journal of the Academy of Natural Sciences of Philadelphia* 7 (1834): 5–60.

"A Description of Some Rarer or Little-known Plants Indigenous to the United States from the Dried Specimens in the Herbarium of the Academy of Natural Sciences of Philadelphia," *Journal of the Academy of Natural Sciences of Philadelphia* 7 (1834): 61–115.

"Collections Towards A Flora of the Territory of Arkansas," *Transactions of the American Philosophical Society*, new series, 5 (1837): 139–203.

"Descriptions of New Species and Genera of Plants in the Natural Order of the *Compositae*, collected in a tour across the continent to the Pacific, a residence in Oregon, and a visit to the Sandwich Islands and upper California, during the years 1834 and 1835," *Transactions of the American Philosophical Society*, new series, 7 (1841): 283–453.

SECONDARY BIBLIOGRAPHY

References

John Bradbury, *Travels in the Interior of North America in the Years 1809, 1810 and 1811* (London: Sherwood, Neely, and Jones, 1819).

Henry Marie Breckinridge, *Journal of a Voyage Up the River Missouri* (Pittsburgh: Cramer, Spear and Eichbaum, 1814).

Richard Henry Dana, *Two Years Before The Mast: A Personal Narrative of Life at Sea* (New York: Harper & Bros., 1840).

Howard Ensign Evans, *Pioneer Naturalists: The Discovery and Naming of North American Plants and Animals* (New York: Henry Holt & Co., 1993), 79–83.

Jeannette E. Graustein, *Thomas Nuttall, Naturalist: Explorations in America, 1808–1841* (Cambridge, MA: Harvard University Press, 1967).

Washington Irving, *Astoria; or, Anecdotes of an Enterprise Beyond the Rocky Mountains* (Philadelphia, Carey, Lea, & Blanchard, 1836).

Joseph Kastner, *A Species of Eternity* (New York: Knopf, 1977): 254–284.

Ian MacPhail, *Thomas Nuttall* (Lisle, Illinois: The Morton Arboretum Press, 1983).

John Moring, *Early American Naturalists: Exploring the American West 1804–1900* (New York: Cooper Square Press, 2002): 48–68.

James L. Reveal, *Gentle Conquest: The Botanical Discovery of North America* (Washington, D.C.: Starwood, 1992).

John Kirk Townsend, *Narrative of a Journey Across the Rocky Mountains* (Philadelphia: H. Perkins, 1839).

Almira Hart Lincoln Phelps
(July 15, 1793–July 15, 1884)

Christine Marie Hilger

Almira Hart Lincoln Phelps, educator, administrator, and author, contributed to the genre of nature writing in historical ways primarily from the late 1820s to the late 1830s. While she did publish in other prose genres (including novel, personal essay, and memoir) and acted as editor for a scholarly work, her inventive contribution to nature writing serves as the focus of her literary legacy. During her lifetime, she achieved national recognition by becoming only the second woman elected to the American Association for the Advancement of Science, in 1859. Her first, and most famous textbook, *Familiar Lectures on Botany* (1829), underwent two major revisions and 39 printings over a 40-year period selling a publisher-estimated 375,000 copies, an amazing accomplishment by nineteenth-century standards. Although her work outside the nature writing genre did not cause a great sensation, Phelps's manner of educating students in the rigors of the natural sciences remains a lasting influence in academic institutions today.

Born in Berlin, Connecticut, on July 15, 1793, Phelps was the youngest of 17 children, seven siblings from her father's previous marriage and ten siblings from the marriage to her mother, Lydia. Their home was a simple three-story farmhouse built around a massive chimney that served not only to warm the

rooms on cold winter nights, but as a focal point of family life. Her father frequently read selections from Shakespeare's plays, Milton's poetry, and Rollins's *Ancient History* in the evenings. A self-educated man, Samuel Hart encouraged his children to be well read and did not fend off lively discussions or divergent opinions. Family members discussed literature as well as politics in an environment that encouraged enlightened thinking. The Hart home became a hub for dissenters within the community as well as a training ground for the Hart children to grow in exposition and rhetorical skill.

Following these evening discussions, the children headed to the staircase for bedrooms found on the second and third floors of the house, as well as in wings constructed onto the main building as the growing family's needs changed. Although some of her half-siblings were grown with children of their own by the time Phelps was born, the enormity of the extended family structure within the large farmhouse required an effective organization and rewarded patience. It also provided the template that would mold Phelps's early academic interests. But because large family environments seldom rely strictly on one mother to supervise and organize the potential chaos of the constant coming and going within the house, Phelps had numerous "mothers" in her older siblings who encouraged intellectual exploration and independence.

She found a substantial role model in her sister Emma Hart. Emma, later Emma Willard, provided the structure for Phelps's own early education. Willard developed into one of the leading female educational reformers striving to spread acceptance within American society for young women to receive the opportunity to achieve greater formal education. Willard was the first to establish female schools offering secondary or college-level courses in this country or in any other. Yet, before she would accomplish those groundbreaking advances, Willard would first help guide her sister's academic interests. Whether in person or by letter, Willard strove to convey to her younger sister the importance of selecting reading material carefully. Not every fictional work had intellectual value, Willard would declare before steering her sister, then age 12, to such works as James Burgh's essays or to the *Strictures on Female Education* by Hannah Moore.

By age 16, Phelps began teaching in district schools as she continued her own education, largely through her sister's Female Academy in Pittsfield, Massachusetts. In 1814, Phelps opened her own boarding school for women at her Connecticut home. Two years later she found herself the principal of a school in Sandy Hill, New York. In 1817, she set aside her professional duties for the duties of a dedicated housewife and mother of three; however, her husband, Simeon Lincoln, editor of *The Connecticut Mirror,* died in 1823. She returned to teaching and became the vice-principal of her sister's renowned Troy Female Seminary in New York.

One particular experience at Troy brought about a change of direction in Phelps's life, leading her into the genre of nature writing. Amos Eaton, cofounder of the Rensselaer School, was lecturing on chemistry, botany, and geology in the Troy area. Eaton, who wrote textbooks, developed teaching theories and methods that focused on supplying an application of the sciences to the common

purposes in life. At that point in history the current method for mastering knowledge in the sciences was to learn everything by rote. By contrast, Eaton's pedagogical ideas emphasized practical application or a learning-by-doing method. His innovative classroom ideas—such as gathering specimens for study during field trips, including students in laboratory experimentation, and adopting the current graduate seminar approach in the classroom, whereby a student prepares and delivers oral presentations while the instructor and other students provide a critique—had a profound effect on Phelps.

She first encountered Eaton at a public lecture in New England where she discovered that his vision of education in the sciences included women equally with men. He did not hold the common exclusionary tone of the day that declared women unfit to learn mathematics, botany, physical geography, or experimental chemistry; instead, he encouraged women to attend his lectures, tutored many, including Phelps, and even allowed women to lecture to men on occasion at the Rensselaer Scientific School at Troy.

Under Eaton's guidance, Phelps pursued her interests in the sciences, especially botany. Her admiration for Eaton's intellect and innovative learning approach to the sciences influenced a personal change in pedagogical direction for Phelps, ruled, as others of her generation had been, by the sterile, rote method of accumulating scientific knowledge. A natural teacher by personality and temperament, Phelps now had a new means by which she could formulate a curriculum for women. Through nature she could design a program able to transform boisterous girls into educated, independently thinking, self-disciplined young women. Her pioneering approach promulgated a general idea of pervasive order in the natural world, while also instructing students to substitute the testing of hypotheses through evidence for the mystical and magical thought processes believed to be characteristic of childhood. Phelps saw botany as a vehicle for improving mental function, intellectual achievement, and spiritual enlightenment. Botany as a scientific discipline required the development of the discerning powers of observation, reasoning, and memory, while promoting intellectual stimulation and a deeper connection to the great "Author," who illustrates the logical divisions of botany and the deepest goodness of God through the fragrance, form, and color of the flowers.

Since textbooks reflecting her inductive, objective teaching style did not exist, Phelps had to compose them herself. As an author she may never have intended to nationalize the study of the natural sciences, but her nature writing found more than an eager, exclusively female audience. Thousands of schoolchildren entered the realm of the natural sciences through Phelps during the latter decades of the nineteenth century. Her textbooks served as a doorway to nature writing for the masses. Because no earlier work had made so much knowledge so accessible to students, her textbooks became a very powerful tool. Phelps served to channel scientific knowledge away from the experts and deliver that knowledge directly to the populace, to take scientific knowledge, left solely to the universities to ponder and probe, and disperse that knowledge to students whose primary intellectual abilities had traditionally been ignored.

When Phelps first wrote *Familiar Lectures on Botany*, her decision to write on the subject of botany as opposed to chemistry or geography followed a logical line of reasoning based on a number of ideological advantages. Botany proved to be the most taxonomically developed of the natural sciences. Wherever students lived, regardless of the region of the country, a plethora of objects could be found to observe and study. A few steps outside of any classroom would easily lead to obtainable specimens. In addition, teachers could avoid the guilt associated with the dissection of an animal. The insentient nature of plants provided students with an introduction to the basic idea of organic nature. By selecting botany as her first endeavor in nature writing, Phelps introduced students to the structure underlying all physiological and anatomical study. Students explored the systems and subsystems of a plant, the organs and reproductive structures, all of the components with their distinctly different and separate functions that contribute to making the plant an entity, a whole.

But to fully understand the depths of Phelps's contribution to nature writing, it is necessary to further define the historical context of her day. The natural sciences were subjects out of the academic reach of most women, but more importantly, those same subjects did not pique the interests of women. Further, men of the era could see no wisdom in allowing women to pursue academic interests in the sciences nor any clear benefit in taking their daughters away from their traditional duties in order to pursue what belonged to a man's world. Phelps faced a formidable challenge in altering the long-established belief that women's intellectual pursuits should include anything other than the education of other women in the areas that would best serve their future husbands and children.

Through *Familiar Lectures on Botany*, Phelps stepped in as intermediary between men and science. She believed in the capabilities and the intellect of women and was well aware of the influence women held not only as representatives of half the population, but also as instructors to sons and companions to husbands. Phelps held firm to the conception that America could not achieve the status of "most modern nation" until the women of America understood the importance of science, the need to appreciate and disseminate science in the context of modernity. *Familiar Lectures on Botany* serves as the declaration of the opportunities awaiting the women willing to step into their new role in science.

As a nature writer, Phelps bridged an enormous gap. Prior to her first textbook, formal training in botany was limited to male medical students and to a simple curriculum requiring the memorization of the medicinal properties of plants. Women were not a part of the sciences, nor did any course of study exist for their inclusion. Phelps argued successfully that botany was a science especially suited for women's capabilities and interests. She rhetorically hushed critics by presenting the education of women in botany as a natural extension of femininity. Following the broad acceptance of *Familiar Lectures on Botany*, coursework available in botany increased in American schools. Phelps became a science popularizer, as well as an advocate proclaiming that women should not be turned away from any of the natural sciences based solely on the fact that they are women.

The text of *Familiar Lectures on Botany* does not change in terms of organization throughout the numerous editions, thus providing further testimony of the contribution Phelps made to nature writing. She designed the textbook for the classroom engaged in botanical activities, not simply a series of monotone lectures made by an instructor. Students reading her text would venture outside for field trips to gather specimens and would be as likely armed with dissection knifes as pencil and paper. The diagrams and numerous pictures appearing on the pages were never intended to substitute for actual contact with nature. Phelps wanted her students to view nature as it appeared around them, not as it appeared in a picture printed in a book. However, since nature was not organized in a way that could be intuited, the book was a necessary resource to deeper study. She encouraged students to work with real plants, to have a full sensory experience with nature by touching specimens, by visually examining them, by smelling them, and by using their developing intellectual skills to best identify a species through the Linnaean system of plant classification.

The ease with which Phelps describes complicated botanical structures further testifies to her skill as a nature writer. Whether defining the divisional system of classes and orders making up the Linnaean system or describing the intricate parts of a flower, Phelps imbues her prose with an ethos that not only displays for students a command of the language, but also clearly demonstrates her expertise in botany as a science. Despite

an authoritative tone, her use of the second-person pronoun "you" brings about a more nurturing feel to the text. In the 1845 edition of *Familiar Lectures on Botany*, Phelps writes, "Before you can learn the principles on which the classification of plants depends, it is necessary that you should become acquainted with the parts of the flower." The maternal appeal to the student of botany clearly demonstrates that there is work to do in mastering the subject in a way that resembles a reminder to a child that the bread will rise, but first it must be thoroughly kneaded.

Phelps initiates this "rising" by avoiding the textual boredom, the mundane, rote pedagogical style considered the standard for textbooks at that time. Her prose presents the physiological and systematic study of plants in a way that enhances, encourages, promotes, and advances not simply student interest in botany or chemistry or geology but also student participation in the wonder and discovery of nature. It is this literary facet of Phelps's writing, the animation of scientific facts, by which she frees her work from the limiting parameters of textbook authors and places her publications clearly into the sphere of nature writing. Through the use of illustrations, diagrams, and a lively narrative style, Phelps creates a soothing textual environment. Here, her motherly resonance in conjunction with her expertise in the sciences forms a mechanism by which the door between student and nature is opened.

In addition to the maternal prodding Phelps uses to encourage her students to study, a multidisciplinary tone echoes throughout the text, which increased with each new edition. Students received detailed botanical glossaries as well as introductions to poetry, physiological descriptions of plant life cycles as well as travel accounts, and physical geography mapping the global distribution of plants as well as relevant histories. This approach clearly added to the likelihood that students would receive their first encounters with nature writing in a "familiar" atmosphere. Following a difficult translation of *Vauquelin's Dictionnaire de Chimie*

(1830), Phelps published several texts in succession that continued to bridge the gap between women and science using the same academic but maternal, discipline-focused but multidisciplinary, style. *A Child's Geology* (1832), *Botany for Beginners* (1833), *Chemistry for Beginners* (1834), *Lectures on Natural Philosophy* (1835), *Lectures on Chemistry* (1837), *Natural Philosophy for Beginners* (1837), and *Familiar Lectures on Natural Philosophy* (1838) all strove to widen the intellectual door first opened to female students through *Familiar Lectures on Botany*.

Many of the subsequent textbooks went into multiedition publication; however, the techniques used by Phelps came up against stiff competition in the personage of Asa Gray. This Harvard professor, who published a textbook of his own on botany in 1836, believed in his approach to science and in his scientific textbook and openly criticized *Familiar Lectures on Botany* for its amateurism. The two texts competed for sales, and although Gray's text outsold Phelps's from beginning to end, the controversy between these two nature writers exposed the larger issue of gender, which had initially set Phelps out on the course of nature writing.

Gray's charge of amateurism epitomizes the defeatist corner women found themselves placed into concerning the exploration of the sciences and the presentation of nature writing in textbooks in the nineteenth century. Gender restriction kept Phelps from obtaining the Harvard degree Gray earned, setting her into a guaranteed perpetual status as amateur. Although quite accomplished in the sciences through self-study, Phelps would always lack the credibility gained by a university degree. Hers would always be a world once removed from the acceptance of "serious" academics.

By consequence of the amateur issue, Phelps found her pedagogical philosophy at odds with Gray's "natural" system. Phelps and her commitment to the Linnaean system of classification came to represent the "popular" method of botany versus Gray's "professional" method. Gray acknowledged the need to categorize and classify but insisted that the Linnaean system hindered rather than advanced scientific progress. Gray's concern centered on the margin of error created by a system organized to determine species by counting stamens (or other parts) without accounting either for variations that occur naturally or for specimens inadvertently damaged in the collection process. Under the Linnaean system, a missing stamen became the decree of a new species, and to Gray this was unacceptable.

His point, valid as the development of botany as a science proved him to be, set into motion the process of returning botany into the exclusive domain of professional scientists. Phelps fought the shift toward the natural system, knowing the complexities involved would discourage the interests of her young, female students. She did not want to see the "New Botany" return the science she and her students loved to the academic elite. As a nature writer, Phelps strove for the connection between plant and student to remain one of discovery and wonder. Her textbooks on botany continued throughout her 50-year career to reflect her original views about botany as a science and about the young women being educated by them. Phelps's interest would not be found in *creating* a science, but in creating a forum, her textbooks, by which her students could *experience* a science.

During a prolific decade of nature writing (1829–1838), Phelps produced a legacy unmatched in scope or depth by other writers of her era. Each of the nineteenth-century sciences, with the exception of astronomy, enjoyed representation in a Phelps textbook. She systematically presented the structures and forms of geology and chemistry to students who otherwise would not have had the chance to explore such expressions of nature. With an encouraging and nurturing tone, she opened students's minds to the secrets of creation and, in her thinking, to the secrets of the Creator.

In 1856, following the accidental death of her daughter, Phelps retired to Baltimore, Maryland. For the next 28 years she wrote, lectured, and revised her textbooks. Her initial belief that botany enlarged and disciplined the minds of her female students grew to include other subjects in science, but unlike the other subjects, botany would remain for Phelps a "female" science. In a later book titled *Hours with My Pupils* (1869), Phelps enters into discourses detailing her fundamental beliefs on women, science, and the future. This collection of essays acts as her testament to her students, to nature, and to the continuing need of science education for women.

Hours with My Pupils provides young women with a template for life and a dialogue of wisdom as well as with encouragement for the difficult road of life ahead, but the text also provides insight into the true motivations for Phelps's nature writing. Phelps makes clear the connection she wants her students to perceive between nature and a divine being, whom she often called the "great Author." She reminds her readers that nature was not responsible for surrounding us with the intricate beauty found in the flowers, nor was it nature that designed the complex seed cones that fall from various trees. For Phelps, the wonders we find in nature came completely through the creative majesty of a supreme being. *Hours with My Pupils* reminds the reader that Phelps's pursuit of nature and her desire to see young women pursue the study of nature held an underlying motivation. Phelps desired to see her students enter into adulthood with not only a firm educational foundation, but also a well-developed spiritual life. Her nature writing was never an attempt to mold young, female scientists, but was to allow women to see, to experiment with, to explore, to be educated by, and to document the overwhelmingly creative work of her "great Author."

Phelps was completely committed to the role of woman as wife, as mother, and as homemaker. In her later years, Phelps found herself risking her reputation as one of the country's famed popularizers of science by taking an antisuffrage stance in a growing women's suffrage climate. While she could easily have used her position as a nature writer, as one of the leading female nature writers of her time, to further any cause she chose, she refused to use her popularity or authority as a nature writer to lend credibility to a movement that opposed her cultural views. The maternal tone of her textbooks and the grandmotherly tone of *Hours with My Pupils* reveal Phelps as a woman truly dedicated to the education of her students but also truly faithful to the benefits her students could receive, not through her politics, but through her conception of nature and the duties of women in relation thereto.

By fulfilling the need to provide female students with textbooks, Phelps unknowingly laid the foundation of what would be her legacy as a writer. While she wrote other morally oriented books such as *Caroline Westerly* (1833), *Ida Norman, Or Trials and Their Uses* (1850), and *Whisper to a Bride and Christian Households* (1860), it was her nature writing that brought spiritual enlightenment and solid educational benefits to generations of students, extending even to the present day. The inclusion of multimedia companion CDs in modern textbooks mirrors the innovative contributions Phelps made to nature writing in terms of graphics and textual presentation. Her work opened the tightly sealed academic doors to the study of nature; she dispelled the long-held misconceptions that women were not capable of mastering subjects in the sciences; and she enhanced the rote methodology of course study with hands-on applications.

Almira Hart Lincoln Phelps will be remembered in the history of nature writing as a woman of firsts. She was the first woman in the United States to write and publish a textbook on a natural science, the first innovator of a textual, hands-on method of nature study, and the first American female popularizer of science. Phelps presented the beauty, wonder, mystery, and spiritual majesty of nature to students in an orderly, multidisciplinary manner that generated an interest in the sciences among female students as had never been experienced before. With a motherly tone and great rhetorical skill, Phelps describes in her nature writing not simply a system of classification (botany), a system of chemical composition (chemistry), or a system of logical reasoning (philosophy), in page after page of her textbooks, but a system for encouraging and enabling young minds to explore and nurture all that nature has to offer.

PRIMARY BIBLIOGRAPHY

Textbooks

Familiar Lectures on Botany (Hartford: F.J. Huntington and Co., Connecticut, 5 printings 1829–1836; New York: Huntington and Savage and Mason Brothers, 22 printings 1837–1860; Philadelphia, 5 printings 1864–1868).

Geology for Beginners (Brattleborough, Vermont: n.p., 1832).

Botany for Beginners (Hartford: F.J. Huntington, 3 printings 1833–1836; New York: Mallory and Co., 17 printings 1837–1857; Philadelphia [titled "New Edition of Botany for Beginners"]: J.B. Lippincott, 7 printings 1864–1891).

Female Student or Fireside Friend (Boston: Leavitt, Lord and Co., 1833).

Lectures to Young Ladies (Boston: Carter, Hendee and Co., 1933; London: Scott, Webster, and Geary, 1838).

Chemistry for Beginners (Hartford: F.J. Huntington, 7 printings 1834–1850; New York: George Savage and Mason and Law, 1852; Philadelphia: J.P. Lippincott, 1875).

Familiar Lectures on Natural Philosophy (New York: F.J. Huntington and Co., 1837).

Lectures on Chemistry (New York: F.J. Huntington, 4 printings 1837–1844).

Natural Philosophy for Beginners (New York: F.J. Huntington and Co., 4 printings 1837–1841; New York: Huntington and Savage, 1842; New York: H.W. Derby and Co., 1850; New York: Sheldon, Lamport and Co. 1856; Philadelphia: J.B. Lippincott, 1866).

Books

Caroline Westerly (New York: Harper's Family Library, 1833).

Ida Norman, Or Trials and Their Uses. Also titled: *Ida Norman, Or The Discipline Of Life* (Baltimore: Cushing, 1848; New York: Lamport and Blackeman, 1855).

Hours with My Pupils (New York: Scribner, 1859).

Whisper to a Bride and Christian Households (New York: Billin and Brother, 1858; New York: D. Dana Jr., 1860; Philadelphia: Cloxton, Remsen and Haffelfinger, 1869).

Reviews and Essays on Art, Literature, and Science (n.p,, 1873).

Translation

Dictionary of Chemistry (New York: G. & C. & H. Cavill, 1830).

Other

Tribute To The Memory of Jane Porter Lincoln (Baltimore: J.D. Toy, 1855).

Mrs. Emma Willard's Theory of Circulation By Respiration (Baltimore: W.K. Boyle, 1870).

A Plea For Cuba; addressed to the Senate and House of Representatives of the United States (Baltimore: W.K. Boyle, 1870).

SECONDARY BIBLIOGRAPHY

References

Lois Barber Arnold, *Four Lives in Science: Women's Education in the Nineteenth Century* (New York: Schocken Books, 1984).

Nina Baym, *American Women of Letters and the Nineteenth-Century Sciences: Styles of Affiliation* (New Brunswick, NJ: Rutgers University Press, 2002).

Emma Lydia Bolzau, *Almira Hart Lincoln Phelps: Her Life and Work* (Philadelphia: University of Pennsylvania, 1936).

Lawrence Cremin, *American Education, the National Experience, 1783–1876* (New York: Harper and Row, 1980).

Carl Kaestle, *Pillars of the Republic: Common Schools and American Society, 1780–1860* (New York: Hill and Wang, 1983).

Emanuel Rudolph, "Botany in American and British Chapbooks before 1860," *Plant Science Bulletin* 19.3 (1973): 34–36.

Emanuel Rudolph, "Learning Botany by Rote, the Way of Nineteenth Century Catechisms," *Plant Science Bulletin* 24.4 (1978): 39–40.

Emanuel Rudolph, "Almira Hart Lincoln Phelps (1793–1884) and the Spread of Botany in Nineteenth Century America," *American Journal of Botany* 71 (1984): 1161–1167.

John Wesley Powell
(March 24, 1834– September 23, 1902)

James Kraus

John Wesley Powell wrote one of the most important first-person narratives in American literature, *The Exploration of the Colorado River and its Canyons* (1875). The book recounts a series of surveying expeditions that began in 1869 and included a dangerous passage through the Grand Canyon by boat. At the time, little was known about the region. His name is profoundly associated with the Grand Canyon and the Grand Canyon National Park, and man-made Lake Powell, in Utah, is named after him. Powell was first and foremost an adventurer; however, as a result of his superb skill at careful observation and classification, he is regarded as one of the most influential scientists and nature writers of his day. As a geologist and geographer, he contributed profoundly to the refinement of old ideas and the development of new ones, especially in the area of geomorphology. As a writer of ethnology about Native Americans, he helped establish the discipline of anthropology. He was appointed to a series of government posts, first as director of the Geographical and Geological Survey of the Rocky Mountain Region, and later as Director of the Smithsonian Institution's Bureau of Ethnology and Director of the U.S. Geological Survey. He was also among the group that in 1888 created the National Geographic Society.

John Wesley Powell was born to Joseph and Mary Dean Powell on March 24, 1834. Joseph was a restless Welsh immigrant and Methodist minister who settled first in New York's Genesee Valley. It was there that Wes, their third child, was born and where his family resided until he was four. Joseph then moved the family to southern Ohio. Mary tutored Wes and his siblings in reading using the Bible as the text, a common practice in the early nineteenth century. Additionally, in Ohio, young Wes was informally tutored by local naturalist George Crookham. Although Wes never acquired the evangelical religious enthusiasm of his father, it is clear from his writings that he looked at the world from a monotheistic perspective and regarded the animistic belief system of the Native Americans he would later write about as superstitious.

The Powells lived in Ohio until 1846, by which time the family's open, abolitionist sympathies made them the target of harassment by proslavery zealots. They then moved to a farm in Walworth County, in southern Wisconsin. It was there that Wes first met

Native Americans—a group of Winnebagos who camped on the family's property and who, he later wrote, stimulated his interest in Native American languages and culture.

In 1850, Wes left his family in search of the education needed to qualify for college admission; however, later that same year he rejoined his family as the Powells moved to northern Illinois. With the encouragement of his mother, Wes began a period of intense self-study, so that by 1852 he was able to find a teaching position and to begin giving public lectures on the subject of geography. In 1855, he was admitted to Illinois College as a first-year science student. When his financial resources ran low, he dropped out to return to live with his family; he was then enrolled at the Illinois Institute, where he was active in the school's literary society and in debating; however, he again dropped out. Subsequently, with his father's support he briefly attended Oberlin College in Ohio. Then he again tried the Illinois Institute, but soon dropped out of college for good. Throughout this period, he spent his free time collecting fossils and exploring nearby rivers, including the Mississippi River.

In 1861, Powell enlisted in the Union Army to fight in the Civil War. He was soon promoted to company commander. Later that year he asked for and received a leave in order to go to Detroit to marry Emma Dean, his first cousin. She returned with him to the war. In April of the next year, at the Battle of Shiloh, Powell was shot in the right arm, and doctors amputated the arm. Emma Dean remained with him, as she would for many of his western expeditions. In 1863, after participating in the Battle of Vicksburg, he returned to Detroit for another operation on his arm. That same year he was promoted to the rank of major.

In 1865, Powell resigned from the Army and took a position as professor of geology at Illinois Wesleyan University, which had awarded him an honorary master's degree while he was at Vicksburg. In 1867, he became curator of the Illinois Natural History Society and organized his first scientific expedition— a party of 12—to Colorado. During this

expedition, Powell and Emma Dean climbed Pike's Peak, she being the first woman to do so. In 1868, he took another expedition to Colorado, this time a party of 23.

In 1869, Powell led an expedition down the Green and Colorado Rivers through the Grand Canyon. The publicity surrounding this accomplishment, ironically including a completely fraudulent report of the expedition's failure published by the *Chicago Tribune*, resulted in Powell's being regarded as a national hero. Consequently, he embarked on an immensely successful lecturing circuit.

Powell's firsthand writings about the expedition consisted of letters and journals. During the early phase of the expedition, he wrote a set of seven letters to the *Chicago Tribune*, as well as several letters to friends. These were mailed from various outposts along the way. During the later part of the expedition, when side trips to outposts were not possible, he wrote a journal on pieces of long brown paper. All of these primary sources were collected in the *Utah Historical Quarterly* in 1947. Powell's journal resides at the National Anthropological Archives.

In 1875, *Scribner's Monthly* published Powell's "The Canyons of the Colorado," a serialization of the journey that ran over several issues. Powell subsequently expanded the *Scribner's* articles to create a government report, *Exploration of the Colorado River and Its Tributaries* (1875), which was first presented to the Smithsonian Institution and later to Congress. During the expedition, Powell also kept a geological journal, excerpts of which are included in the *Utah Historical Quarterly* materials mentioned above.

Some 20 years later, Powell added both geographical material about the landscape and ethnographic material about the Native American tribes of the region, and published the book *Canyons of the Colorado* (1895) as a commercial edition. This edition has subsequently been republished and is the primary basis of Powell's standing as a nature writer.

Powell's account of the expedition and his description of the geology and people of the region achieved much of its force because of his mix of objectivity, optimism and reverence. Powell's objectivity as a naturalist won readers and admirers who already held essentially empirical ideas about nature. His optimism allowed him to promote, organize, and lead his various expeditions. Both of these qualities appealed to politicians and bureaucrats who were eager to exploit whatever resources the new land might hold. But it is Powell's reverence, his sense of awe, at what he encountered and what he and his companions endured, that ultimately explains his continuing popularity. This sensibility is directly connected to the popular nineteenth-century ideas of the sublime. In the concluding paragraph of *The Exploration of the Colorado River and its Canyons*, for example, he writes that one can experience the Grand Canyon from the multiple perspectives permitted only by moving through it and that in this way "a concept of sublimity can be obtained never again to be equaled on the hither side of Paradise." While Powell was utterly pragmatic in the conduct of both his expeditions and his career, he managed in his writing to stop short of sentimental rhapsodizing about nature and on occasion to state in simple direct language that he did not have the words to convey what he felt. Of particular interest in this regard is his acknowledgment in attempting a description of the Canyon of Lodore that the scenery was "beyond the power of the pen to tell." Powell immediately follows this acknowledgment of the limits of his language with a description of the roaring of the water and the assertion that it is in these sounds reverberating through the landscape that he hears "a story of beauty and grandeur." He then immediately follows with a return to his most objective tones, beginning with: "The Canyon Lodore is 20¾ miles in length. It starts abruptly with what we have called the Gate of Lodore, with walls nearly 2,000 feet high."

In 1873, Powell, his wife, and young daughter moved to Washington, D.C., where he worked at directing a survey of the western

United States and researching the problems of the Native Americans. In 1878, he published *Report on the Lands of the Arid Region*, in which he proposed the formation of irrigation districts and the building of small dams as an approach to settlement of the West. His proposals contradicted the Homestead Act of 1862 and were broadly attacked as socialistic.

As a writer of ethnology, Powell's ideas were influenced by Lewis Henry Morgan, who theorized that human culture evolved through stages of savagery, barbarism, and civilization. Thus, Powell's ideas about Native Americans seem racist by modern standards. Nonetheless, his *Introduction to the Study of Indian Languages* (1877) and his numerous periodical publications are important early contributions to the understanding of Native Americans. By 1881, Powell was director of both the Smithsonian Institution's Bureau of Ethnology and the U.S. Geological Survey. These organizations remain today among the most important scientific organizations in the world. Through the last decades of his life, Powell's writing encompassed speculation about the broad relationship of humanity to nature. He died on September 23, 1902.

As a writer about nature, Powell's contribution is primarily in the area of science writing. His skill at careful observation, combined with his ability to develop theories about the unknown that were solidly grounded in fact, resulted in important and influential contributions to the field of geology and anthropology. As George Crosette argues in his introduction to the *Selected Prose of John Wesley Powell* (1970), Powell proved his capacity for accurate scientific analysis when he calculated, contrary to the belief of other scientists, that there would be no impassable waterfalls in the Grand Canyon. So when he and his party successfully completed their journey, Powell became a national hero not only as an adventurer, but as a scientist. The excerpts from Powell's periodical publications Crosette collected serve as an excellent introduction to the full range of Powell's science writing, from ethnographic and linguistic studies of the Hopi, the Utes, and other Western Native American tribes, to comprehensive government-sponsored surveys and plans for the arid regions of the West.

By far the most authoritative and comprehensive study of Powell's life and work is Donald Worster's *A River Running West, the Life of John Wesley Powell* (2001); by virtue of its breadth and its attention to detail, Worster's book supersedes earlier biographies of Powell, including geologist William Culp Darrah's *Powell of the Colorado* (1951) and novelist Wallace Stegner's much acclaimed *Beyond the Hundredth Meridian* (1954). Worster's book places Powell in the context of American nationalism, in this way illustrating the centrality of Western expansionism to the rise of American nature writing. Worster also points to an important contrast between Powell and John Muir, who valued wilderness above civilization. Powell, on the other hand, regarded wilderness, like savagery and barbarism, as something to overcome. Powell would later come into conflict with forest conservationists over the construction of dams, which he strongly supported. This sets Powell apart from nineteenth-century nature writers Henry David Thoreau and John Muir, who were strong advocates for wilderness and for conservation.

Nonetheless, Powell has been well-received by contemporary ecocritics. For example, Rick Van Noy's "Surveying the Sublime: Literary Cartographers and the Spirit of Place" examines Powell's orientation to landscapes in contrast to those of Henry David Thoreau and Clarence King, who preceded Powell as director of the Geological Survey. Explaining that "the sublime" is an essentially emotional experience, sometimes grounded in terror that transforms into awe and reverie, Van Noy argues that Powell's capacity to represent the sublime in landscape results from his ability to experience a place from a variety of interpretive perspectives, often those derived from Native Americans, who he felt were interested in the particulars of a place rather than a generality

delimited by a singular viewpoint. John Tallmadge has pointed out that as a result of actually traveling through the landscape, Powell was uniquely drawn to perspectives that had to do with motion and sound, and ultimately with change itself.

It was Powell's pragmatic, scientific perspective merged with his sense of the sublime that succeeded in securing his place in American literary history. His name is also ensconced in the American memory for its association with the recreational areas of southern Utah and northern Arizona. He had immense influence over the ways in which government supports the study of nature, and thereby also the ways in which government acts to conserve what is of lasting value. He is widely considered to be one of the founders of the American environmental movement.

PRIMARY BIBLIOGRAPHY

Books

Report of Special Commissioners J.W. Powell and G.W. Ingalls on the Condition of the Ute Indians of Utah; the Paiutes of Utah, Northern Arizona, Southern Nevada, and Southwestern California, the Go-si Utes of Utah and Nevada, the Northwestern Shoshones of Idaho and Utah, and the Western Shoshones of Nevada, and Report Concerning Claims of Settlers in the Mo-A-Pa Valley (Southeastern Nevada) (Washington, D.C.: U.S. Government Printing Office, 1874).

Exploration of the Colorado River and Its Tributaries (Washington, D.C.: U.S. Government Printing Office, 1875).

Report on the Geology of the Eastern Portion of the Uinta Mountains and a Region of the Country Thereto (Washington, D.C.: U.S. Government Printing Office, 1876).

Introduction to the Study of Indian Languages (Washington, D.C.: U.S. Government Printing Office, 1877).

Report on the Lands of the Arid Region of the United States, With a More Detailed Account of the Lands of Utah (Washington, D.C.: U.S. Government Printing Office, 1878).

Canyons of the Colorado (Meadville, PA: Flood and Vincent, 1895).

Truth and Error: Or, the Science of Intellection (Chicago: Open Court, 1898).

Editions and Collections

Exploration of the Colorado River, introduction by Wallace Stegner (Chicago: The University of Chicago Press, 1957 [reprint of *Exploration of the Colorado River and Its Tributaries* (1875)]).

The Exploration of the Colorado River and Its Canyons (New York: Dover Publications, 1961 [reprint of *Canyons of the Colorado* (1895)]).

Report on the Lands of the Arid Region of the United States, With a More Detailed Account of the Lands of Utah, ed. Wallace Stegner (Cambridge, MA: Belknap Press, 1962).

Canyons of the Colorado (New York: Argosy Antiquarian, Ltd., 1964 [reprint of *Canyons of the Colorado* (1895)]).

Selected Prose of John Wesley Powell, ed. George Crossette (Boston: David R. Godine, 1970).

Anthropology of the Numa: John Wesley Powell's Manuscripts on the Numic Peoples of Western North American, 1868–1880, ed. Don and Catherine Fowler (Washington, D.C.: Smithsonian Institution, 1971).

The Exploration of the Colorado River and Its Canyons (New York: Penguin, 1987 [reprint of *Canyons of the Colorado* (1895)]).

Other

"Major Powell's Report on His Explorations of the Rio Colorado in 1869," in *New Tracks in North America,* ed. William A. Bell (New York: Scribner, Welford, and Co., 1870), 559–64.

"Indians of North America," in *Johnson's Universal Cyclopedia, Vol. 4* (New York: D. Appleton, 1895), 544–52.

"Physiographic Processes," "Physiographic Features," and "Physiographic Regions of the United States," in *The Physiography of the United States* (New York: American Book Co., 1895), 1–100.

"Relation of Primitive Peoples to Environment," in *Smithsonian Institution, Annual Rpt., 1895* (Washington, D.C.: U.S. Government Printing Office, 1896), 625–37.

"The Scientific Explorer," in *The Grand Canyon of Arizona,* (N.p.: Sante Fe Railroad, 1902), 18–32.

Selected Periodical Publications— Uncollected

"Some Remarks on the Geological Structure of a District of Country Lying to the North of the Grand Canyon of the Colorado," *American Journal of Science and Arts* 5 (1873): 456–65.

"Biographical Notice of Archibald Robertson Marvine," *Philosophical Society of Washington Bulletin* 2 (1875–1880): 53–60.

"Physical Features of the Colorado Valley," *Popular Science Monthly* 7 (1875): 385–99, 531–92, 670–80.

"The Canyons of the Colorado," *Scribner's Monthly* 9 (1875): 293–310, 394–409, 523–37.

"An Overland Trip to the Grand Canyon," *Scribner's Monthly,* 10 (1875): 659–78.

"The Ancient Province of Tusayan," *Scribner's Monthly* 11 (1875): 193–213.

"A Discourse on the Philosophy of the North American Indians," *Journal of American Geographical Society of New York* 8 (1878): 251–68.

"Mythologic Philosophy," *Popular Science Monthly* 15 (1879): 795–808; 16 (1879): 56–66.

"Sketch of Lewis H. Morgan," *Popular Science Monthly* 18 (1880): 114–21.

"Address of Major Powell," *American Institute of Mining Engineers, Trans.* 10 (1881–1882): 232–36.

"Darwin's Contributions to Philosophy," *Biological Society of Washington Proceedings* 1 (1882): 60–70.

"Ward's Dynamic Sociology," *Science* 2 (1883): 45–49, 105–8, 171–74, 222–26.

"The Three Methods of Evolution," *Philosophical Society of Washington Bulletin* 6 (1884): xxvii–lii.

"The Organization and Plan of the United States Geological Survey," *American Journal of Science* 29 (1885): 93–102.

"From Savagery to Barbarism," *Anthropological Society of Washington Trans.* 3 (1885): 173–96.

"The Larger Import of Scientific Education," *Popular Science Monthly* 26 (1885): 452–56.

"The Administration of the Scientific Work of the General Government," *Science* 5 (1885): 51–55.

"Museums of Ethnology and Their Classification," *Science* 9 (1887): 612–14.

"Classification of the Sciences," *American Anthropologist* 1 (1888): 297–323.

"Address of Major Powell in Memory of Professor Baird," *Science* (1888): 25–26.

"The Lesson of Conemaugh," *North American Review* 149 (1889): 150–56.

"Evolution of Music from Dance to Symphony," in *American Association for the Advancement of Science, Proceedings, 38th Meeting* (Salem, MA: AAAS, 1890), 1–21.

"Irrigable Lands of the Arid Region," *Century Magazine* 39 (1890): 766–76.

"The Non-Irrigable Lands of the Arid Region," *Century Magazine*, 39 (1890): 915–22.

"Institutions for the Arid Lands," *Century Magazine* 40 (1890): 111–16.

"Prehistoric Man in America," *Forum* 8 (1890): 489–503.

"Problems of American Archaeology," *Forum* 8 (1890): 638–52.

"The Humanities," *Forum* 10 (1890): 410–22.

"National Agencies for Scientific Research," *Chautauquan* 14 (1891–1892): 37–42, 160–65, 291–97, 422–25, 545–49, 668–73.

"The New Lake in the Desert," *Scribner's Magazine* 10 (1891): 463–68.

"Are Our Indians Becoming Extinct?" *Forum* 15 (1893): 343–54.

"Proper Training and the Future of the Indians," *Forum* 18 (1895): 622–29.

"The Five Books of History," *Science* 1 (1895): 157–61.

"James Dwight Dana," *Science* 3 (1896): 181–85.

"How a Savage Tribe is Governed," *Forum* 25 (1898): 712–22.

"The Evolution of Religion," *Monist* 8 (1898): 183–204.

"Fallacies of Perception," *Open Court* 12 (1898): 720–29.

"Esthetology," *American Anthropologist*, new series, 1 (1899): 1–40.

"Technology," *American Anthropologist*, new series, 1 (1899): 319–49.

"Sociology," *American Anthropologist*, new series, 1 (1899): 475–509, 695–745.

"Reply to Critics," *Science* 9 (1899): 259–63.

"The Lessons of Folklore," *American Anthropologist*, new series, 2 (1900): 1–36.

"Philology," *American Anthropology*, new series, 2 (1900): 603–37.

"Dualism Modernised," *Monist* 10 (1900): 385–96.

"Sophiology," *American Anthropologist*, new series, 3 (1901): 51–79.

"The Categories," *American Anthropologist*, new series, 3 (1901): 404–30.

"Letters of Major J.W. Powell to the *Chicago Tribune* [1869]," *Utah Historical Quarterly* 15 (1947): 73–88.

"Major Powell's Journal," *Utah Historical Quarterly* 15 (1947): 125–31.

"Geological Notes and Sections," *Utah Historical Quarterly* 15 (1947): 134–39.

"John Wesley Powell's Journal: Colorado River Explorations, 1871–1872," *Smithsonian Journal of History* 3 (1968): 1–44.

SECONDARY BIBLIOGRAPHY

Bibliographies

Lawrence F. Schmeckbier, *Catalog and Index of the Hayden, King, Powell and Wheeler Surveys*, U.S. Geological Survey Bulletin 222 (Washington, D.C.: U.S. Government Printing Office, 1904).

P.C. Warman, "Catalogue of the Published Writings of John Wesley Powell," *Proceedings of the Washington Academy of Sciences* 5 (July 1903): 131–87.

Biographies

William Culp Darrah, *Powell of the Colorado* (Princeton: Princeton University Press, 1951).

Mrs. M.D. Lincoln, "John Wesley Powell," Open Court, 16 (December 1902): 705–15; 17 (February 1903): 14–25, 86–93.

Wallace Stegner, *Beyond the Hundredth Meridian: John Wesley Powell and the Second Opening of the West* (Boston: Houghton Mifflin Co., 1954).

Donald Worster, *A River Running West: The Life of John Wesley Powell* (New York: Oxford University Press, 2001).

References

James M. Aton, *Inventing John Wesley Powell: The Major, His Admirers and Cash-Register Dams in the Colorado River Basin*, Southern Utah State College Distinguished Faculty Lecture No. 9 (Cedar City: Southern Utah State College, 1988).

James M. Aton, *John Wesley Powell* (Boise: Boise State University Press, 1994).

"Lost in the Grand Canyon," television, *The American Experience*, PBS/WGBH Educational Foundation, 1999.

John Muir, "The Grand Canyon of the Colorado," *Century Magazine* 65 (1902): 107–16.

Henry Nash Smith, *Virgin Land: The American West as Symbol and Myth* (Cambridge, MA: Harvard University Press, 1951).

John Tallmadge, "Western Geologists and Explorers: Clarence King and John Wesley Powell," in *American Nature Writers, Vol. 2*, ed. John Elder (New York: Charles Scribner's Sons, 1996).

Rick Van Noy, "Surveying the Sublime: Literary Cartographers and the Spirit of Place," *The Greening of Literary Scholarship: Literature, Theory, and the Environment*, ed. Steven Rosendale (Iowa City: University of Iowa Press, 2002), 181–206.

John J. Zernel, "John Wesley Powell: Science and Reform in a Positive Context" (dissertation, Oregon State University, 1983).

Papers

Collections of John Wesley Powell's manuscripts and correspondence are in the American Philosophical Society Library in Phildelphia; the Grand Canyon National Park Museum; Illinois Wesleyan University Library in Bloomington, Illinois; the Library of Congress, Manuscripts Division; the National Archives; Smithsonian Institution, National Anthropoligical Archives; and the Utah State Historical Society in Salt Lake City.

Constantine Samuel Rafinesque (Constantine Samuel Rafinesque Schmaltz) (October 22, 1783– September 18, 1840)

Michael Ziser

Perhaps the most colorful and controversial naturalist in nineteenth-century America, Constantine Samuel Rafinesque possessed a voracious intellectual appetite for knowledge in every field known to science—and in some that were still unknown to it. The subjects of his published works, which number in the hundreds, range from the tiniest minutiae of the natural world (the hinges of freshwater mollusks) to the most intractable problems of human society (the regulation of credit), touching on matters of pure science as well as practical application. All of Rafinesque's scattered projects were motivated by a fierce conviction that the world was full of novel objects and new ways of doing things awaiting discovery: one of the most common phrases in his correspondence and published articles is "all new!" Although Rafinesque's eclecticism and eccentricity earned him a partly deserved reputation in his day and ours as an incompetent scientist, huckster, or even madman, he was in some respects far ahead of his time and made fundamental contributions to many fields, including medicine, botany, zoology, ethnography, and historical linguistics.

The cosmopolitan and peripatetic Rafinesque did not exaggerate when he wrote, as a motto for an abbreviated attempt at autobiography,

> Un voyageur dés le berceau,
> Je le serais jusqu' au tombeau
> (A traveler from the cradle,
> I'll be one to the tomb).

He was born in a suburb of Constantinople (now Istanbul) in 1783 to a Grecian-born mother of German ancestry and a French father in the employ of a mercantile firm. The family moved back to Marseilles when Constantine was an infant, and there he spent much of his boyhood. In 1793 the elder Rafinesque perished of the yellow fever, which he had contracted in Philadelphia during his return from a trading expedition to China. During his absence the family had moved from France to Leghorn (Livorno) in

Italy. In 1796 the family returned to live in the Marseilles household of a grandmother, who passed away four years later. Whether from the confusion created by the French Revolution or from fraudulent treatment by their late father's business partner, Rafinesque and his two siblings never received any inheritance and had to rely on their own resources throughout their lives.

Beginning in Livorno and continuing in Marseilles, Rafinesque enjoyed a haphazard and incomplete formal education superintended by private tutors. French was his first language, though he may have learned some Greek from his mother and as a boy became fluent in Italian. While his only formal language instruction was in English, as a gifted natural linguist Rafinesque quickly mastered several other modern and ancient languages. By his own account he was a voracious reader, first of travel narratives, then of natural histories, books of philosophy, medical texts, and other subjects. As a teenager Rafinesque made a few tentative field explorations around Marseilles, sending bird and plant specimens to established French naturalists. Plans for the young man to enroll in a Swiss college fell through, and after a few years spent honing his trading skills under his mother's new husband, Rafinesque and his brother set sail for the United States in 1802.

The 18-year-old Rafinesque spent his Atlantic crossing examining new fishes, mollusks, and turtles. Arriving in Philadelphia, he made the acquaintance of the eminent Dr. Benjamin Rush, who offered to take him on as a pupil. Rafinesque's yen for exotic adventure apparently outweighed his desire for medical study, for he instead took a position with the Clifford shipping firm in expectation of someday being sent on a voyage. Over the next three years, Rafinesque's work at the Clifford's counting house was repeatedly interrupted by outbreaks of the yellow fever, which forced him to the suburbs. There he fell in with nurserymen who put him in contact with the important American botanists of the day (William Bartram, Frederick Pursh, Benjamin Smith

Barton, Gotthilf Muhlenberg, and others) and began his first systematic study of American plants. Rafinesque officially began his prolific scientific publishing career with brief descriptions of Javanese birds found in the Peale Museum sent to ornithological authorities in France. He soon also undertook a number of botanical tramps through Pennsylvania, New Jersey, Delaware, Maryland, and Virginia, broadening his focus to include birds, animals, minerals, and native American antiquities.

Convinced that opportunities for material advancement in America were few, and apparently intending to travel in Asia, Rafinesque left America for Italy and eventually Sicily, where he settled in Palermo in 1806. Over the next ten years he worked there in a number of employments, the most lucrative of which seems to have been the trade in botanical medicines, especially those derived from squills (sea onions). Most of his time, however, was devoted to scientific pursuits. Rafinesque organized and enlarged his herbarium and zoological collections, publishing descriptions of new species in European and American journals (in particular Samuel Latham Mitchill's *Medical Repository*). The natural history of the island of Sicily in all of its aspects drew his sustained attention, and he published articles and monographs on its abundant sea life (*Indice d' ittiologia siciliana*) as well as more comprehensive accounts of its flora and fauna (*Statistica generale di sicilia*). With *Specchio delle scienza*, an Italian-language *omnium gatherum* of short articles on subjects ranging from microorganisms to medicine to economics, Rafinesque inaugurated a form to which he would return on several occasions later in his career. The most important publications from this period, however, are his theoretical texts, *Principes fondamentaux de somiologie* and *Analyse de la nature*. The former, coining his term "somiology" in the sense of "biology," lays out the principles for the naming of new genera and species, which followed the natural systematics of Tournefort and de Jussieu rather than the more rigid sexual organization of

Linnaeus. The latter work represents Rafinesque's grand systematic division of the entire natural world—animal, vegetable, and mineral. In both cases he reveals himself to be at the cutting edge of natural science as it was practiced in the early nineteenth century.

In 1815 Rafinesque left his wife and daughter in Sicily and headed for New York to set up trade. The ship foundered off of Long Island, and although Rafinesque survived uninjured, all of his saleable merchandise, books, scientific manuscripts, and copperplates were lost along with 50 boxes containing his mineral, fossil, plant, and animal specimens. The catastrophic loss was compounded when Rafinesque's wife, hearing of his misfortune, ran off with a comedic actor in Sicily. Alone and penniless in New York, Rafinesque relied on his scientific acquaintances and a stint as a tutor to see him through until the insurance settlement could be made. Despite, or perhaps because of, this terrible setback, he took up his scientific pursuits with renewed zeal, joining the Academy of Natural Sciences in Philadelphia and helping to establish the Lyceum of New York. Besides writing a few scientific articles during this period, many of them sketchy descriptions of new species and genera drawn from travel accounts rather than from direct experience, Rafinesque critically reviewed the leading botanical works of the day. Though many of his criticisms were valid and even brilliant, Rafinesque developed the unfortunate habit of using his reviews to advance his own taxonomic notions, often claiming priority and proposing at length to split or rename genera or species described in the work under consideration. This did not endear him to fellow naturalists, nor was it good scientific practice to pronounce judgment on natural specimens with which he had little or no experience. The *Florula Ludoviciana*, an extensive revision and completion of an earlier work by C.C. Robin, continued this pattern and introduced chaos into American botanical nomenclature. By the early 1820s many of the major journals of science in America refused, out of a mixture of spite and genuine caution, to accept the flood of manuscripts that Rafinesque pressed upon them.

In 1818 Rafinesque took a fateful trip from Pittsburgh down the Ohio River to its confluence with the Wabash, collecting a large number of fish and mollusk species. From these collections he wrote two of his most enduring natural histories, *Ichthyologia Ohiensis* and "Monographie des coquilles bivalves fluviatiles de la rivière Ohio." It was during this trip that he met up with John James Audubon, who published a fictionalized account of Rafinesque in his *Ornithological Biography*. From 1819 to 1825 Rafinesque secured a professorship at Transylvania University in Lexington, Kentucky. There he gave popular lectures in all branches of science, worked to establish a botanical garden, and published a great deal of scientific work. Barred from the prestigious journals of New York and Philadelphia, Rafinesque turned to more accommodating journals and newspapers in Europe and Kentucky. When even these could not hold his prodigious productions, Rafinesque launched subscription journals of his own. The *Annals of Nature*, discontinued after one issue, was intended to be a forum for Rafinesque's underappreciated innovations in the taxonomy of North American plants and animals. Like the earlier *Specchio delle natura*, *The Western Minerva* was a more ambitious journal showcasing Rafinesque's output in fields ranging from poetry to politics to agriculture and medicine. Though it was printed, the journal was suppressed and never circulated. Rafinesque had begun to take an interest in native American monuments and languages, and in 1824 he began to publish a series of works on comparative native American linguistics whose methods, while crude, nevertheless anticipated later field linguists.

Rafinesque left Transylvania University in 1826 on bad terms and made his way to Philadelphia, where he intended to make a fortune from a new financial vehicle that he had created and patented. The "Divitial Invention" (from the Latin word for money) was a form of coupon based on stocks rather than bonds, and it allowed the bearer to combine the convenience of readily divisible and transferable currency with the equity appreciation of a stock. Rafinesque intended to franchise the business and collect a small commission, but because of the difficulty of calculating the value of a stock-based coupon every time it was converted, the scheme did not succeed and the naturalist temporarily sank into poverty. Much more lucrative for poor Rafinesque was the sale of Pulmel, a tuberculosis remedy whose effectiveness he touted in the self-published book *The Pulmist*. From the sale of his medicine he made enough to publish the richly illustrated *Medical Flora*, a significant textbook still consulted for botanical cures, and to get his scientific collections out of hock.

Supported now by the sales of Pulmel, Rafinesque published a number of minor botanical pieces, including a series of articles in the field of sentimental botany that appeared from 1827 to 1832 in the weekly *Saturday Evening Post* and the monthly *Casket; or Flowers of Literature, Wit, & Sentiment* under the title "The School of Flora." The articles, which present graphic and verbal descriptions of a plant and enumerate both its economic uses and "moral" significance, are the earliest American examples of the tradition of sentimental botany common in Europe. A more significant publication from this time was Rafinesque's *Atlantic Journal, and Friend of Knowledge,* another attempt to establish a journal devoted solely to his own contributions. This time the experiment lasted through six quarterly issues (1832–1833) and was mainly confined to scientific and ethnographic articles (this despite its compendious subtitle: "a Cyclopedic journal and review of Universal Science and Knowledge: historical, natural, and medical art and sciences: industry, agriculture, education, and every kind of Useful Knowledge").

By 1836 another business scheme, the Six Percent Savings Bank, had begun to pay off for Rafinesque, who used the funds to accelerate his publication schedule. Over the next four years he printed around 3,000 pages of

text on many subjects. *The American Nations* and *The Ancient Monuments of North and South America* carried on his researches into native American anthropology and linguistics. The latter included the famous *Walam Olum,* Rafinesque's translation of Lenape pictographs describing the early migrations of their tribe. Long a centerpiece in the study of native American folklore, the *Walam Olum*'s authenticity has recently been strongly disputed, though it remains unclear whether Rafinesque fabricated the text or was the victim of some other unidentified hoaxer. Also published that year was *The World, or Instability,* an unusual mixture of sentimentalism and science in a 5,400 line epic poem tracing the development of the world from the earliest times to the present day. "The great aim of this poem is to prove that *Instability* is as much a law of nature as attraction or gravitation," writes the editor (Rafinesque himself), favorably comparing what follows to Thomson's *Seasons* and Milton's *Paradise Lost*. The connection between this rumination on mutability and Rafinesque's scientific pursuits is made explicit in a footnote to the text that defines "species" as artificial groupings of varied individuals "produced by successive deviations from the original types." This clear challenge to the doctrine of single creation and the immutability of species, bolstered by similarly acute observations in the introduction to the *Flora Telluriana* (1836–1837), have led some scholars to claim that Rafinesque anticipates Darwin's more subtle and systematic evolutionary theory. Also published that year was Rafinesque's abbreviated autobiography (*A Life of Travels and Researches in North America and South Europe,* a major source for all subsequent biographies); the first segments of a multipart botanical project of enormous scope that would come to comprise the *New Flora and Botany of North America; Flora telluriana* (a survey of world botany from the sixth century BCE); *Alsographia Americana* (on trees and shrubs); *Sylva telluriana* (world trees); *American Manual of the Mulberry Trees;* and *Autikon Botanikon* (a collection of Rafinesque's woodcut botanical illustrations).

In the late 1830s Rafinesque acquired a patron, retired chemical manufacturer George Wetherill, with whom he hatched an ambitious development scheme that would transform 100 square miles of Illinois wilderness into a city (Agathopolis), four satellite towns (Industry, Honesty, Benevolence, and Tolerance), and a university. Little came of this plan, though several of Rafinesque's late works are published by the nonexistent "University of Central Illinois" and the affiliated "Eleutherium of Knowledge." The contents of these last publications range from "celestial religion" to the Hebrew Bible to moral economy. One more discontinued annual—*The Good Book, and Amenities of Nature*—rounds out Rafinesque's series of *omnium gatherum* journalistic experiments.

Rafinesque died of stomach cancer in 1840, leaving his fragile reputation in the hands of hostile botanists and bemused biographers. The former mounted a campaign to expunge his name from the records of science, ignoring the many instances where Rafinesque's descriptions were accurate and his claims valid. The latter circulated myths such as the one that, after Rafinesque died alone in an attic, his body narrowly escaped being sold to a medical school by his landlord to cover back rent. Like so much by and about Rafinesque, however, this was not the case. A great field naturalist and theoretical scientist, a paranoid and insensitive individual, the unique Rafinesque and his mixed achievements defy easy appraisal.

PRIMARY BIBLIOGRAPHY

A Note on Rafinesque Bibliography: Rafinesque presents a number of challenges to the bibliographer. The number of his published works (written in at least four languages—Italian, French, Latin, and English—and under several names) runs into the hundreds. Many of his writings, moreover, were published in several formats, often appearing as letters or articles in European or American journals and newspapers before being published—

sometimes revised, sometimes not—as books or pamphlets. These latter were frequently published in very small runs by the author himself; as a result, few or no copies survive of some works. Because Rafinesque projected many works that did not materialize, it is sometimes difficult to distinguish between what has been lost and what never existed. Below is a complete list of Rafinesque's known published books, as well as a very selective offering of his pamphlet and periodical publications. Students interested in delving more deeply into Rafinesque's bibliography are advised to consult Boewe (1982, 2001).

Books

Caratteri di alcuni nuovi generi e nuove specie d'animali e piante della sicilia, as C.S. Rafinesque Schmaltz (Palermo: Sanfilippo, 1809–1810).

Indice d' ittiologia siciliana, as Rafinesque Schmaltz (Messina: Giovanni del Nobolo, 1810).

Statistica generale di sicilia, as Rafinesque Schmaltz (Palermo: Reale Stamperia, 1810).

Specchio delle scienze, o giornale enciclopedico di Sicilia, 2 vols. (Palermo: dalla tipografia di francesco Abate Qm. Domenice, 1814).

Précis des découvertes et travaux somiologiques, as Rafinesque-Schmaltz (Palermo: Royal Military PRess,1814).

Principes fondamentaux de somiologie, as Rafinesque Schmaltz (Palermo: Franc. Abate, 1814).

Analyse de la nature (Palermo: n.p., 1815).

Circular Address on Botany and Zoology (Philadelphia: S. Merritt, 1816).

Florula Ludoviciana; or, a Flora of the State of Louisiana (New York: C. Wiley & Co., 1817).

Annals of Nature (Lexington, KY: Thomas Smith, 1820).

Icthyologia Ohiensis, or Natural History of the Fishes Inhabiting the River Ohio and its Tributary Streams (Lexington: W.G. Hunt, 1820); reprinted with substantial notes by Richard Ellsworth Call (Cleveland: Burrows Brothers Co., 1899).

Prodrome d'une monographie des rosiers de a'Amérique septentrionale, by Rafinesque and J.D. Clifford (Brussels: Weisenbruch, 1820).

Western Minerva, or American Annals of Knowledge and Literature, edited anonymously with eponymous, pseudonymous, and anonymous contributions (Lexington, KY: Thomas Smith, 1821).

Ancient History, or Annals of Kentucky; with a Survey of the Ancient Monuments of North America, and a Tabular View of the Principal Languages and Primitive Nations of the Whole Earth (Frankfort, KY: Printed for the author, 1824).

First Catalogues and Circulars of the Botanical Garden of Transylvania University of Lexington in Kentucky, anonymous (Lexington, KY: Printed for the Botanical Garden Company by John M. M'Calla, 1824).

Medical Flora; or, Manual of the Medical Botany of the United States, 2 vols. (Philadelphia: Atkinson & Alexander, 1828–1830).

The Pulmist: or, Introduction to the Art of Curing and Preventing the Consumption or Chronic Phthisis (Philadelphia: C. Alexander, 1829).

American Manual of the Grape Vines and the Art of Making Wine (Philadelphia: Printed for the author, 1830).

Atlantic Journal, and Friend of Knowledge (Philadelphia: William Sharpless, 1832–1833).

The American Nations; or, Outlines of Their General History, 2 vols. (Philadelphia: F. Turner, 1836).

A Life of Travels and Researches in North America and South Europe (Philadelphia: F. Turner, 1836); the original manuscript upon which this is based was later published as *Précis ou Abrégé des Voyages, Travaux, et Recherches de C.S. Rafinesque (1833): The Original Version of a Life of Travels (1836)*, ed. Charles Boewe, Georges Reynaud, and Beverly Seaton (Amsterdam: North-Holland Publishing Company, 1987).

The World, or Instability: A Poem in Twenty Parts (Philadelphia: J. Dobson; London: O. Rich, 1836).

Flora telluriana (Philadelphia: H. Probasco, 1836–1837).

New Flora and Botany of North America (Philadelphia: Printed for the author, 1836–1837).

Safe Banking, Including the Principles of Wealth (Philadelphia: 1837).

Alsographia Americana; or an American Grove of New or Revised Trees and Shrubs (Philadelphia: n.p., 1838).

The Ancient Monuments of North and South America (Philadelphia: Printed for the author, 1838).

Celestial Wonders and Philosophy, or The Structure of the Visible Heavens (Philadelphia: Printed for the Central University of Illinois, 1838).

Genius and Spirit of the Hebrew Bible (Philadelphia: Printed for the Eleutherium of Knowledge and Central University of Illinois, 1838).

Sylva telluriana (Philadelphia: n.p., 1838).

American Manual of the Mulberry Trees (Philadelphia: printed for the Eleutherium of Knowledge, 1839).

Autikon Botanikon (Philadelphia: n.p., 1839).

The Good Book, and Amenities of Nature, or Annals of Historical and Natural Sciences (Philadelphia: Printed for the Eleutherium of Knowledge, 1840).

The Pleasures and Duties of Wealth (Philadelphia: Printed for the Eleutherium of Knowledge, 1840).

Selected Periodicals—Uncollected

"Survey of the progress and actual state of Natural Sciences in the United States of America, from the beginning of this century to the present time," *The American Monthly Magazine and Critical Review* 2:2 (December 1817): 81–89.

"Monographie des coquilles bivalves fluviatiles de la rivière Ohio," *Annales Générales des Sciences Physiques* 5 (1820); reprinted separately (Paris: A. Franck, 1845); trans. C.A. Poulson as *A Monograph on the Fluviatile Bivalve Shells of the River Ohio* (Philadelphia: J. Dobson, 1832).

"Patent Divitial Invention," *The Saturday Evening Post* 6: 290 (February 17, 1827): 2.

Collections

Arthur Cain, *Constantine Rafinesque Schmaltz on Classification: A Translation of Early Works with Introduction and Notes* (Philadelphia: Academy of Natural Sciences, 1990).

SECONDARY BIBLIOGRAPHY

References

Charles Boewe, ed. *Profiles of Rafinesque* (Knoxville: University of Tennessee Press, 2003).

Richard Ellsworth Call, *Life and Writings of Constantine Rafinesque*, Filson Club Publication No. 10 (Louisville: J.P. Morton & Co., 1895).

Huntley Dupre, *Rafinesque in Lexington, 1819–1826* (Lexington, KY: Bur Press, 1945).

T.J. Fitzpatrick, *Rafinesque: A Sketch of His Life with Bibliography* (Des Moines, IA: The Historical Department of Iowa, 1911).

Asa Gray, "Notice of the Botanical Writings of the Late C.S. Rafinesque," *American Journal of Science* 42 (March 1841): 221–41.

S.S. Haldeman, "Notice of the Zoological Writings of the Late C.S. Rafinesque," *American Journal of Science* 42 (March 1842).

Joan Leopold, *The Prix Volney: Early Nineteenth-century Contributions to General and Amerindian Linguistics: Du Ponceau and Rafinesque* (Dordrecht, Boston: Kluwer Academic Publishers, 1999).

Elmer Merrill, *Index Rafinesquianus: the plant names published by C.S. Rafinesque with reductions, and a consideration of his methods, objectives, and attainments* (Jamaica Plain, MA: Arnold Arboretum of Harvard University, 1949).

Keir B. Sterling, ed., *Rafinesque: Autobiography and Lives* (New York: Arno Press, 1978).

Harry B. Weiss, *Rafinesque's Kentucky Friends* (Highland Park, NJ: Privately printed, 1936).

Bibliographies

Charles Boewe, *Mantissa: A Supplement to Fitpatrick's Rafinesque* (Providence: M & S Press, 2001).

Fitzpatrick's Rafinesque: A Sketch of His Life with Bibliography, revised and enlarged by Charles Boewe (Weston, MA: M & S Press, 1982).

Captain Charles Melville Scammon (May 28, 1825–May 2, 1911)

Daniel Patterson

Captain Charles M. Scammon might justifiably be called "the American Scoresby" after the British whaling captain William Scoresby, whose remarkable *An Account of the Arctic Regions* (1820) clearly served as a model and an inspiration for the account of North American cetology and the Pacific whale fishery that the American whaling captain Scammon would produce half a century after his *The Marine Mammals of the North-western Coast of North America* (1874). Scammon also, however, contributes, in his one book and in his many popular essays, to a rising literature in America that depicts the complex interaction of humans with the physical, untamed natural environment. This literature emerges historically on the East Coast in the hands of such writers as William Bartram, John D. Godman, and Susan Fenimore Cooper. Scammon marks the arrival of that literature on the West Coast.

Charles Melville Scammon was born in Pittston, Maine, on May 28, 1825. His parents were Eliakim and Joanna (Young) Scammon. His father served in the state legislature for many years representing Kennebec County. Joanna Scammon was from Pittston; her father was David Young, a wealthy veteran of the Revolutionary War. It is known that in 1812 the Scammons were farmers in neighboring Whitefield, Maine. His brother Jonathan Young Scammon attended Whitefield College (now Colby College), and his brother Eliakim Parker Scammon attended West Point; Charles Melville, however, was attracted to a life at sea, and he left his family home in Pittston when he was 17 and began his nautical career. When he was 23, he married Susan C. Norris, who would distinguish herself from most nautical wives by joining her husband on many of his voyages. In the same year, 1848, Scammon received his first command out of Bath, Maine; he spent two years with the schooner *Phoenix* trading between Maine and the Carolinas. At this time news and dubious reports from California were firing the imaginations of adventurous Americans in the East, and the young couple appear to have been affected by this. In August 1849, with the 24-year-old Charles in command of the merchant bark *Sarah Moers*, the Scammons departed from Bath to make the long and dangerous voyage around the Horn. They arrived in San Francisco Bay on February 21, 1850. No doubt assisted in many ways by his wife, Scammon began what would be his life's work.

After two years on the California coast, Scammon made a change from merchant captain to whaling captain. In the preface to his major work, *The Marine Mammals of the North-western Coast of North America* (1874), he alludes cryptically to what seems to have been insufficient berths for merchant captains:

> Being on the coast of California in 1852, when the "gold-fever" raged, the force of circumstances compelled me to take command of a brig, bound on a sealing, sea-elephant, and whaling voyage, or abandon sea-life, at least temporarily.

His new command, the brig *Mary Helen*, of 160 tons, departed from San Francisco on April 1, 1852. On August 29, the *Mary Helen* returned with a cargo of 350 barrels of elephant seal oil. It is evident that between this time and 1869, when Scammon began his period of steady publication in the *Overland Monthly*, he kept copious, detailed records of his measurements of the various marine species, kept extensive journals of his travels and whaling, and made many drawings of animals and seascapes. He would draw upon all of these for his essays in the *Overland Monthly* and for his *Marine Mammals*.

Scammon's career as a whaling captain spans from April 1, 1852, to March 21, 1863. During this period, he commanded six different vessels and, in his pursuits of gray and sperm whales, elephant seals, sea lions, and sea otters, he sailed frequently along Mexico's Baja Peninsula, where he introduced whaling to what became known in the 1850s as Scammon's Lagoon. Scammon was the first whaling captain to manage the tricky crossing of the bar at the mouth of the lagoon and in the shallow protected waters there found the calving grounds of the California gray whale. In addition to killing many of them, Scammon was also able to observe the behavior of the species at length. He also pursued his quarry northward, following the coasts of the Northwest to Alaska and the Aleutian Islands, and westward from

there across the Bering Sea to the Kamchatka Peninsula and the Sea of Okhotsk, where he observed, while in pursuit of bowhead whales, the summer destination of the gray whales. Over the course of this commercial voyaging, his abilities as a naturalist evolved with his deepening knowledge of the mammal species he hunted. In his drawings and in his written representations of the animals, he incorporated his carefully recorded measurements of dead individuals as well as his vivid memory of their living behavior.

His opportunities to study the marine mammals continued beyond his career as a whaling captain. Between the spring of 1863 and the winter of 1865, Scammon sailed the seas along the northwest coast in command of the United States Revenue Cutter *Shubrick* for the U.S. Revenue Marine (which would later be incorporated into the U.S. Coast Guard). For two years following this command, he sailed in more northern and western waters as Chief of Marine for the Western Union Telegraph Company, which was attempting to establish a telegraph link between the United States and Europe by way of the Bering Strait, Siberia, and Saint Petersburg. During this time he also met the young explorer and naturalist William Healy Dall (1845–1927), among other scientists, who probably contributed to Scammon's emerging sense of his own possibilities as a naturalist. He had amassed an extensive collection of journals and drawings by this time, which the other naturalists would undoubtedly have found exciting. No one else was in a position to convey so much information about the marine mammals of the nation's northwestern coasts.

In 1867, Scammon resumed his command of U.S. Revenue Marine vessels. For a brief time in the same year, however, he seems to have accompanied J. Ross Browne as a passenger on a voyage from Magdalena Bay on the Baja Peninsula to assist Browne in his preparation of a report for the Lower California Company. Scammon's contribution to Browne's *A Sketch of the Settlement and Exploration of Lower California* (1869) comprises his first publication. He would shortly thereafter develop his descriptive accounts of the lagoons and coasts of the Baja Peninsula into popular articles for the *Overland Monthly and Out West Magazine* and thus begin his career as a naturalist author writing for a general readership. His period of greatest literary productivity begins with this publication and does not slow until a year after the publication of his *Marine Mammals*, that is, until the end of 1875.

In November 1869, Scammon began to publish his essays in the *Overland Monthly and Out West Magazine.* Under the editorship of Bret Harte, the *Overland Monthly* began publication in July 1868, a few months before the completion of the Transcontinental Railroad brought a new dimension of promise to the West generally and to San Francisco in particular, and this new magazine instantly became the region's most important literary and cultural publication. Harte and his readers clearly approved of Scammon's descriptive and narrative essays about marine mammal species and the variety of human cultures along the northwest coast; Scammon was by far the most frequent contributor throughout Harte's two and a half years as editor, which concluded approximately with the February 1871 issue, in which Scammon's tenth essay appeared; several of these essays would be incorporated almost unchanged into his 1874 *Marine Mammals.* It should be noted that the publisher of the *Overland Monthly*, John H. Carmany and Company, also published Scammon's *Marine Mammals.*

Between July 1871 and October 1874, Scammon published serially his "Pacific Sea-Coast Views," parts 1–4. Considered as a whole, this work is quite remarkable among all his literary production, for it provides a sustained description of the Pacific coast and its offings from the Islas Diego Ramirez, the southernmost point of the Americas some 100 kilometers south of Tierra del Fuego, to the Bella Coola River north of Vancouver Island in British Columbia. Scammon was always a superior descriptive writer, but some of his most vivid and coherently dynamic scenes occur in this four-part essay. The

following passage serves to illustrate this commercial whaling captain's skills as a descriptive writer. The dramatic use of light, sounds, and actions in this account of a storm off the coast of Chile—from the shouts of boatmen in the "blinding darkness" to the oppressive crashing of waves on the coast, with the "lurid light" of erupting Aconcagua over a hundred miles distant in the Argentine Andes and nearly 23,000 feet above the ocean, and with the bay about them a "waving sheet of phosphorescent foam"—indicated to Bret Harte and the readers of the *Overland Monthly* the emergence of an accomplished word painter:

> It was a dismal winter evening, in 1851, that we were off the roadstead, anxiously working our ship, with every favoring wind-flaw, toward the anchorage. A heavy swell was heaving in, and the high rollers, beating upon the bold coast, resounded oppressively as the fitful land-breeze filled the light, lofty sails; while the far-off volcanic peak of Aconcagua flashed its lurid light, as if boding disaster. Slowly we coursed along till the signal-lights of the shipping were seen, and the shouts and calls of the boatmen were distinctly heard, as they groped among the numerous fleet in the blinding darkness. We could hear, too, the seamen working with hurry and bustle to secure their ships against the impending storm; for a norther was close upon us. Day dawned, however, before our vessel swung to her anchors; night came again, and with it the gale burst in all its fury. The sea soon arose to a fearful height, and nothing could be heard but the howling of the blast through the rigging, and the washing of the spray over the bow of the ship. Night came again, but the gale was still raging; the whole bay seemed one waving sheet of phosphorescent foam, while ship after ship dragged its anchors and came in collision with some other.

Between November 1869 and December 1875, Scammon published 21 of his descriptive and narrative essays in the *Overland Monthly*, essays in which he treated variously, but always with an engaging intelligence and vivid, dramatic description, the lives of whalemen and sealers, the history and economics of whaling, the cultures of several indigenous peoples, and the natural history of the marine mammals most of his readers knew of only from the oil in the lamps they read by or the bone in their corsets. Scammon's *The Marine Mammals of the North-western Coast of North America* is the culmination of some 26 years at sea and some five years as a writer of the Pacific coast.

In the preface to *Marine Mammals*, Scammon explains the unique position he found himself in shortly after his arrival on the Pacific coast. First of all, he found "great numbers" of all species, and "the opportunities for studying their habits were so good, that I became greatly interested in collecting facts bearing upon the natural history of these animals." He also recognized that his unique position presented a unique opportunity:

> I was the more encouraged to pursue these investigations, because, among the great number of intelligent men in command of whaling-ships, there was no one who had contributed anything of importance to the natural history of the Cetaceans; while it was obvious that the opportunities offered for the study of their habits, to those practically engaged in the business of whaling, were greater than could possibly be enjoyed by persons not thus employed.

Since he knew, admired, and relied upon the contributions to cetology by the British whaling captain William Scoresby, his suggestion that no "intelligent men in command of whaling-ships" had contributed to that branch of zoology suggests that he refers strictly to American captains; thus, in his preface, Scammon prepares the way for his becoming his nation's leading writer on marine mammals, their behavior, and the human hunting of them. He also stresses the difficulty of observing marine mammals: "My own experience has proved that close observation for months, and even years, may be required before a single new fact in regard to their habits can be obtained." He assures his readers, however, that his illustrations and written representations of the animals and their habits are extremely accurate

because of the many years he has observed them at sea, both living and dead.

A recurring motif in American nature writing is the look back on the previously much greater populations of animal species. Scammon regularly includes accounts of the declining populations of marine mammals, thereby bringing these more elusive creatures into the American literature of biologic loss. Where other authors conjured in the minds of readers the formerly vast populations of passenger pigeons, American bison, and Carolina parakeets, Scammon writes of, among other species, the California gray whale herds when the California whale fishery opened 23 years earlier:

> It has been estimated, approximately, by observing men among the shore-whaling parties, that a thousand whales passed southward daily, from the 15th of December to the 1st of February, for several successive seasons after shore-whaling was established, which occurred in 1851.

Without emotion or explicit caveat, Scammon observes, "at the present time the average number seen from the stations passing daily would not exceed forty." More pass than can be observed, he notes, and he estimates that currently "there are probably between 100 and 200 whales going southward daily."

He pairs matter-of-fact accounts of killing the whales with accumulating evidence of their intelligence. The following passage illustrates the passionless description of a typical kill:

> As soon as the boat is fast, the officer goes into the head, and watches a favorable opportunity to shoot a bomb-lance. Should this enter a vital part and explode, it kills instantly, but it is not often this good luck occurs; more frequently two or three bombs are shot, which paralyze the animal to some extent, when the boat is hauled near enough to use the hand-lance. After repeated thrusts, the whale becomes sluggish in its motions; then, going "close to," the hand-lance is set into its "life," which completes the capture. The animal rolls

over on its side, with fins extended, and dies without a struggle.

Scammon's representation of whale intelligence is certainly not intended to evoke compassion for the animals, but rather to enhance the drama of the hunt. Because the gray whales alter their behavior in order to avoid being killed, the whalers find that they have to adopt new hunting and capturing techniques with some regularity. A significant portion of Scammon's treatment of the gray whale is a history of those adaptations. The humans, for example, devised a technique of ambushing whales by waiting in a chase boat atop a kelp bed for whales to pass out of a lagoon, but after the second season of employing this method, "the sagacious creatures" "soon found what would be the consequence of getting too near the long, dark-looking object, as it lay motionless" and successfully avoided such ambushes. Scammon infuses his story of California whaling with the craft and wariness, the ploy and evasion, of hunter and prey.

Scammon frequently brings the animals alive for his readers by portraying, often in quite charming terms, the memorable behavior of an individual he observed. In his account of the gray whale's surprising tendency to spend time in shallow water, Scammon narrates the playful behavior of one whale, revealing about himself that he observed it for fully half an hour; he describes this particular California gray as:

> turning from side to side with half-extended fins, and moved apparently by the heavy ground-swell which was breaking; at times making a playful spring with its bending flukes, throwing its body clear of the water, coming down with a heavy splash, then making two or three spouts, and again settling under water; perhaps the next moment its head would appear, and with the heavy swell the animal would roll over in a listless manner, to all appearance enjoying the sport intensely.

It is not surprising that a whaling captain would frequently describe a whale or other marine mammal strictly in terms of the number of barrels of oil it "yielded," as this captain often does, but Scammon's sensibility runs deeper than such appropriating commodification, and his representations of whales and other species often include evidence that they are conscious, that they "enjoy" their lives.

Many of the observations included in *Marine Mammals* give insights into both whaling lore and whale behavior. He lists the various names sailors have given the gray whale ("Hard-head," "Mussel-digger," "Devil-fish," "Gray-back," and "Rip-sack") as a means of helping his readers imagine the living animals responding to their environment. He explains "Hard-head," for example, with a comparison his readers would be familiar with:

> The first-mentioned misnomer arose from the fact of the animals having a great propensity to root the boats when coming in contact with them, in the same manner that hogs upset their empty troughs.

Part of his work as a writer is to evoke wonder and admiration. In this passage on the "sulphur-bottom," or blue whale, the rhetoric of magnitude seems designed to inspire awe:

> It glides over the surface of the ocean, occasionally displaying its entire length. When it respires, the volume of its vaporous breath ascends to a height which reveals at once, to the observer, the presence of that leviathan of the deep, whose capture baffles the practical skill of the most experienced whalers. When "rounding" to descend to the depths below, it throws its ponderous flukes high above the waves, with a swoop that is well in keeping with its matchless strength and vigor.

In his discussion of the sperm whale, Scammon weaves into his account of their observed behavior the well-known reports of various ships that have been damaged or sunk "by the deliberate assaults of vicious, gray-headed, old Cachalots" (the French term for sperm whale). More so than with any other species, Scammon develops the sperm whale's legendary presence in human culture. After briefly relaying the stories of several ships destroyed by sperm whales, Scammon leaves his readers with this rather gothic suggestion: "And we have no doubt but that many vessels which have sailed from port, and never been heard of after, have suffered wreck through Cachalots."

There is in Scammon's work a call for restraint and conservation, but it is subtle, only rarely explicit. He speaks with the voice of a whaling captain, which lends his observations and natural history credibility, but it also makes him complicit in the commodification of the "monsters of the deep" he clearly admired. He describes the various methods of killing the gray whale, and he narrates the deaths of several individuals in considerable detail—all without exploiting the clear potential for a rhetoric of pathos. Nevertheless, his concern for the survival of the species emerges in the gradual accumulation of references to the possible extinction of gray whales in the final pages of his essay on that species. In his description of their annual migrations up and down the length of North and Central America, he emphasizes the fact that humans in all latitudes, including the "civilized whalemen" and the "savage," are hunting the species—despite its innate "sagacity"—out of existence. More than any other marine mammal, the gray whale is "constantly and variously pursued." He closes his essay on the gray whale with the following chilling, foreboding image:

> The mammoth bones of the California Gray lie bleaching on the shores of those silvery waters, and are scattered along the broken coasts, from Siberia to the Gulf of California; and ere long it may be questioned whether this mammal will not be numbered among the extinct species of the Pacific.

Scammon thus makes his call for restraint implicitly. Nature writing is indeed a subversive genre, as Thomas J. Lyon has written. Perhaps because of the great dependence of his readers on the products and wealth resulting from the whaling industry and because of

his own complicity in the reduction of the gray whale populations himself, Scammon saw that his text, if it were to encourage the conservation of marine mammal species, would have to be quietly subversive.

Among the several other species whose population decline Scammon notes is the sea lion:

> The vast herds of these marine animals, to the far north and south, do not materially diminish, as they are hunted by the natives solely for domestic consumption; but those on our California shores will soon be exterminated by the deadly shot of the rifle, or driven away to less accessible haunts.

Such testimony to population declines constitutes a recurring motif in the first important American study of marine mammals.

Occasionally Scammon sheds light on a sinister or pernicious economic mechanism, whereby the depletion of one species drives humans employed in the marine mammal fishery to seek out other species formerly less desirable, and whereby one human culture endangers another. In the conclusion to his essay on the walrus, for example, he explains that mechanism in a tone of lamentation that is more overt than his usual seeming neutrality:

> Among the numerous enemies of the Walrus, it is to be regretted that the whalers are included, they having been driven to the necessity of pursuing them on account of the scarcity of Cetaceans. Already the animals have suffered so great a slaughter at their hands that their numbers have been materially diminished, and they have become wild and shy, making it difficult for the Esquimaux to successfully hunt them, in order to obtain a necessary supply of food. It is stated that there has been much suffering among those harmless people of the far north, on account of this source for supplying themselves with an indispensable article of sustenance being to an alarming extent cut off.

Here a writer who was himself a whaler regrets the perhaps inevitable consequences of the industry that brought him to his most satisfying engagement in the world, his life's work as a whaler and as a writer of both whalemen and the cetaceans they preyed upon.

In this light, Scammon can be seen to occupy an interesting place in the history of American nature writing. The consequences to the biosphere of unrestrained human exploitation of "natural resources" were becoming ever more apparent in the mid-nineteenth century. George Perkins Marsh's scholarly environmental jeremiad, *Man and Nature: Or, Physical Geography as Modified by Human Action* (New York: Charles Scribner, 1864), was published just ten years before Scammon's *Marine Mammals*. David Lowenthal has described Marsh's work as "the first book to controvert the myth of superabundance and to spell out the need to reform." Marsh reports that whales have "now almost wholly disappeared from many favorite fishing grounds, and in others [are] greatly diminished in numbers." Marsh also reports that the American whaling fleet has been reduced in size over the past "few years" "from more than six hundred whaling ships" to a present count of 353. Thus Scammon's entire career as a whaling captain occurs at a time of the steady reduction of the whaling fleet. Though he himself was successful, he was increasingly aware of the consequences of overhunting, and in his new role as an author who represented the physical environment that all life is dependent upon, he—even an agent of that overhunting—began to speak for restraint. But what emerges over the 300 or so pages is a clear and undeniable fact: practically all of these species are in dramatic, documented decline. In many branches of the natural sciences, the same phenomenon was occurring, and from approximately this time onward, the call for conservation and restraint became one of the most important themes in American nature writing. One has the sense, however, that Scammon himself did not reach this level of urgency and move then to a more overt lamentation until he had written the bulk of his essays.

He exercises a deceptive neutrality in his frequent testimonies to the causes of the massive killings. After describing the notorious method of clubbing fur seals to death by the thousands in their rookeries, Scammon observes:

> As soon as the killing was over, the flaying commenced. Some sealers became great experts in skinning the animals; and the number of skins one would take off in the course of an hour would be a decidedly fishy story to tell. However, to flay fifty seals in a day would be regarded as good work. It will be readily seen that a sealing-ship's crew, numbering twenty or more, would make great havoc among a seal rookery in very short time; and it is no matter of surprise that these valuable fur-bearing animals soon became comparatively scarce.

By bearing apparently disinterested witness to the effects of human excesses, Scammon in essay after essay subtly cautions members of his own species to find ways to reduce their destructive effects on the species of marine mammals.

Following the publication of *Marine Mammals* and his next four essays in the *Overland Monthly*, Scammon published very little. In 1874, Scammon went on "sick leave" and did not command a vessel until 1880, when he began a three-year stint of active duty for the U.S. Revenue Marine, during which he sailed along the coasts of the Gulf of Mexico and developed malaria; from 1883 until his death in 1911, he was listed as inactive in the Revenue Marine for a while, then as retired. From 1883 until 1890, he lived on a farm north of San Francisco in the rural settlement of Sebastopol. In 1890 he moved to what is now East Oakland. By 1908 he was the senior-most officer in the U.S. Revenue Marine and was given the rank of Senior Captain. He was 86 when he died in 1911.

Scammon bears witness to an age of rapid and extensive declines in the populations of practically all the marine mammal species he includes; in fact, it is evident that any species that is included has commercial value.

Eighteen years after he published *Marine Mammals,* for example, no more than 20 elephant seals were known to exist. And in 1911, the year of Scammon's death, an international treaty forbade the killing of sea otters, but it was already feared that the species had been eradicated. None had been seen in California for several decades when, in 1938, a number of otters were observed in the ocean near Carmel. In his writings, Scammon represents, even enacts, the awakening of one of the most biologically destructive of all the human industries, the whaling industry, significantly memorialized in "the great American novel," *Moby-Dick.* Scammon was a whaler himself, and he understood absolutely the great physical courage and the ability to endure and survive some of the harshest conditions the planet can present humans with. Accordingly, there is a clear cord of heroism in his representation of his own profession. There is, however, also the dawning of an awareness, as there was in the nation at large, that Americans were being more destructive to other species than they had been previously aware. This is an awareness that had to develop over time, and it is this awakening environmental ethic that is enacted by the voice of America's most accomplished nineteenth-century cetologist.

PRIMARY BIBLIOGRAPHY

Books

The Marine Mammals of the North-western Coast of North America Described and Illustrated: Together with an Account of the American Whale-Fishery (San Francisco: John H. Carmany and Company; New York: G.P. Putnam's Sons, 1874; facsimile edition, New York: Dover Publications, Inc., 1968; facsimile edition, introduction by Campbell Grant, Riverside, California: Manessier Publication Company, 1969).

Journal Aboard the Bark Ocean Bird *on a Whaling Voyage to Scammon's Lagoon, Winter of 1858–1859,* edited and annotated by David A. Henderson (Los Angeles: Dawson's Book Shop, 1970).

Other

"Report of Captain C.M. Scammon, of the U.S. Revenue service, on the west coast of Lower California," in J. Ross Brown's *A Sketch of the Settlement and Exploration of Lower California* (San Francisco: H.H. Bancroft, 1869); also issued as Part 2 of J. Ross Brown's *Resources of the Pacific Slope* (New York: D. Appleton and Company, 1869), 123–31.

Selected Periodical Publications—Uncollected

"On the Cetaceans of the Western Coast of North America," ed. Edward D. Cope, *Proceedings of the Academy of Natural Sciences of Philadelphia* 21 (April 1869): 13–63.

"Fur Seals," *Overland Monthly and Out West Magazine* 3.5 (November 1869): 393–99.

"In and Around Astoria," *Overland Monthly and Out West Magazine* 3.6 (December 1869): 495–99.

"The Sea Otters," *The American Naturalist* 4 (1870): 65–74.

"Sea-Otters," *Overland Monthly and Out West Magazine* 4.1 (January 1870): 25–30.

"Sea-Elephant Hunting," *Overland Monthly and Out West Magazine* 4.2 (February 1870): 112–17.

"On the Lower California Coast," *Overland Monthly and Out West Magazine* 4.3 (March 1870): 230–38.

"The Pacific Coast Cod-Fishery," *Overland Monthly and Out West Magazine* 4.5 (May 1870): 436–40.

"Lumbering in Washington Territory," *Overland Monthly and Out West Magazine* 5.1 (July 1870): 55–60.

"Seal Islands of Alaska," *Overland Monthly and Out West Magazine* 5.4 (October 1870): 297–301.

"The Aleutian Islands," *Overland Monthly and Out West Magazine* 5.5 (November 1870): 438–43.

"Coast Whaling," *Overland Monthly and Out West Magazine* 6.2 (February 1871): 118–25.

"Northern Whaling," *Overland Monthly and Out West Magazine* 6.6 (June 1871): 548–54.

"Pacific Sea-Coast Views," *Overland Monthly and Out West Magazine* 7.1 (July 1871): 76–84.

"About the Shores of Puget Sound," *Overland Monthly and Out West Magazine* 7.3 (September 1871): 277–86.

"Pacific Sea-Coast Views, No. II," *Overland Monthly and Out West Magazine* 7.5 (November 1871): 393–98.

"Pacific Sea-Coast Views, No. III," *Overland Monthly and Out West Magazine* 8.3 (March 1872): 245–52.

"About Sea-Lions," *Overland Monthly and Out West Magazine* 8.3 (March 1872): 266–72.

"The Orca," *Overland Monthly and Out West Magazine* 9.1 (July 1872): 52–57.

"Pacific Sea-Coast Views, No. IV," *Overland Monthly and Out West Magazine* 13.4 (October 1874): 371–77.

"Pioneer Nig Saul," *Overland Monthly and Out West Magazine* 14.3 (March 1875): 273–76.

"Beacons at the Golden Gate," *Overland Monthly and Out West Magazine* 15.1 (July 1875): 54–57.

"A Russian Boat-Voyage," *Overland Monthly and Out West Magazine* 15.6 (December 1875): 554–57.

"The Sea-Cow," *Overland Monthly and Out West Magazine* 14.84 (December 1889): 581–85.

"About the Stikine," *Overland Monthly and Out West Magazine* 15.87 (March 1890): 253–56.

"About the Stikine: How a Squaw Saved Her Husband," *Overland Monthly and Out West Magazine* 32.187 (July 1898): 24–26.

"On Watch," *Overland Monthly and Out West Magazine* 43.6 (June 1904): 516.

SECONDARY BIBLIOGRAPHY

References

David A. Henderson, *Men and Whales at Scammon's Lagoon* (Los Angeles: Dawson's Book Shop, 1972).

David Lowenthal, "Introduction," in *Man and Nature*, by George Perkins Marsh (Cambridge: Harvard University Press, 1965), ix–xxix.

George Perkins Marsh, *Man and Nature: Or, Physical Geography as Modified by Human Action*, ed. David Lowenthal (Cambridge: Harvard University Press, 1965).

Victor B. Scheffer, Introduction to Charles M. Scammon's *The Marine Mammals of the Northwestern Coast of North America* (New York: Dover Publications, Inc., 1968), v–x.

William Scoresby, *An Account of the Arctic Regions, with a History and Description of the Northern Whale-Fishery*, 2 vols. (Edinburgh: Archibald Constable and Company; London: Hurst, Robinson and Company, 1820).

Alexander Starbuck, *History of the American Whale Fishery from Its Earliest Inception to the Year 1876* (Waltham, MA: The Author, 1878; reprinted, 2 vols.; New York: Argosy-Antiquarian, 1964).

Papers

The Bancroft Library at the University of California at Berkeley houses "The Papers and Correspondence of Charles Melville Scammon."

Henry Rowe Schoolcraft
(March 28, 1793–December 10, 1864)

Donald M. Hassler

In modern views of literary scholars and historians, Henry Rowe Schoolcraft as writer seems at times to resemble the great natural shape-shifters personified in the Algic folktales and legends that he collected and commented on when he worked as Indian Agent in the Michigan Territory. He reinvented and changed himself as an American writer several times from 1818 until his death in the final year of the Civil War. A vital and evolving discussion emerged about how to read Schoolcraft's massive output of work so that in the later nineteenth century he was viewed, in part, as a writer of children's fairy stories until now, in recent decades, his work has come to be seen as seminal both to modern ethnographic research and to the history of American writers attempting to find a voice as Americans. Like the Northwest Territories themselves, his work was always both on the fringe as well as characteristic of a sort of Emersonian self-reliance and stubbornness in the effort to define his own voice. His was a quest of an American scholar, and he was continually conflicted as a writer. His material was distinctly American; and his shape-shifting was as insecure, suspect, and as immensely fertile as the rest of the expanding nation in the early nineteenth century. A century after his death, scholars began to identify and to describe these qualities in what Schoolcraft wrote about the Northwest Territories, especially the Lake Superior region and northern Minnesota and the shifting populations of natives that explorers found there, interacted with, and eventually remade for their own purposes.

Schoolcraft's roots, however, were in the East. He had the rudiments of a classical education in his hometown of Hamilton, New York, in preparation for entering Union College. But he had to go to work instead. Later, he did attend Middlebury College briefly and published poetry as a young man. Whenever he traveled in the West, he tried to purchase books through agents in Detroit and to maintain his book collection. A dissertation on his writing done nearly 200 years after his birth finds, "Books were a part of his life in which he never lost interest even when he moved to the frontier." Also, he used his language and classical studies to highlight some of his best investigative work and ideas. Finally, he returned east in the last two decades of his life to compete vigorously and, for the most part, unsuccessfully in the literary marketplaces of New York and Philadelphia and in the battle for patronage support from the federal government.

But Schoolcraft's classical studies initially were superseded by science, or natural history, and his father's successful glass-making business in upstate New York prompted him to combine studies in mining, geology, and business. He was not successful at business, however, and went West to make use of his knowledge of geology and mining. Indeed, his first publications about mines and geology in the Missouri Territory made him well enough known as a person "acquainted with zoology, botany, and mineralogy" that General Lewis Cass hired him to join his 1819 expedition along the southern shores of Lake Superior in search of mineral resources and to study the native populations. The patron in Washington for this first expedition was John C. Calhoun, and both Schoolcraft's lifelong friendship with Cass and his continual soliciting of the brilliant Calhoun were key influences on the way Schoolcraft operated for the rest of his life. He wrote the campaign biography (apparently he enjoyed writing anything) for the Cass bid for the presidency in 1848. And just as Cass was defeated by the Free Soil movement so Schoolcraft could never shed his allegiance to Democrat principles, originally enthused about the Frontier but soon to be mired in the slave question, and to some of the Calhoun principles about the States. His second wife was a slave owner, and he eventually supported the South in the war. But the major influence on Schoolcraft that derived from his decision to go West and then to join the first Cass expedition into the North came from his meeting the Irish fur trader John Johnston of the Sault and marrying Jane Johnston, who was the daughter of John and a full-blooded Chippewa princess. General Cass had also appointed Schoolcraft Indian Agent for the northern parts of the Territory. So during the 1820s and 1830s, until his wife's death, Schoolcraft made his home at the Sault, or at the Mackinaw straits 40 miles south, and began to collect ideas and literary materials from his numerous native American in-laws and friends.

In his "Preliminary Observations," part of the prefatory material, to his important two-volume work of 1839, Schoolcraft theorizes about why native American "savages" had not before been studied and appreciated as real people. Not only had they threatened all American settlers in what seemed like continual warfare (and as a young man he had heard much about such savagery in upstate New York), but also they had been treated too much as commercial objects in fur trade and land trade. Schoolcraft writes, "This view results from an attentive examination of the earlier voyages and histories of adventure in this hemisphere in which is exhibited the coldest air of mercantile calculation." To correct this cold view, Schoolcraft embarks on a lifelong study of language and culture, rooted in his Chippewa family and then branching to related tribes, in an attempt to categorize the network of Indian nations that had been found from where he was living in the West to the Atlantic in the East. He also had become a strong Christian by this time and so viewed the Indians as fallen and in need of salvation. But mainly he saw them as rounded people and not just as commercial or labor markers.

Schoolcraft the writer, however, can be seen fully operating alongside his seminal work as ethnographic investigator and even as geographic explorer. A later expedition in the big canoes west that took place in 1832, with the blessing of Governor Cass of the Territory, moved from the Sault westward and resulted in Schoolcraft's key discovery of the source of the Mississippi at Lake Itasca in Minnesota. Schoolcraft renamed the lake from earlier "mooselike" names that the trappers had used, and when he did so he used his Latin training: as Philip Mason explains, "... he took the name from the Latin words 'veritas caput.'" The Latin means "true head," and what is fascinating is the Schoolcraft habit of chopping a few letters from the body of a phrase to coin a new word. He did something very similar with language in his Indian studies when he attempts to categorize the related tribes that he finds linked by language and storytelling: according to Curtis Hinsley, "In 1832 he founded the Algic Society—the first use of his neologism that combined 'Algonquin' and 'Atlantic.'" Further, when he writes about his most famous story character, Manabozho, who becomes Longfellow's

Hiawatha, the tone of slight irony he uses resounds with the literary training that permits Schoolcraft the distinct sensibility to appreciate what he has uncovered in his investigations and yet to show a writer's voice, and a Christian voice, of interpretation: "...as Manabozho exercises powers and performs exploits wild or wonderful, the chain of narration which connects them is broken or vague. He leaps over extensive regions of country like an ignis fatuus." Thus, a somewhat ironic and detached rational voice emerges in the mass of Algic materials that were originally published by Schoolcraft the Indian Agent. This voice has classical echoes as well as echoes from the investigators of the Enlightenment whom Schoolcraft must have included among his collections of books. Again, from the Algic researches prefatory material, he sounds almost like an eighteenth-century numismatic collector of Roman coins: "Words are like coins, and may, like them be examined to illustrate history." He recorded many of these words from his Johnston extended family, but he also coined them (and "Englished" them) as though he were chopping up Latin. Hence, in addition to his large label "Algic," which he coined, other labels for parts of the network of tribes spanning the eastern half of the continent spice up his narratives: "Ostic" for one group, "Abanic" for another. Schoolcraft claims to have Englished these labels from native words. He was a working linguist in the field, and he had family to work with in these studies.

More than numismatic coinages and eighteenth-century wit, however, it is the interest in detail and the sense of actually being there as ethnographic explorer and geographic explorer that seems to have warranted the revived interest in Schoolcraft's text. In particular, his narrative of the 1832 expedition to Lake Itasca is packed with information about the big canoes, about food supplies, about costs, and even about native American interpreters. One of the interpreters was Schoolcraft's own brother-in-law, and it is fascinating to modern scholars that in the 1832 publication he is not identified by Schoolcraft as a member of his family, but in the 1850s when Schoolcraft repackaged some of this travel narrative material back east, the Johnston family connections were spoken of more openly by him. On the ground and doing his ethnographic and exploring work, Schoolcraft, like his mentor Cass, may have intended to use data in order to remove the Indians, or at least to convert them. Later, his writings become both more objectively scientific (the Iroquois notes are considered by scholars the most complete in terms of useful data) and more writerly. The raw travel narratives, however, with their details of logistics and "being there" read a bit like accounts from explorers of the Antarctic written 80 years later. Captain Scott had no natives to convert, but he did carry with him copies of Browning's poems.

Finally, in his literary work, Schoolcraft's great nemesis was Henry Wadsworth Longfellow so that in the last two decades of his life while he was gathering together immense amounts of data and publishing it in many volumes, some with government subvention that he had to petition vigorously to get, he also repackaged both original travel writing and Hiawatha writing in an attempt to capitalize on the famous Longfellow poem of 1855. They were not ungenerous to one another. Longfellow fully acknowledged his debt to Algic research, and Schoolcraft praised the poem. But Schoolcraft's writing was never popular and commercially successful. After his death, some of it was repackaged again for children's reading. But the key contrast seems to have been between the ability of the Harvard professor to construct a classic epic poem that pointed toward the Finns and other roots in Europe, on the one hand, and, on the other, the massive investigations and genre-searching work of the former Indian Agent that pointed West.

At the end of his career some of Schoolcraft's large volumes were reviewed with some disdain. Critics were worried about the government expense. His statistical work on the Iroquois, however, probably enjoyed the highest esteem among his contemporary pioneers in ethnography. Also, he did become a close friend of Joseph Henry, the first secretary of the Smithsonian, so that he did influence early policies about collecting ethnographic materials. But as a writer, he seemed continually in search of an audience. Back in New York, he briefly changed his name to "Colcraft" after studying his own family genealogy. Since the 1950s, however, the reach for identity seems to be over. Michigan State University Press has a publishing project to produce well-edited new versions of the Schoolcraft work, and important articles and dissertations are appearing from literary scholars and historians. Schoolcraft is seen now as a pioneer in ethnography but also as an interesting writer of the Northwest. He died in Washington, D.C., just a few months before Lincoln was shot, probably as conflicted as ever about what would become of his writing.

PRIMARY BIBLIOGRAPHY

Books

A View of the Lead Mines of Missouri (New York: Charles Wiley & Co., 1819).

Journal of a Tour into the Interior of Missouri and Arkansaw, from Potosi, or Mine a Burton, in Missouri Territory, in a South-West Direction, Toward The Rocky Mountains: Performed in the Years 1818 and 1819 (London: Sir R. Phillips and Co., 1821).

Narrative Journal of Travels from Detroit Northwest, through the Great Chain of Lakes to the Sources of the Mississippi River in the Year 1820 (Albany: E.E. Hosford, 1821).

Travels in the Central Portions of the Mississippi Valley (New York: Collins and Hannay, 1825).

Narrative of an Expedition Through the Upper Mississippi to Itasca Lake, Performed in 1832 (New York: Harper & Brothers, 1834).

Algic Researches, Comprising Inquiries Respecting the Mental Characteristics of the North American Indians, 2 vols. (New York: Harper & Brothers, 1839).

Oneota, or the Red Race of America, 8 parts (New York: Burgess Stringer, 1844–1845).

Notes on the Iroquois (Albany: Erastus Pease & Co., 1847).

Outlines of the Life and Character of Gen. Lewis Cass (Albany: Joel Munsell, 1848).

Historical and Statistical Information Respecting the History, Conditions, and Prospects of the Indian Tribes of the United States, 6 vols. (Philadelphia: Lippincott, Grambo & Co., 1851–1857).

Personal Memoirs of a Residence of Thirty Years with the Indian Tribes on the American Frontier (Philadelphia: Lippincott, Grambo & Co., 1851).

Western Scenes and Reminiscences: Together with Thrilling Legends and Traditions of the Red Men of the Forest (New York: Burgess Stringer, 1853).

Summary Narrative of an Exploratory Expedition to the Sources of the Mississippi River in 1820 (Philadelphia: Lippincott, Grambo & Co., 1855).

The Myth of Hiawatha and Other Legends, Mythological and Allegoric of the North American Indian (Philadelphia: Lippincott, Grambo & Co., and London: Trubner & Co., 1856).

Other—Selected

"Expedition into Indian Country," *United States House Executive Document* No. 152, Twenty-second Congress, First Session, 1831.

"Report on the Fur Trade," *United States Senate Document* No. 90, Twenty-second Congress, First Session, 1831.

"Report on Expedition among the Northwestern Indians," *United States House Executive Document* No. 125, Twenty-second Congress, Second Session, 1832.

"Senate Communication from Henry R. Schoolcraft relative to private land claims at Sault Ste. Marie in the State of Michigan," *United States Senate Document* No. 425, Twenty-ninth Congress, First Session, 1846.

Selected Periodical Publications— Uncollected

"Schoolcraft's Journal," *North American Review* 15 (1822): 224–50.

"Civilization and Conversion of the Indians," *North American Review* 28 (April 1829): 354–68.

"Sketches of Lake Superior: From Letters Written by Melancthon L. Woolsey to Jane Johnston Schoolcraft," *Southern Literary Messenger* 2 (February 1836): 166–71.

"History and Languages of the North American Tribes," *North American Review* 45 (1837): 34–59.

"A Memoir on the History and Physical Geography of Minnesota," *Minnesota Historical Society Collections* 1 (1872): 108–32.

SECONDARY BIBLIOGRAPHY

References

William M. Clements, *Native American Verbal Arts: Texts and Contexts* (Tucson: The University of Arizona Press, 1996).

John F. Freeman, "Religion and Personality in the Anthropology of Henry Schoolcraft," *Journal of the History of the Behavioral Sciences* 1 (1965): 301–13.

Irving H. Hart, "The Origin and Meaning of the Name 'Itasca,'" *Minnesota History* 12 (September 1931): 225–29.

Curtis M. Hinsley, ed., *Algic Researches: North American Indian Folktales and Legends* (Mineola, NY: Dover Publications, 1999), i–xl.

Andrew C. McLaughlin, *Lewis Cass* (New York: Chelsea House, 1980); originally published 1899.

Philip P. Mason, ed., *Schoolcraft's Expedition to Lake Itasca* (East Lansing: Michigan State University Press, 1993), i–xxvi.

Duane Paul Mosser, *Henry Rowe Schoolcraft: Eyewitness to a Changing Society* (Ann Arbor: UMI, 1992) (dissertation at University of California–Santa Barbara).

Papers

The Library of Congress in its manuscript divisions holds both Schoolcraft papers and the Papers of the United States Office of Indian Affairs, 1797–1920. The Minnesota Historical Society in Saint Paul holds a number of Schoolcraft letters. There are also Schoolcraft manuscripts at the Huntington Library, San Marino, California.

George Washington Sears (Nessmuk)
(December 2, 1821–May 1, 1890)

Tom Murphy

George Washington Sears, who wrote under the name Nessmuk, was an outdoorsman in the classic sense of that word. He loved to camp, canoe, wander through the woods, hunt, and fish. He would frequently leave his family and his shoemaker's shop to camp for days in the woods around his Wellsboro, Pennsylvania, home. He left for months at a time to explore the wilds of Michigan or the Amazon or the Adirondacks or Florida. Though the stereotypical outdoorsman is a big burly man, Sears was probably about five feet, four inches tall and weighed just over 110 pounds. He was plagued his whole life with poor health, often involving his lungs. His desire for adventure in the natural world was stronger than his body, and since he could not overcome nature with strength, he learned to live in it intelligently. As a result, Sears developed an attitude toward living in nature that enabled him to write in his book *Woodcraft* a century before poet Gary Snyder, "Go light."

Sears was born on December 2, 1821, in Oxford Plains (now Webster), Massachusetts. He describes how he was born "on the border of Douglas Woods, within half a mile of Nepmug Pond and within three miles of Junkamuag Lake," in the kind of geography that would define his life. More ominously, his birthplace is also near Slater's Mill, the starting point of the industrial revolution in the United States. Though he worked in a cotton mill as a child, a more formative experience seems to be the time he spent with a Nipmuc Indian called Ja-ha Levi by the non-Native community and Nessmuk by his fellow Nipmucs. The small band of about 36 Nipmucs were not particularly well-thought-of by their neighbors, and Sears tells of being punished after spending time with them. Later, he adopted the name Nessmuk, which he translates as "Wood-duck, or rather Wood-Drake" in Narragansett, as his pen name.

He attended grammar school, but his father and brothers were shoemakers and Sears, too, learned the trade. In 1838, his family moved to Brockport, New York, on the Erie Canal and then nearby to Addison, New York. In August 1841, Sears returned to Massachusetts to sign on as a sailor aboard the whaling ship *Rajah* out of New Bedford. It was to be a three-year voyage to the South Seas, but Sears took ill with a fever and was put ashore on the Portuguese-speaking island of Fayal in the Azores. It took him some months to recover, and when he did the American consul in Fayal arranged for his passage home, the first of his adventures cut short by health problems.

Back in western New York, he continued to spend time in the woods and gained the nickname "Bacchus," which stuck to him through the rest of his life. Part of his extended family had settled in Wellsboro, in north central Pennsylvania, and having discovered the area on his extended hunting trips, he decided in 1848 to settle there, the place he would call home for the next 42 years. He set up a shoemaking business, but he does not seem to have been an aggressive businessman. His interest in how objects are made, however, and his concern for functionality and quality are evident in the way he later describes the tools and equipment used in outings (speaking with special authority about boots) and in his designs for knives, hatchets, tents, canoes, and other gear.

He married Mariette Butler in 1857, and they would eventually have a son and two daughters. She apparently tolerated his absences, though she sometimes had to depend on the help of friends and neighbors to get by when he was gone.

By 1860, he had developed his writing about the outdoors to the point that *Porter's Spirit of the Times*, a sportsman's newspaper published in New York City, printed many articles from him under the Nessmuk name. Since *Porter's* devoted quite a bit of attention to horse racing, its subscribers included many Southerners; when the Civil War broke out in 1861, a Northern magazine dependent on Southern subscribers did not last long. Sears lost his national audience, and temporarily he stopped writing.

Sears volunteered for service in the army, joining Company E of the 13th Pennsylvania Reserves, 42nd Regiment, a group known as "The Bucktails" because of the deer tails worn on their forage caps. Sears was mustered into service in May 1861 as a sergeant, but before he ever saw battle he was discharged by surgeon's certificate in August of the same year. Some sources say that he broke his foot playing ball; others say the cause was trouble with his lungs. Either way, Sears's aspirations

to be part of the regiment of hardy backwoods sharpshooters did not pan out.

Though he lived in a small Pennsylvania town, he did not feel hemmed in by it. In the 1850s Sears had taken some trips to Michigan, where he hunted and camped. On one of these trips he took the ten-day solo trip through the wilderness that he would later describe in *Woodcraft*. In 1866, he and his brother spent time trapping in Minnesota. The next year, Sears spent four months in Brazil, traveling the Amazon. Because he developed what he felt was a better way to process rubber, he returned in 1870, backed by some investors, in an unsuccessful attempt the sell the process to the Brazilians.

In 1871, back in Wellsboro, Sears tried to settle down, taking the job as Items Editor of the *The Tioga County Agitator*. He lasted almost a year on the job, and the Items column is full of Nessmuk-style wit. "But," as the *Agitator* obituary notes, "the close application was distasteful to him, and he resumed his old trade, taking long outings every summer."

The publication that was to give Nessmuk his most consistent and far-reaching arena was *Forest and Stream*, which described itself in 1885 as, "A Weekly Journal of the Rod and Gun, Angling, Shooting, the Kennel, Practical Natural History, Fish Culture, Protection of Game—and the—Inculcation in Men and Women of a Healthy Interest in Out-Door Recreation and Study." The journal was published in a tabloid format on newsprint, and its structure was more like a listserv or an online bulletin board than what we think of as a magazine today. The correspondents were indeed just that—people who corresponded with each other publicly. In its editorial note, *Forest and Stream* boasted that it was "the recognized medium of entertainment, instruction, and information between American Sportsmen." A correspondent would write about an experience or describe a technique or communicate a discovery, and others would expand on it, respond to it, or dispute it. Sears was not alone in using a pseudonym; many of the names of other writers were also derived from

Native American names or from animal species, names like Wawayanda, Issaquena, and Tarpon. The articles were organized into sections, and Nessmuk generally appeared in the "Sportsman Tourist" section. He quickly established himself as an authority on camping and wilderness living.

In his first series of letters, "Rough Notes from the Woods," Nessmuck chronicled the first of his three canoe trips through the Adirondacks, paddling the lakes, carrying his duffle and canoe between lakes and streams, and sometimes camping and sometimes staying in the tourist hotels that dotted the area. Both when he made the trip and when he wrote about it, the canoe he used attracted much attention. An Adirondack guide boat, hefted onto the shoulders of a powerful guide using the built-in yoke, averaged about 75 pounds. In 1880, Sears was 59 years old and suffering from chronic lung problems, probably tuberculosis; he was setting out alone to make a 550-mile trip in a wooden boat that he would need to carry from time to time along with his pack. As a result of a collaboration between Sears and boat builder J. Henry Rushton, Rushton built a canoe— called either "The Nessmuk" or "The Wood-Duck"—which weighed only 17 pounds, 9-1/2 ounces. Sears and Rushton are still legendary among canoeists, but this was just the beginning of their collaboration. The letters Nessmuk wrote about this trip are full of character sketches of guides and tourists, stories of the past and of his activities, and descriptions of the woods and of how his small canoe behaves.

In 1881, he set out again, this time in the 16-pound *Susan Nipper* intending to go 1000 miles through the Adirondacks. That year the rain at the beginning of the summer was incessant, and it seemed to Sears that he was never dry. He ended the trip after only about 200 miles because he had become too ill and weak to go on. He produces some memorable writing, however. Lost in a storm in high water, his canoe becomes wedged between a log and a half-submerged tree top as darkness falls and a violent lightening

storm develops. Freeing himself from the snags, but disoriented, he waits in clear water as the storm rages around him:

> So as there seemed nothing better to do, I sat still and watched the strange, wild scenery, as shown in different colors by electricity. There were white flashes that appeared to dash all over the forest in a broad, white glare of light, with no distinct points of stroke. Pale blue, zig-zag chains that gave a peculiar, ghastly light among the trunks and limbs, and orange colored bolts that seemed to my eye like globes of fire.

He eventually makes shore, builds his camp, and shares the warmth of his fire and of his anger at the commercially motivated damming of the Adirondack waterways, damming that enables the rain to cause such destructive flooding.

Sears would not return to the Adirondacks until the summer of 1883, and this time he used his most famous Rushton boat—*The Sairy Gamp*, weighing 10-1/2 pounds. Rushton wrote to Sears, "Now you must stop with this one. Don't try any smaller one. If you get sick of this as a canoe, use it as a soup dish." But the small boat held up well during the 255-mile trip. He sent the canoe back to Rushton "as tight and staunch as the day I took her at Boonville." But Sears did not look at himself as some kind of daredevil; he hoped "at no distant day to meet independent canoeists, with canoes weighing twenty pounds or less, at every turn in the wilderness, and with no more duffle than is absolutely necessary."

During his last trip through the Adirondacks, Sears had been treated like a celebrity —the famous and knowledgeable woodsman, Nessmuk. After the trip, he returned to Wellsboro and began work on his book, *Woodcraft*. The book is dedicated to "the Grand Army of 'Outers'" who want to spend their vacations camping. In it Nessmuk continued his theme of fitting the equipment to the task by advising, "Go light; the lighter the better, so that you have the simplest material for health, comfort and enjoyment."

But he did not mean that suffering should be part of camping; he comments on the popular phrase "roughing it": "I dislike the phrase. We do not go to the green woods and crystal waters to rough it, we go to smooth it. We get it rough enough at home; in towns and cities; in shops, offices, stores, banks[...]." Like Thoreau, he sees choosing to have only the necessities not as self-denial but as liberation. Thoreau, however, is skeptical of the value of shared experience, and Nessmuk thinks that learning from the experience of others is crucial.

Woodcraft is full of practical camping advice, some of it, of course, outdated, but much of the advice is in stories—the way Native Americans preserve and transmit to the young their ways of doing things. He tells how, as the Old Woodsman, he makes camp for and instructs some young tenderfeet. In the course of the story, he dispenses advice to the reader, contrasting the actions of the inexperienced youths with those of the wise Old Woodsman. He describes how to set up camp, build the cooking fire, prepare the food, and clean up. Nessmuk relishes all the activities of the camp. He notes, "if there is a spot on earth where trifles make up the sum of human enjoyment, it is to be found in a woodland camp." When he is in the woods, the woods become the whole world.

In *Woodcraft*, Nessmuk's attitude toward nature is based on practical experience, not on the romantic notion of a welcoming and protective Mother Nature. Those who have the skills to survive in the solitary wilderness,

> know that nature is stern, hard, immovable and terrible in unrelenting cruelty. When wintry winds are out and the mercury far below zero, she will allow her most ardent lover to freeze on her snowy breast without waving a leaf in pity or offering him a match; and scores of her devotees will starve to death in as many different languages before she will offer a loaf of bread. She does not deal in matches and loaves; rather in thunderbolts and granite mountains.

The practicality of his advice and the wit with which he gives it has kept the book alive with readers even today.

In 1884, he also wrote a series of articles— "The Log of the Bucktail"—about the Pine Creek area, where he had lived and camped for over 30 years. Sears had come to northern Pennsylvania in the late 1840s when lumbering in the area meant selecting the prime old-growth white pines and sending them down Pine Creek to the Susquehanna in rafts. He had seen loggers move on to cutting all the pines and floating them down in massive carpets of logs. He was caught off guard when they started on the hemlocks, stripping them of their bark, to be used in leather tanning. Eventually the dark majestic forests would be gone and much of the area would become a burned-over wasteland. But Sears knew that at least some of the destruction was temporary. In a canoe trip down Pine Creek, he points out, "To note the effect of this constant depletion of green timber is a part of my business." He also notes how, after the inevitable debris fires, the forest succession process begins with blackberry, fire cherry, and poplars. He bemoans the fate of the trout and documents the activities of "trout hogs," who break the law and threaten the struggling fish population. Later, in an article in 1888, he would again bemoan the continued cutting of the hemlocks: "It is beyond question that the hemlocks are fated to fade and fall. But that is an inevitable conclusion. Thank Heaven, the tanneries, too, must go."

In 1886, *Forest and Stream* published by subscription a collection of Nessmuk's poetry—*Forest Runes*. After Sears's death, James Whitcomb Riley wrote a poem called "Nessmuk," which begins,

> I HAIL thee, Nessmuk, for the lofty tone
> Yet simple grace that marks thy poetry!

But the book was never reprinted, and time has not been kind to Nessmuk's poetry. What characterizes the best of his prose is its directness and liveliness, qualities missing from his poetry.

When his declining health made outdoor life in the northern winters too demanding, he accepted an invitation to spend the winters in Florida in 1885 and 1886. During the second trip, he sailed aboard the yacht *Stella* and spent two weeks ashore camping and canoeing alone. He wrote extensively about his Florida experience for *Forest and Stream*, and it was there that he paddled the canoe he called *The Rushton*—six inches shorter and eight ounces lighter than the tiny *Sairy Gamp*.

Though in December 1889 he would publish a 10,000-word article on his Amazon experience, during the previous summer he had been too weak to do any camping. On May 1, 1890, he died in Wellsboro. According to the editors of *Forest and Stream*, he was one of their most popular contributors. *Woodcraft* remained in print until 1920 and was reissued in 1963 and is still available. The *Sairy Gamp* now belongs to the Smithsonian Institution and is on display at the Adirondack Museum.

PRIMARY BIBLIOGRAPHY

Books

Woodcraft (New York: Forest and Stream, 1884; [14 editions, the last in 1920; slightly abridged and edited under the title *Woodcraft and Camping* [New York: Dover, 1963]).

Forest Runes (New York: Forest and Stream, 1886).

Selected Periodical Publications—Collected

Canoeing the Adirondacks with Nessmuk: The Adirondack Letters of George Washington Sears, ed. Dan Brenan (Blue Mountain and Syracuse, NY: Adirondack Museum and Syracuse University Press, 1993) [comprises three series of articles originally published in *Forest and Stream*: "Rough Notes from the Woods" (1880); "Cruise of the Susan Nipper" (1881–1882), and "Cruise of the Sairy Gamp" (1883).

Selected Periodical Publications—Uncollected

"Jack O' the Smithy" [poem], *Atlantic Monthly* 21 (March 1868): 298–99.

"Our Camping-Ground" [poem], *Putnam's Magazine* 14, 19 (1869): 28.

"Local Items," *Tioga County Agitator* (January 3, 1871–December 1871?) [Sears gathered and wrote local stories for the weekly newspaper].

"The Log of the Bucktail: Down the Tiadatto," *Forest and Stream* 23 (1884): 122, 183, 202, 222, 242–43.

"The Bucktail in Florida," *Forest and Stream* 24 (1884): 124, 143, 247, 267, 286–87, 346, 386–87, 486–87; 25 (1885–1886): 2–3.

"Camping in the Keys," *Forest and Stream* 25 (1885): 324–25.

"Some Points in Woodcraft," *Forest and Stream* 26 (1886): 222.

"A Night Among the Keys," *Forest and Stream* 26 (1886): 318.

"Unofficial Log of the Stella," *Forest and Stream* 28 (1887): 2, 22, 62, 174, 224.

"What Shall be the Outcome?" *Forest and Stream* 31 (1888): 142.

"On the Trombetas," *Forest and Stream* 33 (1889): 423–25.

SECONDARY BIBLIOGRAPHY

References

Dan Brenan, "Introduction," in *Canoeing the Adirondacks with Nessmuk: The Adirondack Letters of George Washington Sears* (Blue Mountain and Syracuse, NY: Adirondack Museum and Syracuse University Press, 1993).

"Death of George W. Sears: After Months of Sickness His Lamp of Life Flickers Out," *Tioga County Agitator*, May 6, 1890, 2.

Christine Jerome, *An Adirondack Passage: The Cruise of the Canoe Sairy Gamp* (New York: Harper Collins, 1994).

Robert L. Lyon, *Who Was Nessmuk?* (Wellsboro: Wellsboro Chamber of Commerce, 1971).

Robert L. Lyon, "The Phantom in the Canyon: Nessmuk," *Pennsylvania Game News* (July 1990): 6–11.

Robert L. Lyon, "The Odyssey of Nessmuk," *The Conservationist* (March–April 1992): 32–35.

"Nessmuk," *Forest and Stream* 34 (1890): 372.

James Whitcomb Riley, "Nessmuk," *Green Fields and Running Brooks* (Indianapolis: Bowen-Merrill, 1893).

George Washington Sears, "Nessmuk," in *Forest Runes* (New York: Forest and Stream, 1886), v–xi.

Annie Trumbull Slosson
(May 18, 1838–October 4, 1926)

Rebecca Tolley-Stokes

Annie Trumbull Slosson's literary career spans two centuries, the nineteenth and early twentieth, though most of her work was concentrated in the 1890s and written during her mature years. Slosson's short stories depicting New England village life were published in *Harper's New Monthly Magazine* and the *Atlantic Monthly* while her entomology articles appeared in professional journals including: *Journal of the New York Entomological Society, Bulletin of the Brooklyn Entomological Society, Entomological News, Canadian Entomologist,* and *Entomologica Americana.* Recognized for her local color short stories, and compared with Sarah Orne Jewett, Harriett Beecher Stowe, Mary Wilkins Freeman, and Rose Terry Cooke, founders of the local color movement in the last quarter of the nineteenth century, she was equally acknowledged as a proficient nature writer.

Born May 18, 1838, in Stonington, Connecticut, Anna Trumbull was the ninth child out of ten born to Gurdon and Sarah Ann (Swan) Trumbull. They lived in Stonington until 1852, and moved to Hartford, Connecticut, where Slosson attended public schools. Her father was a merchant and justice of the peace. Though little is known about her education and early writing, a poem she wrote at age 11 was published in a Stonington inspirational newspaper, *Lux*

Mundi. The Trumbull children engaged in lively philosophical and theological discussions, and this environment influenced Slosson's daughter's studies and intellectual development. As one of the youngest surviving children, Slosson was adept at relating to her elders and functioning on their level intellectually, though she was closest to her younger brother Gurdon, Jr.

Though Slosson goes unmentioned as part of the Nook Farm literary circle that flourished in Hartford from the late 1860s into the 1890s, which had close connections with Boston publishers and the New York literary scene, it is likely that she was acquainted with its denizens. No doubt she was influenced by several members of her family who associated with the Farm's luminaries: Samuel Clemens, Harriet Beecher Stowe, and Charles Dudley Warner. Literary, political, and religious personalities and radical Progressive Era thinkers gathered at Nook Farm.

Slosson's elder brothers, James Hammond and Henry Clay, were frequent visitors to Nook Farm. They published books and articles on several subjects. Her sister Mary Hollister married William C. Prime, the editor of New York's *Journal of Commerce.* Mary Prime, whose diary of her travels to Egypt in 1854 was published in 1998, established the Trumbull-Prime rare book collection at the

Wadsworth Athenaeum in Hartford. James Hammond was philologist, historian, authority on American Indian languages, and a librarian who was known as the most learned and acute bibliographer in America. Henry Clay was a Congregational clergyman and chaplain who moved to Philadelphia in 1875, eventually editing the *Sunday School Times* and writing many theological books. Undoubtedly Slosson's older siblings inspired her endeavors in writing and influenced her spiritual and scientific progress.

Slosson married 53-year-old Edward Slosson, a lawyer, notary public, and native of Poughkeepsie, New York, on June 6, 1867. A son of William and Catherine Alice (Shenk), Edward graduated from Columbia College in 1833 with his BA and practiced law in New York. He served as Chairman of the Ninth Ward of the Whig General Committee in September 1852 and appeared on the Regular Whig Ticket for an Assembly position during November 1852. He officiated as a steward at the first Semi Centennial Anniversary of the New York Historical Society dinner held at the Astor House, New York City, on November 20, 1854. In August 1856 he was a delegate to the Old-Line Whigs State Convention at Albany, New York. Two years later he was elected as an inspector for the next election of directors of Citizen's Bank of New York City.

It is possible that she met Edward through her father, Gurdon, who was justice of the peace and merchant in Hartford, though it is more likely that her brother-in-law, William Prime, a lawyer-turned-editor who later served as vice president of the Metropolitan Museum of Art and as Professor of Art History at Princeton University, introduced the couple to each other. They lived in New York during their childless marriage that lasted less than four years. Edward died in Greenwich, Connecticut, November 4, 1871 at their country estate. At the time of his death, Edward practiced law at Slosson, Hutchens, and Platt located on Wall Street, New York City, and owned numerous lots on Broadway, DeKalb Avenue, Reed Avenue, and others.

It is unclear whether Slosson returned to Hartford after her husband's death. One account relates that Mrs. Prime invited Slosson to live in her New York City household, while Hartford city directories suggest that during this period before Slosson's first book was published, she resided at Asylum Avenue a few doors down from her brother James Hammond. After Mrs. Prime's death in 1872, Slosson and William Prime lived together in New York City, using his home as a base for summer trips to Profile House, a resort hotel at Franconia Notch, New Hampshire, and winter trips to Florida. Their relationship was platonic.

Slosson's first book, *The China Hunter's Club*, was published in 1878 when she was 40, but it was published anonymously, credit given to the "youngest member" of the club. Prime wrote the introduction, and illustrations were done by Slosson's younger brother, Gurdon, Jr., an artist known for his paintings of fish and ornithology studies.

China Hunter's Club was a collection of stories on pottery found in New England, specifically Stonington and the Franconia Notch area of New Hampshire's White Mountains. Slosson's blend of history and anecdote derive from fact, though she changed identifying names of the characters. Her clever characterizations and gift for dialect engaged many readers, which was not the case with Prime's foray into the subject *Pottery and Porcelain of All Ages and Nations*, published that same year.

Slosson's fondness for the natural world was limited to flowers and plants, accounts of which she shared with readers of the Franconia and Hartford papers in weekly reports. After 1886 her interest in insects consumed her time and thoughts. She spent more time collecting than writing, though she made scrupulous lists of the insects she found. Slosson sold the unusual specimens and was one of the first entomologists to collect around Miami, Florida, in the early 1890s. Her lists were published annually in entomological journals as well as the Mount Washington weekly newspaper,

Among the Clouds. One hundred of her discoveries were given the suffix *slossonae* in her honor.

Six years marked the time between the publication of *China Hunter's Club* and the appearance of Slosson's first story in *Harper's New Monthly Magazine.* Ruth recalls an amnesiac child's peculiarities in "How Faith Came and Went." Set in Sudbury, a New England town, the girl wanders into Ruth's yard, and she and her brother Max, a doctor, take her in. Ruth and Max come to call this girl Faith after their dead sister, and eventually they move away from their village because Max and Faith have fallen in love. The day of their wedding, she disappears from their lives. The story is charming and lacks the regional dialect that Slosson's later stories feature.

"Aunt Randy" was published in *Harper's* three years later. Slosson's first story includes a brief reference to roses, but in this second story, she describes the early buttercups, tiarella, trilliums, and bunchberry in the first paragraph. Her attention to outdoor settings grounds the reader in the natural world while lending a sensual quality to the story, a technique Slosson uses in her later work. The narrator, sharing an interest in entomology with the author, catches sight of Aunt Randy wielding a butterfly net and asks her companion, Nathan, about the woman. Aunt Randy transforms much like a butterfly, from an isolated widowed woman into someone who takes interest in people after finding solace in naming butterflies and pondering their personalities. Regional dialect appears in this story. Slosson's work collected within *Seven Dreamers* is a fine example of local color stories, the dominant movement in American literature in the 1880s. Slosson's stories are entertaining and particularly marked with eccentric characters with whimsical fancies and dialect specific to New England.

Slosson's signature story "Fishin' Jimmy" appeared in the *Princeton Review* in 1888. That Prime's alma mater published the work suggests that he acted as an agent in placing Slosson's work and in all probability was her greatest champion and supporter. It is telling that her regular literary productivity coincided with the 33 years she and Prime were companions until his death in 1905. Set in Franconia Notch, the character in this morality tale was based on the caretaker at Prime's cabin at Lonesome Lake on the side of Cannon Mountain. The story opens with great attention to the natural surroundings: a cheerful brook, fly casting, spring flowers, and butterflies and moths. The narrator likens Jimmy's fisherman's art to a system of morality, a gospel. Slosson's Congregationalist upbringing endowed her fiction with spiritual themes. It is within this story that Slosson's attention to idiom, pronunciations, and forms of language, all which characterize her mature work, prominently appear in Jimmy's speech.

Naturally this narrative reflected Slosson's spiritual connection with the natural world given the amount of time she spent outdoors. When the story was published in book form the next year by A. D. F. Randolph & Co., its popularity introduced the term "Fishin' Jimmy" to the urbane who used it when referring to mountain rubes.

Slosson placed her first stories in *Harper's New Monthly Magazine,* producing roughly one each year except for a gap between 1892 and 1895, when her entomological endeavors consumed her time. "Butterneggs," "Deacon Pheby's Selfish Nature," and "Speakin' Ghost" appeared in the magazine before they were collected in *Seven Dreamers.* Sometime before 1890 Slosson bought Mount Lafayette House, a hotel in Franconia, New Hampshire. She and Prime built a home on its grounds, which they named "Gale Cottage."

Seven Dreamers, a collection of Slosson's stories, was published in 1891. Including her first five published stories and one new story, the volume includes pantheistic themes filled with disenfranchised characters, her characteristic use of dialect, and details of the natural world. Isolated from his community, the title character in "Botany Bay," a mentally retarded dwarf who makes his living through wild crafting, conceives and communes with an imaginary brother. Slosson creates one of the earliest depictions of transvestitism in American literature in "Deacon Phelby's Selfish Nature." After his sister's death, Phebus wears her clothing, takes on her mannerisms, and becomes a pious churchgoer as a means to soothe his mother's sorrow. Thought charming and clever for their dialect and examples of New England village life, Slosson's stories met with popular success.

The next year, 1892, Slosson helped establish the New York Entomological Society. One of the few women, she was admitted to the Society in 1893 because she garnered the primary financial support for their journal. The Society met in her home in New York until she persuaded the American Museum of Natural History to allow the group to hold their meetings there. The next year, Slosson published the first of many lists of her entomological findings, *Insects Taken in the Alpine Regions of Mt. Washington.*

Slosson spent the winter of 1894 in Florida at Palm Beach on the east side of Lake Worth. For several years she had been collecting in Florida during the first two months of the year. Though there was less insect life this year than in previous ones, she discovered several rare specimens.

Starting in 1896, Slosson corresponded with Sarah Orne Jewett. Two years later, her most acclaimed collection, *Dumb Foxglove, and Other Stories,* was published. A reviewer for the *Atlantic Monthly* compared her work to Jewett's and Freeman's but recognized mystical qualities in her stories that the other writers lacked. The reviewer commented that, despite being burdened with excessive dialect, her stories were quaint and memorable.

"Dumb Foxglove" is the story of a handicapped child, Colossy Bragg, who concocts recipes using ingredients from the Bible. After her death, Mrs. Peavy swears that her cooking is tinged by the child's unearthly presence. A visit from the minister, Mr. Robbins, and Aunt Eunice ends the culinary haunting and life returns to normal. Set in

Stonington, "Apple Jonathan" is the story of the local apple seller's friendship with a physically challenged child and how Jonathan feels in the aftermath of the child's death. It includes Slosson's copious imagery of flowers. "Anna Malann" begins with the narrator's description of goldenrod, sunflowers, and black-eyed Susans by the side of the road but turns into a story about a dying dog and the woman, Anna Malann, who might save it. "Davy's Christmas," "Clavis," and "A Transient" all have male narrators, an unusual choice of departure for Slosson.

In "Aunt Liefy," Slosson charts the transformation of Relief Staples, who was abandoned as a child, from a difficult old maid into an esteemed aunt. In a case of mistaken identity, Relief is included in a family's bereavement. During the burial, she notices the beauty around her: the bees, flowers, bird song. Her appreciation of life broadens afterwards. She engages with nature by planting a garden and feeding the birds and engages with humans by nursing the sick and elderly and looking after eccentric folks. "Aunt Liefy" illustrates the transformative power of human connection and ultimately the affirmative influence of nature appreciation.

Slosson's subsequent books received little popular or critical success. Divorcing herself from the narrow local-color style she worked within was impossible. Her characters, the suffering children that she reverently wrote about, failed to interest a wide audience.

In 1897, a year before *Dumb Foxglove* was published, her eldest brother, James, died. Within the next four years, her other living siblings, Henry and Gurdon, died as well, both in 1903. These deaths certainly affected Slosson's productivity, though *Story-Tell Lib,* a series of stories told by a disease-afflicted child, was published in 1900. *White Christopher,* published the next year, was about a feral albino child whose holiness was sensed throughout the town. Two years later *Aunt Abby's Neighbors* was published, but it met with little acclaim.

Prime's death early in 1905 devastated her, though she wrote the section on Stonington in her brother's biography *The Life Story of Henry Clay Trumbull* later that year, which was written by Philip E. Howard and published by The Sunday School Times Company.

"A Dissatisfied Soul" and "A Prophetic Romancer" were published in 1908, combined in one book, and were also included in Slosson's last collection of short stories *A Local Colorist* (1912). Maria Bliven was "A Dissatisfied Soul" who traveled a circuit among her relative's homes and who, still restless after death, came back to earth. Finally deciding to go back to the afterlife, she consulted the Bible, finding insight for her return trip within. *A Local Colorist* (1912) was faulted for shallow character development and excessive use of dialect. Her last few books had small audiences and have been critically dismissed. *A Little Shepherd of Bethlehem* (1914), *Puzzled Souls* (1915), *Other People* (1918), and *"And Other Folks": The Story of a Little Girl and a Little Sermon* (1918) were all published by The Sunday School Times, with which her late brother Henry Clay was closely associated.

Slosson died at age 89 in her residence at 26 Gramercy Park, New York City, on Monday, October 4, 1926. Funeral services were held at St. George's Chapel, and she was buried in Hartford, Connecticut.

Although Slosson has been critically acclaimed for her collection *Dumb Foxglove, and Other Stories*, her other work has fallen into obscurity. Recognized for her writing aptitude while alive, her reputation has not outlived her. A regionalist, Slosson has received little scholarly attention regarding her literary production though she published in two genres; fiction and nonfiction. Criticism focuses on her short stories, and no work has examined her nonfiction writing.

Slosson was one of the first authors writing in the local color or regional realist genres. Instead of negating the male-identified world within her stories, Slosson created another world that nurtured women and gave importance to insects, animals, and the natural world. Though she was from New England, her class and education ideo-logically separated her from the rural people on whom she based her stories; this is typical within the "village tradition," as Slosson's specific school is known. In many of her tales, Slosson's narrators are outsiders much like herself. Her outsiders are compelled to inquire about the curious folks whom they encounter. Slosson's focus on collecting insects as a field naturalist began later in life. Known for authentic regional detail and inhabited by women and their experiences, her contribution to the feminine literary tradition of other local colorists lacked serious attention for half a century, though Jewett, Stowe, Phleps, and Cook received critical attention from scholars. The leading authority of the genre, Perry D. Westbrook, dismisses her as a short-story writer of little talent and criticizes the sentimentality of her themes, the gushiness of her narrative, her fixation with nature study, and her excessive use of dialect.

PRIMARY BIBLIOGRAPHY

Books

The China Hunters Club, by the youngest member (New York: Harper & Brothers, 1878).

Fishin' Jimmy (New York: A.D.F. Randolph & Co., 1889).

Seven Dreamers (New York: Harper & Brothers, 1890).

Aunt Liefy (New York: A.D.F. Randolph & Co., 1892).

The Heresy of Mehetable Clark (New York: Harper, 1892).

Anna Malann (Hartford, CT: Press of the Case, Lockwood, and Brainard, Co., 1894).

Dumb Foxglove, and Other Stories (New York: Harper & Bros., 1898).

Story-tell Lib (New York: C. Scribner's Sons, 1900).

White Christopher (New York: James Pott & Company, 1901).

Aunt Abby's Neighbors (New York: F.H. Revell Company, 1902).

Simples from the Master's Garden (Philadelphia: The Sunday School Times Company, 1907).

A Dissatisfied Soul, and a Prophetic Romancer (New York, Bonnell, Silver & Co., 1908).

A Local Colorist (New York: C. Scribner's Sons, 1912).

A Little Shepherd of Bethlehem (Philadelphia: Sunday School Times Company, 1914).

Puzzled Souls (Philadelphia: Sunday School Times, 1915).

"And Other Folks": The Story of a Little Girl and a Little Sermon (Philadelphia: Sunday School Times, 1918).

Other People (Philadelphia: Sunday School Times, 1918).

Other

The Shepherd Boy's Carol ([privately printed, folded sheet] 1900, 1926).

December Nineteenth MDCCCCX (Boston: Merrymount Press, 1910).

Selected Periodical Publications— Uncollected

Poetry

"Uncle Jotham's Boarder," *New York Times,* October 29, 1895, 10.

"Puzzled," *Outlook,* 91, February 20, 1909, 388.

Fiction

"How Faith Came and Went," *Harper's New Monthly Magazine* 70 (April 1885): 799–806.

"Aunt Randy: An Entomological Sketch," *Harper's New Monthly Magazine* 75 (July 1887): 303–9.

"Butterneggs: A Story of Heredity," *Harper's New Monthly Magazine* 79 (October 1889): 693–703.

"Deacon Pheby's Selfish Nature," *Harper's New Monthly Magazine* 80 (April 1890): 709–20.

"A Speakin' Ghost," *Harper's New Monthly Magazine* 82 (December 1890): 137–48.

"Dumb Foxglove," *The Atlantic Monthly* 75 (April 1895): 466–77.

"Clavis," *Harper's New Monthly Magazine* 76 (December 1896): 150–55.

"Davy's Christmas," *The Wave* (December 31, 1898): 23–31.

"The Boy That Was Scaret o' Dyin'," *Outlook* 66 (October 27, 1900): 211–12.

"A Local Colorist," *Harper's New Monthly Magazine* 120 (1901): 84–94.

"A Dissatisfied Soul," *The Atlantic Monthly* 94 (July 1904): 114–24.

"Portents," *The Atlantic Monthly* 96 (October 1905): 567–70.

Nonfiction

"May Moths in Northern New Hampshire," *Entomological News and the Proceedings of the Entomological Section Academy of Natural Sciences* 1 (February 1890): 2–19.

"Winter Collecting in Florida, Part I," *Entomological News and the Proceedings of the Entomological Section Academy of Natural Sciences* 1 (June 1890): 81–83.

"Winter Collecting in Florida, Part I," *Entomological News and the Proceedings of the Entomological Section Academy of Natural Sciences* 1 (September 1890): 101–2.

"Collecting on Mt Washington, Part I," *Entomological News and the Proceedings of the Entomological Section Academy of Natural Sciences* 4 (October 1893): 249–52.

"Collecting on Mt Washington, Part II," *Entomological News and the Proceedings of the Entomological Section Academy of Natural Sciences* 4 (October 1893): 287–92.

"Coleoptera of Lake Worth, Florida," *Canadian Entomologist* 27 (1895): 9–10.

"Collecting at Lake Worth, Fla.," *Entomological News and the Proceedings of the Entomological Section Academy of Natural Sciences* 6 (5 May 1895): 5, 134–136.

"Collecting on Biscayne Bay," *Entomological News and the Proceedings of the Entomological Section Academy of Natural Sciences* 10 (April 1899): 94–96.

"Collecting on Biscayne Bay, Part II" *Entomological News and the Proceedings of the Entomological Section Academy of Natural Sciences* 10 (April 1899): 124–126.

"A Few Memories," *Journal of the New York Entomological Society* 23 (June 1915): 85–91.

"Experiences of a Collector," *Bulletin of the Brooklyn Entomological Society* 12 (April 1917): 25–29.

Selected Publications—Collected

Short Stories, ed. Mrs. Burton Harrison (New York: Harper & Brothers, 1893).

Library of the World's Best Literature: Ancient and Modern, Vol. 34, SHE-SOP (New York: J.A. Hill, 1902).

The Golden Staircase: Poems and Verses for Children (New York: G.P. Putnam's Sons, 1907).

Short Stories of America (New York: Houghton Mifflin Company, 1921).

Representative Modern Short Stories, ed. Alexander Jessup (New York: The Macmillan Co., 1923).

Representative Modern Short Stories, ed. Alexander Jessup (New York: The Macmillan Co., 1929).

Golden Tales of New England, ed. May Lamberton Becker (New York: Dodd, Mead, & Company, 1939).

Representative Modern Short Stories, ed. Alexander Jessup (New York: The Macmillan Co., 1949).

Short Story Index Reprint Series (Manchester, NH: Ayer Company Publishers, Incorporated, 1969).

The Scribner Treasury: 22 Classic Tales, ed. J.G.E. Hopkins (New York: Charles Scribner's Sons, 1953).

American Women Afield: Writings by Pioneering Women Naturalists, ed. Marcia Bonta (College Station: Texas A&M, 1995).

Restless Spirits: Ghost Stories by American Women, 1872–1926, ed. Catherine E. Lundie (Amherst: University of Massachusetts Press, 1996).

SECONDARY BIBLIOGRAPHY

References

Martha J. Bailey, *American Women in Science: A Biographical Dictionary* (Denver: ABC-CLIO, 1994), 360–61.

Barbara Blair, "'Ties of Blood and Bonds of Fortune': The Cultural Construction of Gender in American Women's Fiction: An Interdisciplinary Analysis" (dissertation, Brown University, 1984).

Julie Boardman, *When Women and Mountains Meet: Adventures in the White Mountains* (Etna, New Hampshire: Durand Press, 2001).

James Boylan, "Annie Trumbull Slosson: A Local Colorist from Cannon Square," *Historical Footnotes: Bulletin of the Stonington Historical Society* 22 (August 1985): 1–11.

"A Group of Recent Novels," *Atlantic Monthly*, 83 (February 1899): 287.

Barbara A. Johns, "The Spinster in Five New England Regionalists" (dissertation, University of Detroit, 1979).

"New England in the Short Story," *Atlantic Monthly*, 67 (June 1891): 846–47.

Caroline Preston, "Annie Trumbull Slosson," in *American Women Writers: A Critical Reference Guide From Colonial Times to the Present* (New York: Ungar, 1994), 97–98.

Jeffery S. Wallner, "Butterflies and Trout: Annie Trumbull Slosson and W.C. Prime," *Historical New Hampshire* 32 (1977): 129–43.

Marek Wilczynski, "From Edwards to Slosson: Typology, Nature, and the New England Domestic Gothic," *Studia Anglica Posnaniensia: International Review of English Studies Annual* (2001): 303–310.

Letters

Letters to Philip Powell Calvert, Library of the Academy of Natural Sciences, Philadelphia, PA; letters to William T. Davis, Museum of Staten Island Archives and Library, Staten Island Institute of Arts and Sciences, Staten Island, New York; letters to Harrison Gray Dyar, Special Collections in the Smithsonian Institution Archives, Washington, D.C.; letters to Katherine Seymour Day, Harriett Beecher Stowe Center, Hartford, Connecticut; letters to Sarah Orne Jewett, Houghton Library, Harvard College Library, Cambridge, Massachusetts; letters to John D. Sherman, Jr., Special Collections in the Smithsonian Institution Archives, Washington, D.C.; letters to Henry Skinners Library of the Academy of Natural Sciences, Philadelphia, Pennsylvania.

Papers

While there is no collection of Slosson's papers, she left entomological collections to the American Museum of Natural History in New York, which houses the Slosson Collection of Diptera. Slosson also left items to the Harvard Museum of Comparative Zoology.

Celia Laighton Thaxter
(June 29, 1835–August 25, 1894)

Jessie Ravage

Celia Thaxter lived virtually all of her life within the coastal region of New England bounded on the north by the Piscataqua River, which delineates the boundary between Maine and New Hampshire, and on the south by Boston, Massachusetts. Born in 1835, she was first published in *The Atlantic Monthly* in 1861. She became one of that magazine's "stable" of writers and its "lady poet" during the Civil War period and later. She also wrote for many other popular periodicals and published volumes of poetry and prose. Much of her work is characterized as "local color" or "regional" writing as the bulk of her poetry and essays focused primarily on natural occurrence and observation of locale, especially the Isles of Shoals, taking in also the customs and habits of the region's inhabitants. She also wrote about music, gardening, and other topics. Her work was praised during her writing career, which spanned nearly 35 years, from 1861 to 1894. Some of her contemporaries collected her letters and most of her previously published poetry and published them posthumously with additional introductory materials.

Thaxter's friends, nearly all part of an intellectual circle based in Boston, admired her also for her embodiment of a Victorian ideal of womanhood. She encouraged others in their creative efforts, and, in her own parlor on the Isles of Shoals, provided an informal salon where many writers, artists, musicians, academicians, and others found lively discussion and music. In addition to her writing, Celia Thaxter gained a livelihood from that most feminine of pursuits, china painting. Her work includes meticulously observed plant specimens and seascapes. She also illustrated her own books on commission. Beyond this, she was a notable gardener in the developing nostalgic idiom, an outgrowth of the larger Colonial Revival taste of the late nineteenth century. Her garden, about which she wrote her last book, is restored on Appledore Island.

Celia Laighton Thaxter was born in Portsmouth, New Hampshire, on June 29, 1835, the daughter of Thomas and Eliza Rymes Laighton. Her father came from a shipping family based in Portsmouth; he was also involved in local politics at the time. A capable entrepreneur, he enjoined his brother Joseph to purchase Hog, Smuttynose, and Malaga islands, three of the Isles of Shoals group off the coast of Portsmouth in 1839. Following his defeat in a local election for selectman the same year, he moved his wife Eliza and their two children, four-year-old Celia and three-month-old Cedric, to White Island late that year where he took up the position of lighthouse keeper.

The Isles of Shoals are nine low-lying, treeless islands ranging in size from a few acres to roughly a mile across, lying off the meeting of the New Hampshire and Maine coastlines. To understand Celia Thaxter's work, one must have some knowledge of this small archipelago because they fill the dual roles of setting and characters in much of her writing. Named for the large shoals, or schools, of fish found there, the Shoals, as they were often known colloquially, were known by European fishermen before the turn of the seventeenth century. Champlain charted them in 1605, and Captain John Smith described them in his account of the North Atlantic coast. The islands were inhabited at first on a seasonal basis by fishermen, but by the eighteenth century, full time residents gained a livelihood from the fishery. The largest of the islands were called Star and Hog, later more picturesquely renamed Appledore by Thomas Laighton. The smaller ones are still known as Duck, White, Seavey, Lunging (thought to be derived from the word Londoner), Malaga, Cedar, and Smutty-nose.

When the Laightons moved to the Isles of Shoals, a small fishing community was based at Gosport on Star Island. These families of Shoalers, as they were known, clung to the way of life carried on by their ancestors. Later, a small group of Norwegian fisherfolk resided on Smutty-Nose. Thomas Laighton hoped to revive the failing fishing industry based on the islands he owned, and White Island provided a good place to watch over his investment.

The 1840s were an exceedingly busy time for the Laighton family. The family grew to three children with the birth of Oscar on June 30, 1841. The same year, Thomas Laighton was elected to a two-year term in the New Hampshire legislature. The family moved to the Haley House, built by entrepreneur Samuel Haley from the wreck of a Spanish ship in 1813, on Smutty-nose. Eliza Laighton put the large house in order and opened its remaining rooms as a summer inn for the 1841 season. This foray launched the Laighton family's long association with the

summer resort hotels on the Isles of Shoals, among the earliest, and eventually one of the most successful, along the New England coast.

Lodgers in the Laightons' inaugural summer at Haley House included John Greenleaf Whittier's younger sister, Lizzie; her friend Margie Curzon; John Weiss, a young man studying to be a minister; and his friend, Levi Lincoln Thaxter. Harvard-educated, Thaxter (b. 1824) was one of a group of young Boston literati called the "Brothers and Sisters." They included James Russell Lowell and Thomas Wentworth Higginson. Thaxter, Lowell, and Higginson were Harvard friends; Lowell became one the mid-nineteenth century's foremost writers and editors. Higginson was slightly less prominent, but he played an important role in bringing Emily Dickinson to light. This group of people and their larger circle of friends were destined to play significant roles in Celia Laighton's personal and artistic life.

When Thomas Laighton completed his term in the legislature, the family returned to White Island light. Thomas Laighton seized the opportunity to liquidate his Portsmouth property to the railroad in 1847, providing the initial capital for building a large hotel on Hog Island. Levi Thaxter, who came from a banking family in Watertown, Massachusetts, convinced his parents to visit the Shoals in 1847 to look over the project. They agreed to put up the remaining funds, and on September 10, Thaxter and Laighton became partners in building a large frame summer hotel on Hog Island, which Laighton renamed Appledore.

In September 1847, the Laightons moved permanently to Appledore to oversee the building project, which took less than a year. The four-story Appledore House, able to accommodate 130 guests, opened June 15, 1848. That winter, Thaxter also became the Laighton children's tutor. Despite summer visitors, the Laighton children had grown up in comparative isolation. In his *American Notebooks*, Nathaniel Hawthorne called Celia Laighton Thaxter the "Miranda of the Isles," an allusion to Miranda in

Shakespeare's *Tempest,* who grows up with only her father and the native sprites of their island as her teachers. Thaxter, with undergraduate and law degrees from Harvard University, altered this circumstance. He continued as the children's tutor through the winter of 1848–1849. In November 1849, Thaxter and Laighton dissolved their partnership and divided the property with Laighton retaining the hotel buildings, and Celia continued her education for a short time at the Mount Washington Female Seminary in Boston, Massachusetts, in 1849–1850. Celia returned to the Shoals, and on September 31, 1851, at age 16, she married Thaxter in the parlor at Appledore House.

As soon as they were married, the Thaxters moved to Watertown, Massachusetts. They returned to the Shoals in 1852 for the birth of their first child, Karl, in June. He suffered a mishap in the birth, and was born with a crippled foot. He suffered emotional troubles, too, and would end up occupying considerable amounts of his mother's attention with his requirements for all of her life. The young family spent 1853 on Star Island, as Levi was the temporary pastor of the Stone Chapel and schoolmaster for the children of Gosport, the village on Star. After that position was filled permanently, the Thaxters moved back to the mainland in 1854, with Celia carrying their second child. They lived with the Curzon family at Mill House in Newburyport, where John Thaxter was born on November 29. Celia developed a close friendship with Margie Curzon; her letters to Margie are the first transcribed in the book of letters published posthumously by Annie Fields and Rose Lamb. Celia Thaxter may have first met John Greenleaf Whittier, a prominent member of the Boston Transcendentalist circle, in Newburyport. He became one of Celia's regular correspondents and played a leading role in encouraging her to write about the Shoals and her life there.

After the autumn of 1855, Levi Thaxter was reluctant to return to the Shoals after he nearly drowned in a fall storm, and he sold his Appledore property to Thomas Laighton. With the help of Levi's parents, the Thaxters acquired a house in Newtonville, Massachusetts, in 1855. On August 28, 1858, Celia bore her third and last child, Roland. By the following year, Levi was unemployed, and the family was scrambling financially following a national economic downturn of the previous year. Economic difficulties became a pattern for the Thaxters. This often strained their relationship and may have increased Celia's longing to be on the Shoals. But from the time of his near death onwards, Levi avoided going to the Shoals again.

Thaxter expressed her deep homesickness for the ocean and sense of entrapment among the low-lying hills west of Boston in a poem entitled "Land-locked." Without her knowledge, James Russell Lowell published it anonymously in *The Atlantic Monthly* in March 1861 and launched her professional writing career. *The Atlantic* was conceived in 1857 as a monthly journal of American belles lettres and politics. James T. Fields was its first editor, followed by Lowell. William Dean Howells succeeded to the editorship in 1871, serving first as an editorial assistant from 1866. Howells guided the magazine's tastes toward the developing American realism of the post–Civil War period as well as scientific interests, like anthropology and geology. Howells recognized and published Bret Harte, Mark Twain, Sarah Orne Jewett, Mary Murfee, and others now described as local color or regional writers and realists.

From 1861 to 1865, Thaxter's poetry was published anonymously in *The Atlantic*. After that and through the mid-1880s, she wrote under her own name for *The Atlantic Monthly.* She also published in several other popular American periodicals, including *Scribner's Magazine, Harper's New Monthly Magazine, The Century, The New England Magazine,* and children's periodicals *St. Nicholas Magazine* and *Youth's Companion.* This income sometimes provided her family with necessary income as her husband earned money only intermittently. Possibly most important for Thaxter herself, it eventually paid for a house maid and a sewing machine. Thaxter's letters from this period speak often of exhaustion from keeping a house entirely by herself. She wrote to editor James Fields in October 1862 that her poems were "evolved among the pots and kettles....Verses can grow where prose cannot."

Not only were her family's needs pressing; Thomas Laighton's health was failing after he suffered paralytic strokes in the winter of 1862–1863. At the same time, her brothers had undertaken to expand the hotel. The summer of 1863 revealed that their staff and kitchens were inadequate, and Thaxter worked the entire summer to make ends meet while also helping take care of her father. In her correspondence, she reported a temporary distaste for people brought on by overwork and overexposure. Indeed, the hotel guest registers reveal an overwhelming array of visitors that included the period's best known artists, authors, academicians, and musicians. At the same time as Celia Thaxter's reputation as a poet was established, she was also expanding her friendships and artistic relationships, both in summer at the Shoals and in winter in Newtonville, where the Thaxters were part of the literary social round centered on *The Atlantic Monthly* and its publisher, James Fields.

With Thomas Laighton's death in May 1866 and Levi Thaxter's first attack of what he called rheumatism of the chest in 1869, Celia's residential pattern shifted again. To avoid the harsh New England winter, Levi took sons John and Roland with their schoolbooks and camping paraphernalia to Florida; Celia took Karl to Appledore to keep her mother company and help with the winter work involved in keeping the hotel operating. For the next eight years, she spent much of each winter on the Shoals. During this first winter, she made time to write the prose her friends had urged her to compose since the mid-1860s. This effort produced four essays published in *The Atlantic* under the title "Among the Isles of Shoals I–IV" in the August 1869 and January, February, and May 1870 numbers. Thaxter's text moves easily from natural history to geology to

history to architecture, describing and placing in context the details of the place, as if she is walking over the islands with a companion and yarning off what comes to mind as she goes. Her description of local customs, which were disappearing with the concurrent development of the summer resort, is related to the developing discipline of cultural anthropology. Thaxter chronicled these patterns before they faded away, fixing meaning to them and establishing their historical importance at least in a local way. The American literary community praised the essays. Whittier wrote to Thaxter that Horace Greeley, editor of the influential *New York Tribune* called her essays "the best prose writing I have seen for a long while.... Her pen pictures are wonderfully well-done."

Her reputation established, Thaxter's writing was collected and published in many different editions during the 1870s. Her first volume of poetry was published in 1872; an enlarged edition with 28 new poems came out in 1874. These volumes collected poetry previously published in periodicals with additional unpublished work. Levi Thaxter managed the selection and publication of the first volume, which included "Land-Locked" and "Offshore" and also five new poems. The Shoals essays were collected in book form with eight woodcut illustrations commissioned by the publisher James R. Osgood in 1873. *Stories and Poems for Children* followed in 1875. *Drift-Weed*, a second collection of poems, was published in 1878. She defended the title *Drift-Weed* to James Fields, saying "these little verses sprang out of the rock and never knew cultivation." Thaxter's range of subject matter remained variable throughout her career. Stories of the sea and seaside observations predominated, but her love of music and admiration of the poetry of Robert Browning intersected in sonnets about composers and singers. Her stories for children were praised for their lack of moralizing, but she also wrote her share of what modern critics characterize as sentimental poetry, often expressing conventional religious beliefs, even though Thaxter herself never joined any church. Her wide popularity probably rested as much with the latter part of her canon: such poetry expressed the ethos of the age. By the end of the decade, she was generally considered one of America's best-loved poets. Her name recognition was considerable and went well beyond Boston's literary circle to less esoteric realms like popular sheet music.

With the gift of a box of water colors during the summer season of 1874, Thaxter tried painting from nature. She wrote to her regular confidante Annie Fields, wife of publisher James Fields and an author in her own right, that she had "been in a new world. I thought I knew every leaf, flower, bud, grass-stem, seed vessel, but I find I make their acquaintance all over again." By the summer of 1877, she was taking lessons from the well-known American painter John Appleton Brown. Later, she would study with William Morris Hunt, another noted American painter. Both were regular visitors at the Shoals. Thaxter's painting, primarily of botanical specimens, survives both on porcelain blanks, of which she recorded painting over 100 one winter on Appledore and copies of her own books that she illuminated for individual clients. This talent allowed her dual livelihoods of paint and writing.

The 1870s brought much change in the Laighton family's affairs on the Shoals. In 1872, John Poore built a rival hotel, the Oceanic, on Star Island. It burned in 1874, and Poore rebuilt it immediately. Oscar and Cedric Laighton bought the rebuilt hotel and took over its operation the following year. This established the Laighton brothers as the sole proprietors of a very large resort. Already a popular spot, the clientele only grew, and many of New England's literary, artistic, and intellectual circle spent time there. The seeds of friendships Thaxter planted in the 1850s and 1860s matured and strengthened in the 1870s, 1880s, and 1890s. Her own circle of regular correspondents included Annie Fields; author and resident of nearby Berwick, Maine, Sarah Orne Jewett; and the well-known poet and writer, and later editor of the *Atlantic*, Thomas

Bailey Aldrich. These friendships gave her strength when, in November 1877, Eliza Laighton died in Portsmouth, New Hampshire, after a decline of several years.

With her mother's death, Celia faced whether she would return to Newtonville that winter, where housework unaided by a servant awaited her. The Thaxter family summered in 1879 in Celia's cottage on Appledore, brought together by the convalescence of artist and family friend Hunt. His death ruptured the tenuous peace, and they decided to put the house in Newtonville up for sale, acknowledging that it was no longer a family home. Roland was attending Harvard, and John was a farmer's apprentice in West Virginia. Celia had little wish to return to Newtonville, and Levi spent only a portion of each year there himself. Karl, it was assumed, would follow Celia, as Levi seemed unable to admit that his eldest son would always require care. Levi Thaxter bought a farm at Kittery Point, Maine, overlooking the Isles of Shoals and renamed the property Champernowne for one of its seventeenth-century owners. John moved there in 1880 to try farming on his own. In October 1880, Celia went abroad with her brother Oscar, who suffered a mental collapse after a failed love affair the previous summer. They returned in February 1881. Cedric, the older of her two brothers, married Julia Stowell later the same year.

The early 1880s found Thaxter dividing her time between Champernowne in the early spring and fall, the Shoals in late spring to help ready the hotels and then to stay for the summer season, and Boston in winter. Levi Thaxter died of chronic peritonitis on June 1, 1884. Both John and Roland Thaxter married in 1887, John to Mary Stoddard and Roland to Mabel Freeman. With each of these events, Celia's family responsibilities diminished considerably. She published a third volume of poetry, *The Cruise of the Mystery, and other Poems,* in 1886. She noted to Annie Fields that about half of them were love songs, "a new departure." Embarking on a different subject, Thaxter wrote "Woman's Heartlessness" for the first number of the Audubon Society's magazine, published in February 1887. In this, she called for women to rethink their taste for bird plumage to decorate their headgear.

Celia Thaxter suffered ill health in 1888 and 1889, when nervous prostration laid her low during the winter months. She spent winters in Portsmouth, whence she could easily travel by train to Boston or to Kittery Point by carriage. After this, she rarely published in periodicals. Literary tastes were shifting away from the finely observed sketches and poems at which she excelled. *The Atlantic* itself grew more conservative as it neared its fiftieth year, drawing from a time-honored stable of male essayists.

Thaxter's final book, *An Island Garden*, was published in the spring of 1894. It was a collaborative effort between her and American Impressionist Childe Hassam, who spent many summers on Appledore. Hassam provided full-page plates and illuminations for chapter heads, while Thaxter wrote the text describing and discussing her 15-by-50-foot garden on Appledore in front of her cottage. Thaxter describes the labor and ingenuity she applied to creating a garden on the windswept rocks of the Shoals and explains how she uses the flowers to decorate her cottage. Her choice of plants reflected an interest in the gardens of earlier generations, especially of the early American era. Her garden also provided her with a respite from the busy rounds of running her family's hotels and with a way of bringing pleasure to her friends. While she complained to Sarah Orne Jewett in 1893 of how difficult she found it to write prose as she was preparing the text, prose allowed her to exercise her ability for close observation. Though broken into chapters, her free-flowing text moves from subject to subject with comparatively little structure, echoing her earlier *Among the Isles of Shoals* essays and that of other writers' village sketches. The publisher, Houghton Mifflin, lavished attention on the book. All of Hassam's illustrations were reproduced using chromolithography, making the run of a thousand very costly to produce. It was well received, and the publisher released an additional thousand copies in November 1894 after Thaxter's death.

After a brief illness, Celia Thaxter died on Appledore on August 25, 1894. She is buried on the Isles of Shoals near her parents. During the next two years, her friends Sarah Orne Jewett, Annie Fields, and Rose Lamb worked to bring out complete editions of Thaxter's poetry and letters. Jewett wrote introductions to posthumous editions of *The Poems of Celia Thaxter* and *Stories and Poems for Children* during the winter of 1894–1895; Fields appears to have written the introduction for *The Letters of Celia Thaxter*. Thaxter's personality, admired and revered by her friends and family, gave rise to further publications related to her life and work well into the twentieth century including additional volumes of letters and a biography by her granddaughter.

PRIMARY BIBLIOGRAPHY

Books

Poems (New York: Hurd and Houghton, 1872, 1874, 1876).

Among the Isles of Shoals (Boston: J.R. Osgood, 1873).

Drift-Weed (Boston: Houghton and Osgood, 1879; Houghton Mifflin, 1894).

Poems for Children (Boston: Houghton Mifflin, 1883, 1884).

The Cruise of the Mystery, and Other Poems (Boston: Houghton Mifflin, 1886).

Idyls and Pastorals: A Home Gallery of Poetry and Art (Boston: D. Lothrop, 1886).

Yule Log (Boston: L. Prang, 1889).

My Lighthouse, and Other Poems (Boston: L. Prang, [1890]).

Verses (Boston: D. Lothrop, 1891).

An Island Garden (Boston: Houghton Mifflin, 1894).

Letters of Celia Thaxter, edited by Annie Fields and Rose Lamb (Boston: Houghton Mifflin, 1895, 1897).

Stories and Poems for Children, preface by Sarah Orne Jewett (Boston: Houghton Mifflin, 1895, 1896, 1906).

The Poems of Celia Thaxter, preface by Sarah Orne Jewett, Appledore Edition (Boston: Houghton Mifflin, 1896, 1899, 1902, 1906).

The Heavenly Guest, edited by Oscar Laighton (Andover, MA: Smith and Coutts, 1935).

Sandpiper, and Sandalphon (Taylorville, IL: Parker Publishing, n.d.).

Maize, The Nation's Emblem (Taylorville, Illinois: Parker Publishing, n.d.).

Selected Periodical Publications— Uncollected

"Child-Life at the Isles of Shoals," *Atlantic Monthly* 31 (May 1873): 532–39.

"A Memorable Murder," *Atlantic Monthly* 35 (May 1875): 602–15.

"Maize for the Nation's Emblem," *New England Magazine* 14 (May 1893): 304.

SECONDARY BIBLIOGRAPHY

References

John Albee, "Memories of Celia Laighton Thaxter," *New England Magazine* 24 (1901): 166–72.

S.G.W. Benjamin, *The Atlantic Islands as Resorts of Health and Pleasure* (New York: Harper and Bros., 1878).

Van Wyck Brooks, *New England Indian Summer* (New York: E.P. Dutton, 1952).

Lawrence Buell, *New England Literary Culture: From Revolution to Renaissance* (Cambridge: Cambridge University Press, 1986).

S.A. Drake, *Nooks and Corners of the New England Coast* (New York: Harper and Bros., 1875).

Annie Fields, *Whittier: Notes of His Life and Friendships* (New York: Harper and Bros., 1893).

Annie Fields and Rose Lamb, eds., *Letters of Celia Thaxter* (Boston and New York: Houghton Mifflin, 1895).

Allen Lacy, introduction to reprint edition of *An Island Garden* (Boston, MA: Houghton Mifflin Company, 1988), iii–xiv.

Cedric Laighton, *Letters to Celia* [1860–1875] (Boston, MA: Star Island Corporation, 1972).

Oscar Laighton, ed., *The Heavenly Guest* [reprints of essays by friends and contemporaries] (Andover, MA: South and Coutts, 1935).

Oscar Laighton, *Ninety Years at the Isles of Shoals* (Boston: Beacon Press, 1930).

Vera Norwood, *Made From This Earth: American Women and Nature* (Chapel Hill: University of North Carolina Press, 1993).

Lyman Rutledge, *The Isles of Shoals in Lore and Legend* (Boston: Star Island Corporation, 1965).

Rosamond Thaxter, *Sandpiper: The Life and Letters of Celia Thaxter* (Francestown, NH: The Golden Quill Press, 1963; Portsmouth, NH: Peter E. Randall, 1999).

Jane E. Vallier, *Poet on Demand: The Life, Letters, and Work of Celia Thaxter* (Camden, ME: Down East Books, 1982; Portsmouth, NH: Peter E. Randall, 1994).

Papers

Celia Laighton Thaxter corresponded with many people, and an unusually large proportion of these letters survives. Letters between her and John Greenleaf Whittier as well as editorial correspondence with various members of the Houghton publishing entities are preserved at the Houghton Library of Rare Books at Harvard. Other material, including photographs and related correspondence, is located at Colby College; the Huntington Library in Pasadena, California; the Boston Public Library of Rare Books; the J.P. Morgan Library of New York; the Public Libraries of New York and Providence; the Essex Institute in Salem, Massachusetts; the Portsmouth Athenaeum and Portsmouth Public Library in New Hampshire; and the Boston Athenaeum.

Edith M. Thomas
(August 12, 1854–
September 13, 1925)

Kevin De Ornellas

Edith Matilda Thomas was a prolific and acclaimed poet, but has been virtually forgotten since her death. Her work's declining status may be gauged by the contrasting treatment of her by the editors of the *Dictionary of American Biography* (1928 —1936) and of its successor, *American National Biography* (1999): in the former, a fulsome, appreciative article by Harry Shaw, Jr., is included; in the latter, Thomas has been excluded, ignored. Edith M. Thomas's poetry has long been out of favor. Barriers exist to render it unpalatable to latter-day readers: the poems are ornate, ordered, neat, and rigidly crafted, lacking the free-flowing, liberated shapelessness of much post-War American and English poetry. Thomas, provocatively referred to by F.L. Pattee as "more Greek than American," saturates her poetry in classical allusion, thereby further impeding the understanding of her work by post-1960s generations who have had little exposure to the Greek and Roman greats. But Thomas wrote in another genre: nonfictional prose. In 1886, her one book of nature essays was published; later essays were published as journal articles. With their concern for the interrelatedness between humans and their natural surroundings, and her sensitivity to how these delicate connections are threatened by careless interference, Thomas's essays speak to twenty-first century readers in a way that her poems do not.

Edith M. Thomas's father, Frederick J. Thomas, was the son of Welsh immigrants to New York; her mother, Louisa Sturges, was born in Connecticut to descendants of English settlers. Having married, Thomas and Sturges became established in Chatham, Ohio, at a time when such locations were still thought of as "Western" by the white settlers. Thomas worked as a school teacher and as a farmer. The couple's daughter, Edith Matilda, was born on August 12, 1854. The family moved again, first to Kenton, and then to Bowling Green, where Frederick J. Thomas died during 1861. Almost immediately, his widow brought her daughters (Edith had one sister) on the eastwards journey to Geneva, where the family remained for over two decades. Although still in Ohio, Geneva has a markedly different environment from Edith M. Thomas's previous places of residence. Geneva is very close to the southern shore of Lake Erie. Thus, from the age of seven onwards, Thomas could view the spectacular sights of nature, and witness the ever-changing force of the natural elements and their effect on human activity as well as on farmed and wild vegetation and fauna.

Seeming set on a career in teaching, the bookish, Greek-learning Edith graduated from a normal institute in 1872, but her subsequent few months teaching at Oberlin College left her frustrated and unfulfilled. Thomas dabbled in the production and marketing of typesetting for a number of months, but, in effect, became wholly dedicated to literature during the mid-1870s. Throughout this decade, she contributed poems to local newspapers and journals in Geneva and in the nearby Great Lakes city, Cleveland. Her father's brother, James Thomas (whose wealth derived from speculation in the Californian gold rush), greatly encouraged Edith, supplying her with books, with financial assistance, and with morale-boosting plaudits. The uncle brought Edith on a visit to New York in the early 1880s, in a move that would expose her successfully to the literati of America's then cultural capital.

In New York, the poet Helen Hunt Jackson took an instant interest in Thomas and in her poems, and agitated for a selection of her work to be published in *Scribner's Magazine*. The association with Thomas and this journal continued—further Thomas verses were published after its name was changed to *The Century*. Many other newspapers and magazines printed Thomas's poetry—a preliminary list would cite *The Critic*, *Harper's*, and *The Nation*. Corresponding from Geneva, and traveling when she could to the east coast, Thomas supplied many more poems to her main supporting publication, *The Atlantic Monthly*. Her acceptance by the literary establishment, and physical distance from it, can be seen in an apologetic letter of 1882, when she regretfully declines an invitation to attend a celebratory gathering for Harriet Beecher Stowe. Critics were excited by Thomas's person as well as by her tightly measured poems: a (male) writer in *Graphic* wrote that Thomas "has one of the most striking faces ever bestowed on a woman...beautiful in its refined intelligence." In short, Thomas became a slightly enigmatic, minor literary celebrity.

After four years of numerous and manifold contributions to these high-ranking periodicals, Thomas's first book of poetry, *A New Year's Masque, and Other Poems*, was published by Houghton Mifflin during 1885 —with typical gratitude from Thomas, the book was prefaced with a poem dedicated to the recently deceased Helen Hunt Jackson. A year later, *The Round Year*, her first—and last—book of prose was published. But, still, Thomas continued—in her own words from *The Round Year*—"Living not far from a great lake." After a lengthy illness, Thomas's mother died in 1887. With her main familial tie to Ohio now cut off, Edith M. Thomas moved to New York permanently, where she would remain until her death in 1925. The essays in *The Round Year* derive from Thomas's biographical circumstances. She was conscious not only of the Great Lake and rural surroundings of Geneva, but also of the axiomatic differences between this country way of living and the urban speed of New York. *The Round Year* captures a moment when an inherently emotional, sensitive writer is being tempted away from her naturally abundant, bucolic environment, one that she knows she will miss after living there for most of her young life. It is small wonder, then, that the book poignantly celebrates every conceivable attribute, large and small, of northern Ohio's landscape and its natural animals and plants.

The Round Year was published by Houghton Mifflin in Boston and New York in 1886. Now a rare and expensive book, it has never been reprinted. It is austere in appearance—none of the 300 pages in octavo format is illustrated. Ten of the 22 essays had appeared in *The Atlantic Monthly* between February 1882 and September 1885. The few variants between the periodical versions and *The Round Year* versions are, for the most part, insignificant. One essay, however, "A Summer Holinight," had been published in *Century* with substantial variants. Sequenced carefully in the book, the essays are arranged to reflect the changing seasons (flux is a recurring theme throughout the collection). A trajectory moves from the promise of spring, onto the excitement of summer, through the colors of autumn, and concludes with descriptions of harsh, winter times. Each essay concentrates on the flourishes or struggles of wildlife and/or humans at a particular time of year. The effects of seasonal meteorological phenomena on man and on wildlife are also addressed.

If obstacles exist to deter later readers from Edith M. Thomas's poetry, then some other obstacles may impede engagement with these unapologetically subjective essays. Thomas can be willfully unscientific in approach: at one stage, she asks the naïve question, "Do dolphins inhabit fresh water?" Because support for the threatened natural world of the twenty-first century needs to be knowledgeable to be credible, such self-declared ignorance may not appeal to modern environmentalists. Almost invariably, Thomas eschews Latin species nomenclature and taxonomic details, preferring to cite common English and sometimes local names for animals and plants. In addition, Thomas frequently anthropomorphizes not only birds and mammals, but insects, flowers, and even lakes. The most trivial of the 22 essays is "Frost and Moonshine," which, basically, creates the fantasy of the personified beings of Frost and Moonshine debating a rather elusive issue. To give another, smaller, instance of this anthropomorphizing tendency, Thomas writes about the plumage of a Kingfisher "that accomplished angler"—as if it consciously decided upon its appearance: it wears a "helmet" of feathers, and wears a "dark-blue glossy coat" and, like a dining gentleman, a "white neck-cloth." Plant biology is also referred to in human terms, as Thomas refers to the "quick-closing eyelids" of chickweed and dandelion flowers

Thomas's prose is repeatedly broken by poetic extracts, some of which derive from her own works, but many of which are extracted from works by the Greek and Roman ancients, canonical Medieval and Renaissance writers, English Romantics (particularly Keats, whose combination of subjective observation and allusive literariness inspired Thomas more than any other writer), and nineteenth-century Americans.

Although most can now be traced through simple Internet searches, few of the quotations are credited. Thus, the unaccounted-for extracts may create a barrier for a fuller appreciation of Thomas's motives and impassioned depth of feeling and intellectual endeavor. These obstacles, combined with the inaccessibility of the book, can hinder an introduction to *The Round Year*. But the book has a lot to offer in the present. Its difficulties are dwarfed by the attractiveness of many of its preoccupations. Many of Thomas's observations of, and anxieties for, the natural world speak to us. These attractions include, but are not limited to: her delight in even the most common, humble, or minute aspects of wild life; the insistence that organisms must be studied whilst alive and in their natural habitat's context; the connections between fauna and flora and between humans and their surroundings (Thomas's "biocentrism," as Lorraine Anderson and Thomas S. Edwards term it); the vulnerability of much natural phenomena to human recklessness; and, finally, the fact that Thomas betrays a wicked, satirical sense of humor.

In *The Round Year*, Thomas celebrates massive and tiny natural creatures and landscapes. A blade of grass is lavished with the same heightened, appreciative observance as the tidal patterns of the "fresh-water sea," Lake Erie. Writing about maize, Thomas insists that each corn plant "possesses presence and dignity no less than does the oak itself. It stands erect, poised, sufficient." Even though it is very common and "unkempt" in appearance, Thomas writes "In praise of the Blackberry," lauding its hardiness and its usefulness for fruit-loving birds and humans. Thomas's imperative to celebrate the familiar is complemented by the drive to observe nature very closely, to approach it and to concentrate on its possibilities with a disciplined, patient eye. A tree has a notable, changing character throughout the year— "he has hardly become acquainted with the whole tree who has known it only in its summer months." Finding it "strange that not more is said about the beauty of

blackberry flowers," Thomas acclaims overlooked bounties, such as the "recondite loveliness" of grass-plant flowers, which, she
claims, are seen only by "the faithful, refined,
and loving eye, patient to investigate." For
nature to be understood, it must be seen, living, in its natural habitat. Dead, cut flowers,
"lying in faded state" are no more useful for
Thomas than "mummified Egyptian royalty."
Specimen gathering is castigated, as it disas-
sociates the once-living artifact from the
thriving ecosystems from which they derive
—"a 'dry garden' and a case of still-life are
poor showings for the true natural history of
flower or bird," Thomas asserts. In the biologically straitened world of the twenty-first
century, with its declining biodiversity and
almost nonexistent wildernesses, the rousing
call for the celebration and protection of
all wildlife, however unspectacular, surely
appeals.

All human and nonhuman life is connected in the formulations set down by
Thomas. Birds and humans will both greedily
consume nutritious blackberries; during
summer nights, human voices are responded
to by wild creatures' "murmurous responses
and expostulations"; and within Thomas's
anthropomorphized, nonhuman world, flowers and insects deliberately collaborate,
fanned by the "friendly goddesses" of Fauna
and Flora. At this period of history, after half
a century of intensive, wildlife-hindering
farming, Thomas's claim that agriculture
and birds work to each other's benefit seems
dated but also warming. Blackbirds and robins follow the plough, "ready to share the
toils and profits of tillage," while farmers
should be grateful for the avian appetite for
pests such as "cutworm, slug, beetle, and mis-
chievous larvae." Although seemingly sentimental, the implicit, material point is that
rather than treating natural creatures as competitors to human interests, society should
see wild fauna as kindred spirits and maybe
even as willing partners. Thomas abhors
any killing of animal or plant life that she
does not regard as absolutely necessary. She
can enjoy observing fish, just as much as a
competent angler, but without "indulging in
his cruelty or forerelish of the table." With
mock hysteria, Thomas refers to farmer-
bothering birds as a "horde of feathered
trespassers," and lambasts trigger-happy bird
killers as mere "boys with a shot-gun."

Despairingly, Thomas bewails "the inroad
that has been made upon the timber during
the fall and winter months." With controlled, yet emotive, repetitive language, she
observes that "Down go the beech, down go
the oak, and the ash; down goes the maple."
Guiltily writing about the domestic comforts
of a home fire, Thomas worries that all coal
burning is really tree burning ("coal miners
may be reckoned as woodmen"), and that
someday the vulnerable, "superficial forests
[will] have been quite stripped away by the
careless generations." Thus, in calling for sustainable uses of naturally formed products,
Thomas expresses anxieties that we are now
alarmingly familiar with. Thomas states that
it is in man's "self-interest" to "stay his
inroads upon the sylvan territory" of forests.
But any anachronistic suspicion that Thomas
is a mere "shallow ecologist" is negated by
the abundant evidence that Thomas values
all fauna and flora for their inherent qualities,
not merely because of their uses for humans.
Thomas sometimes turns a sharp, biting
humor against persons who murderously
attack natural creatures. Killing a bird, a
mammal, or an insect are crimes that are all
equal for Thomas.

The bitterest, but also the most amusing,
chapter in *The Round Year* is a brazenly
sarcastic tribute to a man who kills any fly
that approaches him. Mockingly castigated
as an intellectually limited know-all, the pro-
vider of the "useful service" of insect killing
is "a hard-working, rheumatism-plagued,
weather-forecasting, one-newspaper-reading,
politics-and-theology-debating" nobody.
Thomas ironically acclaims as "indeed wonderful" the fact that the truculent, opinion-
ated killer can "carry on an argumentative
discourse and at the same time attend to
the flies." He can speak and move his
arms at the same time. Thomas scorns the

"satisfaction a supreme being must take in dooming its abject creatures," and excoriates the unnecessary killing done by "our hero." For Thomas, even lesser creatures are to be studied and learned from, not destroyed for ephemeral, questionable pleasures or purposes.

Between January 1887 and December 1895, Thomas published 14 further prose essays in the *Atlantic Monthly*, 11 of which develop, elaborate, or repeat the preoccupations with nature that are accounted for above. But, perhaps influenced by an *Atlantic Monthly* review that advised "Miss Thomas" not "to lose herself in prose," because verse "is her natural expression," Edith M. Thomas never produced another full-length prose work. Apparently, after 1897, she reneged on prose writing altogether, continuing to produce considerable amounts of poetry—much of which dwells on her lifelong engagement with nature. From 1888 onwards, Thomas lived and worked (as a reader for *Harper's Magazine* and as a clerk for the *Century Dictionary*) in various offices and residences of New York. When living in the Staten Island home of the retired oculist and patron of the arts, Dr. Samuel Elliott, her room's view of the Kill Van Kull's water reminded her of, but also contrasted with, her views of Lake Erie from Geneva.

When Thomas was in her early seventies, her prose had already been forgotten, but the still-active writer was acclaimed by literary conservatives for the learned, measured style of her ever-careful poems. Robert Underwood Johnson prized her as a yardstick and as a bulwark against the perceived sloppiness and "lawlessness" of the increasingly popular free verse of the period. Thomas died on September 13, 1925; her passing was marked by an adulatory obituary in *The New York Times*. Her *Selected Poems* were published in 1926. The poems were introduced by an affectionate memoir by Jessie B. Rittenhouse—this remains the major source for information about Thomas's life. But, rather than inspiring new interest in Thomas's career, the *Selected Poems* edition seems rather to have closed the book on this Ohio-born writer's work. Little interest has been shown in her poetry ever since; and her prose has been almost completely buried.

However, in 2000, an anthology of American women's nature writing, *At Home on This Earth*, was published—three well-chosen essays from *The Round Year* were included. The editors, Lorraine Anderson and Thomas S. Edwards, also provide a brief but cogent statement of the possible benefits of reading Thomas's prose in the new millennium. In addition, all of Thomas's poetic and prose contributions to *The Atlantic Monthly* can now be read for free on the World Wide Web. Cornell University Library's "Making of America" project (http://cdl.library.cornell.edu/moa) makes Thomas's works available in a way that they were not for many decades. If a new edition of *The Round Year* itself could be published and read by sensitive, ecocritical scholars and an environmentally concerned, general readership, Edith M. Thomas could once again become something of a valuable and appreciated, albeit minor, literary celebrity.

PRIMARY BIBLIOGRAPHY

Books

A New Year's Masque, and other Poems (Boston and Cambridge: Houghton Mifflin & Co., 1885).

The Round Year (Boston and Cambridge: Houghton Mifflin & Co., 1886).

Lyrics and Sonnets (Boston and Cambridge: Houghton & Co., 1887).

Children of Autumn (New York: F.A. Stokes & Brother, 1888).

Children of Spring (New York: F.A. Stokes & Brother, 1888).

Children of Summer (New York: F.A. Stokes & Brother, 1888).

Children of Winter (New York: F.A. Stokes & Brother, 1888).

Babes of the Year, illustrated by Maud Humphrey (New York: F.A. Stokes & Brother, 1889).

Heaven and Earth (New York: F.A. Stokes & Brother, 1889).

Tiny Folk of Sunny Days (New York: F.A. Stokes & Brother, 1889).

Tiny Folk of Wintry Days (New York: F.A. Stokes & Brother, 1889).

The Inverted Torch (Boston: Houghton & Co., 1890).

Fair Shadow Land (Boston: Houghton Mifflin, 1893).

In Sunshine Land, illustrated by Katharine Pyle (Boston: Houghton Mifflin, 1895).

A Winter Swallow, with other Verse (New York: C. Scribner, 1896).

In the Young World (Boston: Houghton Mifflin, 1896).

The Dancers, and other Legends and Lyrics (Boston: R.G. Badger, 1903).

Cassia and Other Verse (Boston: R.G. Bader, 1905).

Children of Christmas (Boston: R.G. Badger, 1907).

The Guest at the Gate (Boston: R.G. Badger, 1909).

The Flower from the Ashes (Portland: T.B. Mosher, 1915).

The White Messenger, and other War Poems (Boston: R.G. Badger, 1915).

Selected Poems, Edited, with a Memoir, by Jessie B. Rittenhouse (New York: Harper & Bros., 1926).

SECONDARY BIBLIOGRAPHY

References

Lorraine Anderson and Thomas S. Edwards, eds., *At Home on This Earth: Two Centuries of U.S. Women's Nature Writing* (Hanover, NH: University Press of New England, 2002).

Claire Buck, *Bloomsbury Guide to Women's Literature* (London: Bloomsbury, 1992).

Lawrence Buell, *The Environmental Imagination: Thoreau, Nature Writing, and the Formation of American Culture* (Cambridge, MA: Belknap Press, 1998).

Joseph G.E. Hopkins, ed., *Concise Dictionary of American Biography,* 2nd ed. (New York: Charles Scribner's Sons, 1977).

Stanley J. Kuntz and Howard Haycroft, *American Authors, 1600–1900* (New York: H.W. Wilson, 1938).

Sherry Lee Linkon, *In Her Own Voice: Nineteenth-Century Women Essayists* (New York: Garland, 1997).

Cynthia Ozick, "Against Modernity: the American Academy in the '20s," *New Criterion* 13.1 (1994), www.newcriterion.com/archive/13/sept94/ozick.htm (accessed January 23, 2004).

F.L. Pattee, *A History of American Literature Since 1870* (New York: Century Co., 1915).

Harry Shaw, Jr., "Edith Matilda Thomas," *Dictionary of American Biography,* 20 vols., ed. Dumas Malone and Humphrey Milford (London: Oxford University Press; New York: Charles Scribner's Sons, 1928–1936), 18: 428–29.

Who Was Who in America, Volume 1: 1897–1942 (Chicago: A.N. Marquis, 1943), 1229.

J.G. Wilson, and J. Fiske, eds., *Appleton's Cyclopedia of American Biography,* 6 vols. (New York: D. Appleton & Co., 1887–1889), 6: 78.

Papers

The Geneva Branch of the Ashtabula County District Library, Ohio, has a number of unpublished documents and scrapbooks in its Edith M. Thomas Collection; autographed letters by Thomas feature in the Richard Walter Gilder Manuscripts and the James Whitcomb Riley papers, Indiana University Bloomington Library; in the Thomas Mosher Bird Papers, Houghton Library, Harvard College; and in the Mary Mapes Dodge Collection, Princeton University Library.

Henry David Thoreau
(July 12, 1817–May 6, 1862)

Bryan L. Moore

Contrary to popular belief, Henry David Thoreau was not the first American nature writer. Anne Bradstreet, William Bartram, Philip Freneau, and William Cullen Bryant, not to mention the American Indians, produced what could accurately be termed "nature writing" before Thoreau was born. Yet Thoreau has without question dominated the genre since his untimely death in 1862, and he has largely defined what nature writing would be for those who followed him. No writer more eloquently explored the place of humanity in the rest of nature, but, of course, Thoreau is not *just* a nature writer. Outside the genre, his contribution to the development of the personal essay is considerable. His work stands as the greatest example in American literature on how to live deliberately, actively, and simply, and his "Resistance to Civil Government" is among the most important statements regarding the pre-eminence of the individual conscience.

American writers before Thoreau had extolled the value of wild nature and questioned unlimited wilderness development, Manifest Destiny, and the ambition for wealth as noble or even desirable goals. But Thoreau's writings are unique in proclaiming the value of untamed wilderness by showing how it is an inextricable part of humanity. More than any other writer, in his philo-sophical essays Thoreau personalized the relationship between the natural world and the human inner world and dramatized the correlation between wild nature and the essential wildness of humans. And he did so with great wit and learning, with a unique ability to extol the wonders and mysteries of the natural world, and to critique—sometimes gently, sometimes bitterly—the human culture that detracts from self-discovery. While Thoreau's greatest radicalism lies in his views on how we might live more principled, productive—and not merely materialistic—lives, his writings continue to stand as an eloquent argument for preserving wild areas over the clamorous, unending demands of industry and profit. More than anyone else in his time, Thoreau was keenly aware of the dangers of human encroachment on nature. Though the preservation of wild places is a relatively minor theme in Thoreau's work, the ramifications of his oft-quoted statement "in Wildness is the preservation of the World" reverberated in the writings of John Muir, Aldo Leopold, Loren Eiseley, Edward Abbey, Annie Dillard, Terry Tempest Williams, and scores of others from the nineteenth century to the present who write in celebration and defense of wilderness.

Thoreau was born David Henry Thoreau (he would switch the first and middle names when he was 20 years old) on July 12, 1817, in Concord, Massachusetts, where he would live almost all his life. He inherited his wit and social conscience from his mother, Cynthia (Dunbar). His father, John Thoreau, a Harvard graduate of French ancestry, worked a variety of jobs until he established himself in his pencil-making business. With three siblings—two sisters, Helen and Sophia, and a brother, John—Henry Thoreau's family was tightly knit. Until the 1850s the family frequently had a hard time financially. The family took in boarders for supplemental income. After grammar school, Henry attended the newly built college preparatory school, the Concord Academy, from 1828 until 1833. Shy and fond of reading but not particularly studious, as a young boy he did not make a strong impression on his schoolmates or teachers. He was, like many boys, drawn to the outdoors, but even in childhood, Thoreau was unusually enthusiastic in learning about the world around him and had excellent observation skills. It was said that he had an uncanny ability to find an arrowhead in the forest almost at will. He was also unusually good with his hands, at doing carpentry work and building small boats.

Though John seemed to be the more promising of the two brothers, Henry was the more scholarly, and so the family decided to send him, in his father's footsteps, to Harvard. Thoreau had difficulty passing the entrance examinations, but soon after entering the college in 1833 he began to excel in languages, classics, and English poetry. Although he belittled his education at Harvard, he would later acknowledge that he learned to write at college. Graduating in 1837, Thoreau returned to Concord and taught at the public school, Concord Center School, but he lasted less than two weeks, at least in part because he refused to cane his students. He would later open a tiny school with his brother, John, but over the next months, as he unsuccessfully sought another teaching position (an economic depression was on that lasted into the 1840s), it became clear that he would not have a career as a teacher. For the rest of his life, Thoreau made money off and on by working in his father's pencil factory and as a land surveyor. Though both trades may be considered mundane and constricting for America's greatest nature writer, in his own way he excelled at both trades. Through Henry's innovations, the Thoreau pencils became the best in the region, and his precision and skill as a surveyor placed him in demand; in 1856 he traveled to New Jersey for work. Despite Thoreau's talent for making pencils and surveying, they were merely means, not ends. In 1841, in a letter to his friend Lucy Brown, he wrote,

> I dream of looking abroad summer and winter, with free gaze, from some mountain-side, while my eyes revolve in an Egyptian slime of health,—I to be nature looking into nature with such easy sympathy as the blue-eyed grass looks in the face of the sky.

A decade later, he would note in his journal that his profession is "to find God in nature." These were Thoreau's true occupations.

The effort to teach ended in failure, but the return to Concord precipitated interests that were to stay with Thoreau for the rest of his life. He went on long walks virtually every day, drinking in nature, even though his health was not good for much of his life. He also took boating trips, one in 1837 by steamer to Maine to attempt (unsuccessfully) to secure a teaching job and another, in the summer of 1839, with his brother in a homemade boat on the Concord and Merrimack Rivers (the subject of his first book). Over the course of his life, he succeeded in scaling some 20 New England mountains. In the late 1830s, Thoreau began to forge a friendship with Ralph Waldo Emerson, who, though 14 years older than Thoreau, became the most important friendship of his life. Already established as one of the prominent thinkers in New England, Emerson shared and fostered the younger man's social views and his love of nature, reading tastes, and Transcendental philosophy. Coming out of Harvard, Thoreau was already interested in writing, but in addition to inspiring Thoreau with his organic, idealistic world view, Emerson provided Thoreau the crucial encouragement to work hard at his writing and reading. He recommended that Thoreau begin keeping a journal—a practice Emerson had observed for some time—and for almost the rest of his life, from October 1837 until November 1861, Thoreau religiously filled up notebooks with entries. (The 1906 edition of his journals totals about 6,000 printed pages.) He kept several additional notebooks in which to record ideas, data, and quotations —his notes on aboriginal America is contained in 12 separate notebooks of about 3,000 manuscript pages. The journal became his chief means of recording and storing ideas for later writing projects. Thoreau would regularly cut out pages of his journal in drafting various projects, but in late 1850, realizing that the journal was becoming a grand literary project of its own, he ceased this practice and began dating his entries more carefully.

Thoreau and Emerson would have disagreements, and it is a mistake to assume they held precisely the same views about art and the world in general, but their influence on one another is difficult to overestimate. Emerson's *Nature*, which set forth the principles of New England Transcendentalism, was particularly instrumental in showing Thoreau, fresh out of college, that he could shape his own life. In determining how to live, in coming to know oneself, Emerson's little book suggests one look to nature for answers:

> But the best read naturalist who lends an entire and devout attention to truth, will see that there remains much to learn of his relation to the world, and that it is not to be learned by any addition or subtraction or other comparison of known quantities, but is arrived at by untaught sallies of the spirit, by a continual self-recovery, and by entire humility. He will perceive that there are far more excellent qualities in the student than preciseness and infallibility; that a guess is often more fruitful than an indisputable affirmation, and that a dream may let us deeper into the secret of nature than a hundred concerted experiments.

Most of the major Transcendentalists were, like Emerson, well-educated, liberal Unitarians from East Massachusetts who knew one another personally and by reputation. Transcendentalism—a philosophy, an epistemology, and a major American literary movement—is not composed of a neat set of tenets and can be difficult to pin down, but most of its major practitioners held that God exists within the individual soul, that all humans, through intuition, are capable of transcending the limitations of the senses and logic and of corresponding with the divine being to receive higher truths and knowledge. The Transcendentalists were deeply dissatisfied with the sterility of materialistic society and were generally opponents of Manifest Destiny. They were skeptical toward inherited beliefs, including those handed down from Puritan orthodoxy. Socially, many Transcendentalists were reformers and staunch abolitionists, and some, Thoreau included, took active roles in opposing the Fugitive Slave Law and helping runaway slaves escape.

For some but not all of its practitioners, the Transcendental movement was an expression of discontent with Unitarianism—even though Unitarian (as well as Puritan, Deistic, and Quaker) traces are discernible in the movement. Emerson had been a Unitarian minister until 1832, when, feeling constricted by the church's reliance on formalities, he resigned. Thoreau was baptized and buried as a Unitarian, but one does not need to read deeply in his writings to understand that he did not, in any conventional sense, adhere to any organized religion. In addition to Unitarianism, Transcendentalists borrowed freely from a wide array of sources. From Hinduism, other Eastern religions, and the ancient Stoics of Greece and Rome, they appropriated the belief that the universe is governed by a set of laws that apply to all of nature. Kant, Plato, and the Neoplatonists were key sources for the philosophical idealism central to the belief in higher laws that transcend the material world. They adopted for their own the ideas of the European Romantics, who democratized literary subject matter, language, and form and who espoused a pantheistic view of nature. Goethe's holistic, dynamic view of nature was a major influence on the Transcendentalists, as were Coleridge and Wordsworth, especially their *Lyrical Ballads*. Romanticism was, of course, the larger movement to which the New England Transcendentalists, including Emerson and Thoreau, were a part.

Thoreau's reading over the years was wide, deep, and eclectic, ranging from ancient to contemporary, from New England to the Far East. He had little use for fiction, but virtually everything else struck his interest at some point in his life. In grammar school, he had been exposed to the Bible (the language of which he appropriates freely in his writings) and English classics. At the Concord Academy, under the tutelage of Phineas Allen, he read Homer, Euripides, Virgil (whose *Georgics* would remain a favorite), Sallust, Cicero, Molière, and Voltaire, all in their original languages. Thoreau learned something about the niceties of language from reading Milton and Chaucer and about Northern European myth and primitivism from Longfellow, who had taken a position at Harvard in 1840. Of course, Emerson's writings, which Thoreau began to read at the end of his Harvard days, had an enormous and lasting effect. To a lesser extent, so did the writings of Emerson's friend Thomas Carlyle and the English Romantics (especially Samuel Coleridge but also William Wordsworth). Goethe's *Italian Journey* (1816–1817), which combined a romantic artistic view with a social sense, was an early favorite. He admired Herman Melville's *Typee* (1846)—an autobiographical novel, but one that most people in the day (including Thoreau) read as a piece of travel writing on a primitive culture. Though he did not care much for the open sexuality of *Leaves of Grass*, Thoreau came to be a great admirer of Walt Whitman, whom he met in Brooklyn in 1856. Two of his favorite writers were William Gilpin and John Ruskin, English writers concerned with perception and the artistic representation of nature. Gilbert White's

The Natural History of Selborne (1788), which, like *Walden*, is largely concerned with a relatively small area of land, held a similar value. He greatly admired John Evelyn's *Sylvan* (1664), a book on arboriculture that makes some early quasi-conservationist statements.

Though he learned much from the natural history writings of Louis Agassiz, he disputed Agassiz's theory of special creation. On the other hand, he appreciated the writings of Charles Darwin as fully as anyone in his day, and he came to embrace what would later be called evolutionary theory. Later in life, a survey of trees entitled *A Report on the Trees and Shrubs Growing Naturally in the Forests of Massachusetts* (1846) by George B. Emerson (a distant cousin of Ralph Waldo Emerson) was a major model for Thoreau in his own work in natural history. In addition, Thoreau read scores of books on travel and exploration, philosophy (especially the Stoics and Aristotle), language, botany, zoology, natural history, Hindu, and other Eastern religions. Thoreau kept copious notes on much of his reading. For example, his "Indian Books"— the 11 notebooks he filled with quotations and responses from books on American Indians—is culled from over 270 different sources. As is true of Montaigne's *Essais*, much of Thoreau's own writings allude to or quote directly from an extensive range of material, but Thoreau's words and ideas, rooted in his own personal experience, are always front and center.

In November 1840 Thoreau proposed marriage to a family friend named Ellen Sewall, but she rejected him, most likely because of her father's reservations about the Thoreau boys. (Earlier that year, John Thoreau had also proposed to her, but after initial encouragement, he too was rejected.) Apparently, he developed an affection for at least a few women he encountered in Concord, including Emerson's wife Lidian, and Lucy Brown, a longtime boarder with the Thoreau family and 19 years Henry's senior. After Ellen, Thoreau never again proposed marriage. Nor did he maintain a romantic relationship with a woman; he almost certainly went to his grave a virgin. (There is little evidence to support the claim that Thoreau was homosexual.) By the mid-1840s, it became clear to Thoreau that he was married to nature, to his work as writer and observer; years later, in 1856, he would write in his journal, "all nature is my bride."

For the first few years after college, Thoreau began working hard on becoming a good writer. His earliest post-Harvard essays betray an Emerson enthusiast trying to find his own voice. He became involved in the Concord Lyceum, serving as its curator off and on until 1845 and giving lectures there (20 times from 1838 to 1860). But Thoreau's chief interest early on lay in writing poetry. He wrote most of his best verse while he was in his twenties. Virtually all of his poetry is romantic and deeply personal; some of it is memorable, but some of it is hackneyed and uninteresting. On Thoreau the poet, Hyatt H. Waggoner writes, "As with Melville, there is vastly more and better poetry, and even better rhythms, in his prose." Though he would later say that Thoreau's verses were "often rude and defective," Emerson was Thoreau's greatest source of encouragement as a writer, and he praised the younger man's poetry. Later he would suggest that one looking for Thoreau's autobiography should read his poetry. Thoreau published several poems in the short-lived but influential journal *The Dial*, which began in 1840. The journal's first editor, Margaret Fuller, was never enthusiastic about Thoreau's verse; Emerson's enthusiasm would eventually cool.

Had Thoreau left us with nothing but his poetry, he would be a minor figure in the history of American letters, but he would be a remembered figure nonetheless. Although much of his verse is mediocre, some of it establishes nature themes that would occupy Thoreau for the rest of his life. Always seeking an emergence with nature, his poem "Great Friend" dramatizes a Thoreau unable to look upon the face of his brother and best friend John, who died in 1842. The poet thus seeks the face of nature, "the person in her mask":

> The center of this world,
> The face of nature,
> The site of human life,
> Some sure foundation
> And nucleus of a nation—
> At least a private station.

Some of Thoreau's poems address feelings the poet had for Ellen Sewall and a few other women who took his interest in Concord. "Sic Vita" (also known as "I Am a Parcel of Vain Strivings") expresses, in part, frustration over the lack of a clearly established career, but the poem also looks forward to his later prose operation of employing metaphors from nature to dramatize human mortality. Many of Thoreau's poems announce the author's growing pantheism and Transcendental sensibility. One of his better poems, "Inspiration," does so by appropriating Puritan language in order to immolate Puritanism. "Smoke" (or "Light-Winged Smoke"), which found its way into *Walden*, follows a similar vein; though the poet cites the pagan "gods," there is no mistaking his wish to mock the Puritan belief in the essential wickedness of the human soul:

> Go thou my incense upward from this hearth,
> And ask the gods to pardon this clear flame.

In another poem, not feeling bound for the promised land, instead, Thoreau feels compelled to write,

> I am bound, I am bound, for a distant shore,
> By a lonely isle, by a far Azore,
> There it is, there it is, the treasure I seek,
> On the barren sands of a desolate creek.

In his apostrophe to "Nature," the poet requests a minor role in the course of things, preferring to be a minute part of nature over sharing "the city's year forlorn." "Winter Memories" is a poem about life and death that employs an ironic set of lines

> (So by God's cheap economy made rich
> To go upon my winter's task again)

that anticipates Emily Dickinson and indicates that, even early on, Thoreau's views of nature were more complicated than some may expect.

In the premiere issue of *The Dial*, Thoreau published his first essay, which is concerned with showing the value the Latin satirical poet Persius had for his day. The enduring values between the ages, antiquity and modern, was a common theme with Thoreau, as it was with Emerson. In the spring of 1841, Thoreau moved into Emerson's house and lived there for two years, working in the garden, overseeing the household, and developing an attraction to Lidian while Emerson was away giving lectures. It was while Thoreau lived with Emerson, in 1842, that his brother John developed lockjaw and died. Thoreau was so affected that he developed a sympathetic lockjaw himself. Even more tragic, only a few days after John Thoreau's death, Emerson's five-year-old son, Waldo, became ill and died. The deaths threw Thoreau into grief and into an extended illness, but it was shortly after these disasters that he began to find his niche as a writer and his early work began to fall into place.

After succeeding Margaret Fuller as editor of *The Dial* in 1842, Emerson published Thoreau's "Natural History of Massachusetts." The essay departs from its original purpose —a review of five different books on flora and fauna—and draws from journal entries to identify nature as beneficent, healthful, the source of all life and all law. Like much of his prose work, "Natural History" is interspersed with Thoreau's own poetry (some of it having been rejected by Fuller for publication), and is an interesting snapshot of the writer in his growing transition from poet to essayist. Some of the essay's ideas (e.g., "is not Nature, rightly read, that of which she is commonly taken to be the symbol merely?") veer closely to a mature Thoreau. Because the ambition overruns the form, the essay is not completely successful, but it helped Thoreau establish his chief concerns as a writer.

In May 1843, he left Emerson's house for Staten Island, where he lived with Emerson's brother, William, ostensibly to tutor his children. More specifically, Thoreau moved to New York to establish himself in a literary career. He met *New York Tribune* founder Horace Greeley (who would later be an important promoter of Thoreau's writing), Henry James, Sr., and others, but the move did not provide the desired career boost; times were hard and especially so for those trying to make a living from writing. The sojourn in New York, which lasted a little over a half year, was, however, fairly productive. He continued work on an anthology of English poetry, a project he never finished. He wrote the memorable "Paradise (to be) Regained," a long, part skeptical, part admiring review of a book by J.A. Etzler called *The Paradise within the Reach of all Men, without Labor, by Powers of Nature and Machinery*, which had been reprinted in 1842. In the *Boston Miscellany* he published "A Walk to Wachusett," which, though still a relatively mediocre Thoreau essay, is notable in part because it is his first publication that is essentially a narrative of an excursion into the wilds. In later works he would find this form well-suited to his talents.

Most importantly, while in New York Thoreau wrote the essay that many scholars regard as Thoreau's first mature work of prose, "A Winter Walk." As with most of his work, this essay is derived in large part from his journals, the source for many of his best ideas. The first person plural ("we") suggests a melding of narrator and reader to a deliberately unnamed frozen country road, woodland, and lake. The senses are open and alive in this pastoral travel guide, which leads the reader through a beneficent natural world. It evokes and celebrates "the wonderful purity of nature," and though nature is superior to culture, humanity is a part of, and not apart from, nature: "There is a slumbering fire in nature which never goes out"; the same "subterranean fire has its altar in each man's breast." Nature is necessary not only for its raw materials but also for its ability to inspire and renew us. He asks, "What would human life be without forests, those natural cities?" But he still believes that human encroachment is easily absorbed by the forest, which "cheerfully and unsuspiciously echoes the strokes of the axe that fells it."

The essay visits an important theme that recurs throughout Thoreau's work—the idea that nature is filled with metaphors and other tropes that enlighten our own lives and can show us how to live. Thoreau had read and digested Emerson's *Nature*, which proclaims that "Words are signs of natural facts," and that "every word which is used to express a moral or intellectual fact...is found to be borrowed from some material appearance." In "A Winter Walk" and elsewhere, Thoreau takes Emerson's dictum and makes it his own, often by his use of gentle personifications. He notes certain "fantastic forms...across the dusky landscape, as if Nature had strewn her fresh designs over the fields by night as models for man's art." For the first time in an essay, Thoreau successfully makes the landscape itself an important part of the subject matter, and this is an accomplishment he would perfect in future writings, including *Walden* and "Walking." Further, the essay marks Thoreau's trademark of addressing multiple themes simultaneously. As an analogue to life itself, which does not make neat demarcations, in this essay and others his ideas tend to intermingle indirectly.

Unable to establish himself in New York, Thoreau moved back to Concord in late 1843. He would never make much money in his life and very little from his writing. Some of the citizens of Concord began to call Thoreau "Dolittle" and a loafer. Possessed of extraordinary powers of observation, a holistic, transcendental point of view, a lucid, direct (a few would say supercilious) writing style, and an unquenchable thirst for knowledge gained through his readings and experiences, Thoreau was preoccupied and thus limited in other ways. Some of the townsfolk of Concord noted that not only was Thoreau unproductive but neither was he all that personally engaging. Nathaniel Hawthorne, who lived in Concord for a time in the 1840s, wrote to publisher Evert Duyckinck that

Thoreau "is the most unmalleable fellow alive—the most tedious, tiresome, and intolerable—the narrowest and most notional—and yet, true as all this is, he has great qualities of intellect and character."

Though he could be prickly and contentious, Thoreau was, in fact, a sociable person, even chatty with neighbors. Thoreau was at home in Concord, and he developed several close friendships outside of his family. William Ellery Channing, a poet, early biographer of Thoreau, and fellow Concord underachiever, was a close companion for much of Thoreau's life. They often went on walks and other excursions together, even though Thoreau did not care much for Channing's crude talk or his unsolicited commentaries on his own marriage problems. Though he was 18 years older than Thoreau and not possessed of conservationist ideas toward the wilderness, Amos Bronson Alcott called Thoreau "a friend who comes never too often nor stays too long." After Thoreau read Alcott his 1848 essay "Friendship," Alcott declared that it was superior to anything he had ever heard. The Thoreau-Emerson friendship went through some rough periods. Emerson thought Thoreau was hardhearted, too unambitious, and too much given to argument for its own sake. Thoreau's declaration in *Walden* that "the old have no very important advice to give to the young" must have stung Emerson, who had for years been the younger man's chief mentor and patron. Yet Emerson always considered Thoreau his best friend. Near the end of his life, stricken with Alzheimer's, Emerson would ask his wife, "What was the name of my best friend?" "Henry Thoreau," she would answer. "Oh, yes, Henry Thoreau."

What was likely the most embarrassing event of Thoreau's life occurred in the spring of 1844, when he and a companion, Edwin S. Hoar, went on a rowboat expedition on the Sudbury River, which joins with the Assabet to form the Concord River. They caught a mess of fish, and, sitting on the bank of Fair Haven Bay, they made a fire to cook them. The woods being exceedingly dry, the fire got out of hand quickly. Before the fire was finally put out, it had burned over 300 acres. Thoreau never discussed the incident in his public writing, and could not manage to write about it privately for six more years. In 1850 he wrote in his journal that he had expected to be condemned for starting the fire, and though some called him names, he found that the townspeople "did not sympathize with the owners of the wood, but were in fact highly elate and as it were thankful for the opportunity which had afforded them so much sport." In retrospect, he could write, with some justification, that "The locomotive engine has since burned over nearly all the same ground and more...."

At the end of March 1845, Thoreau borrowed an axe and began building a small cabin on land Emerson owned next to Walden Pond. The little cabin was not located in what could, with much accuracy, be called a wilderness setting. It was located minutes away from the heart of Concord, and a little over a mile from the town railroad station. But the setting was wild enough, removed enough to serve Thoreau in his experiment in living simply, freely, and, in a relative way, independently in nature. *Walden* is also the recording of an attempt by Thoreau to live an idea, to live as a Transcendentalist. If Emerson is the founder of New England Transcendentalism, Thoreau is its great practitioner. *Walden*, published nine and a half years after borrowing the axe, is the heart of Thoreau, and it is an endlessly rich, complex, often elusive text (Barbara Johnson addresses the work's "obscurity"), the product of seven drafts of fastidious labor by one of the world's great prose stylists and individualists. It is his most important statement on living consciously, in step with oneself, even if out of step with everyone else, with senses open to nature and its changing seasons in order to understand one's own wildness. He writes that he moved to the cabin "by accident...on Independence Day, or the fourth of July" that year. Always aware of national affairs—the growing abolitionist movement, the controversial war with Mexico over Texas, the utopian communal experiments at Brook Farm, Fruitlands, and

elsewhere, the westward movement of settlers and speculators—it is highly unlikely that Thoreau's move to the cabin on Independence Day was "by accident." *Walden* is only in part Thoreau's "declaration of independence" from society, but the "accident" may have other meanings. As Thoreau reminds the reader in a throwaway phrase, the Revolutionary War began in Concord, only a few miles from Thoreau's cabin, but now, 60 years after the Declaration of Independence, Thoreau could call America only a "comparatively free country." Thoreau's move to Walden was a conscious experiment in freedom, a conspicuous gesture of withdrawal from society into nature and the self.

One of the main goals of the long opening chapter "Economy" is to untangle life's true necessities (one of the key words in the chapter) from those things that are merely luxuries, which he maintains "are not only not indispensable, but positive hindrances to the elevation of mankind" and "improved means to an unimproved end." His move to the cabin, then, is a conscious attempt "to transact some private business with the fewest obstacles." Thoreau sets out almost immediately in the book to critique what he sees as a society obsessed with money and uninterested in cultivating the treasures within themselves. His response to being regarded by some Concord citizens as a loafer is to satirize the preoccupation with climbing the social ladder: for years, he writes, he "was self-appointed inspector of snow storms and rain storms," yet after a time "it became more and more evident that my townsmen would not after all admit me into the list of town officers, nor make my place a sinecure with a moderate allowance." He states that earlier in his life he had considered picking huckleberries for a living ("that surely I could do, and its small profits might suffice,—for my greatest skill had been to want but little...") or other similar jobs, "But," he writes, "I have since learned that trade curses every thing it handles...."

Beyond Concord, "Economy" may also be read as a repudiation of Benjamin Franklin, for whom industry, distinction, wealth, and felicity are the ends of human existence. His meticulously itemized tables of expense for the cabin materials burlesque business transactions, but they also show that one can, in fact, live cheaply by simplifying and eschewing luxuries, and he writes that he could cover all his expenses by working only about six weeks per year. However supercilious or preachy Thoreau may seem to some readers, he does not wish for his readers to emulate him and live in a small cabin by a lake: "I would have each one be very careful to find out and pursue *his own* way...."

Living simply and without excessive regard for material possessions pervades the entirety of *Walden,* for it is in the context of a materialistic society that Thoreau is compelled to live in the woods. Thus, in the next chapter, "Where I Lived and What I Lived For," when considering what trees, if any, he ought to chop down, he decides to leave them all alone, "for a man is rich," he writes, "in proportion to the number of things which he can afford to let alone." As some readers of Thoreau have noted, this statement—perhaps more so now than when Thoreau wrote it—stands as a concise explanation of the conservation ethic. Not only is Thoreau retreating *from* material society, he writes that his experiment is a "conscious endeavor" to elevate himself, "to live deliberately, to front only the essential facts of life, and see if I could not learn what it had to teach, and not, when I came to die, discover that I had not lived." He wants to reduce life "to its lowest terms" and "Simplify, simplify." The chapter concludes with a remarkable passage ("Time is but the stream I go a-fishing in") in which extended metaphorical language renders the writer merged with the wildness for which he so urgently yearns.

Thoreau, an enthusiastic, prolific reader, does not neglect books in his experiment; they are, in fact, essential in his elevation. As art, the written word is the most "universal," the "nearest to life itself." Nevertheless, in "Sounds" he writes, "I did not read books the first summer; I hoed beans." The railroad is a constant presence all around the Concord

area, its whistle reminding him of commerce even when he is in the woods. Walden cannot provide a refuge from the forces of technology and change. The train is distracting and an unignorable reminder of gogetterism, yet Thoreau is not completely anti-railroad, nor is he anti-commerce. Echoing a similar statement in Emerson's *Nature*, Thoreau writes, "Commerce is unexpectedly confident and serene, alert, adventurous, and unwearied. It is very natural in its methods withal" and he is "refreshed and expanded when the freight train rattles past" him. Yet Thoreau, Leo Marx points out, is "skeptical about the compatibility of the pastoral ideal and industrial progress," and he realizes that industry is "making nonsense of the popular notion of a 'pastoral life.'" It is only after the train has gone that he can hear the town bells, cows, birds, wagons crossing bridges, and bullfrogs.

Upon moving to the woods, Thoreau feels lonesome only once ("for an hour"), but a gentle rain makes him "suddenly sensible of such sweet and beneficent society in nature" and "aware of the presence of something kindred to me, even in scenes which we are accustomed to call wild and dreary...." He writes that he loves to be alone, that he "never found the companion that was so companionable as solitude," and he dramatizes the point by personifying natural objects more regularly than in past chapters (which have dealt more with society). The title of the chapter "Solitude" is itself ironic because Thoreau personifies the natural world so heavily in it that he is scarcely ever "alone." He writes, for example, "our great-grandmother Nature" offers "such health... such cheer...and such sympathy" for the human race

that all Nature would be affected and the sun's brightness fade, and the winds would sigh humanely, and the clouds rain tears, and the woods shed their leaves and put on mourning in midsummer, if any man should ever for a just cause grieve. Shall I not have intelligence with the earth? Am I not partly leaves and vegetable mould myself?

By contrast, in the succeeding chapter, "Visitors," he writes that when people would come to see him "we often parted without being aware that we had come very near to one another." And generalizing, he claims that the businessmen, farmers, and ministers ("who spoke of God as if they enjoyed a monopoly of the subject"), among others, do not like the woods, though children like it, as do many others—including the unnamed, woodchuck-eating Canadian woodsman—"who came out to the woods for freedom's sake...."

Inspired in part from his readings in the agricultural works of Virgil and Cato, "The Bean-Field" is, among other things, *Walden*'s statement on the "sacredness" of the farmer's calling. Writing more than a century before Wendell Berry would write on the same subject, Thoreau maintains that in modern times farming has lost that sacredness:

> By avarice and selfishness, and a grovelling habit, from which none of us is free, of regarding the soil as property, or the means of acquiring property chiefly, the landscape is deformed, husbandry is degraded with us, and the farmer leads the meanest of lives. He knows Nature but as a robber.

In planting and tending the rows of his bean field, which he claims, "added together, was seven miles already planted," Thoreau is planting not just beans but tropes: he is "making the earth say beans instead of grass." A few pages later he states (figuratively, though not ironically) that he will not "plant beans or corn with so much industry another summer, but such seeds, if the seed is not lost, as sincerity, truth, simplicity, faith, innocence, and the like, and see if they will not grow in this soil...." Returning mid-chapter to the woods, he comments indirectly on the war with Mexico as from a distance he hears the patriotic celebration of "great guns, which echo like pop guns to these woods"; he facetiously feels with a swell of pride that he "could spit a Mexican with good relish," and he looks "for a woodchuck or a skunk I could exercise my chivalry upon." He visits the

village often to hear gossip and news, this being "as refreshing in its way as the rustle of leaves and the peeping of frogs," but toward evening he is ready to head back to the woods. Not as misanthropic as he is anti-institutional, Thoreau alludes to his own arrest for not paying the poll tax to support the war and concludes that "wherever a man goes, men will pursue and paw him with their dirty institutions, and, if they can, constrain him to belong to their desperate odd-fellow society."

"The Ponds" records the exploration and technical description of Walden and other ponds in the region, but it is also a subjective, poetic description that expresses the link between humans and nature. The bodies of water he describes are living beings: a lake, he writes, is "earth's eye, looking into which the beholder measures the depth of his own nature"; the trees on the shore are its eyelashes, and "the wooded hills and cliffs around are its overhanging brows." He laments the chopping down of the forest around Walden ("How can you expect the birds to sing when their groves are cut down?"), but he is confident that the forest will renew itself: "where a forest was cut down last winter another is springing up by its shore lustily as ever...." He ridicules the name of Flint's Pond and the presumption that anyone would believe they truly owned such a place and should give it his name "—him who thought only of its money value; whose presence perchance cursed all the shore...." "Baker's Farm" continues the exploration of the landscape, though its focus is more on the narrator. It paganizes Christian terms in an effort to reclaim nature from Puritan industriousness: certain trees he visits are "shrines," and, reflecting on how he once found himself inside a rainbow's arch, he says he wondered "at the halo of light around my shadow, and would fain fancy myself one of the elect." After a discussion with his neighbor in the woods, John Field, an Irishman who toils with his family in poverty by working in bogs, Thoreau's inner "Good Genius" appropriates Ecclesiastes—"Remember thy

Creator in the days of thy youth"—and advises him, "Let not to get a living be thy trade, but thy sport. Enjoy the land, but own it not."

At the opening of "Higher Laws," which posits that nature is the source and teacher of morality, Thoreau proclaims his increased state of wildness; he sees a woodchuck and is "strongly tempted to seize and devour him raw...for that wildness he represents." Noting that fishermen, hunters, woodsmen, and the like "are often in a more favorable mood for observing [nature]...than philosophers or poets, even," he states, "No humane being, past the thoughtless age of boyhood, will wantonly murder any creature, which holds its life by the same tenure that he does." He eats little meat not for health reasons but for ethical ones, and he predicts a day when people will no longer eat meat. The diet represents restraint and self-purification, the will to satiate bodily needs in terms as simple as materialistic needs, as outlined in "Economics." The next chapter, "Brute Neighbors," asserts that animals are conscious, kindred creatures, and several anecdotes underscore this idea. The eyes of a young partridge reflect "intelligence" and "suggest not merely the purity of infancy, but a wisdom clarified by experience." The less peaceful red and black ants engage, "as if they had been men" in their own Trojan War with swarming Myrmidons and an ant Achilles returning to the war to avenge the killing of Patroclus. Playing what resembles a game of chase with a loon on the pond, Thoreau reasons, "While he was thinking one thing in his brain, I was endeavoring to divine his thought in mine."

The first of *Walden*'s four winter chapters, "House-Warming" laments our increased separation, by technology, from the wildness that is the basis for civilization. He notes that chestnuts "now sleep their long sleep under the railroad," and the groundnut, in "these days of fatted cattle and waving grainfields... is quite forgotten." A return to a world in which "wild Nature reign[s]" would, in Thoreau's unique vision, simultaneously result in "the reign of poetry." Nature, increasingly

distant, has the power to transform and invigorate our words and our thinking:

> our lives pass at such remoteness from its symbols, and its metaphors and tropes are necessarily so far fetched, through slides and dumb-waiters, as it were; in other words, the parlor is so far from the kitchen and workshop. ...As if only the savage dwelt near enough to Nature and Truth to borrow a trope from them.

"Former Inhabitants; and Winter Visitors" evokes the memory of former human residents of the area, but he concludes, "Alas! how little does the memory of these human inhabitants enhance the beauty of the landscape!" "Winter Animals" opens with Thoreau walking to give a town lecture (presumably on his Walden experiment), but the chapter otherwise has very little "action." The chapter is filled with the author's observations (auditory and visual) of various animals in the winter landscape, and (anticipating Aldo Leopold's *A Sand County Almanac*) some of the observations question an anthropocentric view of history (e.g., "if we take the ages into our account, may there not be a civilization going on among brutes as well as men?"). One of the main ideas in "The Pond in Winter" is that a precise, scientific knowledge of nature is necessary to balance our imaginative understanding of it. As he would discover more so later in life, for Thoreau science and poetry are vital and complementary. Balanced between the realms of the imagination and natural history, he criticizes the townsfolk for their laziness and naivete in believing "in the bottomlessness of a pond without taking the trouble to sound it," yet Thoreau is nothing if not a champion of the imagination: "I am thankful that this pond was made deep and pure for a symbol. While men believe in the infinite some ponds will be thought to be bottomless."

"Spring" describes the breaking up of the ice that has covered the surface of Walden Pond all winter. Thoreau uses metaphors to show that the pond is not static, but a giant living being. The branches in streams are "blood vessels," while the water deposits a "bony system" and a "fleshy fibre or cellular tissue." To underscore the idea, one of *Walden*'s major themes, that the earth is a kindred, living creature, Thoreau explains his metaphor with more metaphors:

> The earth is not a mere fragment of dead history, stratum upon stratum like the leaves of a book, to be studied by geologists and antiquaries chiefly, but living poetry like the leaves of a tree, which precede flowers and fruit,—not fossil earth, but a living earth; compared with whose great central life all animal and vegetable life is merely parasitic.

The gentle personifications continue throughout the chapter illustrating how the spring reveals the earth as infantile, beneficent, innocent, and restorative to the human soul: "In a pleasant spring morning all men's sins are forgiven." Anticipating the important ideas he would lay out a few years later in his great essay "Walking," in the last few paragraphs of "Spring," Thoreau articulates directly why wildness is crucial for humans. "Our village life would stagnate," he writes, "if it were not for the unexplored forests and meadows which surround it. We need the tonic of wildness." In the last sentence of the chapter, Thoreau notes that he left Walden on September 6, 1847, and in the "Conclusion," he explains that he had other "lives to live, and could not spare any more time than that one." *Walden*'s "Conclusion" is, among other things, a call for readers not to allow themselves to be tossed around and shaped by seasonal fluxes but to live life courageously and imaginatively, whether in the woods or in the city. In "Economy" Thoreau had stated (in a famous phrase) that "The mass of men lead lives of quiet desperation." In "Conclusion," he returns to the idea in an equally famous passage:

> Why should we be in such desperate haste to succeed, and in such desperate enterprises? If a man does not keep pace with his companions, perhaps it is because he hears a different

drummer. Let him step to the music which he hears, however measured or far away.

When Thoreau left Walden, he had lived there a little over two years and two months. After leaving Walden, he sold his cabin to Emerson and, from 1847 to 1848, he lived again in the Emerson house while its owner was lecturing in Europe. *Walden* would not be published for another seven years. When it was published by Ticknor and Fields on August 9, 1854, it found an audience that his first book, *A Week on the Concord and Merrimack Rivers*, had not found. *Walden* (sometimes titled *Walden; or, Life in the Woods*) sold all but 256 copies of the original printing of 2,000, and it made Thoreau a minor celebrity in New England, where he was sought out by many admirers. The book went out of print in 1859, but Thoreau persuaded Ticknor and Fields to reprint it, and a second edition appeared a few weeks after Thoreau's death. The book has become one of the most beloved in the American literary canon and has not been out of print ever since.

By the late 1840s, Thoreau had published relatively little, but this would soon change. At Walden Thoreau had been productive writing what would become major works. In addition to his journals, which functioned, in part, as a compost of ideas, and other prose works, while living in the cabin he completed the earliest draft of *Walden*, an advanced draft of *A Week on the Concord and Merrimack Rivers*, he wrote out "Ktaadn" (later collected as part of *The Maine Woods*), and he began writing the important essay "Resistance to Civil Government," also called "Civil Disobedience," which he published in May 1849. On one level, this essay may be read as Thoreau's response to spending a night in jail for refusing to pay the poll tax in support of what he thought was not only an immoral war with Mexico over Texas but also an attempt to extend slavery in the United States. On another, it may be read more broadly as a clarification of the line between the authority of government and the rights of the governed. Thoreau's act of civil disobedience combined with the essay he wrote about it are the bases of American political and social activism. Thoreau's most famous and influential essay deeply affected Tolstoy, and it helped show Gandhi and Martin Luther King, Jr., how to conduct their own acts of civil disobedience on much larger scales. Though it is by no means a piece of nature writing, "Resistance to Civil Government" continues to show protesters —including those demonstrating dissatisfaction with the governmental and commercial exploitation of land communities—how to stage acts of civil disobedience.

Thoreau had begun working hard on *A Week on the Concord and Merrimack Rivers* in the fall of 1844, and after almost endless revision it was published with Thoreau's own money in 1849. It sold only 219 copies in four years. Though the book is purportedly the record of a river trip Thoreau took with his brother, John, the travel narrative, which is pleasant, is merely a framework for a series of interpolations—a collection of poems, essays, translations, and quotations that demonstrates Thoreau's scholarship in classical literature and history. But critics have noted that the interpolations have little (or worse, at points a *forced*) connection with the narrative portions of the book. Thoreau's first book does succeed in articulating an idea central to all his other work: the kinship of human law to the law of nature. The landscape, including the river, is a perfect analogue to the human mind. Much of the language of the book is mystical ("And in the heavens there are rivers of stars and milky ways....And our thoughts flow and circulate—and seasons lapse into the current year"), and Thoreau does tend in the book toward a sort of pantheism when (for example) he announces that "what in other men is religion is in me love of nature." (Such phrases were troubling to Concord churchgoers, including some in Thoreau's own family.) The book received mixed reviews. Horace Greeley himself allegedly wrote the lengthy review for the *New York Tribune*; the review gives the book modest praise as "a fresh, original, thoughtful work," but it also states that its "Pantheistic egotism does *not* delight us." All in all, for an unknown writer, the book received fairly wide attention, even in England. Thoreau found himself in debt for publishing the book, but it certainly encouraged him to keep writing.

"Ktaadn," most of the first draft of which is contained in his 1846 journal, is the first and best known of the three long excursion essays that would make up *The Maine Woods*. (*The Maine Woods* and *Cape Cod* were edited by Sophia Thoreau and Ellery Channing and published in 1864 and 1865, respectively.) Thoreau travels from Concord by boat to Bangor, where he, his cousin George Thatcher (not mentioned by name in the essay), and two men with logging interests travel by coach north to Mattawamkeag, where the road ends. They take a batteau up the Penobscot River into lands uninhabited and so wild that it is scarcely ever visited by humans. Much of the piece may be described as travel writing combined with anthropological observations on the loggers, settlers, and Indians of the area—how and where they live, what they eat, how they hunt. Thoreau's encounters with the Indians in "Ktaadn" tend to express frustration. In all his mature work, the Indian is a symbol for wildness, a being as intimate with wilderness on a daily basis as are moose, bears, and other animals. And yet upon approaching civilization on the return trip, Thoreau is disappointed to find that the Indians there resemble "the sinister and slouching fellows whom you meet picking up strings and paper in the streets of a city." European encroachment has degraded not only the Indians and their way of life, but even nature as it was before the white men. Floating toward the mountain, Thoreau notes,

> The Indians say that the river once ran both ways, one half up and the other down, but that, since the white man came, it all runs down, and now they must laboriously pole their canoes against the stream, and carry them over numerous portages.

Despite occasional passages such as this, "Ktaadn" has little commentary, giving way instead to a straight narrative. Along the way to Mount Ktaadn (now spelled "Katahdin" and at 5,267 feet the highest point in Maine), they pick up settlers George McCauslin and Tom Fowler, who serve as guides, and float down a series of rivers and lakes until coming at last to the mountain itself.

One of the most widely discussed passages in all of Thoreau's work is his experience on the summit of the mountain. Hiking alone upwards, but seemingly back in time past "ancient black spruce trees, old as the flood" into an alien, unpastoral landscape, he finds himself enclosed in clouds, mist, and wind, with only an occasional view of inhospitable crags around him. On the summit he finds not a kindly Mother Nature but rather a personified force hostile to humans:

> Vast, Titanic, inhuman Nature has got him at disadvantage, caught him alone, and pilfers him of some of his divine faculty. She does not smile on him as in the plains. She seems to say sternly, Why came ye here before your time. This ground is not prepared for you. Is it not enough that I smile in the valleys? I have never made this soil for thy feet, this air for thy breathing, these rocks for thy neighbors. I cannot pity nor fondle thee here, but forever relentlessly drive thee hence to where I *am* kind. Why seek me where I have not called thee, and then complain because you find me but a stepmother? Shouldst thou freeze or starve, or shudder thy life away, here is no shrine, nor altar, nor any access to my ear.

Though it is couched in the third person, the account of the summit takes an unmistakably grim view of nature quite out of step with most of the rest of "Ktaadn" and with almost all his other work, as well as his overall transcendent view of nature as beneficent. A few pages later, Thoreau's view of a friendly nature is clearly shaken ("There was there felt the presence of a force not bound to be kind to man"), and he indicates that his relationship with nature is more precarious than he might otherwise acknowledge:

> Think of our life in nature,—daily to be shown matter, to come in contact with it,—

rocks, trees, wind on our cheeks! the *solid* earth! the *actual* world! the *common sense!* *Contact! Contact! Who* are we? *where* are we?

Despite such questions, which seem to strike at the heart of his point of view, Thoreau does not directly mention his harrowing experience again in his account of the excursion after the summit or anywhere else, and it seems to have had little effect on his romantic view of the world. For the sake of context, it may be relevant to note that Thoreau was drafting "Ktaadn" and the earliest version of *Walden* in the same year, at the time he was living his serene life at Walden Pond.

An almost compulsive walker, Thoreau made the first of four walking trips (two of them with Ellery Channing) to Cape Cod— the "bare and bended arm of Massachusetts"—in 1849. Some of the Cape Cod pieces that came out of the walks were published in *Putnam's Monthly Magazine* in 1855, but when the editor tried to censor Thoreau, he withdrew the rest. Three of the trips were knit together to make the posthumous book *Cape Cod.* Some have described the book as lighthearted: the book's setting is full of sunshine, sand, and ocean, and there is a good amount of humor. "The Wellfleet Oysterman" is satisfyingly amusing in its one-liners ("There are many Herring Rivers on the Cape; they will, perhaps, be more numerous than herrings soon"), its character sketches, in Thoreau's observations, and in the conversations with the 88-year-old title character, who is, Thoreau writes, "the merriest old man that we had ever seen, and one of the best preserved. His style was coarse and plain enough to have suited Rabelais."

Yet, as it is in "Ktaadn," the natural world of *Cape Cod* is often devoid of pastoral charm and gentleness toward humanity. In the opening section, "The Shipwreck," Thoreau stops in Boston on the way to Cape Cod to hear news that a steamer has wrecked, killing 145 passengers (mostly Irish emigrants), in a violent storm at Cohasset, a town on the western side of Cape Cod Bay. Thoreau describes with almost journalistic detachment how he arrives in Cohasset to find the beach crowded with coffins and people searching for bodies and looking through fragments of the wrecked steamer. Meanwhile, Thoreau notes, "the sea was still breaking violently on the rocks." He comes across the body of a drowned girl,

> gashed by the rocks or fishes, so that the bones and muscle were exposed, but quite bloodless —merely red and white—with wide-open and staring eyes, yet lusterless, dead-lights; or, like the cabin windows of a stranded vessel, filled with sand.

Moving along, he observes a 40 foot chunk of the vessel resting on the rocks and suggests that "no material could withstand the power of the waves," yet the people he encounters seem to be as emotionally detached from the scene as the ocean itself. After describing the stark scene, Thoreau inserts two long paragraphs of pure stoicism ("If this was the law of Nature, why waste any time in awe or pity?") and the defiant conclusion only an individualist of Thoreau's depth could muster: "A just man's purpose cannot be split on any Grampus or material rock, but itself will split rocks till it succeeds."

Nine months after his first trip to Cape Cod, in July 1850, Thoreau would witness the aftermath of another shipwreck, this one the brig *Elizabeth*, which sunk off Fire Island. On board the ship was Margaret Fuller with her new husband and infant son, all of whom perished in the accident. At Emerson's request, Thoreau went to the scene of the accident to search for her body. Unsuccessful in his search, he recorded his thoughts in his journal, and eventually they found their way into *Cape Cod*. The shipwrecks and the summit of Ktaadn, among other experiences, challenged Thoreau's belief in the essential goodness of nature. Though his intellectual interests shifted (more or less cyclically) throughout his life, he never completely abandoned his transcendentalism or his belief in the sacredness and the essential beneficence of nature. Yet he acknowledged

time and again that nature has a dark side that is capable of great harshness and utter indifference to humans. A man of considerable experience—even if he did stay close to Concord his whole life—Thoreau confronted nature on some hostile terms, far removed from the tranquility of Walden Pond.

In 1848, Thoreau had begun a correspondence with Harrison Gray Otis Blake, who became a close friend in person as well as through the exchange of letters, that would last until 1861. Composed of a total of 50 letters (published in 2004 as *Letters to a Spiritual Seeker*), his correspondence with Blake would be the most important of Thoreau's life. H.G.O. Blake was the ideal audience for the letters: he was honest, well-informed, and inquisitive—the perfect sounding board for Thoreau, who wrote in one of the letters, "You will perceive that I am as often talking to myself, perhaps, as speaking to you." If Thoreau's poetry was the autobiography of the young man, his collection of letters to Blake was the autobiography of Thoreau in his prime and up to near the end of his life. Some of these letters record some extraordinarily personal thoughts. A week after his futile search for Fuller's remains, he wrote to Blake, "Our thoughts are the epochs in our lives: all else is but as a journal of the winds that blew while we were there."

Thoreau's sole trip out of the United States took place in September and October 1850, when he and Channing journeyed by train to Quebec. The trip resulted in *A Yankee in Canada*, a five-part account of around a hundred pages published in part in 1853. He enjoyed seeing a great variety of trees along the way to Canada by way of Vermont, but once across the border he was not particularly impressed with anything he saw, much preferring his home turf instead. Though he greatly admired the St. Lawrence River, which he calls "the most splendid river on the globe," he has very little positive to say about this land full of nuns, priests, and soldiers. Montreal struck him as being "considerably Americanized....you felt as if a French revolution might break out any moment." Though he was of French ancestry, he felt no kinship to French Canada; he truly *was* a Yankee in Canada. The piece's opening statement may be the most succinct way of summing up the overall tone of the book: "I fear that I have not got much to say about Canada, not having seen much; what I got by going to Canada was a cold." Eventually, though, as Robert D. Richardson points out, the trip would transform Thoreau's view of North America's history, as he would assert that the French, more than the Pilgrims, deserve the credit for establishing America. As Thoreau writes, "the Englishman's history of New England commences only when it ceases to be New France."

Thoreau worked up a lecture entitled "The Wild" and delivered it the first of several times in April 1851. In 1862, not long before his death, he finally got around to combining with it another lecture and preparing it for publication under the title "Walking." As *Walden* is Thoreau's most important book, "Walking" is, at least as a piece of nature writing, his most important essay. He asks at one point, "Where is the literature which gives expression to Nature?" On the most literal level, essays such as "Walking" answer that question; more than any other American writer, Thoreau himself is the "poet who could impress the winds and streams into his service, to speak for him; who nailed words to their primitive senses...." Wildness, he declares throughout the essay, is central to our existence. The opposite of civilization, it has a unique, irreplaceable moral value. He writes that "there is a subtle magnetism in Nature, which, if we unconsciously yield to it, will direct us aright." Continuing a line of argument from *Walden*, many of our so-called necessities only have the effect of isolating us from the natural world and taking away the essential freedom that is based in nature. In walking "westward"—into the wild—we recover our freedom. Thoreau's "West" is not a literal one or an endorsement of the march of civilization. On the contrary, it represents the intuition in all humans to recognize and follow the wildness within

them: "The West of which I speak is but another name for the Wild; and what I have been preparing to say is, that in Wildness is the preservation of the World."

In his analysis of Thoreau's contribution to the concept of wilderness in America, Roderick Nash discusses the importance of these last eight words:

> Americans had not heard the like before. Previous discussion of wilderness had been mostly in terms of Romantic or nationalistic cliches. Thoreau tossed these aside in an effort to approach the significance of the wild more closely. In doing so he came to grips with issues which others had only faintly discerned. At the same time he cut channels in which a large portion of thought about wilderness subsequently flowed.

The prototypical American preservationist statement is not particularly specific as a policy proposal: in what sense is the world's "preservation" contingent on "Wildness"? Thoreau goes on to give clues. As the New England forests are being chopped down for human use, "fewer pigeons visit us every year." With nature, again, serving as a trope for the human mind, he continues:

> So, it would seem, few and fewer thoughts visit each growing man from year to year, for the grove in our minds is laid waste—sold to feed unnecessary fires of ambition, or sent to mill—and there is scarcely a twig left for them to perch on.

So nature, relatively untouched by human hand, is necessary as the "raw material of life," for our own elevation as a species, for imagination, renewal, and recreation.

We are drawn to nature because we "have a wild savage in us" and because we are "a part and parcel of nature." He alleges that "Life consists with wildness. The most alive is the wildest," even as he acknowledges that "few are attracted strongly to Nature." Throughout the essay he is clearly aware that humans are capable of obliterating wilderness. He metaphorically but also literally envisions a country in which "part will be tillage, but the greater part will be meadow and forest." In his view,

> all man's improvements, so called, such as the building of houses and the cutting down of the forest and of all large trees, simply deform the landscape, and make it more and more tame and cheap. A people who would begin by burning the fences and let the forest stand!

Though the essay's message carries more than a little urgency, the writing is full of play and flourishes of humor to elaborate important ideas:

> Yes, though you may think me perverse, if it were proposed to me to dwell in the neighborhood of the most beautiful garden that ever human art contrived, or else of a Dismal Swamp, I should certainly decide for the swamp. How vain, then, have been all your labors, citizens, for me!

The second essay that would eventually go into *The Maine Woods*, "Chesuncook," is an account of an 1853 trip Thoreau took with George Thatcher (again, not mentioned by name) to hunt moose in the Chesuncook Lake region of Maine. Meeting Thoreau in Maine is Joe Aitteon, the Indian son of the governor, lumberman, hunter, and paid guide. Toward the end of the essay, Thoreau tells an Indian he has made the excursion "partly to see where the white-pine, the Eastern stuff of which our houses are built, grew," and he spends much time, by choice, with various Indians, with whom he discusses the land, moose, and their language. Thoreau, a nonhunter, has also come back to Maine for the experience:

> Though I had not come a-hunting, and felt some compunctions about accompanying the hunters, I wished to see a moose near at hand, and was not sorry to learn how the Indian managed to kill one. I went as reporter or chaplain to the hunters—and the chaplain has been known to carry a gun himself.

When Joe kills a moose, Thoreau helps him carry its carcass to the canoe, but when Joe begins to skin the moose, Thoreau feels sympathy for the animal—"a tragical business it was,—to see that still warm and palpitating body pierced with a knife...." A few pages later, Thoreau has "had enough of moose-hunting," and he bemoans the fact that few people, even among the Indians, experience the wilderness out of a noble motive. "But pray," he asks,

> could not one spend some weeks or years in the solitude of this vast wilderness with other employments than these—employments perfectly sweet and innocent and ennobling? For one that comes with a pencil to sketch or sing, a thousand come with an axe or rifle.

Thoreau states that in order to understand and participate in the "true and highest use" of a pine tree, one must come to understand "a higher law affecting our relation to pines as well as to men. A pine cut down, a dead pine, is no more a pine than a dead human carcass is a man." It is not the lumberman or the tanner but the poet "who makes the truest use of the pine." In a direct expression of the human kinship with nature, he posits that the pine "is immortal as I am, and perchance will go to as high a heaven, there to tower above me still." In the closing pages of "Chesuncook," Thoreau comments more directly on the need to preserve forests from human use, other than for study and recreation. Writing almost two decades before the first national park, Yellowstone, was authorized in 1872, the concluding passages comprise one of the earliest, most important statements in the conservation movement. Thoreau lays out in plain language the unique value of public wilderness areas and an argument for democratic "national preserves." Unlike the woods around Concord, in the Maine woods "you are never reminded that the wilderness which you are threading is, after all, some villager's familiar woodlot...." Having witnessed firsthand the human encroachment on forests (and examples of it were everywhere in nineteenth-century New England, even more so than now), Thoreau suggests that "Maine, perhaps, will soon be where Massachusetts is. A good part of her territory is already as bare and commonplace as much of our neighborhood." Thoreau is glad to be back home after two weeks in the wilderness, even as it is (echoing a similar statement in "Walking"), "necessary" as "resource and a background, the raw material of all our civilizations."

By the mid-1850s Thoreau was in some demand as a lecturer. Many of the talks he gave at this time eventually found their way into essays, some of which are among his best work. In 1854, he gave two very different lectures that were both published posthumously in *The Atlantic Monthly* in 1863. "Life without Principle," one of Thoreau's best known pieces, is a direct, unsubtle attack on the shortsightedness, meanness, and destructiveness of materialism. "I think there is nothing, not even crime, more opposed to poetry, to philosophy, ay, to life itself, than this incessant business." Not only does "incessant business" keep one from living well, it brutalizes others and robs them of their individualism. And, of course, its demands are too often at odds with wildness:

> If a man walk in the woods for love of them half of each day, he is in danger of being regarded as a loafer; but if he spends his whole day as a speculator, shearing off those woods and making earth bald before her time, he is esteemed an industrious and enterprising citizen. As if a town had no interest in its forests but to cut them down!

Though rousing and full of memorable prose, it is also rather preachy and lacks the subtle humor *Walden* employs to strike the same target.

Invited to give a lecture at Plymouth, Thoreau delivered the less known but notable "Night and Moonlight" there in October 1854. Thoreau announces at the outset that the speech concerns "another side of Nature"—not the sunny world of Walden Pond, but the dark, night side of nature. By "dark," Thoreau does not mean Ktaadn-like malignancy so much as *literal* darkness, the absence of light. Like many of Thoreau's

pieces, "Night and Moonlight" is about seeing things from a different perspective, examining assumptions, and understanding nature on its own terms. For example, Thoreau gently takes issue with the casual use of the word "moonshine" to denote ideas that are empty, nonsensical, or "loony" (accusations commonly lobbed at the Transcendentalists):

> They are moonshine, are they? Well, then, do your night-travelling when there is no moon to light you; but I will be thankful for the light that reaches me from the star of least magnitude. Stars are lesser or greater only as they appear to us so.

"The Allegash and East Branch," the final and longest section of *The Maine Woods*, is an account of what could well have been Thoreau's most arduous excursion—a 325-mile canoe trip up the West Branch of the Penobscot River across a large swamp and down the East Branch to Mount Katahdin in June 1857. Accompanying Thoreau was Edwin Hoar (with whom Thoreau had accidently set the woods of Concord on fire years before) and Joe Polis, a chief of the Penobscot tribe and guide. The damp Maine woods the three endured were as wild as any place Thoreau had ever been. Constantly harassed by mosquitoes, they traveled through black, harsh swamplands full of fallen timber. The wilderness was not just inhospitable; at some points it was full of terror. Confronting the swamp at Mud Pond, Thoreau writes (in retrospect) that "a howling wilderness does not howl: it is the imagination of the traveller that does the howling." Since much of the route was unnavigable, they often had to carry heavy loads for miles. (The trip made both Hoar and Polis ill, though Thoreau, who had only recently recovered from an extended illness, was not affected.) The piece is largely focused on Joe Polis, who, though having experienced civilization rather fully in Washington, where he represented his tribe, he did not, like many Indians, lose touch with his heritage or cease to use his woodcraft skills, and he taught Thoreau as much of his language—and more importantly, about a sympathetic communion with wilderness—as possible over the course of the excursion.

Thoreau's final Maine essay reflects his intense interest in botany in the late 1850s, and it is full of detailed botanical descriptions as well as ruminations on wildness itself and an examination of the differing values of scientific and transcendent observation. Thoreau's greatest discovery on the excursion occurs late one evening as the wood in the campfire Polis had made burns out. Thoreau, rising in the middle of the night, finds that the logs are shining in "a perfectly elliptical ring of light." Concluding that the logs must be phosphorescent wood, which he has heard about but had not seen, he revels in the phenomenon. "It could hardly have thrilled me more," he writes, "if it had taken the form of letters, or of the human face." The next morning, after inquiry, Polis tells Thoreau the Indian word for the phenomenon and says that Indians frequently encounter this and similar occurrences. The incident leads Thoreau to an important insight, that "Nature must have made a thousand revelations to [the Indians] which are still secrets to us." The Indians, Thoreau posits, have much to teach our white scientists about sympathetic observation.

"Autumnal Tints" is the essay version of a lecture Thoreau originally delivered in Worcester on February 22, 1859. One of Thoreau's best nature pieces, the essay was influenced to a large degree by John Ruskin's *The Elements of Drawing* and volume four of *Modern Painters*. The essay takes as its subject the ever-changing colors of the leaves on various trees and plants in and around Concord, from late August through October, "the month of painted leaves." The piece is largely descriptive, reflecting Thoreau's recently deepened interest in botany (and in Ruskin's books on art). But "Autumnal Tints" is more so about seeing, perspective, and living deliberately, and it further develops the Thoreauvian themes of nature as a valued kindred and a depository of tropes for human living. Where in "Chesuncook" he states that it is the poet, not the lumberman

or tanner, "who makes the truest use of the pine," in "Autumnal Tints" one who cuts down plants to feed his cattle has only a coarse understanding of the plants:

> Yet if he ever favorably attends to them, he may be overcome by their beauty. Each humblest plant, or weed, as we call it, stands there to express some thought or mood of ours; and yet how long it stands in vain!

The fallen leaves, he writes, "teach us how to die." Thoreau discusses the characteristics of plant species in general terms, but he also describes individual trees with which he is familiar in Concord, as if they were individual townsfolk. He has, over time, observed a specific red maple whose leaves invariably change colors earlier than its "fellows"; "I should be sorry, " he continues, "if it were cut down." Anticipating the sermonic nature writing of John Muir, he writes that the sugar maples

> are cheap preachers, permanently settled, which preach their half-century, and century, ay, and century-and-a-half sermons, with constantly increasing unction and influence, ministering to many generations of men; and the least we can do is to supply them with suitable colleagues as they grow infirm.

The love and study of nature is, for Thoreau, an alternative to the pieties of Puritanism as well as melancholy, and the trees are steady reminders that their nature is much the same as our own.

Since Thoreau, throughout his body of work, is concerned with the liberating potential in wildness, it is not surprising that Thoreau would write a handful of often impassioned essays on abolition, which stood for a more basic sort of freedom. Both Thoreau and Emerson had been opposed to slavery their entire adult lives, but they had a distinct distaste for the narrow-minded world of politics. Even so, the Fugitive Slave Law of 1851 moved both men firmly into the abolitionist camp. Thoreau gave his strongly worded, militant (but not quite pro-violence) "Slavery in Massachusetts" talk in

Farmingham on July 4, 1854. John Brown, who would attempt to lead an insurrection against the slave states by raiding the federal armory at Harpers Ferry, Virginia, visited Concord in 1857 and again in 1859, a few months before the raid, to raise money for his activities. Thoreau met him and thought him heroic. He made a small contribution, though he was not told directly what the money was for. Emerson was also impressed with Brown, as was Thoreau's friend and early biographer Franklin Sanborn, who was one of the "secret six" who diverted funds to support Brown in his militant endeavors. When in the fall of 1859 Thoreau heard of the raid a few days after it took place, convinced that Brown was in the right and the government was in the wrong, he became one of Brown's most passionate defenders, delivering a few weeks later "A Plea for Captain Brown," a speech that made a stir in New England. After Brown was hanged, he declined to speak at a memorial for Brown, instead sending in "The Last Days of John Brown." One more piece on the matter, "After the Death of John Brown," is the text of remarks Thoreau made in Concord on the day of Brown's execution.

Thoreau would live eight more years after the publication of *Walden* in 1854. In these years he concentrated increasingly on what may now be called ecological matters. (The word "ecology," or rather "Oecologie," was first applied by the German Darwinist Ernst Haeckel in 1866.) His planned work, as recorded in journals and other documents, was nothing less than an attempt to account for the natural world in and around Concord. Donald Worster writes that Thoreau's most important contribution to ecological science, conservation, and agriculture lies in his first-hand research and writings (mostly entries in his journal) on forest succession in the Concord area. Lumber being a vital raw material in the nineteenth century, management of forests was an important but misunderstood science in the day. Few had even an incipient understanding of forest ecology, and no one could explain how new trees were

planted to replace the ones cut down for lumber. In September 1857, after observing a squirrel bury some hickory nuts in a group of hemlocks, Thoreau noted in his journal, "This, then is the way forests are planted." Since squirrels will not recover all the nuts they cache, some of the nuts, if buried at the right depth, will sprout and grow. Most predators having been trimmed back in previous generations, farmers in the day had recklessly shot such "vermin" on sight, ignorant of the symbiotic relationship between them and the trees. Thoreau wrote that it would have been "far more civilized and humane, not to say godlike" to honor the squirrel for "the great service it performs, in the economy of the universe." In 1860, Thoreau expanded these journal entries into a lecture, "The Succession of Forest Trees," which he delivered in Concord at the annual cattle show of the Middlesex Agricultural Society. Some writers, the popular nature writer John Burroughs for one, have contested Thoreau's abilities as a naturalist. In his essay "The Art of Seeing Things" he writes that Thoreau's observations of the natural only "at times fitted things closely." But others have jumped to Thoreau's defense. Worster notes that Thoreau was a superior field naturalist to Louis Agassiz, the well-known Harvard zoologist:

> So resourceful was he that a twentieth-century scientist could find the limnological studies Thoreau carried out at Walden Pond to be truly "original and genuine," still reliable a hundred years later, despite his makeshift equipment and lack of professional training.

In his last years, Thoreau learned how to read a natural environment, its history, and its development. He was in some ways ambivalent about science, which, by the mid-nineteenth century had come to reject any knowledge derived through sympathetic intuition. Thoreau had no patience for such a position; in his journal he wrote, "Our science, so called, is always more barren and mixed up with error than our sympathies are." By attempting to be value-free and "objective," science had the result of devaluing nature. Such an attitude was at odds with Thoreau's own near-pantheistic, if not out and out pagan, view of the natural world. Despite his reservations about modern science—he was, after all, an excellent amateur scientist himself and elected a corresponding member of the Boston Society of Natural History in 1850—he believed that a more scientific understanding of the land would lead to better stewardship of it. A wiser, more scientific use of the forest would result in the forest's regeneration. Much of his late work is committed to the notion that the forest around Concord could and should be regenerated. Thoreau did not, however, primarily wish for a "wise use" policy so much as a restored wildness, a forest unused for the needs of industry. Restating an idea similar to ones presented earlier in "Chesuncook" and elsewhere, in his manuscript for *Wild Fruits* he writes,

> I think that each town should have a park, or rather a primitive forest, of five hundred or a thousand acres, either in one body or several, where a stick should never be cut for fuel, not for the navy, nor to make wagons, but stand and decay for higher uses—a common possession forever, for instruction and recreation.

In the late 1850s, Thoreau began working on two massive projects which were evidently a part of the proposed grand study of the Concord woods. *The Dispersion of Seeds*, left as a 354-page manuscript, reflects Thoreau's interest in the evolution of forests. The work makes use of observations and data culled from years of work recorded in notebooks, and it includes most of "The Succession of Forest Trees" as well as a much longer work, *Faith in a Seed*. *The Dispersion of Seeds* is an ecological work by a writer-scientist on the growth and evolution of land communities. Since very few of us are aware of how forests grow and "we hardly associate seeds with trees," the work, he writes, is a minute study of "how, according to my observations, our forest trees and other vegetables

are planted by Nature." Thoreau proceeds to discuss the natural planting of the pitch pine, the white pine, the birch, the alder, and several other trees, and he explains the roles of animals and birds in the process. Though the manuscript of *The Dispersion of Seeds* is not without poetic and philosophical language, it is much more scientific than *Walden*, and it is much less about the self than about the natural neighborhood. The entirety of *The Dispersion of Seeds* has not, to date, been published, but a part of it was published under the (slightly misleading) title *Faith in a Seed* in 1993.

Thoreau drafted the other, larger, work entitled *Wild Fruits* (sometimes called "Notes on Fruits") from 1859 until May 1861. Where *The Dispersion of Seeds* focuses mainly on the succession of forest trees, the unfinished 631-page manuscript of *Wild Fruits* is devoted to both an objective cataloguing of the wild fruits around Concord and to a subjective narrative and philosophical commentary. Ultimately, one of Thoreau's chief purposes in the study seems to have been similar to that of "Autumnal Tints"—to awaken himself (and others) to the "little oases" of nature, the everyday wildness that is an inextricable part of civilization. Thus he writes in the opening paragraph,

> Most of us are still related to our native fields as the navigator to undiscovered islands in the sea. We can any afternoon discover a new fruit tree which will surprise us by its beauty or sweetness. So long as I saw in my walks one or two kinds of berries whose names I did not know, the proportion of the unknown seemed indefinitely, if not infinitely, great.

Sailing "the unexplored sea of Concord," Thoreau draws freely from information recorded in notebooks over the years to convey his observations on the various fruits—when they bloom and ripen, how they taste, what colors they are—elaborated with personal narratives and information from other sources, both ancient and contemporary. Like *The Dispersion of Seeds*, the whole of

Wild Fruits has not been published; a generous portion of the work was published under the title *Wild Fruits* in 2000.

One day in December 1860, while conducting studies on trees, Thoreau came down with a severe cold, which he called "an influenza." Despite his illness, he kept a lecture engagement at Waterbury, Connecticut. When he returned to Concord, the cold turned into bronchitis, and he was housebound for the winter. Unable to go outside, he worked on his papers, Alcott said, "as if he had a new book in mind." As news of the Civil War circulated through Concord, bronchitis weakened Thoreau, though the underlying illness was tuberculosis, which killed a great number of people in Thoreau's time. (In 1849 his sister Helen had died of the disease, which was not called tuberculosis until 1882.) Advised by his doctors to convalesce in a better climate, Thoreau took a trip to Minnesota with Horace Mann, Jr., son of the famous educator. The trip proved to be futile, though Thoreau did see Chicago, St. Paul, Milwaukee, and the Mississippi River. He witnessed a ceremonial Indian dance and saw Chief Little Crow, who a year later would lead the great Sioux uprising, which resulted in the massacre of 800 Minnesota pioneers.

Long a great lover of apples—their look and smell as much as their taste—Thoreau gave inventive names to scores of apples in the Concord area (e.g., the "Railroad-apple" grows in locales where passengers may have thrown out cores). Based in part on journal entries from the early 1850s, on February 8, 1860, Thoreau delivered "Wild Apples," his final lecture before the Concord Lyceum. An audience member would write that the lecture received "long continued applause." Thoreau revised this familiar essay several times until near the end of his life (it refers to the writer's visit to Minnesota, where he saw a "Crab-Apple" in May 1861). Full of humor and wordplay ("apples not of Discord, but of Concord!") and an impressive display of knowledge of the fruit, he draws his characteristic lesson from nature:

There is thus about all natural products a certain volatile and ethereal quality which represents their highest value, and which cannot be vulgarized, or bought and sold. No mortal had ever enjoyed the perfect flavor of any fruit, and only the god-like among men begin to taste its ambrosial qualities. For nectar and ambrosia are only those fine flavors of every earthly fruit which our coarse palates fail to perceive,—just as we occupy the heaven of the gods without knowing it.

Here once again Thoreau displays his virtually endless ability to squeeze tropes from nature and apply them to the act of seeing things from a fresh perspective. True wealth lies in understanding our natural relationship with the universe and not in the love of money or in exploiting nature haphazardly. As he does in "Autumnal Tints" and in virtually all his nature pieces, Thoreau attempts to speak up for the neglected and unloved. It is easy to sing the praises of domestic apples, but Thoreau's main concern is always the wild, the uncivilized.

Returning to Concord in July 1861, Thoreau stayed as active as his illness would allow. There is evidence that he continued working on his Concord project as late as January 1862. Aware that he would not live much longer, Thoreau accepted a solicitation to prepare some of his better lectures for publication. From February to early April he sent off the manuscripts for "Autumnal Tints," "Life without Principle," "Walking," and "Wild Apples" to James Russell Lowell's new magazine, *The Atlantic Monthly*. Thoreau was fairly well known by the time of his death. His sickness had been reported in the newspapers. He spent his last days at home, bedridden and surrounded by family. Though he remained in good spirits, he was no longer able to read or write, and by April 1862 he could only whisper. When his Aunt Louisa asked him if he had made his peace with God, Thoreau answered, "I did not know we had ever quarrelled." Thoreau died at nine in the morning on May 6; his last words were, reportedly, "moose" and "Indian." Thoreau had been less than ingratiating to many of the Concord townsfolk, but his friends made sure that the Concord children were dismissed from school so they could attend his funeral, and obituaries appeared in several newspapers and magazines in New England. At the funeral, Emerson read a long, brilliant eulogy, which was later published in *The Atlantic Monthly* under the simple title "Thoreau."

PRIMARY BIBLIOGRAPHY

Books

A Week on the Concord and Merrimack Rivers, 1849, ed. Carl F. Hovde (Princeton: Princeton University Press, 1980).

Walden, 1854, ed. J. Lyndon Shanley (Reprint, Princeton: Princeton University Press, 1971).

The Maine Woods, 1864, ed. Joseph J. Moldenhauer (Reprint, Princeton: Princeton University Press, 1972).

Cape Cod, 1865, ed. Joseph J. Moldenhauer (Reprint, Princeton: Princeton University Press, 1988).

The Writings of Henry D. Thoreau, Walden edition, 6 vols. (Boston: Houghton Mifflin, 1903).

The Journal of Henry Thoreau, ed. Bradford Torrey and Francis H. Allen, 14 vols. (Boston: Houghton Mifflin, 1906).

Collected Poems of Henry Thoreau, ed. Carol Bode (Chicago: Packard, 1943); Enlarged edition, ed. Carl Bode (Baltimore: The Johns Hopkins Press, 1965).

The Correspondences of Henry David Thoreau, ed. Walter Harding and Carl Bode (New York: New York University Press, 1958)

Thoreau's Minnesota Journey: Two Documents, ed. Walter Harding ([Concord, NH:] Thoreau Society, 1962).

Huckleberries, ed. Leo Stoller (Iowa City and New York: Windhover and New York Public Library, 1970).

Journal, Volume 3: 1848–1851, ed. Robert Sattlemeyer et al. (Princeton: Princeton University Press, 1990).

Journal, Volume 5: 1852–1853, ed. Patrick F. O'Connell (Princeton: Princeton University Press, 1990).

Journal, Volume 4: 1851–1852, ed. Leonard N. Neufeldt and Nancy Craig Simmons (Princeton: Princeton University Press, 1992).

Faith in a Seed: The Dispersion of Seeds and Other Late Natural History Writings, ed. Bradley P. Dean (Covelo, CA: Island, 1993).

Wild Fruits, ed. Bradley P. Dean (New York: Norton, 2000).

Letters to a Spiritual Seeker, ed. Bradley P. Dean (New York: Norton, 2004).

SECONDARY BIBLIOGRAPHY

References

Lawrence Buell, *The Environmental Imagination: Thoreau, Nature Writing, and the Formation of American Culture* (Cambridge: Harvard University Press, 1995).

Lawrence Buell, *Literary Transcendentalism: Style and Vision in the American Renaissance* (Ithaca, NY: Cornell University Press, 1973).

John Burroughs, *Birch Browsings: A John Burroughs Reader*, ed. Bill McKibben (New York: Penguin, 1992).

Stanley Cavell, *The Senses of Walden: An Expanded Edition* (Chicago: University of Chicago Press, 1992).

Ralph Waldo Emerson, *Nature. Ralph Waldo Emerson: A Critical Edition of the Major Works* (Oxford: Oxford University Press, 1990), 2–36.

Edwin Fussell, *Frontier: American Literature and the American West* (Princeton: Princeton University Press, 1965).

Walter Harding, *The Days of Henry Thoreau* (New York: Knopf, 1966).

Walter Harding, ed., *Thoreau as Seen by His Contemporaries* (New York: Dover, 1960).

Edward Hoagland, "Introduction," in *The Maine Woods* (New York: Penguin, 1988), ix–xxxiii.

Barbara Johnson, "A Hound, a Bay Horse, and a Turtle Dove: Obscurity in *Walden*," *A World of Difference* (Baltimore: Johns Hopkins University Press, 1987), 49–56.

Leo Marx, *The Machine in the Garden: Technology and the Pastoral Ideal in America* (London: Oxford University Press, 1964).

F.O. Matthiessen, *American Renaissance: Art and Expression in the Age of Emerson and Whitman* (London: Oxford University Press, 1941).

James McIntosh, *Thoreau as Romantic Naturalist: His Shifting Stance toward Nature* (Ithaca, NY: Cornell University Press, 1974).

Roderick Nash, *Wilderness and the American Mind*, 3rd ed. (New Haven: Yale University Press, 1982).

Joel Myerson, ed., *The Transcendentalists: A Review of Research and Criticism* (New York: MLA, 1984).

Sherman Paul, *The Shores of America: Thoreau's Inward Exploration* (Urbana: University of Illinois Press, 1958).

Robert D., Richardson, Jr., *Henry Thoreau: A Life of the Mind* (Berkeley: University of California Press, 1986).

Richard J. Schneider, ed., *Thoreau's Sense of Place* (Iowa City: University of Iowa Press, 2000).

Hyatt H. Waggoner, *American Poets: From the Puritans to the Present*, rev. ed. (Baton Rouge: Louisiana State University Press, 1984).

Donald Worster, *Nature's Economy: A History of Ecological Ideas* (San Francisco: Sierra, 1977).

Papers

The largest holdings of Thoreau's manuscripts are in Harvard University's Houghton Library, The Huntington Library, The New York Public Library's Berg Collection of English and American Literature, and The Morgan Library and Museum. Other holdings can be found in William Howarth's *The Literary Manuscripts of Henry David Thoreau* (Columbus: Ohio State University Press, 1974).

Bradford Torrey
(October 9, 1843–October 7, 1912)

Kevin E. O'Donnell

Though his work first appeared in print when he was already 39 years old, Bradford Torrey produced 13 books of nature writing in the subsequent 28 years of his life. Those books are mainly collections of essays he wrote for the *Atlantic Monthly*. Torrey was among the most popular of the Houghton and Mifflin Company's travel and "outdoor" writers at the end of the nineteenth century. (Other outdoor writers then in the Houghton Mifflin stable include H.D. Thoreau, John Burroughs, and John Muir.) Torrey also wrote, for a time, a weekly nature column for a Boston daily newspaper. A close observer of nature, and a master of the nature "ramble" when that literary form was at the height of its popularity, Torrey blended the nature ramble with travel writing, to introduce readers to emerging vacation destinations in the United States, while also promoting bird-watching and amateur nature study.

In addition to his newspaper columns and *Atlantic Monthly* articles, Torrey wrote numerous essays and field observations for ornithological publications such as *Bird-Lore*, *The Auk*, and *The Condor*, and for non-scientific periodicals such as *Youth's Companion* and the *Christian Endeavor World*. He was also an energetic promoter of Henry David Thoreau's work. He edited a "deluxe" edition of *Walden* in the 1890s, and he edited the first version of *Thoreau's Journal*, in 14 volumes, as part of the 20-volume "Manuscript Edition" of Thoreau's *Complete Works*, issued by Houghton Mifflin in 1906. (Torrey's friend and assistant, Francis H. Allen, though not credited as co-editor in the 1906 edition, does receive credit in later editions.)

Some of Torrey's best work appears in his last book, *Field Days in California*, published a few months after his death in 1912. However, by that time Torrey's readership had been in decline for ten years or more. In a sense, Torrey outlived his audience. After his death, literary critics largely ignored his work. Twentieth-century readers and critics alike came to reject the polite, gentle, and genteel literary traditions with which Torrey was associated. Yet for a period at the end of the nineteenth century—while the genteel nature ramble still had a following, and before bird-watching became a subject for satire—Torrey's writings had broad influence.

Despite the decline in his reputation, twenty-first-century readers will find appealing qualities beneath the polite veneer of Torrey's prose. At a time when science had begun policing the boundaries between amateur and professional discourse, Torrey wrote with the precision of a scientist, yet insistently rejected professionalization. At a time when even prominent conservationists and ornithologists were hunters, Torrey railed acidly against gunning. Torrey's writings include surprisingly modern commentary on the nature of observation, seeing, and perception. And they are informed by some idiosyncratic and distinctly ungenteel notions, including the belief that birds, insects, and even plants have souls. Torrey considered birds to be individuals, as well as representatives of their species, and he sometimes wrote commentary about individual birds' musical performances that borders on music criticism.

Very little biographical information about Torrey has been published. The best source is a brief though lovingly rendered account of his life, written by his colleague and friend Francis H. Allen, which appeared in *The Auk* (*The Bulletin of the Nuttall Ornithological Club*) three months after Torrey's death. As a result of the lack of information, misconceptions about Torrey's life have disseminated among students of American nature writing— including the erroneous notion that Torrey retired, Thoreau-like, to an isolated cabin in California. That error probably originated with a *Dictionary of American Biography* article written by Henry S. Chapman in the 1920s. In actual fact, Torrey retired to a Santa Barbara hotel. As his essays and correspondence show, he lived an active and sociable life in that California city in the years preceding his death. His essays also show that, unlike John Muir and other outdoor writers of the period, Torrey had no enthusiasm for "roughing it," though he was an exuberant advocate of foot travel, even as the automobile began to gain widespread use.

From the information available, however, Torrey does emerge as a solitary figure. He was a confirmed, lifelong bachelor. His letters show he had a lively and far-flung network of correspondents (including Celia Thaxter, with whom he conducted an energetic correspondence—see Marion Titus's collection of Thaxter's letters to Torrey). Yet the few written accounts of Torrey suggest that he was a shy man who kept to himself. John Burroughs remarks in a letter to a friend that Torrey was "a fine-souled fellow [who] suggests a bird with his bright eyes and shy ways and

sensitiveness." Francis H. Allen, in his obituary for Torrey, remarks that, "in his social relations [Torrey] was too modest and retiring to form a wide acquaintance, but he was much loved by the small circle of his more intimate friends."

Only the broad outlines are known of Torrey's life before he began publishing. Torrey was born in Weymouth, Massachusetts, to Samuel and Sophronia (Dyer) Torrey, on October 9, 1843. His own writings suggest a boyhood filled with nature rambles on his father's land and adjoining property in what was then a largely rural area outside Boston. Torrey graduated from Weymouth public schools at the age of 18 and worked briefly in a shoe factory, then taught school for a brief time, before entering what Allen describes as "positions with two business houses in Boston." Though Torrey was of the right age to serve in the Civil War, none of his obituaries mentions service. Around 1870, Torrey took a position in the office of the Treasurer of the American Board of Commissioners for Foreign Missions, in Boston, where he remained for about 16 years. In 1886, he obtained a position with *Youth's Companion*, a popular magazine that was then rising to the height of its influence. There Torrey edited the "Miscellany" section of the magazine. He remained on the *Youth's Companion* editorial staff until 1901, which is around the time he began work on Thoreau's journal, and also around the time that he began his newspaper column.

Torrey belongs among a group of late-nineteenth-century writers "whose essays laid the spiritual foundation for an age of suburbs," as Peter Schmitt observes in his classic 1969 study of American attitudes toward nature. That is, Torrey's writings both shaped and reflected what Schmitt calls the middle-class "Arcadian myth" that emerged at the end of the century. Unlike an earlier, Romantic point of view, this myth or viewpoint does not reject urbanism. Instead, it is more concerned with joining the benefits of urban culture with the advantages of country living. Accordingly, then, Torrey's first published essay, "With the Birds on Boston Common," which appeared in the *Atlantic Monthly* in February 1883, shows the narrator discovering nature study in an urban setting —namely, on Boston Common, the historic, urban green space outside the Park Street offices of the *Atlantic Monthly* itself. Torrey's audience, in this and many of his early essays, is explicitly the urban commuter, much like the person he mentions in a typical aside from one of his newspaper articles: "Only last night a man took a seat by me in an electric car and said...that he and his family, who live in a desirably secluded, woody spot, had never before seen so many birds, especially so many warblers" (*Clerk of the Woods*, 10).

This urban audience is implied by the title of Torrey's turn-of-the-century newspaper column: "The Clerk of the Woods." The title joins an urban, white-collar, middle-class occupation ("The Clerk"), with nature study ("The Woods"). Torrey wrote the column for the Boston *Evening Transcript* (it also appeared in the New York *Mail and Express*), at a time when the *Transcript* was read daily by "all proper Bostonians," according to one resident of Wellesley, Massachusetts, who was an enthusiastic follower of Torrey's column. Torrey delighted readers with the notion that they could become observers of the natural world, even in the city. His urban nature rambles—with their genial, polished charm and astute natural history observa- tions—found an enthusiastic audience among readers of the *Atlantic Monthly* in the 1880s and 1890s. Bliss Perry, one-time editor of that magazine, remarks in his memoirs that "anything from Bradford Torrey...[was] sure of an appreciative response" from readers during this period. Torrey's first two books quickly went through multiple "editions." (What publishers then called "editions" are now called "printings.")

Some modern commentators still consider Torrey to be an exclusively urban writer. An author of a recent study of John Burroughs, for instance, mistakenly observes that "Tor- rey never took his readers more than ten miles from downtown." It is true that most of the essays in Torrey's first three books are set in and around Boston and eastern Massa- chusetts. Yet those books also include essays from New Hampshire's White Mountains. And in the early 1890s, Torrey began roam- ing farther afield. He traveled south—to Florida, east Tennessee, western North Caro- lina, Arizona, California—at a time when those regions were being developed as vaca- tion destinations, and just as vacation travel was becoming more affordable for middle- class Americans.

The depth of Torrey's nature observations developed dramatically during this period, and his writings about the American south- east "represent the first major work on southern nature since Bartram, Wilson, and Audubon," according to one twentieth- century reader. Unlike John Burroughs, who claimed that he felt out of place whenever he left his native rural New York, Torrey shows himself to be an alert and sympathetic traveler. And in a later essay, "Friends on the Shelf," he launches a spirited defense of travel writing: "the value of such literature depends on the observer's alertness, fairness, good sense...rather than upon the length and leisureliness of his journey," as well as of the "scribbling tourist": "those who know a place or person best," writes Torrey, para- phrasing Bagehot, "are not those most likely to describe it best."

Torrey's narrative persona, in his first few books, is personable and agreeable, occasion- ally scripture-quoting, and with a touch of moralizing and didacticism. Torrey began writing about birds in the 1880s, at the begin- ning of a movement that, by the turn of the century, would come to associate bird- watching with character development. For example, in an essay from his first book, enti- tled "Character in Feathers," Torrey writes about chickadees as models of personal behavior because of their good cheer in the face of hardships:

> Their [chickadees'] example might well be heeded by those who suffer from fits of depression...[the bird's song] would most likely send them home in a more Christian mood. The time will come, we may hope,

when doctors will prescribe bird gazing instead of blue-pill.

Torrey's anthropomorphizing is the sort of thing modern readers can find cloying. Yet Torrey is aware of, and self-deprecating about, this tendency, upon which he remarks in an essay entitled "Butterfly Psychology" after speculating about a butterfly's inner life:

> It is my private heresy, perhaps, this strong anthromorphic [sic] turn of mind, which impels me to assume the presence of a soul in all animals, even in these airy nothings; and, having assumed its existence, to speculate as to what goes on within it.

Though he is often apologetic about it, this "anthropomorphic turn of mind" allows Torrey to consistently entertain what modern readers might call a "non-human" point of view. In an essay entitled "Flowers and Folk," for instance, Torrey imagines a study of "the human nature of plants." The work he has in mind would be a different kind of botany, which would "deal not so much with our likeness to tree and herb as with the likeness of tree and herb to us."

This anthropomorphic turn likewise leads him to critique, gently but persistently, Emerson's dichotomy between man and nature. That critique in turn leads him to consider —if always ever so politely—the serious ethical questions raised by nonhuman perspectives. In an essay entitled "Autumnal Moralities," for instance, Torrey observes two old white oaks, two trees he has long known, and he wonders if these trees do not enjoy each other's company. "Who knows— putting the matter on grounds of pure science—whether they do not enjoy each other's companionship? Who knows that trees have no kind of sentience? Not I." Farther along in this same nature ramble, along a semirural "old path," Torrey sees a stand of old pines. Addressing an imaginary property owner, he writes of the trees:

> These tall pine trees are yours. You have sovereignty over them, to use a word that is just now sweet in the American mouth. . . . You

may turn all their beauty to ashes, and it will be nobody's business to remonstrate. The trees are yours. I hope, notwithstanding, that you do not quite think so. I would rather believe that you look upon your so-called proprietorship as little more than a convenient legal fiction. . . .

That passage appeared in a Boston newspaper at a time when growing American imperialist-expansionist sentiment had led to the Spanish-American War. During the same era, industrial logging practices had already begun that would, within the decade, lead to the clear-cutting of most of the old-growth forests in New Hampshire's White Mountains, as well as in the mountains of the Southeast. Torrey's anthropomorphic turn of mind, then, leads him to a critique that links the two phenomena—imperialism, on the one hand, and imprudent natural-resource extraction on the other. Torrey was by no means a political activist, however. His calls for conservation, though consistent throughout his work, are gentle, even timid, in comparison with those of, say, John Muir, his contemporary. Nevertheless, with his appeals to personal sensitivity, Torrey persistently nudges his readers in the direction of political awareness. Typical are his remarks in an article entitled "An Idler on Missionary Ridge." Following his comments on the song of the thrasher, Torrey writes,

> The thrasher is to a peculiar degree a bird of passion; ecstatic in song, furious in anger, irresistibly pitiful in lamentation. How any man can rob a thrasher's nest with that heartbroken whistle in his ears is more than I can imagine.

Torrey's anthropomorphism likewise leads him to a critique of the scientific perspective: he observes that

> one may become so zealous a botanist as almost to cease to be a man. The shifting panorama of the heavens and the earth no longer appeals to him. He is now a specialist, and go where he will, he sees nothing but specimens.

As philosophy, this thought is fairly conventional. But it leads Torrey to nature observations that would have been challenging to many nineteenth century readers, as when Torrey considers birds as individuals:

> [the scientific classification of species] rates birds as bodies, and nothing else: while to the person of whom we are speaking [that is, "the person whose interest in birds is friendly rather than scientific"] birds are, first of all, souls; his interest in them is, as we say, personal.

Yet even while flaunting his anthropomorphism and his personal connections to individual birds, Torrey retained a scientific frame of mind. He took his nature study seriously, and especially in his later writings he is careful and precise, even while retaining an insistence on the importance of intuition in nature study. In "Some Tennessee Bird Notes," for example, he concludes, after listening to oven birds singing, that those birds are not migrating but are, rather, native to the region. His conclusion is based on intuition, as he explains:

> Birds which are at home have, as a rule, an air of being at home; a certain manner hard to define, but felt, nevertheless, as a pretty strong kind of evidence—not proof—by a practiced observer.

In 1903, John Burroughs wrote what was to become a famous critique of what he considered sensationalistic nature writers, including Jack London and William L. Long, for their anthropomorphic conceits. Burroughs's article initiated a debate that came to be known as the "nature faker" controversy, a controversy that remained in the public eye for years and that eventually involved public commentary from Theodore Roosevelt, even as Roosevelt was president of the United States. Yet, while Burroughs takes nature writers to task for their too-fanciful anthropomorphism, he begins the article by singling out Bradford Torrey, not for criticism, but rather for praise:

But before I proceed with this discussion, let me briefly speak of the books that have lately appeared in this field that are real contributions to the literature of the subjects of which they treat. All of Mr. Bradford Torrey's bird studies merit this encomium.

Despite Torrey's consistent entertainment of nonhuman perspectives, then, Torrey retains Burroughs's approval because of his accuracy, close observation, and respect for facts.

In later essays, Torrey comes close to adopting the pose of the late-Victorian aesthete. He refers to himself as a "rambler," an "idler," and a "bird-gazer." ("Our creed is more frankly hedonistic," he remarks at one point, when comparing himself and a companion to entomologists on a vacation trip.) Yet even while posing as an aesthete, he retains a peculiar, New-England-style industriousness and didacticism. He writes, in *Footing It in Franconia*, for example, of his "industrious indolence." The didactic aim of Torrey's travel writing is to tutor his middle-class audience in how to enjoy their travel and leisure in refined ways. In *Clerk of the Woods*, for example, he educates his middle-class audience in the discourse of the "picturesque" so that they may properly enjoy the scenery, when visiting the North Shore. Here he provides an easy, practical take on the transcendentalist version of the picturesque, in order to justify repeated visits to a North Shore vacation destination: "The eye is the lens, the mind is the plate. The landscape prints itself upon the mind, through the eye. But the mind must be sensitive and still, and —what is oftener forgotten—the exposure must be sufficiently prolonged." Elsewhere he tells his New England audience how to travel to popular Southern vacation destinations while distinguishing themselves from the herd of common tourists. He provides advice on clothing and deportment for New Englanders wintering in Daytona Beach, Florida, for instance. And he instructs the White Mountain vacationer on how to enter the "noble fraternity of saunterers." "I speak of those of us who foot it," he writes, in *Footing It in Franconia:* "To plod through the mud is more exhilarating than to sit before a fire; and we leave the question of reasonableness and comfort on one side."

After Torrey took on the project of editing *Thoreau's Journals*, around 1900, his own productivity declined, though he continued to produce some first-rate work. With the rising popularity of nature writing during that period, Houghton Mifflin appears to have made an attempt to include Torrey in a developing nature-writing cannon. Houghton Mifflin editors included his work in a 1909 anthology, for example, that includes the work of six writers under contract to that publisher. The writers' work is apparently arranged according to what editors then decided was their order of importance: Henry D. Thoreau, John Burroughs, John Muir, Bradford Torrey, Dallas Lore Sharp, Olive Thorne Miller. Of those six, however, only the first three would be widely known a century later. As mentioned earlier, Torrey had lost his popularity even before his death. As John Burroughs remarked, in a letter to a friend, after hearing of Torrey's death:

> He was a rare spirit and a maker of pure literature. His style has an ease and flexibility and a conversational charm that I wish I might inherit. Yet Clifton Johnson says his books have little sale. What a criticism of the readers of nature books!

Though ignored by literary critics, Torrey's work has continued to serve as primary source material for naturalists, cultural historians, and, more recently, environmental historians. In recent years, attention to his writing has been revived by students of American attitudes toward nature, and by students of Thoreau's canonization. Also recently, selections from Torrey's writing have been reprinted in regional nature writing and travel writing collections.

PRIMARY BIBLIOGRAPHY

Books

Birds in the Bush (Boston: Houghton Mifflin and Co., 1885).

A Rambler's Lease (Boston: Houghton Mifflin and Co., 1889).

The Foot-Path Way (Boston: Houghton Mifflin and Co., 1892).

A Florida Sketch-Book (Boston: Houghton Mifflin and Co., 1894).

Spring Notes from Tennessee (Boston: Houghton Mifflin and Co., 1896).

A World of Green Hills: Observations of Nature and Human Nature in the Blue Ridge (Boston: Houghton Mifflin and Co., 1898).

Everyday Birds: Elementary Studies [juvenile], *With Twelve Illustrations in Color after Audubon, and Two from Photographs* (Boston: Houghton Mifflin and Co., 1901).

Footing It in Franconia (Boston: Houghton Mifflin and Co., 1901).

The Clerk of the Woods (Boston: Houghton Mifflin and Co., 1903).

Nature's Invitation; Notes of a Bird-Gazer North and South (Boston: Houghton Mifflin and Co., 1904).

Friends on the Shelf (Boston: Houghton Mifflin and Co., 1906).

Field-Days in California (with Illustrations from Photographs) (Boston: Houghton Mifflin, 1913).

Selected Essays, Collected and Uncollected

"With the Birds on Boston Common," *Atlantic Monthly* 51 (February 1883): 203–8.

"The Bird of Thanksgiving," *Youth's Companion* 61 (November 29, 1888): 605–8.

"The 'Booming' of the Bittern," *The Auk* (*The Bulletin of the Nuttall Ornithological Club*) [Cambridge MA] 6 (1889): 1–8.

"Watching the Bittern 'Pump'," *Bird-Lore: An Illustrated Bi-Monthly Magazine Devoted to the Study and Protection of Birds* 1 (August 1899): 123–25.

"Introduction," in *The Journal of Henry D. Thoreau*, 14 vols., ed. Bradford Torrey and Francis H. Allen (Boston: Houghton Mifflin, 1906), xix–li.

"Introduction," in *Birds of the Boston Public Garden: A Study in Migration; with an Introduction by Bradford Torrey and Illustrations*, by Horace Winslow Wright (Boston: Houghton Mifflin, 1909), xv–xviii.

"Scraping Acquaintance (from *Birds in the Bush*)" and "An Old Road (from *A Rambler's Lease*)," *In American Fields and Forests: Henry D. Thoreau, John Burroughs, John Muir, Bradford Torrey, Dallas Lore Sharp, Olive Thorne Miller; with Illustrations from Photographs by Herbert W. Gleason* (Boston: Houghton Mifflin, 1909), 271–90; 290–309.

Works by Thoreau, Edited by Torrey

Henry David Thoreau, *Walden, with an Introduction by Bradford Torrey; Illustrated with Photogravures, in 2 volumes* ["deluxe" edition] (Boston: Houghton Mifflin, 1897).

Henry David Thoreau, *Excursions*, ed. Bradford Torrey and Francis H. Allen (Boston: Houghton Mifflin, 1906).

Henry David Thoreau, *The Journal of Henry David Thoreau, in 14 Volumes,* ed. Bradford Torrey and Francis H. Allen, from *The Writings of Henry David Thoreau, in Twenty Volumes* [Manuscript Edition] (Boston: Houghton Mifflin and Co., 1906).

Reprints in Regional Travel and Nature Writing Collections, Selected

From "Birds, Flowers, and People" [*A World of Green Hills*], in *North Carolina Nature Writing: Four Centuries of Personal Narratives and Descriptions*, ed. Richard Rankin (Winston-Salem, NC: John F. Blair Publisher, 1996), 87–95.

From "At Natural Bridge" [*A World of Green Hills*], in *The Height of Our Mountains: Nature Writing from Virginia's Blue Ridge Mountains and Shenandoah Valley*, ed. Michael P. Branch and Daniel J. Philippon (Baltimore, MD: Johns Hopkins University Press, 1998), 200–204.

"A Week on Walden's Ridge I" [*Spring Notes from Tennessee*], in *Seekers of Scenery: Travel Writing from Southern Appalachia, 1840–1900*, ed. Kevin E. O'Donnell and Helen Hollingsworth (Knoxville: University of Tennessee Press, 2004), 83–96.

SECONDARY BIBLIOGRAPHY

References

Francis H. Allen, "Bradford Torrey [obituary—in 'Notes and News']," *The Auk (The Bulletin of the Nuttall Ornithological Club)* [Cambridge MA] 30 (1913): 157–59.

Clara Barrus, *The Life and Letters of John Burroughs*, 2 vols. (Boston: Houghton Mifflin, 1925).

Paul Brooks, *Speaking for Nature: How Literary Naturalists from Henry Thoreau to Rachel Carson Have Shaped America* (Boston: Houghton Mifflin, 1980).

John Burroughs, "Real and Sham Natural History," *Atlantic Monthly* 91 (March 1903): 298–309.

Robert C. Cottrell, *Roger Nash Baldwin and the American Civil Liberties Union* (New York: Columbia University Press, 2000).

Felton Gibbons and Deborah Strom, *Neighbors to the Birds: A History of Birdwatching in America* (New York: Norton, 1988).

Peggy Lamson, *Roger Baldwin: Founder of the American Civil Liberties Union* (Boston: Houghton Mifflin, 1976).

Ralph H. Lutts, *The Nature Fakers: Wildlife, Science, and Sentiment* (Golden, CO: Fulcrum, 1990).

Perry Miller, "A Note on the Editing," *Consciousness in Concord: The Text of Thoreau's hitherto "Lost Journal" (1840–41),* by H.D. Thoreau [*Thoreau's Journal,* July 30, 1840–January 22, 1841—the portion omitted from Torrey's 1906 edition], ed. Perry Miller (Boston: Houghton Mifflin, 1958), 128–30.

Bliss Perry, *And Gladly Teach: Reminiscences* (Boston: Houghton Mifflin, 1935).

Edward J. Renehan, Jr., *John Burroughs: American Naturalist* (Hensonville, NY: Black Dome Press, 1998).

Peter J. Schmitt, *Back to Nature: The Arcadian Myth in Urban America, 1900–1930* (London: Oxford University Press, 1969).

Donna Marion Titus, ed., *By This Wing: Letters by Celia Thaxter to Bradford Torrey about Birds at the Isles of Shoals, 1888 to 1894* (Manchester, NH: J. Palmer Publisher, 1999).

Robert Henry Welker, *Birds and Men: American Birds in Science, Art, Literature and Conservation, 1800–1900* (Cambridge: Belknap of Harvard University Press, 1955).

Papers

Torrey was an energetic and prolific letter writer. Most of his letters are apparently widely scattered. The most extensive collection is in the William Brewster Collection at Harvard University's Museum of Comparative Zoology. Torrey corresponded regularly with Brewster over a period of 25 years. Brewster, curator of mammals and birds, Museum of Comparative Zoology, Harvard, from 1885 to 1900, was well-known for his ornithological expeditions, and Torrey's writings about the American Southeast, especially, are informed by Brewster's observations.

The Houghton Library at Harvard University holds a number of letters from Torrey to his editors at the publishing firm of Houghton Mifflin, and to editors at the *Atlantic Monthly*, regarding the preparation and publication of his work.

Another notable cluster of letters, written to Joseph Grinnell, is held in the Joseph Grinnell papers at the Bancroft Library, University of California,

Berkeley. These letters regard mainly behavior and identification of species of birds native to the western United States. Joseph Grinnell, an influential ecologist and officer in the Cooper Ornithological Club (not to be confused with Joseph Bird Grinnell, the well-known ornithologist from the same period), was active in wildlife protection and conservation in the West and was director of the Museum of Vertebrate Zoology at the University of California from 1908 until his death in 1939.

Torrey carried on a lively, flirtatious correspondence with Celia Thaxter from 1888 to Thaxter's death in 1894. Thaxter's letters to Torrey were selected and published in 1999. According to Donna Marion Titus, the editor of that volume, Torrey's letters to Thaxter are lost. But much can be inferred about Torrey's work and personality from Thaxter's side of the correspondence. (See Titus in References.)

The following letters also survive:

Sixty-five letters to William Brewster, 1884–1909 (bBr 661.10.1); William Brewster Collection, Museum of Comparative Zoology, Harvard University.

Twenty-two letters to and from the Houghton Mifflin Company, 1886–1903 (bMS Am 1925: I. A., item 1791); eight Letters to *The Atlantic Monthly*, 1900–1903 (bMS Am 1925.1, item 115); Houghton Mifflin Collection, Houghton Library, Harvard University.

Seventeen letters to Joseph Grinnell, 1905–1907; Joseph Grinnell papers (BANC MSS C-B 995); The Bancroft Library, University of California, Berkeley.

John Kirk Townsend
(October 10, 1809–February 6, 1851)

Michael P. Branch

Ornithologist and explorer John Kirk Townsend was among the first professional naturalists to cross the American continent, traveling westward in 1834 along the overland route later known as the Oregon Trail. Many of the birds Townsend collected on his travels were new to science, and his account of his remarkable adventures, *Narrative of a Journey across the Rocky Mountains to the Columbia River...* (1839), is among the most engaging and interesting nineteenth-century accounts of the landscapes and fauna of the American West. Despite his scientific and literary accomplishments, there are two primary reasons why Townsend has remained obscure: first, most of his ornithological discoveries were published by his rival, John James Audubon, before he could return from his travels to receive credit for his own ambitious fieldwork; and, second, his overland journal has long been considered a work of frontier history rather than a richly literary or environmental text. However, in its ethical and aesthetic engagement with the natural world, its often unprecedented observations of western species, and its unusually lively prose, Townsend's *Narrative* is certainly an important work of pre-Thoreauvian American nature writing.

Although there remains some argument about the date of his birth, it is probable that

John Kirk Townsend was born in Philadelphia on October 10, 1809. As the son of Charles Townsend and Priscilla Kirk, John was a member of a family of Quakers distinguished for their intellectual, philanthropic, and scientific activity. John took an early interest in natural history, a passion shared by his sister, Mary, who later wrote *Life in the Insect World* (1844). He was educated at the Quaker school in Westtown, Pennsylvania, where the curriculum of natural history studies had nurtured entomologist Thomas Say and other American naturalists. As a teenager John became a proficient ornithologist and taxidermist, and in 1833 he collected what appeared to be a new species of bird. Townsend wished to name the discovery in honor of John James Audubon, to whom he showed the unusual specimen; in describing the bird in his *Ornithological Biography* (vol. 2, 1834), however, Audubon instead named it *Emberiza townsendi*, Townsend's Bunting. The bird was never seen again, and some scientists maintain that Townsend collected the type of a now extinct species.

Townsend's great opportunity came the following year, when botanist Thomas Nuttall invited Townsend to join him on Nathaniel J. Wyeth's second transcontinental expedition. Captain Wyeth was a businessman whose goal was to establish a fur-trading company on the west coast and, if possible, help claim Oregon for America by competing successfully with the established commercial empire of the British-sponsored Hudson's Bay Company. Nuttall was an itinerant naturalist of considerable skill and legendary tenacity, a zealous collector in a variety of fields, and had published *A Journal of Travels into the Arkansa Territory* in 1821 and the widely used volumes of the *Manual of the Ornithology of the United States and Canada* in 1832 and 1833. Having examined plants brought back from the first Wyeth expedition (1833), Nuttall could not resist the temptation of new western plants, and so had resigned his position at Harvard to accompany Wyeth's second expedition in 1834. Although he was also an ornithologist, Nuttall intended to devote his journey to botanizing, and so invited Townsend along to study and collect the little-known birds of the western territories. The 24-year-old Townsend enthusiastically accepted, and he immediately sought funding from the Academy of Natural Sciences and the American Philosophical Society in Philadelphia, each of which provided him $125 in exchange for his promise to gather specimens for their collections. In March 1834, Townsend left Philadelphia with Nuttall on the stage for Pittsburgh. He would not return until November 1837, after the three and a half years of adventures that took him across the continent, to Hawai'i, South America, and around Cape Horn.

From Pittsburgh, Townsend and Nuttall traveled down the Ohio by boat to St. Louis, and from there walked to Independence, Missouri. On April 28, 1834, the Wyeth expedition—complete with 250 horses and 70 men —left Independence bound for the Pacific. Rather than travel along the earlier, Missouri River route, the party would go overland through the South Pass of Wyoming and down the Columbia River along the route that was to become the Oregon Trail.

Traveling west across the prairies, Townsend soon found himself in scientific terra incognita, where he delighted in the wildness of the prospect and the diversity and beauty of the unfamiliar birds—many of which were as yet undescribed. He remarked on the large flocks of (now extinct) passenger pigeons, and enthusiastically described places where the bare ground was "literarally covered" with "thousands of golden plovers." He saw for the first time "vast numbers of the beautiful parrot of this country" (the Carolina parakeet, also now extinct), and he studied the large ravens that scoured the party's camps. But Townsend's adventures were not exclusively ornithological: he also weathered a storm of hailstones "as large as musket balls" and survived a wild stampede in which more than a hundred horses crashed through the camp of sleeping men.

By mid-May Wyeth's group was far enough west that Townsend could report seeing first wolves, then antelope, and, at last, vast herds of bison. "Towards evening, on rising a hill, we were suddenly greeted by a sight which seemed to astonish even the oldest amongst us," wrote Townsend on May 20.

> The whole plain, as far as the eye could discern, was covered by one enormous mass of buffalo. Our vision, at the very least computation, would certainly extend ten miles, and in the whole of this great space...there was apparently no vista in the incalculable multitude. It was truly a sight that would have excited even the dullest mind to enthusiasm.

Much like the experiences of early European explorers in the wilderness of eastern North America, Townsend's encounter with the landscapes and creatures of the great West is animated by a sense of the newness, strangeness, and grandeur of nature—the thrill of enthusiasm that gives his *Narrative* much of its power and interest.

Unlike James Fenimore Cooper, who romanticized Western landscapes in his 1826 novel *The Prairie*, or Washington Irving, who recorded his observations of the Great Plains in *A Tour on the Prairies* (1835), Townsend was no literary romanticizer or tourist. He was a devoted naturalist, and his passion for science is another source of his book's impressive energy. As the party traveled along the Platte River, for example, Townsend was ecstatic about his opportunities to collect birds, and heartbroken that the pace of the party prevented him from undertaking exhaustive studies. "I think I never before saw so great a variety of birds within the same space," he wrote on the first of June.

> All were beautiful, and many of them quite new to me; and after we had spent an hour amongst them, and my game bag was teeming with its precious freight, I was still loath to leave the place, lest I should not have procured specimens of the whole.

Townsend lamented that other members of the party could neither appreciate nor accommodate his scientific activities. He reflected in his journal that

> [n]one but a naturalist can appreciate a naturalist's feelings—his delight amounting to ecstasy—when a specimen such as he has never before seen, meets his eye, and the sorrow and grief which he feels when he is compelled to tear himself from a spot abounding with all that he has anxiously and unremittingly sought for.

As this passage suggests, Townsend often used impassioned literary language to place the natural world in the conventional place of the human beloved—a technique widely adopted by nature writers who followed him, but rarely employed in science writing, either during the nineteenth century or since.

It was in the service of science that Townsend endured the many hardships of the trail: rough traveling, occasional hunger and thirst, bad weather, fear of Indian attack, even being charged by an enraged grizzly bear. He likewise endured frustrations to his enterprise as a collector: on one occasion he lost a valuable field journal while swimming his horse across the Green River; on another he returned to camp to discover some of the party feasting on an owl he had collected as a specimen; on yet another he found that several of the men had drunk the preservative whiskey from his bottle of reptile specimens,

noting with disappointment that "Thornburg had decanted the liquor from the precious reptiles which I had destined for immortality, and he and one of his pot companions had been 'happy' upon it for a whole day." Townsend speculated that a proper scientific expedition might transcend many of these difficulties, and he was among the first to propose that government-sponsored collecting parties be sent west:

> What valuable and highly interesting accessions to science might not be made by a party, composed exclusively of naturalists, on a journey through this rich and unexplored region! The botanist, the geologist, the mamalogist [sic], the ornithologist, and the entomologist, would find a rich and almost inexhaustible field for the prosecution of their inquiries.

Townsend's *Narrative* is also distinguished by an unusual interest in what we now call "environmental ethics." Throughout the book he struggles to determine, to his own satisfaction, the circumstances under which the killing of animals is ethically acceptable. Unlike many explorers and scientists of his day, Townsend was a thoughtful man whose developing ethical sensibility—and his unfortunate lapses from it—anticipate the environmental concerns and insights so important to contemporary nature writing. For example, Townsend strongly objects to the killing of more pronghorn antelope than are needed for food: "A number are, however, slaughtered every day, from mere wantonness and love of killing, the greenhorns glorifying in the sport, like our striplings of the city, in their annual murdering of robins and sparrows." He is likewise scandalized by the profligate wasting of buffalo, a form of killing he indignantly condemns as a "useless and unwarrantable waste of the goods of Providence." It is noteworthy that Townsend is alone among his compatriots in objecting to the improvident killing of bison.

> I have seen dozens of buffalo slaughtered merely for the tongues, or for practice with the rifle; and I have also lived to see the very perpetrators of these deeds, lean and lank with

famine, when the meanest and most worthless parts of the poor animals they had so inhumanly slaughtered, would have been received and eaten with humble thankfulness.

And Townsend is quite capable of making careful ethical distinctions: he rarely objects to the killing of animals for specimens or for food, but he often decries cruelty and waste. As an example, he notes in his journal that he relishes the flavor of dog meat (a food common on the Western trail), but he explains that he is "always unwilling, unless when suffering absolute want, to take the life of so noble and faithful an animal." Townsend's emergent ethical sensibility makes his *Narrative* especially interesting as the record of a developing, individual environmental ethic.

As nature writing, the *Narrative* is perhaps most impressive when Townsend's own behavior is least laudable. For rather than simply chastising others as ethically degenerate, he also examines his own behavior, and has the moral courage to admit when that behavior is condemnable. In one powerful example of this ethical growth, Townsend confesses that "I committed an act of cruelty and wantonness, which distressed and troubled me beyond measure, and which I have ever since recollected with sorrow and compunction." He first explains that a beautiful doe antelope had been following the party, and then confesses that his "evil genius and love of sport triumphed," and he shoots her without cause. Stricken with guilt, Townsend approaches his victim while in the agony of her death throes. "[A]s I stood over her, and saw her cast her large, soft, black eyes upon me with an expression of the most touching sadness," he writes, "I felt myself the meanest and most abhorrent thing in creation." Embracing the animal, Townsend drives his knife to her heart in order to end her suffering. This is a powerful moment in Townsend's book, and it is remarkably similar to the famous passage in *A Sand County Almanac* (1949) in which Aldo Leopold deeply regrets killing a wolf as he watches the "green fire" dying in its eyes. In both

cases the writer has the courage to question his own environmental values and to learn from his mistakes. Townsend rides away from the doe's body with, he says, "feelings such as I hope never to experience again." "For several days the poor antelope haunted me," he concludes, "and I shall never forget its last look of pain and upbraiding."

Despite his developing ethical relationship to the nonhuman natural world, Townsend had considerably less compunction in his approach to Native Americans. Although his reflections on Indian life and culture are less narrowly racist than those of most other commentators of the period, his lust for collecting unfortunately extended beyond birds and reptiles. On one occasion Townsend removed the embalmed corpse of an Indian woman from her ceremonial burying ground, and on another he robbed Indian graves of four skulls that he carried away for further study. In a particularly chilling observation about Indian children, he writes that

> I have often been evilly disposed enough to wish, that if in the course of events one of these little beings should die, I could get possession of it. I should like to plump the small carcass into a keg of spirits, and send it home for the observation of the curious.

Like many earlier American naturalists, Townsend considered Native Americans a fit subject for the study of natural history; as such, they were fair game for collection as specimens, even by a scientist who remained haunted by his unethical treatment of an antelope.

The Wyeth party successfully crossed the Wind River Range in present-day Wyoming before establishing Fort Hall on the Snake River and then following the Columbia River all the way to Fort Vancouver, where their five-month crossing of the continent ended on September 16, 1834. Soon after, Townsend paid respects to his most renowned predecessors by visiting the ruins of the house at Fort Clatsop where Lewis and Clark spent the dreary winter of 1805–1806. Although his great transcontinental adventure was over, for the next two years Townsend lived in the Pacific Northwest, basing out of Fort Vancouver but making collecting trips into the Blue Mountains, up the Columbia and Willamette Rivers, along the Pacific coast, and even in Hawai'i (then the Sandwich Islands), where he collected for four months during early 1835. On these trips, which are also recounted in the *Narrative*, Townsend discovered a number of bird species that were new to science; so extensive were his ornithological studies in the region that among the Northwest Indians Townsend became known as the "bird chief."

Thomas Nuttall sailed for Boston in September 1835, taking with him for safekeeping the treasure of Townsend's Western bird specimens. Townsend, however, remained in Oregon, serving for a time as surgeon at Fort Vancouver, and continuing to explore afield and to collect the birds of the coastal Northwest. At the end of November 1836 Townsend at last left Oregon, from which he sailed first to Hawai'i, then Tahiti, and then Valparaiso, Chile, where he remained seriously ill for several weeks. He left Chile on August 22, rounded Cape Horn in early September, and arrived safely back in Philadelphia on November 14, 1837.

One of the most fascinating aspects of Townsend's life and legacy as a naturalist concerns the unusual fate of his great Western collections and the bearing that fate had upon the rest of his short life. Long before Townsend returned to Philadelphia, his collections were the subject of intense interest in the scientific community. His specimens, which were cared for by Nuttall, had been safely deposited at the Academy of Natural Sciences in Philadelphia in early summer of 1836. So significant was Townsend's collection of Western birds that John James Audubon, then at work on the final volumes of *The Birds of America* (1827–1838), became desperate to gain access and to depict Townsend's birds in his great book. Audubon had long wished to make a Western collecting journey himself, but he now realized that time and age would prevent such a trip, and he urgently needed the Western

birds to complete his magnum opus. In September Audubon rushed to Philadelphia to examine the collection, but was coolly received by Townsend's friends at the Academy. Audubon was allowed to briefly examine the specimens but was not permitted to draw any. Writing of Townsend's collection that "its value cannot be described," Audubon tried first persuasion and then outright purchase to obtain the Western birds.

When the naturalists at the Academy still refused, claiming a need to protect Townsend's discoveries until he returned from the Pacific, the tireless Audubon went to Boston, where he successfully enlisted Thomas Nuttall in his cause. Nuttall first gave Audubon some of his own duplicate skins of new Western birds and further promised to intervene with the Academy. With Nuttall's involvement, eventually a deal was struck: the Academy would sell Audubon duplicates from their Townsend collection with the understanding that Audubon and Nuttall would prepare a paper claiming discovery of the new species in Townsend's name. Audubon thus captured one of the greatest prizes in the history of American ornithology, and by late October could gloat ecstatically in a letter to his friend and collaborator John Bachman:

> Read aloud!! quite aloud!!!—I have purchased *Ninety Three Bird Skins!* Yes 93 Bird Skins!— Well what are they? Why nought less than 93 Bird Skins sent from the Rocky Mountains and the Columbia River by Nuttal [sic] & Townsend!—Cheap as Dirt too....Such beauties! such rarities! Such Novelties! Ah my Worthy Friend how we will laugh and talk over them!—

As Townsend sailed the Pacific on his long route home, Audubon was at Bachman's home in Charleston rushing to draw Townsend's hard-won Western birds for his own *Birds of America*.

By the time Townsend returned to Philadelphia in November 1837, Audubon had finished with the first group of Western birds and was anxious for the additional species Townsend had brought home with him and deposited at the Academy. Knowing that Townsend was in poor financial condition, Audubon once again moved to buy him out, writing to a friend that he did not think Townsend could afford to "publish [the new birds] himself under his present (I am sorry to say) embarrassed pecuniary circumstances." Townsend, of course, had returned to Philadelphia to find that the new species sent home with Nuttall had already been described by Audubon. Given this missed opportunity and his bad financial straits, he now had little choice but to sell Audubon his additional specimens. On the eve of the completion of *Birds of America,* Audubon thus came into possession of another cache of Townsend birds; Audubon expanded his project to accommodate the new species, which were subsequently included in the final volume of *Birds.*

Despite these setbacks, Townsend's hopes were not all lost. In 1839 he published his *Narrative,* which contained a scientific appendix but was written more as a Western adventure story than as a bird book. Nor had Townsend's losses to Audubon yet forced him to relinquish his ambitions as a naturalist, for Audubon's double elephant folio edition of *Birds of America* was so expensive as to be inaccessible to most bird enthusiasts. If he could publish an affordable book of American birds, Townsend reasoned, he might yet make his mark. Working with the talented natural history artist J. B. Chevalier, Townsend set to work on his *Ornithology of the United States,* the first volume of which was published in an affordable octavo edition later in 1839. It is a beautiful pamphlet, well written and graced with four superb plates depicting condors and vultures. However, Townsend's bad luck was to continue. The first volume of Audubon's octavo edition of *Birds of America*—which contained 508 bird species, 74 of which were collected by Townsend—carried an 1840 publication date but was available in late 1839. The book went on to become the best-selling natural history book ever published up to that time. Audubon was a step ahead of Townsend once

again. Presumably recognizing the octavo edition of *Birds* as a direct and undefeatable competitor, Townsend relinquished his own project, thus making the sole volume of *Ornithology of the United States* one of the rarest of American natural history books, fewer than a half dozen copies of which are believed to exist. When Audubon had completed the octavo *Birds,* he began his great mammal book, *Viviparous Quadrupeds of North America* (1845–1848). His engraver on the project was J. B. Chevalier, whose services were no longer needed by Townsend, and contained within its pages were previously undescribed Western mammals drawn from specimens purchased from their discoverer, John Kirk Townsend.

His prospects for publishing the results of his own discoveries now lost, Townsend accepted a position as curator at the Academy of Natural Sciences in Philadelphia, where his work consisted largely of preparing bird specimens for study and display. During the early 1840s he relocated and did similar work at the National Institution for the Promotion of Science (precursor to the Smithsonian) in Washington, D.C. However, he was soon caught up in a disagreement between the Institute and Charles Wilkes, the commander of the United States Exploring Expedition, and was discharged from his position in 1843. Townsend returned home to Philadelphia, where he resumed work at the Academy and also studied dentistry, though apparently without ever practicing. Although he was often in poor health, Townsend agreed to serve as naturalist on a U.S. naval ship that was to sail, in 1851, to explore the east coast of Africa. But Townsend was too ill to join the expedition, and died shortly before the voyage, on February 6, 1851. He was only 41 years old, and his death is attributed to the cumulative poisoning caused by the arsenic powder he used to preserve bird specimens.

Despite the numerous misfortunes that kept him hidden in the long shadow of his rival, John James Audubon, Townsend left a rich legacy. The freshness of his observations, the energy of his prose, and the ethical sensitivity of his engagement with nature make the account of his great adventure, *Narrative of a Journey across the Rocky Mountains*, a classic of nineteenth-century Western exploration and nature writing. And while most of Townsend's scientific discoveries were published by others, his legacy is preserved in the names of many of the Western species he was the first to collect, including Townsend's Warbler, Townsend's Solitaire, Townsend's Chipmunk, Townsend's Ground Squirrel, and the White-tailed Jackrabbit (*Lepus townsendi*).

PRIMARY BIBLIOGRAPHY

Book

Narrative of a Journey across the Rocky Mountains, to the Columbia River, and a Visit to the Sandwich Islands, Chili, &c., with a Scientific Appendix (Philadelphia: Henry Perkins, 1839; reprinted as *Sporting Excursions in the Rocky Mountains, Including a Journey to the Columbia River, and a Visit to the Sandwich Islands, Chili &c.*, 2 vols. [London: Henry Colburn, 1840]; abridged edition, ed. Ruben G. Thwaites, in vol. 11 of *Early Western Travels, 1748–1846* [Cleveland: Arthur H. Clark, 1905]; an edition of the full 1839 text, ed. George A. Jobanek [Corvallis: Oregon State University Press, 1999]).

Other

Ornithology of the United States of North America; or, Descriptions of the birds inhabiting the states and territories of the Union: with an accurate figure of each, drawn and coloured from nature, vol. 1 (Philadelphia: J. B. Chevalier, 1839) [no subsequent volumes were issued].

Articles

"Description of Twelve New Species of Birds, chiefly from the vicinity of the Columbia river," *Journal of the Academy of Natural Sciences of Philadelphia* 7 (1837): 187–93 [probably written in Townsend's name by Thomas Nuttall and John James Audubon].

"Description of the Birds of the Columbia River Region," published in Samuel Parker, *Journal of an exploring tour beyond the Rocky Mountains* (Ithaca, NY: published by the author, 1838), 338–40; reprinted in George A. Jobanek and David B. Marshall, "John K. Townsend's 1836 Report of the Birds of the Lower Columbia River Region, Oregon and Washington," *Northwestern Naturalist* 73 (1992): 1–14.

"Description of a New Species of *Cypcelus*, from the Columbia River," *Journal of the Academy of Natural Sciences of Philadelphia* 8 (1839): 148.

"Description of a New Species of *Sylvia*, from the Columbia River," *Journal of the Academy of Natural Sciences of Philadelphia* 8 (1839): 149–50.

"List of the Birds Inhabiting the Region of the Rocky Mountains, the Territory of the Oregon, and the North West Coast of America," *Journal of the Academy of Natural Sciences of Philadelphia* 8 (1839): 151–58.

"Note on *Sylvia* Tolmoei [sic]," *Journal of the Academy of Natural Sciences of Philadelphia* 8 (1839): 159.

"Sketches of a voyage, and residence in the South Sea Islands," *Literary Record* of the Linnaean Association of Pennsylvania College, Gettysburg 3.4 (February 1847): 88–92, 113–20, 121–26.

"Popular Monograph of the Acciptrine Birds of North America; no. 1: The Condor of the Andes (*Cathartes gyphus*)," *Literary Record* of the Linnaean Association of Pennsylvania College, Gettysburg 4.11 (September 1848): 249–55, 265–72.

"On the giant wolf of North America, Lupus gigas," *Journal of the Academy of Natural Sciences of Philadelphia* 2 (1850): 75–79.

SECONDARY BIBLIOGRAPHY

References

Roland H. Alden and John D. Ifft, *Early Naturalists in the Far West* (San Francisco: California Academy of Sciences, 1943).

Richard G. Beidleman, "John K. Townsend on the Oregon Trail," *Audubon Magazine* 59 (March–April 1957): 64–65, 83, 88.

Alice Ford, *John James Audubon* (Norman: University of Oklahoma Press, 1964).

Jeannette E. Graustein, *Thomas Nuttall, Naturalist: Explorations in America, 1808–1841* (Cambridge: Harvard University Press, 1967).

Francis H. Herrick, *Audubon the Naturalist: A History of his Life and Time* (New York: D. Appleton and Co., 1917).

George A. Jobanek, "John Kirk Townsend in the Northwest," *Oregon Birds* 12.4 (1986): 253–76.

George A. Jobanek, "Introduction to John Kirk Townsend," *Narrative of a Journey Across the Rocky*

Mountains to the Columbia River (Corvallis: Oregon State University Press, 1999): xiii–xxix.

George A. Jobanek and David B. Marshall, "John Kirk Townsend's 1836 Report of the Birds of the Lower Columbia River Region, Oregon and Washington," *Northwestern Naturalist* 73 (1992): 1–14.

Barbara and Richard Mearns, *Audubon to Xántus: The Lives of Those Commemorated in North American Bird Names* (London: Academic Press, 1992).

John I. Merritt, III. "Naturalists Across the Rockies: The 1834 Journey of John Kirk Townsend and Thomas Nuttall," *The American West: The Magazine of Western History* 14.2 (March/April 1977): 4–9, 62–63.

Elizabeth Stevenson, *Figures in a Western Landscape: Men and Women of the Northern Rockies* (Baltimore: Johns Hopkins University Press, 1994).

Witmer Stone, "John Kirk Townsend," *Cassinia: Proceedings of the Delaware Valley Ornithological Club* 7 (1903): 1–5.

Papers

Most of Townsend's extant manuscripts and letters are in the John Kirk Townsend Papers at the Academy of Natural Sciences in Philadelphia.

Mary (Davis) Treat
(September 7, 1830–April 11, 1923)

Tina Gianquitto

Mary Davis Treat was best known to her neighbors in Vineland, New Jersey, as both a shy, retiring nature lover and a prolific chronicler of the plant, bird, and insect life of the New Jersey pine barrens. The scientific world outside the small agricultural community of Vineland, however, regarded Treat as an accomplished entomologist and botanist, a peer, and a valued correspondent. She was an acknowledged authority on harvesting ants, insectivorous plants, and burrowing spiders and was frequently consulted by the world's eminent botanists and entomologists, including Charles Darwin, Asa Gray, Charles Sprague Sargent, Auguste Henri Forel, and Gustav Mayr.

Treat was intrepid in her pursuit of knowledge. She writes of fording streams and slogging through marshes in pursuit of rare specimens and of suffering chills from long nights observing them under her microscope. But her sufferings came with the reward of recognition: Treat discovered a rare amaryllis lily (*Zepharanthes treatae*), an equally rare fern (*Schizaea pusilla*), two species of spider (*Tarantula tigrina* and *Tarantula turricula*), and a new species of an orange aphid. In addition, she is credited with rediscovering a yellow water lily that was considered extinct. Gustav Mayr, the Viennese entomologist, named a new harvesting ant (*Aphaenogaster*

treatae) for Treat in honor of her work on that species, while the Swiss naturalist Auguste Forel named the cynipid oak fig root gall (*Belonocnema treatae*) for her after she discovered it while on a trip to Florida.

Treat enjoyed the fame that such recognition brought her in scientific circles, but she relied on her success as a professional writer to guarantee her income. She contributed frequently to the most influential literary and scientific magazines of the period, and her articles knowingly appealed to the growing public interest in scientific topics. Her remarkable talent lay in her ability to translate dry scientific observation into narratives that captured the imagination of a wide audience. Throughout her career, Treat successfully bridged the growing rift between hard scientific investigation and popular nature writing by developing a complex understanding of both the market and multiple audiences for her work. Her success at this task, in addition to the sheer volume of her literary output, guaranteed Treat a comfortable income well into her old age.

Mary Davis was born on September 7, 1830, in Trumansville, Tompkins County, New York, to Isaac M. and Eliza Davis. Isaac Davis, an itinerant Methodist minister, moved his family to Ohio in 1839, where Mary remained throughout her adolescence. Little is known about her early life or education, except that she attended public schools before studying for a short time at a girl's academy. Her formal knowledge of plant science, as demonstrated in her articles on botany, is not surprising given the fact that she attended school at a time when botany dominated science curricula at girls' schools. After several years in Ohio, Mary returned to New York where she lived for a time with a sister.

Davis's career as a professional scientist and author began with her marriage to Dr. James Burrel Treat in 1861. Treat, like his wife, was the child of a minister and was deeply interested in the sciences, and he even gave frequent public lectures on scientific topics, including astronomy. Treat was also politically active in antislavery causes and became a nurse during the Civil War. His abiding interest in business and agriculture brought the couple to Iowa shortly after their marriage, where they lived for several years before moving to a more permanent home in Vineland, New Jersey. Mary Treat's interest in participating in public discussions of plants and insects appears to have begun in Iowa in 1864, when she contributed grass specimens for an article in *The Horticulturist*.

This modest beginning put Treat on a path she would follow for years, and for the next four decades, she published numerous articles in publications as diverse as *American Entomologist and Botanist*, *St. Nicholas Magazine* (a children's magazine), *Lippincott's*, *Harper's New Monthly Magazine*, and *Atlantic Monthly*. By the 1870s Treat was publishing the results of original experiments and observations, despite her standing as an amateur. Treat's earliest articles, a three-part series entitled "Botany for Invalids" (1866), however, are not quite as daring as the ones she published later in her career. In these articles, she presents topics that were well known by the 1860s—the importance of the study of botany for invalids and young girls. Indeed, Treat echoes other popular writers like Elizabeth C. Wright and Almira Phelps, author of the best-selling botany textbook of the mid-nineteenth century, *Familiar Lectures in Botany*, when she argues that botanical excursions are good for the mind and the body. She writes: "If weak, nervous, dyspeptic invalids know how much might be benefited by the study of Botany, that it is almost a panacea for many of their diseases, would it not be more generally prosecuted?" Although these overtly moralistic articles bear little resemblance to Treat's later work, they do display her abiding interest in both botany and entomology.

When her "Botany for Invalids" series was published, Treat was living in Hammonton, New Jersey, and was active in local garden clubs, where, on occasion, she was introduced to well-known botanists, some of whom she would remain in contact with for years to come. In 1868, the Treats moved again—first to the relatively isolated Mays Landing, then shortly thereafter to the more populated town of Vineland. Vineland, established as a fruit-producing agricultural community, was well suited to the Treats' interests. They soon developed a small orchard on the grounds of their modest property and contributed notes and articles on the insects that attacked those orchards to prominent entomological journals. By late 1869 these articles had attracted the attention of Charles Riley and Benjamin Walsh, America's leading entomologists, and both wrote encouraging Mary to continue publishing the results of her observations. In 1870, Riley nominated Mary Treat to the American Association for the Advancement of Science. The public accolades Treat garnered during these years may have upset the balance of her private life; Joseph left Mary and Vineland and moved to New York City, where he remained until his death in 1878. Treat lived on her own in Vineland until Joseph's death; from 1878 until roughly 1885, she shared a house with the Campbell family while her own property, The Cedars, was completed.

Treat's reaction to her husband's departure is unknown, but if her publishing record is any indication, she found either emotional solace or intellectual freedom in her new domestic arrangement. She began publishing in earnest in the early years of the 1870s, tackling topics as diverse as determining sex in butterfly larvae to the nest-making habits of birds. Treat's article, "Controlling Sex in Butterflies" (1873), is particularly notable among her early work. In this piece, Treat made public the controversial results of her experiments on the relation of the sex of a butterfly to the nutrition of the larvae. Riley, among others, chastised Treat for publishing results that had not been confirmed by experts. Treat, confidant in her observations, was unmoved by the criticism, even though she would wait 30 years for her findings to be validated.

Treat's interests continued to broaden, and by 1875 she discovered that she could earn a living writing for both scientific and popular journals. Natural history, she likewise found, could be tailored to suit wide audiences, and she translated her love of nature into a series of popular books and articles. Her children's stories on the wonders of the microscopic world appeared in *St. Nicholas Magazine* and *Youth's Companion*, while her ornithological notes appeared in magazines such as *Harper's*, *Atlantic Monthly*, *Lippincott's*, and *Hearth and Home*. Her entomological studies continued to appear in respected scientific journals such as *American Naturalist*.

In the 1870s Treat's concurrent interests in insects and plants brought her almost naturally to the topic that would define her career: insectivorous plants. These plants that eat insects first came to her attention as early as 1869; she mentions them as a curiosity in her "Botany for Invalids" articles. By the early 1870s she had begun a systematic study of the plants, hoping to answer a question that had long vexed her fellow botanists: By what mechanism did insectivorous plants capture and ingest their prey? Through Asa Gray, Treat learned that Darwin was also working on the problem, and she began an extensive correspondence with him that lasted from 1871 to 1876. The news that Darwin was working on the species caught her by surprise, and, worried that he would come to a conclusion before her, she began working feverishly, often until late at night, observing

the mechanisms of the plant. Treat, as she notes in 1885s *Home Studies in Nature*, even used her finger as bait for the carnivorous plant in order to test a hypothesis on the potency of the plant's digestive fluids.

Treat's efforts were again well rewarded: in his *Insectivorous Plants* (1874), Darwin credits her for successfully observing traits that had escaped his, and others', notice: "Mrs. Treat of New Jersey," he writes, "has been more successful than any other observer, and has often witnessed in the case of *Utricularia clandestina* the whole process....Mrs. Treat's excellent observations have already been largely quoted." Treat's lay audience found the topic as intriguing, and she sold several articles on the subject to *Harper's* and *American Naturalist*.

The years 1876, 1877, and 1878 were productive for Treat. She wintered during these years in Florida, investigating the plants and insects along the St. Johns River. During these excursions, Treat discovered several of the species that were later named in her honor. She became especially interested in the habits of large burrowing spiders she saw building nests along the banks of remote parts of the river. She transported several specimens back to the "arachnidan menagerie" she had built on the grounds of her New Jersey home, where she could examine their habits more closely. Treat's backyard observatory, which she describes in *Home Studies in Nature*, consisted of a large space enclosed by "a dense circular hedge of arborvitae, fifteen feet in height and a hundred and fifty feet in circumference." Here, Treat sat among the spiders and birds that inhabited the space, silently watching their nest-building behaviors. She describes the communities she saw in the menagerie in a series of articles for the *Atlantic Monthly*, *Harper's*, and *Lippincott's*.

When Treat began publishing books in the 1880s, she was already a well-known figure. She was elected a corresponding member of the New York Entomological Club (1881), and in 1884 and 1885 she received requests from the "Woman's Department" of the World Exposition for books to be placed on display. Her early books, including *Chapters on Ants* (1879) and *Home Studies in Nature* (1885) were collections of essays, most of which had been previously published in *Harper's*. In 1882, Treat brought out her main entomological work, *Injurious Insects of Farm and Garden,* which went through five editions, with new chapters added to each but the second. *Injurious Insects of Farm and Garden* is in many ways a collaborative work, as Treat borrowed liberally and verbatim, often without citing her sources, from the entomological reports of John Comstock, of the United States Department of Agriculture, and the *Annual Reports* of Charles Riley, state entomologist of Missouri from 1879 to 1881.

Treat collaborated with Samuel Wells and Frederick Leroy Sargent for a small book on microscopes, *Through a Microscope* (1886), and in 1887 she wrote the last of her insect books, *My Garden Pets,* in which she describes the habits of the spiders, ants, and wasps that inhabited her menagerie. Treat's last book is a short biography of Asa Gray, which she prepared to give as a lecture to the Brooklyn Ethical Association in 1890, two years after the botanist's death. Treat's *Asa Gray: His Life and Work* congratulates Gray on his staunch defense of Darwin and evolution at a time when his views were unpopular. Gray's defense was important to Treat, who was also a proponent of Darwin's theories.

In the 1890s Treat returned to writing for periodicals, and during this time composed a popular series on the seasonal plants of the pine barrens for *Garden & Forest,* a fashionable landscape architecture journal. Treat appears to have briefly held a position as an assistant editor of the magazine, then under the direction of Charles Sprague Sargent. Throughout the 1890s Treat received several more petitions for lectures: in 1893 the Brooklyn Ethical Association requested a paper on "evolutionary principles," while the World's Columbian Exposition asked her to present a paper to the Committee on Philosophy and Science. She also read a

paper entitled "The Way of Climbing Plants" at the National Science Club in Washington, D.C., in April 1897. Treat, who was still receiving royalties from *Home Studies in Nature* in 1907, wrote her last article for *Forest & Stream* in 1910, at 80 years old. She continued living in her home in Vineland until she was crippled by a fall and could no longer care for herself. Treat sold her house and moved in with relatives in Akron, New York, with whom she lived until her death on April 11, 1923. She is buried in Siloam Cemetery in Vineland.

Mary Treat is an exceptional figure in the history of women in literature and the sciences. Treat successfully navigated the breach between the private and public spheres by crafting a public persona in line with conventional domestic ideology. Her public knew her as a woman who stayed home watching the nest-building activities of birds and insects. People who knew Treat more intimately, however, especially the scientists with whom she corresponded on a regular basis, knew that Treat was far more than a conventionally domestic woman performing role-appropriate observations. She was one of only a few women publishing the results of original experiments in leading popular and scientific journals. She was also one of only a small community of scientists who read the natural world according to the terms of Darwin's evolutionary biology. She fused sentiment and science in her popular writings, and in doing so, secured for herself an independent intellectual life.

PRIMARY BIBLIOGRAPHY

Books

Two Chapters on Ants (New York: Harpers, 1879).

Injurious Insects of the Farm and Garden (New York: Orange Judd, 1882).

Home Studies in Nature (New York: American Book Company, 1885).

Through a Microscope; Something of the Science Together with Many Curious Observations Indoor and Out and Directions for a Home-made Microscope (with Samuel Wells and Frederick Leroy Sargent) (Chicago: Interstate Publishing, 1886).

My Garden Pets (Boston: Lothrop Publishing, 1887).

Asa Gray: His Life and Work (Boston: James H. West, 1890).

Selected Periodical Publications—Uncollected

"Botany for Invalids," *Herald of Health* 8 (1866): 39–40.

"Botany for Invalids, No. II," *Herald of Health* 8 (1866): 70–72.

"Botany for Invalids, No III," *Herald of Health* 8 (1866): 125–27.

"Are Tomato Worms Poisonous?" *Herald of Health* 14 (1869): 277–78.

"My Summer Pets," *Lippincott's Magazine* 4 (1869): 55–58.

"Parasitic Mites on the House Fly," *American Entomologist* 2 (1869–1870): 87.

"Plant Lice and Their Enemies," *American Entomologist* 2 (1869–1870): 141–43.

"White Grub Fungus," *American Entomologist* 2 (1869–1870): 53.

"The Tomato Worm," *American Entomologist* 2 (1869–1870): 87.

"Polyphemus Moth," *American Entomologist* 2 (1869–1870): 88.

"Notes on Birds," *Hearth & Home* (July 5, 1870).

"Pupa of the Girdled Sphinx," *American Entomologist & Botanist* 2 (1870): 241.

"My Raspberry and Verbena Moths and What Came of Them," *American Entomologist & Botanist* 2 (1870): 241.

"To Kill the Pea Weevil," *American Entomologist & Botanist* 2 (1870): 241.

"Pine Barren Plants," *American Entomologist & Botanist* 2 (1870): 318–19.

"Freaks of Birds," *Hearth & Home* (December 4, 1871).

"Drosera (Sundew) as Fly-catcher," *American Journal of Science* 2 (1871): 463–64.

"Controlling Sex in Butterflies," *American Naturalist* 7 (1873): 129–32; *Entomologist* 6 (1873): 372–75.

"Observations on the Sundew: Drosera filiformis," *American Naturalist* 7 (1873): 705–8.

"The Enemies of the Oak," *American Agriculturist* 33 (1874): 344.

"Plants that Eat Animals," *American Naturalist* 9 (1875): 658–62.

"Do Birds Improve as Architects?" *Harper's New Monthly Magazine* 51 (1875): 127–30.

"The Water Bear," *St. Nicolas Magazine* 2 (March 1875): 274–75.

"The Cyclops," *St. Nicolas Magazine* 2 (September 1875): 686–87.

"Is the valve of the Utricularia sensitive?" *Harper's New Monthly Magazine* 52 (1876): 382–87.

"Carnivorous Plants of Florida," *Harper's New Monthly Magazine* 53 (1876): 546–48, 710–14.

"The Floscule," *St. Nicolas Magazine* 3 (March 1876): 300–301.

"The Microscopic Brick Maker," *St. Nicolas Magazine* 3 (April 1876): 374–75.

"Our Mocking Bird," *Forest & Stream* 8 (March 1877): 112–13.

"Florida Fishers," *St. Nicolas Magazine* 4 (May 1877): 490–91.

"Our Familiar Birds," *Harper's New Monthly Magazine* 54 (1877): 656–64, 785–91.

"Home Observations in Florida," *Harper's New Monthly Magazine* 55 (1877): 365–68.

"The Harvesting Ants of Florida," *Lippincott's Magazine* 22 (1878): 555–62.

"Some Fishing Birds of Florida," *St. Nicolas Magazine* 5 (February 1878): 282–83.

"The Microscope and What I Saw Through It," *St. Nicolas Magazine* 6 (December 1878): 116–17.

"The Habits of the Tarantula," *American Naturalist* 13 (1879): 485–89.

"Notes on the Slave-Making Ant (F. sanguinea)," *American Naturalist* 13 (1879): 707–8.

"A Chapter in the History of Ants," *Harper's New Monthly Magazine* 58 (1879): 176–84.

"Notes on the Intelligence of Birds," *Lippincott's Magazine* 24 (September 1879): 359–64.

"Notes on Harvesting Ants in New Jersey," *American Entomologist* 1 (1880): 225–26.

"Home Studies in Nature," *Harper's New Monthly Magazine* 60 (1880): 710–18, 857–62.

"A Phase of Life in Florida," *Lippincott's Magazine* 25 (1880): 460–66.

"The Great-Crested Flycatcher," *American Naturalist* 15 (1881): 601–4.

"Slave-Making Ants," *Lippincott's Magazine* 2 (1881): 7.

"Our Winter Birds," *Atlantic Monthly* 49 (1882): 381–86.

"In the Pines," *Harper's New Monthly Magazine* 65 (1882): 65–72.

"Under the Maples," *Atlantic Monthly* 54 (1884): 326–33.

"Behavior of *Dolomedes tenebrosus*," *Science* 3 (1884): 214–18.

"Argiope riparia, var. multiconcha," *American Naturalist* 21 (1887): 1122.

"Insects," *Chautauquan* (1887).

"Our Cuckoos and Cowbirds," *Youth's Companion* (1887).

"April in the Pine Barrens," *Garden & Forest* 1, no. 11 (1888): 124.

"The Pine Barrens in May," *Garden & Forest* 1, no. 16 (1888): 182.

"Among the Pines in June," *Garden & Forest* 1, no. 21 (1888): 243.

"The Pines in July," *Garden & Forest* 1, no. 25 (1888): 290–91.

"August in the Pines," *Garden & Forest* 1, no. 31 (1888): 362–63.

"The Pines in October," *Garden & Forest* 1, no. 37 (1888): 435; 6, no. 266 (1893): 142.

"The Pines in Mid-November," *Garden & Forest* 1, no. 42 (1888): 494–95.

"Christmas in the Pines," *Garden & Forest* 1, no. 44 (1888): 518–19; 8 (1895): 3.

"Curculio and Injury to Cherries," *Prairie Farmer* (1888): 538.

"Botanical Names," *Garden & Forest* 3, no. 113 (1890): 206–7.

"The Wild Garden," *Garden & Forest* 3, no. 133 (1890): 442.

"September in the Pines," *Garden & Forest* 3, no. 135 (1890): 463.

"October in the Pines," *Garden & Forest* 3, no. 140 (1890): 524.

"Ornamental Fruits in the Pines," *Garden & Forest* 3, no. 141 (1890): 534.

"Evergreens in the New Jersey Pine Region," *Garden & Forest* 3, no. 142 (1890): 546–47.

"The Pines at Christmas-time," *Garden & Forest* 4, no. 151 (1891): 14.

"Insect Enemies of the Pitch Pine," *Garden & Forest* 4, no. 155 (1891): 62–63.

"How to Make a Wild Garden," *Garden & Forest* 4, no. 165 (1891): 188–89.

"Notes from a Wild Garden," *Garden & Forest* 4, no. 179 (1891): 351.

"Spring in the New Jersey Pines," *Garden & Forest* 5, no. 220 (1892): 220.

"Weeds in Southern New Jersey," *Garden & Forest* 5, no. 226 (1892): 292; 10, no. 494 (1897): 313–14.

"Water-plants in Southern New Jersey," *Garden & Forest* 5, no. 232 (1892): 363.

"Water-Plants in the Pines," *Garden & Forest* 5, no. 235 (1892): 400.

"Edible Fruits in the Pines," *Garden & Forest* 5, no. 238 (1892): 435–36.

"Late Autumn in the Pines," *Garden & Forest* 5, no. 249 (1892): 567–68.

"Native Plants for Winter Decoration," *Garden & Forest* 6, no. 266 (1893): 141.

"Summer in the Pines," *Garden & Forest* 6, no. 283 (1893): 314.

"Late Summer in the Pines," *Garden & Forest* 6, no. 290 (1893): 382–83.

"Some Injurious Insects of the Orchard and Garden," *New York Entomological Society Journal* 1 (1893): 16–20.

"Winter-blooming Plants in the Pines," *Garden & Forest* 7, no. 316 (1894): 102.

"March in the Pines," *Garden & Forest* 7, no. 320 (1894): 142.

"A New Jersey Garden in Spring," *Garden & Forest* 7, no. 327 (1894): 212–13.

"Early June in the Pines," *Garden & Forest* 7, no. 330 (1894): 243–44.

"Wayside Plants in the Pines," *Garden & Forest* 7, no. 336 (1894): 302–3.

"November in a New Jersey Garden," *Garden & Forest* 7, no. 351 (1894): 458.

"Late Autumn in the Pines," *Garden & Forest* 7, no. 354 (1894): 482–83.

"Troublesome Grasses in Southern New Jersey," *Garden & Forest* 8, no. 368 (1895): 103–4.

"In the Pines," *Garden & Forest* 8, no. 378 (1895): 203–4.

"Early Summer in the Pines," *Garden & Forest* 8, no. 384 (1895): 262–63.

"The Pines in a Dry Summer," *Garden & Forest* 8, no. 394 (1895): 362–63.

"Autumn Color in the Pines," *Garden & Forest* 8, no. 403 (1895): 452.

"The Heaths among the Pines in Early Winter," *Garden & Forest* 8, no. 407 (1895): 492–93.

"Spring in the Pines," *Garden & Forest* 9, no. 427 (1896): 173.

"The Pines in August," *Garden & Forest* 9, no. 443 (1896): 332–33.

"Early Autumn in the Pines," *Garden & Forest* 9, no. 451 (1896): 412.

"Climbing Plants in the Pines," *Garden & Forest* 9, no. 459 (1896): 492–93.

"Cruelty of Asclepias," *Garden & Forest* 10, no. 497 (1897): 341.

"Autumn Flowers in the Pines," *Garden & Forest* 10, no. 504 (1897): 411–12.

"Autumn Fruits in the Pines," *Garden & Forest* 10, no. 510 (1897): 471–72.

"Some Microscopic House-Builders," *Godey's Magazine* 138, no. 815 (1898): 535–37.

"Some Solitary Wasps," *Forest & Stream* 75 (1910): 690–91.

SECONDARY BIBLIOGRAPHY

References

Marcia Myers Bonta, *Women in the Field: America's Pioneering Women Naturalists* (College Station: Texas A&M University Press, 1991).

Marcia Myers Bonta, *American Women Afield: Writings by Pioneering Women Naturalists* (College Station: Texas A&M University Press, 1995).

Mary Creese, *Ladies in the Laboratory? American and British Women in Science, 1800–1900* (Lanham, MD: The Scarecrow Press, 1998).

John W. Harshberger, *The Botanists of Philadelphia and Their Work* (Philadelphia: T.C. Davis and Sons, 1899).

Vera Norwood, *Made from this Earth: American Women and Nature* (Chapel Hill: University of North Carolina Press, 1993).

Mary Treat, "Botany for Invalids," *Herald of Health* 8 (1866): 39–40.

Henry Wilbur, "World's Most Famous and Industrious Woman Naturalist," *Philadelphia Public Ledger*, October 5, 1913.

Papers

The bulk of Treat's papers and private correspondence are held at the Vineland Historical Society, Vineland, New Jersey.

Alexander Wilson
(July 6, 1766–August 23, 1813)

Michael Ziser

Over the course of a life and career curtailed by poverty and illness, Alexander Wilson fashioned himself from an untutored Scottish weaver into one of the preeminent men of science, art, and letters in the early American republic. Although overshadowed today by the better-publicized work of John James Audubon, the achievement of Wilson's watershed nine-volume work on American birds has led many historians to call him "the father" of the long and deep tradition of American ornithology. In addition to showcasing its author's considerable skill in carefully observing, sensitively describing, and precisely rendering the creatures that absorbed the attention of his last decade, *American Ornithology* draws together the strands of folk poetry, democratic advocacy, and love of the Scottish and American landscapes that run through Wilson's entire body of work.

Wilson was born into a family of Paisley silk weavers who had only recently left behind the more ancient local professions of illicit smuggling and distilling. The trade in silk gauze was booming, and during Alexander's childhood the Wilson family enjoyed a materially comfortable existence enlightened by the many weavers' societies that formed to discuss fields of common interest, particularly liberal politics and natural history. Alexander, the youngest of five

children, spent his days studying at the Paisley Grammar School, rambling through the countryside, and swimming and fishing in the River Cart. Among his closest schoolboy friends were the sons of the Reverend Dr. John Witherspoon, the foremost minister in the country, a well-known advocate for democratic reform in the Church of Scotland, and later the president of Princeton College and a signer of the American Declaration of Independence.

Wilson's association with the Witherspoons was just the first of many indications that his fate was linked to America. His tenth birthday was marked by the death of his mother and by the signing of the Declaration of Independence, both of which in the short term led to a steep drop in his fortunes. The beginning of the war interrupted trade with the colonies, and the Paisley silk weavers suffered from the loss of their most dependable customers. Wilson's father, who had quickly remarried a widow and was now saddled with eight children, pulled Alexander out of school and sent him to work as a cowherd on a farm ten miles from town. The three years of lonely work in uninhabited fields gave the young Wilson ample time to read and daydream and sharpened his attachment to the natural landscape and its wild inhabitants.

In the summer of 1779, Wilson was indentured as an apprentice in his brother-in-law's weaving shop, his first formal induction into a profession he would come to loathe. As soon as his three-year contractual obligation was fulfilled, Wilson rejoined his family, who were now living in the ancient Tower of Auchinbathie and had taken up their old livelihoods of smuggling and distilling. Throughout the 1780s, Wilson continued his self-education while he worked as a journeyman weaver in shops around Paisley. He also began to work as a peddler carrying woven goods from the family looms throughout the Scottish countryside. The long rambles allowed Wilson to indulge his interest in the various personalities of rural Scotland, and he often made side trips to learn from the local botanists, poets, and musicians. The spirit of these expeditions is preserved in Wilson's "Journal as a Pedlar," a prose piece included in his first book of poems and an important harbinger of the socially and scientifically sensitive travel narratives to come.

Wilson's earliest poetic influences were John Milton and Alexander Pope, whose works he committed to memory and imitated in the largely derivative verse of his youth. He studied Goldsmith's poetry closely, one indication of his interest in village themes. The greatest influence on Wilson, however, was the 1786 publication of Robert Burns's *Poems, Chiefly in the Scottish Dialect*. The example of Burns encouraged the use of Scottish diction and native subject matter. In Wilson's case that meant not only the agrarian scenes of Burns's poetry but also the quasi-urban intrigues of Paisley and its weaving sheds. Wilson's early poems, which have much in common with other Burns imitators of his era, are remarkable for the way they combine conventional regard for the countryside with evident approval of the mechanization then sweeping over the mill towns.

Wilson's first book, published in 1790, is evenly divided between poems written in standard poetic English and those written in the Scottish dialect. For the most part, the English poems hewed very closely to the originals they imitated: the elegies of Thomas Gray, the seasonal poems of William Cowper, the rural polemic of Oliver Goldsmith, Alexander Pope's fables and verse epistles, and the pastoral odes of Milton and William Collins. In other cases Wilson seems a harbinger of literary events to come. "Hardyknute; or, The Battle of Largs" mines Scottish history for epic subject matter as Sir Walter Scott would later do in prose. Both "Thunder-storm" and "Lines Written on a Summer's Evening," in which the author "feels emotions words can ne'er express" in the presence of a sublime natural landscape, can be seen as faint precursors of Wordsworth. Wilson did manage to break free of English classical tradition at a few points. "Lochwinnoch," a descriptive poem about a town near Paisley, proceeds largely according to pastoral conventions, but mixed in among the swains are unprecedented positive descriptions of contemporary industry from a man who knew the value of laborsaving machinery:

> wheels turning wheels in mystic throngs appear,
> to twist the thread or tortur's cotton tear,
> While toiling wenches songs delight the
> list'ning ear.

One other poem, "Address to Calder Banks," reveals Wilson's more conventionally Romantic attraction to unstoried wilderness. The poet asks the remote brook:

> Strayed e'er a bard along this hermit shore?
> Alas! Methinks the weeping rocks around,
> And the lone stream, that murmurs far below;
> And trees and caves, with solemn hollow sound,
> Breathe out one mournful melancholy "No."

The Scottish poems in this first collection are considerably more personal. Many are epistolary addresses to friends and patrons in and around Paisley. Others cast in verse local events and scandals. "Elegy on the Long-Expected Death of a Wretched Miser," for example, tells the sordid tale of the marriage of 75-year-old John Craig, an unloved local landlord, to the unscrupulous 15-year-old Meg Duncan. A small number of moral fables drawn from local experiences give some indication of Wilson's sensitivity to the ethical questions surrounding human labor in the natural world. "Verses on Seeing Two Men Sawing Timber," for instance, warns against attempting to defy the power of nature. "Rabby's Mistake," about a relentless hunter who accidentally kills his own sow, argues for restraint in light of the fact that "short is the far'est fouk can see." Many of the remaining poems in the volume—in particular "The Pack," "Daybreak," "Achtertool"—are complaints about the impoverished and difficult life of the weaver and peddler, which grew ever more chafing to Wilson over the 1780s. The only bird poem in this earliest collection, "The Disconsolate Wren," is a transcription of a wren's lament at the loss of her brood when their nest fell to earth. It reveals a sympathetic Wilson steeped in bird lore but as yet without much ornithological knowledge.

While his collection was still in the planning stages, Wilson wrote and published "The Hollander, Or Light Weight," a thinly veiled and caustic attack on Paisley silk manufacturer William Henry. The poem accuses Henry of cheating his laborers out of their rightful pay. Mindful of revolutionary events in France and concerned about unrest in his factories, Henry lodged charges of libel and incitement to unrest against Wilson. For unknown reasons, these charges were later withdrawn, but not before Wilson had made a name for himself as a rabble-rousing, working-class poet at a time when the industrial order was just coming into being.

The Scottish countryside was in financial straits during the early 1790s, and Wilson found it exceedingly difficult to gain new subscriptions to his book. In debt to his printers and with little hope of emancipation from the loom, Wilson fell into a depression and serious physical illness. Wilson's fortunes soon took a turn for the better, however, with the magazine publication of "The Solitary Philosopher," which sketches the life of an untutored hermit of "universal genius"—"at once by nature botanist, philosopher, naturalist, and physician"—who is able to draw morals from the "common occurrences of nature." Even more encouraging was the acclaim that came to Wilson after his performance in an Edinburgh contest in oratory. Wilson's address, later printed as "The Laurel Disputed," defended the merits of Rab Fergusson, who wrote in the Scottish vernacular and had been a major influence on Robert Burns. Having gained a notoriety in the capital, Wilson arranged to have the unsold copies of his 1790 collection reissued with a few changes in a new edition, which were soon sold out.

Taking his cue from the homespun vernacular realism of Fergusson and Burns, especially the latter's "Tam o' Shanter," Wilson next wrote what would become his most popular poem. "Watty and Meg" tells the story of a shrewish wife whose husband threatens to enlist in the army to escape her nagging. The poem eventually sold over 100,000 copies, though Wilson himself saw little profit from its success beyond the retirement of his printing debts.

In May 1792, just as his prospects were brightening, Wilson committed a lapse of judgment that landed him in jail and eventually forced him to leave Scotland forever. Wilson had become active in political activities, perhaps even having a hand in the composition of the calls for Scottish constitutional reform modeled after Thomas Paine's *The Rights of Man* (1791). At the same time, he apparently resumed his attacks on corrupt silk manufacturers in Paisley with the composition of "The Shark; Or Lang Mills Detected." This time his target was William Sharp, and the charge was the shortchanging of mill workers paid by the piece. Perhaps at the urging of local radicals James and William Mitchell, Wilson took the wholly uncharacteristic step of using the inflammatory poem to extort money from Sharp. Sharp retaliated with a legal complaint, and the next two years of Wilson's life were spent in the courts and jails of Paisley. Though Wilson was fined, jailed, and forced publicly to burn the remaining copies of "The Shark," he was much more fortunate than some other Scottish reformers of his day, many of whom were exiled to penal colonies or even burned alive and disemboweled. After several subsequent tangles with the law over his participation in reformist activities, Wilson resolved to protect himself and the friends and family members who had signed bonds for him over the past two years. Together with a young cousin, William Duncan, he set sail from Belfast to Philadelphia in late May 1794.

Because of the 1793 yellow fever epidemic, all ships bound for Philadelphia were required to unload at Newcastle on the shores of the Delaware. After disembarking and looking in vain for work in Wilmington weaving shops, Wilson and Duncan continued by foot to Philadelphia. The 35-mile walk to America's then-capital city was Wilson's first introduction to the American landscape, and it happened to coincide with the period of highest activity among resident birds and spring migrants on the Atlantic flyway. Wilson took his first specimen on this journey, a brilliant red-headed woodpecker.

After brief stints in engraving and weaving shops and an unsuccessful venture to Virginia, Wilson took up his peddler's pack once again and made a tour of New Jersey that left him richer both in money and in knowledge about American society and natural history. The journal from this period, an extension of his Scottish journal and a forerunner of his later travel reports, has been lost. Eventually Wilson settled in Milestown, Pennsylvania, and began a new career as a schoolmaster, staying up late to keep one lesson ahead of his pupils. During the five years he stayed in Milestown, Wilson also helped his cousin establish a farm near Ovid, New York, to which other family members could emigrate from Scotland. His writings and letters from this time period—most not published until 1816—are sparse and deal with just three main subjects: the hardships of life as schoolmaster ("The Solitary Tutor," "The Dominie"), Republican politics and the election of 1800 ("Jefferson and Liberty," "Oration on the Power and Value of National Liberty"), and a love affair with an unidentified woman ("Lavinia," "Elegy").

His time in Milestown came to an abrupt and mysterious end in 1801 when Wilson fled in anticipation of a scandal (which never materialized) over a love affair with either a married woman of the town or a student in his school. Shortly thereafter, he found his way to a new post at the Union School in Gray's Ferry outside Philadelphia. The foremost naturalist of the day, William Bartram, lived and kept his famous garden nearby, a fortuitous circumstance that allowed Wilson to undertake his great ornithological work.

The precise point at which Wilson resolved to catalog the birds of America is not clear. He had apparently begun to admire them as soon as he arrived in the country, perhaps beginning a more systematic study during his tenure as schoolmaster in Milestown. It was only in Gray's Ferry, however, that Wilson let his interest be publicly known. At first he enlisted the aid of his students in collecting specimens for examination, even keeping a number of live animals (including a hummingbird and a woodpecker) for study. Later he approached William Bartram, a major authority on matters ornithological as well as botanical, for information about bird names and guidance with bird illustration, which Wilson was teaching himself nights with the help of a small owl he had stuffed and mounted for the purpose. Bartram's romantic view of nature and sensitivity to the living animal in its native habitat reinforced Wilson's own predisposition, and under Bartram's tutelage Wilson soon became the unrivalled master of bird observation in America. He often astonished visitors, for instance, with his ability to mimic the calls and songs of almost all North American birds. It is this kind of intimacy with the living creature—not taxonomic rigor—that accounts for Wilson's continued popularity among readers and ornithologists.

Wilson's first explicit birding trip, a 1200 mile journey to Niagara Falls, was documented with painstaking detail in Wilson's "The Foresters," a long poem unusual in American literature for its frontier realism. The experience Wilson had acquired during his periods of itinerant salesmanship in

Scotland and New Jersey served him well on this trip, and his 2,200 line poem is crammed with the details of social life and natural history gleaned along his route.

Back at Gray's Ferry, Wilson circulated the bird drawings he had made on his Niagara trip among interested naturalists. These included President Jefferson, whom Wilson pressed in vain for a position on the Pike expedition to the Red River country of what is now Oklahoma. Around this time the publishing house of Bradford and Inskeep hired Wilson as an assistant editor for natural sciences on Ree's *New Cyclopaedia*. The generous salary allowed Wilson to quit his post at the Union School and move to Philadelphia. More than that, he found in Samuel Bradford a publisher with both the technical capability and the enthusiasm to publish his grand *American Ornithology*, which he projected at ten volumes illustrated with ten hand-colored engravings each. Bradford agreed to publish 200 sets of the series provided that Wilson could come up with 200 subscribers. In order to have an example of his work to persuade subscribers to part with the $120 cost of the full set, Wilson quickly got together the first volume of *The American Ornithology*. It fulfilled its promise of scientific thoroughness and painterly precision, to which was added the considerable bonus of Wilson's firsthand, folksy, and loving writing about birds. By the time volume two was published, there were orders for 500 copies.

The amount of work Wilson accomplished over the last five years of his life is prodigious by any measure. Wilson combined five long birding expeditions to areas stretching from Maine to Georgia with visits to knowledgeable naturalists (including John Abbott, Meriwether Lewis, and Samuel Latham Mitchill) and canvassing trips for new subscribers. In between these busy trips he worked long hours in Philadelphia writing verbal accounts and drawing as well as supervising the engraving and coloring of the plates for the next volume. In the end this incredible pace contributed to his early death, at age 47, of dysentery. The last volume of *The American Ornithology* was completed under the direction of Wilson's friend and biographer, George Ord.

Although John James Audubon's *Birds of America* is without question a greater artistic achievement than Wilson's *American Ornithology*, the latter is technically more accurate both in the visual renderings and the verbal descriptions. Wilson had more firsthand knowledge of bird behavior than Audubon, and his writing, too, is more accomplished: simultaneously fired by folk knowledge, field experience, and sympathetic enthusiasm for the subject, it is burnished with a considerable literary flair. Some of the best-informed bird lyrics in American letters are sprinkled throughout *The American Ornithology* (see especially the learned "Tyrant Fly-Catcher," the folksy "Fish-Hawk," and the bedazzled "Hummingbird"), and the prose is frequently as notable for its execution as for the memorable anecdotes it sets forth.

PRIMARY BIBLIOGRAPHY

Books

Poems (Paisley: J. Nielson, 1790).

Poems, Humorous, Satirical and Serious (Edinburgh: P. Hill, 1791).

The American Ornithology, 9 vols. (Philadelphia: Bradford and Inskeep, 1808–1814).

Poems Chiefly in the Scottish Dialect by Alexander Wilson with an Account of His Life and Writings (Paisley: J. Neilson, 1816).

The Poetical Works of Alexander Wilson (Belfast: John Henderson, 1844).

The Poems and Literary Prose of Alexander Wilson, 2 vols., ed. The Reverend Alexander B. Grosart (Paisley: Alexander Gardner, 1876).

SECONDARY BIBLIOGRAPHY

References

Elsa Guerdrum Allen, "The History of American Ornithology Before Audubon," *Transactions of the American Philosophical Society*, New Series, XLI, No. 3 (1951): 387–591.

Michael Branch, "Indexing American Possibilities: The Natural History Writing of Bartram, Wilson, and Audubon," in *The Ecocriticism Reader: Landmarks in Literary Ecology*, ed. Cheryll Glotfelty and Harold Fromm (Athens: University of Georgia Press, 1996), 282–302.

Robert Brown, *Paisley Poets*, 2 vols. (Paisley: J. & J. Cook, 1889).

Robert Cantwell, *Alexander Wilson: Naturalist and Pioneer* (Philadelphia: J.B. Lippincott, 1961).

Thomas Crichton, *Biographical Sketch of the Late Alexander Wilson to a Young Friend* (Paisley: J. Neilson, 1819).

William T. Hamilton, "Alexander Wilson's America" (dissertation, University of Minnesota, 1971).

Clark Hunter, *The Life and Letters of Alexander Wilson* (Philadelphia: American Philosophical Society, 1983).

George Ord, *Sketch of the Life of Alexander Wilson* (Philadelphia: Harrison Hall, 1828).

Laura Rigal, "Empire of Birds: Alexander Wilson's American Ornithology," in *Art and Science in America*, ed. Amy R.W. Meyers (San Marino: The Huntington Library, 1998), 61–96.

Robert Henry Welker, *Birds and Men: American Birds in Science, Art, Literature, and Conservation* (Cambridge, MA: Harvard University Press, 1955), 18–58.

Theodore Winthrop
(September 22, 1828–June 10, 1861)

Paul Lindholdt

Theodore Winthrop, born in New Haven, Connecticut, had the expectation of literary greatness thrust upon him. His family traced a line of inheritance that stems back on his father's side to John Winthrop, the first governor of the Massachusetts Bay Colony, who delivered his lay sermon entitled "A Modell of Christian Charity" in 1630 aboard the flagship *Arbella* en route to New England. On his mother's side, Theodore's forebears included the Puritan evangelical Jonathan Edwards—the foremost theologian-philosopher in America, whose extant works during the Great Awakening (ca. 1740) include some 1,300 sermons—as well as Timothy Dwight, a member of the literary group at Yale College known as the Connecticut Wits. Theodore Winthrop, scion of New England gentry and descendant of six college presidents, graduated at the top of his Yale class in 1848. During the next 13 years of his short life, he traveled, worked abroad, tried his hand at practicing law, socialized with painters, and composed the four novels and three works of nonfiction on which his slender reputation rests. His most significant contributions to American nature writing may be found in his nonfiction books.

A grand tour of Europe followed his college graduation. That tour took him through the western European countries. It also permitted him a polyglot's ostentation, heightened his taste for art and cuisine, and ran up tailor bills that embarrassed him after his return. Winthrop would have flourished as a gentleman of leisure and independent wealth. Instead, he needed to earn a living.

In Paris he met American millionaire William H. Aspinwall, who became his employer from 1851 to 1855. Winthrop tutored Aspinwall's son in New York in 1851, then headed back to Europe to secure the pupil a place at a Swiss school. Soon thereafter, Winthrop clerked within the Pacific Mail Steamship Company founded by Aspinwall, a job that took him to Panama, where he sold tickets, guarded supplies and gold going to and from California, and suffered fevers in the tropical heat. The job did not advance him as he hoped, so he made his way up the western seaboard, exploring California, Oregon, Washington, and Victoria, B.C., always keeping an eye on possible ways to make his fortune. He considered investing in cattle, gold, coal, and real estate in the territories. At Fort Dalles, though, on the Columbia River, the 24-year-old traveler contracted smallpox. He lay in quarantine for several weeks, a convalescence that allowed him to germinate his later narratives and poems in the journals and letters he drafted to his beloved sisters and mother. (His father had died when Theodore was 12 years old.) An accomplished equestrian, he made his way on horseback via the Oregon Trail to St. Louis, an adventure that he drew upon for his novel *John Brent*. The narrator of that prototypal Western, presaging the author's death very early in the Civil War, remarks, "It is easier to die for a holy cause than to find one's way along through life."

In 1855 Winthrop was admitted to the New York bar; in 1856 he hit the campaign trail for John Frémont of the newly organized Republican party; in 1857 he practiced law in St. Louis, before returning to New York to stay. From the late 1850s on, until he was killed in battle in 1861, Winthrop wrote feverishly, an occupation that suited him much better than politics or legal work.

By all accounts the man was never well. Spiritually or physically at odds, a valetudinarian perhaps, he was preoccupied with his health. In nineteenth-century terms, he was dyspeptic—a disorder of the digestive function—but also emotionally unstable. One biographer called Winthrop's condition a "delicately constructed conscience that had not yet come to terms with itself." Another named him a "semi-invalid," a man who managed nonetheless to sprint across the Washington Territory in record time. While traveling the Oregon Trail home, still fragile from the smallpox, he reported in his journal that he had luckily acquired "a little laudanum [&] a cholera powder   some saleratus [or baking soda]" to dose himself with. Like many of his Puritan ancestors, Winthrop struggled earnestly with his faith. During college, as one biographer reports, "He experienced a religious conversion and spent so many hours praying in his room that his sisters feared he was losing his mind." In later years "Nervous exhaustion, vague and unlocalized illnesses, stomach pains and recurring attacks of crushing despondency alternated with brief periods of feverish sociability and enthusiasm." When he confessed to his mother from afar that his Christian faith was faltering, she grieved openly to family friends, whereupon he became the subject of much gossip in New York, New Haven, and Boston.

One relative, George Templeton Strong, reported that Theodore, back in New York,

> was always letting off gas about atheism, and propounding horrible paradoxes. He takes every opportunity of giving judgment on heaven and earth and all things visible and invisible, and generally puts their alleged Creator out of court in a summary way.

His journal reveals a spiritual man who held a hopeful belief in a kind of interspecies evolution to which humanity must yield. We live in an "unfinished world and when next great convulsions come we shall give place to other beings more advanced than us [;] who knows what places we shall take." He was also a proponent of civilization, for whom nature embodied a great national potential.

Winthrop's interest in nature deepened through exposure to the English Romantic poets and the American landscape painters of his time. His education had steeped him in the classics; Greek and Roman mythologies influenced him profoundly. Water nymphs haunted the streams in his travels, Indian spirits populated mountaintops, and forests harbored sylphs or genius loci. These deities are as vigorous in his writing as they are in Edmund Spenser and in John Milton, both of whom the bookish Winthrop clearly had enjoyed. Allusion for allusion, though, William Wordsworth exerted the greatest romantic sway over Winthrop's imagination, particularly the philosophical Wordsworth of "Tintern Abbey." But the most surprising aesthetic inspiration for Winthrop's work, however hard it is to measure with certainty, were the great painters of nature in his century, most notably his intimate friend and traveling companion Frederic Edwin Church.

Winthrop was writing at the height of the glory of American landscape painting, typified in the productions of the Hudson River School and the luminists. In Paris following college, he spent time with his college classmate Richard Morris Hunt, then studying architecture, and with Richard's brother, William Morris Hunt, who was busy studying art. Both men would go on to make enduring reputations for themselves in their respective fields. Meantime, in 1850, Winthrop was planning a book on art and delivered a lecture entitled "The Fine Arts in America" in 1856. In New York, at the Tenth Street Studio Building where he rented work space, painters Frederic Church and Sanford R. Gifford likewise kept studios. Winthrop watched Church paint *The Heart of the Andes* (1859), which was later displayed in that same space, where a skylight complemented the commercially triumphant painting with natural illumination. The entrepreneurial Church arranged for the concurrent publication of descriptive pamphlets of his painting by Winthrop and the Reverend Louis LeGrand. Winthrop and Church made journeys together to Maine, moreover, one account of which Winthrop wrote up as "Life in the Open Air," naming his companion "Iglesias," Spanish for "church." On this visit also, which took the men high up Mount Ktaadn, Winthrop watched Church work and praised his technique. If art history has been ungenerous to the landscape painters, often cheapening them as agents of manifest destiny, literary history has shortchanged Winthrop's writings even more. Today, only one of his books is in print in its entirety. *The Canoe and the Saddle* appeared in a critical edition in 2006.

Much of Winthrop's nonfiction remains nonetheless valuable today for its study of landscapes, its documentation of bygone folkways, its movement toward a bioregional ethic, its formulation of an environmental philosophy, and its passionate discussions of place names.

The narrative of his trip to Maine, "Life in the Open Air," shows some of the ways that well-heeled aesthetes communed with the natural world. They were a scrupulous crew. "Iglesias bore an umbrella, our armor against what heaven could do with assault of sun or shower." Winthrop, finicky about passengers who spat from the coach, describes an amateur hunter, who yearns to "let out the caged savage within him for a tough struggle with Nature." Winthrop and Church sip straight from rivers, innocent of pathogens, partaking joyfully of "that most ethereal tipple, the mingled air and water of electric bubbles, as they slid brightly toward our lips." Yet the lot of the artist is harsh, he attests. "To be conscious of the highest beauty demands an involuntary intentness of observation so fanatically eager that presently we are prostrated and need stimulants." Church might have bankrolled this junket through Maine, for the painter claims a bunk at an inn the third night out, while Winthrop "mummied myself in my blankets and did penance upon a bench."

The essay contains keen observations of nature and humankind: the birch canoes made by the Indians proved indispensable for travelers where the stage lines ended, for Maine rivers are erratic channels: "Sometimes you have a foamy rapid, sometimes a broad shoal, sometimes a barricade of boulders with gleams of white water springing through or leaping over its rocks." Swiftwater paddlers today can appreciate the details of Winthrop's reports: "A birch thirty feet long, big enough for a trio and their traps [i.e., gear], weighs only seventy-five pounds." Moose, too, quicken the Maine landscape, and Winthrop's report of moose antlers owes as much to the imagination as to observation and study. The head of the bull moose is crowned with palmations, "strange excrescences," "like fronds of a tree-fern, like great corals or sea fans"—analogies that demonstrate how well Winthrop's global travels served him. The moose in spring, having lost one antler, is out of whack: "For a few days he steers wild; in this ill-balanced course his lone horn strikes every tree on this side as he dodges from that side; the unhappy creature is staggered, body and mind." In his lopsided misfortune, the moose is a "tragicomedy of decoronation and recoronation" every year.

This trip with Frederic Edwin Church may be placed at 1856. Winthrop mentions that he "had three years before floated down the magnificent Columbia to Vancouver, bedded on bales of beaver skins"—a jaunt with trappers that took place in the summer of 1853, journal entries show, just weeks before the events described in *The Canoe and the Saddle*.

Henry David Thoreau's essay on Mount Ktaadn had appeared in 1848, and although there is no evidence Winthrop had read it, his reflections on the region bring to mind Thoreau. Hunting for bears while Frederic Church paints, Winthrop flags in pursuit of his quarry and wryly admits, "I begin to fear that I shall slay no other than my proper personal bearishness." His would-be prey has more sense than to spend its time on a chase, Winthrop speculates. The bear he seeks "had not long ago decamped, and was now, perhaps, sucking the meditative paw hard-by in an arbor of his bear-garden." This ancient image of the bear (originally a misunderstanding of its posture while hibernating) has been handed down by generations of nature writers—from Pliny the Elder, to John Josselyn, to Winthrop and Thoreau. Winthrop here laments also that he may not convey the full loveliness of nature, which ought to be the proper object of his devotion. While Church sketches, Winthrop "repented more bitterly of my momentary falseness to Beauty while I saw him so constant." A man of action, a hunter and traveler, Winthrop yearned also to be a thrall to eternal elegance and truth.

Winthrop's most extended work of nature writing, published posthumously, as were all his books, is *The Canoe and the Saddle,* a title imposed by James T. Fields at Ticknor and Fields, the Boston publishing house that handled many authors of this time. Winthrop's working title for the book had been "Klallam and Klickatat," after the Indian tribes that guided him down Puget Sound in their 40-foot dugout canoe, then across the rugged Naches Pass on horseback. The date of this trip was August 21–31, 1853. The book was composed in 1858, although it did not come out until 1862, after its author had died in a botched battle that he helped plan. *The Canoe and the Saddle* has gone through more printings than honestly can be counted. During an era when Ralph Waldo Emerson,

Thoreau, and Whitman were touting the grandeur of the American West, Winthrop actually was living in that land, witnessing its grandeur firsthand. Too long have we glorified Europe, he wrote; "Let us, therefore, develop our own world. It has taken us two centuries to discover our proper West across the Mississippi...." To fulfill the nascent but enormous potential of the nation, he held, all of the American landscape deserves the attention of people around the world.

If the Hudson River School painters of Winthrop's time loved mountains—the Andes, the Catskills, the Adirondacks, the Rockies, and the Sierras—Winthrop brings the Cascades to the page. His lengthy narrative of a summer thunderstorm atop 5,000-foot Naches Pass is a model piece of nature writing, reminiscent of Thomas Cole and Albert Bierstadt: "A gloomy purple storm lay over the Cascades, vaster than they." Winthrop, his "trio of mustangs," and a Yakama guide, weary from a long day's ride, watch dark clouds advance from the direction they had come:

> Beside that envelope of storm hiding the west from floor to cope, there was only to be seen, now softened with dull violet haze, the large, rude region of my day's gallop—thirty miles of surging earth, seamed with frequent valleys of streams flowing eastward, where scanty belts of timber grew by the water-side.

A landscape of such scale might have astounded many of his readers. There is no cover to be had; the cavalcade stands vulnerable to the storm.

> Fitful bursts of weeping rain were now coming thicker, until control ceased, and the floods fell with no interval, borne on furiously, dashing against every upright object as great crushing wave-walls smite on walls of cliff by the sea-side.

This is the sublime, as the landscape painters beheld it and depicted it—so vast, grand, and perilous that it must inspire fear, awe, and veneration: "There were sudden clefts, and ravines with long sweeping flanks, and chasms where a cloud mountain-side had fallen in, leaving a precipice all ragged and ruinous, ready itself to fall." The sublime also carries connotations of landscapes that are harsh, antisocial, and even masculine. Magnificent and threatening at once, the scene recalls the many paintings of storms and mountains in the century.

Literally and aesthetically, Mount Rainier looms over Winthrop's account. At 14,411 feet (4,392 meters), it is the highest peak in the contiguous United States. The natives knew it only as Tacoma, an appellation that Winthrop strongly sanctioned, today the name of Washington's second-largest city nearby. "It was a giant mountain dome of snow," Winthrop says of his first glimpse of the peak from the Indian canoe, "swelling and seeming to fill the aerial spheres as its image displaced the blue deeps of tranquil water." The daydreaming young traveler, suddenly viewing this image reflected in the calm of Puget Sound, thinks he is hallucinating. He could be nasty and ethnocentric in writing about the Indians he met, but Winthrop often had high regard for their culture and folkways. The word for the peak in Chinook jargon rings "melodiously," and it is wrong to call it Rainier, the name that certain "Christians have dubbed it, in stupid nomenclature perpetuating the name of somebody or nobody." He argues, moreover, that mountains exert an "ennobling influence" over humankind. Judging by his writing at this time, he feels nobler and more at peace in the peak's shadow, where "The summer evening air enfolded me sweetly, and down from the cliffs and snowy mounds of Tacoma a cool breeze fell like the spray of a cascade." Aesthetically the mountain shares both male and female qualities, in the serene time of year that he passed through; there is "feminine beauty in the cones, and more of masculine force and hardihood in the rough pyramids...."

The Canoe and the Saddle is characterized by a painterly sensitivity, one that pays attention to color, to the light and the dark. Winthrop studies Mount Rainier from many angles, systematically as painters do, first from the north and then from east and south, as he circumnavigated the peak on his journey to Fort Dalles. Here is a colorful and exacting view of what would later be named the Winthrop Glacier on the mountain:

> The blue haze so wavered and trembled into sunlight, and sunbeams shot glimmering over snowy brinks so like a constant avalanche, that I might doubt whether this movement and waver and glimmer, this blending of mist with noontide flame, were not a drifting smoke and cloud of yellow sulphurous vapor floating over some slowly chilling crater far down in the red crevices.

While not an expert in the earth sciences, Winthrop composed commendable word paintings of the peak. On the Naches Trail, preparing dinner for his Klickitat guide, he shares another painterly perception, this one of a salmon he had propped up to roast:

> The colors that are encased within a salmon, awaiting fire that they may bloom, came forth artistically. On the toasted surface brightened warm yellows, and ruddy orange; and delicate pinkness, softened with downy gray, suffused the separating flakes.

His outsider's objectivity, suggestive of Alexis de Tocqueville, adds grace and force to the book. Nature, not an impediment or antagonist in Winthrop's haste to meet his traveling companions, functions as a beneficent presence in the timeless summer of his 1853 visit.

Had he not traveled Europe for a year and a half after graduating from Yale, Winthrop might have kept his Christian faith intact. Had he not fraternized with landscape painters in New York City, he might never have drifted toward the nature fascination that characterizes his best work. Had he found success in the steamship business, or gold in California, or a willing wife in Washington Territory, he might not have landed in the Staten Island home of his mother and rented the New York City studio to compose his seven books. Had he not hailed from a line of military officers, he might never have plunged to the forefront of an early Civil War battle at the age of 32, where he became the first Union officer to die, before he could realize any of his aspirations as an author. His enormously popular writings all appeared posthumously. His post-mortem fame prompted publishers to rush into print his books without the mature revision and editing that might have toned down the smack of melodrama in some of the novels, the preciosity in some of the nonfiction, and the ethnocentric sneers in nearly all his work. What remains of the Winthrop corpus are seven sometimes brilliant but always uneven volumes, best sellers produced with no evident input from his literary coevals working at the height of the American Renaissance.

PRIMARY BIBLIOGRAPHY

Books

A Companion to the Heart of the Andes (New York: Appleton, 1859).

Cecil Dreeme (Boston: Ticknor and Fields, 1861; Edinburgh: Paterson, 1883).

The Canoe and the Saddle: Adventures Among the Northwestern Rivers and Forests; and Isthmiana (Boston: Ticknor and Fields, 1862; London: Low, 1863; Tacoma, WA: John H. Williams, 1913; Portland, OR: Binford & Mort, 1957); republished in part as *Saddle and Canoe* (Glasgow, KY: Long Riders Guild, 2001); *The Canoe and the Saddle: A Critical Edition*, ed. Paul J. Lindholdt (Lincoln. University of Nebraska Press, 2006).

Edwin Brothertoft (Boston: Ticknor and Fields, 1862; Edinburgh: Paterson, 1883).

John Brent (Boston: Ticknor and Fields, 1862; Edinburgh: Paterson, 1883).

Life in the Open Air, and Other Papers (Boston: Ticknor and Fields, 1863); republished in part as *Love and Skates* (New York: Putnam, 1902).

The Life and Poems of Theodore Winthrop, ed. Laura Winthrop Johnson (New York: Holt, 1884).

Mr. Waddy's Return, ed. Burton E. Stevenson (New York: Holt, 1904).

SECONDARY BIBLIOGRAPHY

References

Robert Cantwell, *The Hidden Northwest* (Philadelphia: J.B. Lippincott, 1972).

George Templeton Strong, *The Diary of George Templeton Strong*, vol. 2 (1850–1859), ed. Allan Nevins and Milton Halsey Thomas (New York: Macmillan, 1952).

John H. Williams, Introduction and Notes, *The Canoe and the Saddle; or Klalam and Klickitat, to Which Are Now First Added His Western Letters and Journals*, ed. John H. Williams (Tacoma, WA: John H. Williams, 1913).

Eugene T. Woolf, *Theodore Winthrop: Portrait of an American Author* (Washington D.C.: University Press of America, 1981).

Papers

The vast majority of Winthrop's surviving manuscripts, including the journals and letters, are in the New York Public Library. They include personal correspondence to Winthrop's mother from Europe, Panama, California, Oregon, Washington, and British Columbia. They also include journals, academic papers from his years at Yale College, and holographic manuscripts of his published and unpublished works. For a list of the complete papers, which measure two linear feet and six inches and are contained within eight archival boxes and one bound volume, see Nick Tucker, "Theodore Winthrop Papers, 1844–1860," The New York Public Library, Manuscripts and Archives Division, printed March 1997.

Elizabeth C. Wright
(ca. 1832–?)

Daniel Patterson

Of all the forgotten and neglected early American nature writers, none is less well known or more deserving of recovery, republication, and scholarly attention than Elizabeth C. Wright. Her only book, *Lichen Tufts, from the Alleghanies* (1860), is one of the earliest literary treatises on nature published in the United States, and the very first by a woman. One would probably have to look ahead a hundred years to the work of Rachel Carson to find the next female naturalist and writer who attempted so comprehensively to represent the whole of nature as a system. No one in the nineteenth century wrote more engagingly about the social aspects of a camping trip. And no one in the century produced a fuller analysis of the social implications of the essentialist theory of biology promulgated by Harvard's Louis Agassiz and others. Wright was also the first literary naturalist to incorporate responses to Thoreau's *Walden* (1854) in her published work. Published a few months after Darwin's *On the Origin of Species* (1859), *Lichen Tufts* gives literary expression to the essentialist biology that Darwin's theory of speciation by natural selection challenged and eventually undermined. Wright's treatise nonetheless comprises a significant cultural moment at the beginnings of the Thoreauvian tradition in American nature writing.

Elizabeth C. Wright's identity remains an enticing and important mystery in the history of American nature writing. So far as is currently known, she left behind very little evidence of her existence. The likeliest candidate uncovered so far is an Elizabeth Wright listed in the 1860 U.S. census as 29 years old, born in New York state, and married to one Henry C. Wright, a book dealer. Elizabeth and Henry were living in Dunkirk, New York, with their two children at the time of the census. A later census record suggests that the Wrights moved to St. Louis, Missouri, one would suppose following the Civil War. The 1880 U.S. census lists an Elizabeth Wright as married to Henry C. Wright, who had become Superintendent of Letter Carriers. The 1890 census shows Henry as General Manager of the U.S. Stenograph Company. The only other clues to her biography show up as several references within her published work. A passage in *Lichen Tufts* tells us that Wright lived in Illinois (which she dubs "prairie land") for two years in the late 1850s before returning, as a result of "ague," to her beloved Allegany Mountains in New York state. A poem printed in the second half of *Lichen Tufts* bears the heading "Lexington, Ill., *Christmas Eve*, 1857." This poem, "Anniversary Letter," tells us also that she missed her native

New York tremendously. In her only known magazine article, published in 1859, she refers to herself as offering public classes in botany. If the Elizabeth Wright listed in the 1860 census is the correct one, she would have taught these botany classes in the area of Dunkirk, New York. Although several notices of *Lichen Tuft*'s publication appeared in the leading literary magazines of the day, no review is known to have been published. The search for this American nature writer is still on.

Other than a single poem in *The Ladies' Repository* of 1855, Wright's first known publication is an 1859 essay in which she argues that mycology, the study of fungi, should become as popular as botany. In "Something about Fungi," Wright intends to train her readers to "perceive," not merely *see,* what is already visible before them in the natural environment. She notes that people do not observe the wonders of the variety of fungi only because they have not trained their eyes to see them:

> If you begin to explore this field and fail, at first, to see the wonders of which we read, remember, "The eye sees only what it brings with it the power to see," and be not discouraged. *Keep looking,* and by-and-by you will see. Sooner or later we find what we look for in this world. But the eye must be educated.

As part of her encouragement, she narrates her own beginnings as a mycologist. For two years she conducted her study of local fungi "without guide or guide-book," yet she "collected and described one hundred and fifty species within the radius of half a mile." Just as she trained her eyes, so could her readers train theirs. For Wright, however, the highest purpose of all nature study—as it was for the natural theologians and the essentialist biologists—was to gain insight into the divine "principle of LIFE." The reproductive spore of a fungus, she writes,

> contains within itself the inscrutable, grand mystery of life. This little cell, like any other vital cell, or seed, or egg, has in itself, hidden beyond all finding, that fixed law of

development which makes each of these primitive beginnings grow "after its kind."

Wright clearly aligns herself in opposition to those naturalists (early among whom was Charles Darwin's paternal grandfather, Erasmus Darwin) who had begun to claim that only matter exists, that all phenomena have only material causes, not spiritual or divine:

> But they cannot use the commonest speech, nor recognize the difference between the living and the not alive, without measurably recognizing the perpetual miracle of the Incarnation; which makes any living thing allied to the Infinite, and worth more in itself, for the sake of the wonder of its being alive, than any inanimate things can be.

As a premise for her nature writing, this statement effectively unifies Wright's science, religion, and art. In a memorable, taunting jab, she writes: "Let a chemist try to extract an epos from the brains of a dead poet!"

Even though so little is known about Wright, she seems to fit an interesting cultural profile of the nineteenth century: that of the female naturalist passionately and expertly pursuing her chosen branch of the natural sciences despite the total absence of professional or semiprofessional positions for women in science. A significant number of nineteenth-century American "ladies" altered their dress, their manner of travel and lodging, and in some cases even their conception and valuation of marriage in order to satisfy their irrepressible desire to study their world scientifically. Florence Merriam Bailey, Olive Thorne Miller, Neltje Doubleday, and Mabel Osgood Wright became accomplished ornithologists. Almira Phelps became a general natural philosopher, but also a botanist. Mary (Davis) Treat and Annie Trumbull Slosson developed as both botanists and entomologists. But only Elizabeth C. Wright moved into mycology.

When considered together with her advocacy of sleeping outdoors, adopting Thoreau's "deliberate philosophy," and botanizing off-trail for women in *Lichen Tufts*, it seems clear that from the beginning of her publishing career, regardless of how short it was, Wright was not only an accomplished naturalist but also an original thinker interested in leading her readers to deeper and surprising insights about nature. No one else in the popular press was advocating for mycology at this time. The originality of "Something about Fungi" bears a further interesting relation to her major work, *Lichen Tufts,* since lichens were classified as fungi at the time. (We now know lichens to be organisms formed of a photosynthetic partnership between fungi and green algae.)

Only recently was *Lichen Tufts* brought into the scholarly discussion of the history of American nature writing. When Lawrence Buell came upon a copy in an antiquarian bookshop in Chapel Hill, North Carolina, he was quickly impressed by several of its qualities: "Thumbing through it, my attention was immediately caught by both its earliness and by the fact that the author was a woman with a zest for Thoreau and for being contrarian." Over the next several years, Professor Buell included discussions of Elizabeth C. Wright in his influential studies of nineteenth-century environmental writing, and now to find a copy of *Lichen Tufts* available for sale in the United States is very difficult. Despite the sketchy and cryptic nature of the biographical information about her, Wright clearly has entered the canon of American nature writers because of the qualities of her literary treatise on nature.

Like much of American nature writing, as Thomas J. Lyon characterizes it, *Lichen Tufts* is essentially subversive in purpose; that is, Wright expresses her view that her culture as she knows it is deficient in several ways, that her contemporaries' ideas about nature are the chief causes of those deficiencies, and that the "nature cure" that the treatise describes, theorizes, and advocates could correct the cultural weaknesses she perceives. Wright's text reveals that its author clearly believed that a literary representation of the natural environment and of the proper human relation to it could contribute to her

nation's physical, intellectual, and moral well-being.

In *Lichen Tufts,* Wright devises two main strategies whereby to accomplish her cultural work. First, she makes figurative use of Protestant typology and several New Testament passages in order to imply that a thorough knowledge of one's local ecology can cure a person of moral and intellectual weaknesses. Second, she dramatizes the healing power that this knowledge of one's home environment has by means of her narrative persona who is so imbued by her deep and experiential knowledge of her Allegheny bioregion that the persona is able to exhibit a fulfilled self and thereby model the desired cultural transformation.

Wright appeals to her largely Protestant readers by drawing upon the New England tradition of reading the Bible typologically, that is, as a divinely inspired text the first portion of which, the Old Testament, anticipates and foreshadows the second, the New Testament. According to this method of exegesis, figures and events occurring in the Old Testament are designed by God as "shadows" or "types" of Christ and events in his life related in the New Testament. Thus, for example, circumcision among the tribes of Israel shadows forth the Christian sacrament of baptism, and Adam is seen as a type of Christ. Typology was a means devised by Protestants to make the Old Testament more clearly relevant to their conception of the History of Redemption. The Puritans brought a knowledge and regular practice of typology to New England in the seventeenth century and Protestants maintained it well into the nineteenth century. Wright shows a familiarity with this tradition and makes literary use of it to appeal to her readers while simultaneously implying that a kind of redemption is at stake in the cultural work *Lichen Tufts* is designed to accomplish.

Wright's employment of Christian soteriology (that is, the doctrine of salvation through a savior) as a trope in her nature writing begins in the jaunty opening narrative essay, "Into the Woods." Here she dichotomizes, in the traditional terms of saved and damned souls, those persons who profess to love nature but will not venture away from their home comforts to experience it directly from those who are hearty and inspired enough to endure the discomfort that might accompany a camping trip. Wright's satirical voice ridicules her "sentimental" and "croaking neighbors" who "professed to love poetry, and to appreciate the enthusiasm of the poet-lovers of Nature" but who avoided encounters with the realities of the natural environment. As she advances her narrative, she leaves these benighted neighbors behind while she and her spirited companions escape the confining city and make for the woods, where they will dwell for a while amidst the "divine poem" of nature. Wright thus challenges her own readers to put down their anthologies of nature poetry and go into the woods,

> into the forests and grottoes where the air breathes poetry, and all the elements of grander dramas than ever we have enacted, are created and exhaled by rock, and tree and moss—by cool spring and shady river—by many-toned birds, and bright-hued insects, and shy wild beasts—by fog, and cloud, and wind, sunshine, and rain, and dew.

Wright's equation of nature, truth, and poetry is conventionally romantic, but her emphasis on the diversity of phenomena in the passage above reflects her emerging ecological conception of the natural realm as composed of myriad relationships, interactions, and interdependencies. Her suggestion that this dynamic, other-than-human world is "grander" than any of the comedies and tragedies ever enacted by humans marks the beginning of her attempt to persuade her readers to adopt a humbler ethical posture toward nature. She continues her persuasive work by drawing upon Christian soteriology in the following passage:

> It was utterly delightful to let ourselves loose, and live freely; to have no rules for coming in or going out, for rising up or sitting down; to be emancipated from the bondage of the

ceremonial law, and do what pleased us best was paradisiacal enough.

The allusion to "ceremonial law" creates a trope by the terms of which Wright and her companions, in being "emancipated" from the Old Testament prescriptions for worship, are associated with Christians, and their nature-poetry-loving neighbors snug in their homes are associated with the Tribes of Israel. The savior of these blessed campers is nature. The clear implication of Wright's trope is that nature, and only nature, can save human civilization from its own corrupting influences.

Later in *Lichen Tufts*, Wright develops this conceit to an extreme political position. In the third essay, "The Nature Cure.—For the Mind," the tone of which is polemical rather than comical and satirical, the neighbors left behind in cities have become "poor mammon-ridden wretches," no longer treated as merely dim-witted. Similarly, those saved by nature are transformed in this essay from simple blessed souls to individuals liberated from all cares about what others think about one's affinity for nature: "By and by you get the habit if being free, even among your fellows." In the next step of her argument, Wright widens the gap between the saved and the damned even farther by means of a dichotomy between "we, the working people" and the "aristocrats." In this polemical essay, the followers of nature are rendered as a social class oppressed by the followers of Mammon, the privileged, affluent ruling class. The working people, she writes, are capable of making "ourselves the peers of any class we please." By adding the concept of oppression, Wright politicizes her treatise on nature and condemns the aristocrats' insistence that "it is necessary to have a privileged class to do the learning and thinking, leaving another class to perform all labor; for labor, they say, is incompatible with study and thought." The clear message to her readers is that the aristocrats act in concert to set obstacles between workers and the study of nature and that workers can be free only if they act deliberately to overcome these obstacles. And Wright's nature is radically democratic, standing ready to offer her "treasures" to anyone who seeks them, even if only in "the odd scraps of half worn hours, and the fag end of holidays." Seen in the light of this later argument, Wright's advocacy for the study of botany by young women is an advocacy for, not only their intellectual, but also their political liberation.

Wright's treatise on nature is also a treatise on individuation, the fulfillment of the self. Through her persona, Wright develops a model of the fulfilled individual whose fulfillment is achieved by means of a close knowledge of the ecology of one's home place. It is by means of the close study of nature that women and men can raise themselves to the highest moral and intellectual levels. A deep knowledge of her local ecology is a chief identifying characteristic of Wright's persona. Early in *Lichen Tufts*, the persona announces her affinity for her Allegany woods:

> I had grown up in woods like these, and they were home to me. I had been absent from them two years in the west, and had longed with more unspeakable homesickness for the evergreen woods and mountain air, than for home or friends.

The native flora receives her special attention; she goes "'maundering' about, greeting my old friends beside every log and under every bank." Wright develops this connectedness to place at one point to the extreme of suggesting a vaguely causal relation between one's personal health and one's native place. We learn that the persona's recent return to western New York state was prompted by an illness she acquired on the Illinois prairies; a week after returning to her native place, she was cured:

> When I lay sick and fevered by the Mississippi, drinking warm wiggling water, I felt as though the cool springs and clear air of these hills would cure me at once—but it took more than one week.

Wright develops this affinity further by showing her narrative self's knowledge of place to be deeply rooted in childhood perceptions of ecological relationships. In one passage, she recounts a childhood memory of regularly hearing the display drumming of a grouse on a log near a black birch among a stand of sugar maples:

> We very rarely saw him, for he was a shy bird, but we heard him many times a day in his season, and found his tracks there. We children used to tap the old birch and catch its profuse sweetish sap in a little trough, to drink of its diluted spicery; and that draught and its neighborhood, and the tremulous thunder of the grouse's wings, with the hum of the wild bees which used to drink at the same place, are all called up by the birch's voice, and become part and parcel of it, past the power of analysis to separate them.

Her representation of nature in this passage reflects an ecological conception of the environment in which entities (grouse, tree, bee, human child, sap) are rendered as relationships in a complex web. Later in the work, Wright takes the connection between place and self to its most profound level. She writes: "Our thoughts are us. What we *think*, we *are*. What we *know*, we *are*. What we learn becomes part of our minds." By this reasoning, a knowledge of one's home place is much more than a body of memorized, discrete facts, ecological relationships, and observations; this knowledge shapes a new personal identity, an identity that Wright very closely associates with the higher moral and intellectual levels she encourages her readers to strive for. With her consistent emphasis on knowing one's home place, Wright is one of the earliest nature writers to develop a bioregional ethic. In this regard, she follows very closely her contemporaries, Susan Fenimore Cooper and Henry David Thoreau.

The major obstacle to the fulfillment of self, especially for young women, that Wright chooses to expose is the way in which botany was popularly presented to female students. Flower language books were extremely popular, and Wright saw them as damaging her culture. These books were designed for women and offered them a floral world as an alternative to human society, weaving dubious botany with folklore, poetry, bits of personal narrative, and horticulture. About one such book entitled the *Floral Diadem,* Wright remarks, "If the Diadem's piety, which it professes to teach, is as bogus as its botany, we wish it a speedy death." Wright's concern was that a society that was trained to view nature through such a distorting lens as these books presented and not through the clarifying lens of accurate natural history could never stand in a proper relationship to its natural environment. On the other hand, too often the books that presented botany with greater scientific accuracy were written in an obscure style. Wright refers to these as "mechanical" botanies:

> There are a class of botanists of the mechanical sort, who are to science what the patent-note singing books are to music—mechanical, soulless anatomists of parts, and dictionary-like vocabularies of technology, who perceive no laws, conceive of no causes nor forces not laid down in the text-books....These scientific bores disgust those who *love* flowers and trees for the sake of their beauty and poetry; and so, because some scientific prattlers are stupid and prosy, they think that the science of plants itself is unlovely and undesirable.

Thus Wright points out to her largely female readers that they are deluded and patronized on the one hand and repelled and discouraged on the other. Speaking from within the tradition of women botanizers, she calls for a literature of nature that blends art and science.

Wright also called for reform in the ways that young women are represented in the popular literature. The women she is writing for were victimized, she argued, by the romanticization of both nature and women in romantic fiction. Although she chided her female readers for their own complicity in this victimization, she exposed and condemned this romanticization as a means to keep women from nature study:

> Young ladies in their teens, who have resolution enough to defy parental advice and authority, and run away with some perfumed popinjay, to be "married in haste to repent at leisure," have not moral force nor physical courage enough to put on a pair of calfskin shoes, and a dress short and loose enough to climb hills in without stepping on the skirts, or gasping for the breath they have no room for in their dress waists; and then, thus equipped, to take rambles, and even scrambles, in places rough and smooth in pursuit of those objects of beauty or curiosity, of scientific or artistic interest, which are always accessible in the woods and fields.

The authors of the popular fiction are to blame for actively discouraging women from the study of nature:

> *Scientific young ladies are never the heroines of novels!* They are absurd and unfashionable, and are supposed always to have ragged blue stockings, inky fingers, and dowdy hair....All the oracles of romance have shown that women never take to science or art, except from starvation or disappointment.

Wright would transform her culture in such ways that women could acquire the "gumption," "moral force," and "physical courage" to improve themselves and thereby their culture by means of the close study of their local ecologies.

To some extent *Lichen Tufts* is allied to the symbolic and teleological theory of nature put forth by the essentialists such as Louis Agassiz and Hugh Miller, but her representation of nature consistently reflects a more phenomenological and ecological conception of her world. The disparity between these two modes of thought about nature in Wright's book reflects a change that was occurring at this time in American culture. More and more people were becoming informed by the rising influence of ecological science and finding the explanations that relied purely on Christian teleology less satisfying. At least in part, this is the cultural moment of *Lichen Tufts.*

It is surprising that Elizabeth C. Wright has remained so obscure a figure when one considers how original she was. In 1876, America's most famous and successful female scientist of the nineteenth century, Vassar's professor of astronomy Maria Mitchell, gave a talk entitled "The Need for Women in Science," in which she encouraged women who labored to popularize the sciences by writing textbooks and essays for the lay reader. Mitchell knew better than most how rare an event it was for a woman to gain a professional position as a scientist. But, as Nina Baym explains, if women "became scientifically competent enough to lecture in schools and in public, to write for periodicals, to translate, their work might make it easier for future women to become professional scientists as a matter of course." Nearly 20 years before Wright could hear such encouragement, she was teaching classes in botany, and probably in mycology as well, publishing in periodicals, and writing the first treatise on nature by a woman in this country up in the relative remoteness of northwestern New York state. Wright also can be seen as belonging to a triad of nature writers suggesting a bioregional ethic as an antidote to the two forces that were ripping people away from their home places: industrialization and western expansionism. Together with Susan Fenimore Cooper's *Rural Hours* (1850) and Henry David Thoreau's *Walden* (1854), *Lichen Tufts* asks Americans to slow down, stay put, and learn the land for the good of the culture.

PRIMARY BIBLIOGRAPHY

Book

Lichen Tufts, from the Alleghanies (New York: M. Doolady, 1860).

Other

At Home on This Earth: Two Centuries of U.S. Women's Nature Writing, ed. Lorraine Anderson and Thomas S. Edwards, selection from Wright (Hanover, NH: University of New England Press, 2002), 41–53.

Sisters of the Earth: Women's Prose and Poetry about Nature, 2nd ed., ed. Lorraine Anderson, selection from Wright (New York: Vintage, 2003), 206–9.

Periodical Publications—Uncollected

"Phantom Building," *The Ladies' Repository* 15.5 (May 1855): 263.

"Something about Fungi," *Putnam's Monthly Magazine* 22 (October 1859): 431–35.

SECONDARY BIBLIOGRAPHY

References

Nina Baym, *American Women of Letters and the Nineteenth-century Sciences: Styles of Affiliation* (New Brunswick, NJ: Rutgers University Press, 2001).

Lawrence Buell, "American Pastoral Ideology Reappraised," *American Literary History* 1 (1989): 1–29.

Lawrence Buell, *The Environmental Imagination: Thoreau, Nature Writing, and the Formation of American Culture* (Cambridge: Harvard University Press, 1995).

Thomas J. Lyon, "Nature Writing as a Subversive Activity," *North Dakota Quarterly* 59.2 (1991): 6–16.

Daniel Patterson, "'I commend you to Allegany underbrush': The Subversive Place-made Self in Elizabeth C. Wright's Treatise on Nature, *Lichen Tufts*," *Legacy: A Journal of American Women Writers* 17.1 (2000): 33–47.

Beverly Seaton, *The Language of Flowers: A History* (Charlottesville: University Press of Virginia, 1995).

Mabel Osgood Wright ("Barbara")
(January 26, 1859–July 16, 1934)

Melissa Moore

Mabel Osgood Wright's literary career flourished for 35 years, extending from the late nineteenth century into the first third of the twentieth century. Wright was a prolific and versatile writer whose body of work reflects a diversity of interests. Her publications span a broad generic range, but the most significant have proved to be those centered on nature. Acute observations of the natural world provided her with material for poetic essays, field guides, educational children's books, and articles advancing environmental concerns. She also composed several more conventional novels, which were only moderately popular with contemporary audiences and have attracted no attention from modern scholars. Though she was widely known during her life as an author as well as an environmental activist, her reputation today is not commensurate with her many achievements. Wright is presently being rediscovered, however, and her contributions to the environmental advocacy movement are of especial interest in this process.

Mabel Gray Osgood was born on January 26, 1859, to Ellen Haswell Murdoch and Samuel Osgood. She had been preceded in birth by her sisters Agnes and Bertha. Her mother was the great-niece of Susanna Rowson, author of the enormously successful *Charlotte Temple,* and her father was a respected Unitarian minister. The family enjoyed a comfortable middle-class existence, spending winters in their Greenwich Village home, and vacationing during the summer months at their large second home in Fairfield, Connecticut. Young Mabel's upbringing was guided by the conservative Victorian principles espoused by her father. This may account for her limited formal education, which was received at Miss Lucy Green's School for girls.

Wright recounts close relationships with both parents, but it is clear that her father, in particular, exerted tremendous influence in her life. While serving for 20 years as a Unitarian pastor, Osgood edited two religious periodicals, published multiple collections of his sermons and essays, and contributed to many popular magazines. His evident passion for intellectual pursuits doubtless affected Wright, who would exhibit a similar scope and sedulousness in her work. Certainly, the father's endeavors also imbued in his daughter a profound appreciation for the act of writing.

Perhaps the most important value Osgood modeled for his youngest child was love for the natural world. He was an avid gardener and designed the grounds at Mosswood, the family's summer estate. The result was a space that accommodated humans and nature simultaneously. Walkways were created for accessibility and decorative ornaments were added to the natural landscape, while abundant trees and flowers invited wildlife. As a girl, Wright adored the extensive grounds and the opportunities afforded for observing plants and animals. She would later write (in *The Friendship of Nature*), "The garden's growth was nowhere warped or stunted by tradition; there was no touch of custom's bondage to urge this or that." Although the garden layout was the outcome of planning and not a tract of pristine wilderness, Wright conceived of it as a natural space. This conception of nature would distinguish her in the conservation movement. Mosswood would also become her home and the subject of her first book.

In 1884 Mabel Gray Osgood married the Englishman James Osborne Wright. Wright's father, who died before the marriage, had introduced the two. James, seven years Wright's senior, shared her two great loves: books and nature. The newlyweds lived in the Osgood family home and continued the ritual of spending summers in Fairfield. Wright became a housewife, though never a mother. She had finally assumed the role for which her upbringing had prepared her, yet she felt unfulfilled. She experienced a waxing desire to write and expressed to her husband interest in a literary vocation. James did not initially take her ambition seriously. When Wright exhibited potential for success, however, he became wholly supportive of her endeavors and proved instrumental in launching her career.

Wright's debut into the literary world was initially unheralded. She published brief nature writings in *The New York Evening Post;* but the submissions were always anonymous. Eventually, she revealed her secret efforts to friends and family who offered their encouragement and assistance. James arranged for an acquaintance, the president of McMillan's, to read Wright's works. He agreed

and subsequently published her first book. *The Friendship of Nature: A New England Chronicle of Birds and Flowers* was composed of Wright's anonymous pieces, several new essays, and her own amateur photographs. The book appeared in 1894, when Wright was 35 years old.

The Friendship of Nature, Wright's most enduring literary accomplishment, contained her observations of the natural environment at Mosswood. Eleven chapters documented the changes an annual cycle wrought on the property. The marriage of poetic language with keen ornithological and botanical insights was the most noted feature of the work at its time of publication. On a recommended summer reading list in *The Chautauquan*, the book was described as "a portfolio filled with flower pieces, bird representations, and bits of landscape, done not in water colors, pastels, or oils, but in word painting." Wright remarked on subjects such as the varying hues of bird plumage, saying: "How the bird colours ebb and flow from spring until autumn! The grays of March and April are glinted by flying colour, though the earliest birds are more soberly clad than those that arrive when the leafage has grown." An oriole was presented as "the fiery hang-bird who, wearing Lord Baltimore's colours, flits about the sweeping elm branches in May, searching for a wand both strong and supple where he may safely anchor his sky cradle." Exhibiting the same acumen and artistry she recognized the sequence in which types of roses bloomed: "The wild rose, token of simple-hearted love, that stars the unmown edges of the fields and rocky banks, is the first of the wild tribe, coming before its paler swamp sister unfurls, or even the hardy little sand-rose bush has budded." Her lyrical treatment of natural history earned the praise of such prominent figures as Harriet Prescott Spofford and Oliver Wendell Holmes.

While the favorable contemporary reception of *The Friendship of Nature* was based mainly on style, modern attention has been directed toward the conceptions of nature that underlie the text. Mosswood covered eight acres and was inherently connected with humans. During a period in which vast tracts of land were being protected as National Parks, Wright was expounding on the intimate details of the local landscape. In the literary treatment of her relatively small suburban backyard as a natural space, she elevated its status. By including humans in her pastoral portraits, Wright was advocating an ecological consciousness. She realized that people's use of the land had consequences in the natural world. For Wright, nature could be close to home, crossed by roads, visited by hunters, and used for agricultural purposes. These traits served only to enhance the need for careful stewardship. Relation to a natural place was more important than its size or primitivism.

Wright's inaugural effort was succeeded the following year by *Birdcraft: A Field Book of Two Hundred Song, Game, and Water Birds* (1895), a very different project. *Birdcraft* was intended to provide scientifically accurate ornithological information to a lay public. Contemporary reviews recognized it as satisfying the need for an accessible field guide to birds. Data were presented in such a way that the information could be useful to amateur and inexperienced birders. The book was also inexpensive, and therefore allowed a larger segment of the population to participate in informed bird watching. A profusion of quality illustrations were included to aid in bird identification. A reviewer for *The Bookman* wrote:

> Those who have read the author's former chronicle of birds and flowers in *The Friendship of Nature* will meet here with the same fresh delight in open-air life, the same qualities of rare insight, felicitous expression, and racy New England humor.

Birdcraft proved so popular that it was reprinted through 1936. It is a significant work in Wright's career as it reflects her concern with disseminating environmental information, a concern that developed into a lifelong mission for the writer and activist.

Never committed to a single genre, Wright next turned to the publication of children's books. She adapted her style to a new juvenile audience, but nature remained the clear focus of her writing. Without exception, Wright's children's books were designed to inform young readers about the natural world. The stories relied on anthropomorphization to present material, but the technique was adroitly and carefully employed. Wright's tone was vivacious and entertaining, while the information she included regarding plants and animals was sophisticated and accurate. Wright made her foray into the field of children's literature with *Tommy-Anne and the Three Hearts* (1896). A review of the story appearing in *The Literary World* recognized it as containing "a great deal of pretty and curious information" and declared that children would find it "as instructive as delightful." Wright continued to publish children's books for 17 years. Her efforts in the genre consistently received warm praise.

In 1898 Wright accepted the presidency of the newly formed Audubon Society of Connecticut. The environmentalist sentiments evinced in her literary works became the principles that would guide her leadership of the society. Under her direction the institution lobbied for the protection of threatened bird species and initiated educational programs. The Audubon Society had formed in opposition to the harvesting of birds for their fashionable feathers, and the Connecticut chapter challenged the fashion industry, particularly the millinery trade, by distributing petitions and pamphlets. Members sought to accomplish the goal of educating young people by visiting classrooms, supplying informational books and materials to schools, and hosting walks and lectures. Wright's administrative assistance was indispensable in these activities. She held the presidential post for 26 years before resigning.

Wright again expanded her professional scope in 1899. While continuing to publish books and perform her responsibilities with the Audubon Society of Connecticut, she embarked on a new career as assistant editor for the journal *Bird-Lore*. For her first seven years with the publication Wright was assigned to the Audubon section. This department helped to unify the various chapters of the society by announcing updates on the activities of each and identifying issues that warranted their combined attention. From this platform Wright offered advice on the structuring of meetings, solicited funds from readers, and encouraged societies to value quality of membership over quantity. In this capacity she was clearly writing to achieve political aims rather than to entertain.

The turn of the century was also a turning point in Wright's literary career. In 1901 she published her final work of nonfiction and her first of ten novels. *Flowers and Ferns in their Haunts* was the botanical equivalent of *Birdcraft* and was received with similar enthusiasm. Again, readers appreciated the combination of artistry and accuracy Wright achieved. *The Garden of a Commuter's Wife,* published under the pseudonym "Barbara," was much less successful. A reviewer for *Current Literature* noted that it was "not especially original in character of treatment, nor in theme," but went on to acknowledge "several interesting and delightful characters" as well as "a sunny humor." The novels Wright produced would never earn acclaim comparable to that inspired by her other works. Wright's involvement in the Audubon Society increased in the early 1900s as the group expanded and grew more powerful. As president of the Connecticut chapter Wright automatically became a member of the National Association of Audubon Societies when it was established in 1901. In 1905 she took a seat on the Board of Directors. During these years she continued to support and strengthen the institution through her *Bird-Lore* editorials. Her tireless devotion to the Society, combined with the similar efforts of many others, helped it to evolve into a politically potent organization. Legislative victories included laws protecting endangered species of birds, licensing regulations for hunters, and the establishment of preserves and parks on state and national levels.

Over the years Wright's contributions to *Bird-Lore* changed. In 1907 she became editor of the magazine's school department rather than the Audubon department. For the next three years she used the new position to emphasize the necessity of teaching young people about the environment, recognizing that the advances made by such institutions as the Audubon Society would require the support of the next generation if they were to endure. Wright became a general contributor to the journal in 1910.

The Audubon Society of Connecticut purchased a ten-acre parcel of land in 1914, and an enterprise that Wright had long advocated finally commenced. The property was to be transformed into a bird sanctuary: a refuge for indigenous songbirds and an educational avian exhibit for the community. Wright had first proposed the sanctuary more than a decade earlier. Her appeals for its realization became more ardent as she witnessed the effects of urbanization and deforestation on the local landscape and its animal populations. The small tract was located in Fairfield across the road from Mosswood, Wright's home at the time. Her proximity to and passion for the undertaking made her an ideal director for the project. She oversaw the design process and its implementation. The sanctuary was to embody the environmental ideals outlined in her writing. It was a natural space within the city that could both shelter birds and educate the public. In her honor, the facility was christened Birdcraft Museum and Sanctuary. Birdcraft opened its gates to the first wave of visitors in 1915.

Birdcraft Sanctuary was an enormously popular attraction, but it holds a complicated place in the history of conservationism. It was a clear symbol of progress for the developing environmental movement, but the management practices would be troubling to today's environmentalists. The founding of the sanctuary was important as it attested to the efficacy of grassroots environmentalism. Birdcraft, conceived of by Wright, was the first privately owned sanctuary in the nation.

It served as an example to other groups and landowners concerned with preserving wildlife. The value of action at the community level was part of what Wright wished to illustrate with the project. Birdcraft was located on Main Street, indicating that any space, even one in the midst of a town, could become a nature refuge. Guests were taught about the birds that nested in their own backyards. This allowed them to appreciate and understand the ways in which they might contribute to the cause at home. At a time when the National Park system was expanding, Wright offered a reminder that intimate and immediate forms of nature also deserved attention.

While Birdcraft was the result of progressive environmental ethics, it was maintained with the help of conventional techniques. The caretakers at the sanctuary engaged in highly invasive control methods to protect the birds within. Wright both suggested and supported the tactics employed. The property was bounded by a fence to prevent the entrance of cats and other potential predators. Authorization was granted for the extermination of animals that threatened birds within the sanctuary, either as predators or competitors for food. Squirrels, weasels, cats, snakes, sparrows, crows, and more were victims of the strict policies. Songbirds did thrive in the park, so Wright's primary objective was achieved, but this was not accomplished without some cost to other species.

A year after the opening of Birdcraft, the Wrights sold Mosswood and established residence at a house across the street. Wright remained near the sanctuary that was her passion, and the upkeep required by the new, smaller home was less taxing on the aging couple. Little information is available regarding Wright's personal life, but it can be assumed that her marriage was a happy one. For, when James died in 1920, Wright mourned deeply. She stayed two more years at the home they had shared, but her declining health then prompted her to secure a more manageable cottage nearby.

Until the end of her life, Wright continued to publish novels and articles. In 1926 she released a partially fictionalized autobiography entitled *My New York*, which related her childhood experience in the city. After 1914 her contributions to *Bird-Lore* increasingly addressed the process of establishing bird sanctuaries and the specific developments at Birdcraft. Her final novel, *Eudora's Men*, appeared in 1931. Wright was 75 when she passed away on July 16, 1934.

Mabel Osgood Wright made many literary contributions to the environmental cause during her long writing career. She composed political articles for numerous periodicals, educational books for children and adults, and essays reflecting her personal environmental philosophy, such as those that appeared in *Bird-Lore* and her pinnacle work: *The Friendship of Nature*. It is primarily for the latter that she has been acknowledged by the modern literary community. Several of these works have been anthologized in four recent collections of nature writing. Her treatment of limited suburban landscapes as natural places is today recognized as the most relevant feature of her work. Only in the backyard can the "friendship" with a place that her writings illustrate be achieved, and it is friendship with a place that inspires one to protect it. In a natural place devoid of people, individual actions matter little, but in small, local fragments of nature, Wright demonstrated through her activism and art, their efforts can have substantial impact. Mabel Osgood Wright does not yet occupy a secure position in the evolutionary history of nature writing, but the process of locating her in that history has clearly begun.

PRIMARY BIBLIOGRAPHY

Books

The Friendship of Nature: A New England Chronicle of Birds and Flowers (New York: The Macmillan Company, 1894; Baltimore: Johns Hopkins University Press, 1999, edited by Daniel J. Philippon).

Birdcraft: A Field Book of Two Hundred Song, Game and Water Birds (New York: The Macmillan Company, 1895).

Tommy-Anne and the Three Hearts (New York: The Macmillan Company, 1896).

Citizen Bird: Scenes from Bird-life in Plain English for Beginners, with Elliott Coues (New York: The Macmillan Company, 1897).

Four-footed Americans and their Kin, ed. Frank Chapman (New York: The Macmillan Company, 1898).

Wabeno the Magician: The Sequel to "Tommy-Anne and the Three Hearts" (New York: The Macmillan Company, 1899).

The Dream Fox Story Book (New York: The Macmillan Company, 1900).

Flowers and Ferns in Their Haunts (New York: The Macmillan Company, 1901).

The Garden of a Commuter's Wife, as Barbara (New York: The Macmillan Company, 1901).

Dogtown: Being Some Chapters from the Annals of the Waddles Family, Set Down in the Language of Housepeople (New York: The Macmillan Company, 1902).

Aunt Jimmy's Will (New York: The Macmillan Company, 1903).

People of the Whirlpool: From the Experience Book of a Commuter's Wife, as Barbara (New York: The Macmillan Company, 1903).

First Reader: Stories of Earth and Sky (New York: The Macmillan Company, 1904).

Second Reader: Stories of Plants and Animals (New York: The Macmillan Company, 1904).

Third Reader: Stories of Birds and Beasts (New York: The Macmillan Company, 1904).

The Woman Errant: Being Some Chapters from the Wonder Book of Barbara, the Commuter's Wife, as Barbara (New York: The Macmillan Company, 1904).

At the Sign of the Fox: A Romance, as Barbara (New York: The Macmillan Company, 1905).

The Garden You and I, as Barbara (New York: The Macmillan Company, 1906).

The Heart of Nature (New York: The Macmillan Company, 1906).

Gray Lady and the Birds: Stories of the Bird Year for Home and School (New York: The Macmillan Company, 1907).

The Open Window: Tales of the Months (New York: The Macmillan Company, 1908).

Poppea of the Post Office (New York: The Macmillan Company, 1909).

Princess Flower Hat: A Comedy from the Perplexity Book of Barbara, the Commuter's Wife (New York: The Macmillan Company, 1910).

The Love that Lives (New York: The Macmillan Company, 1911).

The Stranger at the Gate: A Story of Christmas (New York: The Macmillan Company, 1913).

My New York (New York: The Macmillan Company, 1926).

Captains of the Watch of Life and Death (New York: The Macmillan Company, 1927).

Eudora's Men (New York: The Macmillan Company, 1931).

Translation

Charles Nodier, *Bibliomaniac* (New York: J.O. Wright, 1894).

Selected Periodical Publications— Uncollected

"Life Outdoors and Its Effect Upon Literature," *Critic* 42 (April 1903): 308–11.

"The Truce of the Year: Winter, Dogs, and Books," *Critic* 44 (February 1904): 138–46.

"Beagle as a Family Dog," *Country Calendar* 1 (June 1905): 161–62.

"Poor Man's Paradise," *Country Calendar* 1 (August 1905): 339–43; 1 (September 1905): 431–34; 1 (October 1905): 557–61.

"Birds We Ought to Know," *Delineator* 73 (June 1909): 779.

"House Wren," *Bird-Lore* 11 (July 1909): 183–86.

"Bird-Cities-of-Refuge," *Bird-Lore* 12 (July 1910): 159–60.

"Little Christmas Sermon for Teachers," *Bird-Lore* 12 (November 1910): 253–54.

"Birds and Seasons in My Garden," *Bird-Lore* 13 (January 1911): 1–7; (March 1911): 67–74; (May 1911): 128–34; (July 1911): 179–86; (September 1911): 229–35; (November 1911): 279–84.

"Ruby Throated Hummingbird," *Bird-Lore* 14 (May 1912): 186–89.

"How to Make a Thrashery," *Bird-Lore* 15 (November 1913): 362–63.

"Making of Birdcraft Sanctuary," *Bird-Lore* 17 (July 1915): 263–73.

"Three Years After," *Bird-Lore* 20 (May 1918): 201–210.

"Homeland and the Birds," *Bird-Lore* 20 (November 1918): 406–8.

"Our Responsibility," *Bird-Lore* 21 (January 1919): 6–10.

"Stories from Birdcraft Sanctuary," *Bird-Lore* 24 (July 1922): 193–95; 24 (September 1922): 253–55; 25 (January 1923): 1–4; 25 (May 1923): 176–79; 25 (November 1923): 367–71; 26 (March 1924): 104–7.

"Fence and the Fox: What is a Sanctuary?" *Bird-Lore* 29 (November 1927): 403–4.

"Philosophy of a Sanctuary," *Bird-Lore* 31 (September 1929): 315–18.

"Pastoral: The Winter Rest," *Bird-Lore* 32 (January 1930): 1–3.

"Birdcraft Sanctuary," *Bird-Lore* 32 (November 1930): 401–3.

"Silver Flight: An Idyl of the Mourning Dove," *Bird-Lore* 34 (May 1932): 186–88.

"Peep o' Day," *Bird-Lore* 35 (July 1933): 199–200.

"What is a Bird Sanctuary," *Bird-Lore* 36 (July 1934): 280.

References

Lorraine Anderson, ed., *Sisters of the Earth* (New York: Vintage, 2003).

Lorraine Anderson and Thomas Edwards, eds., *At Home on This Earth: Two Centuries of U.S. Women's Nature Writing* (Hanover, NH: University Press of New England, 2002).

Anonymous, "Summer Books," *The Chautauquan* 19.4 (July 1894): 484.

Anonymous, "Current Fiction," *The Literary World* 28.1 (January 9, 1897): 12.

Anonymous, "Another Garden Story," *Current Literature* 31.6 (December 1901): 762.

Robert Finch and John Elder, eds., *Nature Writing: The Tradition in English* (New York: W.W. Norton & Company, 2002).

Linda Forbes and John Jermier, "The Institutionalization of Bird Protection," *Organization & Environment* 15.4 (December 2002): 458–65.

Karen Knowles, ed., *Celebrating the Land: Women's Nature Writings 1850–1991* (Flagstaff, AZ: Northland Publishing, 1992).

Ralph Lutts, *The Wild Animal Story* (Philadelphia: Temple University Press, 1998).

David Mazel, ed., *A Century of Early Ecocriticism* (Athens: University of Georgia Press, 2001).

Daniel Philippon, *Conserving Words: How American Nature Writers Shaped the Environmental Movement* (Athens: University of Georgia Press, 2004).

Daniel Philippon, Introduction, *The Friendship of Nature: A New England Chronicle of Birds and Flowers,* by Mabel Osgood Wright, ed. Daniel Philippon (Baltimore: Johns Hopkins University Press, 1999), 1–27.

Mabel Osgood Wright, *Birdcraft: A Field Book of Two Hundred Song, Game and Water Birds* (New York: The Macmillan Company, 1895).

Mabel Osgood Wright, *Citizen Bird: Scenes from Bird-life in Plain English for Beginners,* with Elliott Coues (New York: The Macmillan Company, 1897).

Mabel Osgood Wright, "The Conducting of Audubon Societies," *Bird-Lore* 1.2 (April 1899): 64–65.

Mabel Osgood Wright, *Flowers and Ferns in Their Haunts* (New York: The Macmillan Company, 1901).

Mabel Osgood Wright, *The Garden of a Commuter's Wife,* as Barbara (New York: The Macmillan Company, 1901).

Mabel Osgood Wright, *My New York* (New York: The Macmillan Company, 1926).

Mabel Osgood Wright, *The Friendship of Nature,* ed. Daniel Philippon (Baltimore: Johns Hopkins University Press, 1999).

Further Reading

Adams, Agatha Boyd. *Nature Writers in the United States*. Chapel Hill, NC: The University of North Carolina Extension Publication, X, 2 (April 1944).

Adams, Alexander B. *Eternal Quest: The Story of the Great Naturalists*. New York: Putnam, 1969.

Adams, Cass, ed. *The Soul Unearthed: Celebrating Wildness and Personal Renewal Through Nature*. New York: Putnam's, 1996.

Adams, Stephen. *The Best & Worst Country in the World: Perspectives on the Early Virginia Landscape*. Charlottesville: University of Virginia Press, 2001.

Adamson, Joni. *American Indian Literature, Environmental Justice, and Ecocriticism*. Tucson: University of Arizona Press, 2001.

Albanese, Catherine. *Nature Religion in America: From the Algonkian Indians to the New Age*. Chicago: University of Chicago Press, 1990.

Allister, Mark. *Refiguring the Map of Sorrow: Nature Writing and Autobiography*. Charlottesville: University Press of Virginia, 2001.

Anderson, Lorraine, ed. *Sisters of the Earth: Women's Prose and Poetry about Nature*. Second edition. New York: Vintage, 2003.

Anderson, Lorraine, and Thomas S. Edwards, eds. *At Home on This Earth: Two Centuries of U.S. Women's Nature Writing*. Hanover, NH: University of New England Press, 2002.

Armbruster, Karla, and Kathleen Wallace, eds. *Beyond Nature Writing: Expanding the Boundaries of Ecocriticism*. Charlottesville: University Press of Virginia, 2001.

Ballowe, James. "Loving the World: Nature Writers/Writing." *North Dakota Quarterly* 60.3 (Summer 1992): 72–79.

Barber, Lynn. *The Heyday of Natural History, 1820–1870*. New York: Doubleday, 1980.

Bates, Marston. *The Nature of Natural History*. New York: Scribner's, 1950.

Bateson, Gregory. *Mind and Nature: A Necessary Unity*. New York: Bantam Books, 1979.

Baym, Nina. *American Women of Letters and the Nineteenth-Century Sciences: Styles of Affiliation*. New Brunswick, NJ: Rutgers University Press, 2002.

Belsey, Catherine. *Critical Practice*. London: Methuen, 1980.

Bercovitch, Sacvan. *The Puritan Origins of the American Self*. New Haven: Yale University Press, 1975.

Bercovitch, Sacvan. *The American Jeremiad*. Madison: University of Wisconsin Press, 1978.

Bercovitch, Sacvan, gen. ed. *The Cambridge History of American Literature*, 4 volumes. Cambridge: Cambridge University Press, 1994–2002.

Bigwood, Carol. *Earth Muse: Feminism, Nature, and Art*. Philadelphia: Temple University Press, 1993.

Bennett, Michael, and David Teague, eds. *The Nature of Cities: Ecocriticism and Urban Environments*. Tucson: University of Arizona Press, 1999.

Blum, Ann Shelby. *Picturing Nature: American Nineteenth-Century Zoological Illustrations*. Princeton: Princeton University Press, 1993.

Bonta, Marsha Meyers. *Women in the Field: America's Pioneering Women Naturalists*. College Station: Texas A&M University Press, 1991.

Bonta, Marcia Meyers. *American Women Afield: Writings by Pioneering Women Naturalists*. College Station: Texas A&M University Press, 1995.

Bradford, Robert W. "Journey into Nature: American Nature Writing, 1733–1860." Dissertation, Syracuse University, 1957.

Bramwell, Anna. *Ecology in the Twentieth Century: A History*. New Haven: Yale University Press, 1989.

Branch, Michael P., ed. *Reading the Roots: American Nature Writing before Walden.* Athens: University of Georgia Press, 2004.

Branch, Michael P., Rochelle Johnson, Daniel Patterson, and Scott Slovic, eds. *Reading the Earth: New Directions in the Study of Literature and the Environment.* Moscow, ID: University of Idaho Press, 1999.

Branch, Michael P., and Daniel J. Philippon, eds. *The Height of Our Mountains: Nature Writing from Virginia's Blue Ridge Mountains and Shenandoah Valley.* Baltimore: Johns Hopkins University Press, 1998.

Brooks, Paul. *Speaking for Nature: How Literary Naturalists from Henry Thoreau to Rachel Carson Have Shaped America.* San Francisco: Sierra Club, 1980.

Brooks, Van Wyck. *The Flowering of New England 1815–1865.* New York: Dutton, 1936.

Bryant, Paul T. "Nature as Picture/Nature as Milieu." *CEA-Critic* 54.1 (Fall 1991): 22–34.

Bryson, Michael A. *Visions of the Land: Science, Literature, and the American Environment from the Era of Exploration to the Age of Ecology.* Charlottesville: University Press of Virginia, 2002.

Buell, Lawrence. *New England Literary Culture from Revolution through Renaissance.* New York: Cambridge University Press, 1986.

Buell, Lawrence. *The Environmental Imagination: Thoreau, Nature Writing, and the Formation of American Culture.* Cambridge, MA: Harvard University Press, 1995.

Buell, Lawrence. "The Ecocritical Insurgency." *New Literary History* 30.3 (Summer 1999): 699–712.

Buell, Lawrence. "Environment and the Literary Landscape." *Chronicle of Higher Education* 47(38) (2001 June 1): B15.

Buell, Lawrence. *Writing for an Endangered World: Literature, Culture, and the Environment in the U.S. and Beyond.* Cambridge: Harvard University Press, 2001.

Burton, Katherine. *Paradise Planters: The Story of Brook Farm.* London: Longmans, Green, 1939.

Callicott, J. Baird. "Hume's Is/Ought Dichotomy and the Relation of Ecology to Leopold's Land Ethic." *Environmental Ethics* 4 (1982): 163–74.

Callicott, J. Baird, and Roger T. Ames, eds. *Nature in Asian Traditions of Thought.* Albany: State University of New York Press, 1989.

Carroll, Joseph. *Evolution and Literary Theory.* Columbia: University of Missouri Press, 1995.

Carroll, Peter N. *Puritanism and the Wilderness: The Intellectual Significance of the New England Frontier, 1629–1700.* New York: Columbia University Press, 1969.

Cartmill, Matt. *A View to a Death in the Morning: Hunting and Nature through History.* Cambridge: Harvard University Press, 1993.

Cason, Jacqueline J. "Nature Writer as Storyteller: The Nature Essay as a Literary Genre." *CEA-Critic* 54.1 (Fall 1991): 12–18.

Clemmons, Linda M. "'Nature Was Her Lady's Book': Ladies' Magazines, American Indians, and Gender, 1820–1859." *American Periodicals* 5 (1995): 40–58.

Clough, Wilson O. *The Necessary Earth; Nature and Solitude in American Literature.* Austin: University of Texas Press, 1964.

Coates, Peter. *Nature: Western Attitudes Since Ancient Times.* Berkeley: University of California Press, 1998.

Conlogue, William. *Working the Garden: American Writers and the Industrialization of Agriculture.* Chapel Hill: University of North Carolina Press, 2001.

Cooley, John. ed. *Earthly Words: Essays on Contemporary American Nature and Environmental Writers.* Ann Arbor: University of Michigan Press, 1994.

Cotgrove, Stephen. *Catastrophe or Cornucopia.* Chicester: John Wiley & Sons, 1982.

Cowley, Malcolm. "Naturalism in American Literature." reprinted in *Evolutionary Thought in America,* edited by Stow Persons. New York: George Braziller, 1956.

Cronon, William. *Changes in the Land: Indians, Colonists, and the Ecology of Colonial New England.* New York: Hill and Wang, 1983.

Cronon, William. "A Place for Stories: Nature, History, and Narrative." *Journal of American History* (1992): 1347–1346.

Cronon, William, ed. *Nature Writings.* New York: Library of America, 1997.

Daniels, Stephen. *Fields of Vision: Landscape Imagery and National Identity in England and the United States.* Princeton, NJ: Princeton University Press, 1993.

Dean, John. "The Uses of Wilderness in American Science Fiction." *Science Fiction Studies* 9:1 (26) (1982 March): 68–81.

Denall, Bill, and George Sessions. *Deep Ecology.* Salt Lake City: Gibbs Smith, 1985.

Dixon, Melvin. *Ride Out the Wilderness: Geography and Identity in Afro-American Literature.* Urbana: University of Illinois Press, 1987.

Dunsmore, Roger. "Earth's Mind," *Studies in American Indian Literature* 10 (1986 Fall): 187–202.

Edwards, Thomas S., and Elizabeth A. DeWolfe, eds. *Such News of the Land: U.S. Women Nature*

Writers. Hanover, NH: University Press of New England, 2001.

Egerton, Frank N., ed. *History of American Ecology*. New York: Arno Press, 1977.

Ekrich, Arthur A., Jr. *Man and Nature in America*. New York: Columbia University Press, 1963.

Elder, John, ed. *American Nature Writers*. Two volumes. New York: Scribner's, 1996.

Elgin, Don D. "What is Literary Ecology?" *Humanities in the South: Newsletter of the Southern Humanities Council* 57 (Spring 1983): 7–9.

Elgin, Don D. *The Comedy of the Fantastic: Ecological Perspectives on the Fantasy Novel*. Westport, CT: Greenwood Press, 1985.

Elliot, Emory, gen. ed. *Columbia Literary History of the United States*. New York: Columbia University Press, 1988.

Elman, Robert. *First in the Field: America's Pioneering Naturalists*. New York: Mason/Charter, 1977.

Evans, Howard Ensign. *Pioneer Naturalists: The Discovery and Naming of North American Plants and Animals*. New York: Henry Holt and Company, 1993.

Farber, Paul Lawrence. *Finding Order in Nature: The Naturalist Tradition from Linnaeus to E.O. Wilson*. Baltimore: Johns Hopkins University Press, 2000.

Finch, Robert, and John Elder, eds. *The Norton Book of Nature Writing*. New York: Norton, 1990.

Fitter, Chris. *Poetry, Space, Landscape: Toward a New Theory*. New York: Cambridge University Press, 1995.

Foerster, Norman. *Nature in American Literature: Studies in the Modern View of Nature*. New York: Russell & Russell, 1923.

Foster, Edward Halsey. *The Civilized Wilderness: Backgrounds to American Romantic Literature, 1817–1860*. New York: Free Press, 1875.

Fowles, John. "Seeing Nature Whole." *Harper's* 259 (November 1979): 66.

Francis, Richard. *Transcendental Utopias: Individual and Community at Brook Farm, Fruitlands, and Walden*. Ithaca, NY: Cornell University Press, 1997.

Franklin, Wayne. *Discoverers, Explorers, Settlers: The Diligent Writers of Early America*. Chicago: University of Chicago Press, 1979.

Franklin, Wayne, and Michael Steiner. *Mapping American Culture*. Iowa City: University of Iowa Press, 1992.

Fritzell, Peter. *Nature Writing and America: Essays Upon a Cultural Type*. Ames: Iowa State University Press, 1990.

Frothingham, Octavius Brooks. *Transcendentalism in New England: A History*. New York: Putnam, 1876.

Fussell, Edwin. *Frontier: American Literature and the American West*. Princeton: Princeton University Press, 1965.

Gangewere, Robert J., ed. *The Exploited Eden: Literature on the American Environment*. New York: Harper & Row, 1972.

Glotfelty, Cheryll, and Harold Fromm, eds. *The Ecocriticism Reader: Landmarks in Literary Ecology*. Athens: University of Georgia Press, 1996.

Goetzmann, William H. *Exploration and Empire: The Explorer and the Scientist in the Winning of the American West*. Austin: Texas State Historical Association, 1993.

Hall, Dewey W. "From Edwards to Emerson: A Study of the Teleology of Nature." *Early Protestantism and American Culture*, edited by Michael Schuldiner. Lewiston, NY: Mellen, 1995.

Hallock, Thomas. *From the Fallen Tree: Frontier Narratives, Environmental Politics, and the Roots of a National Pastoral, 1743–1826*. Chapel Hill: University of North Carolina Press, 2003.

Halprin, Lawrence. "Nature into Landscape into Art." *Landscape in America*, edited by George F. Thompson and Charles E. Little, 241–50. Austin: University of Texas Press, 1995.

Hanley, Wayne. *Natural History in America: From Mark Catesby to Rachel Carson*. New York: Quadrangle, 1977.

Harris, Wendell V. "Toward an Ecological Criticism: Contextual Versus Unconditional Literary Theory." *College English* 48:2 (1986 February): 116–131.

Hazard, L.L. *The Frontier in American Literature*. Chicago: Cornwell, 1927.

Henly, Don, and Dave Marsh, eds. *Heaven is Under Our Feet*. New York: Berkley, 1991.

Hicks, Philip Marshal. *The Development of the Natural History Essay in American Literature*. Philadelphia: University of Pennsylvania Press, 1924.

Hilbert, Betsy, ed. "The Literature of Nature." *CEA-Critic* 54.1 (Fall 1991). Special Edition.

Hitt, Christopher. "Toward an Ecological Sublime." *New Literary History* 30.3 (Summer 1999): 603–23.

Hodder, Alan. *Emerson's Rhetoric of Revelation: Nature, the Reader, and the Apocalypse Within*. University Park: Pennsylvania State University Press, 1989.

Hodder, Alan. *Thoreau's Ecstatic Witness*. New Haven: Yale University Press, 2001.

Hoffman, Michael J. *The Subversive Vision: American Romanticism in Literature.* Port Washington, NY: Kennikat Press, 1972.

Hogan, Linda, and Brenda Peterson, eds. *The Sweet Breathing of Plants: Women Writing on the Green World.* New York: North Point Press, 2001.

Howarth, William. "Literature of Place, Environmental Writers." *Isle* 1.1 (Spring 1993): 167–78.

Howarth, William. "Thoreau and the Cultural Construction of Nature." *Isle* 2.1 (Spring 1994): 85–89.

Howarth, William. "Ego or Eco Criticism? Looking for Common Ground." *Reading the Earth: New Directions in the Study of Literature and Environment,* edited by Michael P. Branch et al., 3–8. Moscow, ID: University of Idaho Press, 1998.

Howarth, William. "Imagined Territory: The Writing of Wetlands." *New Literary History* 30.3 (Summer 1999): 509–39.

Huth, Hans. *Nature and the American: Three Centuries of Changing Attitudes.* Berkeley: University of California Press, 1957.

Hyde, Anne Farrar. *An American Vision: Far Western Landscape and National Culture, 1820–1920.* New York: New York University Press, 1990.

Irmscher, Christoph. *The Poetics of Natural History: From John Bartram to William James.* New Brunswick: Rutgers University Press, 1999.

Jenkins, Alan C. *The Naturalists: Pioneers of Natural History.* New York: Mayflower, 1978.

Kastner, Joseph. *A Species of Eternity.* New York: Knopf, 1977.

Katz, Eric. *Nature as Subject: Human Obligation and Natural Community.* Lanham, MD: Rowman & Littlefield, 1997.

Keeney, Elizabeth B. *The Botanizers: American Scientists in Nineteenth-Century America.* Chapel Hill: University of North Carolina Press, 1992.

Keith, W. J. *The Poetry of Nature: Rural Perspectives in Poetry from Wordsworth to the Present.* Toronto: University of Toronto Press, 1980.

Kerridge, Richard, and Neil Sammells, eds. *Writing the Environment: Ecocriticism and Literature.* London: Zed, 1998.

Killingworth, M. Jimmie, and Jacqueline S. Palmer. *Ecospeak: Rhetoric and Environmental Politics in America.* Carbondale: Southern Illinois University Press, 1992.

Knott, John R. *Imagining Wild America: Wilderness and Wildness in the Writings of John James Audubon, Henry David Thoreau, John Muir, Edward Abbey, Wendell Berry and Mary Oliver.* Ann Arbor: University of Michigan Press, 2002.

Kollin, Susan. *Nature's State: Imagining Alaska and the Last Frontier.* Chapel Hill: University of North Carolina Press, 2001.

Kolodny, Annette. *The Lay of the Land: Metaphor as Experience and History in American Life and Letters.* Chapel Hill: University of North Carolina Press, 1975.

Kolodny, Annette. *The Land Before Her: Fantasy and Experience of the American Frontiers, 1630–1860.* Chapel Hill: University of North Carolina Press, 1984.

Kroeber, Karl. *Ecological Literary Criticism: Romantic Imagining and the Biology of Mind.* New York: Columbia University Press, 1994.

Krutch, Joseph Wood, ed. *Great American Nature Writing.* New York: William Sloane, 1950.

Langbaum, Robert. "The New Nature Poetry." In his *The Modern Spirit: Essays on the Continuity of Nineteenth- and Twentieth-Century Literature.* New York: Oxford University Press, 1970.

Larson, James. *Interpreting Nature: The Science of Living Form from Linnaeus to Kant.* Baltimore: Johns Hopkins University Press, 1994.

Lawson-Peebles, Robert. *Landscape and Written Expression in Revolutionary America: The World Turned Upside Down.* Cambridge: Cambridge University Press, 1988.

Lewis, R.W.B. *The American Adam: Innocence, Tragedy, and Tradition in the Nineteenth Century.* Chicago: University of Chicago Press, 1955.

Locke, David. *Science as Writing.* New Haven: Yale University Press, 1992.

Love, Glen A. "Revaluing Nature: Toward an Ecological Criticism." *Western American Literature* 25 (1990): 201–15.

Love, Glen A. "Ecocriticism and Science: Toward Consilience?" *New Literary History* 30.3 (Summer 1999): 561–76.

Love, Glen A. *Practical Ecocriticism: Literature, Biology, and the Environment.* Charlottesville: University of Virginia Press, 2003.

Low, Anthony. *The Georgic Revolution.* Princeton, NJ: Princeton University Press, 1985.

Luke, Timothy W. "On Environmentality: Geo-Power and Eco-Knowledge in the Discourses of Contemporary Environmentalism." *Cultural Critique* 31 (Fall 1995): 57–81.

Lutwack, Leonard. *The Role of Place in Literature.* Syracuse: Syracuse University Press, 1984.

Lyon, Thomas J. *This Incomperable Lande: A Book of American Nature Writing.* Boston: Houghton Mifflin, 1989.

Malamud, Randy. *Reading Zoos: Representations of Animals and Captivity.* New York: New York University Press, 1998.

Marx, Leo. *The Machine in the Garden: Technology and the Pastoral Ideal in America.* New York: Oxford University Press, 1964.

Matthiessen, F.O. *American Renaissance: Art and Expression in the Age of Emerson and Whitman.* New York: Oxford University Press, 1941.

Mazel, David. *American Literary Environmentalism.* Athens: University of Georgia Press, 2000.

Mazel, David, ed. *A Century of Early Ecocritism.* Athens: University of Georgia Press, 2001.

McKusick, James. *Green Writing: Romanticism and Ecology.* New York: St. Martins, 2000.

Meeker, Joseph W. *The Comedy of Survival: Studies in Literary Ecology.* New York: Scribner's, 1972.

Meisel, Max. *A Bibliography of American Natural History: The Pioneer Century, 1769–1865.* 3 volumes. Brooklyn, NY: Premier, 1924–1929.

Mendelson, Donna. "'Transparent Overlay Maps': Layers of Place Knowledge in Human Geography and Ecocriticism." *Interdisciplinary Literary Studies* 1.1 (Fall 1999): 81–96.

Merchant, Carolyn. *The Columbia Guide to American Environmental History.* New York: Columbia University Press, 2002.

Merchant, Carolyn. *Ecological Revolutions: Nature, Gender, and Science in New England.* Chapel Hill: University of North Carolina Press, 1989.

Meyers, Amy R. *Art and Science in America: Issues of Representation.* San Marino: Huntington Library Press, 1998.

Miall, Louis Compton. *The Early Naturalists: Their Lives and Work (1530–1789).* London: Macmillan, 1912.

Miller, Perry. *Nature's Nation.* Cambridge, MA: Harvard University Press, 1967.

Mitchell, Lee Clark. *Witnesses to a Vanishing America: The Nineteenth-Century Response.* Princeton: Princeton University Press, 1981.

Mumford, Lewis. *The Golden Day: A Study in American Experience and Culture.* New York: Boni & Liveright, 1926.

Murphy, Patrick D. *Literature, Nature, and Other: Ecofeminist Critiques.* Albany: SUNY Press, 1995.

Murphy, Patrick D., ed. *Literature of Nature: An International Sourcebook.* Chicago: Fitzroy Dearborn, 1998.

Murphy, Patrick D. *Farther Afield in the Study of Nature-Oriented Literature.* Charlottesville: University Press of Virginia, 2000.

Naess, Arne. "The Shallow and the Deep, Long-Range Ecology Movement: A Summary." *Inquiry* 16 (1973): 95–100.

Nash, Roderick. *Wilderness and the American Mind.* New Haven: Yale University Press, 1967.

Nash, Roderick. *The Rights of Nature: A History of Environmental Ethics.* Madison: University of Wisconsin Press, 1989.

Newman, Lance. "The Politics of Ecocriticism." *Review* 20 (1998): 59–72.

Newton, L.H., and C.K. Dillingham. *Watersheds: Classic Cases in Environmental Ethics.* Belmont, CA: Wadsworth, 1994.

Norwood, Vera. *Made from This Earth: American Women and Nature.* Chapel Hill: University of North Carolina Press, 1993.

Novak, Barbara. *Nature and Culture: American Landscape and Painting, 1825–1875,* revised edition. New York: Oxford University Press, 1995.

Oelschlaeger, Max. *The Idea of Wilderness from Prehistory to the Age of Ecology.* New Haven: Yale University Press, 1991.

O'Grady, John P. *Pilgrims to the Wild: Everett Ruess, Henry David Thoreau, John Muir, Clarence King, Mary Austin.* Salt Lake City: University of Utah Press, 1993.

Pachter, Marc, and Frances Wein, eds. *Abroad in America: Visitors to the New Nation, 1776–1914.* Reading, MA: Addison-Wesley, 1976.

Parrington, Vernon Lewis. *The Romantic Revolution in America 1800–1860.* New York: Harcourt, Brace, 1927.

Parrish, Susan Scott. *American Curiosity: Cultures of Natural History in the Colonial British Atlantic World.* Chapel Hill: University of North Carolina Press, 2006.

Pattee, Fred Lewis. *The First Century of American Literature 1770–1870.* New York: Appleton-Century, 1935.

Paul, Sherman. *For the Love of the World: Essays on Nature Writers.* Iowa City: University of Iowa Press, 1992.

Payne, Daniel G. *Voices in the Wilderness: American Nature Writing and Environmental Politics.* Hanover, NH: University Press of New England, 1996.

Peattie, Donald Culross. *Green Laurels: The Lives and Achievements of the Great Naturalists.* New York: Simon and Schuster, 1936.

Persons, Stow. *American Minds: A History of Ideas.* New York: Holt, 1958.

Phillips, Dana. "Ecocriticism, Literary Theory, and the Truth of Ecology." *New Literary History* 30.3 (Summer 1999): 577–602.

Pojman, Louis P., ed. *Environmental Ethics: Readings in Theory and Application*. 2nd ed. Belmont, CA: Wadsworth, 1998.

Porter, Charlotte. *The Eagle's Nest: Natural History and American Ideas, 1812–1842*. Tuscaloosa: University of Alabama Press, 1986.

Rankin, Richard, ed. *North Carolina Nature Writing: Four Centuries of Personal Narratives and Descriptions*. Winston-Salem: John F. Blair, Publisher, 1996.

Regis, Pamela. *Describing Early America: Bartram, Jefferson, Crèvecoeur, and the Rhetoric of Natural History*. DeKalb: Northern Illinois University Press, 1992.

Richardson, Robert D., Jr. *Myth and Literature in the American Renaissance*. Bloomington: Indiana University Press, 1978.

Rogers, Robert Emmons. *The Voice of Science in Nineteenth-Century Literature*. Boston: Atlantic Monthly Press, 1921.

Rosen, Susan A.C., ed. *Shorewords: A Collection of American Women's Coastal Writings*. Charlottesville: University of Virginia Press, 2003.

Rosendale, Steven, ed. *The Greening of Literary Scholarship: Literature, Theory, and the Environment*. Iowa City: University of Iowa Press, 2002.

Rosenthal, Bernard. *City of Nature: Journeys to Nature in the Age of American Romanticism*. Newark: University of Delaware Press, 1980.

Ross, Carolyn. *Writing Nature: An Ecological Reader for Writers*. New York: St. Martin's Press, 1995.

Ross-Bryant, Lynn. "The Self in Nature: Four American Autobiographies." *Soundings* 80.1 (Spring 1997): 83–104.

Ryden, Kent C. *Mapping the Invisible Landscape: Folklore, Writing, and the Sense of Place*. Iowa City: University or Iowa Press, 1993.

Ryden, Kent C. "Landscape with Figures: Nature, Folk Culture, and the Human Ecology of American Environmental Writing." *Isle* 4.1 (Spring 1997): 1–28.

Savage, Henry, Jr. *Lost Heritage: Wilderness America through the Eyes of Seven Pre-Audubon Naturalists*. New York: William Morrow, 1970.

Savage, Henry, Jr. *Discovering America, 1700–1875*. New York: Harper and Row, 1979.

Schama, Simon. *Landscape and Memory*. New York: Knopf, 1995.

Schmitt, Peter J. *Back to Nature: The Arcadian Myth in Urban America*. New York: Oxford University Press, 1969.

Schweighauser, Charles A. "'Know Thyself' Study Nature: The Contemporary Scientist's Dilemma."

The Delegated Intellect: Emersonian Essays on Literature, Science, and Art in Honor of Don Gifford, edited by Donald E. Morse, 109–24. New York: Peter Lang, 1995.

Schweninger, Lee. "Writing Nature: Silko and Native Americans as Nature Writers." *MELUS* 18.2 (1993): 47–60.

Sears, John F. *Sacred Places: American Tourist Attractions in the Nineteenth Century*. New York: Oxford University Press, 1989.

Seelye, John. *Prophetic Waters: The River in Early American Life and Literature*. New York: Oxford University Press, 1977.

Seelye, John. *Beautiful Machine: Rivers and the Republican Plan: 1755–1825*. New York: Oxford University Press, 1991.

Serafin, Steven R., gen. ed. *Encyclopedia of American Literature*. New York: Continuum, 1999.

Shepard, Paul. *Man in the Landscape: A Historic View of the Esthetics of Nature*. New York: Ballantine, 1967.

Shi, David. *The Simple Life: Plain Living and High Thinking in American Culture*. New York: Oxford University Press, 1985.

Sibum, Heinz O. "The Bookkeeper of Nature: Benjamin Franklin's Electrical Research and the Development of Experimental Natural Philosophy in the Eighteenth Century." *Reappraising Benjamin Franklin: A Bicentennial Perspective*, edited by J.A. Leo Lemay, 221–42. Newark: University of Delaware Press, 1993.

Slotkin, Richard. *Regeneration through Violence: The Mythology of the American Frontier, 1600–1860*. Middletown, CT: Wesleyan University Press, 1973.

Slovic, Scott. *Seeking Awareness in American Nature Writing: Henry Thoreau, Annie Dillard, Edward Abbey, Wendell Berry, Barry Lopez*. Salt Lake City: University of Utah Press, 1992.

Slovic, Scott. "Nature Writing and Environmental Psychology: The Interiority of Outdoor Experience." *The Ecocriticism Reader: Landmarks in Literary Ecology*, edited by Cheryll Glotfelty and Harold Fromm, 351–70. Athens: University of Georgia Press, 1996.

Slovic, Scott, ed. *Getting over the Color Green: Contemporary Environmental Literature of the Southwest*. Tucson: University of Arizona Press, 2001.

Smallwood, William Martin, and Mabel Sarah Coon Smallwood. *Natural History and the American Mind*. New York: Columbia Press, 1941.

Smith, Henry Nash. *Virgin Land: The American West as Symbol and Myth*. New York: Vintage Books, 1957.

Smithline, Arnold. *Natural Religion and American Literature*. New Haven, CT: College and University Press, 1966.

Soule, Michael E., ed. *Reinventing Nature?: Responses to Postmodern Deconstruction*. Washington, DC: Island Press, 1995.

Spiller, Robert E. *The Cycle of American Literature*. New York: Macmillan, 1956.

Spiller, Robert E., and others. *Literary History of the United States*, 2 volumes, 4th edition, revised. New York: Macmillan, 1974.

Spirn, Anne Whiston. *The Granite Garden: Urban Nature and Human Design*. New York: Basic Books, 1984.

Spirn, Anne Whiston. *The Language of Landscape*. New Haven: Yale University Press, 1998.

St. Armand, Barton L. "The Book of Nature and American Nature Writing: Codex, Index, Contexts, Prospects." *Isle* 4.1 (Spring 1997): 29–42.

Stearns, Raymond Phineas. *Science in the British Colonies of America*. Urbana: University of Illinois Press, 1970.

Steinberg, Ted. *Down to Earth: Nature's Role in American History*. New York: Oxford University Press, 2002.

Stewart, Frank. *A Natural History of Nature Writing*. Washington, D.C.; Covelo, CA: Island; Shearwater, 1995.

Stuckey, Ronald L. *Development of Botany in Selected Regions of North America before 1900*. New York: Arno Press, 1978.

Sweet, Timothy. *American Georgics: Economy and Environment in Early American Literature, 1580–1864*. Philadelphia: University of Pennsylvania Press, 2002.

Tallmadge, John, and Henry Harrington, eds. *Reading Under the Sign of Nature: New Essays in Ecocriticim*. Salt Lake City: University of Utah Press, 2000.

Taplin, Kim. *Tongues in Trees: Studies in Literature and Ecology*. Bideford, Devon: Green Books, 1996.

Taylor, David, ed. *South Carolina Naturalists: An Anthology, 1700–1860*. Columbia: University of South Carolina Press, 1996.

Teague, David W. *The Southwest in American Literature and Art: The Rise of a Desert Aesthetic*. Tucson: University of Arizona Press, 1997.

Thacker, Robert. *The Great Prairie Fact and Literary Imagination*. Albuquerque: University of New Mexico Press, 1989.

Thomas, Keith. *Man and the Natural World: A History of the Modern Sensibility*. New York: Pantheon, 1983.

Tichi, Cecelia. *New World, New Earth: Environmental Reform in American Literature from the Puritans through Whitman*. New Haven: Yale University Press, 1979.

Tidwell, Paul L. "Academic Campfire Stories: Thoreau, Ecocriticism, and the Fetishism of Nature." *Isle* 2.1 (Spring 1994): 53–64.

Tinling, Marion, ed. *With Women's Eyes: Visitors to the New World, 1775–1918*. Norman: University of Oklahoma Press, 1993.

Tuan, Yi-fu. *Topophilia: A Study of Environmental Perception, Attitudes, and Values*. New York: Columbia, 1990.

Tucher, Andrea J. *Natural History in America, 1609–1860; Printed Works in the Collections of the American Philosophical Society, the Historical Society of Pennsylvania, the Library Company of Philadelphia*. New York: Garland, 1985.

Tucker, Herbert F. "Ecocriticism." *New Literary History* 30.3 (Summer 1999). Special Edition.

Turner, Frederick. *Spirit of Place: The Making of an American Literary Landscape*. San Francisco: Sierra Club, 1989.

Ulman, H. Lewis. "Seeing, Believing, Being, and Acting: Ethics and Self-Representation in Ecocriticism and Nature Writing." *Reading the Earth: New Directions in the Study of Literature and Environment*, edited by Michael P. Branch et al., 225-33. Moscow, ID: University of Idaho Press, 1998.

Vogel, Steven. *Against Nature: The Concept of Nature in Critical Theory*. New York: State University of New York Press, 1996.

Wall, Derek, ed. *Green History: A Reader in Environmental Literature, Philopsophy and Politics*. London: Routledge, 1993.

Walls, Laura Dassow. *Seeing New Worlds: Henry David Thoreau and Nineteenth-Century Natural Science*. Madison: University of Wisconsin Press, 1995.

Welch, Margaret. *The Book of Nature: Natural History in the United States, 1825–1875*. Boston: Northeastern University Press, 1998.

Wendell, Barrett. *A Literary History of America*. New York: Scribner's, 1900.

West, Michael. *Transcendental Wordplay: America's Romantic Punsters & the Search for the Language of Nature*. Athens: Ohio University Press, 2000.

Westbrook, Perry D. *A Literary History of New England*. Bethlehem, PA: Lehigh University Press, 1988.

Westling, Louise H. *The Green Breast of the New World: Landscape, Gender, and American Fiction*. Athens: University of Georgia Press, 1998.

White, Morton. *Science and Sentiment in America.* New York: Oxford University Press, 1972.

Wilson, Alexander. *The Culture of Nature: North American Landscape from Disney to the Exxon Valdez.* New York: Between the Lines, 2001.

Wilson, David Schofield. *In the Presence of Nature.* Amherst: University of Massachusetts Press, 1978.

Wilson, Eric. *Romantic Turbulence: Chaos, Ecology, and American Space.* New York: St. Martins, 2000.

Wilson, E.O. *Biophilia.* Boston: Harvard University Press, 1986.

Worster, Donald. *Nature's Economy: A History of Ecological Ideas.* Cambridge: Cambridge University Press, 1977.

Index

About the Editors and Contributors

THE EDITOR

Daniel Patterson is an early Americanist in the English Department of Central Michigan University, where he teaches a variety of courses that investigate manifestations of environmental awareness and conceptions of nature in cultural forms. His scholarship grows from this intellectual center. Currently he is preparing a new edition of Audubon's 1826 Journal.

THE CONTRIBUTING EDITORS

Scott Bryson (Mount St. Mary's College in Los Angeles) is the author of *The West Side of Any Mountain: Place, Space, and Ecopoetry* (University of Iowa Press, 2005). He has also edited or co-edited several collections of criticism on nature writing. His current scholarship focuses on urban theory and Los Angeles literature.

Roger Thompson is Associate Professor of English and Fine Arts at VMI. He is co-editor of several books, and his work on American literature and rhetoric has appeared in *College English* and *Pedagogy*.

THE CONTRIBUTORS

Elizabeth Addison, PhD Duke University, is active in the Ralph Waldo Emerson Society and has been working on Emerson and his Quaker contacts for more than 25 years. She teaches American literature and heads the Department of English at Western Carolina University.

Jennifer Dawes Adkison is Assistant Professor of English at Idaho State University. She has published on topics ranging from nineteenth-century nature writer Susan Fenimore Cooper to authenticity in twentieth-century depictions of Western women. She recently completed a new scholarly edition of '49er Sarah Royce's memoir of life on the overland trail and in early California.

Patricia Kennedy Bostian teaches at Central Piedmont Community College in Charlotte, North Carolina. Recent scholarship has appeared in *The Critical Companion to Henry James*, *World Popular Culture*, and *Reading in America Today*. She is the editor of *Teaching American Literature: A Journal of Theory and Practice* and *The Wild Goose Poetry Review*.

Michael P. Branch is Professor of Literature and Environment and Director of Graduate Studies at the University of Nevada, Reno. He has published five books and more than 100 articles, essays, and reviews on American environmental literature. His most recent book is *Reading the Roots: American Nature*

Writing before Walden (University of Georgia Press, 2004).

Angela Courtney is the Librarian for English Literatures, Theatre, Film Studies, and Philosophy at Indiana University, Bloomington. She is currently writing research guides on American Nationalism and Romanticism and the literature of Australia and New Zealand for the Scarecrow Press series, *Literary Research: Strategies and Sources*.

John D. Cox, Assistant Professor of English at Georgia College & State University, is the author of *Traveling South: Travel Narratives and the Construction of American Identity*, published by the University of Georgia Press in 2005. He currently serves as the Director of the Center for Georgia Studies and is Associate Editor of the *Flannery O'Connor Review*.

Kevin De Ornellas lectures on English and American literature and ecocriticism at the University of Ulster.

Winter Elliott is currently Assistant Professor of English at Brenau University in Gainesville, Georgia. Her interests include Medieval and Early Modern literature and early American writers.

Patrick M. Erben is completing a manuscript entitled "A Harmony of the Spirits: Multilingualism, Translation, and the Language of Community in Early Pennsylvania." He teaches early American literature at the University of West Georgia. His upcoming projects include a selective edition of Francis Daniel Pastorius's manuscripts and a monograph on the formation of a "German Atlantic World."

David Finney is a novelist currently completing graduate work in fiction at Johns Hopkins University. He has also published journalism and nonfiction. He graduated from Yale University with a degree in English literature and creative writing. For his work on Clarence King, Finney was awarded an Elmore A. Willets Prize.

E. Frances Frame is Associate Professor of English at The Citadel in Charleston, South Carolina. Her 2007 publications include "Anxious Allusions: The Bible in Thomas Carlyle's Correspondence" in *Literature and Belief* and an article on Matthew Arnold in *Victorian Poetry*. Her book, *Thomas and Jane Welsh Carlyle*, will appear in 2008.

April D. Gentry is Assistant Professor of American literature at Savannah State University. She received her PhD from Southern Illinois University in 2003 and also holds an MA from Ohio University (1998) and a BA from MacMurray College (1996). Her research interests include gender studies, nineteenth- and twentieth-century American literature and culture, and postcolonial studies.

Tina Gianquitto is Assistant Professor of English at the Colorado School of Mines. She authored *Good Observers of Nature: American Women and the Scientific Study of the Natural World, 1820–1885* and is currently working on a book, *Dear Mr. Darwin: Women and the Epistolary Tradition in the Nineteenth-Century Sciences*.

Donald M. Hassler is Professor of English at Kent State University. He is executive editor of the journal *EXTRAPOLATION*, which is devoted to the study of modern science fiction. He has published books on Erasmus Darwin, Isaac Asimov, and the lesser-known science fiction writer Hal Clement.

Christine Marie Hilger is a doctoral student at Texas Women's University and a lecturer in rhetoric at Southern Methodist University.

Tom J. Hillard is Assistant Professor of English at Boise State University and Co-Editor of the Boise State University Western Writers Series. His research interests include early American nature writing, western American literature, and the literary Gothic. He is working on a book about fears of nature in American literature and culture.

Christoph Irmscher is Professor of English and Adjunct Professor of American Studies at Indiana University, Bloomington. He is the author of several books, among them *The Poetics of Natural History* and *Longfellow Redux*, and has edited *Audubon's Writings and Drawings*. His work in progress is a biography of Louis Agassiz.

Peter T. Koper is Professor of English at Central Michigan University, where he teaches writing, classics in translation, and university program courses in the humanities. His research interests include the history of rhetoric, the work of René Girard, and the American tradition of nature writing.

James Kraus is Professor of English at Chaminade University in Honolulu. His critical work and poetry have appeared in *American Writers, Virginia Quarterly Review, Pequod, Bamboo Ridge*, and elsewhere. He is currently editor of *Chaminade Literary Review* and working on a book project, "Poetry and the Ethics of Ecology."

Deborah Lawrence is the author of *Writing the Trail: Five Women's Frontier Narratives* (University of Iowa Press, 2006). She is currently working on a collection of interviews with authors of western expansion.

Kim Leeder is Reference Librarian at Albertson College of Idaho in Caldwell. In addition to an MLS, she holds a Master's degree in Literature and Environment (English) from the University of Nevada, Reno, where she wrote a thesis on the exploration journals of John C. Frémont.

Anne-Marie Libério is a doctoral student in American Studies and Brazilian History at Paris IV–Sorbonne. Her research compares the interactions between Native groups and missionaries in the Atlantic regions of the United States and Brazil from the 1640s to the 1830s.

Paul Lindholdt is Professor of English at Eastern Washington University, where he teaches literary studies. His recent work includes *The Canoe and the Saddle: A Critical Edition* (University of Nebraska Press, 2006), a novelized memoir by Theodore Winthrop set in the Cascades during the early months of the Washington Territory.

Nancy McKinney is an independent scholar living in Taylorville, Illinois. She earned BA and MA degrees in English from the University of Illinois at Springfield and has done graduate study at Southern Illinois University, Carbondale. She currently teaches English as an adjunct instructor at area colleges.

Bryan L. Moore is Associate Professor of English at Arkansas State University. He has published articles on Robinson Jeffers, Edward Abbey, and Charles Portis as well as pieces of rhetorical criticism and reference articles. He is currently completing his first book. Bryan lives in Jonesboro, Arkansas, with his wife, two children, and many animals.

Melissa Moore holds an MA in English Language and Literature from Central Michigan University. She has written for *The Dictionary of Literary Biography* and *Foreward Magazine*.

Tom Murphy is Associate Professor of English at Mansfield University of Pennsylvania. Beginning as a medievalist, he discovered nature writing almost 20 years ago when he moved to the rural mountains of northern Pennsylvania. He writes nature essays and teaches both the literature and craft of nature writing.

Katrina Neckuty resides in Rochester, Minnesota, and is a Student Service Coordinator for the Minnesota School of Business. She completed her MA in English, with an emphasis in Literature and the Environment, at the University of Nevada, Reno, in 2004.

In her free time, Kat enjoys exploring the north shore of Minnesota.

Stuart Noble-Goodman earned his undergraduate degree in English at UC-Berkeley and a PhD in American Literature from Duke. His research interests include Robinson Jeffers, Emerson, and the rhetorical strategies of environmental nonfiction. A member of the Center for Environmental Studies, he currently serves as dean of the School of Business at the University of Redlands.

Mary DeJong Obuchowski is a retired Professor of English at Central Michigan University. She has written mainly on Midwestern and women writers who are also environmentalists, and is the editor of *Field o' Dreams: The Collected Poems of Gene Stratton-Porter*. She lives in Mt. Pleasant, Michigan, with her husband and two sons.

Kevin E. O'Donnell teaches English and directs the Environmental Studies minor at East Tennessee State University. He is co-editor of *Seekers of Scenery: Travel Writing from Southern Appalachia, 1840–1900* (University of Tennessee Press, 2004).

Thomas Patchell co-edited *Veterans of War Veterans of Peace* with Maxine Hong Kingston. He teaches creative writing and composition at Cuesta College in California.

Linda Elizabeth Peterson teaches composition at Central Michigan University. Her essays of memoir and place can be found in the anthologies *Black Earth and Ivory Tower: New American Essays from Field and Classroom* and *What Wildness Is This: Women Write About the Southwest*.

Bernie Quetchenbach is the author of *Back from the Far Field: American Nature Poetry in the Late Twentieth Century* and a number of poems, essays, and critical articles. He is an assistant professor of English at Montana State University–Billings.

Jessie Ravage is a historical research consultant residing in Cooperstown, New York. She specializes in nineteenth-century vernacular architecture, especially agricultural and resort buildings. She wrote her master's thesis on nineteenth-century authors, including Celia Thaxter, who popularized the Piscataqua region in New Hampshire and Maine as a summer retreat.

Susan A.C. Rosen is Professor of English and Women's Studies at Anne Arundel Community College. She lives by the Little Magothy River near where Dr. John Godman took some of his rambles. She is also the editor of *Shorewords: A Collection of American Women's Coastal Literature*.

Gloria Shearin received a PhD in English with a specialty in Composition and Rhetoric from the University of South Carolina. She is Associate Professor at Savannah State University where she teaches courses in freshman and advanced composition, creative nonfiction, American literature, and Zora Neale Hurston. Her research interests are nineteenth- and early twentieth-century literature, especially African American literature, and eighteenth- and nineteenth-century rhetoric.

Kandi Tayebi received her PhD in English literature from the University of Denver. She is currently Associate Dean of Humanities and Social Sciences at Sam Houston State University. Her research focuses on ecological studies, Romantic women writers, and feminist theory. She has published articles on Romanticism, ecology, and pedagogy.

Alan C. Taylor teaches Rhetoric and American literature at Boston University. He is currently writing a cultural history of the United States that examines the role of surveying in the territorial reconfiguration of North America between 1785 and the conclusion of the nineteenth century.

Rebecca Tolley-Stokes is Associate Professor and Librarian at East Tennessee State University. She has contributed to several encyclopedias and reference works including *Dictionary of American History, Biographical Dictionary of Literary Influences: The Twentieth Century, Encyclopedia of the Gilded Age & Progressive Era*, and *The Encyclopedia of Appalachia*.

David Visser earned his BA from Florida State University, his MA from Central Michigan University, and he is currently a literature instructor and PhD candidate at the University of Colorado at Boulder. An Ecocritic, his dissertation dissects the manner in which nineteenth-century descriptions of space reflect the amorphous American identity.

Michael Ziser is Assistant Professor in the English Department at the University of California, Davis, where he also teaches in the Nature and Culture Program.